shelly & cashman

ADVANCED STRUCTURED COBOL

Program Design and File Processing

ADVANCED STRUCTURED COBOL

Program Design and File Processing

By:

Gary B. Shelly
Educational Consultant
Fullerton, California

&

Thomas J. Cashman, CDP, B.A., M.A.
Long Beach City College
Long Beach, California

ANAHEIM PUBLISHING COMPANY
2632 Saturn, St., Brea, CA 92621
(714) 993-3700

Seventh Printing
June 1981

Library of Congress Catalog Card Number 78-62480

ISBN 0-88236-112-0

Printed in the United States of America

10 9 8 7 6 5 4 3

PREFACE

One of the most significant developments in the history of computer programming has been the acceptance and use of structured programming as a methodology for the improvement of the quality of software. Of equal importance has been the practical implementation of the theory of structured design, in conjunction with structured programming, to assist in the improvement of the quality of computer programs. It is now generally recognized that structured design is the basis for the writing of "good" structured programs. This textbook is designed to serve as an advanced textbook in STRUCTURED COBOL PROGRAMMING and STRUCTURED DESIGN.

A minimum of two COBOL courses is commonly offered in data processing curriculums. The first course usually covers the basic language elements of COBOL and provides the student with programming skills necessary to produce a wide variety of business reports using sequential input files. The second, or advanced course, commonly covers processing involving magnetic tape and magnetic disk and includes such topics as input editing, sequential file updating, and the creation, updating, and retrieval of indexed sequential files.

Several approaches are possible in a textbook in advanced COBOL programming and design. One approach uses simplified programs to teach the new elements of COBOL that are required for the processing of magnetic tape and magnetic disk files. This method provides the student with an overview of the various file processing techniques. Unfortunately, this approach fails to provide the student with a realistic understanding of the scope of file processing activities within a business environment, and fails to provide the student with the technical skills necessary to write "realistic" COBOL programs as might be encountered in industry.

The second approach in the teaching of an advanced COBOL programming class, and the approach advocated by the authors of this textbook, teaches not only the new language elements required for the various types of file processing, but teaches these concepts in the context of significant business applications in which the programs used to illustrate file processing concepts closely approximate the types of programs students will encounter in industry as entry-level programmers. It is the authors' opinion that the second approach, the use of comprehensive applications that illustrate "realistic" programming techniques, is the only valid approach to the teaching of an advanced course in COBOL programming because an important objective of this course should be to provide students with the necessary COBOL language and design skills to enter industry as entry-level programmers.

In discussions with industry representatives from data processing, a common complaint voiced concerning students emerging from programming classes is that, although most students have been adequately trained in the syntax of programming languages, most students have never been exposed to programs that even remotely approximate the level of difficulty, or are comprised of the number of COBOL statements, that are encountered by students entering industry as entry-level programmers. Far too often students, even in advanced classes, are given programs that illustrate the "advanced" concepts of sequential file updating and the use of indexed sequential files in applications that require, perhaps, 75 - 100 COBOL statements; yet even the smallest of programs that the entry-level programmer will normally be given to analyze, read, understand, and maintain ranges from 500 to over 5,000 statements in length. Because of this fact, an important objective of this textbook is to provide students with the opportunity to analyze, read, and understand programs that illustrate comprehensive, realistic programming techniques for various applications; and also to permit the student, as time allows, to write programs of increasingly great difficulty and length that more closely approximate the type of activity that might be encountered in industry.

Another common comment concerning student programming is that the coding written by students is poorly done and is not easily read and understood. Too often, students and instructors are more concerned with the time to keypunch a COBOL program than with producing a quality program which will be easy to modify and maintain. As a result, programs are written with cryptic data-names, poor indentation, no comments, and a general disregard for good program coding standards. Teachers who allow programs to be written in this manner are failing to provide students with the good habits and skills needed to achieve success in the programming profession.

Much of this lack of good code may be attributed to the use of textbooks which treat the writing of good code with disdain, and are only concerned with teaching the syntax of the language. The intent of this textbook, on the other hand, is not only to teach the syntax of the language, but also the methods of using the language to produce a quality program. Each program illustrated in this book has been meticulously coded with the intent of presenting model code which the student can and should emulate. In addition, Appendix B contains Coding Standards which are applied to every program in the text. It is strongly suggested that instructors introduce these standards at the beginning of the course and insist upon strict adherence throughout the course. By doing this, a better quality of programmer will be produced.

Every effort has been made to present the concepts of file processing techniques in as clear a manner as possible through the use of realistic problems, numerous illustrations and examples, and completely documented, designed, structured programs. The approach used in the textbook is to first introduce the student to a typical application, explain the design of the program through the use of IPO Charts and Pseudocode Specifications, and then explain the necessary COBOL statements required to process the data. Each chapter then concludes with a complete listing of the source program that solves the problem. Each of the programs illustrated has been run and tested on an IBM System/370 computer using an ANSI Compiler.

The advanced design and programming concepts in the textbook are illustrated through the use of two major "systems"; thus, the textbook is divided into two major parts. Part I consists of three programs in a system that illustrate the following concepts: (1) Input editing, sequential disk output; (2) Use of two input files and matching; (3) Sequential file updating. Part II consists of two programs in a system that illustrate: (1) Creation of an indexed sequential file; (2) Random updating and retrieval of an indexed sequential file.

To assist the student in mastering the material contained within the textbook, the chapters on computer programming contain Review Questions covering the important concepts discussed within the chapter and Programming Assignments to be completed by the student. The first programming assignment in each chapter has been designed to give the student a programming activity that is somewhat less extensive than the application discussed within the textbook for that chapter. The first assignment can be assigned if shortness of time is a consideration or if the instructor wishes the student to experience program maintenance. It is a complete program within itself. The second programming assignment is an addition to the first programming assignment; it can be assigned either after the first programming assignment has been completely designed, coded, and tested, as a program maintenance exercise; or it can be assigned in conjunction with the first programming assignment in order to present an activity that equals or exceeds the difficulty level of the sample program within the chapter. It is suggested that at least the first programming assignment in each chapter be completed by the student and, if time allows, the second programming assignment should also be completed, either in conjunction with Programming Assignment 1 or as a maintenance exercise for the student. The method of assignment is left to the discretion of the instructor and should be based upon the availability of data entry devices, the time available for laboratory-type activities, and related problems commonly found in an academic environment.

A comprehensive set of appendices is included for student reference covering such topics as disk/tape concepts, COBOL Format Summary, COBOL Reference Summary, and COBOL Coding Standards. These appendices are intended to serve as reference material, but it is suggested that the student be introduced to this material, particularly the COBOL Coding Standards, so that it can be used in a meaningful manner throughout the course.

It is strongly recommended that structured walkthroughs be utilized throughout the course. After a program has been designed by the student through the use of IPO Charts and Pseudocode, the design should be reviewed by two other "peer" programmers who will make up a programming team. When the team is certain that the design will produce the required output, the program should then be coded. After the program is coded, but before the program is compiled and executed, a walkthrough should be conducted of the COBOL code to ensure that there are no syntax errors and that the logic of the program has been properly implemented in COBOL. In addition, this review should ensure that the coding follows the Coding Standards which should be enforced within the classroom. When the members of the team are certain that the program will compile and execute properly, the program should be compiled and executed.

When the student has completed the study of the material contained in the textbook, the student should have gained a firm foundation in the design and programming of applications requiring the use of sequential and indexed sequential file processing concepts.

This textbook when used in conjunction with the previous volume, INTRODUCTION TO COMPUTER PROGRAMMING — STRUCTURED COBOL, should provide schools with a comprehensive set of instructional materials for an in-depth course of instruction in Structured Design and Structured COBOL programming. In addition, the ideas and techniques presented in this text should be of value to the experienced programmer seeking information relative to structured design and structured programming.

The authors would like to thank the many data processing instructors from across the country who have made constructive criticism of the authors' previous works. Many of their suggestions have been incorporated into the current text. In addition, we would like to thank Mrs. Marilyn Martin who typeset the manuscript, Mr. Michael Broussard who designed the cover and layout of the textbook, and Mr. Steve Juarez who prepared the coding forms used in the text.

Gary B. Shelly

Thomas J. Cashman

ACKNOWLEDGEMENT

The following information is reprinted from **COBOL** Edition 1965, published by the Conference on Data Systems Languages (CODASYL).

"Any organization interested in reproducing the COBOL report and specifications in whole or in part, using ideas taken from this report as the basis for an instruction manual or for any other purpose is free to do so. However, all such organizations are requested to reproduce this section as part of the introduction to the document. Those using a short passage, as in a book review, are requested to mention "COBOL" in acknowledgement of the source, but need not quote this entire section.

"COBOL is an industry language and is not the property of any company or group of companies, or of any organization or group of organizations.

"No warranty, expressed or implied, is made by any contributor or by the COBOL Committee as to the accuracy and functioning of the programming system and language. Moreover, no responsibility is assumed by any contributor, or by the committee, in connection therewith.

"Procedures have been established for the maintenance of COBOL. Inquiries concerning the procedures for proposing changes should be directed to the Executive Committee of the Conference on Data Systems Languages.

"The authors and copyright holders of the copyrighted material used herein

> **FLOW-MATIC (Trademark of Sperry Rand Corporation), Programming for the Univac (R) I and II, Data Automation Systems copyrighted 1958, 1959, by Sperry Rand Corporation; IBM Commercial Translator Form No. F28-8013, copyrighted 1959 by IBM, FACT, DSI 27A5260-2760, copyrighted 1960 by Minneapolis-Honeywell**

have specifically authorized the use of this material in whole or in part, in the COBOL specifications. Such authorization extends to the reproduction and use of COBOL specifications in programming manuals of similar publications."

TABLE OF CONTENTS

CHAPTER

Designing and Writing Good Programs

1

> *"There is a world of difference between a correct program and a good program."*[1]

INTRODUCTION

Computer programming as a human activity has been in existence for approximately thirty years. During that time, programmers have developed hundreds of thousands of programs, ranging in size from programs with a few instructions, such as might be required to produce mailing labels, to extremely complex programs requiring thousands of instructions, such as those found in airline reservation systems and on-line order entry systems. Historically, if a program produced correct output when given correct input, the program was considered to be a "good" program. Since the early 1970's, however, great interest has been shown by computer scientists and others in determining more precisely the qualities of a "good" program. It has become evident that producing correct output when given correct input is only one of the ways in which the quality of a program should be measured.

The reason this has become evident is that, in reviewing the development of software and the life cycle of software projects, two factors have been found to have a direct influence upon the quality of software projects. These factors are:

1. Programs remain in operation for many years.

2. Programs require continuous maintenance.

These two factors, it has been found, should be given serious consideration when designing and writing programs for use in a business environment because they have serious implications concerning the quality and "goodness" of a program.

---

1 *G. M. Weinberg, S. E. Wright, R. Kauffman, M. A. Goetz, High Level COBOL Programming, Winthrop Publishers, Inc., 1977.*

PROGRAMS REMAIN IN OPERATION FOR MANY YEARS

Most programs written for business applications remain in operation for many years. Although there occasionally may be a need to write a program that produces a "one-time" report, most computer programs, even those which supposedly were written for one-time operation, are used to process data repeatedly within an organization for long periods of time. It is not unusual to find programs which were written over ten years ago still operational today; indeed, this is the norm, not the exception. Therefore, it is important for the programmer to realize that programs which are being developed today will, in all likelihood, be utilized to process data some 10 - 15 years in the future.

Thus, when writing a program, consideration must be given to the consequences which arise because of the longevity of computer programs. Some of these consequences are:

1. Program reliability is very important since the programs are run over a period of years.

2. Programs which are in operation for long periods of time are likely to require changes to them during this period of time.

Because of these factors, it is important that a programmer approach the designing and writing of a program with reliability uppermost in mind. In addition, changes which are made to a program are normally not made by the programmer who originally wrote the program; therefore, the programmer must write programs which are well documented, readable, and easy to modify and maintain.

PROGRAMS REQUIRE CONTINUOUS MAINTENANCE

As noted, one of the consequences of programs remaining in operation for a long time is that there is a good likelihood that changes will have to be made to the program. Even programs which are not operational for a long period of time within a data processing installation will likely have changes made to them during their lifetime. Program maintenance is that activity which must be performed to make changes to programs which are in a production environment. Program maintenance must be performed for four primary reasons:

1. Outside influences, such as governmental or legal requirements

2. Changes in computer hardware or software

3. The user of the output of the program wants changes made in order to produce more usable output

4. The program must be changed because the program is unreliable, and either produces incorrect output or unexpectedly fails during execution

Changes Due to Outside Influences

In most business organizations, computers are used to process data and produce output which is either required for local, state, or federal governments, or which is regulated by some type of legal or governmental agency. Frequent changes in government regulations or laws require that programs based upon these regulations or laws be changed. One of the classic examples of changes required to computer programs because of governmental regulations is found in payroll applications.

Each year, changes are made in tax laws, Social Security deductions, and other areas involving payroll programs processed on the computer. All such changes require modification to existing programs which are used for the processing of the payroll. In addition, with the strong influence of unions and union contracts, additional changes may be necessary to payroll programs. Thus, as can be seen, it is extremely important that payroll programs be written in a fashion that permits easy modification, as most payroll programs require some form of maintenance each year. This holds true for programs in other application areas as well.

Changes Due to New Hardware or Software

New, better, and less expensive computer hardware and software are constantly made available to the business community. In order to implement this new hardware and software, many times changes are required to existing programs in the installation. Some changes may be as simple as merely respecifying device assignments, while other changes may require rewriting the program in another programming language. In between these two extremes fall many changes which may have to be made to take advantage of the capabilities of the new hardware or software. Since programs last a long time in an installation, there is every likelihood that new hardware and software will be implemented within the lifetime of any program. Therefore, again, it is important that programs be written in a way that allows for easy modification and maintenance.

Changes Due to User Requests

There is an adage in computer programming that a program is obsolete even before it is placed into production. Although this is perhaps too strong a statement, it is nonetheless true that users of computer programs constantly request changes to the programs which produce output they use.

The primary reason for these user requests for changes is that although the output which is produced from the programs may conform to the programming specifications, it may not be as useful as other output which could be produced because the information needs of a company may, in fact, have changed between the time when the user was initially contacted to the time that the program to produce the original output was operational. Another reason may be that in preparing the original program specifications, the users were not aware of their exact needs or were not aware of the capabilities of the computer in producing certain types of output or particular types of information.

In most data processing installations, therefore, user changes are constantly being received by the data processing department. Some requests for change will be denied because they are not practical or economical; but in many cases, the programmers within a department are required to make changes to programs to satisfy the needs of the user.

Changes Due to Unreliable Programs

As noted previously, since programs remain in production for long periods of time, it is quite important that they be reliable; that is, they produce the correct output and they do not fail in execution, regardless of the conditions which occur within the program.

Although any program which is written should be reliable, the need for reliability becomes more apparent when programs remain in operation for long periods of time. Because of the time involved and the number of times the program will be executed, more opportunities for not being able to process all types of data and more opportunities for discovering errors within the program are presented.

Unfortunately, in many cases, programs which are placed into production are written to only process "routine" data correctly and do not always accurately process all of the data which might be input to the program. As a consequence, incorrect output will occasionally be produced by a program. In addition, programs have been known to fail and cease execution in the middle of a run because of either faulty data or errors within the logic of the program which have not been previously detected. Programs which do not consistently produce correct output or which cease execution because of errors within the program or errors in the data are termed UNRELIABLE. Newspaper articles such as "Voting System Felled by Programming Error" and "Computer Issues $250,000.00 Welfare Check" are too often typical, and serve to point out the unreliability of the software which is being produced today.

It should be evident that unreliable programs are not desirable; yet in many instances, programs are not designed and written to be reliable. Instead, the programmer begins coding the program immediately upon receiving the program specifications with little or no consideration for all of the possible conditions which may occur. When this approach is taken, there is very little possibility that the program will be reliable and produce the correct results each time the program is run.

Thus, as can be seen, one of the characteristics of a "good" program is that the program must be reliable, and one of the primary responsibilities of a computer programmer is to produce a reliable program; that is, one which will produce the correct output and will never fail once it is placed in a production environment.

The fact remains, however, that many unreliable programs have been produced in the past; and until programmers adopt structured design and structured programming techniques together with an attitude of writing "good" programs which can be properly and easily maintained, there will continue to be unreliable programs which must be maintained. With this in mind, it can been seen how important it is that programs be designed and written with maintenance as a primary factor in determining the "goodness" of a program.

PROBLEMS WITH PROGRAM MAINTENANCE

Because programs have been written with little consideration for maintenance and modification, there have been considerable problems when the maintenance programmer was required to make changes to a program. These problems have centered around two primary areas:

1. Changes are difficult to make properly

2. Program maintenance has become very costly both in terms of money and in terms of programmer time

Difficulty in Making Changes

Program maintenance has proven to be a difficult and time-consuming task. It has been found in recent studies, in fact, that the probability of making a change to a program, and having that change work properly the first time the program is executed, is at best 50%. In most cases, the probability is considerably less. This is illustrated in the following chart.

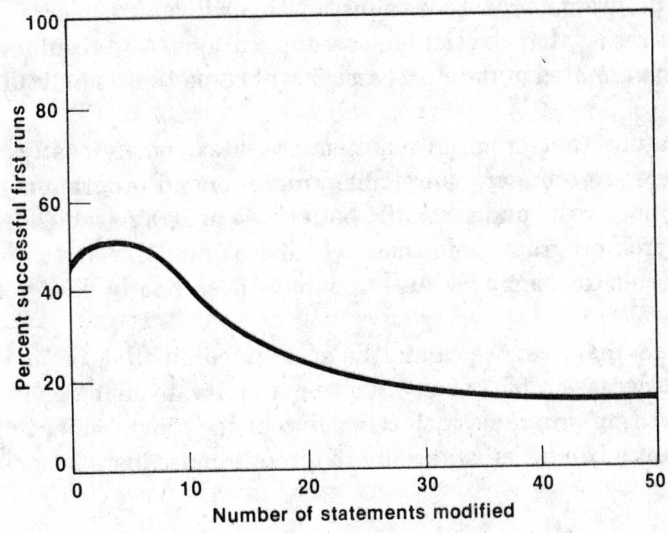

Figure 1-1 Probability of Success in Fixing Bug[1]

Note from the chart in Figure 1-1 that the best chance of correcting a bug or making a change within a program correctly the first time is about 50%, and this occurs when approximately five statements within the program must be changed. If fewer statements must be changed, it has been found that the programmer is often careless when making the change; and, therefore, the program is not correct in the first attempt. When more statements must be changed, it has been found that a change in one part of the program will often cause unpredictable results because the change unexpectedly affects other parts of the program.

---

1 Barry Boehm, "Software and Its Impact: A Quantitative Study," Datamation, Vol. 19, No. 5 (May 1973), pp. 48-59.

Undoubtedly, the primary reason that changes cannot be made properly the first time is that most computer programs are not written with maintenance in mind; that is, they are written only to produce the correct output (many times without achieving this goal), and no consideration is given to the fact that the program will have to be maintained throughout its life. Therefore, when the programmer attempts to make a change, it is many times an arduous task to even identify where within the program the change must be made, let alone make the change properly.

Cost of Program Maintenance

In addition to the fact that making corrections is difficult, and in part because of that fact, great amounts of time and money are being spent on program maintenance. It has been estimated that in 1978, approximately 50% of every data processing installation's time and money, in terms of its programming effort, is spent in program maintenance; that is, half of the programmers in an installation spend their time correcting and modifying existing programs rather than writing new programs for new applications. In some installations, the estimate is as high as 80%; and it has been predicted that within the early 1980's, some installations will be spending 100% of their time and money resources on program maintenance. This means that all programmers within an installation will spend their time making changes to existing programs rather than developing new applications. As a result, innovation and progress within the software area of data processing will come to a standstill.

The primary reasons that program maintenance is extremely costly have already been identified. First, there are too many unreliable programs and programmers must spend too much time "putting out fires;" and secondly, both those programs which legitimately require changes, such as payroll programs, and those which are unreliable and must be corrected are often extremely difficult to change because they have been poorly designed and written.

Although program maintenance cannot be entirely eliminated, because changes in computer programs are a necessary part of any business activity, by using good design techniques and designing and writing programs with the maintenance programmer in mind, the amount and cost of maintenance can be substantially reduced in most installations.

DESIGNING AND WRITING GOOD PROGRAMS

In the previous pages it has been pointed out that when designing and writing computer programs, two important factors must be considered:

1. Programs must be written that are reliable
2. Programs must be written that are easy to modify and maintain

Together with producing correct output, these factors go together to determine whether or not a good program has been designed and written.

Structured Design Theory

To ensure that a program is reliable and will produce the proper output, the program must be properly designed. This design must be correct in both the structure of the program and the logic for each of the modules within the structure of the program. The theory of the design methodology termed "Structured Design," which forms the basis for determining and evaluating the design of a program, is often credited to Wayne Stevens, Glenford Myers, and Larry Constantine, all formerly of International Business Machines, Inc.

In 1974, a classic article appeared in the IBM Systems Journal entitled "Structured Design" by Stevens, Myers, and Constantine. In this article, the theoretical basis for designing programs was presented. The authors defined "Structured Design" as "a set of proposed general program design considerations and techniques for making coding, debugging, and modification, easier, faster, and less expensive by reducing complexity."[2] These design theories were further amplified by Yourdon and Constantine in their book, Structured Design, published in 1975.[3] These two early works have provided the theoretical basis for structured design as it is now practiced in many data processing installations.

Based upon structured design theory, the determination of the quality of the design in terms of the maintainability of the program requires that the design be analyzed within the context of the following measuring tools:

1. Cohesion
2. Coupling
3. Module Size
4. Span of Control

---

2 W. P. Stevens, G. J. Myers, and L. L. Constantine, "Structured Design," IBM Systems Journal, Vol. 13, No. 2 (1974).

3 E. Yourdon, and L. L. Constantine, Structured Design, Yourdon, Inc., 1975 and Second Edition, 1978.

Each of these measuring tools is explained in the following paragraphs.

COHESION

Cohesion is a term applied to a method of evaluating each module within a program. Its formal definition is "Cohesion is a measurement of the strength of association between elements within a module." An element within a module can be an instruction, a group of instructions, or submodules to the module being examined. The primary goal is to have a module with HIGH COHESION; that is, all elements within the module are dedicated to accomplishing one, and only one, task within the program.

Functional Cohesion

A module in which all elements within the module are dedicated to accomplishing one, and only one, task within the program is said to be a FUNCTIONALLY COHESIVE module. Ideally, all modules should be functionally cohesive. For example, a module which determines the square root of a number has high cohesion because all of the instructions (elements) within the module are dedicated to one function — determining the square root. Thus, the square root module is said to be functionally cohesive. As previously stated, this is the best type of cohesion which can be obtained when designing a program.

The following is an example of the COBOL coding for a module whose function is to determine the lowest monthly sales within a year. It is a functionally cohesive module because each of the instructions within the module is dedicated to performing one and only one task — that of determining the lowest monthly sales.

EXAMPLE

```
 CØ1Ø-DETERMINE-LOWEST-MONTH.

     MOVE 1 TO LOW-SUBSCRIPT.
     PERFORM CØ11-LOW-LOOP-PROCESSING
         VARYING SEARCH-SUBSCRIPT FROM 2 BY 1
         UNTIL SEARCH-SUBSCRIPT IS GREATER THAN 12.



 CØ11-LOW-LOOP-PROCESSING.

     IF SALES-INPUT (LOW-SUBSCRIPT) IS GREATER THAN
             SALES-INPUT (SEARCH-SUBSCRIPT)
         MOVE SEARCH-SUBSCRIPT TO LOW-SUBSCRIPT.
```

Figure 1-2 Example of Functionally Cohesive Module

Functional cohesion is desirable within modules because if a programmer must, at some later time in the life of the program, make a change, then it is quite easy to determine where the change should be made. In addition, a change which is made to the module will be a proper change for the function being performed by the module; and such a change should not affect any other module within the program. The ability to identify where the changes should be made in the program and then being able to make the changes without affecting other parts of the program is a major consideration when designing a program for ease of maintenance.

Coincidental Cohesion

As previously stated, when designing a program the programmer should strive to develop the structure of the program in such a manner that all modules are functionally cohesive. On the opposite end of the scale of "goodness" in evaluating modules is what is known as COINCIDENTAL COHESION. In a coincidentally cohesive module, there is no relationship between the elements within a module. The example in Figure 1-3 illustrates the difficulties that can arise when modules are Coincidentally Cohesive rather than Functionally Cohesive.

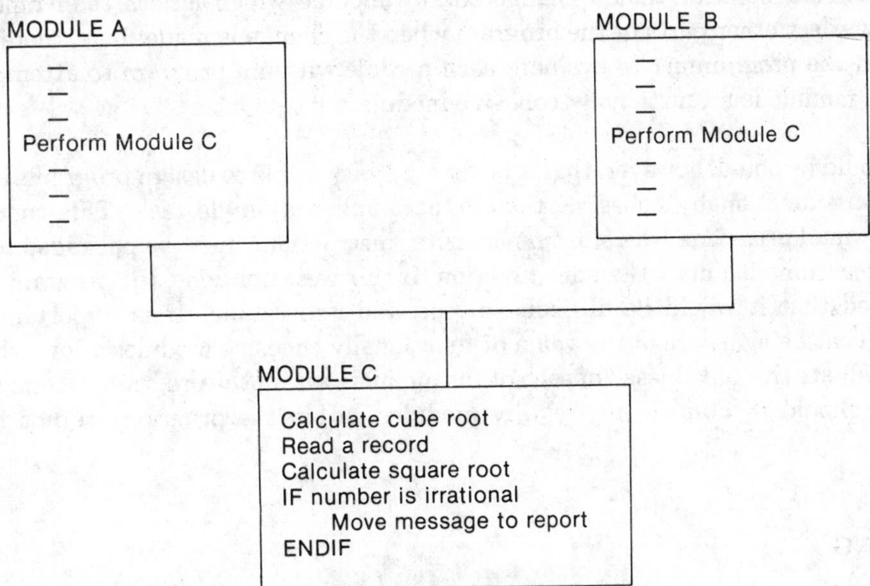

Figure 1-3 Example of Coincidental Cohesion

In Figure 1-3, Module C is the module which is to be evaluated in terms of cohesion. In this example, the only reason that Module C was created was that the instructions in Module C were utilized in both Module A and Module B in the same sequence. Rather than repeating these instructions in both Module A and Module B, the programmer decided to make these instructions into a separate module called Module C. Note that there is no single function which is being accomplished by the instructions in Module C - the only reason these instructions have been made into a separate module is because "coincidentally" they happened to be required in both Module A and Module B.

The problem with Module C, as illustrated in Figure 1-3, is that when a change must be made to this module, there is every likelihood that the change will adversely affect other modules within the program. For example, if a change were required in Module B which stated that two records must be read after the cube root is calculated, but before the square root is calculated, the maintenance programmer would first examine Module B to determine how the change should be made. Upon reviewing Module B, it would be clear that the coding which must be changed is in Module C. Therefore, the maintenance programmer would inspect Module C and determine that another Read Statement should be inserted in Module C. The change would be made, and Module B and Module C would be tested. They would perform properly, provided the change was made properly.

But what about Module A? It also uses Module C; but it did NOT require a change to read two records after calculating the cube root, but before calculating the square root. Since, however, the change was made to Module C for the purpose of modifying Module B, the change will also affect Module A. In fact, it affects it adversely because now it will cause Module A to execute improperly. As can be seen, since Module C was not a functional module, any change to it may adversely affect other modules referencing it — in this case, Module A. Thus, it should be clear that a change to any module which is less than functional may adversely affect other parts of the program when the change is made. It is, therefore, incumbent upon the programmer to evaluate each module within a program to attempt to ensure that each module is a functionally cohesive module.

It should be noted, however, that it is not always possible to design programs in which all modules are functionally cohesive, that is, accomplish a single task. This condition often occurs in small programs where, from necessity, instructions must be packaged together in a module to accomplish more than one function. If this were not done, the program would be so fragmented that it would be difficult to read and understand. It is important to realize, however, that being aware of the value of functionally cohesive modules allows the programmer to evaluate the "goodness" of each of the modules within the program design; and the programmer should be able to justify why modules within the program are not functionally cohesive.

COUPLING

Another method which is used in conjunction with cohesion to evaluate the "goodness" of a program design and subsequent maintainability is the measuring tool called COUPLING. Coupling is the measure of the strength of association between modules within a program.

When a program consists of a series of modules, these modules will normally interact with one another in order to carry out the job which must be done by the program. Ideally, each module in a program should be independent of any other module within the program. When modules are independent of one another, a change to one module will have no effect on any of the other modules within the program. Thus, it is said that a program should be loosely coupled; that is, a change to one module should have as little impact on another module as possible.

In program design, the goal is to strive for the independence of modules. Although complete independence is not possible, a program design goal should be to write programs which are loosely coupled.

Coupling involves two elements:

1. The type of connection between the modules

2. The type of information flowing along the connection between the modules within the program

Coupling — Type of Connection Between Modules

The type of connection between modules refers to the method in which a module communicates with another module in terms of passing control and receiving control back. The general rule is this: Every module in a program is entered at the beginning of the module and exits at the end of the module; and a module is only entered by a module directly above it in the hierarchy chart. This rule is illustrated below.

EXAMPLE

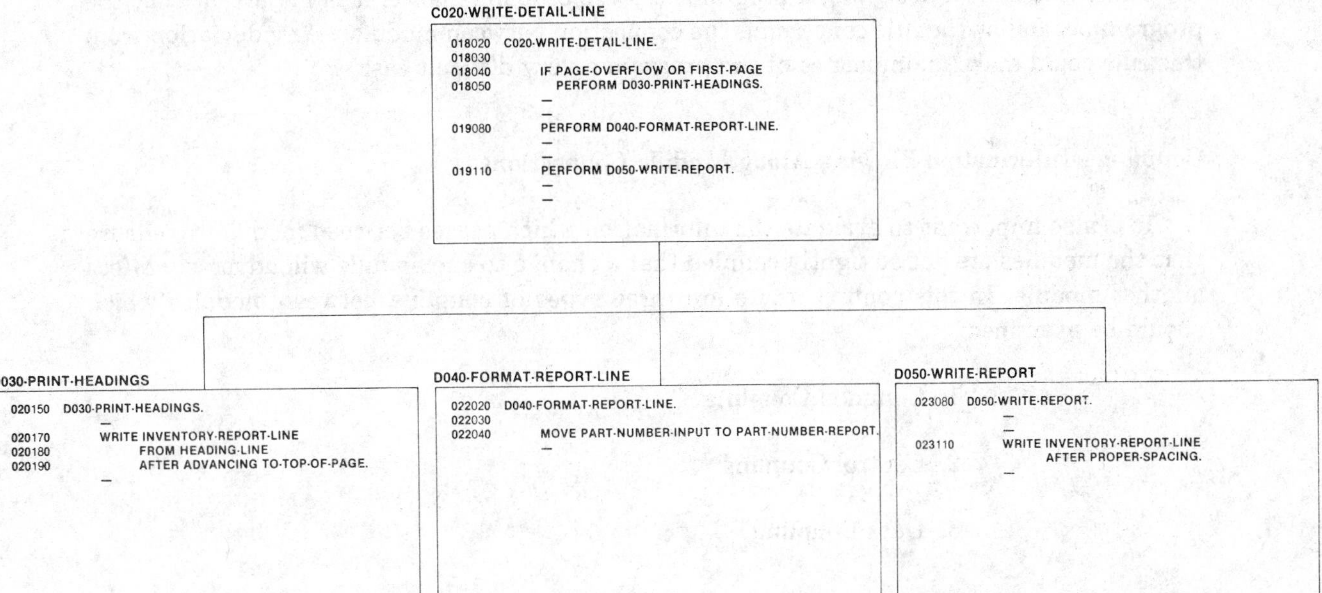

Figure 1-4 Example of Module Connections

Note from Figure 1-4 that there are four modules in the example - C020-WRITE-DETAIL-LINE, D030-PRINT-HEADINGS, D040-FORMAT-REPORT-LINE, and D050-WRITE-REPORT. The C020-WRITE-DETAIL-LINE module invokes the modules on the lower level through the use of the Perform Statement (lines 018050, 019080, and 019110). Since each Perform Statement specifies the module name, each of the modules is entered at the beginning of the module, as specified by the rule. Each of the modules, D030-PRINT-HEADINGS, D040-FORMAT-REPORT-LINE, and D050-WRITE-REPORT performs its task and then returns to the module which called it (C020-WRITE-DETAIL-LINE). Thus, each of the modules exits at the end of the module, as specified by the rule. In addition, the only way in which the D030-PRINT-HEADINGS, D040-FORMAT-REPORT-LINE, and D050-WRITE-REPORT modules are entered is from the C020-WRITE-DETAIL-LINE module; that is, the three modules on the "D" level of the hierarchy chart do not call or perform each other. They are only entered from the higher-level module in the hierarchy chart. Modules on the same level should never communicate with one another. If modules were allowed to communicate with all other modules within the program, the maintenance programmer would be unable to assess the effect a change in one module might have on other modules within the program; that is, a change could affect many modules in the program. In the example, it can be seen that if there is a change made to the D040-FORMAT-REPORT-LINE module, the only two modules affected would be the D040-FORMAT-REPORT-LINE module itself and the module directly above it in the hierarchy chart which calls it (C020-WRITE-DETAIL-LINE).

Thus, in terms of designing a program for ease of maintenance, it is important that the programmer follow the rule concerning the connection between modules. Any deviation from this rule could make maintenance of the program a very difficult task.

Coupling - Information Flowing Along Module Connections

It is also important to evaluate the information which passes between modules to ensure that the modules are not so tightly coupled that a change to one module will adversely affect another module. In this context, there are three types of coupling between modules which should be examined:

1. Common Coupling
2. Control Coupling
3. Data Coupling

Common Coupling

Common coupling means that many modules have access to the same data in a program. This allows a module to modify some piece of data which may be necessary to the execution of another module within the program without the other module having any idea that this modification has taken place. One of the most widely-used examples of common coupling is the Data Division in the COBOL program. This is illustrated in Figure 1-5.

EXAMPLE

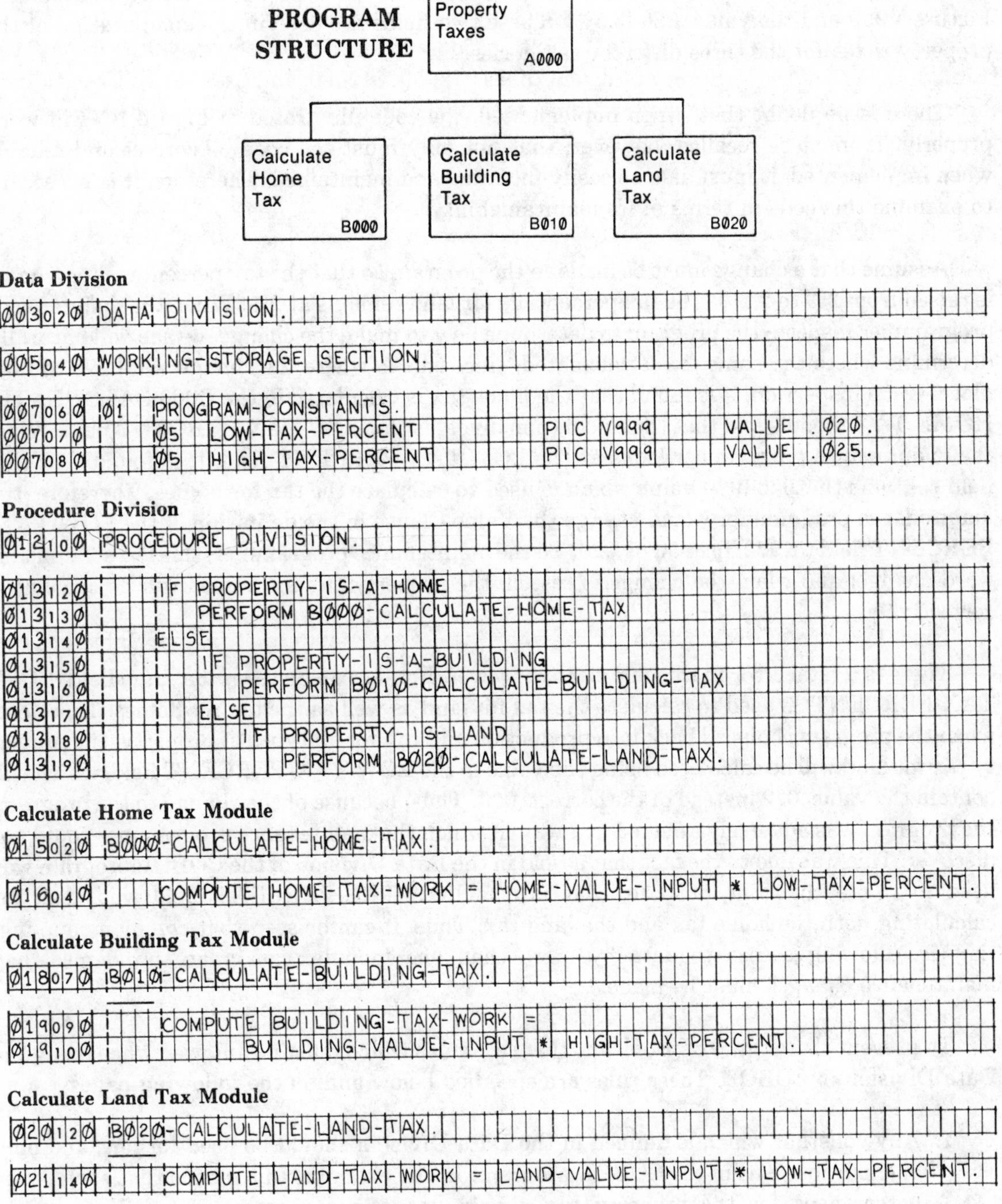

Figure 1-5 Example of Common Coupling

In the example in Figure 1-5, the program is to calculate the property taxes for homes, buildings, and vacant land. As can be seen, there is one module to calculate the home tax, one module to calculate the building tax, and one module to calculate the land tax. The tax percent for homes and land is 2.0%, and the tax percent for buildings is 2.5%.

As can be seen from Figure 1-5, two constants are used in the Data Division for the tax percentages - one constant called LOW-TAX-PERCENT, which contains the Picture V999 and the value .020 (2%); and one constant called HIGH-TAX-PERCENT, which contains the Picture V999 and the value .025 (2.5%). These two fields are used in the computation of the property taxes for the three different categories.

There is no doubt that, when implemented, the code illustrated in Figure 1-5 will work properly. It must be recalled, however, that not only must the code be correct and reliable when implemented, it must also be easily modified and maintained. Therefore, it is necessary to examine this code in terms of its maintainability.

Assume that a change must be made to the program so that the tax percentage for a home is raised from 2% to 2.2%. The tax percentage for land remains at 2%. When the maintenance programmer inspects the program to determine how to make the change, he/she will naturally determine where the home tax is calculated, since this is where the change will have to take place. Upon inspection, it is found that the home tax is calculated in the B000-CALCULATE-HOME-TAX module and that the calculation involves the LOW-TAX-PERCENT field. When the maintenance programmer looks at the LOW-TAX-PERCENT field, it is found that this field contains the .020 (2%) value which is used to calculate the tax for homes. Therefore, the maintenance programmer would change the Value Clause in the definition of the LOW-TAX-PERCENT field to .022, instead of .020. To the maintenance programmer, this is a straightforward change; and when the change is tested, the property tax for homes will be calculated correctly.

There is a fatal error in this approach, however. For, as can be seen, the same field (LOW-TAX-PERCENT) is used to calculate the tax for land as well as the tax for homes. Therefore, when the program is placed back into production and run for all types of property, the property tax for land will be calculated using the value in the LOW-TAX-PERCENT field, which will contain the value .022 instead of the correct .020. Thus, because of the change to the program, the program was adversely affected in a way in which the maintenance programmer could not discover. This was due to the fact that a field in the Data Division of the COBOL program was used for more than one purpose; that is, the LOW-TAX-PERCENT field was used for calculating both the home tax and the land tax. Thus, it can be seen that common coupling, that is, allowing access to data by more than one module, can create problems when maintenance changes must be made.

To prevent these types of problems, there are rules which must be followed when using the Data Division in COBOL. These rules are specified below and on the following pages.

1. Any constant which is defined in the Data Division should be used for one, and only one, purpose within the COBOL program. In the example, this means that each of the percentages for the property tax should be defined separately, as illustrated in Figure 1-6.

EXAMPLE

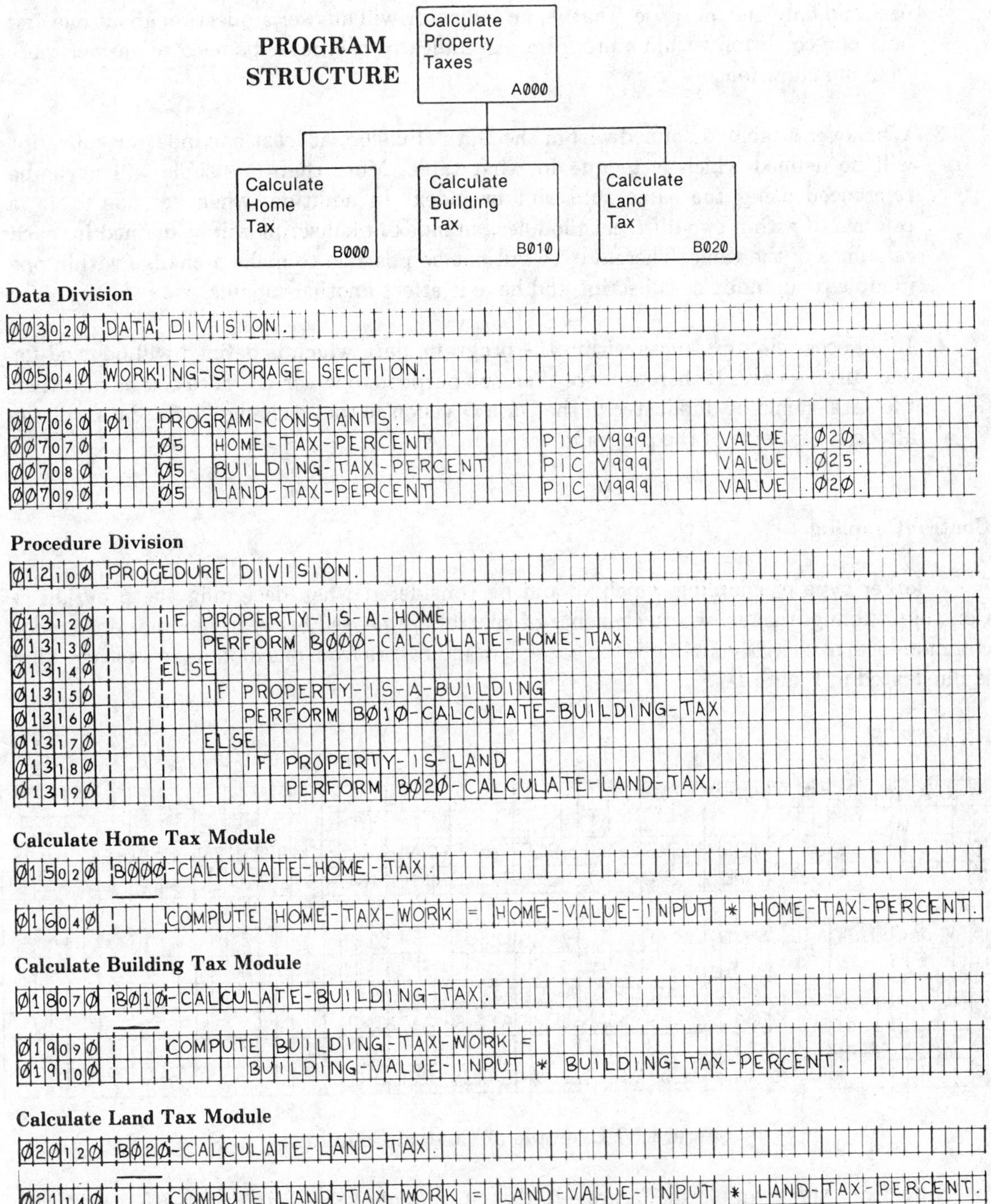

Figure 1-6 Example of Correct Data Definitions in Data Division

Note from Figure 1-6 that three fields are defined for calculating the property tax — one for the home tax (HOME-TAX-PERCENT), one for the building tax (BUILDING-TAX-PERCENT), and one for the land tax (LAND-TAX-PERCENT). It does not matter that the values for both HOME-TAX-PERCENT and LAND-TAX-PERCENT are the same; as was seen previously, the use of a field for more than one purpose within the Data Division of a COBOL program can create difficulties when maintenance must be performed on the program and must, therefore, be avoided.

2. Any indicators which are defined within the Data Division of a program will be used for one, and only one, purpose. That is, an indicator will answer a question about one and only one condition within a program. An indicator can never be used to answer more than one question.

3. Whenever a table is defined within the Data Division, at least one index or subscript will be defined which is unique for that table. More than one table will never be referenced using the same subscript or index. In addition, whenever one table is referenced within two different modules, an index or subscript will be defined for each reference of the table. Therefore, it will not be possible to make a change within one module to an index or subscript and have it affect another module.

4. In all other circumstances within the program, data which is defined will be used for one purpose only. If there is more than one purpose to which the data can be put, then the data should be duplicated in the Data Division so that a change to the data will not affect other parts of the program.

Control Coupling

Another type of coupling which should be considered when designing the program is Control Coupling, that is, where elements of control are passed between modules. The most common form of control coupling is the passing of indicators from one module to another. This is illustrated in Figure 1-7.

EXAMPLE

```
 CØ3Ø-PREPARE-REPORT.

     IF CUSTOMER-NUMBER-INPUT = PREVIOUS-CUSTOMER-NUMBER
        MOVE 'YES' TO ARE-CUSTOMER-NUMBERS-EQUAL.
```

```
 CØ6Ø-UPDATE-MASTER-FILE.

     IF CUSTOMER-NUMBERS-ARE-EQUAL
        PERFORM DØ7Ø-CHANGE-SALES-AMOUNT
     ELSE
        PERFORM DØ8Ø-WRITE-MASTER-RECORD.
```

Figure 1-7 Example of Control Coupling

Note from the example in Figure 1-7 that in module C030-PREPARE-REPORT, the customer number in the current input record (CUSTOMER-NUMBER-INPUT) is compared to the customer number from the previous input record (PREVIOUS-CUSTOMER-NUMBER), and if they are equal, the indicator ARE-CUSTOMER-NUMBERS-EQUAL is set to a value "YES". Thus, this indicator can now be tested in other modules within the program to determine if the customer numbers are equal.

In the example, the indicator is checked in the C060-UPDATE-MASTER-FILE module to determine whether the sales amount should be changed or the master record should be written. Note that the processing which is to occur in the C060-UPDATE-MASTER-FILE module is dependent upon the decision which was made in the C030-PREPARE-REPORT module — this is the reason for the term control coupling. The decision in C030-PREPARE-REPORT controls the processing which is to occur in the C060-UPDATE-MASTER-FILE module.

The reason control coupling is not good again centers around program maintenance. If the maintenance programmer was required to make a change to the C030-PREPARE-REPORT module which affected the IF Statement which compares the customer numbers, then this change could affect the processing which takes place in the C060-UPDATE-MASTER-FILE module. The maintenance programmer, however, would not be aware of this since the C060-UPDATE-MASTER-FILE module has nothing to do with preparing a report. As can be seen, therefore, a change in one part of the program could adversely affect another part of the program because an indicator was set in one module, and another module depended upon that module properly setting the indicator. Thus, these modules are said to be "tightly coupled," since a change to one of the modules may affect the other module.

The general rule, therefore, is to try to avoid passing indicators from module to module whenever possible. To be sure, there are occasions when it is necessary to set an indicator in one module and then test the indicator in another module, but this should be kept to a minimum. In the example in Figure 1-6, control coupling could be avoided by having the C060-UPDATE-MASTER-FILE module make the same comparison as is made in the C030-PREPARE-REPORT module. If this were done, any change to the C030-PREPARE-REPORT module would not affect the other modules within the program. This, of course, is the goal when designing a program.

Data Coupling

A third type of coupling which always occurs within a program is Data Coupling. Data coupling is the passing of data from one module within a program to another module within the program. For example, one module might calculate the gross pay of an employee and then pass the gross pay value to another module which uses the gross pay value to calculate the net pay. Obviously, data coupling will always exist within a program because a module must act upon data in order to produce output useful to the program. The general rule about data, however, is that a module should have access only to that data which it requires in order to perform its function, and it always passes its output back to the module directly above it in the hierarchy chart. In this manner, the problems found with common coupling, as discussed previously, are largely bypassed.

MODULE SIZE

Another means by which programs can be made maintainable is to control the size of the modules which make up the program. If a module is too large, it will normally be quite complex and, therefore, quite difficult to properly modify. The general rule is that a module should be of such a size that it can be easily read and understood "in one sitting." This means that a programmer should be able to read the module; understand the logic and processing which takes place within the module; and, if necessary, be able to identify where in the module a change should be made within no more than a half-hour.

Because of these guidelines, it has been generally agreed that most modules should not exceed 50 COBOL statements, that is, the number of statements which appear on one printed page of the source listing.

There are, of course, certain circumstances where this limit can be exceeded. The most common situation is where there are more than 50 statements required to perform a particular function within a program, and there is no complex logic involved within the module. For example, if 75 Move Statements were required to format a report, then there is very little logic involved within the module; and the programmer should be able to read this module containing 75 statements in one sitting with good understanding. Therefore, this module would be considered acceptable from a size standpoint.

On the other hand, there are situations where a module with 20 statements could be considered too large. For example, if extremely complex logic were involved in the module, it may very well be that a programmer could not understand the logic within the 20 statements; and the module should be broken down into two separate modules so that each module was easily understood.

The programmer must also be aware that modules with too few instructions will cause a program to become so fragmented that it becomes difficult to read and follow. Therefore, a module should generally contain a minimum of 7 - 8 instructions. Again, certain modules may contain fewer statements depending upon the function to be accomplished by the module, but these general guidelines should be followed.

If a module is developed which violates these general guidelines, the programmer must determine if the module should be changed. A module which contains too many statements should be split into two or more modules. It must be cautioned, however, that the arbitrary splitting of modules simply because they contain too many statements is not advised. Instead, the programmer should identify specific functions which can be accomplished by the new modules before splitting the module with too many instructions. Therefore, when splitting a module into two or more modules with less than 50 statements, the programmer must be aware that each of the new modules should be functional in nature.

If a module contains too few instructions, then normally the best way to remedy that situation is to "marry" the lower level module with too few instructions back up into the module which calls it.

As noted, the module size is a guideline to good module design and is not an absolute rule in itself. The measuring tools of coupling and cohesion are the primary tools. If a module has low cohesion or tight coupling, it does not matter what size it is — it is still a bad module.

SPAN OF CONTROL

A module's span of control is the number of modules immediately subordinate to it. In the example in Figure 1-8, the span of control of Module A is three (Module B, Module C, and Module D).

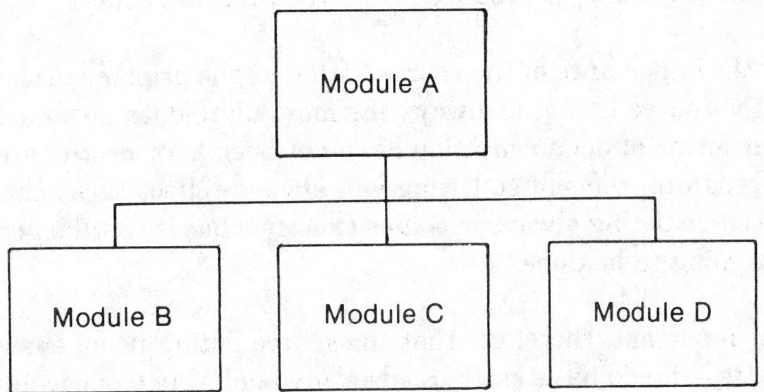

Figure 1-8 Example of Span of Control

Note in Figure 1-8 that there are three modules immediately subordinate to Module A. These are Module B, Module C, and Module D. Therefore, the span of control of Module A is three.

The general rule is that the span of control of a module should be between two and seven. It has been found that if the span of control is greater than seven, the module is too complex because of the logic required to determine which module should be executed. If the span of control is one, many times it is found that the single module can be married back into the higher level module, making a more readable and maintainable module.

As with the other rules, however, there can be exceptions. In some cases a span of control of one is allowable, especially if the single module performs a specific function and the placing of it in the higher level module would create a complex or lengthy module. It is also allowable to have a span of control as high as nine or ten modules in some cases, but the programmer should make every effort to keep the span of control to seven or less in order to keep the complexity of the modules within reason.

PROGRAM DESIGN SUMMARY

Program reliability and program maintainability relies to a large extent on the design of the program. By applying the measuring tools of cohesion, coupling, module size, and span of control, the programmer can determine, as the design is in progress, whether or not the design is a valid and good design. If these guidelines are violated, then the programmer should make every effort to redesign the program so that it obeys the rules specified above.

PROGRAM CODING

As has been emphasized, program design is an extremely important factor in developing reliable and maintainable programs. Another important factor is in the implementation of the design into code, that is, the methods used by the programmer when coding the program.

Obviously, the code which is developed must implement the logic which was developed for each module in the design phase of the program. In addition, however, it is quite important that the program be a document which can be read and understood by any programmer who must reference it. The most important piece of documentation which is developed for a program is the source listing which is produced from the program code.

The reason for the importance of the source listing as the primary piece of documentation is two-fold: First, the source listing is always the most up-to-date documentation of the program. Even if other forms of documentation have not been kept up to date as changes have been made to the program, the source listing will always reflect these changes. The second reason is that the source listing always specifies exactly what is to take place within the program and how it is going to be done.

It is extremely important, therefore, that the source listing be an easily read document. Indeed, a source listing should be as easily read as any book which one would read. It is of little value to design a good program and then code it so poorly that no one can understand what the program does and how it does it.

In order to ensure that good source programs are written, it is necessary to establish and follow well-defined programming standards within an installation. Although certain standards and practices may vary between installations, the overriding concern must be that the programs are written in a manner which can be read and understood by anyone required to examine the program. The standards which are used in programs contained in this textbook are contained in Appendix B. Although there are certain of the standards which may vary from installation to installation, these standards have been developed after considerable experience and experimentation to determine the most effective ways in which to code COBOL programs. It is strongly suggested that these standards be followed unless alternative standards with the same goal of developing readable, understandable programs have been implemented in the installation where the programs are to be written.

It must be realized that following coding standards is not merely a good idea which should be considered when coding a program. They are rules which MUST be followed when coding a program. By following these rules, the programmer will do much to make programs more readable and, therefore, more maintainable. It must be recognized that when coding the program, it is just as easy to follow coding standards as not to follow them. It is only when maintenance must be performed on the program that the maintenance programmer will be grateful that the original programmer followed coding standards, and the value of following them will be realized with easier and less costly maintenance.

PROGRAM REVIEWS

In addition to the techniques of structured design and structured programming, a number of other new approaches to programming have been developed since 1971. One of the most significant in terms of writing reliable, maintainable programs is program reviews and structured walkthroughs.

A structured walkthrough is a "peer" review of both the programmer's design of a program and a review of the actual coding in the program with the purpose of discovering errors which have been made by the programmer. Walkthroughs have been found to be a significant factor in improving the quality of software produced in an installation.

One of the important advantages of a walkthrough is that programs cease being "private works of art" and instead become property of the company for whom the programmer works. In the past, many programmers have felt that their program belonged to them, and that they could develop it in any manner they saw fit. This view has now been recognized to be incorrect; that indeed, a program is a valuable asset of a company, and its development should take place in the same way that other assets of a company are developed. Very few companies will allow an engineer to develop an airplane without reviewing each step in great detail. The same process is applied to programs when walkthroughs are used in reviewing programs. Walkthoughs are so important to the programming process that it has been said, "Any competent professional programmer should know how to conduct a walkthrough, know how to participate in one, and know enough to recognize when one might be valuable."[4]

The primary purpose of a walkthrough is to find errors which have been inadvertently committed by the programmer prior to the time a program is placed on the machine for compilation and execution. It is important, therefore, that all programmers submit their work to other programmers for review so that any errors which have been committed will be found. At the minimum, the program design should be reviewed before coding begins on the portion of the program designed, and the program coding should be reviewed before the program is compiled and executed. The following factors should be reviewed in the design review:

1. Does the design reflect the program requirements as stated in the program specifications?

2. Is the structure of the program a "good" structure from the standpoint of reliability and maintainability?

3. Is the logic correct within each module contained within the program?

4. Will the program do what it is supposed to do?

4 Daniel P. Friedman, and Gerald M. Weinberg, Ethnotechnical Review Handbook, Ethnotech, Inc., Rural Route Two, Lincoln, Nebraska 68505, 1977.

It must be remembered that the design phase of a program is the most important phase in programming - it is in the program design that the structure and logic of the program are determined. At the completion of the design phase of a program, it should be ensured that a correct and good program has been produced. The coding should be merely translating the design into a language which can be processed on the computer. In order to ensure that the program design is correct, it is mandatory that the design which is produced by the programmer be reviewed.

The second phase which must be reviewed is the program code. When reviewing the program code, the following elements are examined:

1. Does the code properly implement the logic which was developed in the design phase?

2. Is the program written in such a way as to be readable and maintainable; that is, are all of the coding rules which have been previously specified being followed?

3. Are there any errors in the code which will prevent it from compiling and executing the first time it is placed on the computer? Included in this question are language syntax errors, misspelled data-names, and other coding errors which may occur.

After the code of the program has been reviewed, there should be no question in either the programmer's mind or in the minds of the people who have reviewed the program that it is syntactically and logically correct; that is, it should compile and execute the first time it is placed on the computer. If there are any doubts, the review process should continue until all doubts are removed. A program should NEVER be placed on the computer with errors in it!

PROGRAMMING ATTITUDE

One of the most popular myths concerning computer programming is that computer programming is a naturally error-prone activity, and that all computer programs will contain errors when they are initially designed and coded. Although computer programming is, without a doubt, complex and challenging, there is absolutely no reason that programs should not be written properly the first time.

In order to write a correct program the first time it is compiled and executed, however, the programmer must approach the task with the attitude that the only way to properly write a program is to write it correctly the first time. Therefore, it cannot be emphasized too much that extraordinary precision and exactness must be used whenever a computer program is being designed and coded. It has been said that computer programming is the most "precise" of all human activities; and although it is true that programming offers many opportunities to make errors, competent professional programmers will not allow this to change their attitude that programs should be written correctly from their inception.

The following list contains some of the elements which must become a part of a programmer's attitude and philosophy in order for that programmer to be considered a competent professional:

1. Any program which is to be written is approached with the attitude that it will be correct from its inception.

2. Any elements of the program which are not clear to the programmer will be clarified before proceeding with the program. A programmer will never assume anything about a program or the programming specifications.

3. During the design of the program, any questionable decisions on the part of the programmer will be checked with others before proceeding.

4. During coding of a program, precision will be the byword; syntax errors or errors of translating logic from design to code WILL NOT OCCUR.

5. Programmers will allow and even encourage reviews of their work at all levels of program development with the hope that any inadvertent errors will be found.

6. A programmer will never allow a program to be placed on the machine without the full confidence that the program is correct. This confidence should be held not only by the programmer who wrote the program but also by others who have had an opportunity to review the program throughout its development.

7. A competent, professional programmer will never allow a program which is being written to become a part of any system without the full knowledge that it is impossible for that program to fail in any production environment, and that the program will be easily maintained when maintenance is required.

These elements are critical when writing programs correctly. If they are followed, the probability is quite good that no errors will be found in the program after it is placed in production, and that the program will be easy to modify and maintain. Therefore, the programmer must conscientiously approach the programming task with an attitude of precision and the realization that the program should work properly the first time it is placed on a machine and never fail subsequently.

SUMMARY

With the advent of structured design, structured programming, and structured walkthroughs, and when programming is approached with an attitude of precision, there is great expectation that the problems which have plagued the software industry for the past decade will cease to be in existence. It is all important, therefore, that programmers dedicate themselves to these ideals and practices every time a program is to be designed or written.

CHAPTER 1

REVIEW QUESTIONS

1. List two factors which have been found to have an influence on the quality of software projects.

2. List four reasons why programs require maintenance.

3. What problems are frequently encountered when maintaining programs?

4. List two important factors which must be considered when designing and writing "good" programs.

5. List four measuring tools which may be used to evaluate the quality of program design.

6. Define and explain the term, COHESION.

7. What is meant by a "functionally cohesive" module?

8. What is meant by "coincidental cohesion"?

9. Define the term COUPLING. List the elements which influence coupling.

10. Briefly explain the general rule related to coupling and the type of connection between modules.

11. Explain the following terms:

    A. Common Coupling

    B. Control Coupling

    C. Data Coupling

12. When designing a program, how many statements should be contained within a module?

13. Explain the term, "Span of Control." What should be the span of control for a module?

14. What is meant by the term, "structured walkthrough"? What factors should be considered in a design walkthrough? What factors should be considered in a program code walkthrough?

Sequential File Processing: Data Editing

> *"The basis for software reliability is design, not testing."*[1]

INTRODUCTION

Although unit record input and output such as punched cards and printers play an important part in recording information which can be processed by a computer program, equally if not more important is the storing of data on auxiliary storage devices such as magnetic tape and direct access storage devices (DASD). These storage devices can be used to store large amounts of data for processing, and form the basis for the systems and programs where large amounts of data must be stored and processed. A detailed description of these devices and the manner in which data is stored on them may be found in **Appendix A**; this chapter will illustrate a program which utilizes the sequential access method when storing data on auxiliary devices.

In Chapter 1 it was pointed out that programmers should approach the task of designing and writing a program with the attitude that the program should work properly the first time it is placed on the computer, and that the program should be designed in such a way as to be both reliable and maintainable.

One of the most likely causes for a program's being unreliable and failing to produce the output expected is that the fields in the input record which are being processed contain invalid data. For example, fields which should contain alphabetic data may have been left blank; numeric fields may erroneously contain alphabetic data or may have been left blank; or the values recorded in these numeric fields may be excessive. These problems may occur because of errors on the original source documents or because of errors made when the input data was prepared. With many programs, when an attempt is made to process this invalid data, the program will either produce incorrect output (garbage in, garbage out), or the program will abnormally terminate. Therefore, one of the more important aspects of processing data using a computer program is the EDITING of the data to be processed.

Editing refers to the process of including in the design of the program the necessary modules and instructions to ensure that only valid and "good" data is allowed to enter the system of computer programs and be subsequently processed. Data which is invalid or incorrect is normally printed on an "exception report," where the data is identified together with a message indicating why the data is in error.

---

1 Harlan Mills, Software Development, IBM Federal Systems, IBM, 1976.

Editing can take many forms and is performed in different places within a system depending upon the particular application; but in all cases, its primary objective is to ensure that only valid data is allowed to enter the system for processing. Some common forms of editing include the following:

1. Checking for blank fields

2. Checking to ensure fields contain only numeric data

3. Checking to ensure a field contains specific values

4. Totaling a series of numeric fields and comparing the total against a predetermined check figure

5. Checking the "reasonableness" of values contained in numeric fields

Although there are other types of editing, the forms of editing listed above are commonly used in computer programs to assist in detecting invalid data.

SAMPLE PROBLEM

In order to illustrate the use of the sequential access method and also to show typical data editing within a program, the sample program in this chapter is designed and programmed to create an Application Program Master File which is to be stored on a direct access device. A master file is a file which contains the current, up-to-date information concerning an application system. In the sample program, the Application Program Master File will contain the current information for all programs which are being designed and written in a data processing installation. The information to create this master file will come from punched cards. Selected fields on the input records will be edited. Those records which contain invalid data will be listed on an exception report. This concept is illustrated in Figure 2-1.

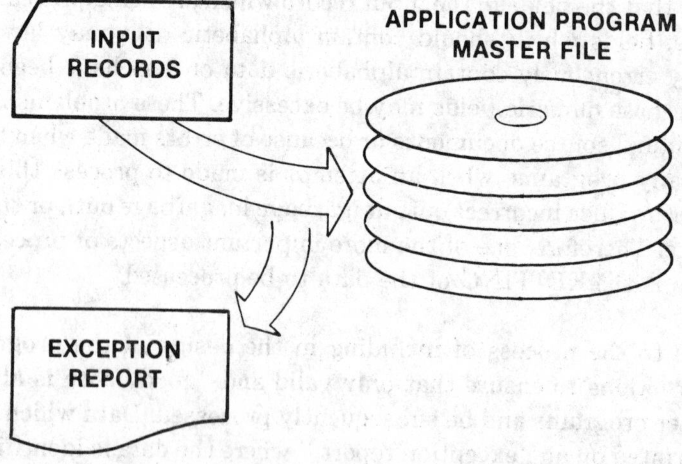

Figure 2-1 Creating a Master File

In the illustration in Figure 2-1, it can be seen that a file of input records stored on punched cards is to be used to create an Application Program Master File which is stored on a magnetic disk direct access device. All input records are to be edited, and those records which contain invalid data will not be recorded in the disk master file, but rather will be listed on an exception report.

The contents of a portion of the master file record are illustrated below. Note that the record contains the Program Identification, Program Description, Programmer Employee Number, Estimated Review Hours, Estimated Design Hours, Estimated Code Hours, Estimated Test Hours, Estimated Implementation Hours, Actual Review Hours, Actual Design Hours, Actual Code Hours, Actual Test Hours, Actual Implementation Hours, and the Status Codes for the Review, Design, Code, Test, and Implementation of the program. Thus, it can be seen that the purpose of the master file is to identify programs which are being designed and written in an installation, and to provide information concerning the estimated and actual time being used to produce the program.

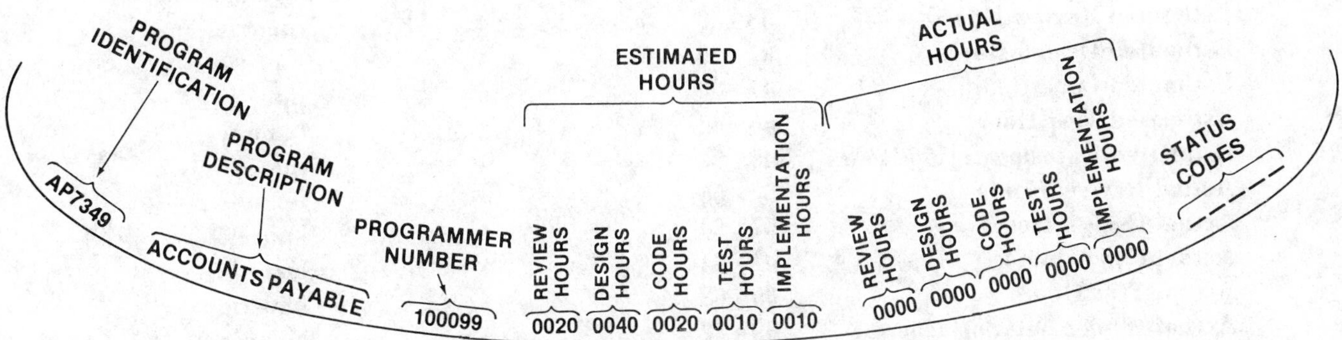

Figure 2-2 Contents of Master File

In the example in Figure 2-2, the program in the record has the program identification AP7349. The description of the program is Accounts Payable, and programmer number 100099 has been assigned to the program. It has been estimated that 20 hours will be required to review the programming specifications, 40 hours will be required to design the program, 20 hours will be required to code the program, 10 hours will be required to test the program, and 10 hours will be required for implementation of the program. No actual work has been performed on the program as of yet.

Master File Format — Output

The master file is to be stored on a direct access device (disk device) using sequential file organization. Sequential file organization means that records within the file are written, stored, and read one after another. The format of each of the records in the Application Program Master File is illustrated below.

Application Program Master File

FIELD	POSITION	NUMBER OF DIGITS	ATTRIBUTES
Program Identification	1 - 6	6	
Application Designation	1 - 2		Alphanumeric
Identification Number	3 - 6		Numeric
Program Description	7 - 26	20	Alphanumeric
Programmer Employee Number	27 - 32	6	Numeric
Estimated Review Hours	33 - 36	4	Numeric
Estimated Design Hours	37 - 40	4	Numeric
Estimated Code Hours	41 - 44	4	Numeric
Estimated Test Hours	45 - 48	4	Numeric
Estimated Implementation Hours	49 - 52	4	Numeric
Actual Review Hours	53 - 56	4	Numeric
Actual Design Hours	57 - 60	4	Numeric
Actual Code Hours	61 - 64	4	Numeric
Actual Test Hours	65 - 68	4	Numeric
Actual Implementation Hours	69 - 72	4	Numeric
Review Status Code	73	1	Alphanumeric
Design Status Code	74	1	Alphanumeric
Code Status Code	75	1	Alphanumeric
Test Status Code	76	1	Alphanumeric
Implementation Status Code	77	1	Alphanumeric

File Information:

Record Length	—	77 characters
Blocking Factor	—	20 records per block
Storage Medium	—	Direct Access Device
Organization	—	Sequential
Access	—	Sequential

Figure 2-3 Application Program Master File Information

As can be seen from Figure 2-3, each record within the Application Program Master File is 77 characters in length. The blocking factor for the file is 20 records per block; thus, there will be 20 logical records in each physical record or block within the file (for an explanation of blocking, see Appendix A). The file will be stored on a direct access device (disk), and the organization and access to the file will be sequential.

The Program Identification field contains both the Application Designation and the Identification Number. The Program Identification field is the Key to the records in the file; that is, the records in the file can be identified by the Program Identification field. In addition, each record in the file will be sorted into an ascending sequence based upon the Program Identification field. This is illustrated below.

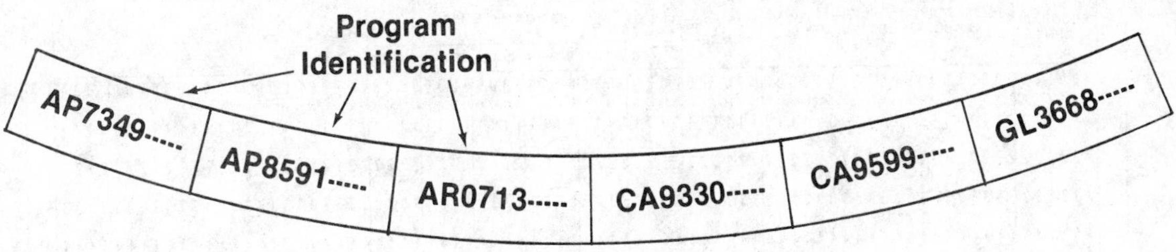

Figure 2-4 Example of Program Identification Field in Master Record

Note in Figure 2-4 that there is a unique Program Identification for each record, and the records are sorted in an ascending sequence based upon the value in the Program Identification field.

The Program Identification field consists of two parts - the Application Designation and the Identification Number. The Application Designation will be one of six values — AP (Accounts Payable), AR (Accounts Receivable), CA (Cost Accounting), GL (General Ledger), IC (Inventory Control), or PA (Payroll). The Identification Number is a unique number which will identify each program within these application areas.

The Program Description field is used to specify a description of the program which is identified by the Program Identification. The Programmer Employee Number identifies the programmer who is assigned to write this program. The Estimated Hours (Review, Design, Code, Test, Implementation) are the hours which are estimated to be required to review, design, code, test, and implement the program. These hours will be placed in the record when the file is initially loaded.

The Actual Hours (Review, Design, Code, Test, Implementation) are the actual hours which are required to perform the specified tasks. These hours are not known at the time the master file is loaded, but will be placed in the master record when the master file is updated (Chapter 4). The Status Codes (Review, Design, Code, Test, Implementation) are used to indicate if the particular task for the program has been completed. If the field contains a blank, the task is not yet completed; if the field contains the character "C," then the task has been completed. These fields will also be changed when the master file is updated.

The Application Program Master File which is created in this chapter will be used as an input file in the programs presented in Chapter 3 and Chapter 4.

Transaction File — Input

The input to the program is the Program Transaction Input File. This file is stored on punched cards. Its format is illustrated in Figure 2-5.

PROGRAM IDENT.	PROGRAM DESCRIPTION	EMPLOYEE NUMBER	TOTAL ESTIMATED HOURS	ESTIMATED HOURS					
				REVIEW	DESIGN	CODE	TEST	IMPLEM.	

Figure 2-5 Transaction File Input Record

The input record illustrated above contains many of the same fields which are in the master record, since the master record is built from this transaction record. The Program Identification, Program Description, and Employee Number are the same as the fields in the Application Program Master File.

The Total Estimated Hours field is the sum of the hours in the Estimated Hours fields (Review, Design, Code, Test, Implementation). It is included in the transaction input record in order to ensure that the proper values are contained in the Estimated Hours fields. Its use will be explained in detail when the editing of the input record is explained. It should be noted that the records in the Transaction Input File will be sorted in an ascending sequence by Program Identification when read by the program.

Processing

As noted, the processing within the program consists basically of reading an input transaction record and, using the information in the transaction record, creating and writing the Application Program Master File. The exact processing to be accomplished, together with the input data editing which must be performed, is explained on the Programming Specification Form in Figures 2-6 through 2-8.

PROGRAMMING SPECIFICATIONS		
SUBJECT Load Application Program Master File	DATE May 2	PAGE 1 OF 4
TO Programmer	FROM Systems Analyst	

A program is to be written to load the Application Program Master File. The format of the input record, the master file record, and the exception report are included as a part of this narrative. The program should be written to include the following processing.

1. The program should read the transaction input file and create the Application Program Master File as illustrated in the description of the master file record. The master record will contain the Program Identification, Program Description, Programmer Employee Number, Estimated Review Hours, Estimated Design Hours, Estimated Code Hours, Estimated Test Hours, Estimated Implementation Hours, Actual Review Hours, Actual Design Hours, Actual Code Hours, Actual Test Hours, Actual Implementation Hours, Review Status Code, Design Status Code, Code Status Code, Test Status Code, and Implementation Status Code.

2. The following fields will come directly from the transaction input record: Program Identification, Program Description, Programmer Employee Number, Estimated Review Hours, Estimated Design Hours, Estimated Code Hours, Estimated Test Hours, and Estimated Implementation Hours. The transaction input records will be in an ascending sequence by Program Identification.

3. The Actual Review Hours, Actual Design Hours, Actual Code Hours, Actual Test Hours, and Actual Implementation Hours should each contain zeros.

4. The Review Status Code, Design Status Code, Code Status Code, Test Status Code, and Implementation Status Code fields should each contain a blank.

5. Before the information in the transaction input record is used to build the Application Program Master File record, the data in the record must be edited. If it passes the following editing criteria, then the data in the transaction input record should be used to create the master record. If any of the following tests is not met by the data in the transaction input record, then the entire transaction record must be rejected and not used to create a master record.

Figure 2-6 Program Specifications (Part 1 of 4)

PROGRAMMING SPECIFICATIONS		
SUBJECT Load Application Program Master File	DATE May 2	PAGE 2 OF 4
TO Programmer	FROM Systems Analyst	

a. Program Identification
   1. The Application Designation must be one of the valid codes: AP (Accounts Payable), AR (Accounts Receivable), CA (Cost Accounting), GL (General Ledger), IC (Inventory Control), PA (Payroll). It should be noted that these application areas may expand, so provision should be made in the program for easily adding new application designation codes.
   2. The Program Identification Number must be numeric.

b. Program Description
   1. The Program Description must be present. If the field is all blanks, it is in error.

c. Programmer Employee Number
   1. The Programmer Employee number must be numeric.

d. Total Estimated Hours
   1. The Total Estimated Hours must be numeric.

e. Estimated Hours (Review, Design, Code, Test, Implementation)
   1. Each field must contain numeric data.
   2. The sum of the Estimated Hours must equal the value in the Total Estimated Hours field.

6. The Estimated Hours fields must also be checked to determine if they contain reasonable values. If it is found that they do not contain reasonable values, an entry should be made on the Exception Report; but the data in the transaction input record should be used to create the master record. The reasonable values for the hours are calculated as follows:

a. Estimated Review Hours
   1. Maximum Reasonable Hours = Total Estimated Hours x 20%
   2. Minimum Reasonable Hours = Total Estimated Hours x 5%

b. Estimated Design Hours
   1. Maximum Reasonable Hours = Total Estimated Hours x 60%
   2. Minimum Reasonable Hours = Total Estimated Hours x 30%

Figure 2-7 Program Specifications (Part 2 of 4)

PROGRAMMING SPECIFICATIONS		
SUBJECT Load Application Program Master File	DATE May 2	PAGE 3 OF 4
TO Programmer	FROM Systems Analyst	

c. Estimated Code Hours
   1. Maximum Reasonable Hours = Total Estimated Hours x 50%
   2. Minimum Reasonable Hours = Total Estimated Hours x 10%

d. Estimated Test Hours
   1. Maximum Reasonable Hours = Total Estimated Hours x 30%
   2. Minimum Reasonable Hours = Total Estimated Hours x 5%

e. Estimated Implementation Hours
   1. Maximum Reasonable Hours = Total Estimated Hours x 20%
   2. Minimum Reasonable Hours = Total Estimated Hours x 0%

If any of the Estimated Hours fields contains a value greater than the maximum reasonable hours or less than the minimum reasonable hours, then the appropriate message should be printed on the Exception Report, but the record should still be loaded onto the Application Program Master File.

7. All fields in each input record should be checked.

8. If any field is found to be in error, the appropriate entry should be made on the Exception Report. The fields on the Exception Report are explained below.

   a. Program I.D. — This field should contain the Program Identification of any record which contains one or more errors. It is to be group indicated on the report; that is, if a single input record contains more than one error, the Program Identification should appear for the first error on the first line only.

   b. Field in Error — This field should identify the field which contains the error. If the error "Sum of Estimated Hours Not = Total Hours" is found, the "Total Estmated Hours" field should be printed as the Field in Error.

   c. Type of Error — This field indicates the type of error which has been found in the input record.

Figure 2-8 Program Specifications (Part 3 of 4)

PROGRAMMING SPECIFICATIONS		
SUBJECT Load Application Program Master File	DATE May 2	PAGE 4 OF 4
TO Programmer	FROM Systems Analyst	

d. Format of report — The report headings and other formatting should be printed as illustrated on the accompanying printer spacing chart.

e. The maximum number of lines on a single page of the Exception Report is forty (40) lines.

9. The program should be written in COBOL.

Figure 2-8 Program Specifications (Part 4 of 4)

Note from the Program Specifications that an Exception Report is to be prepared in order to list those errors which occur within the transaction input data. Exception reports are normally produced from an Edit Program so that the errors produced can be identified and corrected. The format of the Exception Report produced when loading the Application Program Master File is illustrated in Figure 2-9.

Exception Report

PRINTER SPACING CHART

```
 1
 2 XX/XX/XX         APPLICATION PROGRAM MASTER LOAD EXCEPTION REPORT       PAGE XØX
 3
 4 PROGRAM          FIELD                                    TYPE
 5  I.D.          IN ERROR                              OF ERROR
 6
 7 XXXXXX    APPLICATION DESIGNATION           INVALID APPLICATION DESIGNATION
 8           PROGRAM IDENTIFICATION NUMBER     NON-NUMERIC IDENTIFICATION NUMBER
 9           DESCRIPTION                       NO DESCRIPTION PRESENT
10           PROGRAMMER EMPLOYEE NUMBER        NON-NUMERIC PROGRAMMER EMPLOYEE NUMBER
11           TOTAL ESTIMATED HOURS             NON-NUMERIC ESTIMATED HOURS
12           REVIEW HOURS                      SUM OF ESTIMATED HOURS NOT = TOTAL HOURS
13           DESIGN HOURS                      VIOLATES REASONABLENESS CHECK - WARNING ONLY
14           CODE HOURS                        NON-NUMERIC TOTAL ESTIMATED HOURS
15           TEST HOURS
16           IMPLEMENTATION HOURS
17
18 XXXXXX    XXXXXXXXXXXXXXXXXXXXXXXXXXXXXX    XXXXXXXXXXXXXXXXXXXXXXXXXXXXXXXXXXXXXXXXXXXX
```

Figure 2-9 Exception Report

As can be seen from Figure 2-9, the Exception Report contains the fields for Program I.D., the Field in Error, and the Type of Error. The constants contained on the printer spacing chart should be printed as shown. The appropriate message for the Type of Error field should be printed for the error occurring in the Field in Error. For example, for the Test Hours field, the error could be "Non-Numeric Estimated Hours" or "Violates Reasonableness Check — Warning Only," depending upon the error.

EDITING INPUT FIELDS

As noted, it is important that the input fields within the input record be edited to ensure that they contain valid data prior to being placed in the master record. The Programming Specifications listed the types of editing which are to take place on each of the transaction input fields. The following sections examine the editing which is to take place in detail.

Check for Blank Fields and Missing Data

It is commonly required when editing input data that a field contain some data, even though it is not possible to determine exactly what the value of the data should be. For example, in the sample program, it is specified that the Program Description must be present; that is, the field cannot contain all blanks. When programming in COBOL, this test can be easily performed by testing the field for Spaces. This is illustrated below.

EXAMPLE

```
IF PROGRAM-DESCRIPTION-TRANSIN = SPACES
    MOVE PROGRAM-IDENTIFICATION-TRANSIN TO
            PROGRAM-ID-WORK-AREA
    MOVE DESCRIPTION-FIELD-MSG TO FIELD-IN-ERROR-WORK-AREA
    MOVE DESCRIPTION-ERROR-MSG TO TYPE-OF-ERROR-WORK-AREA
    PERFORM UØØØ-WRITE-EXCEPTION-REPORT
    MOVE 'NO ' TO IS-THE-RECORD-VALID.
```

Figure 2-10 Example of Checking for Missing Data

In the example above, the field PROGRAM-DESCRIPTION-TRANSIN is compared to the figurative constant SPACES. If the Program Description field is equal to spaces, it means that there is no data in the Description field, which constitutes an error. Therefore, if the condition is true, the PROGRAM-IDENTIFICATION-TRANSIN, the DESCRIPTION-FIELD-MSG ("DESCRIPTION"), and the DESCRIPTION-ERROR-MSG ("NO DESCRIPTION PRESENT") are moved to the work areas and the Exception Report is written. In addition, an indicator is set to indicate that the input record is not valid.

It should be noted that in order to use the figurative constant, SPACES, the field being checked must be defined as an alphanumeric field (PIC X). Therefore, when checking for the presence of data using this method, the programmer must be aware that the field being checked must be defined as an alphanumeric field.

Checking for Numeric Data

In some applications, it is necessary to check not only for the presence of data, but also that the data present is numeric. This is the case, for example, with the Programmer Employee Number field in the sample program. The COBOL statement to check that the Programmer Employee Number field contains numeric data is illustrated in Figure 2-11.

EXAMPLE

```
Ø19180     IF PROGRAMMER-EMPL-NUMBER-TRANSIN IS NOT NUMERIC
Ø19190         MOVE PROGRAM-IDENTIFICATION-TRANSIN TO
Ø19200                 PROGRAM-ID-WORK-AREA
Ø20010         MOVE PROGRAMMER-EMPL-NUMBER-MSG TO
Ø20020                 FIELD-IN-ERROR-WORK-AREA
Ø20030         MOVE PROGRAMMER-NUMBER-ERROR-MSG TO
Ø20040                 TYPE-OF-ERROR-WORK-AREA
Ø20050         PERFORM U000-WRITE-EXCEPTION-REPORT
Ø20060         MOVE 'NO ' TO IS-THE-RECORD-VALID.
```

Figure 2-11 Example of IF NUMERIC Test

In the example above, the PROGRAMMER-EMPL-NUMBER-TRANSIN field is checked for a numeric value through the use of the IF Statement and the Class Test NUMERIC. If the field does not contain numeric data, then the error messages will be moved to the work areas, a line on the Exception Report will be printed, and the indicator IS-THE-RECORD-VALID will be set to "NO" to indicate that the record is not valid.

The Numeric Class Test performs several functions: First, it tests to determine if there is a value in the field, since a field which contains all blanks would contain non-numeric data. Secondly, it tests to ensure that all data in the field is numeric data.

What data is numeric data and what data is not numeric data can vary, depending upon the way in which the field is defined in the Data Division. If the field being checked is defined as an alphanumeric field, then an operational sign is not allowed in the data; that is, the data must contain absolute numeric values. This is illustrated below for data stored in the EBCDIC format.

EXAMPLE

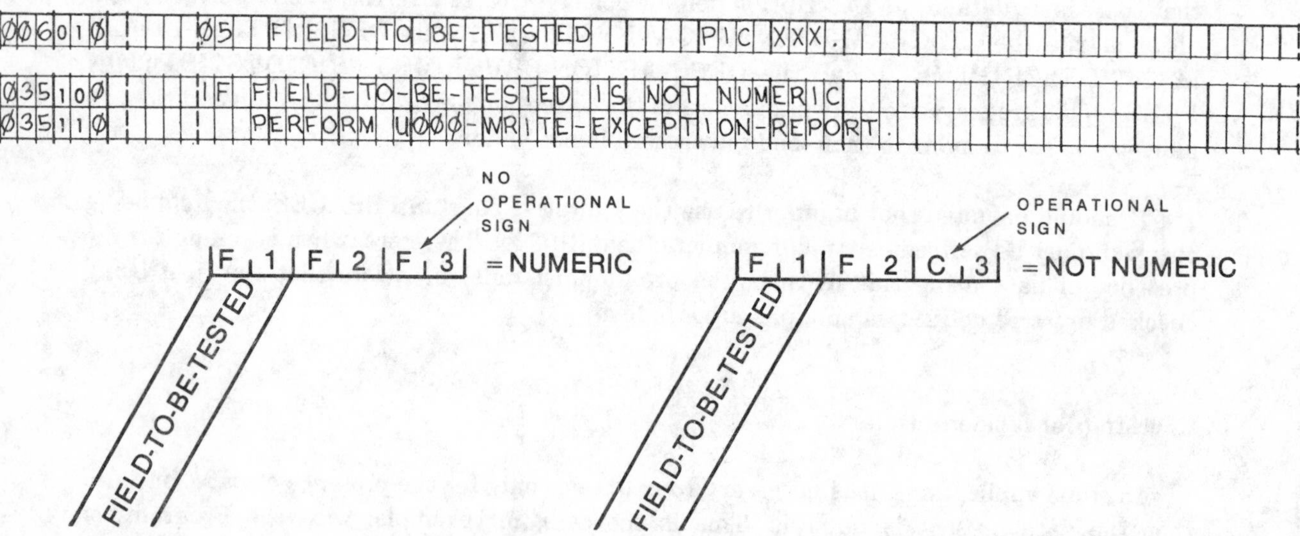

Figure 2-12 IF Numeric Test for Alphanumeric Fields

Note from Figure 2-12 that the field FIELD-TO-BE-TESTED is defined as an alphanumeric field (PIC XXX). Therefore, when the If Numeric Test is performed, there can be no operational sign if the data is to be considered numeric. It can be seen that the field which has no operational sign in the low-order position (Hex 'F1F2F3') is considered numeric while the field which contains an operational sign in the low-order position (Hex 'F1F2C3') is considered not numeric.

If the field to be tested is defined as a numeric field (PIC 9) with no sign, then the If Numeric test performed on it is the same as on an alphanumeric field. If, however, a sign is indicated for the numeric field (PIC S9), then either the absolute sign (Hex 'F') or an operational sign (Hex 'C' or Hex 'D' on the System/360 and Sytem/370) may be contained in the low-order position in order for the data to be considered numeric. This is illustrated in Figure 2-13.

EXAMPLE

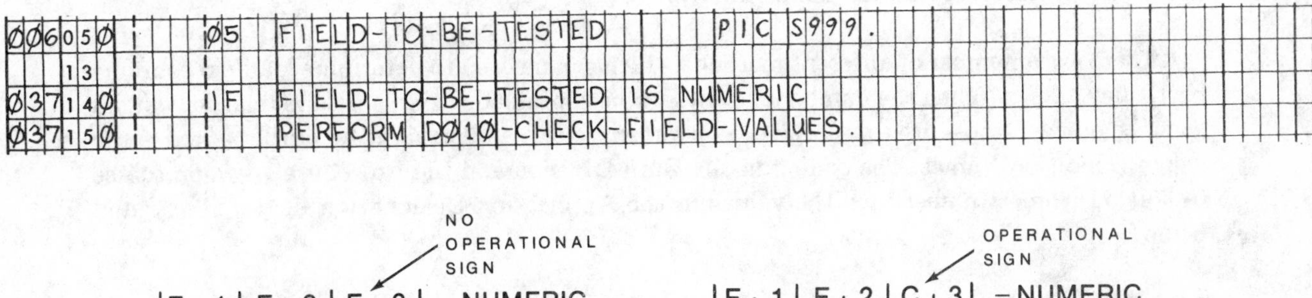

Figure 2-13 IF NUMERIC Test on Signed Numeric Field

Note from Figure 2-13 that FIELD-TO-BE-TESTED is defined as a signed, numeric field. When the If Numeric test is applied to the data in the field, either an operational sign (Hex 'C') or no operational sign (absolute sign of Hex 'F') are valid for numeric data as the sign in the low-order position of field.

The following summarizes the rules for the If Numeric Test:

1. If the field being tested is defined as an Alphanumeric field (Picture X), then it must contain an absolute sign or it will be considered non-numeric. On the System/360 and System/370, the field must contain a hexadecimal 'F' in the zone portion of the low-order byte. The field will be considered non-numeric if it contains the operational signs 'C' or 'D' in the zone portion of the low-order byte.

2. If the field being tested is a numeric field (Picture 9) without the Sign indication, it is treated the same way as a Picture X field.

3. If the field being tested is defined as a Numeric field with a Sign (Picture S9), then the data may contain an absolute sign or an operational sign and be considered numeric. Thus, on the System/360 and System/370, a sign of 'F,' 'C,' or 'D' in the zone portion of the low-order byte will be considered a valid sign for numeric data.

Testing for Specific Values in a Field

In the previous two examples of editing, a check was performed to determine if there was any data in a field, and then a check was performed to determine if the data in a field was numeric. Although these checks are quite helpful and are performed quite frequently in edit programs and modules, neither is concerned with the actual values within the field. In some cases, it is necessary to determine if a field contains specific values; if it does not, then the data in the field is in error.

The Application Designation field in the sample program is an example of a field which requires testing for specific values. It will be recalled that the Programming Specifications state that one of the following six values must be found in the Application Designation field: AP (Accounts Payable), AR (Accounts Receivable), CA (Cost Accounting), GL (General Ledger), IC (Inventory Control), or PA (Payroll). If one of these six values is not contained in the field, then the data in the field is in error.

There are a number of different methods which can be used to determine if a field contains particular values. When the number of values to be contained within a field is relatively small (such as in the sample program), then a convenient, clear, and straight-forward method is the use of Condition Names. The coding in the Data Division and the Procedure Division to use Condition Names to check for the values in the Application Designation field is illustrated below.

EXAMPLE

Data Division

```
       Ø5  PROGRAM-IDENTIFICATION-TRANSIN.
           1Ø  APPL-DESIGNATION-TRANSIN              PIC XX.
               88  APPL-DESIGNATION-IS-VALID         VALUE  'AP',  'AR',
                                                            'GL',  'PA',
                                                            'IC',  'CA'.
```

Procedure Division

```
       IF APPL-DESIGNATION-IS-VALID
           NEXT SENTENCE
       ELSE
           MOVE PROGRAM-IDENTIFICATION-TRANSIN TO
                   PROGRAM-ID-WORK-AREA
           MOVE APPLICATION-DESIGNATION-MSG TO
                   FIELD-IN-ERROR-WORK-AREA
           MOVE APPL-DESIGNATION-ERROR-MSG TO
                   TYPE-OF-ERROR-WORK-AREA
           PERFORM UØØØ-WRITE-EXCEPTION-REPORT
           MOVE 'NO ' TO IS-THE-RECORD-VALID.
```

Figure 2-14 Example of Condition Names

In Figure 2-14 it can be seen that the APPL-DESIGNATION-TRANSIN field is defined as part of the Program Identification. Immediately following the definition of the field is the condition name APPL-DESIGNATION-IS-VALID, followed by the six values which are valid for the Application Designation field.

In the Procedure Division, the IF Statement is used to determine if any of the valid values are present in the field by stating IF APPL-DESIGNATION-IS -VALID. If any of the valid values are in the field, then the condition will be considered true and the NEXT SENTENCE will be executed. If the condition is not true, then the program identification and error messages will be moved to the work areas, the Exception Report will be printed, and it will be indicated that the record is not valid.

It will be noted in Figure 2-14 that the NEXT SENTENCE statement is used when the condition is true. In general, the use of the Next Sentence statement should be restricted and not used very often. Its most common usage is in Nested IF Statements. In this example, however, it is clearer to use it and check if the APPL-DESIGNATION-IS-VALID than to not use it and have the IF Statement read IF NOT APPL-DESIGNATION-IS-VALID. Although this is a valid method to use, it is less clear than using the Next Sentence Clause.

Use of Check Totals

A commonly used method for ensuring that fields contain the proper values is to add the values in the fields and then to check this sum against a separately computed sum. If the sums are equal, then it is likely (although not positive) that the values in the individual fields are correct. If the sums are not equal, then either the values in the individual fields are not correct, or the total sum which is compared is not correct; in either case, there is an error in the input record and the record is rejected.

In the sample program, the Programming Specifications state that the sum of the Estimated Hours (Review, Design, Code, Test, Implementation) must be equal to the value in the Total Estimated Hours field. The method used in the sample program to test this condition is illustrated in Figure 2-15.

Data Division

```
       Ø5  TOTAL-ESTIMATED-HOURS-TRANSIN          PIC 9(4).
       Ø5  ESTIMATED-TASK-HOURS-TRANSIN.
           1Ø  ESTIMATED-REVIEW-HOURS-TRANSIN     PIC 9(4).
           1Ø  ESTIMATED-DESIGN-HOURS-TRANSIN     PIC 9(4).
           1Ø  ESTIMATED-CODE-HOURS-TRANSIN       PIC 9(4).
           1Ø  ESTIMATED-TEST-HOURS-TRANSIN       PIC 9(4).
           1Ø  ESTIMATED-IMPLEM-HOURS-TRANSIN     PIC 9(4).
       Ø5  ESTIMATED-HOURS-TABLE-TRANSIN REDEFINES
              ESTIMATED-TASK-HOURS-TRANSIN        PIC 9(4)
                                                  OCCURS 5 TIMES.
```

```
       Ø5  SUM-OF-ESTIMATED-HOURS-WORK PIC S9(5) VALUE ZERO
                                                  USAGE IS COMP-3.
```

```
       Ø5  SUM-ESTIMATED-HOURS-SUBSCRIPT  PIC S9(8) USAGE IS COMP
                                                    SYNC.
           88  ALL-HOURS-HAVE-BEEN-ADDED            VALUE +6.
```

Procedure Division

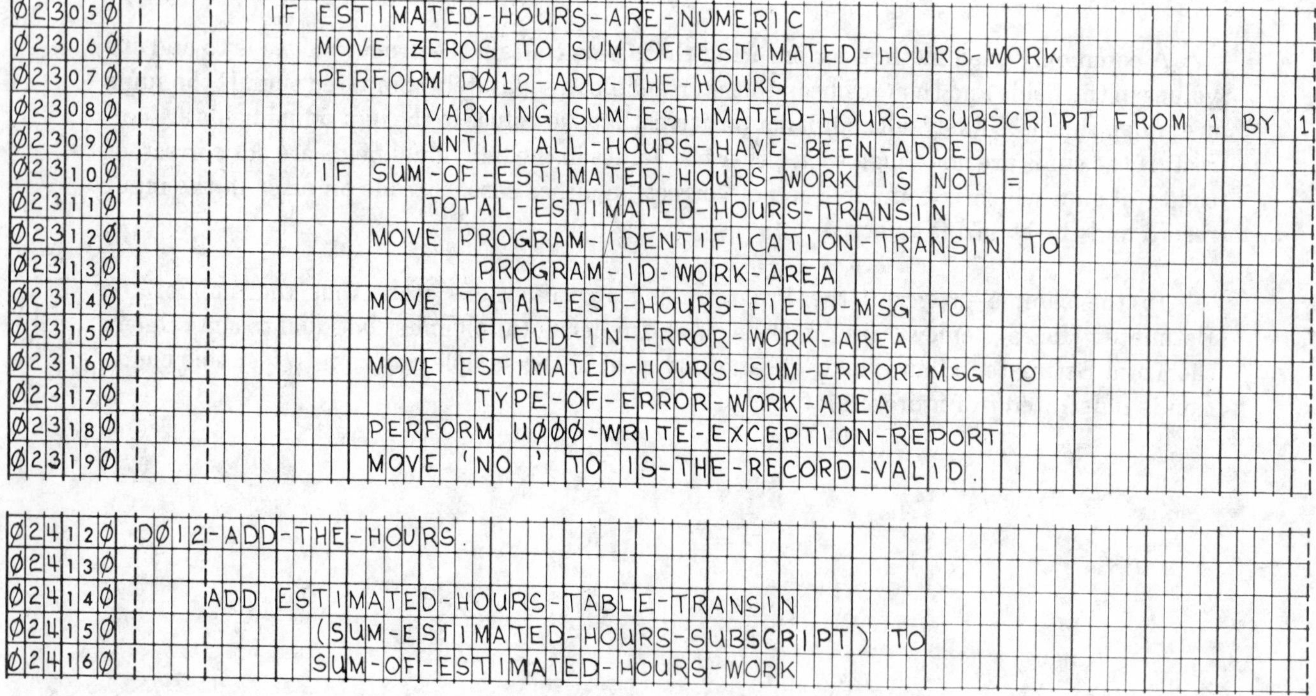

```
           IF ESTIMATED-HOURS-ARE-NUMERIC
               MOVE ZEROS TO SUM-OF-ESTIMATED-HOURS-WORK
               PERFORM DØ12-ADD-THE-HOURS
                   VARYING SUM-ESTIMATED-HOURS-SUBSCRIPT FROM 1 BY 1
                   UNTIL ALL-HOURS-HAVE-BEEN-ADDED
               IF SUM-OF-ESTIMATED-HOURS-WORK IS NOT =
                       TOTAL-ESTIMATED-HOURS-TRANSIN
                   MOVE PROGRAM-IDENTIFICATION-TRANSIN TO
                           PROGRAM-ID-WORK-AREA
                   MOVE TOTAL-EST-HOURS-FIELD-MSG TO
                           FIELD-IN-ERROR-WORK-AREA
                   MOVE ESTIMATED-HOURS-SUM-ERROR-MSG TO
                           TYPE-OF-ERROR-WORK-AREA
                   PERFORM UØØØ-WRITE-EXCEPTION-REPORT
                   MOVE 'NO ' TO IS-THE-RECORD-VALID.
```

```
       DØ12-ADD-THE-HOURS.

           ADD ESTIMATED-HOURS-TABLE-TRANSIN
                   (SUM-ESTIMATED-HOURS-SUBSCRIPT) TO
                   SUM-OF-ESTIMATED-HOURS-WORK
```

Figure 2-15 Example of Check Totals

In the example in Figure 2-15, it can be seen that the TOTAL-ESTIMATED-HOURS-TRANSIN field is defined for the input record. The ESTIMATED-TASK-HOURS-TRANSIN fields are then defined for the Review Hours, the Design Hours, the Code Hours, the Test Hours, and the Implementation Hours. Thus, the individual task hours can be referenced within the Procedure Division by their individual names.

The ESTIMATED-TASK-HOURS-TRANSIN field is then redefined by the ESTIMATED-HOURS-TABLE-TRANSIN field, which is specified as PIC 9(4), occurring five times. Therefore, the individual fields for the estimated task hours can also be referenced through the use of the name ESTIMATED-HOURS-TABLE-TRANSIN and a subscript.

A work area named SUM-OF-ESTIMATED-HOURS-WORK is then defined which will be used to contain the sum of the Estimated Hours. Note that this field is defined as PIC S9(5), even though the Total Estimated Hours (pg/line 004030) is defined as PIC 9(4). It is true that the sum of the Estimated Hours should not be more than four digits in size since this is the maximum size for the Total Estimated Hours field in the transaction input record. It is possible, however, that the sum could be a five digit number; therefore, the total sum field is defined for five digits. If the total sum field was defined with only four digits and a five digit answer developed, the answer certainly would be incorrect in the sum field and, on some computers, would cause the program to terminate abnormally. Defining fields and writing programs which will cover all possible contingencies, even errors in the data or in the processing is called "Defensive Programming" and should always be practiced.

The SUM-ESTIMATED-HOURS-SUBSCRIPT is defined to be used when the fields are added to one another. Note that, as with all subscripts, it is defined as PIC S9(8) USAGE IS COMP, so that the most efficient code possible will be generated when the field is used as a subscript. The condition name ALL-HOURS-HAVE-BEEN-ADDED is used to indicate when all of the fields of the Estimated Hours have been added together.

In the Procedure Division coding, if the Estimated Hours are all numeric (this condition has been previously checked), then the Sum area is set to zeros and the DO12-ADD-THE-HOURS paragraph is performed until all of the hours have been added. Note that the subscript SUM-ESTIMATED-HOURS-SUBSCRIPT is initialized to the value 1 by the Varying Clause of the Perform Statement, and is incremented by one by the Varying Clause each time the DO12-ADD-THE-HOURS paragraph is executed. The loop will be terminated when ALL-HOURS-HAVE-BEEN-PROCESSED, that is, when the value in the SUM-ESTIMATED-HOURS-SUBSCRIPT is equal to 6 (see pg/line 011080).

In the D012-ADD-THE-HOURS paragraph, the Estimated Hours in the transaction record are added to the SUM-OF-ESTIMATED-HOURS-WORK field. The first time the paragraph is executed, the subscript SUM-ESTIMATED-HOURS-SUBSCRIPT contains the value 1, so the Review Hours are added to the work field. The second time the paragraph is executed, the subscript contains the value 2, so the Design Hours are added to the work field. This processing continues until all five fields have been added to the work area.

After the sum of the Estimated Hours has been taken, this sum is compared to the value in the TOTAL-ESTIMATED-HOURS-TRANSIN field (pg/line 023100). If the sums are equal, then it is assumed that there are valid values in the Estimated Hours fields. If they are not equal, then the error messages are moved to the work areas, the Exception Report is written, and the indicator is set to "NO" to show an invalid record has been read.

The method illustrated in Figure 2-15 is a general technique which can be used to accumulate the values in like-sized fields for comparison to a total value — or for any other reason. Note that it does not matter whether there are five fields, such as in the example, or one hundred fields which must be added together. The instructions illustrated in Figure 2-15 may be used; the only variance would be the value of the subscript which would indicate that the summing operation is complete.

Checking Value Reasonableness

In the previous example, the values in the Estimated Hours Fields were added and then compared to a known total to determine if the proper values were stored in the fields. In some instances, it is not possible to determine exactly what values should be in a field, but it is possible to determine that the value in a field extends beyond some reasonable value which should be in the field.

For example, in the sample program, it is not possible to determine exactly what the hours specified for program design should be and then compare that value to the value in the input record. It is possible, however, to indicate that the value in the design input field should not be less than 30% of the total estimated hours nor should it be greater than 60% of the total estimated hours. If the value in the design hours field is less than or greater than these limits, then there is a good possibility that the value in the field is in error.

In the sample program, each of the Estimated Hours fields is to be checked to determine if it contains reasonable values. The values are specified in the Programming Specifications (page 2.8). If the value in any of the fields is not within the reasonable ranges established, an error message is to be written on the Exception Report, but the record is to be placed in the Master File anyway. The module to check the reasonableness of the Estimated Design Hours is illustrated in Figure 2-16.

EXAMPLE

```
 FØ1Ø-CHECK-DESIGN-HOURS.

     IF ESTIMATED-DESIGN-HOURS-TRANSIN IS NUMERIC
         IF ESTIMATED-DESIGN-HOURS-TRANSIN IS GREATER THAN
                 (TOTAL-ESTIMATED-HOURS-TRANSIN *
                 MAXIMUM-PERCENT-FOR-DESIGN) OR
                 IS LESS THAN (TOTAL-ESTIMATED-HOURS-TRANSIN *
                 MINIMUM-PERCENT-FOR-DESIGN)
             MOVE PROGRAM-IDENTIFICATION-TRANSIN TO
                     PROGRAM-ID-WORK-AREA
             MOVE DESIGN-HOURS-FIELD-MSG TO
                     FIELD-IN-ERROR-WORK-AREA
             MOVE REASONABLENESS-CHECK-ERROR-MSG TO
                     TYPE-OF-ERROR-WORK-AREA
             PERFORM UØØØ-WRITE-EXCEPTION-REPORT.
```

Figure 2-16 Example of Reasonableness Check

In the example in Figure 2-16, the function of the F010-CHECK-DESIGN-HOURS module is to check the reasonableness of the Design Hours in the transaction input record. Again, the rule says that the design hours should not exceed 60% of the Total Estimated Hours and should not be less than 30% of the Total Estimated Hours.

The first step in the module is to determine if the value in the Estimated Design Hours is numeric. If the value is not numeric, then the arithmetic statements necessary to determine the reasonableness of the value should not be executed; if they were, and the value was not numeric, there is the possibility that the program would abnormally terminate. Again, this is an example of ''defensive programming'' — attempting to validate the data so that the program will be reliable.

If the data in the field is numeric, then the IF Statement on page/line 027090 is executed. The statement compares the value in the ESTIMATED-DESIGN-HOURS-TRANSIN field with the value calculated by the expression TOTAL-ESTIMATED-HOURS-TRANSIN * MAXIMUM-PERCENT-FOR-DESIGN. As can be seen, this IF Statement is an example of using an arithmetic expression as one of the operands in the IF Statement. If the value in the Design Hours field is greater than the result of the calculation, then the field violates the reasonableness check and an entry is written on the Exception Report.

The IF Statement is also a compound IF Statement since the OR logical operator is used. The second condition which is tested is if the value in the ESTIMATED-DESIGN-HOURS-TRANSIN field is less than the value calculated by the expression TOTAL-ESTIMATED-HOURS-TRANSIN * MINIMUM-PERCENT-FOR-DESIGN. If the value in the Design Hours field is less than the result of the calculation, then the field also violates the reasonableness check and an entry is written on the Exception Report.

It should be noted that a data-name is used for the percent figure in the calculation instead of a literal. In addition, the name selected is MAXIMUM-PERCENT-FOR-DESIGN rather than a name such as SIXTY-PERCENT. The reason for this selection of the name is that if the maximum percent for the design hours would change at a later time, then the name SIXTY-PERCENT would not be reflective of the actual use of the field. In addition, the maintenance programmer may not know the reason for the use of SIXTY-PERCENT, but it is clear what the calculation is doing when the name MAXIMUM-PERCENT-FOR-DESIGN is used, regardless of what value is assigned to the field. Whenever writing a COBOL program, care must be taken when selecting the data-names to be used so that the data-names reflect the function of the data rather than the value contained within the field.

The reasonableness checks for the other four estimated hours fields are accomplished in the same manner as that shown for the Design Hours.

Summary

The previous examples have illustrated some of the techniques which can be used to edit input data in an attempt to ensure that only valid data enters the system. Editing is an important part of the programming effort put forth on any programming project, and the programmer should be familiar with editing techniques and when they should be used.

PROGRAM DESIGN – IPO CHARTS AND HIERARCHY CHART

The definition of the program for this chapter is contained on pages 2.4 through 2.10. It should be recalled that the function of the program is to read a Program Transaction Input File and create the Program Master File on a magnetic disk device. In addition, records in the Program Transaction Input File are to be edited. Records containing errors are to be identified on an Exception Report with an appropriate message describing the error.

When designing this program, the first step is to develop the structure or hierarchy of the program using the IPO Chart as the tool. In developing the structure using the IPO Chart, the programmer must define the output from the program, the input to the program, and the major processing tasks which must be accomplished in order to create the output from the input. The IPO Chart for the top-level module in the program is illustrated in Figure 2-17.

IPO CHART			
PROGRAM: Load Program Master File	PROGRAMMER: Shelly / Cashman		DATE: May 5
MODULE NAME: Load Program Master File	REF: A000	MODULE FUNCTION: Load the Program Master File	
INPUT	PROCESSING	REF:	OUTPUT
1. Program Transaction File	1. Initialize		1. Program Master File
	2. Obtain a valid input record	B000	
	3. Write the master file	B010	
	4. Terminate		

Figure 2-17 IPO Chart for Top-Level Module

In the IPO Chart illustrated in Figure 2-17, it can be seen that the chart is for the program which is to Load the Program Master File. The programmers are Shelly and Cashman, and the date on which the IPO Chart was prepared was May 5. The name of the module is Load Program Master File; it is referenced with number A000, and its function is to Load the Program Master File.

The output specified for the program is the Program Master File (see Figure 2-3 for its format). It should be noted that the Exception Report to be produced from the program is not specified as output from the program even though it will be produced together with the Master File. The reason that it is not specified as output from the program in the top-level module is the role that the Exception Report plays in the program: It is produced to indicate errors which have occurred within the program (in this case, errors in the input data). It is not produced as information which is used by the user, such as the information which is placed in the master file for use in other programs. Generally, an Exception Report which is produced as a result of errors within the program is not specified as primary output from the program. Instead, it will be specified as output from those modules which directly produce the report. In this program, it will be the modules which edit the input record.

The input to the program is the Program Transaction File, which contains the transactions that are used to load the Program Master File. The four major processing tasks which must be accomplished to load the master file are Initialize, Obtain a Valid Input Record, Write the Master File, and Terminate.

The Initialize task is required in order to prepare the files for processing. Obtaining a Valid Input Record is required because without a valid input record, the master file cannot be created. The Master File must be written; and the processing required to Terminate the program must be accomplished.

After identifying those major processing tasks which are required to produce the Program Master File from the Program Transaction File, the programmer must determine which of the major processing tasks is large enough or complex enough to justify a separate module within the program. The Initialize task involves only the preparation of the files for processing (Open Statements). Therefore, it does not justify a separate module. The task, Obtain a Valid Input Record, involves not only reading an input record, but also the editing of the input record to determine that it is a valid record. This involves significant processing and, therefore, should be a separate module. Note that this is indicated on the IPO Chart by noting the reference number of the module which is to perform this processing — B000. The task of Writing the Master Record (including formatting the master record and actually writing the record) will require more than a few statements within the program, so it will be made a separate module referenced by B010. The Terminate task requires only the closing of the files and stopping of the program, so it does not require a separate module. As a result of this analysis, the Hierarchy Chart illustrated in Figure 2-18 would be developed.

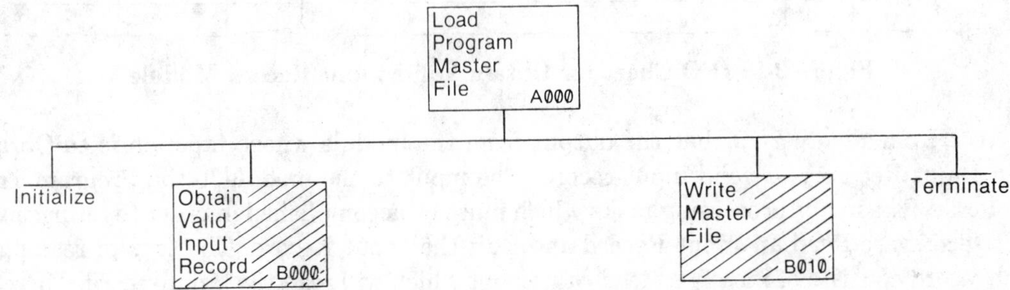

Figure 2-18 Example of Hierarchy Chart

Note from Figure 2-18 that the module on the top level has the function, Load Program Master File. Its reference number is A000, as illustrated in the IPO Chart in Figure 2-17. The two major processing tasks which required separate modules were Obtain a Valid Input Record and Write the Master File. These separate modules are illustrated in Boxes on the second level of the hierarchy chart. In addition to the separate modules, the major processing tasks which did not require a separate module — Initialize and Terminate — are also illustrated on the hierarchy chart, but they are not enclosed within boxes. This procedure is followed so that each task which is to be accomplished within the program will be visible to a maintenance programmer inspecting the hierarchy chart for the program. In small programs, it may not be necessary that all of these tasks are apparent upon the hierarchy chart. In larger programs, however, the hierarchy chart serves as a "map" to anyone inspecting the program to point out where tasks are accomplished within the program. Even if a task is not accomplished in a separate module, but instead is included within a module, the maintenance programmer inspecting the program should be able to observe where the tasks within the program are being accomplished. Therefore, each major processing task listed on the IPO Chart will be included on the Hierarchy Chart, regardless of whether it is performed in a separate module or within the module. In order to illustrate that a major processing task is included within a module, it will not be specified within a box; instead, it will be written below a small horizontal line as illustrated in Figure 2-18. Thus, from Figure 2-18, it can be seen that the Initialize Task and the Terminate Task will be included in the Load Program Master File module, while the Obtain Valid Input Record and Write Master File tasks are in separate modules.

It should be noted also in Figure 2-18 that the B000 and B010 modules are shaded. This is done to show which modules within the program structure have not yet been evaluated through the use of the IPO Chart. It is used within this book to guide the reader through the design of the program; it is NOT USED when actually designing the program. Again, the shading is merely a tool used in the book to aid the reader in following the analysis and design of the modules within the program.

To continue the design of the program, an IPO Chart for the module whose task is to Obtain a Valid Input Record must be developed. This IPO Chart is illustrated below.

IPO CHART			
PROGRAM: Load Program Master File	PROGRAMMER: Shelly/Cashman		DATE: May 5
MODULE NAME: Obtain Valid Input Record	REF: BØØØ	MODULE FUNCTION: Obtain a Valid Input Record	
INPUT	**PROCESSING**	**REF:**	**OUTPUT**
1. Program Transaction File	1. Read an input record		1. Valid Input Record
	2. Edit the input record	CØØØ	

Figure 2-19 IPO Chart for Obtain Valid Input Record Module

Note from Figure 2-19 that the output from the module whose function is to Obtain a Valid Input Record is a valid input record. The input to the module is the Program Transaction File. The major processing tasks which must be accomplished in order to return a valid input record are Read an Input Record and Edit the Input Record. The task of reading the input record consists of merely a Read Statement which will read the input record. Therefore, this task does not require a separate module. The other task, Edit the Input Record, is an involved process since there are a number of fields which must be edited within the input record. Therefore, this task will be a separate module with the reference number C000. This is illustrated in the hierarchy chart in Figure 2-20.

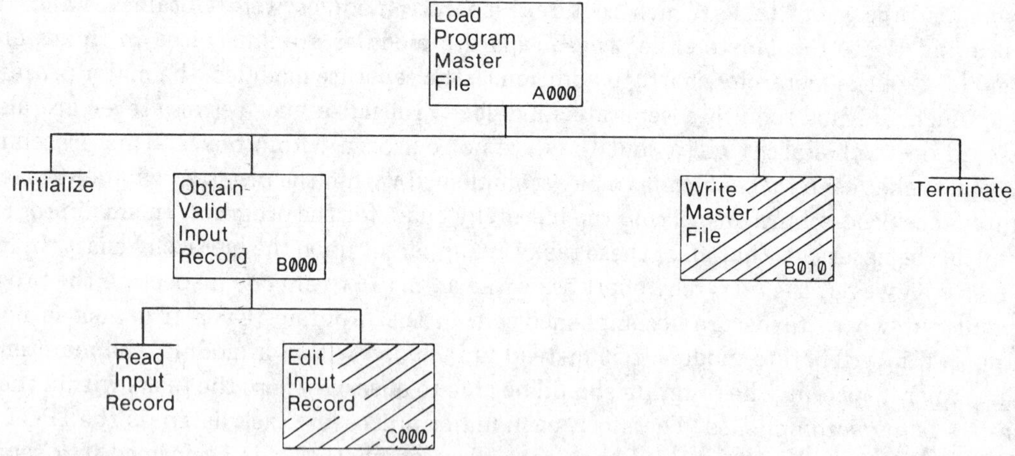

Figure 2-20 Hierarchy Chart

As can be seen, the major processing task of Read Input Record is not a separate module within the module whose function is to Obtain a Valid Input Record, but rather is contained within that module. The function of Editing the Input Record, on the other hand, is a separate module with the reference number C000.

As noted previously, the second module on the second level of the hierarchy chart is the module whose function is to write the master file. The IPO Chart for this module is illustrated in Figure 2-21.

IPO CHART

PROGRAM:	PROGRAMMER:	DATE:
Load Program Master File	Shelly/Cashman	May 5

MODULE NAME:	REF:	MODULE FUNCTION:
Write Master File	BØ1Ø	Write the Program Master File

INPUT	PROCESSING	REF:	OUTPUT
1. Master Load Data	1. Format master record		1. Program Master File
	2. Write master record		

Figure 2-21 IPO Chart for Module to Write the Master File

The output from the module is the Program Master File. The input is the Master Load Data produced elsewhere in the program. The major processing tasks required to create the output are Format the Master Record and Write the Master Record. A series of Move statements, neither lengthy nor complex, are required to format the master record. Therefore, this task does not require a separate module. The task of writing the master record requires only a single Write statement; therefore, it is not made a separate module. Thus, there will be no separate modules from the module whose function is to write the program master file. These major processing tasks will be illustrated on the hierarchy chart, however, as shown in Figure 2-22.

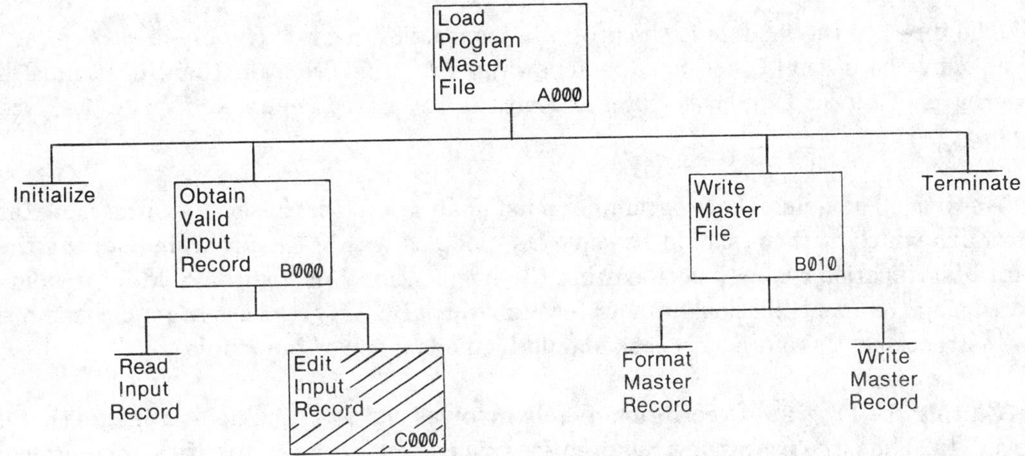

Figure 2-22 Hierarchy Chart

Note from Figure 2-22 that even though the major processing tasks required to write the master file do not require separate modules, they are still illustrated on the hierarchy chart so that a maintainence programmer would be able to easily identify where within the program these tasks are accomplished. As can be seen, by including these tasks on the hierarchy chart, it is readily apparent where in the program various tasks are being performed.

On the third level of the hierarchy chart, the only module which must be evaluated using an IPO Chart is the module whose function is to edit the input record. The IPO Chart for this module is illustrated below.

IPO CHART			
PROGRAM: Load Program Master File	PROGRAMMER: Shelly/Cashman		DATE: May 5
MODULE NAME: Edit Input Record	REF: CØØØ	MODULE FUNCTION: Edit the Input Record	
INPUT	**PROCESSING**	**REF:**	**OUTPUT**
1. Program Transaction Record	1. Edit program identification	DØØØ	1. Edited Fields
	2. Edit description		2. Exception Report
	3. Edit employee number		
	4. Edit estimated hours	DØ1Ø	
	5. Write exception report	UØØØ	

Figure 2-23 IPO Chart for Edit Input Record Module

The output from the module whose function is to edit the input record is the edited fields and the exception report. The edited fields are produced not because of some specific processing which makes them, but rather from the processing which ensures that the fields contain valid data. The Exception Report is produced out of this module because if an error is found in one of the input fields, this fact must be recorded on the exception report.

The input to the module is the program transaction record. The major processing tasks which must be accomplished are the following: Edit the Program Identification, Edit the Description, Edit the Employee Number, Edit the Estimated Hours, and Write the Exception Report.

As with all modules, the programmer must analyze each of these major procesing tasks to determine which of them should be separate modules within the program. Editing the Program Identification requires both editing the Application Designation field for a valid value and editing the Identification Number for numeric data. This appears to require more than a few instructions; therefore, this task should be made a separate module.

Editing the Program Description merely involves checking the field to ensure that it contains data. Thus, the processing required for this editing does not justify a separate module. The editing for the Employee Number requires that the field be checked for numeric data. Again, this is simple processing which is not lengthy, so a separate module is not required for this editing.

The Estimated Hours must be edited for several different criteria — they must be numeric, they must add up to the Total Estimated Hours, the Total Estimated Hours must be numeric, and the Estimated Hours for each task must be reasonable values. Since there is considerable processing to be done when editing the Estimated Hours, this processing should take place in a separate module.

The last major processing task is to write the Exception Report. This report must be written because if an error is found, then an entry must be made on the Exception Report. Since the printing of the Exception Report involves considerable processing, it will be a separate module. It will be noted that the reference number for the module which writes the Exception Report is U000. The "U" stands for Utility, and is used with the exception report writing module because this module will be used in more than one place within the program; that is, it will be invoked by more than one module in the program. Whenever a module is invoked in more than one place in the program, it should be given a reference number beginning with the letter "U."

The hierarchy chart for the program now appears as illustrated in Figure 2-24.

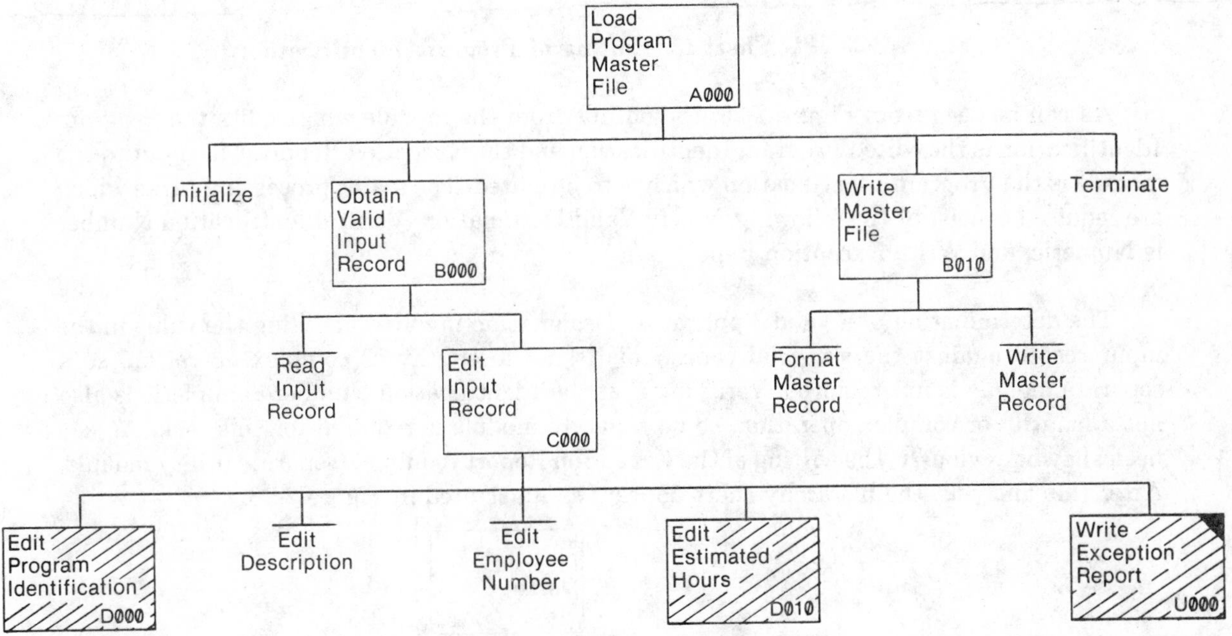

Figure 2-24 Hierarchy Chart

Note from Figure 2-24 that the five major processing tasks specified for the editing of the input record have been included on the hierarchy chart. The tasks, Edit Program Identification, Edit Estimated Hours, and Write Exception Report, will be separate modules; while the tasks, Edit Description and Edit Employee Number, will be contained within the C000-EDIT-INPUT-RECORD module.

It should be noted also that the rectangle for the module, Write Exception Report, is shaded in the upper right-hand corner. This shading indicates that the module is to be invoked from more than one module within the program, as was discussed previously. Thus, whenever a module is to be invoked from more than one module within the program, it should contain a reference number beginning with the letter "U," and the box on the hierarchy chart should be shaded in the upper right-hand corner as illustrated in Figure 2-24.

As can be seen from the hierarchy chart in Figure 2-24, there are now three more modules which must be examined by specifying their output, their input, and the major processing tasks required on IPO Charts. The IPO Chart for the module which edits the program identification is illustrated in Figure 2-25.

IPO CHART				
PROGRAM: Load Program Master File		PROGRAMMER: Shelly/Cashman		DATE: May 5
MODULE NAME: Edit Program Identification	REF: DØØØ	MODULE FUNCTION: Edit the Program Identification		
INPUT	PROCESSING		REF:	OUTPUT
1. Program Identification Field	1. Verify valid designation			1. Edited Program Identification
	2. Verify identification number is numeric			2. Exception Report
	3. Write exception report		UØØØ	

Figure 2-25 IPO Chart for Editing of Program Identification

As can be seen from Figure 2-25, the output from the module which edits the Program Identification is the edited Program Identification and the Exception Report. The input to the module is the Program Identification which is to be edited. The major processing tasks which are required consist of the following: Verify Valid Designation, Verify Identification Number is Numeric, and Write Exception Report.

The determination of a valid Application Designation involves checking the value in the input record against the six valid codes; this is not a lengthy or complex operation, so a separate module is not required. Verifying that the Identification Number is numeric is also not a lengthy or complex operation, so no separate module is required for this task. As has been shown previously, the writing of the Exception Report requires a separate utility module. After this analysis, the hierarchy chart appears as illustrated in Figure 2-26.

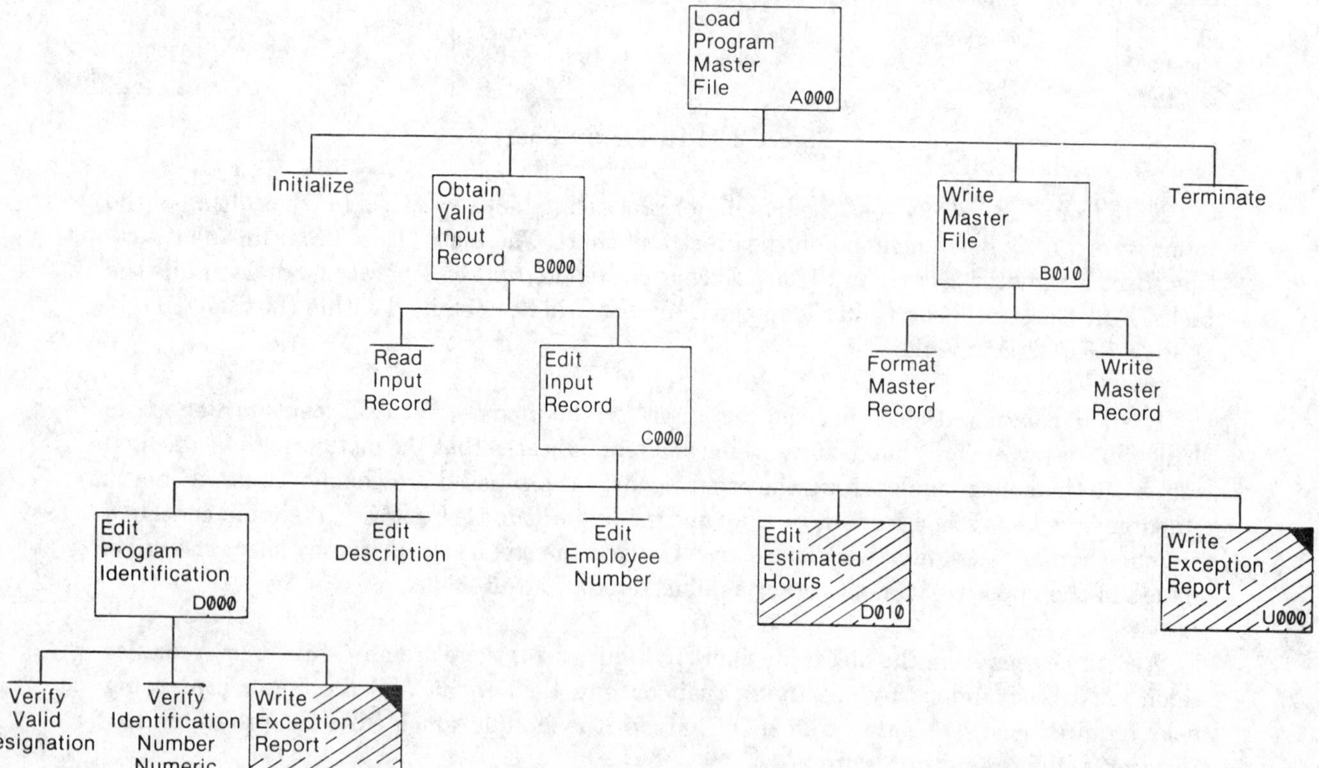

Figure 2-26 Hierarchy Chart

From the hierarchy chart in Figure 2-26, it can be seen that verifying the valid Designation and verifying that the Identification Number is numeric will not be separate modules. A separate module is required to write the Exception Report, but it will be recalled that this is a separate utility module. Thus, it is included on the hierarchy chart with a shaded upper right-hand corner to illustrate that it is called from more than one module within the program.

The next analysis must take place on the module whose function is to Edit the Estimated Hours. The IPO Chart for this module is contained in Figure 2-27.

IPO CHART			
PROGRAM: Load Program Master File	PROGRAMMER: Shelly/Cashman		DATE: May 5
MODULE NAME: Edit Estimated Hours	REF: DØ1Ø	MODULE FUNCTION: Edit the Estimated Hours	
INPUT	**PROCESSING**	**REF:**	**OUTPUT**
1. Total Estimated Hours Field	1. Ensure hours are numeric		1. Edited Estimated Hours Fields
2. Estimated Hours Fields	2. Verify valid total hours		2. Exception Report
	3. Check hour reasonableness	EØØØ	
	4. Write exception report	UØØØ	

Figure 2-27 IPO Chart for Editing of Estimated Hours

Note in Figure 2-27 that the output from the module is the edited Estimated Hours fields and the Exception Report. The input to the module is the Total Estimated Hours field and the Estimated Hours fields. The major processing tasks required to produce the output from the input are as follows: Ensure Hours are Numeric, Verify Valid Total Hours, Check Hour Reasonableness, and Write Exception Report.

Ensuring that the fields contain numeric data is not a long or complex task; therefore, a separate module is not required for that task. Similarly, verifying that the sum of the Estimated Hours is equal to the Total Estimated Hours merely involves adding the Estimated Hour fields and comparing them to the Total Estimated Hours field, and is neither lengthy nor complex; thus, no separate module is required for this major processing task.

The checking of the hours for reasonable values, on the other hand, requires that each field be checked against maximum and minimum values. This would appear to be more than a trivial task; therefore, it will be a separate module. The Exception Report is written by the utility module which has been described previously.

The hierarchy chart for the program after this analysis is illustrated in Figure 2-28.

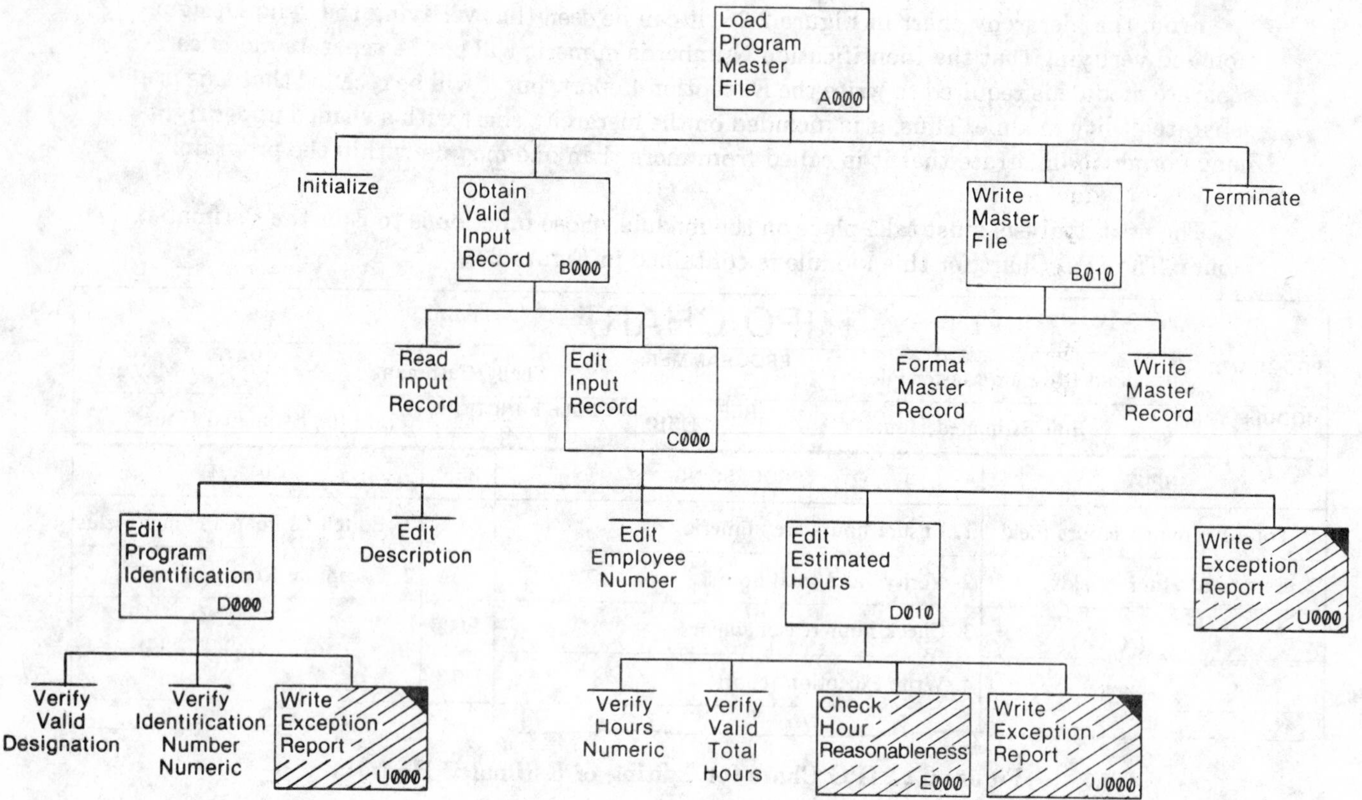

Figure 2-28 Hierarchy Chart

Again it can be seen that those major processing tasks which are not to be separate modules are included on the hierarchy chart without a box. Those tasks which are to be separate modules are included within a box. Note that the module to check the hour reasonableness (E000) has been added, as well as those other tasks which are required to edit the Estimated Hours.

The utility module required to write the Exception Report must also be analyzed to determine the major processing tasks required. The IPO Chart for this module is shown in Figure 2-29.

IPO CHART

PROGRAM: Load Program Master File		PROGRAMMER: Shelly/Cashman	DATE: May 5
MODULE NAME: Write Exception Report	REF: UØØØ	MODULE FUNCTION: Write the Exception Report	

INPUT	PROCESSING	REF:	OUTPUT
1. Program Identification	1. Print headings	UØ1Ø	1. Detail Line on Report
2. Field In Error	2. Format detail line		
3. Type of Error	3. Write detail line		

Figure 2-29 IPO Chart for Writing the Exception Report

As shown in the IPO Chart in Figure 2-29, the output from the module is the detail line on the report. The input to the module is the Program Identification, the Field in Error, and the Type of Error. It will be noted that these are the three fields which are printed on the Exception Report (see Figure 2-9). The major processing tasks required to produce the output from the input are the following: Print the Headings, Format the Detail Line, and Write the Detail Line. In analyzing each of these tasks, it is found that printing the headings may require more than just a few statements, so this major processing task will take place in a separate module. The formatting of the detail line consists of several Move statements, and the writing of the detail line will require a single Write statement. Therefore, neither of these tasks will be performed in separate modules. The hierarchy chart after this analysis appears in Figure 2-30.

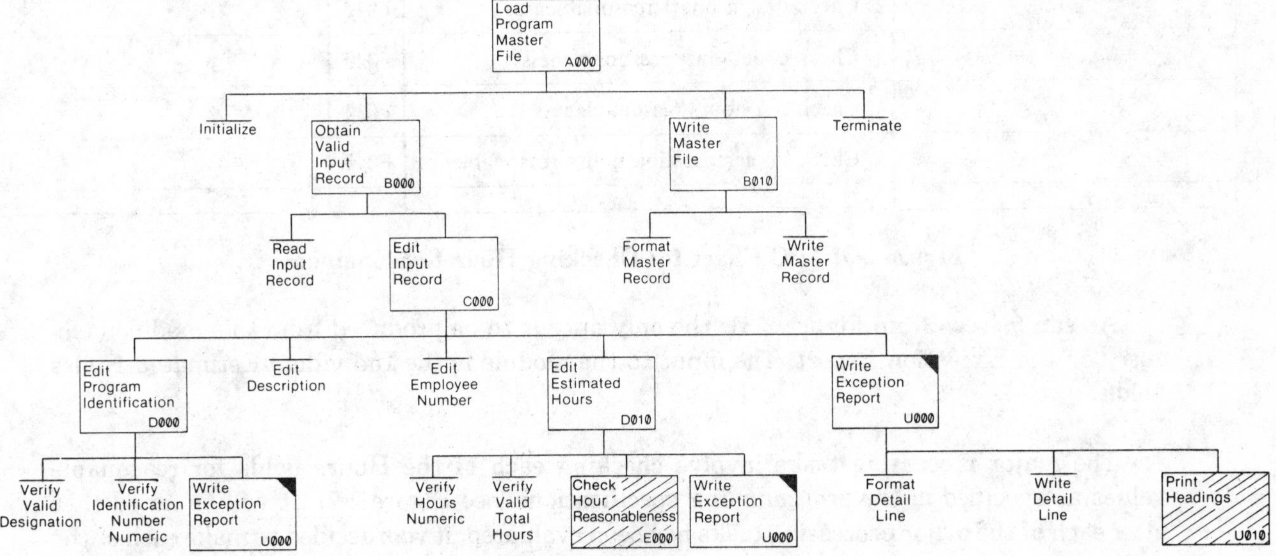

Figure 2-30 Hierarchy Chart

Note in Figure 2-30 that the major processing task of Printing the Headings is made a separate module, but the tasks of formatting the detail line and writing the detail line are not separate modules. This conforms to the analysis performed on the module above. It should be noted also that even though the module which writes the Exception Report is used at different points within the program, it is necessary to show the submodules and tasks only one time; that is, wherever the function of writing the Exception Report is required, only the box specifying that the Exception Report must be written need be shown. The tasks of formatting the detail line, writing the detail line, and printing the headings should not be shown each time the Exception Report is to be written.

The next module to evaluate is the module whose function is to check the Estimated Hour reasonableness. The IPO Chart for this module is illustrated below.

IPO CHART			
PROGRAM: Load Program Master File	PROGRAMMER: Shelly/Cashman		DATE: May 5
MODULE NAME: Check Hour Reasonableness	REF: EØØØ	MODULE FUNCTION: Check the Reasonableness of the Estimated Hours	
INPUT	**PROCESSING**	**REF:**	**OUTPUT**
1. Individual Estimated Hours	1. Check review hours reasonableness	FØØØ	1. Exception Report
	2. Check design hours reasonableness	FØ1Ø	
	3. Check code hours reasonableness	FØ2Ø	
	4. Check test hours reasonableness	FØ3Ø	
	5. Check implementation hours reasonableness	FØ4Ø	

Figure 2-31 IPO Chart for Checking Hour Reasonableness

As can be seen from Figure 2-31, the only output to be produced from this module is an entry on the Exception Report. The input to the module is the Individual Estimated Hours fields.

The major processing tasks involve checking each of the Hours fields for reasonable values as specified in the programming specifications (see Figure 2-7). It will be noted that after each of the major processing tasks has been evaluated, it was decided to make each of the tasks a separate module within the program. The reason that each of the tasks was made a separate module was not based only upon the size or complexity of each of the tasks; checking for the reasonableness involves only computing the reasonable maximum and minimum values and then comparing the value in the field to these computed values.

Instead, consideration was given to the fact that the program may, at some future time, have to be modified. If all of the reasonableness checks were performed in the single module, then it is likely that any changes which must be made would affect other parts of the module, making the change more difficult to make. If each of the checks were done in separate modules, on the other hand, a change to one of the checks would not affect other processing. For example, it is conceivable that at some later time, a change could specify that a sixth category, walkthrough and program review hours, would be added to the hours which need to be checked for reasonableness. If all of the hours were checked in the same module, then the maintenance programmer would have to search the module to determine where the check should be placed and how it would affect other parts of the module. When each of the checks is in a separate module, however, the maintenance programmer need only write another separate module which checks the walkthrough hours, and then call that module from the E000 module illustrated above.

Thus, it can be seen that when designing the program, the programmer must always be aware of the effect the program design will have upon future program maintenance.

The hierarchy chart after the analysis of the module which checks the reasonableness of the Estimated Hours is illustrated below.

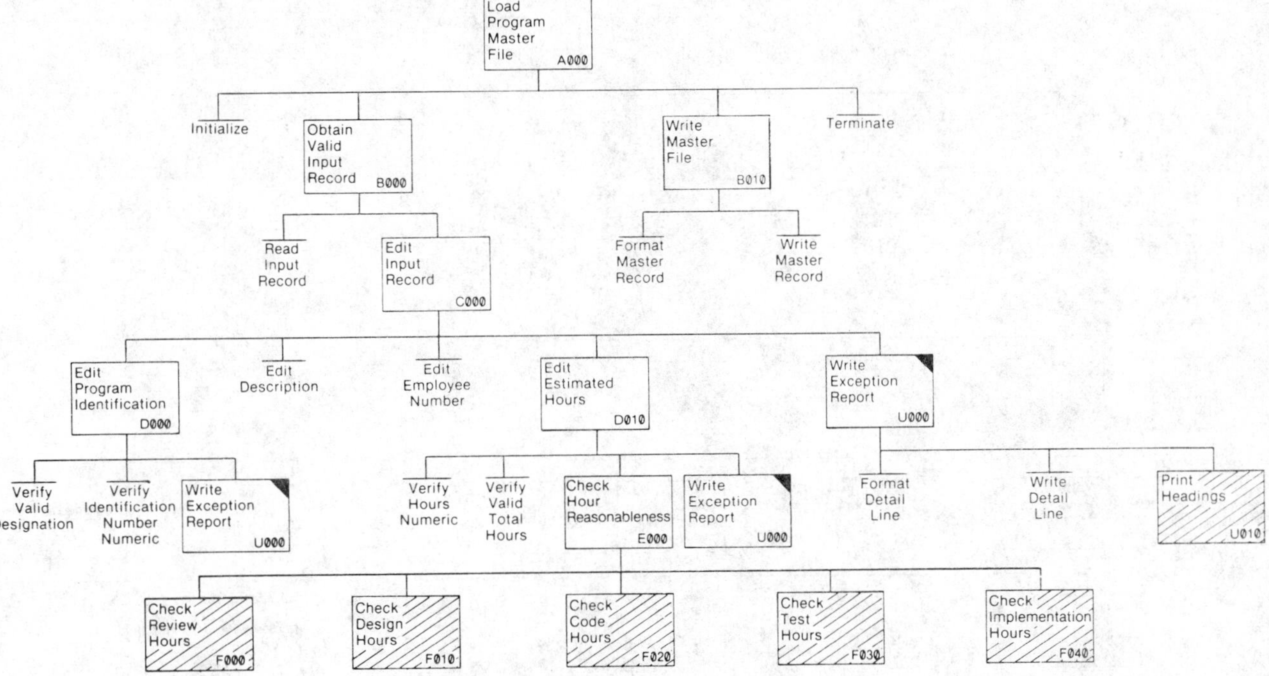

Figure 2-32 Hierarchy Chart

Note from Figure 2-32 that the five modules which check the reasonableness of each of the hours have been added to the hierarchy chart.

The next module to be evaluated is the module which prints the headings on the Exception Report. The IPO Chart for this module is illustrated in Figure 2-33.

IPO CHART			
PROGRAM: Load Program Master File	PROGRAMMER: Shelly/Cashman		DATE: May 5
MODULE NAME: Print Headings	REF: U010	MODULE FUNCTION: Print the Exception Report Headings	
INPUT	PROCESSING	REF:	OUTPUT
	1. Format headings		1. Exception Report Headings
	2. Write headings		

Figure 2-33 IPO Chart for Print Headings Module

As can be seen, the output from the module are the Exception Report headings. The major processing tasks which must be accomplished to create this output are format the headings and write the headings. It will be noted that there is no input specified for the heading module. This is because there is no data which is passed from the module which calls this module that is required in order to create the report headings. Thus, it is not necessary to specify any input to the module.

The hierarchy chart after the IPO Chart for the heading module has been prepared is illustrated in Figure 2-34.

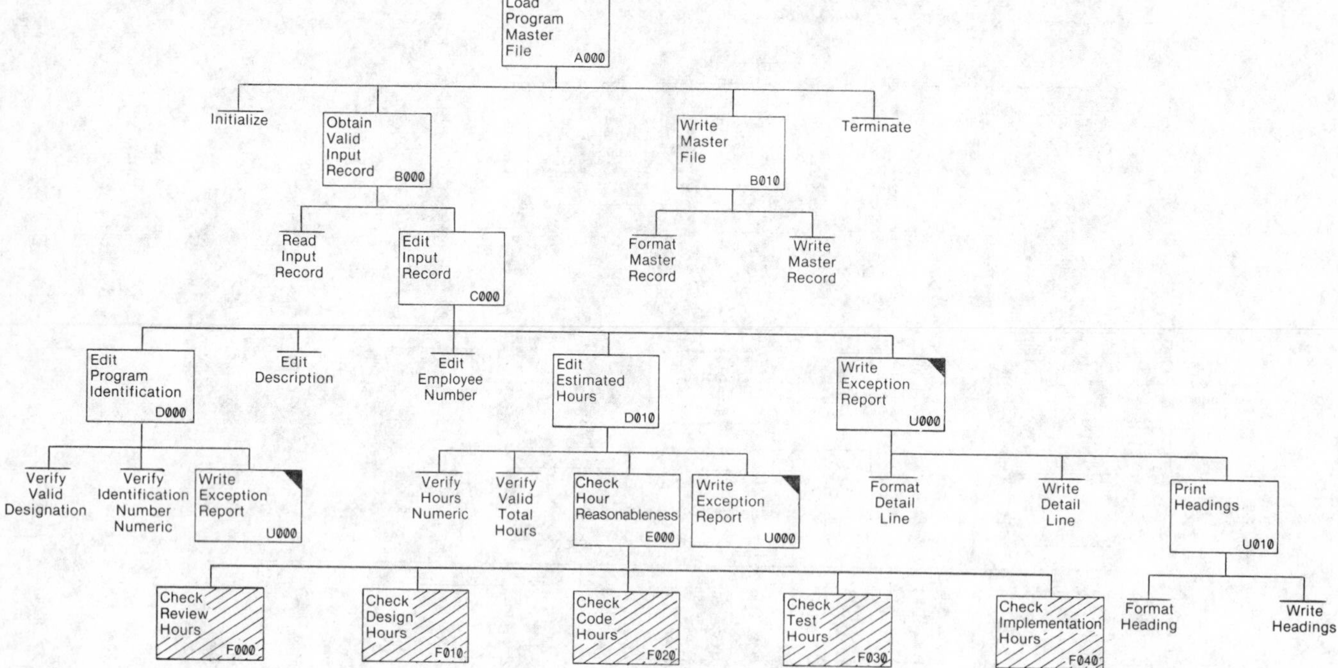

Figure 2-34 Hierarchy Chart

Note in Figure 2-34 that the major processing tasks required to print the headings are included on the hierarchy chart, but they are not separate modules. This is because an analysis of these tasks indicated that neither was of sufficient size or complexity to justify separate modules.

The modules remaining to be analyzed at this point are those modules whose functions are to check the Estimated Hours for reasonableness. The IPO Charts for these modules are illustrated in Figure 2-35.

Note that output from each of the modules is an entry on the Exception Report. The input to the modules is the Total Estimated Hours field and the respective Estimated Hours field which is to be checked. The major processing tasks required include Calculating the reasonable hours, Determining if the Estimated Hours are within the bounds of the reasonable values, and Writing the Exception Report. Calculating the reasonable hours and the determining if the hours in the field are reasonable are not lengthy or complex tasks, so neither requires a separate module.

The Exception Report will be written by a separate utility module, as noted previously.

After this analysis, the hierarchy chart appears as illustrated in Figure 2-36.

IPO CHART

PROGRAM: Load Program Master File	PROGRAMMER: Shelly / Cashman	DATE: May 8
MODULE NAME: Check Review Hours	REF: FØØØ	MODULE FUNCTION: Check Reasonableness of Review Hours

INPUT	PROCESSING	REF:	OUTPUT
1. Estimated Review Hours	1. Calculate reasonable hours		1. Exception Report
2. Total Estimated Hours	2. Determine if estimated review hours		
	are reasonable		
	3. Write exception report	UØØØ	

IPO CHART

PROGRAM: Load Program Master File	PROGRAMMER: Shelly / Cashman	DATE: May 8
MODULE NAME: Check Design Hours	REF: FØ1Ø	MODULE FUNCTION: Check Reasonableness of Design Hours

INPUT	PROCESSING	REF:	OUTPUT
1. Estimated Design Hours	1. Calculate reasonable hours		1. Exception Report
2. Total Estimated Hours	2. Determine if estimated design hours		
	are reasonable		
	3. Write exception report	UØØØ	

IPO CHART

PROGRAM: Load Program Master File	PROGRAMMER: Shelly / Cashman	DATE: May 8
MODULE NAME: Check Code Hours	REF: FØ2Ø	MODULE FUNCTION: Check Reasonableness of Code Hours

INPUT	PROCESSING	REF:	OUTPUT
1. Estimated Code Hours	1. Calculate reasonable hours		1. Exception Report
2. Total Estimated Hours	2. Determine if estimated code hours		
	are reasonable		
	3. Write exception report	UØØØ	

IPO CHART

PROGRAM: Load Program Master File	PROGRAMMER: Shelly / Cashman	DATE: May 8
MODULE NAME: Check Test Hours	REF: FØ3Ø	MODULE FUNCTION: Check Reasonableness of Test Hours

INPUT	PROCESSING	REF:	OUTPUT
1. Estimated Test Hours	1. Calculate reasonable hours		1. Exception Report
2. Total Estimated Hours	2. Determine if estimated test hours		
	are reasonable		
	3. Write exception report	UØØØ	

IPO CHART

PROGRAM: Load Program Master File	PROGRAMMER: Shelly / Cashman	DATE: May 8
MODULE NAME: Check Implementation Hours	REF: FØ4Ø	MODULE FUNCTION: Check Reasonableness of Implementation Hours

INPUT	PROCESSING	REF:	OUTPUT
1. Estimated Implementation	1. Calculate reasonable hours		1. Exception Report
Hours	2. Determine if estimated implementation		
2. Total Estimated Hours	hours are reasonable		
	3. Write exception report	UØØØ	

Figure 2-35 IPO Charts for Estimated Hours Reasonableness Checks

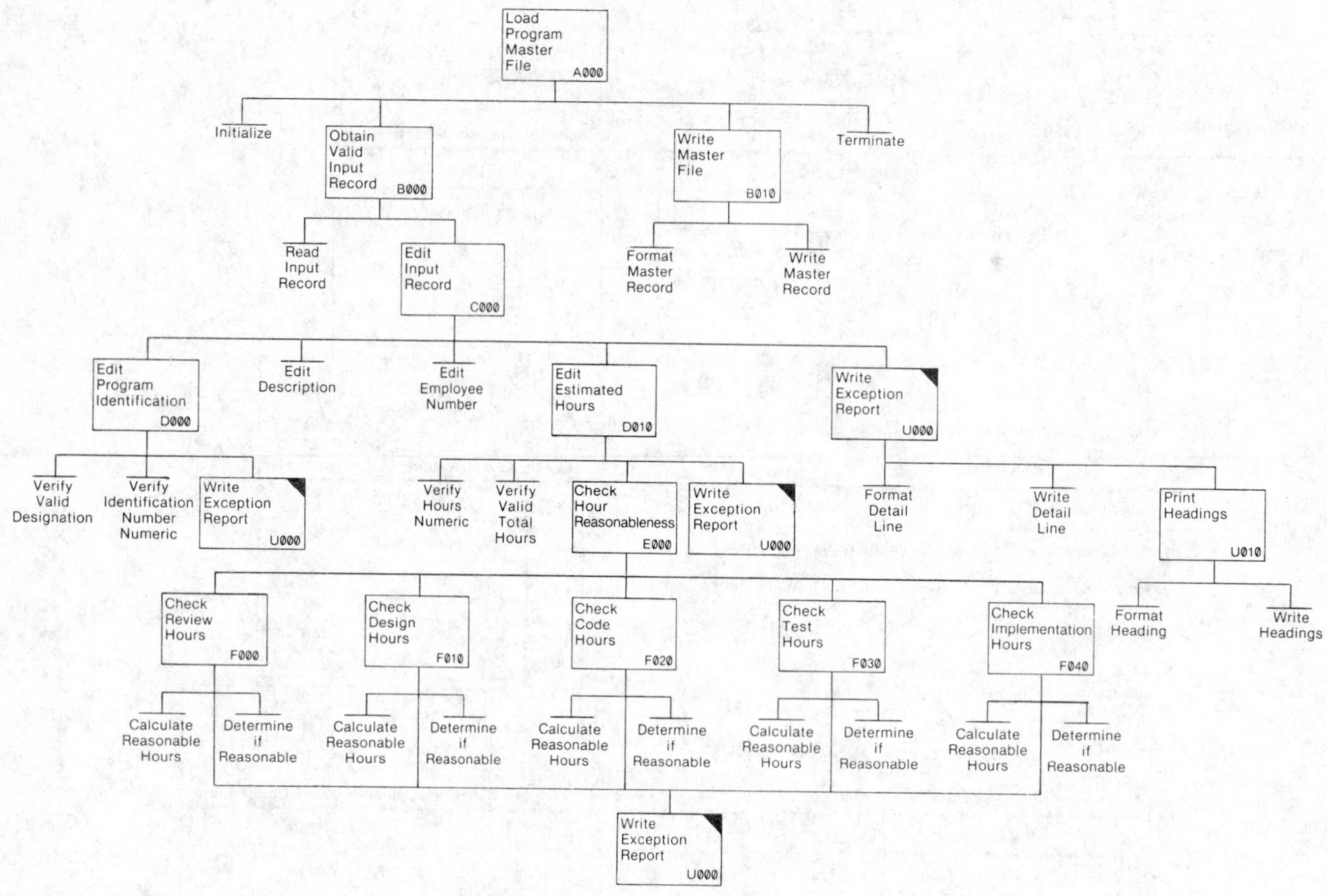

Figure 2-36 Hierarchy Chart

In the hierarchy chart above, it will be noted that each of the major processing tasks required for checking the hour reasonableness is included below the modules which do this processing; but there are not separate modules required. Thus, since there are no more separate modules required for the program, the design of the structure of the program is complete.

Summary

It will be noted that the sequence which was used to identify the modules within the program was a top-to-bottom, left-to-right sequence. It is not always necessary or even desirable that this sequence be used. Indeed, the programmer can choose the appropriate sequence in which to evaluate the need for modules within the program, based upon a number of factors, such as difficulty of the various legs within the hierarchy chart or upon the needs of users. Whatever sequence is used, however, is not so important as the fact that lower-level modules cannot be developed until the modules above them have been developed. For example, in Figure 2-36, it is not possible to develop the submodules to the module, Edit Estimated Hours, until the Edit Input Record and Edit Estimated Hours modules have been developed. Therefore, even if a single "leg" is followed all the way down (for example, the modules are developed in this sequence — Load Program Master File, Obtain Valid Input Record, Edit Input Record, Edit Estimated Hours, Check Hour Reasonableness, Check Code Hours), it still is necessary to evaluate those tasks which are necessary to accomplish a given function before being able to further design the program. Thus, the "top-down" approach to designing the program ensures that all functions within the program will be identified in the proper sequence and manner.

After the design of the program structure is complete, it is many times necessary and advisable to have a structured walkthrough to ensure that the design is a good design from a maintenance standpoint, and that all functions have been accounted for in the design. The programmer would then begin to develop the logic for each of the modules in the structure of the program.

PROGRAM DESIGN — PSEUDOCODE SPECIFICATIONS

After the structure of the program has been determined, it is necessary to develop the logic for each of the modules within the program. This logic is developed by using Pseudocode. The Pseudocode Specifications for the top-level module whose function is to load the program master file is illustrated below.

Pseudocode Specifications — Load Program Master FIle

PSEUDOCODE SPECIFICATIONS		
PROGRAM: Load Program Master File	PROGRAMMER: Shelly/Cashman	DATE: May 9
MODULE NAME: Load Program Master File	REF: AØØØ	MODULE FUNCTION: Load the Program Master File

PSEUDOCODE	REF:	FILES, RECORDS, FIELDS REQUIRED
Open the files		Program transaction file
Obtain a valid input record	BØØØ	Program master file
PERFORM UNTIL there are no more records		Exception report file
Write master file	BØ1Ø	No more records indicator
Obtain a valid input record	BØØØ	
ENDPERFORM		
Close the files		
Stop run		

Figure 2-37 Pseudocode Specifications for Load Program Master File Module

In the Pseudocode Specifications above, the files (Program Transaction File, Program Master File, and Exception Report File) are opened. A valid input record is then obtained. Note that this processing is to be done by the module with the reference number B000. A loop is then entered which will continue until there are no more records. In this loop, the master file is to be written by module B010 and then another valid input record is to be obtained. When this loop is terminated because there are no more input records, the files are closed and the program is terminated.

Pseudocode Specifications — Obtain Valid Input Record

The next module whose logic must be determined is the module whose function is to obtain a valid input record. The pseudocode for this module is illustrated in Figure 2-38.

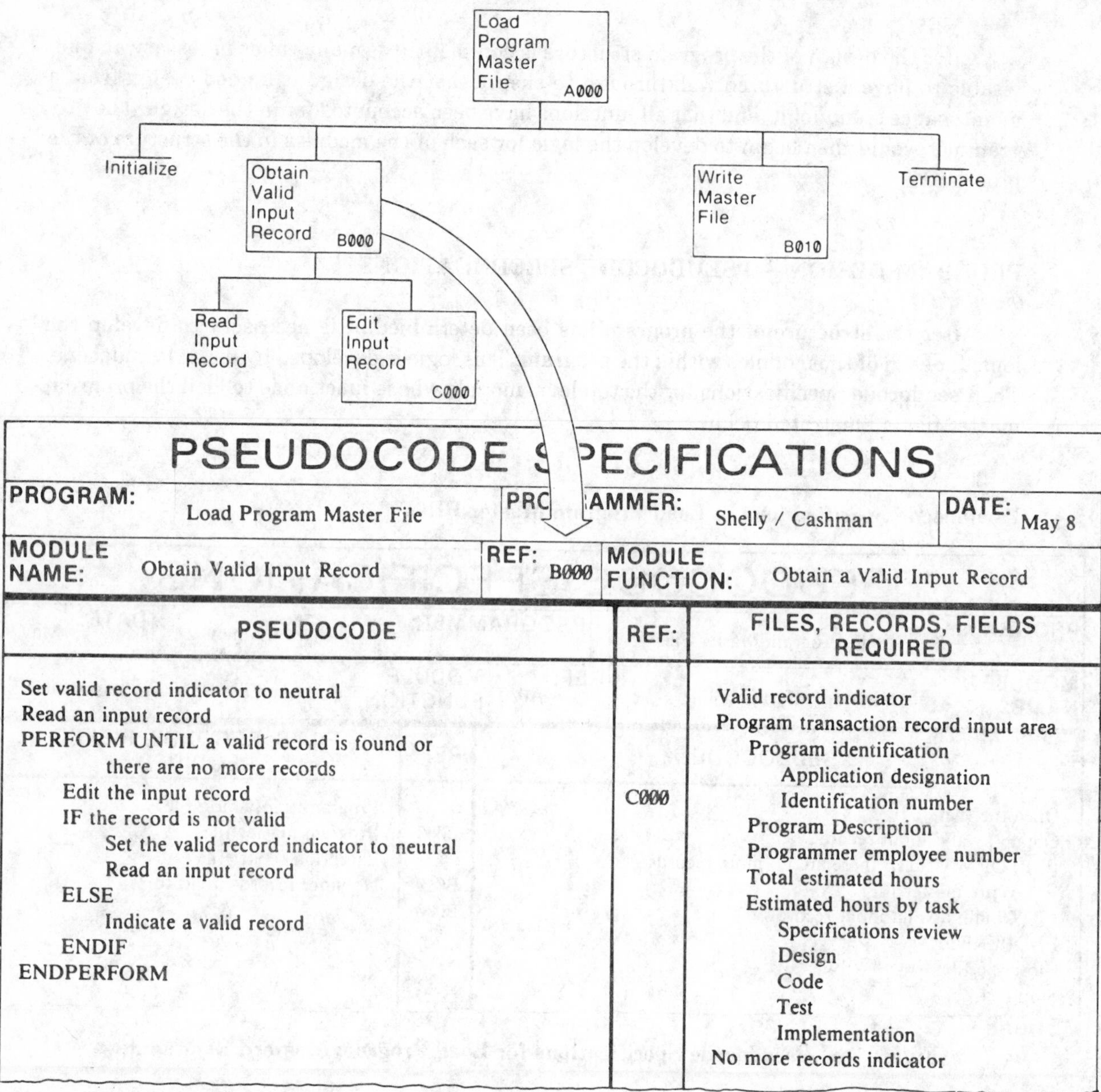

Figure 2-38 Pseudocode for Obtain Valid Input Record Module

The first operation which must be executed upon entry to the module whose function is to obtain a valid input record is the setting of a valid record indicator to a "neutral" status. This means that an indicator should be set so that neither a valid record nor an invalid record is indicated by the indicator. In many instances where indicators are used in a module within a program, it is necessary to set the indicator to a certain status before the processing within the module begins. One of the most frequent errors which occurs when writing programs is that indicators are set to a given value and then are not reset prior to the next time they are tested; this results in processing being performed which should not be. Therefore, it is very important when designing the logic for a module to, at the outset, determine if any of the indicators which will be used within the module should be initialized to a certain value before processing begins. The valid record indicator must be set to a neutral status because it will be tested for both a valid record and an invalid record within the module. Thus, it must have a neutral status prior to beginning the processing within the module.

An input record is then read and a loop is entered, as indicated by the PERFORM UNTIL Statement. Processing in the loop will continue until either a valid record is found or there are no more input records. Note that there are two conditions, either of which may cause the processing in the loop to be terminated. Upon entry to the loop, the first processing which takes place is the editing of the input record. The processing associated with Editing the Input Record will be contained in a separate module, as indicated by the entry C000 in the REF. column. As the input record is being edited, if any field does not pass the edit, that is, if the field contains invalid data, an indicator will be set which specifies an invalid record has been found. After all of the fields in the input record have been checked, control returns to the statement following the pseudocode statement "Edit the input record." At this point, a test is made to determine if the record is valid or not valid. If the record is not valid, the valid record indicator is again set to a neutral status and another input record is read. Control will then be passed back to the Perform Until Statement where the conditions for the loop processing will again be checked. If a valid record was not found, and there are more input records, then the loop will be executed again, with the record just read being edited.

If a valid record was found, then the valid record indicator is set to indicate a valid record was found. Control is then passed back to the Perform Until Statement, where the condition for a valid record is satisfied. Therefore, the loop will be terminated, and control will pass back to the higher-level module which called this module. Upon return to module A000 (see Figure 2-37), the module to write the master file will be executed.

Pseudocode Specifications — Write Master File

The next module for which the logic must be designed is the module whose function is to write the master file. The pseudocode for this module is illustrated below.

PSEUDOCODE SPECIFICATIONS

PROGRAM: Load Program Master File	PROGRAMMER: Shelly/Cashman	DATE: May 9
MODULE NAME: Write Master File	REF: BØ1Ø	MODULE FUNCTION: Write the Program Master File

PSEUDOCODE	REF:	FILES, RECORDS, FIELDS REQUIRED

Move program identification to output area
Move description to output area
Move employee number to output area
Move specs review, design, coding, testing, and
    implementation estimated hours to output area
Set specs review, design, coding, testing, and
    implementation actual hours to zero
Set status fields for all tasks to blank
Write the master record
		Program identification
		Description
		Employee number
		Estimated hours
		Master output area
		    Program identification
		    Program description
		    Programmer employee number
		    Estimated hours
		    Actual hours
		    Completion code

Figure 2-39 Pseudocode for Write Master File Module

As can be seen from Figure 2-39, the processing in the module which writes the master file consists of formatting the master record by moving the fields from the transaction record to the master record, setting the actual hours to zero, setting the status code fields to blanks, and writing the master record.

Pseudocode Specifications — Edit Input Record

The pseudocode for the module which edits the input record is illustrated in Figure 2-40.

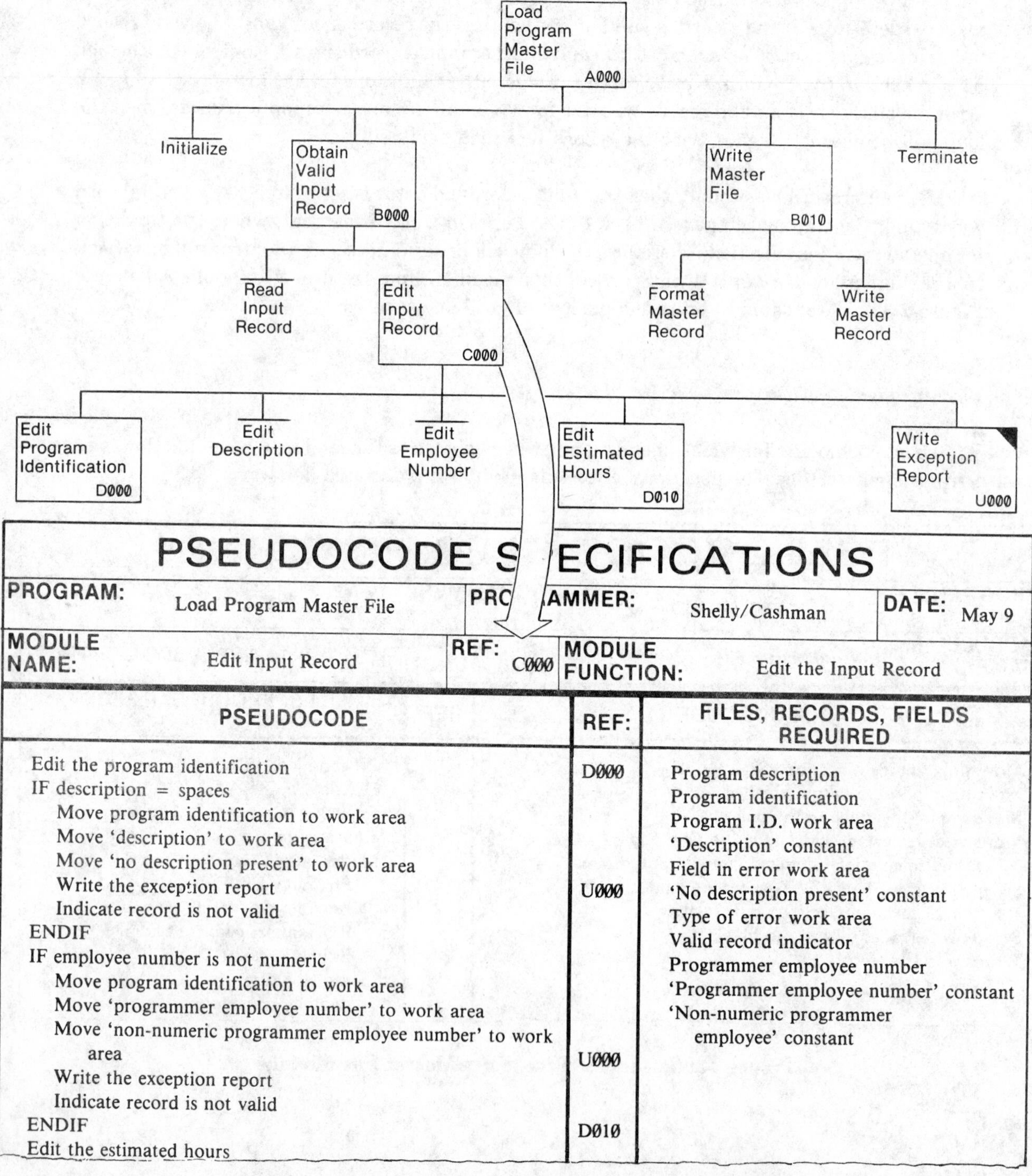

PSEUDOCODE SPECIFICATIONS

PROGRAM: Load Program Master File	PROGRAMMER: Shelly/Cashman	DATE: May 9
MODULE NAME: Edit Input Record	REF: C000	MODULE FUNCTION: Edit the Input Record

PSEUDOCODE	REF:	FILES, RECORDS, FIELDS REQUIRED
Edit the program identification	D000	Program description
IF description = spaces		Program identification
Move program identification to work area		Program I.D. work area
Move 'description' to work area		'Description' constant
Move 'no description present' to work area		Field in error work area
Write the exception report	U000	'No description present' constant
Indicate record is not valid		Type of error work area
ENDIF		Valid record indicator
IF employee number is not numeric		Programmer employee number
Move program identification to work area		'Programmer employee number' constant
Move 'programmer employee number' to work area		'Non-numeric programmer employee' constant
Move 'non-numeric programmer employee number' to work area		
Write the exception report	U000	
Indicate record is not valid		
ENDIF		
Edit the estimated hours	D010	

Figure 2-40 Pseudocode for Edit Input Record Module

In the pseudocode illustrated in Figure 2-40, it can be seen that the first step is to edit the Program Identification. This is performed by the module with the reference number D000. The editing in this module is discussed later in this chapter. The Description field is then checked for spaces. It will be recalled that the editing to be performed on the Description field is to determine if it contains data. If it contains data, it is considered valid. If it does not contain data, that is, if it is blank, then it is in error. Therefore, if the Description field is equal to spaces, it is in error; a message should be written on the Exception Report, and an indicator should be set to show that the record is invalid (see Figure 2-9 for an illustration of the Exception Report).

As can be seen from Figure 2-40, if the Description is equal to spaces, the Program Identification, the constant "description," and the constant "no description present" are moved to work areas. The Exception Report is then written by module U000, and the indicator is set to indicate that the record is not valid. It is important to note that the values which are to appear on the Exception Report are moved to special work areas rather than directly to the printer output area. These work areas are then referenced in the module which writes the Exception Report in order to format the detail line. The reason this is done is that, as will be recalled, one of the tasks which must be accomplished by the Exception Report is to format the detail line (see Figure 2-29). The formatting of the detail line should not be done in any of the modules involved with editing the input record. In order to format the detail line in the Write Exception Report module, the module must have available to it the Program Identification, the name of the field in error, and the type of error. Since the Exception Report module is a utility module and will be entered from more than one module within the program, there is no practical way the Exception Report module can know which module has called it, and what the error and field in error are unless it receives this data through the special work areas. Thus, the module which calls the Exception Report module must place the information required for formatting the report detail line in the work areas; and the Exception Report module can then reference the work areas in order to format the line.

A second reason for using work areas has to do with good program design and the concept of coupling. It will be recalled from Chapter 1 that common coupling is where data is stored in a "common" region, and that data is available to any of the modules within the program. As noted in Chapter 1, it is advisable to keep this common coupling to a minimum so that each of the modules within a program is as independent as possible. One of the ways to do this is to pass data which is required for a module in work areas, and then design the called module to reference only that data which is passed to it in the work areas. The Exception Report module needs the Program Identification, the name of the field in error, and the type of error so that it can format the report line. By designing the module which writes the Exception Report to reference the Program Identification, name of the field in error, and the type of error in only the work areas, coupling is reduced since the module is not referencing data fields used by other modules.

This same reasoning explains why the data required for the report line is not moved directly to the report output area from the various modules within the program. If there were to be a change to the report format, then many modules would be affected. By placing the data in work areas and passing it to the Exception Report module, any changes to the report format would only affect one module.

After the Description field is edited, the Employee Number field is checked for numeric data. It will be recalled that this field must contain numeric data, or it is in error. If the Employee Number is not numeric, then the Program Identification and the error messages are moved to the work areas; and a line is printed on the Exception Report. An invalid record is also indicated.

The last step illustrated in Figure 2-40 is to Edit the Estimated Hours. This is accomplished by the D010 module, as indicated by the D010 entry in the REF column.

Upon completion of this module, control will be returned to the module which called it, the B000-OBTAIN-VALID-INPUT-RECORD module. If an invalid record has been indicated by any of the editing modules, then another input record will be read (see Figure 2-38). If the record is valid, then it will be written on the master file.

Pseudocode Specifications — Edit Program I.D.

The next module for which logic should be developed is the module whose function is to edit the Program Identification. This editing consists of verifying a valid Application Designation and ensuring the Identification Number is numeric. The pseudocode for this module is contained in Figure 2-41.

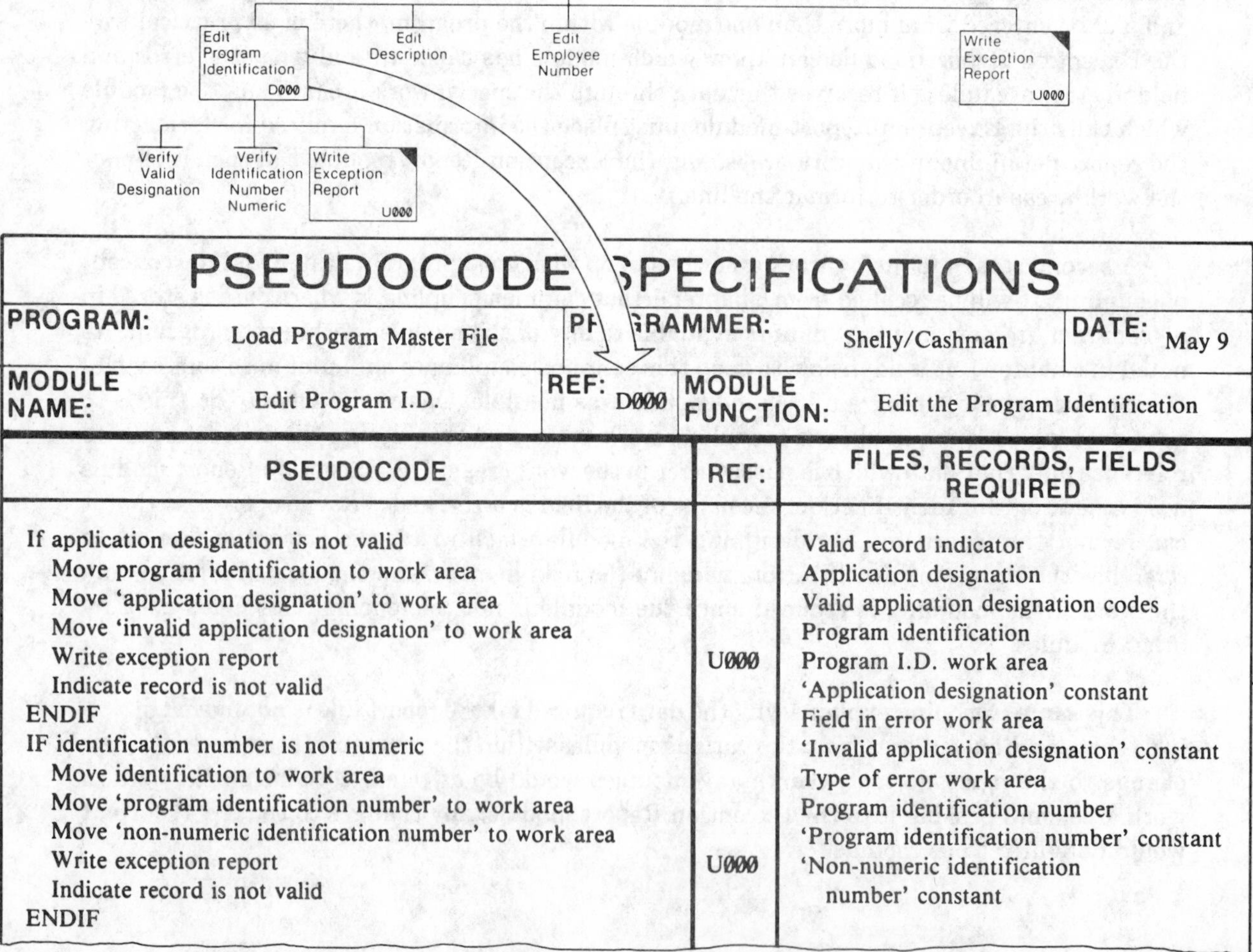

PSEUDOCODE SPECIFICATIONS

PROGRAM:	Load Program Master File	PROGRAMMER:	Shelly/Cashman	DATE:	May 9
MODULE NAME:	Edit Program I.D.	REF: D000	MODULE FUNCTION:	Edit the Program Identification	

PSEUDOCODE	REF:	FILES, RECORDS, FIELDS REQUIRED
If application designation is not valid		Valid record indicator
Move program identification to work area		Application designation
Move 'application designation' to work area		Valid application designation codes
Move 'invalid application designation' to work area		Program identification
Write exception report	U000	Program I.D. work area
Indicate record is not valid		'Application designation' constant
ENDIF		Field in error work area
IF identification number is not numeric		'Invalid application designation' constant
Move identification to work area		Type of error work area
Move 'program identification number' to work area		Program identification number
Move 'non-numeric identification number' to work area		'Program identification number' constant
Write exception report	U000	'Non-numeric identification
Indicate record is not valid		number' constant
ENDIF		

Figure 2-41 Pseudocode for Edit Program Identification Module

Note from Figure 2-41 that if the Application Designation is not valid, the Program Identification and error messages are moved to the work area, the Exception Report is written, and it is indicated that the record is invalid. Similarly, if the Identification Number is not numeric, the same error processing takes place. The checking of these two fields constitutes the editing of the Program Identification.

Pseudocode Specifications — Edit Estimated Hours

The next task is to develop the pseudocode for the module which edits the Individual and Total Estimated Hours fields. It should be recalled that in this module the Individual and Total Estimated Hours are verified numeric, the total of the Individual Estimated Hours is compared to the Total Estimated Hours field in the input record, and the reasonableness of the Individual Estimated Hours is checked (see Figure 2-7). The pseudocode for this module is shown below.

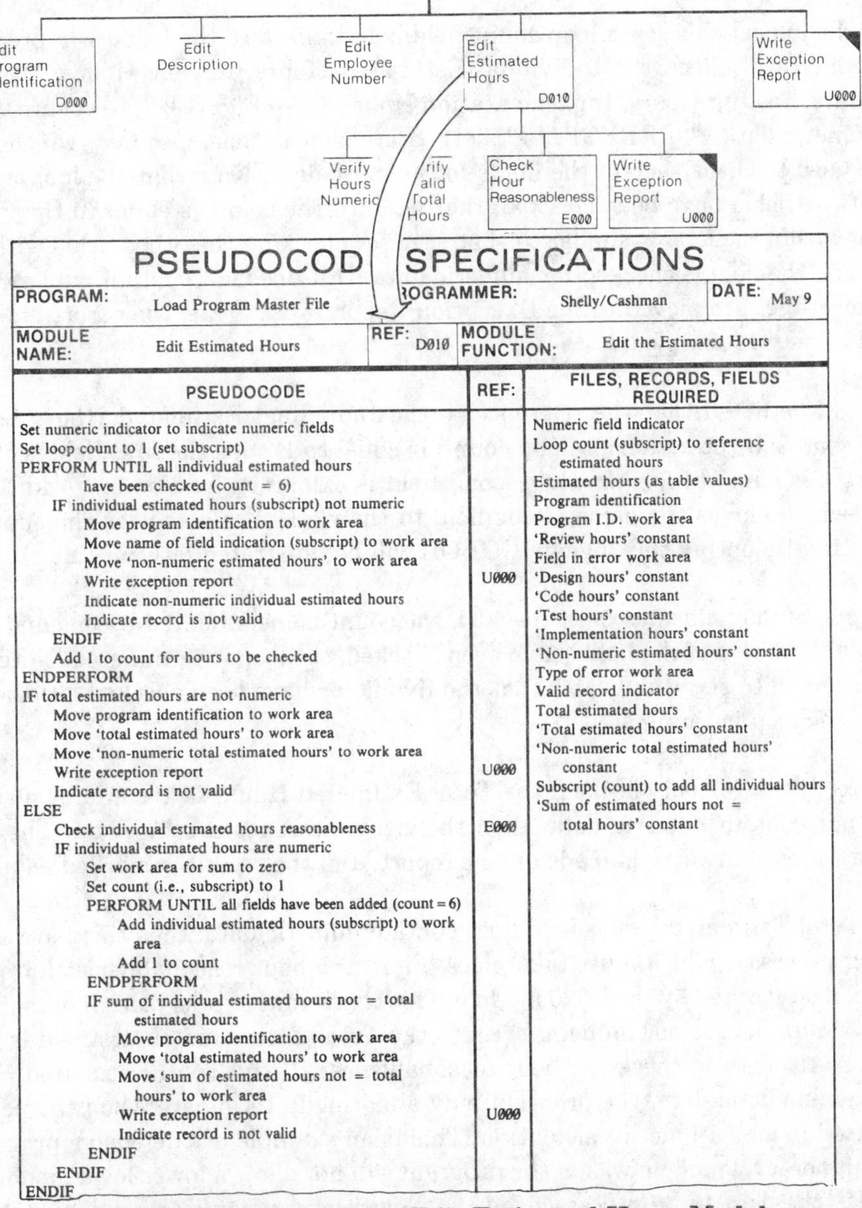

PSEUDOCOD SPECIFICATIONS

PROGRAM: Load Program Master File	ROGRAMMER: Shelly/Cashman	DATE: May 9
MODULE NAME: Edit Estimated Hours	REF: D010	MODULE FUNCTION: Edit the Estimated Hours

PSEUDOCODE	REF:	FILES, RECORDS, FIELDS REQUIRED
Set numeric indicator to indicate numeric fields		Numeric field indicator
Set loop count to 1 (set subscript)		Loop count (subscript) to reference estimated hours
PERFORM UNTIL all individual estimated hours have been checked (count = 6)		Estimated hours (as table values)
IF individual estimated hours (subscript) not numeric		Program identification
Move program identification to work area		Program I.D. work area
Move name of field indication (subscript) to work area		'Review hours' constant
Move 'non-numeric estimated hours' to work area		Field in error work area
Write exception report	U000	'Design hours' constant
Indicate non-numeric individual estimated hours		'Code hours' constant
Indicate record is not valid		'Test hours' constant
ENDIF		'Implementation hours' constant
Add 1 to count for hours to be checked		'Non-numeric estimated hours' constant
ENDPERFORM		Type of error work area
IF total estimated hours are not numeric		Valid record indicator
Move program identification to work area		Total estimated hours
Move 'total estimated hours' to work area		'Total estimated hours' constant
Move 'non-numeric total estimated hours' to work area		'Non-numeric total estimated hours' constant
Write exception report	U000	
Indicate record is not valid		Subscript (count) to add all individual hours
ELSE		'Sum of estimated hours not = total hours' constant
Check individual estimated hours reasonableness	E000	
IF individual estimated hours are numeric		
Set work area for sum to zero		
Set count (i.e., subscript) to 1		
PERFORM UNTIL all fields have been added (count = 6)		
Add individual estimated hours (subscript) to work area		
Add 1 to count		
ENDPERFORM		
IF sum of individual estimated hours not = total estimated hours		
Move program identification to work area		
Move 'total estimated hours' to work area		
Move 'sum of estimated hours not = total hours' to work area		
Write exception report	U000	
Indicate record is not valid		
ENDIF		
ENDIF		
ENDIF		

Figure 2-42 Pseudocode for Edit Estimated Hours Module

The first step in the logic for the Edit Estimated Hours module is to set an indicator to indicate that there is valid numeric data in the Individual Estimated Hours fields. When this module is entered, it must be "assumed" that all fields contain valid numeric data. This is specified by the setting of the indicator. As will be recalled, it is sometimes necessary to set an indicator to a particular value prior to beginning the processing within a module; such is the case here. It should be noted that in some instances it is not possible to know, at the start of the design of the logic of a module, that a particular indicator must be set to a given value. Therefore, it is possible that only after some or all of the logic for a module has been designed will the programmer know which indicators must be initialized at the beginning of the module. There is nothing wrong with this, provided the programmer returns to the start of the logic of the module and specifies that the indicator must be set to the value. As has been noted previously, program design is an iterative process wherein it is likely that several "passes" through the program design will be required before the design is correct. It is important to realize, however, that all of these changes and modifications to make the program correct should take place during the design phase of the program, not in the coding phase.

After the indicator is set, a loop count field is initialized to the value 1 in preparation for the loop which will check the Individual Estimated Hours (Review Hours, Design Hours, Coding Hours, Testing Hours, Implementation Hours — see Figure 2-7) to ensure that they all contain numeric data. A PERFORM UNTIL Statement is then specified, which defines the loop to be used to check each of the fields for numeric data. Note that the loop will continue until all of the fields have been checked; that is, until the count is equal to the value 6. The processing within the loop is similar to that seen for checking the other fields within the program; that is, the field is checked for numeric data. If it does not contain numeric data, then the error messages are moved to the Exception Report work areas, the report is written, and the record is marked as invalid.

It should be noted that the reference to the Individual Estimated Hours fields uses a subscript; that is, if the subscript (loop count) is equal to 1, then the first field is examined; if the subscript is equal to 2, then the second field is examined; and so on. Additionally, the statement which moves the name of the field to the work area also uses the subscript. The method for implementing this logic in COBOL will be illustrated later in this chapter.

After one of the fields has been checked, the count is incremented by one and the loop is repeated. After all five of the fields have been checked, the loop is terminated. Note that when the count is equal to six, it indicates that the five fields have been checked. As there is not a sixth field, the loop is terminated.

The next IF Statement checks if the Total Estimated Hours field contains numeric data. If it does not contain numeric data, then the error messages are moved to the Exception Report work areas, an entry is made on the report, and the record is marked as invalid.

If the Total Estimated Hours field does contain numeric data, then there are several further editing processes which must take place. First, the hour reasonableness for each of the five fields can be checked by the E000 module. This check cannot take place if data in the Total Estimated Hours field is not numeric because the Total Estimated Hours field is utilized in arithmetic statements to check the hour reasonableness. If the Total Estimated Hours field contained non-numeric data, the program may abnormally terminate when the non-numeric data was used in an arithmetic calculation. This is an example of "defensive programming" wherein a higher-level module within the program will not allow a lower-level module to be invoked unless the data to be processed by that lower-level module is valid data and should always be done.

After the reasonableness of each of the five fields has been checked, control returns to this module. If the Individual Estimated Hours fields contain numeric data (this was determined previously within this same module), then the values in the Individual Estimated Hours fields must be added together to determine if their sum is equal to the Total Estimated Hours in the transaction input record. Again, this check cannot take place if the Individual Estimated Hours fields contain non-numeric data because adding non-numeric data will cause abnormal program termination on many systems and, in any event, will not yield proper results. This is another example of defensive programming which should always be practiced when designing the structure and logic of a program.

Provided the Individual Estimated Hours fields contain numeric data, a work area to contain the sum of the fields is set to zero, a count or subscript field is set to the value 1, and a loop is invoked which will add the Individual Estimated Hours fields to the work area. Note that this loop will continue until all of the fields have been added to the work area.

After the sum has been obtained, this sum in the work area is compared to the Total Estimated Hours in the transaction record. If they are not equal, it indicates there is an error in the record. Therefore, the error fields are moved to the work areas, the Exception Report is written, and the indicator is set to show an invalid input record.

Pseudocode Specifications — Write Exception Report

The next module to be examined is the module which writes the Exception Report. Closely associated with that module is the module which writes the headings on the report. The pseudocode for these two modules is illustrated in Figure 2-43.

PSEUDOCODE SPECIFICATIONS

PROGRAM: Load Program Master File	PROGRAMMER: Shelly/Cashman	DATE: May 9
MODULE NAME: Write Exception Report	REF: UØØØ	MODULE FUNCTION: Write the Exception Report

PSEUDOCODE	REF:	FILES, RECORDS, FIELDS REQUIRED

IF first page or lines printed ≧ page size
  Print the headings
  Clear the report area
  Move identification number to report area
ENDIF
IF current program identification is not = previous
    program identification
  Move current identification to report area
  Move current identification to compare area
  Set spacing for double spacing
ENDIF
Move name of field in error to report area
Move type of error to report area
Write report line
Add spacing to line count
Set spacing for single spacing
Clear the report area
	
	UØ1Ø
		First page indicator
		Number of lines printed counter
		Page size constant (40)
		Detail line output area
		  Program identification
		  Field in error
		  Type of error
		Identification number work area
		Previous identification number (compare area)
		Spacing control area
		Double spacing constant
		Field in error work area
		Type of error work area
		Single spacing constant

PSEUDOCODE SPECIFICATIONS

PROGRAM: Load Program Master File	PROGRAMMER: Shelly/Cashman	DATE: May 9
MODULE NAME: Print Headings	REF: UØ1Ø	MODULE FUNCTION: Print the Exception Report Headings

PSEUDOCODE	REF:	FILES, RECORDS, FIELDS REQUIRED
Move the current date to the first heading line Move the page number to the first heading line Write the first heading line Add 1 to the page number count Write the second heading line Write the third heading line Set the lines printed counter to zero Set spacing for double spacing		Current date First heading line Page number count Second heading line Third heading line Number of lines printed counter Spacing control area Double spacing constant

Figure 2-43 Pseudocode for Exception Report and Headings Modules

From the pseudocode for the Exception Report module in Figure 2-43, it can be seen that the first test in the module is to determine if headings should be printed on the report. If it is the first page on the report or if the number of lines printed on the report are equal to or greater than the number of lines to be printed on the page (page size), then the headings are printed on the report. Note that they will be printed by the module with the reference number U010. After the headings are printed, the report area will be cleared ; and the Identification Number for the record in error will be moved to the detail line. This is done so that the first line on any new page will contain the Program Identification number of the record in error, and is normally done when a report is group-indicated.

The next IF Statement determines if the current Program Identification, that is, the Program Identification of the record which is to be printed on the Exception Report, is equal to the Program Identification of the previous record which was printed on the report. When processing the first record, the previous Program Identification will contain low-values; therefore, the Program Identification will not be equal to the previous Program Identification. If they are equal, then the record being processed has more than one error in it. Since the report is group indicated, the Program Identification should be printed only for the first error in a record; and the Program Identification should not be moved to the detail line. If they are not equal, it indicates that this is the first error for the record being processed; therefore, the current Program Identification is moved to detail line. In addition, the current identification is moved to the compare area, so that it can be compared to the next record which will be processed. The spacing is then set for double spacing so that the first line for a new record will be double spaced.

The name of the field in error and the type of error are then moved to the report area. It will be recalled that the name of the field in error and the type of error will be contained in a work area passed by the module which calls the Exception Report module. The record is then written on the report, the line count is incremented, spacing is set for single spacing, and the report area is set to blanks.

In the module which prints the headings on the report, the Current Date and Page Number are moved to the first heading line and the line is printed. The Page Number is then incremented by one, the second and third lines are printed, the line counter is reset to zero, and the spacing is set for double spacing.

Pseudocode Specifications — Check Hour Reasonableness

The next module for which the logic must be developed is the module whose function is to check the reasonableness of the values in the Individual Estimated Hours fields. The pseudocode for this module is illustrated in Figure 2-44.

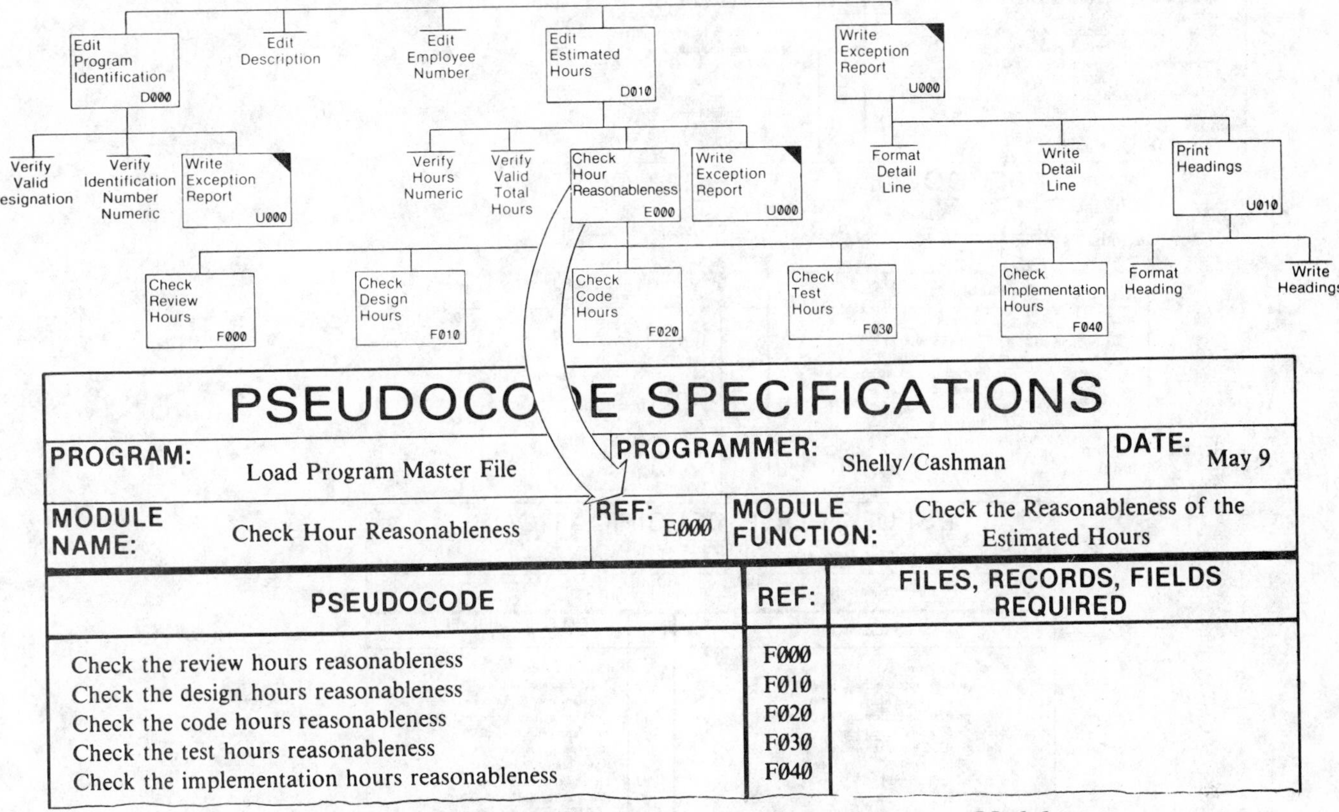

PSEUDOCODE SPECIFICATIONS

PROGRAM: Load Program Master File	PROGRAMMER: Shelly/Cashman	DATE: May 9
MODULE NAME: Check Hour Reasonableness	REF: E000	MODULE FUNCTION: Check the Reasonableness of the Estimated Hours

PSEUDOCODE	REF:	FILES, RECORDS, FIELDS REQUIRED
Check the review hours reasonableness	F000	
Check the design hours reasonableness	F010	
Check the code hours reasonableness	F020	
Check the test hours reasonableness	F030	
Check the implementation hours reasonableness	F040	

Figure 2-44 Pseudocode for Check Hour Reasonableness Module

The logic for the module which checks the reasonableness of the Individual Estimated Hours fields consists of merely calling each of the separate modules which check each of the fields for reasonable values. Thus, there is very little processing required in the module illustrated in Figure 2-44.

It may, therefore, be asked whether the processing in the module in Figure 2-44 should be incorporated back into the module which calls it; that is, should the processing in the E000 module be incorporated into the D010 module which calls it. In this case, the answer is no for several reasons. First, checking the Individual Estimated Hour reasonableness is a specific function which must be performed within the program; thus, the module is a functionally cohesive module. Second, as has been noted previously, there is the possibility that at some future time the processing which must be done to check the Individual Estimated Hour reasonableness could be changed. Since this is the case, and since the module above is functionally cohesive, it makes better sense in terms of the program design to leave the module above as is. Any future modifications which may be required will be easier to make with the above processing in a separate module than if it were incorporated back into the module which calls it.

As can be seen from Figure 2-44, the last modules for which the logic must be developed are the modules which check each of the Estimated Hours fields. The pseudocode for these modules is illustrated in Figure 2-45.

PSEUDOCODE SPECIFICATIONS

PROGRAM: Load Program Master File	PROGRAMMER: Shelly/Cashman	DATE: May 9
MODULE NAME: Check Review Hours	REF: F000	MODULE FUNCTION: Check the Reasonableness of the Review Hours

PSEUDOCODE	REF:	FILES, RECORDS, FIELDS REQUIRED

IF review hours is numeric
  IF review hours > (total hours × 20%) or
        < (total hours × 5%)
    Move program identification to work area
    Move 'review hours' to work area
    Move 'violates reasonableness check-
        warning only' to work area
    Write exception report
  ENDIF
ENDIF
	
	U000
		Estimated review hours
		Total Estimated hours
		Constant max % for review (20%)
		Constant min % for review (5%)
		Program identification
		Program I.D. work area
		'Review hours' constant
		Field in error work area
		'Violates reasonableness check-
		warning only' constant
		Type of error work area

PSEUDOCODE SPECIFICATIONS

PROGRAM: Load Program Master File	PROGRAMMER: Shelly/Cashman	DATE: May 9
MODULE NAME: Check Design Hours	REF: F010	MODULE FUNCTION: Check Reasonableness of the Design Hours

PSEUDOCODE	REF:	FILES, RECORDS, FIELDS REQUIRED

IF design hours is numeric
  IF design hours > (total hours × 60%) or
        < (total hours × 30%)
    Move program identification to work area
    Move 'design hours' to work area
    Move 'violates reasonableness check-
        warning only' to work area
    Write exception report
  ENDIF
ENDIF
	
	U000
		Estimated design hours
		Total estimated hours
		Constant max % for design (60%)
		Constant min % for design (30%)
		Program identification
		Program I.D. work area
		'Design hours' constant
		Field in error work area
		'Violates reasonableness check-
		warning only' constant
		Type of error work area

PSEUDOCODE SPECIFICATIONS

PROGRAM: Load Program Master File	PROGRAMMER: Shelly/Cashman	DATE: May 12
MODULE NAME: Check Code Hours	REF: F020	MODULE FUNCTION: Check the Reasonableness of the Code Hours

PSEUDOCODE	REF:	FILES, RECORDS, FIELDS REQUIRED

IF code hours is numeric
  IF code hours > (total hours × 50%) or
        < (total hours × 10%)
    Move program identification to work area
    Move 'code hours' to work area
    Move 'violates reasonableness check-
        warning only' to work area
    Write exception report
  ENDIF
ENDIF
	
	U000
		Estimated code hours
		Total estimated hours
		Constant max % for code (50%)
		Constant min % for code (10%)
		Program identification
		Program I.D. work area
		'Code hours' constant
		Field in error work area
		'Violates reasonableness check-
		warning only' constant
		Type of error work area

PSEUDOCODE SPECIFICATIONS

PROGRAM: Load Program Master File	PROGRAMMER: Shelly/Cashman	DATE: May 12
MODULE NAME: Check Test Hours	REF: F030	MODULE FUNCTION: Check the Reasonableness of the Test Hours

PSEUDOCODE	REF:	FILES, RECORDS, FIELDS REQUIRED

IF test hours is numeric
  IF test hours > (total hours × 30%) or
        < (total hours × 5%)
    Move program identification to work area
    Move 'test hours' to work area
    Move 'violates reasonableness check-
        warning only' to work area
    Write exception report
  ENDIF
ENDIF
	
	U000
		Estimated test hours
		Total estimated hours
		Constant max % for test (30%)
		Constant min % for test (5%)
		Program identification
		Program I.D. work area
		'Test hours' constant
		Field in error work area
		'Violates reasonableness check-
		warning only' constant
		Type of error work area

PSEUDOCODE SPECIFICATIONS

PROGRAM: Load Program Master File	PROGRAMMER: Shelly/Cashman	DATE: May 12
MODULE NAME: Check Implem Hours	REF: F040	MODULE FUNCTION: Check the Reasonableness of the Implementation Hours

PSEUDOCODE	REF:	FILES, RECORDS, FIELDS REQUIRED

IF implementation hours is numeric
  IF implementation hours > (total hours × 20%) or
        < (total hours × 0%)
    Move program identification to work area
    Move 'implementation hours' to work area
    Move 'violates reasonableness check-
        warning only' to work area
    Write exception report
  ENDIF
ENDIF
	
	U000
		Estimated implementation hours
		Total estimated hours
		Constant max % for implementation (20%)
		Constant min % for implementation (0%)
		Program identification
		Program I.D. work area
		'Implementation hours' constant
		Field in error work area
		'Violates reasonableness check-
		warning only' constant
		Type of error work area

Figure 2-45 Pseudocode for Checking Reasonableness of Individual Hours

From Figure 2-45, it can be seen that the logic for each of the modules is basically the same. The first test is to determine if the field being checked contains numeric data. If it does not, then no further check will be performed on the field. The reason no further check is performed is that a numeric comparison is to be done on the data in the field; that is, the value in the field is to be compared to a numeric value calculated in the If Statement. If the data in the field to be checked is not numeric, then a numeric comparison will likely cause the program to be abnormally terminated, since a valid sign is required for a numeric comparison. Again, "defensive programming," that is, ensuring that the processing within a program will be performed properly, is very necessary in developing reliable programs. Whenever arithmetic operations, report editing, or numeric comparisons are to be performed on a field, the data in that field must be numeric.

As was illustrated previously in Figure 2-16, an arithmetic expression is used in the If Statement which determines if the value in the field falls within the range of reasonable values. If it does not, then the error messages are moved to the work areas for the Exception Report, and the Exception Report is printed. If the values do fall within the range of reasonable values, then no further processing takes place.

It should be noted that there are no instructions to indicate that an invalid record has been read. This is because the programming specifications required only that a warning message be printed on the Exception Report if reasonable values were not contained within these fields. The record is still to be written on the Program Master File.

Summary of Pseudocode

As can be seen from the previous examples, the development of the logic for each of the modules within the program took place in a top-to-bottom, left-to-right sequence. As with the development of the structure of the program, this sequence may vary depending upon the requirements of the program. For example, it may be determined that it is more critical that the logic for the input editing be designed before the logic required for the Exception Report or writing the master file. Therefore, the logic for the modules on the sixth level of the structure (reference numbers F000-F040) may be developed before the logic for writing the master file. With rare exceptions, however, the logic for a module should not be developed until the logic for the module which calls it has been developed. Thus, the logic for module F020 should not be developed until the logic for module E000, which calls it, has been developed.

After the logic for the modules within the program has been developed, each of the modules should be subjected to a structured walkthrough so that the logic can be reviewed. If errors are found in any of the logic by the team of reviewers, they should be corrected prior to beginning the coding of the program.

PROGRAM CODING

Once the design of the program is completed, the programmer should begin coding the program. The following pages contain an explanation of the methods and techniques which are required to code the COBOL program.

Definition of Sequential Disk Output File

As with card and printer files, the Program Master File, which is to be stored as a sequential disk file, must be defined in the Environment Division and Data Division of the COBOL program. The following example illustrates the entries used in the sample program.

EXAMPLE

Environment Division

```
           SELECT PROGRAM-MASTER-OUTPUT-FILE
               ASSIGN TO DA-S-PGMMSTR.
```

Data Division

```
       FD  PROGRAM-MASTER-OUTPUT-FILE
             BLOCK CONTAINS 20 RECORDS
             RECORD CONTAINS 77 CHARACTERS
             LABEL RECORDS ARE STANDARD
             DATA RECORD IS PROGRAM-MASTER-OUTPUT-RECORD.

       01  PROGRAM-MASTER-OUTPUT-RECORD.
           05  PROGRAM-IDENTIFICATION-MSTROUT.
               10  APPL-DESIGNATION-MSTROUT                 PIC XX.
               10  IDENTIFICATION-NUMBER-MSTROUT            PIC X(4).
           05  PROGRAM-DESCRIPTION-MSTROUT                  PIC X(20).
           05  PROGRAMMER-EMPL-NUMBER-MSTROUT               PIC X(6).
           05  ESTIMATED-TASK-HOURS-MSTROUT.
               10  ESTIMATED-REVIEW-HOURS-MSTROUT           PIC 9(4).
               10  ESTIMATED-DESIGN-HOURS-MSTROUT           PIC 9(4).
               10  ESTIMATED-CODE-HOURS-MSTROUT             PIC 9(4).
               10  ESTIMATED-TEST-HOURS-MSTROUT             PIC 9(4).
               10  ESTIMATED-IMPLEM-HOURS-MSTROUT           PIC 9(4).
           05  ACTUAL-TASK-HOURS-MSTROUT.
               10  ACTUAL-REVIEW-HOURS-MSTROUT              PIC X(4).
               10  ACTUAL-DESIGN-HOURS-MSTROUT              PIC X(4).
               10  ACTUAL-CODE-HOURS-MSTROUT                PIC X(4).
               10  ACTUAL-TEST-HOURS-MSTROUT                PIC X(4).
               10  ACTUAL-IMPLEM-HOURS-MSTROUT              PIC X(4).
           05  TASK-STATUS-INDICATORS-MSTROUT.
               10  REVIEW-STATUS-MSTROUT                    PIC X.
               10  DESIGN-STATUS-MSTROUT                    PIC X.
               10  CODE-STATUS-MSTROUT                      PIC X.
               10  TEST-STATUS-MSTROUT                      PIC X.
               10  IMPLEM-STATUS-MSTROUT                    PIC X.
```

Figure 2-46 Definition of Disk Output File

Note from Figure 2-46 that the Select Statement is used to assign the filename PROGRAM-MASTER-OUTPUT-FILE. The Assign Clause specifies that the file is to be stored on a direct access device (DA), the file is to be organized and processed as a sequential file (S), and the system name is PGMMSTR. The system name is used to identify the file on the job control cards which are necessary to define the file on a direct access device. It should be noted that this Assign Clause is utilized with the System/370 Operating System; different operating systems and compilers may require different entries in the Assign Clause.

The File Definition (FD) statement is used to give the attributes of the file. The BLOCK CONTAINS 20 RECORDS clause specifies that there will be 20 logical records in each physical record or block which is written on the disk. Each logical record will contain 77 characters, as specified by the RECORD CONTAINS 77 CHARACTERS Clause. Any file which is stored on a direct access device must have standard labels associated with it. Therefore, the clause LABEL RECORDS ARE STANDARD must be included. Finally, the name of the data record associated with the master file is PROGRAM-MASTER-OUTPUT-RECORD.

As can be seen, the output record is defined in the same format as was specified at the beginning of the chapter (see Figure 2-3). Each of the data-names selected for the fields is as meaningful as possible within the constraints of a maximum of 30 characters per data-name. Note also that each data-name contains the suffix MSTROUT, which identifies the field as a member of the master output record.

Open Statement

Before any file in a COBOL program can be processed, it must be opened. This is, of course, true for disk output files. The Open Statement from the sample program is illustrated below.

EXAMPLE

```
014090     OPEN INPUT  PROGRAM-TRANSACTION-INPUT-FILE
014100          OUTPUT PROGRAM-MASTER-OUTPUT-FILE
014110                 EXCEPTION-REPORT-FILE.
```

Figure 2-47 Example of OPEN Statement

Note from Figure 2-47 that the Open Statement is specified as has been seen in previous programs. The input file is the PROGRAM-TRANSACTION-INPUT-FILE. There are two output files in this program — the PROGRAM-MASTER-OUTPUT-FILE and the EXCEPTION-REPORT-FILE. Note that if there is more than one file, then the names of the files follow the keyword OUTPUT. All files which are going to be processed within the program must be opened before being read or written.

Writing a Disk Output File

In order to record a record on a disk file, the Write Statement is used. The following example illustrates the Write Statement used in the sample program to write the Program Master File.

EXAMPLE

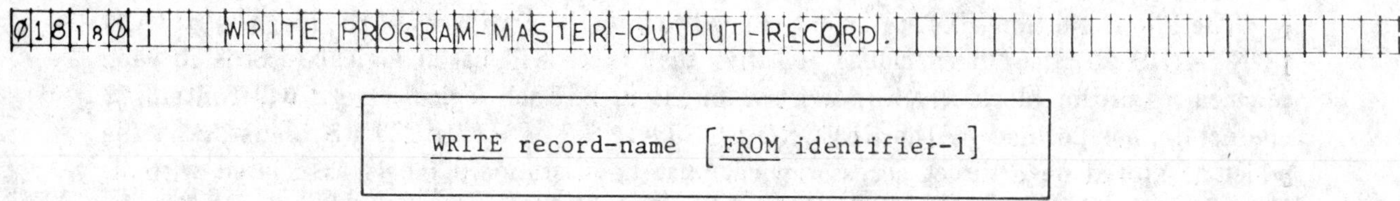

Figure 2-48 Example of Write Statement for Disk Output File

In the example above, it can be seen that the verb WRITE is specified together with the name of the output record (see Figure 2-46). It should also be noted, although not shown in the example, that the optional FROM word can be used to specify an area in Working-Storage from which the data to be written will be taken; this is shown in the format notation in Figure 2-48.

Closing a Disk Output File

A disk output file is closed in the same manner as other files. The statement to close the files in the sample program is illustrated below.

EXAMPLE

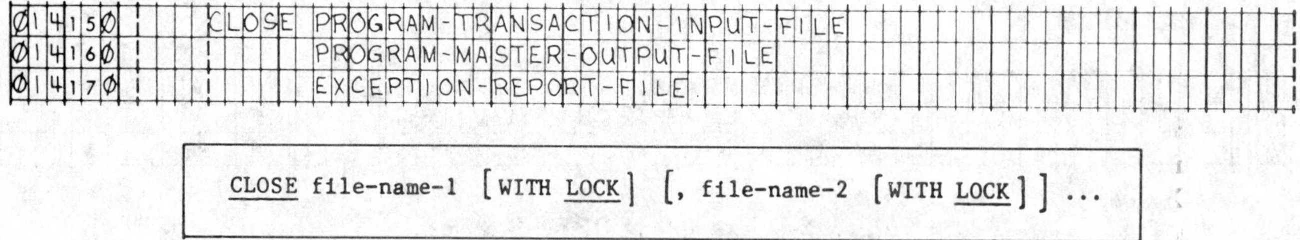

Figure 2-49 Example of Close Statement

As can be seen from Figure 2-49, the Close verb is specified together with the names of the files. When utilizing a direct-access output file, the WITH LOCK option can be used. This option, if specified, will prevent the program from reopening a file which has previously been closed. It is possible, if this option is not used, to open a file after it has been closed. For example, an output file may be closed and reopened as an input file so that it can be read and processed further. If the "WITH LOCK" option is used, the file cannot be reopened after it has been closed.

Multiple Conditions on Perform Statement

As was noted when the pseudocode for the module which obtains a valid input record was explained (see Figure 2-38), it is required that a loop be established which will terminate when one of two conditions occurs. Specifically, an input record will be edited; and then another one will be read until either a valid input record is found or there are no more input records. The Perform Statement to implement this logic is illustrated below.

EXAMPLE

```
Ø1601Ø     PERFORM BØØ2-EDIT-AND-READ
Ø1602Ø             UNTIL A-VALID-RECORD-IS-FOUND OR
Ø1603Ø                   THERE-ARE-NO-MORE-RECORDS.
```

Figure 2-50 Example of Multiple Conditions on Perform Statement

In the example above, the B002-EDIT-AND-READ paragraph will be performed. It will be performed until one of two conditions occurs — when A-VALID-RECORD-IS-FOUND or when THERE-ARE-NO-MORE-RECORDS, the looping will be terminated. Note that these two conditions are specified in the Until Clause of the Perform Statement, together with the OR logical operator. Thus, as can be seen, the OR logical operator and the AND logical operator can be used to specify compound or complex conditions under which a loop implemented by the Perform Statement will be terminated.

Setting Indicators to a Neutral Status

In the discussion of the pseudocode, it was noted that on occasion it is necessary to set an indicator to a neutral status prior to entering a module so that the indicator does not indicate an erroneous condition. When programming in COBOL, the best way to implement this is to move spaces to the indicator, as illustrated in Figure 2-51.

EXAMPLE

Data Division

```
ØØ705Ø     Ø5  IS-THE-RECORD-VALID          PIC XXX   VALUE SPACES.
ØØ706Ø         88  A-VALID-RECORD-IS-FOUND              VALUE 'YES'.
ØØ707Ø         88  THE-RECORD-IS-NOT-VALID              VALUE 'NO '.
```

Procedure Division

```
Ø1517Ø     MOVE SPACES TO IS-THE-RECORD-VALID.
```

Figure 2-51 Example of Setting Indicator

Note in Figure 2-51 that the indicator IS-THE-RECORD-VALID is defined as PIC XXX with the VALUE SPACES. The condition names are specified for when the field contains the value "YES" and value "NO." When the indicator contains spaces, it is in a "neutral status;" that is, it does not indicate that A-VALID-RECORD-IS-FOUND or that THE-RECORD-IS-NOT-VALID. Therefore, in order to set the indicator to a neutral status, the instruction on line 015170 is used to place spaces in the indicator field.

Use of Subscripted Fields

When the Estimated Hours fields are checked for numeric values, it is possible to use subscripts and a loop to check them since they all are of the same size. The definition of the fields to be checked, the corresponding field messages to be placed on the Exception Report, and the routine to check these fields for numeric values are illustrated in the following example.

EXAMPLE

Data Division — Input Record

```
004040        05  ESTIMATED-TASK-HOURS-TRANSIN.
004050            10  ESTIMATED-REVIEW-HOURS-TRANSIN    PIC 9(4).
004060            10  ESTIMATED-DESIGN-HOURS-TRANSIN    PIC 9(4).
004070            10  ESTIMATED-CODE-HOURS-TRANSIN      PIC 9(4).
004080            10  ESTIMATED-TEST-HOURS-TRANSIN      PIC 9(4).
004090            10  ESTIMATED-IMPLEM-HOURS-TRANSIN    PIC 9(4).
004100        05  ESTIMATED-HOURS-TABLE-TRANSIN REDEFINES
004110                ESTIMATED-TASK-HOURS-TRANSIN      PIC 9(4)
004120                                                  OCCURS 5 TIMES.
```

Data Division — Working-Storage

```
009020        05  ESTIMATED-HOURS-FIELD-MSGS.
009030            10  REVIEW-HOURS-FIELD-MSG     PIC X(30) VALUE
009040                                'REVIEW HOURS                  '.
009050            10  DESIGN-HOURS-FIELD-MSG     PIC X(30) VALUE
009060                                'DESIGN HOURS                  '.
009070            10  CODE-HOURS-FIELD-MSG       PIC X(30) VALUE
009080                                'CODE HOURS                    '.
009090            10  TEST-HOURS-FIELD-MSG       PIC X(30) VALUE
009100                                'TEST HOURS                    '.
009110            10  IMPLEM-HOURS-FIELD-MSG     PIC X(30) VALUE
009120                                'IMPLEMENTATION HOURS          '.
009130        05  ALL-ESTIMATED-HOURS-FIELD-MSGS REDEFINES
009140                ESTIMATED-HOURS-FIELD-MSGS PIC X(30) OCCURS 5 TIMES.

011040        05  HOURS-NUMERIC-CHECK-SUBSCRIPT   PIC S9(8) USAGE IS COMP
011050                                                      SYNC.
011060            88  ALL-HOURS-HAVE-BEEN-CHECKED           VALUE +6.
```

Procedure Division

```
022110        PERFORM D011-CHECK-FOR-NUMERIC-HOURS
022120            VARYING HOURS-NUMERIC-CHECK-SUBSCRIPT FROM 1 BY 1
022130            UNTIL ALL-HOURS-HAVE-BEEN-CHECKED.

024030    D011-CHECK-FOR-NUMERIC-HOURS.
024040
024050        IF ESTIMATED-HOURS-TABLE-TRANSIN
024060                (HOURS-NUMERIC-CHECK-SUBSCRIPT) IS NOT NUMERIC
024070            MOVE PROGRAM-IDENTIFICATION-TRANSIN TO
024080                    PROGRAM-ID-WORK-AREA
024090            MOVE ALL-ESTIMATED-HOURS-FIELD-MSGS
024100                    (HOURS-NUMERIC-CHECK-SUBSCRIPT) TO
024110                    FIELD-IN-ERROR-WORK-AREA
024120            MOVE ESTIMATED-HOURS-ERROR-MSG TO
024130                    TYPE-OF-ERROR-WORK-AREA
024140            PERFORM U000-WRITE-EXCEPTION-REPORT
024150            MOVE 'NO ' TO ARE-ESTIMATED-HOURS-NUMERIC
024160            MOVE 'NO ' TO IS-THE-RECORD-VALID.
```

Figure 2-52 Example of the Use of Subscripted Fields

In the example in Figure 2-52, the ESTIMATED-TASK-HOURS-TRANSIN field contains all of the hours for each of the Estimated Task Hours. This field is then redefined by the field ESTIMATED-HOURS-TABLE-TRANSIN field, which occurs 5 times. Note, therefore, that the Estimated Task Hours can be referenced either by name (ESTIMATED-REVIEW-HOURS-TRANSIN, ESTIMATED-DESIGN-HOURS-TRANSIN, etc.) or through the use of the field ESTIMATED-HOURS-TABLE-TRANSIN and a subscript.

The field messages for these fields are defined in a similar manner. The ESTIMATED-HOURS-FIELD-MSGS field contains all of the messages which are used to identify which field is in error on the Exception Report. This field is then redefined by the ALL-ESTIMATED-HOURS-FIELD-MSGS field, which occurs 5 times. Thus, these messages can be referenced either by name (REVIEW-HOURS-FIELD-MSG, etc.) or through the use of the ALL-ESTIMATED-HOURS-FIELD-MSGS field with a subscript.

A subscript is defined on line 011040 to be used in this processing. The name of the subscript is HOURS-NUMERIC-CHECK-SUBSCRIPT. Note in addition that the condition name ALL-HOURS-HAVE-BEEN-CHECKED is specified for this field, with the value 6 being required for the condition to be true.

In the Procedure Division, these Estimated Hours fields are going to be checked for numeric values through the use of a Perform loop. Note on pg/line 022110 the Perform Statement which performs the D011-CHECK-FOR-NUMERIC-HOURS paragraph until ALL-HOURS-HAVE-BEEN-CHECKED. Note also that the Perform Statement includes a Varying Clause, which will cause the subscript HOURS-NUMERIC-CHECK-SUBSCRIPT to be initially set to the value 1, and the subscript will be incremented by 1 each time the loop is performed. When the value in the subscript becomes 6, the loop will be terminated because of the condition specified.

In the D011-CHECK-FOR-NUMERIC-HOURS paragraph, the If Statement checks the value in the ESTIMATED-HOURS-TABLE-TRANSIN field, modified by the subscript HOURS-NUMERIC-CHECK-SUBSCRIPT. It will be recalled that this subscript field is initially set to 1 by the Perform Varying Statement on pg/line 022110. Therefore, the first time the loop is entered, the If Statement will reference the first occurrence in the ESTIMATED-HOURS-TABLE-TRANSIN field. As can be seen from Figure 2-52, this corresponds to the ESTIMATED-REVIEW-HOURS-TRANSIN field (pg/line 004050). If the field being checked is not numeric, then the error messages are moved to the exception report work areas in a manner similar to the other routines which have been examined. One difference is when the field in error message is moved (pg/line 024090). Note that a specifically named field is not moved; rather, the field ALL-ESTIMATED-HOURS-FIELD-MSGS, modified by the subscript HOURS-NUMERIC-CHECK-SUBSCRIPT is moved. Thus, if the subscript contains the value 1, then the message corresponding to the REVIEW-HOURS-FIELD-MSG will be moved to the work area.

On the second pass through the loop, the value in the HOURS-NUMERIC-CHECK-SUBSCRIPT will be set to 2 by the Varying Clause of the Perform Statement (pg/line 022110). Therefore, when the If Statement takes place, the second occurrence of the ESTIMATED-HOURS-TABLE-TRANSIN will be used for the numeric check. Similarly, the second occurrence of the ALL-ESTIMATED-HOURS-FIELD-MSGS will be used if the field is not numeric (pg/line 024090). This second occurrence corresponds to the Design Hours fields (pg/line 004060 and 009050). This looping will continue until all five fields have been checked; that is, until the value 6 appears in the HOURS-NUMERIC-CHECK-SUBSCRIPT. At that time, the ALL-HOURS-HAVE-BEEN-CHECKED condition (pg/line 011060 and 022130) will be true and the looping will terminate.

This method of looping through processing and using subscripts to reference fields defined with the Occurs Clause is quite a common technique, and the programmer should consider this technique whenever similarly defined fields must be checked or processed by the same logic.

SAMPLE PROGRAM

The source listing for the sample program is contained on the following pages.

```
PP 5740-CB1 RELEASE 1.2  DEC 15, 1976              IBM OS/VS COBOL                              8.45.34  DATE JUN 16,1978

   1              8.45.34        JUN 16,1978

001010 IDENTIFICATION DIVISION.                                              LOADMSTR
001020                                                                       LOADMSTR
001030 PROGRAM-ID.     LOADMSTR.                                             LOADMSTR
001040 AUTHOR.         SHELLY AND CASHMAN.                                   LOADMSTR
001050 INSTALLATION.   ANAHEIM.                                              LOADMSTR
001060 DATE-WRITTEN.   05/10/78.                                             LOADMSTR
001070 DATE-COMPILED.  JUN 16,1978.                                          LOADMSTR
001080 SECURITY.       UNCLASSIFIED.                                         LOADMSTR
001090                                                                       LOADMSTR
001100*****************************************************************     LOADMSTR
001110*                                                               *     LOADMSTR
001120*  THIS PROGRAM LOADS THE APPLICATION PROGRAM MASTER FILE. IT   *     LOADMSTR
001130*  READS THE TRANSACTION FILE AND EDITS THE FIELDS WITHIN THE   *     LOADMSTR
001140*  RECORD TO ENSURE THAT THEY CONTAIN VALID DATA. IF ALL THE    *     LOADMSTR
001150*  FIELDS CONTAIN VALID DATA, THE RECORD IS WRITTEN ON THE      *     LOADMSTR
001160*  APPLICATION PROGRAM MASTER FILE. IF ANY ERRORS (EXCEPT       *     LOADMSTR
001170*  REASONABLENESS CHECKS ON TASK HOURS) ARE FOUND, THE RECORD   *     LOADMSTR
001180*  IS NOT WRITTEN ON THE MASTER FILE. WHEN AN ERROR OR          *     LOADMSTR
001190*  VIOLATION OF THE REASONABLENESS CHECK OCCURS, A LINE IS      *     LOADMSTR
001200*  WRITTEN ON THE APPLICATION PROGRAM MASTER LOAD EXCEPTION     *     LOADMSTR
002010*  REPORT. ALL FIELDS ARE CHECKED IN EACH TRANSACTION.          *     LOADMSTR
002020*                                                               *     LOADMSTR
002030*****************************************************************     LOADMSTR
002040                                                                       LOADMSTR
002050                                                                       LOADMSTR
002060                                                                       LOADMSTR
002070 ENVIRONMENT DIVISION.                                                 LOADMSTR
002080                                                                       LOADMSTR
002090 CONFIGURATION SECTION.                                                LOADMSTR
002100                                                                       LOADMSTR
002110 SOURCE-COMPUTER. IBM-370.                                             LOADMSTR
002120 OBJECT-COMPUTER. IBM-370.                                             LOADMSTR
002130 SPECIAL-NAMES.    C01 IS TO-THE-TOP-OF-THE-PAGE.                      LOADMSTR
002140                                                                       LOADMSTR
002150 INPUT-OUTPUT SECTION.                                                 LOADMSTR
002160                                                                       LOADMSTR
002170 FILE-CONTROL.                                                         LOADMSTR
002180     SELECT PROGRAM-TRANSACTION-INPUT-FILE                             LOADMSTR
002190         ASSIGN TO UR-S-SYSIN.                                         LOADMSTR
002200     SELECT PROGRAM-MASTER-OUTPUT-FILE                                 LOADMSTR
003010         ASSIGN TO DA-S-PGMMSTR.                                       LOADMSTR
003020     SELECT EXCEPTION-REPORT-FILE                                      LOADMSTR
003030         ASSIGN TO UR-S-SYSOUT.                                        LOADMSTR
```

Figure 2-53 Source Listing (Part 1 of 10)

```
     2                    8.45.34          JUN 16,1978

003050 DATA DIVISION.                                                   LOADMSTR
003060                                                                  LOADMSTR
003070 FILE SECTION.                                                    LOADMSTR
003080                                                                  LOADMSTR
003090 FD  PROGRAM-TRANSACTION-INPUT-FILE                               LOADMSTR
003100         RECORD CONTAINS 80 CHARACTERS                            LOADMSTR
003110         LABEL RECORDS ARE OMITTED                                LOADMSTR
003120         DATA RECORD IS PROGRAM-TRANSACTION-INPUT-REC.            LOADMSTR
003130                                                                  LOADMSTR
003140 01  PROGRAM-TRANSACTION-INPUT-REC.                               LOADMSTR
003150     05  PROGRAM-IDENTIFICATION-TRANSIN.                          LOADMSTR
003160         10  APPL-DESIGNATION-TRANSIN          PIC XX.            LOADMSTR
003170             88  APPL-DESIGNATION-IS-VALID      VALUE 'AP', 'AR', LOADMSTR
003180                                                     'GL', 'PA',  LOADMSTR
003190                                                     'IC', 'CA'.  LOADMSTR
003200         10  IDENTIFICATION-NUMBER-TRANSIN     PIC X(4).          LOADMSTR
004010     05  PROGRAM-DESCRIPTION-TRANSIN           PIC X(20).         LOADMSTR
004020     05  PROGRAMMER-EMPL-NUMBER-TRANSIN        PIC X(6).          LOADMSTR
004030     05  TOTAL-ESTIMATED-HOURS-TRANSIN         PIC 9(4).          LOADMSTR
004040     05  ESTIMATED-TASK-HOURS-TRANSIN.                            LOADMSTR
004050         10  ESTIMATED-REVIEW-HOURS-TRANSIN    PIC 9(4).          LOADMSTR
004060         10  ESTIMATED-DESIGN-HOURS-TRANSIN    PIC 9(4).          LOADMSTR
004070         10  ESTIMATED-CODE-HOURS-TRANSIN      PIC 9(4).          LOADMSTR
004080         10  ESTIMATED-TEST-HOURS-TRANSIN      PIC 9(4).          LOADMSTR
004090         10  ESTIMATED-IMPLEM-HOURS-TRANSIN    PIC 9(4).          LOADMSTR
004100     05  ESTIMATED-HOURS-TABLE-TRANSIN REDEFINES                  LOADMSTR
004110             ESTIMATED-TASK-HOURS-TRANSIN      PIC 9(4)           LOADMSTR
004120                                                OCCURS 5 TIMES.   LOADMSTR
004130     05  FILLER                                PIC X(24).         LOADMSTR
004140                                                                  LOADMSTR
004150 FD  PROGRAM-MASTER-OUTPUT-FILE                                   LOADMSTR
004160         BLOCK CONTAINS 20 RECORDS                                LOADMSTR
004170         RECORD CONTAINS 77 CHARACTERS                            LOADMSTR
004180         LABEL RECORDS ARE STANDARD                               LOADMSTR
004190         DATA RECORD IS PROGRAM-MASTER-OUTPUT-RECORD.             LOADMSTR
004200                                                                  LOADMSTR
005010 01  PROGRAM-MASTER-OUTPUT-RECORD.                                LOADMSTR
005020     05  PROGRAM-IDENTIFICATION-MSTROUT.                          LOADMSTR
005030         10  APPL-DESIGNATION-MSTROUT          PIC XX.            LOADMSTR
005040         10  IDENTIFICATION-NUMBER-MSTROUT     PIC X(4).          LOADMSTR
005050     05  PROGRAM-DESCRIPTION-MSTROUT           PIC X(20).         LOADMSTR
005060     05  PROGRAMMER-EMPL-NUMBER-MSTROUT        PIC X(6).          LOADMSTR
005070     05  ESTIMATED-TASK-HOURS-MSTROUT.                            LOADMSTR
005080         10  ESTIMATED-REVIEW-HOURS-MSTROUT    PIC 9(4).          LOADMSTR
005090         10  ESTIMATED-DESIGN-HOURS-MSTROUT    PIC 9(4).          LOADMSTR
005100         10  ESTIMATED-CODE-HOURS-MSTROUT      PIC 9(4).          LOADMSTR
005110         10  ESTIMATED-TEST-HOURS-MSTROUT      PIC 9(4).          LOADMSTR
005120         10  ESTIMATED-IMPLEM-HOURS-MSTROUT    PIC 9(4).          LOADMSTR
005130     05  ACTUAL-TASK-HOURS-MSTROUT.                               LOADMSTR
005140         10  ACTUAL-REVIEW-HOURS-MSTROUT       PIC X(4).          LOADMSTR
005150         10  ACTUAL-DESIGN-HOURS-MSTROUT       PIC X(4).          LOADMSTR
005160         10  ACTUAL-CODE-HOURS-MSTROUT         PIC X(4).          LOADMSTR
005170         10  ACTUAL-TEST-HOURS-MSTROUT         PIC X(4).          LOADMSTR
005180         10  ACTUAL-IMPLEM-HOURS-MSTROUT       PIC X(4).          LOADMSTR
005190     05  TASK-STATUS-INDICATORS-MSTROUT.                          LOADMSTR
005200         10  REVIEW-STATUS-MSTROUT             PIC X.             LOADMSTR
006010         10  DESIGN-STATUS-MSTROUT             PIC X.             LOADMSTR
006020         10  CODE-STATUS-MSTROUT               PIC X.             LOADMSTR
006030         10  TEST-STATUS-MSTROUT               PIC X.             LOADMSTR
006040         10  IMPLEM-STATUS-MSTROUT             PIC X.             LOADMSTR
006050                                                                  LOADMSTR
006060 FD  EXCEPTION-REPORT-FILE                                        LOADMSTR
006070         RECORD CONTAINS 133 CHARACTERS                           LOADMSTR
006080         LABEL RECORDS ARE OMITTED                                LOADMSTR
006090         DATA RECORD IS EXCEPTION-REPORT-LINE.                    LOADMSTR
006100                                                                  LOADMSTR
006110 01  EXCEPTION-REPORT-LINE.                                       LOADMSTR
006120     05  CARRIAGE-CONTROL                      PIC X.             LOADMSTR
006130     05  PROGRAM-IDENTIFICATION-REPORT         PIC X(6).          LOADMSTR
006140     05  FILLER                                PIC X(4).          LOADMSTR
006150     05  FIELD-IN-ERROR-REPORT                 PIC X(30).         LOADMSTR
006160     05  FILLER                                PIC X(4).          LOADMSTR
006170     05  TYPE-OF-ERROR-REPORT                  PIC X(45).         LOADMSTR
006180     05  FILLER                                PIC X(43).         LOADMSTR
006190                                                                  LOADMSTR
006200 WORKING-STORAGE SECTION.                                         LOADMSTR
007010                                                                  LOADMSTR
007020 01  PROGRAM-INDICATORS.                                          LOADMSTR
007030     05  ARE-THERE-MORE-RECORDS      PIC XXX   VALUE 'YES'.       LOADMSTR
007040         88  THERE-ARE-NO-MORE-RECORDS         VALUE 'NO '.       LOADMSTR
007050     05  IS-THE-RECORD-VALID         PIC XXX   VALUE SPACES.      LOADMSTR
007060         88  A-VALID-RECORD-IS-FOUND           VALUE 'YES'.       LOADMSTR
007070         88  THE-RECORD-IS-NOT-VALID           VALUE 'NO '.       LOADMSTR
007080     05  ARE-ESTIMATED-HOURS-NUMERIC PIC XXX   VALUE 'YES'.       LOADMSTR
007090         88  ESTIMATED-HOURS-ARE-NUMERIC       VALUE 'YES'.       LOADMSTR
007100                                                                  LOADMSTR
007110 01  EXCEPTION-REPORT-COMPARE-AREA.                               LOADMSTR
007120     05  PREVIOUS-PROGRAM-ID         PIC X(6) VALUE LOW-VALUES.   LOADMSTR
007130                                                                  LOADMSTR
007140 01  PROGRAM-WORK-AREAS.                                          LOADMSTR
007150     05  PROGRAM-ID-WORK-AREA        PIC X(6).                    LOADMSTR
007160     05  FIELD-IN-ERROR-WORK-AREA    PIC X(30).                   LOADMSTR
007170     05  TYPE-OF-ERROR-WORK-AREA     PIC X(45).                   LOADMSTR
007180     05  SUM-OF-ESTIMATED-HOURS-WORK PIC S9(5) VALUE ZERO         LOADMSTR
007190                                        USAGE IS COMP-3.          LOADMSTR
008040                                                                  LOADMSTR
```

Figure 2-54 Source Listing (Part 2 of 10)

```
    3                      8.45.34        JUN 16,1978

008050 01  PROGRAM-CONSTANTS.                                                    LOADMSTR
008060     05  DESCRIPTION-FIELD-MSG         PIC X(30) VALUE                     LOADMSTR
008070                                  'DESCRIPTION                  '.LOADMSTR
008080     05  DESCRIPTION-ERROR-MSG         PIC X(45) VALUE                     LOADMSTR
008090               'NO DESCRIPTION PRESENT                          '.LOADMSTR
008100     05  PROGRAMMER-EMPL-NUMBER-MSG  PIC X(30) VALUE                       LOADMSTR
008110                                  'PROGRAMMER EMPLOYEE NUMBER   '.LOADMSTR
008120     05  PROGRAMMER-NUMBER-ERROR-MSG PIC X(45) VALUE                       LOADMSTR
008130               'NON-NUMERIC PROGRAMMER EMPLOYEE NUMBER          '.LOADMSTR
008140     05  APPLICATION-DESIGNATION-MSG PIC X(30) VALUE                       LOADMSTR
008150                                  'APPLICATION DESIGNATION      '.LOADMSTR
008160     05  APPL-DESIGNATION-ERROR-MSG  PIC X(45) VALUE                       LOADMSTR
008170               'INVALID APPLICATION DESIGNATION                 '.LOADMSTR
008180     05  IDENTIFICATION-NUMBER-MSG    PIC X(30) VALUE                      LOADMSTR
008190                                  'PROGRAM IDENTIFICATION NUMBER '.LOADMSTR
008200     05  IDENTIFICATION-NUMBER-ERR-MSG PIC X(45) VALUE                     LOADMSTR
009010               'NON-NUMERIC IDENTIFICATION NUMBER               '.LOADMSTR
009020     05  ESTIMATED-HOURS-FIELD-MSGS.                                       LOADMSTR

    4                      8.45.34        JUN 16,1978

009030         10  REVIEW-HOURS-FIELD-MSG  PIC X(30) VALUE                       LOADMSTR
009040                                  'REVIEW HOURS                 '.LOADMSTR
009050         10  DESIGN-HOURS-FIELD-MSG  PIC X(30) VALUE                       LOADMSTR
009060                                  'DESIGN HOURS                 '.LOADMSTR
009070         10  CODE-HOURS-FIELD-MSG    PIC X(30) VALUE                       LOADMSTR
009080                                  'CODE HOURS                   '.LOADMSTR
009090         10  TEST-HOURS-FIELD-MSG    PIC X(30) VALUE                       LOADMSTR
009100                                  'TEST HOURS                   '.LOADMSTR
009110         10  IMPLEM-HOURS-FIELD-MSG  PIC X(30) VALUE                       LOADMSTR
009120                                  'IMPLEMENTATION HOURS         '.LOADMSTR
009130     05  ALL-ESTIMATED-HOURS-FIELD-MSGS REDEFINES                          LOADMSTR
009140         ESTIMATED-HOURS-FIELD-MSGS PIC X(30) OCCURS 5 TIMES.              LOADMSTR
009150     05  ESTIMATED-HOURS-ERROR-MSG   PIC X(45) VALUE                       LOADMSTR
009160               'NON-NUMERIC ESTIMATED HOURS                     '.LOADMSTR
009170     05  TOTAL-EST-HOURS-FIELD-MSG   PIC X(30) VALUE                       LOADMSTR
009180                                  'TOTAL ESTIMATED HOURS        '.LOADMSTR
009190     05  TOTAL-EST-HOURS-ERROR-MSG   PIC X(45) VALUE                       LOADMSTR
009200               'NON-NUMERIC TOTAL ESTIMATED HOURS               '.LOADMSTR
009210     05  ESTIMATED-HOURS-SUM-ERROR-MSG PIC X(45) VALUE                     LOADMSTR
009220               'SUM OF ESTIMATED HOURS NOT = TOTAL HOURS        '.LOADMSTR
009230     05  MAXIMUM-PERCENT-FOR-REVIEW  PIC V99   VALUE .20                   LOADMSTR
010010                                            USAGE IS COMP-3.               LOADMSTR
010020     05  MINIMUM-PERCENT-FOR-REVIEW  PIC V99   VALUE .05                   LOADMSTR
010030                                            USAGE IS COMP-3.               LOADMSTR
010040     05  MAXIMUM-PERCENT-FOR-DESIGN  PIC V99   VALUE .60                   LOADMSTR
010050                                            USAGE IS COMP-3.               LOADMSTR
010060     05  MINIMUM-PERCENT-FOR-DESIGN  PIC V99   VALUE .30                   LOADMSTR
010070                                            USAGE IS COMP-3.               LOADMSTR
010080     05  MAXIMUM-PERCENT-FOR-CODE    PIC V99   VALUE .50                   LOADMSTR
010090                                            USAGE IS COMP-3.               LOADMSTR
010100     05  MINIMUM-PERCENT-FOR-CODE    PIC V99   VALUE .10                   LOADMSTR
010110                                            USAGE IS COMP-3.               LOADMSTR
010120     05  MAXIMUM-PERCENT-FOR-TEST    PIC V99   VALUE .30                   LOADMSTR
010130                                            USAGE IS COMP-3.               LOADMSTR
010140     05  MINIMUM-PERCENT-FOR-TEST    PIC V99   VALUE .05                   LOADMSTR
010150                                            USAGE IS COMP-3.               LOADMSTR
010160     05  MAXIMUM-PERCENT-FOR-IMPLEM  PIC V99   VALUE .20                   LOADMSTR
010170                                            USAGE IS COMP-3.               LOADMSTR
010180     05  MINIMUM-PERCENT-FOR-IMPLEM  PIC V99   VALUE .00                   LOADMSTR
010190                                            USAGE IS COMP-3.               LOADMSTR
010200     05  REASONABLENESS-CHECK-ERROR-MSG PIC X(45) VALUE                    LOADMSTR
011010               'VIOLATES REASONABLENESS CHECK - WARNING ONLY '.LOADMSTR
011020                                                                           LOADMSTR
011030 01  PROGRAM-SUBSCRIPTS.                                                   LOADMSTR
011040     05  HOURS-NUMERIC-CHECK-SUBSCRIPT  PIC S9(8) USAGE IS COMP            LOADMSTR
011050                                                  SYNC.                    LOADMSTR
011060         88  ALL-HOURS-HAVE-BEEN-CHECKED          VALUE +6.                LOADMSTR
011070     05  SUM-ESTIMATED-HOURS-SUBSCRIPT  PIC S9(8) USAGE IS COMP            LOADMSTR
011080                                                  SYNC.                    LOADMSTR
011090         88  ALL-HOURS-HAVE-BEEN-ADDED            VALUE +6.                LOADMSTR
011100                                                                           LOADMSTR
011110 01  PRINTER-CONTROL.                                                      LOADMSTR
011120     05  PROPER-SPACING           PIC 9.                                   LOADMSTR
011130     05  SPACE-ONE-LINE           PIC 9          VALUE 1.                  LOADMSTR
011140     05  SPACE-TWO-LINES          PIC 9          VALUE 2.                  LOADMSTR
011150     05  NUMBER-OF-LINES-PRINTED PIC S999        VALUE ZERO                LOADMSTR
011160                                                 USAGE IS COMP-3.          LOADMSTR
```

Figure 2-55 Source Listing (Part 3 of 10)

```
5                     8.45.34         JUN 16,1978

011170      05  PAGE-SIZE                  PIC 999        VALUE 40              LOADMSTR
011180                                                    USAGE IS COMP-3.      LOADMSTR
011190      05  PAGE-NUMBER-COUNT          PIC S999       VALUE +1              LOADMSTR
011200                                                    USAGE IS COMP-3.      LOADMSTR
012010          88  THIS-IS-THE-FIRST-PAGE                VALUE +1.             LOADMSTR
012020                                                                          LOADMSTR
012030 01   HEADING-LINES.                                                      LOADMSTR
012040      05  FIRST-HEADING-LINE.                                             LOADMSTR
012050          10  CARRIAGE-CONTROL       PIC X.                               LOADMSTR
012060          10  CURRENT-DATE-HDG1      PIC X(8).                            LOADMSTR
012070          10  FILLER                 PIC X(9)       VALUE SPACES.         LOADMSTR
012080          10  FILLER                 PIC X(12)      VALUE                 LOADMSTR
012090                                                   'APPLICATION '.        LOADMSTR
012100          10  FILLER                 PIC X(8)       VALUE 'PROGRAM '.     LOADMSTR
012110          10  FILLER                 PIC X(7)       VALUE 'MASTER '.      LOADMSTR
012120          10  FILLER                 PIC X(5)       VALUE 'LOAD '.        LOADMSTR
012130          10  FILLER                 PIC X(10)      VALUE 'EXCEPTION '.   LOADMSTR
012140          10  FILLER                 PIC X(6)       VALUE 'REPORT'.       LOADMSTR
012150          10  FILLER                 PIC X(8)       VALUE SPACES.         LOADMSTR
012160          10  FILLER                 PIC X(5)       VALUE 'PAGE '.        LOADMSTR
012170          10  PAGE-NUMBER-HDG1       PIC ZZ9.                             LOADMSTR
012180          10  FILLER                 PIC X(51)      VALUE SPACES.         LOADMSTR
012190      05  SECOND-HEADING-LINE.                                            LOADMSTR
012200          10  CARRIAGE-CONTROL       PIC X.                               LOADMSTR
013010          10  FILLER                 PIC X(7)       VALUE 'PROGRAM'.      LOADMSTR
013020          10  FILLER                 PIC X(10)      VALUE SPACES.         LOADMSTR
013030          10  FILLER                 PIC X(5)       VALUE 'FIELD'.        LOADMSTR
013040          10  FILLER                 PIC X(37)      VALUE SPACES.         LOADMSTR
013050          10  FILLER                 PIC X(4)       VALUE 'TYPE'.         LOADMSTR
013060          10  FILLER                 PIC X(69)      VALUE SPACES.         LOADMSTR
013070      05  THIRD-HEADING-LINE.                                             LOADMSTR
013080          10  CARRIAGE-CONTROL       PIC X.                               LOADMSTR
013090          10  FILLER                 PIC X          VALUE SPACE.          LOADMSTR
013100          10  FILLER                 PIC X(4)       VALUE 'I.D.'.         LOADMSTR
013110          10  FILLER                 PIC X(10)      VALUE SPACES.         LOADMSTR
013120          10  FILLER                 PIC X(8)       VALUE 'IN ERROR'.     LOADMSTR
013130          10  FILLER                 PIC X(34)      VALUE SPACES.         LOADMSTR
013140          10  FILLER                 PIC X(8)       VALUE 'OF ERROR'.     LOADMSTR
013150          10  FILLER                 PIC X(67)      VALUE SPACES.         LOADMSTR

6                     8.45.34         JUN 16,1978

013170 PROCEDURE DIVISION.                                                      LOADMSTR
013180                                                                          LOADMSTR
013190***************************************************************           LOADMSTR
013200*                                                             *           LOADMSTR
014010*   THE FUNCTION OF THIS MODULE IS TO LOAD THE APPLICATION    *           LOADMSTR
014020*   PROGRAM MASTER FILE. IT IS ENTERED FROM AND EXITS TO THE  *           LOADMSTR
014030*   OPERATING SYSTEM.                                         *           LOADMSTR
014040*                                                             *           LOADMSTR
014050***************************************************************           LOADMSTR
014060                                                                          LOADMSTR
014070 A000-LOAD-PROGRAM-MASTER-FILE.                                           LOADMSTR
014080                                                                          LOADMSTR
014090     OPEN INPUT  PROGRAM-TRANSACTION-INPUT-FILE                           LOADMSTR
014100          OUTPUT PROGRAM-MASTER-OUTPUT-FILE                               LOADMSTR
014110                 EXCEPTION-REPORT-FILE.                                   LOADMSTR
014120     PERFORM B000-OBTAIN-VALID-INPUT-RECORD.                              LOADMSTR
014130     PERFORM A001-WRITE-AND-READ                                          LOADMSTR
014140         UNTIL THERE-ARE-NO-MORE-RECORDS.                                 LOADMSTR
014150     CLOSE PROGRAM-TRANSACTION-INPUT-FILE                                 LOADMSTR
014160           PROGRAM-MASTER-OUTPUT-FILE                                     LOADMSTR
014170           EXCEPTION-REPORT-FILE.                                         LOADMSTR
014180     STOP RUN.                                                            LOADMSTR
014190                                                                          LOADMSTR
014200                                                                          LOADMSTR
015010                                                                          LOADMSTR
015020 A001-WRITE-AND-READ.                                                     LOADMSTR
015030                                                                          LOADMSTR
015040     PERFORM B010-WRITE-MASTER-FILE.                                      LOADMSTR
015050     PERFORM B000-OBTAIN-VALID-INPUT-RECORD.                              LOADMSTR
```

Figure 2-56 Source Listing (Part 4 of 10)

```
7                        8.45.34         JUN 16,1978

******************************************************************  LOADMSTR
*                                                                *  LOADMSTR
*  THE FUNCTION OF THIS MODULE IS TO OBTAIN A VALID PROGRAM      *  LOADMSTR
*  TRANSACTION INPUT RECORD. IT IS ENTERED FROM AND EXITS TO     *  LOADMSTR
*  THE A000-LOAD-PROGRAM-MASTER-FILE MODULE.                     *  LOADMSTR
*                                                                *  LOADMSTR
******************************************************************  LOADMSTR
                                                                    LOADMSTR
B000-OBTAIN-VALID-INPUT-RECORD.                                     LOADMSTR
                                                                    LOADMSTR
    MOVE SPACES TO IS-THE-RECORD-VALID.                             LOADMSTR
    PERFORM B001-READ-A-TRANSACTION-RECORD.                         LOADMSTR
    PERFORM B002-EDIT-AND-READ                                      LOADMSTR
        UNTIL A-VALID-RECORD-IS-FOUND OR                            LOADMSTR
              THERE-ARE-NO-MORE-RECORDS.                            LOADMSTR
                                                                    LOADMSTR
                                                                    LOADMSTR
                                                                    LOADMSTR
B001-READ-A-TRANSACTION-RECORD.                                     LOADMSTR
                                                                    LOADMSTR
    READ PROGRAM-TRANSACTION-INPUT-FILE                             LOADMSTR
        AT END                                                      LOADMSTR
            MOVE 'NO ' TO ARE-THERE-MORE-RECORDS.                   LOADMSTR
                                                                    LOADMSTR
                                                                    LOADMSTR
                                                                    LOADMSTR
B002-EDIT-AND-READ.                                                 LOADMSTR
                                                                    LOADMSTR
    PERFORM C000-EDIT-INPUT-RECORD.                                 LOADMSTR
    IF THE-RECORD-IS-NOT-VALID                                      LOADMSTR
        MOVE SPACES TO IS-THE-RECORD-VALID                          LOADMSTR
        PERFORM B001-READ-A-TRANSACTION-RECORD                      LOADMSTR
    ELSE                                                            LOADMSTR
        MOVE 'YES' TO IS-THE-RECORD-VALID.                          LOADMSTR

8                        8.45.34         JUN 16,1978

******************************************************************  LOADMSTR
*                                                                *  LOADMSTR
*  THE FUNCTION OF THIS MODULE IS TO WRITE THE APPLICATION       *  LOADMSTR
*  PROGRAM MASTER FILE. IT IS ENTERED FROM AND EXITS TO THE      *  LOADMSTR
*  A000-LOAD-PROGRAM-MASTER-FILE MODULE.                         *  LOADMSTR
*                                                                *  LOADMSTR
******************************************************************  LOADMSTR
                                                                    LOADMSTR
B010-WRITE-MASTER-FILE.                                             LOADMSTR
                                                                    LOADMSTR
    MOVE PROGRAM-IDENTIFICATION-TRANSIN TO                          LOADMSTR
            PROGRAM-IDENTIFICATION-MSTROUT.                         LOADMSTR
    MOVE PROGRAM-DESCRIPTION-TRANSIN TO                             LOADMSTR
            PROGRAM-DESCRIPTION-MSTROUT.                            LOADMSTR
    MOVE PROGRAMMER-EMPL-NUMBER-TRANSIN TO                          LOADMSTR
            PROGRAMMER-EMPL-NUMBER-MSTROUT.                         LOADMSTR
    MOVE ESTIMATED-REVIEW-HOURS-TRANSIN TO                          LOADMSTR
            ESTIMATED-REVIEW-HOURS-MSTROUT.                         LOADMSTR
    MOVE ESTIMATED-DESIGN-HOURS-TRANSIN TO                          LOADMSTR
            ESTIMATED-DESIGN-HOURS-MSTROUT.                         LOADMSTR
    MOVE ESTIMATED-CODE-HOURS-TRANSIN TO                            LOADMSTR
            ESTIMATED-CODE-HOURS-MSTROUT.                           LOADMSTR
    MOVE ESTIMATED-TEST-HOURS-TRANSIN TO                            LOADMSTR
            ESTIMATED-TEST-HOURS-MSTROUT.                           LOADMSTR
    MOVE ESTIMATED-IMPLEM-HOURS-TRANSIN TO                          LOADMSTR
            ESTIMATED-IMPLEM-HOURS-MSTROUT.                         LOADMSTR
    MOVE ZERO TO ACTUAL-REVIEW-HOURS-MSTROUT                        LOADMSTR
                 ACTUAL-DESIGN-HOURS-MSTROUT                        LOADMSTR
                 ACTUAL-CODE-HOURS-MSTROUT                          LOADMSTR
                 ACTUAL-TEST-HOURS-MSTROUT                          LOADMSTR
                 ACTUAL-IMPLEM-HOURS-MSTROUT.                       LOADMSTR
    MOVE SPACES TO REVIEW-STATUS-MSTROUT                            LOADMSTR
                   DESIGN-STATUS-MSTROUT                            LOADMSTR
                   CODE-STATUS-MSTROUT                              LOADMSTR
                   TEST-STATUS-MSTROUT                              LOADMSTR
                   IMPLEM-STATUS-MSTROUT.                           LOADMSTR
    WRITE PROGRAM-MASTER-OUTPUT-RECORD.                             LOADMSTR
```

Figure 2-57 Source Listing (Part 5 of 10)

```
9                    8.45.34        JUN 16,1978

018200*****************************************************************  LOADMSTR
019010*                                                                *  LOADMSTR
019020*  THIS MODULE EDITS THE TRANSACTION INPUT RECORD. IT IS         *  LOADMSTR
019030*  ENTERED FROM AND EXITS TO THE B000-OBTAIN-VALID-INPUT-RECORD*  LOADMSTR
019040*  MODULE.                                                       *  LOADMSTR
019050*                                                                *  LOADMSTR
019060*****************************************************************  LOADMSTR
019070                                                                    LOADMSTR
019080 C000-EDIT-INPUT-RECORD.                                            LOADMSTR
019090                                                                    LOADMSTR
019100     PERFORM D000-EDIT-PROGRAM-ID.                                  LOADMSTR
019110     IF PROGRAM-DESCRIPTION-TRANSIN = SPACES                        LOADMSTR
019120         MOVE PROGRAM-IDENTIFICATION-TRANSIN TO                     LOADMSTR
019130             PROGRAM-ID-WORK-AREA                                   LOADMSTR
019140         MOVE DESCRIPTION-FIELD-MSG TO FIELD-IN-ERROR-WORK-AREA     LOADMSTR
019150         MOVE DESCRIPTION-ERROR-MSG TO TYPE-OF-ERROR-WORK-AREA      LOADMSTR
019160         PERFORM U000-WRITE-EXCEPTION-REPORT                        LOADMSTR
019170         MOVE 'NO ' TO IS-THE-RECORD-VALID.                         LOADMSTR
019180     IF PROGRAMMER-EMPL-NUMBER-TRANSIN IS NOT NUMERIC               LOADMSTR
019190         MOVE PROGRAM-IDENTIFICATION-TRANSIN TO                     LOADMSTR
019200             PROGRAM-ID-WORK-AREA                                   LOADMSTR
020010         MOVE PROGRAMMER-EMPL-NUMBER-MSG TO                         LOADMSTR
020020             FIELD-IN-ERROR-WORK-AREA                               LOADMSTR
020030         MOVE PROGRAMMER-NUMBER-ERROR-MSG TO                        LOADMSTR
020040             TYPE-OF-ERROR-WORK-AREA                                LOADMSTR
020050         PERFORM U000-WRITE-EXCEPTION-REPORT                        LOADMSTR
020060         MOVE 'NO ' TO IS-THE-RECORD-VALID.                         LOADMSTR
020070     PERFORM D010-EDIT-ESTIMATED-HOURS.                             LOADMSTR

10                   8.45.34        JUN 16,1978

020090*****************************************************************  LOADMSTR
020100*                                                                *  LOADMSTR
020110*  THE FUNCTION OF THIS MODULE IS TO EDIT THE PROGRAM           *  LOADMSTR
020120*  IDENTIFICATION. IT IS ENTERED FROM AND EXITS TO THE          *  LOADMSTR
020130*  C000-EDIT-INPUT-RECORD.                                       *  LOADMSTR
020140*                                                                *  LOADMSTR
020150*****************************************************************  LOADMSTR
020160                                                                    LOADMSTR
020170 D000-EDIT-PROGRAM-ID.                                              LOADMSTR
020180                                                                    LOADMSTR
020190     IF APPL-DESIGNATION-IS-VALID                                   LOADMSTR
020200         NEXT SENTENCE                                              LOADMSTR
021010     ELSE                                                           LOADMSTR
021020         MOVE PROGRAM-IDENTIFICATION-TRANSIN TO                     LOADMSTR
021030             PROGRAM-ID-WORK-AREA                                   LOADMSTR
021040         MOVE APPLICATION-DESIGNATION-MSG TO                        LOADMSTR
021050             FIELD-IN-ERROR-WORK-AREA                               LOADMSTR
021060         MOVE APPL-DESIGNATION-ERROR-MSG TO                         LOADMSTR
021070             TYPE-OF-ERROR-WORK-AREA                                LOADMSTR
021080         PERFORM U000-WRITE-EXCEPTION-REPORT                        LOADMSTR
021090         MOVE 'NO ' TO IS-THE-RECORD-VALID.                         LOADMSTR
021100     IF IDENTIFICATION-NUMBER-TRANSIN IS NOT NUMERIC                LOADMSTR
021110         MOVE PROGRAM-IDENTIFICATION-TRANSIN TO                     LOADMSTR
021120             PROGRAM-ID-WORK-AREA                                   LOADMSTR
021130         MOVE IDENTIFICATION-NUMBER-MSG TO                          LOADMSTR
021140             FIELD-IN-ERROR-WORK-AREA                               LOADMSTR
021150         MOVE IDENTIFICATION-NUMBER-ERR-MSG TO                      LOADMSTR
021160             TYPE-OF-ERROR-WORK-AREA                                LOADMSTR
021170         PERFORM U000-WRITE-EXCEPTION-REPORT                        LOADMSTR
021180         MOVE 'NO ' TO IS-THE-RECORD-VALID.                         LOADMSTR
```

Figure 2-58 Source Listing (Part 6 of 10)

```
 11                    8.45.34         JUN 16,1978

 021200*****************************************************************  LOADMSTR
 022010*                                                               *  LOADMSTR
 022020*  THIS MODULE EDITS THE ESTIMATED HOURS IN THE INPUT RECORD.   *  LOADMSTR
 022030*  IT IS ENTERED FROM AND EXITS TO THE C000-EDIT-INPUT-RECORD   *  LOADMSTR
 022040*  MODULE.                                                      *  LOADMSTR
 022050*                                                               *  LOADMSTR
 022060*****************************************************************  LOADMSTR
 022070                                                                   LOADMSTR
 022080 D010-EDIT-ESTIMATED-HOURS.                                        LOADMSTR
 022090                                                                   LOADMSTR
 022100     MOVE 'YES' TO ARE-ESTIMATED-HOURS-NUMERIC.                    LOADMSTR
 022110     PERFORM D011-CHECK-FOR-NUMERIC-HOURS                          LOADMSTR
 022120             VARYING HOURS-NUMERIC-CHECK-SUBSCRIPT FROM 1 BY 1     LOADMSTR
 022130             UNTIL ALL-HOURS-HAVE-BEEN-CHECKED.                    LOADMSTR
 022140     IF TOTAL-ESTIMATED-HOURS-TRANSIN IS NOT NUMERIC               LOADMSTR
 022150         MOVE PROGRAM-IDENTIFICATION-TRANSIN TO                    LOADMSTR
 022160                 PROGRAM-ID-WORK-AREA                              LOADMSTR
 022170         MOVE TOTAL-EST-HOURS-FIELD-MSG TO                         LOADMSTR
 022180                 FIELD-IN-ERROR-WORK-AREA                          LOADMSTR
 022190         MOVE TOTAL-EST-HOURS-ERROR-MSG TO                         LOADMSTR
 022200                 TYPE-OF-ERROR-WORK-AREA                           LOADMSTR
 023010         PERFORM U000-WRITE-EXCEPTION-REPORT                       LOADMSTR
 023020         MOVE 'NO ' TO IS-THE-RECORD-VALID                         LOADMSTR
 023030     ELSE                                                          LOADMSTR
 023040         PERFORM E000-CHECK-HOUR-REASONABLENESS                    LOADMSTR
 023050         IF ESTIMATED-HOURS-ARE-NUMERIC                            LOADMSTR
 023060             MOVE ZEROS TO SUM-OF-ESTIMATED-HOURS-WORK             LOADMSTR
 023070             PERFORM D012-ADD-THE-HOURS                            LOADMSTR
 023080                     VARYING SUM-ESTIMATED-HOURS-SUBSCRIPT FROM 1 BY 1LOADMSTR
 023090                     UNTIL ALL-HOURS-HAVE-BEEN-ADDED               LOADMSTR
 023100             IF SUM-OF-ESTIMATED-HOURS-WORK IS NOT =               LOADMSTR
 023110                     TOTAL-ESTIMATED-HOURS-TRANSIN                 LOADMSTR
 023120                 MOVE PROGRAM-IDENTIFICATION-TRANSIN TO            LOADMSTR
 023130                         PROGRAM-ID-WORK-AREA                      LOADMSTR
 023140                 MOVE TOTAL-EST-HOURS-FIELD-MSG TO                 LOADMSTR
 023150                         FIELD-IN-ERROR-WORK-AREA                  LOADMSTR
 023160                 MOVE ESTIMATED-HOURS-SUM-ERROR-MSG TO             LOADMSTR
 023170                         TYPE-OF-ERROR-WORK-AREA                   LOADMSTR
 023180                 PERFORM U000-WRITE-EXCEPTION-REPORT               LOADMSTR
 023190                 MOVE 'NO ' TO IS-THE-RECORD-VALID.                LOADMSTR
 023200                                                                   LOADMSTR
 024010                                                                   LOADMSTR
 024020                                                                   LOADMSTR
 024030 D011-CHECK-FOR-NUMERIC-HOURS.                                     LOADMSTR
 024040                                                                   LOADMSTR
 024050     IF ESTIMATED-HOURS-TABLE-TRANSIN                              LOADMSTR
 024060             (HOURS-NUMERIC-CHECK-SUBSCRIPT) IS NOT NUMERIC        LOADMSTR
 024070         MOVE PROGRAM-IDENTIFICATION-TRANSIN TO                    LOADMSTR
 024080                 PROGRAM-ID-WORK-AREA                              LOADMSTR
 024090         MOVE ALL-ESTIMATED-HOURS-FIELD-MSGS                       LOADMSTR
 024100                 (HOURS-NUMERIC-CHECK-SUBSCRIPT) TO                LOADMSTR
 024110                 FIELD-IN-ERROR-WORK-AREA                          LOADMSTR
 024120         MOVE ESTIMATED-HOURS-ERROR-MSG TO                         LOADMSTR
 024130                 TYPE-OF-ERROR-WORK-AREA                           LOADMSTR
 024140         PERFORM U000-WRITE-EXCEPTION-REPORT                       LOADMSTR
 024150         MOVE 'NO ' TO ARE-ESTIMATED-HOURS-NUMERIC                 LOADMSTR
 024160         MOVE 'NO ' TO IS-THE-RECORD-VALID.                        LOADMSTR

 12                    8.45.34         JUN 16,1978

 024170                                                                   LOADMSTR
 024180                                                                   LOADMSTR
 024190                                                                   LOADMSTR
 024200 D012-ADD-THE-HOURS.                                               LOADMSTR
 024210                                                                   LOADMSTR
 024220     ADD ESTIMATED-HOURS-TABLE-TRANSIN                             LOADMSTR
 024230             (SUM-ESTIMATED-HOURS-SUBSCRIPT) TO                    LOADMSTR
 024240             SUM-OF-ESTIMATED-HOURS-WORK.                          LOADMSTR

 13                    8.45.34         JUN 16,1978

 025010*****************************************************************  LOADMSTR
 025020*                                                               *  LOADMSTR
 025030*  THIS MODULE CHECKS THE REASONABLENESS OF THE ESTIMATED HOURS*  LOADMSTR
 025040*  IN THE INPUT RECORD. IT IS ENTERED FROM AND EXITS TO THE     *  LOADMSTR
 025050*  D010-EDIT-ESTIMATED-HOURS MODULE.                            *  LOADMSTR
 025060*                                                               *  LOADMSTR
 025070*****************************************************************  LOADMSTR
 025080                                                                   LOADMSTR
 025090 E000-CHECK-HOUR-REASONABLENESS.                                   LOADMSTR
 025100                                                                   LOADMSTR
 025110     PERFORM F000-CHECK-REVIEW-HOURS.                              LOADMSTR
 025120     PERFORM F010-CHECK-DESIGN-HOURS.                              LOADMSTR
 025130     PERFORM F020-CHECK-CODE-HOURS.                                LOADMSTR
 025140     PERFORM F030-CHECK-TEST-HOURS.                                LOADMSTR
 025150     PERFORM F040-CHECK-IMPLEM-HOURS.                              LOADMSTR
```

Figure 2-59 Source Listing (Part 7 of 10)

```
14                    8.45.34        JUN 16,1978

025170**************************************************************** LOADMSTR
025180*                                                             * LOADMSTR
025190*  THIS MODULE CHECKS THE REVIEW HOURS FOR REASONABLENESS. IT  * LOADMSTR
025200*  IS ENTERED FROM AND EXITS TO THE                            * LOADMSTR
026010*  E000-CHECK-HOUR-REASONABLENESS MODULE.                      * LOADMSTR
026020*                                                             * LOADMSTR
026030**************************************************************** LOADMSTR
026040                                                                 LOADMSTR
026050 F000-CHECK-REVIEW-HOURS.                                        LOADMSTR
026060                                                                 LOADMSTR
026070     IF ESTIMATED-REVIEW-HOURS-TRANSIN IS NUMERIC                LOADMSTR
026080         IF ESTIMATED-REVIEW-HOURS-TRANSIN IS GREATER THAN       LOADMSTR
026090                (TOTAL-ESTIMATED-HOURS-TRANSIN *                 LOADMSTR
026100                MAXIMUM-PERCENT-FOR-REVIEW) OR                   LOADMSTR
026110                IS LESS THAN (TOTAL-ESTIMATED-HOURS-TRANSIN *    LOADMSTR
026120                MINIMUM-PERCENT-FOR-REVIEW)                      LOADMSTR
026130            MOVE PROGRAM-IDENTIFICATION-TRANSIN TO               LOADMSTR
026140                    PROGRAM-ID-WORK-AREA                         LOADMSTR
026150            MOVE REVIEW-HOURS-FIELD-MSG TO                       LOADMSTR
026160                    FIELD-IN-ERROR-WORK-AREA                     LOADMSTR
026170            MOVE REASONABLENESS-CHECK-ERROR-MSG TO               LOADMSTR
026180                    TYPE-OF-ERROR-WORK-AREA                      LOADMSTR
026190            PERFORM U000-WRITE-EXCEPTION-REPORT.                 LOADMSTR
```

```
15                    8.45.34        JUN 16,1978

027010**************************************************************** LOADMSTR
027020*                                                             * LOADMSTR
027030*  THIS MODULE CHECKS THE REASONABLENESS OF THE DESIGN HOURS.  * LOADMSTR
027040*  IT IS ENTERED FROM AND EXITS TO THE                         * LOADMSTR
027050*  E000-CHECK-HOUR-REASONABLENESS MODULE.                      * LOADMSTR
027060*                                                             * LOADMSTR
027070**************************************************************** LOADMSTR
027080                                                                 LOADMSTR
027090 F010-CHECK-DESIGN-HOURS.                                        LOADMSTR
027100                                                                 LOADMSTR
027110     IF ESTIMATED-DESIGN-HOURS-TRANSIN IS NUMERIC                LOADMSTR
027120         IF ESTIMATED-DESIGN-HOURS-TRANSIN IS GREATER THAN       LOADMSTR
027130                (TOTAL-ESTIMATED-HOURS-TRANSIN *                 LOADMSTR
027140                MAXIMUM-PERCENT-FOR-DESIGN) OR                   LOADMSTR
027150                IS LESS THAN (TOTAL-ESTIMATED-HOURS-TRANSIN *    LOADMSTR
027160                MINIMUM-PERCENT-FOR-DESIGN)                      LOADMSTR
027170            MOVE PROGRAM-IDENTIFICATION-TRANSIN TO               LOADMSTR
027180                    PROGRAM-ID-WORK-AREA                         LOADMSTR
027190            MOVE DESIGN-HOURS-FIELD-MSG TO                       LOADMSTR
027200                    FIELD-IN-ERROR-WORK-AREA                     LOADMSTR
027210            MOVE REASONABLENESS-CHECK-ERROR-MSG TO               LOADMSTR
027220                    TYPE-OF-ERROR-WORK-AREA                      LOADMSTR
028010            PERFORM U000-WRITE-EXCEPTION-REPORT.                 LOADMSTR
```

```
16                    8.45.34        JUN 16,1978

028030**************************************************************** LOADMSTR
028040*                                                             * LOADMSTR
028050*  THIS MODULE CHECKS THE CODE HOURS FOR REASONABLE VALUES. IT * LOADMSTR
028060*  IS ENTERED FROM AND EXITS TO THE                            * LOADMSTR
028070*  E000-CHECK-HOUR-REASONABLENESS MODULE.                      * LOADMSTR
028080*                                                             * LOADMSTR
028090**************************************************************** LOADMSTR
028100                                                                 LOADMSTR
028110 F020-CHECK-CODE-HOURS.                                          LOADMSTR
028120                                                                 LOADMSTR
028130     IF ESTIMATED-CODE-HOURS-TRANSIN IS NUMERIC                  LOADMSTR
028140         IF ESTIMATED-CODE-HOURS-TRANSIN IS GREATER THAN         LOADMSTR
028150                (TOTAL-ESTIMATED-HOURS-TRANSIN *                 LOADMSTR
028160                MAXIMUM-PERCENT-FOR-CODE) OR                     LOADMSTR
028170                IS LESS THAN (TOTAL-ESTIMATED-HOURS-TRANSIN *    LOADMSTR
028180                MINIMUM-PERCENT-FOR-CODE)                        LOADMSTR
028190            MOVE PROGRAM-IDENTIFICATION-TRANSIN TO               LOADMSTR
028200                    PROGRAM-ID-WORK-AREA                         LOADMSTR
028210            MOVE CODE-HOURS-FIELD-MSG TO                         LOADMSTR
028220                    FIELD-IN-ERROR-WORK-AREA                     LOADMSTR
029010            MOVE REASONABLENESS-CHECK-ERROR-MSG TO               LOADMSTR
029020                    TYPE-OF-ERROR-WORK-AREA                      LOADMSTR
029030            PERFORM U000-WRITE-EXCEPTION-REPORT.                 LOADMSTR
```

Figure 2-60 Source Listing (Part 8 of 10)

```
17                          8.45.34        JUN 16,1978

029050**************************************************************** LOADMSTR
029060*                                                              * LOADMSTR
029070*  THIS MODULE CHECKS THE TEST HOURS FOR REASONABLENESS. IT IS * LOADMSTR
029080*  ENTERED FROM AND EXITS TO THE E000-CHECK-HOUR-REASONABLENESS* LOADMSTR
029090*  MODULE.                                                     * LOADMSTR
029100*                                                              * LOADMSTR
029110**************************************************************** LOADMSTR
029120                                                                 LOADMSTR
029130 F030-CHECK-TEST-HOURS.                                          LOADMSTR
029140                                                                 LOADMSTR
029150     IF ESTIMATED-TEST-HOURS-TRANSIN IS NUMERIC                  LOADMSTR
029160         IF ESTIMATED-TEST-HOURS-TRANSIN IS GREATER THAN         LOADMSTR
029170                 (TOTAL-ESTIMATED-HOURS-TRANSIN *                LOADMSTR
029180                 MAXIMUM-PERCENT-FOR-TEST) OR                    LOADMSTR
029190                 IS LESS THAN (TOTAL-ESTIMATED-HOURS-TRANSIN *   LOADMSTR
029200                MINIMUM-PERCENT-FOR-TEST)                        LOADMSTR
030010             MOVE PROGRAM-IDENTIFICATION-TRANSIN TO              LOADMSTR
030020                     PROGRAM-ID-WORK-AREA                        LOADMSTR
030030             MOVE TEST-HOURS-FIELD-MSG TO                        LOADMSTR
030040                     FIELD-IN-ERROR-WORK-AREA                    LOADMSTR
030050             MOVE REASONABLENESS-CHECK-ERROR-MSG TO              LOADMSTR
030060                     TYPE-OF-ERROR-WORK-AREA                     LOADMSTR
030070             PERFORM U000-WRITE-EXCEPTION-REPORT.                LOADMSTR

18                          8.45.34        JUN 16,1978

030090*************************************************************** LOADMSTR
030100*                                                             * LOADMSTR
030110*  THIS MODULE CHECKS THE REASONABLENESS OF THE IMPLEMENTATION * LOADMSTR
030120*  HOURS. IT IS ENTERED FROM AND EXITS TO THE                 * LOADMSTR
030130*  E000-CHECK-HOUR-REASONABLENESS MODULE.                     * LOADMSTR
030140*                                                             * LOADMSTR
030150*************************************************************** LOADMSTR
030160                                                                LOADMSTR
030170 F040-CHECK-IMPLEM-HOURS.                                       LOADMSTR
030180                                                                LOADMSTR
030190     IF ESTIMATED-IMPLEM-HOURS-TRANSIN IS NUMERIC               LOADMSTR
030200         IF ESTIMATED-IMPLEM-HOURS-TRANSIN IS GREATER THAN      LOADMSTR
030210                 (TOTAL-ESTIMATED-HOURS-TRANSIN *               LOADMSTR
030220                 MAXIMUM-PERCENT-FOR-IMPLEM) OR                 LOADMSTR
030230                 IS LESS THAN (TOTAL-ESTIMATED-HOURS-TRANSIN *  LOADMSTR
030240                 MINIMUM-PERCENT-FOR-IMPLEM)                    LOADMSTR
031010             MOVE PROGRAM-IDENTIFICATION-TRANSIN TO             LOADMSTR
031020                     PROGRAM-ID-WORK-AREA                       LOADMSTR
031030             MOVE IMPLEM-HOURS-FIELD-MSG TO                     LOADMSTR
031040                     FIELD-IN-ERROR-WORK-AREA                   LOADMSTR
031050             MOVE REASONABLENESS-CHECK-ERROR-MSG TO             LOADMSTR
031060                     TYPE-OF-ERROR-WORK-AREA                    LOADMSTR
031070             PERFORM U000-WRITE-EXCEPTION-REPORT.               LOADMSTR
```

Figure 2-61 Source Listing (Part 9 of 10)

```
 19                8.45.34        JUN 16,1978

031090******************************************************************* LOADMSTR
031100*                                                                 * LOADMSTR
031110*  THIS MODULE IS ENTERED TO PRINT THE EXCEPTION REPORT. IT IS    * LOADMSTR
031120*  A UTILITY MODULE AND IS ENTERED FROM AND EXITS TO SEVERAL      * LOADMSTR
031130*  MODULES WITHIN THE PROGRAM (SEE HIERARCHY CHART).               * LOADMSTR
031140*                                                                 * LOADMSTR
031150******************************************************************* LOADMSTR
031160                                                                    LOADMSTR
031170 U000-WRITE-EXCEPTION-REPORT.                                       LOADMSTR
031180                                                                    LOADMSTR
031190     IF THIS-IS-THE-FIRST-PAGE OR                                   LOADMSTR
031200            NUMBER-OF-LINES-PRINTED IS = PAGE-SIZE OR               LOADMSTR
032010            IS GREATER THAN PAGE-SIZE                               LOADMSTR
032020         PERFORM U010-PRINT-HEADINGS                                LOADMSTR
032030         MOVE SPACES TO EXCEPTION-REPORT-LINE                       LOADMSTR
032040         MOVE PROGRAM-ID-WORK-AREA TO                               LOADMSTR
032050                 PROGRAM-IDENTIFICATION-REPORT.                     LOADMSTR
032060     IF PROGRAM-ID-WORK-AREA NOT = PREVIOUS-PROGRAM-ID              LOADMSTR
032070         MOVE PROGRAM-ID-WORK-AREA TO                               LOADMSTR
032080                 PROGRAM-IDENTIFICATION-REPORT                      LOADMSTR
032090         MOVE PROGRAM-ID-WORK-AREA TO PREVIOUS-PROGRAM-ID           LOADMSTR
032100         MOVE SPACE-TWO-LINES TO PROPER-SPACING.                    LOADMSTR
032110     MOVE FIELD-IN-ERROR-WORK-AREA TO FIELD-IN-ERROR-REPORT.        LOADMSTR
032120     MOVE TYPE-OF-ERROR-WORK-AREA TO TYPE-OF-ERROR-REPORT.          LOADMSTR
032130     WRITE EXCEPTION-REPORT-LINE                                    LOADMSTR
032140          AFTER PROPER-SPACING.                                     LOADMSTR
032150     ADD PROPER-SPACING TO NUMBER-OF-LINES-PRINTED.                 LOADMSTR
032160     MOVE SPACE-ONE-LINE TO PROPER-SPACING.                         LOADMSTR
032170     MOVE SPACES TO EXCEPTION-REPORT-LINE.                          LOADMSTR
```

```
 20                8.45.34        JUN 16,1978

032190******************************************************************* LOADMSTR
032200*                                                                 * LOADMSTR
033010*  THIS MODULE PRINTS THE HEADINGS ON THE EXCEPTION REPORT. IT    * LOADMSTR
033020*  IS ENTERED FROM AND EXITS TO THE U000-WRITE-EXCEPTION-REPORT   * LOADMSTR
033030*  MODULE.                                                        * LOADMSTR
033040*                                                                 * LOADMSTR
033050******************************************************************* LOADMSTR
033060                                                                    LOADMSTR
033070 U010-PRINT-HEADINGS.                                               LOADMSTR
033080                                                                    LOADMSTR
033090     MOVE CURRENT-DATE TO CURRENT-DATE-HDG1.                        LOADMSTR
033100     MOVE PAGE-NUMBER-COUNT TO PAGE-NUMBER-HDG1.                    LOADMSTR
033110     WRITE EXCEPTION-REPORT-LINE FROM FIRST-HEADING-LINE            LOADMSTR
033120          AFTER ADVANCING TO-THE-TOP-OF-THE-PAGE.                   LOADMSTR
033130     ADD 1 TO PAGE-NUMBER-COUNT.                                    LOADMSTR
033140     WRITE EXCEPTION-REPORT-LINE FROM SECOND-HEADING-LINE           LOADMSTR
033150          AFTER ADVANCING 2 LINES.                                  LOADMSTR
033160     WRITE EXCEPTION-REPORT-LINE FROM THIRD-HEADING-LINE            LOADMSTR
033170          AFTER ADVANCING 1 LINES.                                  LOADMSTR
033180     MOVE ZERO TO NUMBER-OF-LINES-PRINTED.                          LOADMSTR
033190     MOVE SPACE-TWO-LINES TO PROPER-SPACING.                        LOADMSTR
```

Figure 2-62 Source Listing (Part 10 of 10)

CHAPTER 2

REVIEW QUESTIONS

1. What is meant by the term "Editing"?

2. List five types of "editing."

3. Write the COBOL statement to edit the field EMPLOYEE-NAME to determine if the field is blank. If the field is blank, the field EMPLOYEE-NAME should be moved to the work area, EMPLOYEE-NAME-WORK-AREA, and the literal "NO" should be moved to IS-THE-RECORD-VALID.

4. When the figurative constant, spaces, is referenced in a comparing operation, how must the field be defined that is being compared to SPACES?

5. Write the COBOL statement to determine if the field EMPLOYEE-NUMBER is numeric. If the data contained in the field is not numeric, EMPLOYEE-NUMBER should be moved to the work area EMPLOYEE-NUMBER WORK and the literal "NO" should be moved to IS-THE-RECORD-VALID.

6. In the following examples indicate whether the field AMOUNT-WORK would be considered numeric or not numeric, and the reason for your answer.

EXAMPLE 1:

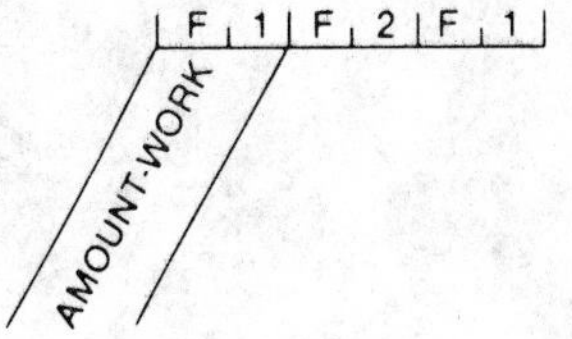

F 1	F 2	F 1

AMOUNT-WORK

```
05 AMOUNT-WORK                    PIC XXX.

IF AMOUNT-WORK IS NOT NUMERIC
   PERFORM U000-WRITE-EXCEPTION-REPORT.
```

ANSWER____________________REASON ____________________

EXAMPLE 2:

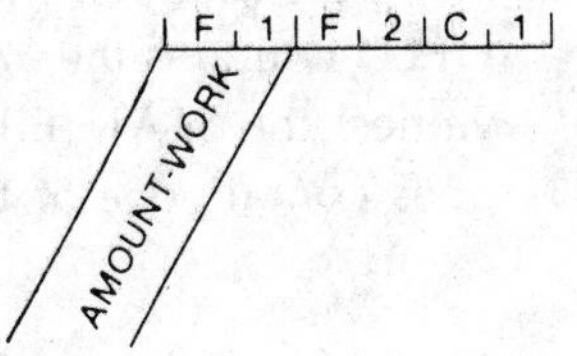

F 1	F 2	C 1

AMOUNT-WORK

```
05 AMOUNT-WORK                    PIC XXX.

IF AMOUNT-WORK IS NOT NUMERIC
   PERFORM U000-WRITE-EXCEPTION-REPORT.
```

ANSWER____________________REASON ____________________

EXAMPLE 3:

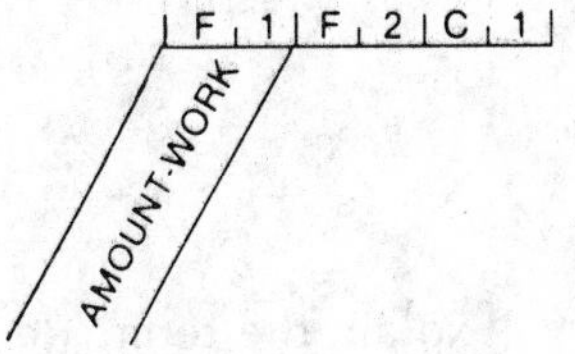

F 1	F 2	C 1

AMOUNT-WORK

```
05 AMOUNT-WORK                    PIC 999.

IF AMOUNT-WORK IS NOT NUMERIC
   PERFORM U000-WRITE-EXCEPTION-REPORT.
```

ANSWER____________________REASON ____________________

EXAMPLE 4:

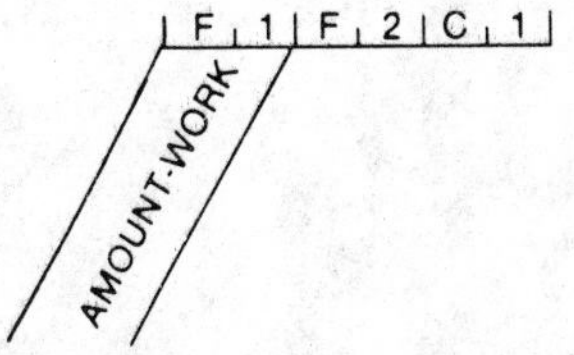

F 1	F 2	C 1

AMOUNT-WORK

```
05 AMOUNT-WORK                    PIC S999.

IF AMOUNT-WORK IS NOT NUMERIC
   PERFORM U000-WRITE-EXCEPTION-REPORT.
```

ANSWER____________________REASON ____________________

7. Summarize the rules for the If Numeric Test.

8. Write the required statements in the Data Division and Procedure Division to check if STATE-FIELD contains the values CA, AZ, NV, or OR. If STATE-FIELD does not contain one of these values, the STATE-FIELD is to be moved to STATE-FIELD-WORK-AREA. If the STATE-FIELD does contain one of these values, the next statement in the program is to be executed.

9. Explain the term "Reasonableness Test."

CHAPTER 2

PROGRAMMING ASSIGNMENT 1

OVERVIEW — PROGRAMMING ASSIGNMENTS

The programming assignments in Chapter 2 consist of two parts: 1) The design and programming of an application which creates a Decathlon Master File; 2) The maintenance of the program which creates the Decathlon Master File. Three approaches are possible when utilizing these programming assignments:

1. Only Programming Assignment 1 is assigned. This approach results in the design and coding of a relatively small program which illustrates the basic concepts discussed in the chapter.

2. Programming Assignment 1 may be assigned. After this program has been designed, coded, and tested, Programming Assignment 1A may be assigned. Assignment 1A involves the revision and maintenance of the program completed in Assignment 1. Upon completion of Assignment 1A, the student will have completed a program of the approximate difficulty of the program contained in the chapter.

3. Programming Assignment 1 and Programming Assignment 1A may be viewed as one large programming project and be written as a single assignment.

The method of assigning the program is at the option of the instructor.

INSTRUCTIONS

The decathlon is a sporting event in which the participant competes in ten different track and field events and receives an individual score for each event based upon his performance in the event. The scores for each individual event are then added, and the participant with the highest total score is judged to be the winner.

A program should be written to read a series of Decathlon Score Records stored on punched cards and create a Decathlon Master File stored on magnetic disk. A Hierarchy Chart, IPO Charts, and Pseudocode Specifications should be used when designing the program. Test data is contained in Appendix D.

INPUT

Each input record, stored on a punched card, will contain an Athlete Number, Athlete Name, a Coach Number, and the athlete's Total Decathlon Score. The format of the input records is illustrated below.

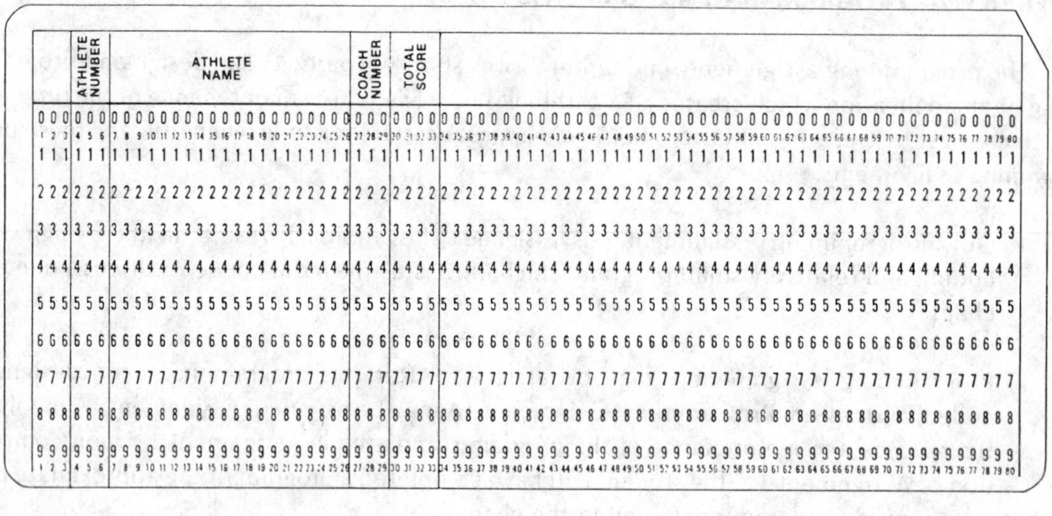

ATHLETE NUMBER
ATHLETE NAME
COACH NUMBER
TOTAL SCORE

OUTPUT

The output from the program is the Decathlon Master File which is to be stored sequentially as a disk file. The format of the Decathlon Master Record to be stored in the file should be as follows:

FIELD	POSITION	NUMBER OF DIGITS	ATTRIBUTES
Athlete Number	1-3	3	Numeric
Athlete Name	4-23	20	Alphanumeric
Coach Number	24-26	3	Numeric
Total Decathlon Score	27-30	4	Numeric

The input records are sorted in sequence by Athlete Number prior to being read by the program; therefore, the Decathlon Master File will be stored on disk in Athlete Number sequence. Twenty logical records should be stored in a block.

PROCESSING

The records in the input file are to be read, and the data in these records is to be used to create the Decathlon Master File. Before the data can be used, however, it must be edited to ensure that only valid data is loaded into the Decathlon Master File.

The editing which must take place within the program is as follows:

1. Athlete's Number — This field must contain numeric data.
2. Athlete's Name — This field must contain data. If the field contains all blanks, it is in error.
3. Coach Number — The data in this field must be numeric.
4. Total Decathlon Score — The data in this field must be numeric. In addition, the value must not be greater than 9000 or less than 5000.

If a record contains any data which does not pass the above editing criteria, then the record should not be written in the Decathlon Master File. All fields in error should be listed on the Exception Report.

EXCEPTION REPORT

Records which contain invalid data should be listed on the Exception Report and SHOULD NOT be written in the Decathlon Master File. The Exception Report should contain the Athlete Number, the name of the field in error, and the type of error. The format of the Exception Report is illustrated below.

PRINTER SPACING CHART

```
          1111111111222222222233333333334444444444555555555566
 1234567890123456789012345678901234567890123456789012345678901
 1
 2XX/XX/XX   DECATHLON MASTER LOAD EXCEPTION REPORT    PAGE XØX
 3
 4ATHLETE        FIELD                      TYPE
 5 NUMBER      IN ERROR                   OF ERROR
 6
 7  XXX     ATHLETE NUMBER      FIELD CONTAINS NON-NUMERIC DATA
 8          ATHLETE NAME        NO NAME PRESENT
 9          COACH NUMBER        VIOLATES REASONABLENESS CHECK
10          TOTAL SCORE
11
12  XXX     XXXXXXXXXXXXXXX     XXXXXXXXXXXXXXXXXXXXXXXXXXXXXXX
13          XXXXXXXXXXXXXXX     XXXXXXXXXXXXXXXXXXXXXXXXXXXXXXX
14
```

Note from the printer spacing chart above that the Exception Report contains the Athlete Number, the Field in Error, and the Type of Error. The messages under the Type of Error illustrate the three different error messages which should appear on the report as a result of input editing and are not necessarily horizontally aligned with the Field in Error. If an input record has more than one field in error, the Athlete Number should be group-indicated on the report.

NOTE: After the Decathlon Master File has been created, a utility program should be used to "dump" the file to ensure that all valid data has been properly stored in the file.

Upon completion of this assignment, the program should be retained for use in Chapter 3 and Chapter 4.

CHAPTER 2

PROGRAMMING ASSIGNMENT 1A

INTRODUCTION

At the discretion of the instructor, this assignment may be completed in combination with Programming Assignment 1, or may be assigned only after Assignment 1 has been completely designed, coded and tested.

INSTRUCTIONS

A request for some modifications to the program in Assignment 1 have been received by the data processing department. The three requested changes are:

1. A School Identification (I.D) Code should be included in the Decathlon Master Record to identify the school which the athlete attends.

2. Each master record should contain the individual scores which were scored in the ten events when the athlete's total score was obtained.

3. Each master record should contain the athlete's highest score in each event that he has ever obtained in his career.

IMPLEMENTATION OF CHANGES

After considering the modifications requested, the following changes were made to the input, output, and processing steps specified for Assignment 1.

INPUT

The modified input record is illustrated below.

SCHOOL I.D.	ATHLETE NUMBER	ATHLETE NAME	COACH NUMBER	TOTAL SCORE	100 METERS	LONG JUMP	SHOT PUT	HIGH JUMP	400 METERS	110 METER HURDLES	DISCUS	POLE VAULT	JAVELIN	1500 METERS	
1 2 3	4 5 6	7 8 9 10 11 12 13 14 15 16 17 18 19 20 21 22 23 24 25 26	27 28 29	30 31 32 33	34 35 36 37	38 39 40 41	42 43 44 45	46 47 48 49	50 51 52 53	54 55 56 57	58 59 60 61	62 63 64 65	66 67 68 69	70 71 72 73	74 75 76 77 78 79 80

Note from the input record illustrated that the School I.D. field and fields for each of the individual scores have been added to the input record. The School I.D. field will contain a 3-digit code which will identify the school that the athlete attends. The individual scores for each event which comprise the total score the athlete has obtained will be contained in each of the fields as indicated on the input record.

OUTPUT

The output from the program will be the Decathlon Master File. The new format of the file is specified below.

FIELD	POSITION	NUMBER OF DIGITS	ATTRIBUTES
School Identification	1-3	3	Alphanumeric
Athlete Number	4-6	3	Numeric
Athlete Name	7-26	20	Alphanumeric
Coach Number	27-29	3	Numeric
100 Meters Score	30-33	4	Numeric
Long Jump Score	34-37	4	Numeric
Shot Put Score	38-41	4	Numeric
High Jump Score	42-45	4	Numeric
400 Meters Score	46-49	4	Numeric
110 Meter Hurdles Score	50-53	4	Numeric
Discus Score	54-57	4	Numeric
Pole Vault Score	58-61	4	Numeric
Javelin Score	62-65	4	Numeric
1500 Meters Score	66-69	4	Numeric
Best Score-100 Meters	70-73	4	Numeric
Best Score-Long Jump	74-77	4	Numeric
Best Score-Shot Put	78-81	4	Numeric
Best Score-High Jump	82-85	4	Numeric
Best Score-400 Meters	86-89	4	Numeric
Best Score-110 Meter Hurdles	90-93	4	Numeric
Best Score-Discus	94-97	4	Numeric
Best Score-Pole Vault	98-101	4	Numeric
Best Score-Javelin	102-105	4	Numeric
Best Score-1500 Meters	106-109	4	Numeric

Note from above that the Decathlon Master Record has been modified considerably from Program Assignment 1. The School Identification field has been added, the Total Decathlon Score field has been removed, the fields for the individual event scores which comprise the total score have been added, and the fields for the best score ever in each event have been added.

The blocking factor for this file should remain at 20 records per block.

Processing

The following processing must take place, in addition to that processing specified in Programming Assignment 1, in order to create the Decathlon Master File.

1. The School Identification code in the input record must be one of the following: STA (Stanford), USC (University of Southern California), UCL (UCLA), UCB (University of California at Berkeley), ORS (Oregon State University), ORU (University of Oregon), WAS (Washington State University), or WAU (University of Washington).
2. The individual event scores must be numeric.
3. The sum of the individual event scores must be equal to the Total Score in the input record, and this sum cannot be greater than 9000 or less than 5000.
4. Each of the decathlon event fields should be edited for reasonableness. No score in any single event should be greater than 2000 or less than 500.
5. The individual scores in each event (columns 34 - 73 in the input record) are to be placed in the individual scores fields in the master record. They are also to be placed in the best score fields in the master record (positions 70 - 109). These fields will be updated in Chapter 4.
6. If any record contains a field which fails to pass the editing specified, then the record should not be placed in the Decathlon Master File. This includes the reasonableness editing specified in #3 and #4 above.
7. Any errors found in the input records should be recorded on the Exception Report.

Exception Report

The modified format of the Exception Report is illustrated below.

PRINTER SPACING CHART

```
 1
 2 XX/XX/XX        DECATHLON MASTER LOAD EXCEPTION REPORT          PAGE XØX
 3
 4 ATHLETE            FIELD                                  TYPE
 5  NUMBER          IN ERROR                               OF ERROR
 6
 7   XXX      SCHOOL IDENTIFICATION          INVALID SCHOOL IDENTIFICATION
 8            ATHLETE NUMBER                 FIELD CONTAINS NON-NUMERIC DATA
 9            ATHLETE NAME                   NO NAME PRESENT
10            COACH NUMBER                   VIOLATES REASONABLENESS CHECK
11            TOTAL SCORE                    SUM OF INDIVIDUAL SCORES NOT = TOTAL SCORE
12            1ØØ METERS
13            LONG JUMP
14            SHOT PUT
15            HIGH JUMP
16            4ØØ METERS
17            11Ø METER HURDLES
18            DISCUS
19            POLE VAULT
20            JAVELIN
21            15ØØ METERS
22
23   XXX      XXXXXXXXXXXXXXXXXXXXXXXXX      XXXXXXXXXXXXXXXXXXXXXXXXXXXXXXXXXXXXXXXXXXXXX
24            XXXXXXXXXXXXXXXXXXXXXXXXX      XXXXXXXXXXXXXXXXXXXXXXXXXXXXXXXXXXXXXXXXXXXXX
```

NOTE: After the Decathlon Master File has been created, a utility program should be used to "dump" the file to ensure that all valid data has been properly stored in the file. Upon completion of this assignment, the program should be retained for use in Chapter 3 and Chapter 4.

Sorting; Multiple Input Files

> *"The real objective in programming should be to write correct programs from the start — not merely to emerge from debugging with no errors."[1]*

INTRODUCTION

In the program in Chapter 2, it will be recalled that there were two output files (the Program Master File, stored on magnetic disk, and the Exception Report), but there was only one input file (Program Transaction File). It is common when processing business applications to utilize two or more input files to produce the required output from a program. When this occurs, the files are normally processed in conjunction with one another; that is, data from the records of each file are used in producing output from the program. In the sample program in this chapter, two input files will be used to produce a printed report.

Whenever two or more sequential input files are used in a program, it is normally required that each of the files be arranged in such a way that data from both of the files can be coordinated and used. The most frequent method of arranging the files is to have them sorted on a given "key" within the records of the files. The "key" of a record refers to a field within the record that is used as a controlling field. When processing two input files, it is necessary to compare the key of a record from one file to the key of a record from the other file. When equal "keys" are found, the data in the related records can be extracted for use. This concept is illustrated in Figure 3-1.

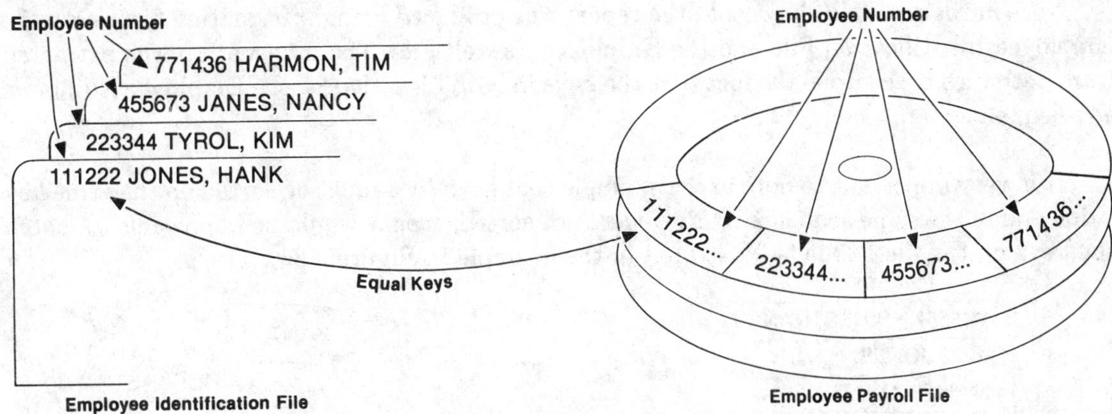

Figure 3-1 Example of Processing Sorted Records

Note from Figure 3-1 that there are two input files illustrated — the Employee Identification File and the Employee Payroll File. The Employee Identification File is stored on punched cards and contains the Employee Number and the Employee Name. The key to the file is the Employee Number. Note that the records in the Employee Identification File are sorted in an ascending sequence by the Employee Number; that is, Employee Number 111222 is the lowest key in the file and it is the first record. It is followed by records with Employee Number 223344, 455673, and 771436.

---

1 Harlan Mills, How to Write Correct Programs and Know it IBM Federal Systems Division, IBM, February 1973.

The records in the Employee Payroll File, which are stored on disk, are also sorted in an ascending sequence based upon Employee Number. When the files are processed together, it can be seen that the first record from the Employee Identification File, with Employee Number 111222, can be read, and then the first record from the Employee Payroll File, with Employee Number 111222, can be read and compared. As these records have the same key, they will contain related information which can then be processed in the program.

For example, the Employee Identification File contains the Employee Number and Employee Name. The Employee Payroll File could contain the Employee Number, the Pay Rate, and the Year-To-Date Earnings of the employee. By combining the information from both of the records, a report can be produced with the Employee Number and the Employee Name being obtained from the Employee Identification File; and the Pay Rate and Year-To-Date Earnings being obtained from the Employee Payroll File. A sample report is illustrated below.

EXAMPLE REPORT

EMPLOYEE NUMBER	EMPLOYEE NAME	EMPLOYEE PAY RATE	YEAR-TO-DATE EARNINGS
111222	JONES, HANK	4.50	8,980.00
223344	TYROL, KIM	7.50	13,987.09
455673	JANES, NANCY	3.80	6,908.00
771436	HARMON, TIM	5.45	10,873.00

Figure 3-2 Example of Report Produced from Two Input Files

Note in the example above that the report was produced using information from both the Employee Identification File and the Employee Payroll File. The information was extracted from both files based upon the fact that the keys in both files, that is, the Employee Numbers, were equal.

It is very important to note in the example that both files must be sorted on the same key value and in the same sequence. If they were not sorted, then it would be impossible to match the keys on the files. This is illustrated in the example in Figure 3-3.

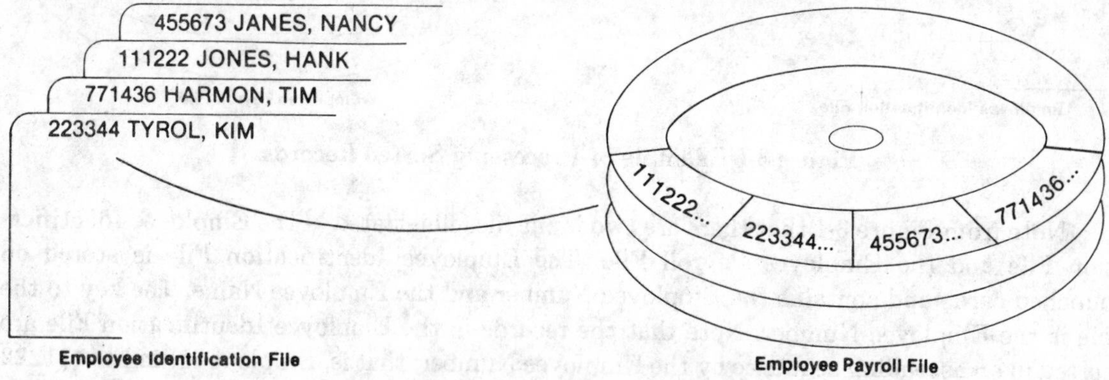

Figure 3-3 Example of Unsorted Files

Note in Figure 3-3 that the Employee Payroll File is sorted in an ascending sequence by Employee Number, but the Employee Identification File is not. When the two sequential files are read, it will not be possible to match them based upon Employee Number. For example, the first record in the Employee Identification File contains Employee Number 223344. When the first record in the Employee Payroll File is read, it is found that it contains the Employee Number 111222. Since there is not a match, the Employee Payroll File will have to be read again. The second record in the Employee Payroll File contains the Employee Number 223344, so the records can be processed. The next record from the Employee Identification File contains Employee Number 771436. Again, two records must be read from the Employee Payroll File before a match is found.

The next record in the Employee Identification File contains the Employee Number 111222. This record, however, has already been read from the Employee Payroll File and was not processed. When both files are organized and processed sequentially, as in the example, it is not possible to go backwards and retrieve the record with the key 111222; once it has been read, the only way to read it again is to reread the entire file, starting with the first record in the file. When files contain thousands of records, this is obviously not a feasible way to solve the problem. Therefore, whenever two or more sequential files are to be input to a program and are to be processed against one another, they must be sorted in the same sequence based upon a common key.

SAMPLE PROGRAM

In order to illustrate the use of two sequential input files and extracting information from the records of each of the files, the sample program in this chapter will produce an Application Programmer Status Report from the Program Master File created in Chapter 2 and an Employee Identification File. The format of this report is illustrated in Figure 3-4.

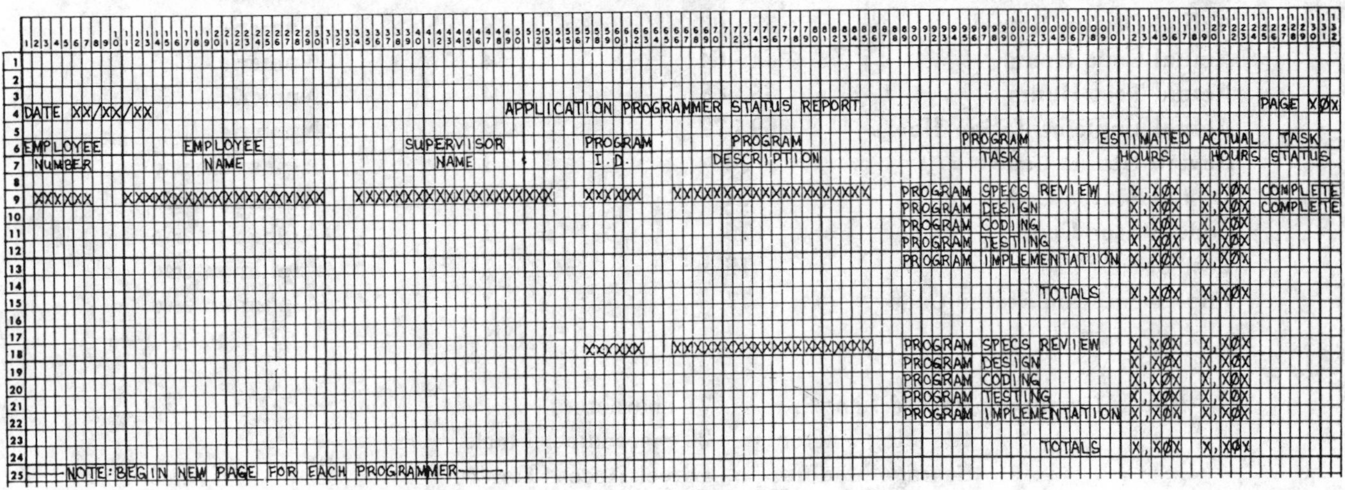

Figure 3-4 Application Programmer Status Report Format

Note from Figure 3-4 that the report contains the Employee Number, the Employee Name, the Supervisor Name, the Program I.D., the Program Description, the Program Task, the Estimated Hours, the Actual Hours, and the Task Status. For each employee, the Employee Number, Employee Name, and Supervisor Name are group-indicated. If a programmer has more than one program assigned, then the Program I.D. and Program Description for each of the programs is group-indicated.

Input

The input to the program consists of two input files — the Program Master File and the Employee Identification File. The Program Master File was created in Chapter 2 and is stored on disk. Its format is illustrated below.

Application Program Master File

FIELD	POSITION	NUMBER OF DIGITS	ATTRIBUTES
Program Identification	1 - 6	6	
Application Designation	1 - 2		Alphanumeric
Identification Number	3 - 6		Numeric
Program Description	7 - 26	20	Alphanumeric
Programmer Employee Number	27 - 32	6	Numeric
Estimated Review Hours	33 - 36	4	Numeric
Estimated Design Hours	37 - 40	4	Numeric
Estimated Code Hours	41 - 44	4	Numeric
Estimated Test Hours	45 - 48	4	Numeric
Estimated Implementation Hours	49 - 52	4	Numeric
Actual Review Hours	53 - 56	4	Numeric
Actual Design Hours	57 - 60	4	Numeric
Actual Code Hours	61 - 64	4	Numeric
Actual Test Hours	65 - 68	4	Numeric
Actual Implementation Hours	69 - 72	4	Numeric
Review Status Code	73	1	Alphanumeric
Design Status Code	74	1	Alphanumeric
Code Status Code	75	1	Alphanumeric
Test Status Code	76	1	Alphanumeric
Implementation Status Code	77	1	Alphanumeric

File Information: Record Length — 77 characters
Blocking Factor — 20 records per block
Storage Medium — Direct Access Device
Organization — Sequential
Access — Sequential

Figure 3-5 Format of Program Master File

Note from the report format in Figure 3-4 and the file format illustrated in Figure 3-5 that the Program I.D., Program Description, Estimated Hours, Actual Hours, and Task Status field on the report will be retrieved from the Program Master File. The Program Task field will be printed from program constants.

The format of the Employee Identification File, which is stored on punched cards, is illustrated below.

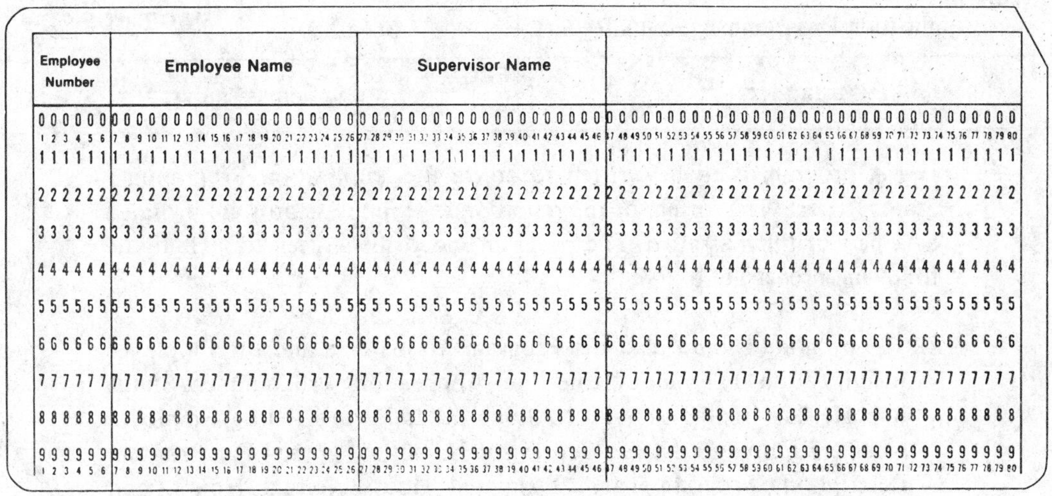

Employee Number	Employee Name	Supervisor Name	

Figure 3-6 Format of Employee Identification File

As can be seen from Figure 3-6, the Employee Identification File contains the Employee Number, Employee Name, and Supervisor Name. The Employee Name and Supervisor Name will be placed on the Application Programmer Status Report.

It should be noted that in order to produce the Application Programmer Status Report, information from both the Employee Identification File and the Program Master File will be used. Therefore, both of these files must be sorted on a given key, so that they can be processed properly, as discussed previously. The common key for both of these files, and the proper sequence for the report, is the Employee Number. Therefore, both the Employee Identification File and the Program Master File must be in ascending employee number sequence.

The Employee Identification File will be in employee number sequence when it is read by the program. It will be recalled, however, that the Program Master File was created and stored in Program Identification sequence. Therefore, it is necessary to re-sort the Program Master File into the proper sequence before it can be processed in this program.

The Programming Specifications for this program are illustrated on the following pages.

PROGRAMMING SPECIFICATIONS		
SUBJECT Application Programmer Status Report	**DATE** May 2	**PAGE** 1 **OF** 2
TO Programmer	**FROM** Systems Analyst	

A program is to be written to create the Application Programmer Status Report. The format of the report and the input records are included as a part of this narrative. The program should be written to include the following processing.

1. The program should read the Program Master File and the Employee Identification File and create the Application Programmer Status Report. The report should contain the following fields: Employee Number, Employee Name, Supervisor Name, Program I.D., Program Description, Program Task, Estimated Hours, Actual Hours, and Task Status.

2. The Employee Number, Program I.D., Program Description, Estimated Hours, and Actual Hours are taken directly from the Program Master File.

3. The Employee Name and Supervisor Name are taken directly from the Employee Identification File.

4. The records from the Program Master File and the Employee Identification File must be matched on the Employee Number. Thus, the Program Master File must be in an ascending sequence by Employee Number. The Employee Identification file is already stored in this sequence.

5. The following are the conditions under which the files are to be processed:

   a. Every record in the Program Master File has a matching record in the Employee Identification File; that is, for each Employee Number in the Program Master File, there is a corresponding record in the Employee Identification File.

   b. It is possible that a programmer is not assigned to a program. Therefore, there may be records in the Employee Identification File for which there are not matching records in the Program Master File.

   c. It is possible that a programmer is assigned to two or more programs. In this case, there will be more than one record in the Program Master File which matches a record in the Employee Identification File.

Figure 3-7 Programming Specifications (Part 1 of 2)

PROGRAMMING SPECIFICATIONS		
SUBJECT Application Programmer Status Report	DATE May 2	PAGE 2 OF 2
TO Programmer	FROM Systems Analyst	

d. All records which are contained in the Program Master File are to be reported on the Application Programmer Status Report. There is the possibility that one or more records in the Employee Identification File will not be contained on the report because the programmer is not assigned to a program.

6. The Application Programmer Status Report is to be printed according to the printer spacing chart which is included as a part of this narrative. The Employee Number, Employee Name, and Supervisor Name are to be group-indicated for each employee. The Program I.D. and Program Description are to be group-indicated for each program.

7. If the programmer is assigned to more than one program, the Program I.D., Program Description, the Program Tasks, Estimated Hours, Actual Hours, and Task Status fields should be printed for each program. The spacing should be as shown on the printer spacing chart.

8. Each programmer should be printed on a separate page. Therefore, whenever a different programmer is to be printed, new page headings should be printed.

9. The task status field should contain either the word "COMPLETE" or be blank. If the status field in the Program Master File record contains the value "C," then the task should be indicated as complete. Otherwise, the task status field should be blank on the report.

10. The Program Task field on the report will contain constants identifying each task.

11. Totals should be taken for the Estimated Hours and the Actual Hours and should be printed on the report as illustrated on the printer spacing chart.

12. The program should be written in COBOL

Figure 3-8 Programming Specifications (Part 2 of 2)

SORTING DATA

As has been noted previously, one of the requirements within the program is to sort the Program Master File in an ascending sequence based upon the Employee Number so that it will be able to be matched against the Employee Identification File. When programming in COBOL, a common method which is used to sort files is the Sort Verb and the associated processing required with it.

The processing which will be accomplished by the Sort Verb and the routines used with the Sort Verb are illustrated in the following example.

Step 1: The Program Master File records which are on disk are read one at a time and are placed in a "work file" on a separate area of the disk.

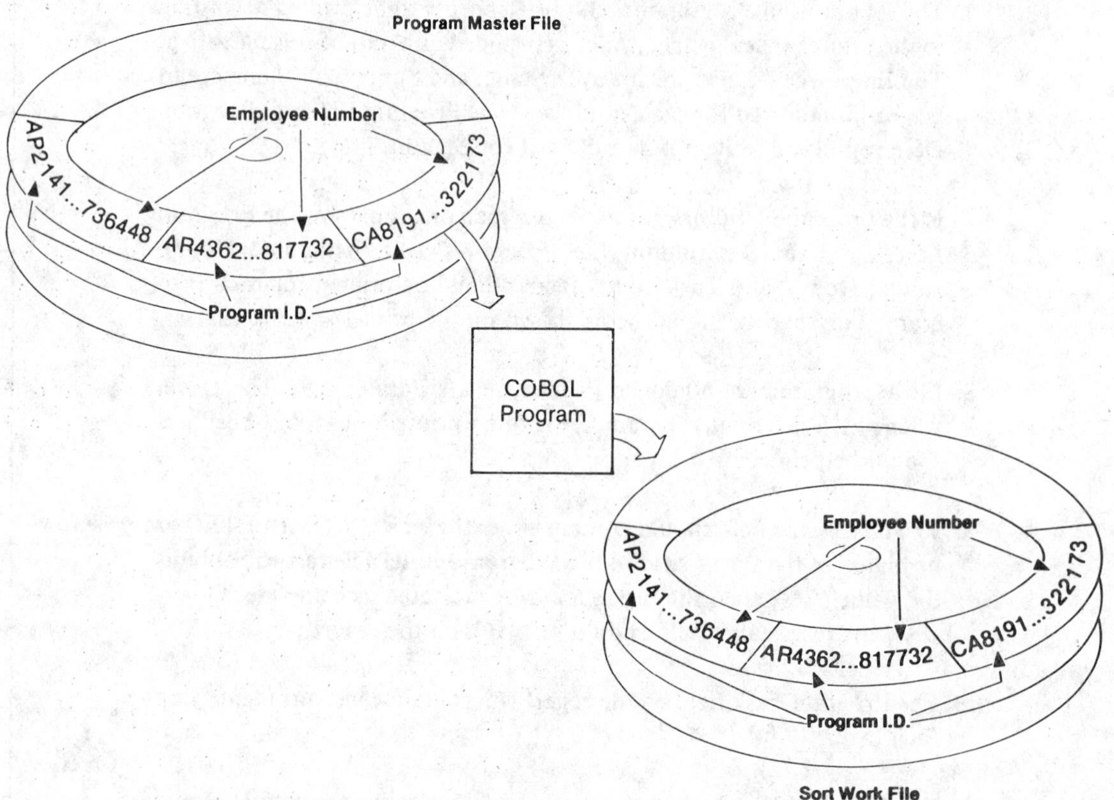

Figure 3-9 Example of Placing Data in Sort Work File

Note from the example above that the records in the Program Master File are read by the program and are stored on a disk device in a Sort Work File in the same sequence in which they are read, that is, in Program I.D. sequence. The Sort Work File must be defined within the COBOL program for use with the Sort Verb, as must the Program Master File.

After the data is placed in the Sort Work File, it is then available to be sorted. This step is illustrated in Figure 3-10.

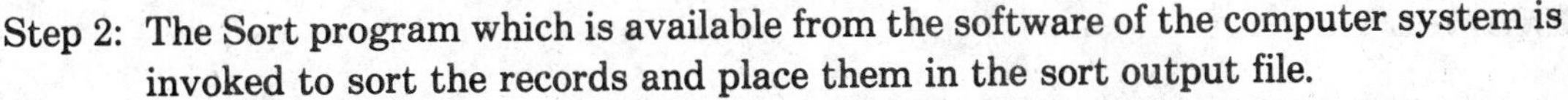

Step 2: The Sort program which is available from the software of the computer system is invoked to sort the records and place them in the sort output file.

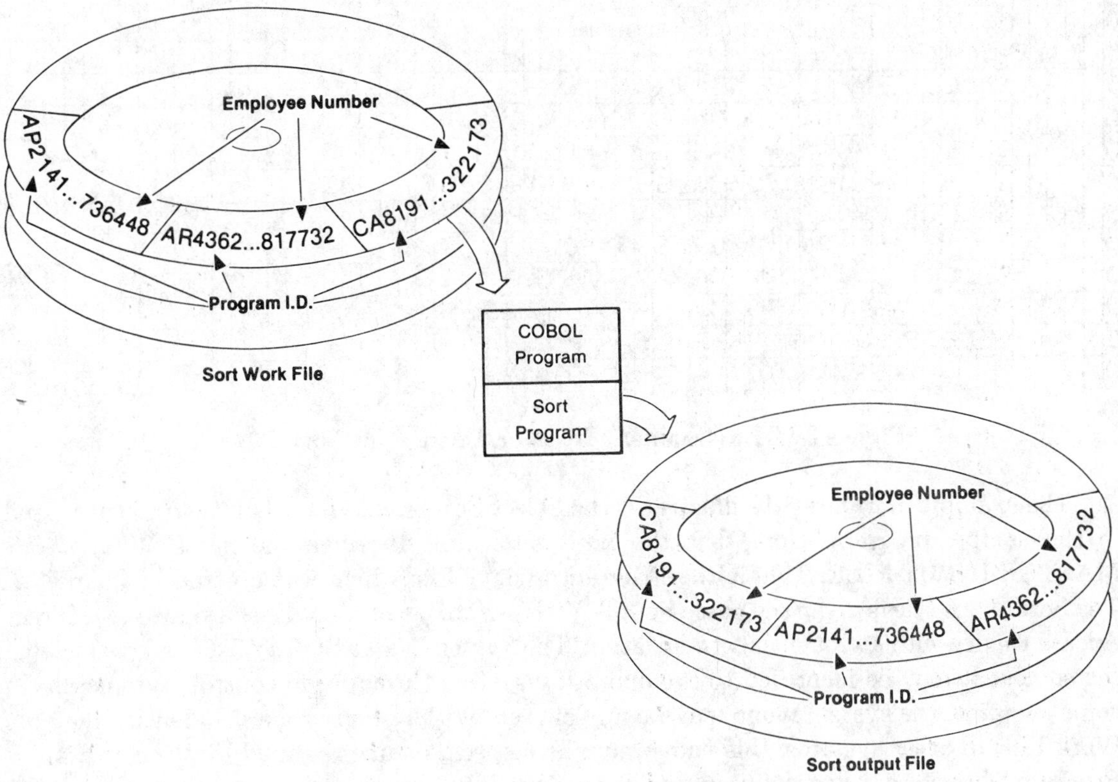

Figure 3-10 Example of Sorting the Data

Note from the example above that the data which is stored in the Sort Work File is read by the Sort Program and is sorted into the desired sequence. In this program, the data is to be sorted into an ascending sequence based upon the Employee Number. As can be seen, after the sorting is complete, the Sort Output File contains the record in an ascending sequence by Employee Number. It should be noted that the Sort Work File and the Sort Output File will be on separate areas of the disk, or possibly on different disk packs.

The Sort Output File must also be defined within the COBOL program. After it has been created, it can be opened as an input file and be processed within the COBOL program. In the sample program, it will be used to match against the Employee Identification File and create the Application Programmer Status Report.

ENVIRONMENT DIVISION

In order to use the Sort Verb to sort the data as illustrated, certain files must be defined in the Environment Division and the Data Division. As can be seen, the Program Master File must be defined so that it can be input to the sorting process. In addition, a Sort Work File must be defined, and the Sort Output File must be defined. The entries in the Environment Division to define these files are illustrated in Figure 3-11.

EXAMPLE

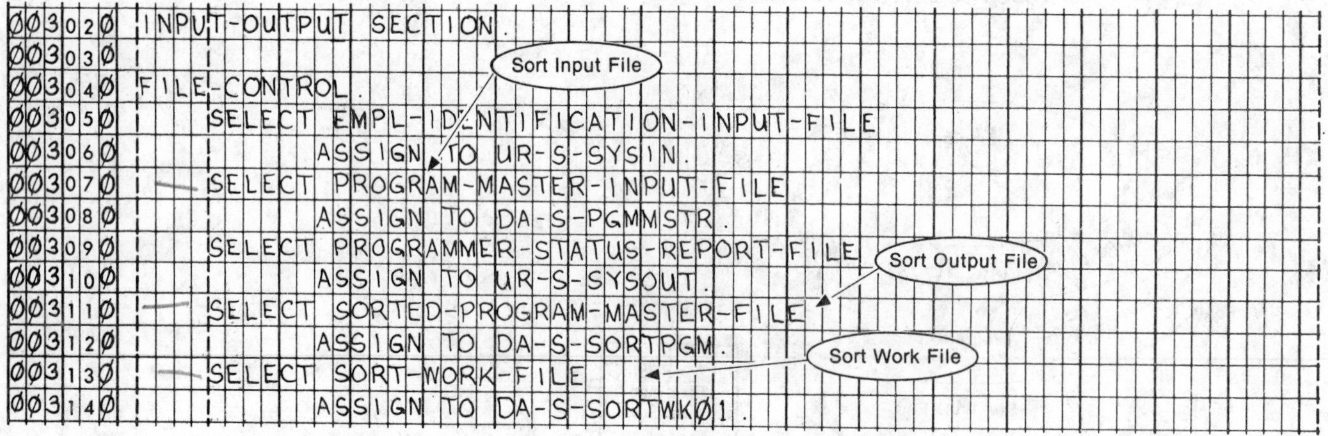


```
003020 INPUT-OUTPUT SECTION.
003030
003040 FILE-CONTROL.
003050     SELECT EMPL-IDENTIFICATION-INPUT-FILE
003060         ASSIGN TO UR-S-SYSIN.
003070     SELECT PROGRAM-MASTER-INPUT-FILE
003080         ASSIGN TO DA-S-PGMMSTR.
003090     SELECT PROGRAMMER-STATUS-REPORT-FILE
003100         ASSIGN TO UR-S-SYSOUT.
003110     SELECT SORTED-PROGRAM-MASTER-FILE
003120         ASSIGN TO DA-S-SORTPGM.
003130     SELECT SORT-WORK-FILE
003140         ASSIGN TO DA-S-SORTWK01.
```

Figure 3-11 Environment Division Entries for Sort Files

The example in Figure 3-11 illustrates the Select Statements for all of the files to be used in the sample program. Note that the Sort Input File is given the name PROGRAM-MASTER-INPUT-FILE. This is the Program Master File which was created in Chapter 2. The Sort Work File is given the name SORT-WORK-FILE. Note that it is assigned to a Direct Access Device with a sequential organization. The System Name SORTWK01 is given to this file so that it may be identified to the operating system through job control statements. In some systems, the system name may be any chosen by the programmer to identify the Sort Work File; in other systems, this name must be a specific name required by the Sort Utility Program. Therefore, when defining this Sort Work File, the programmer should ensure that the proper system name is being used.

The Sort Output File is given the name SORTED-PROGRAM-MASTER-FILE. It is to be stored on a direct access device with sequential organization and is identified to the operating system with the system name SORTPGM.

DATA DIVISION

As with other files to be used in the program, those files which are concerned with sorting data must also be defined in the Data Division. The definition of these files in the Data Division is illustrated in Figure 3-12.

EXAMPLE

```
FD  PROGRAM-MASTER-INPUT-FILE
        BLOCK CONTAINS 2Ø RECORDS
        RECORD CONTAINS 77 CHARACTERS
        LABEL RECORDS ARE STANDARD
        DATA RECORD IS PROGRAM-MASTER-INPUT-RECORD.

Ø1  PROGRAM-MASTER-INPUT-RECORD                        PIC X(77).
```

```
FD  SORTED-PROGRAM-MASTER-FILE
        BLOCK CONTAINS 2Ø RECORDS
        RECORD CONTAINS 77 CHARACTERS
        LABEL RECORDS ARE STANDARD
        DATA RECORD IS SORTED-MASTER-INPUT-RECORD.

Ø1  SORTED-MASTER-INPUT-RECORD.
    Ø5  PROGRAM-IDENTIFICATION-SORTMST                 PIC X(6).
    Ø5  PROGRAM-DESCRIPTION-SORTMST                    PIC X(2Ø).
    Ø5  PROGRAMMER-EMPL-NUMBER-SORTMST                 PIC X(6).
    Ø5  ESTIMATED-TASK-HOURS-SORTMST OCCURS 5 TIMES
                                                       PIC 9(4).
    Ø5  ACTUAL-TASK-HOURS-SORTMST    OCCURS 5 TIMES
                                                       PIC 9(4).
    Ø5  TASK-STATUS-INDICATORS-SORTMST OCCURS 5 TIMES
                                                       PIC X.
        88  TASK-IS-COMPLETE                           VALUE 'C'.
```

```
SD  SORT-WORK-FILE
        RECORD CONTAINS 77 CHARACTERS
        DATA RECORD IS SORT-WORK-RECORD.

Ø1  SORT-WORK-RECORD.
    Ø5  FILLER                                         PIC X(26).
    Ø5  PROGRAMMER-EMPL-NUMBER-SORTWK                  PIC X(6).
    Ø5  FILLER                                         PIC X(45).
```

```
[SD file-name

    [; RECORD CONTAINS [integer-1 TO] integer-2 CHARACTERS]

    [; DATA {RECORD IS  } data-name-1 [, data-name-2] ... ]
            {RECORDS ARE}
```

Figure 3-12 Data Division File Definitions

In the example in Figure 3-12, the input file to the sort is the PROGRAM-MASTER-INPUT-FILE. Note that the definition of this file is the same as the definition of the PROGRAM-MASTER-OUTPUT-FILE in Chapter 2; that is, since the file which was created in Chapter 2 is the input to this program in Chapter 3, the blocking factor and record length must be the same. It should also be noted that the input area for the file, PROGRAM-MASTER-INPUT-RECORD, is specified as 77 characters in length (PIC X(77)), but there are no detailed field definitions. This is because the fields within the record are not going to be referenced in the program; the fields will be referenced only for the output of the Sort.

The output file from the sort is the SORTED-PROGRAM-MASTER-FILE. This is the file which will be produced as a result of the sort processing, as illustrated in Figure 3-10. It contains the same blocking factor and record length as the PROGRAM-MASTER-INPUT-FILE, that is, the input file to the sort, because the same records are contained in this file as are contained in the PROGRAM-MASTER-INPUT-FILE. The only difference between the two files is that the records in the PROGRAM-MASTER-INPUT-FILE are stored in Program I.D. sequence while the records in the SORTED-PROGRAM-MASTER-FILE will be stored in Employee Number sequence as a result of the sort processing.

The record identification for the SORTED-PROGRAM-MASTER-FILE contains a detailed definition of each of the fields in the record. This is because it is the record in the SORTED-PROGRAM-MASTER-FILE, that is, the sort output file, which will be processed within the program. Note that the definitions of the fields correspond to the definitions of the fields in Chapter 2 where the Program Master File was created. Whenever a disk or tape file is used as input to a program, the definition of the record should be equivalent to that specified when the file was created so that the data can be referenced properly.

The Sort Work File must be defined with a special entry in Area A of the coding form. Instead of the more familiar "FD" entry, the entry "SD" is required. This is because a sort work file is being defined. Note from the general format illustrated that two optional entries may be included — the Record Contains Clause and the Data Record Is Clause. These two entries are optional with the FD Statement as well. It is suggested, however, that the clauses be included for documentation purposes. In the example, the Record Contains Clause specifies that there will be 77 characters in the sort work record. This is because there are 77 characters in the records to be sorted; that is, in the records contained in the PROGRAM-MASTER-INPUT-FILE, which is the input file to the sort program. The Data Record is SORT-WORK-RECORD, which is defined on line 007060.

It will be noted also that the Block Contains Clause is not included for the Sort Work File even though the input and output files for the sort are blocked files. This is because the Sort program will use its own blocking factor depending upon the format of the records to be sorted; therefore, this entry may not be included in the definition of the Sort Work File.

It should be noted that within SORT-WORK-RECORD, only one field is defined — PROGRAMMER-EMPL-NUMBER-SORTWK. The rest of the record is specified as Filler. The reason that the Programmer Employee Number is specified is that this is the field on which the sort is to take place. The only fields which must be specified for the sort record are the fields which are to act as the keys when sorting. Since the Programmer Employee Number is the only field on which the sort is to take place, it must be specified in the Sort Work Record.

SORT STATEMENT

In order to cause the records in the input file to be read into the program, the records sorted, and the sorted output file to be created, the Sort Verb must be specified in the Procedure Division of the COBOL program. The Sort Statement used in the sample program is illustrated in Figure 3-13.

EXAMPLE

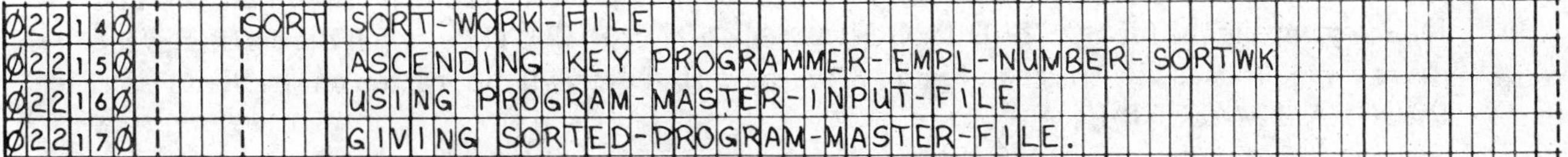

```
       SORT SORT-WORK-FILE
            ASCENDING KEY PROGRAMMER-EMPL-NUMBER-SORTWK
            USING PROGRAM-MASTER-INPUT-FILE
            GIVING SORTED-PROGRAM-MASTER-FILE.
```

```
SORT file-name-1 ON {ASCENDING | DESCENDING} KEY data-name-1 [, data-name-2] ...

USING file-name-2 [, file-name-3] ...

GIVING file-name-4
```

Figure 3-13 Example of Sort Verb

Note from Figure 3-13 that the Sort Statement begins with the SORT verb. It is followed by the name SORT-WORK-FILE, which corresponds to the "file-name-1" entry in the general format illustrated. The file-name-1 is always the sort work file which is defined with the SD entry in the Data Division.

The next entry in the general format is the optional word ON followed by one of the required words, either ASCENDING or DESCENDING. This word is used to indicate the sequence in which the particular field specified by data-name-1 is to be sorted. The word ASCENDING specifies that the data is to be sorted in an ascending sequence. It should be noted that most Sort programs will also allow the data to be sorted in a descending sequence, and this is specified by the word DESCENDING. In the example above, the word ASCENDING is specified, indicating that the file is to be sorted in an ascending sequence. The optional word KEY can then be specified to make the statement easier to read.

As noted, the data-name entry following either Ascending or Descending specifies the data name of the control field in the record to be sorted as specified in the File Section for the SD file. In the example in Figure 3-13, this field is PROGRAMMER-EMPL-NUMBER-SORTWK because the records are to be sorted on the programmer employee number. It will be recalled that this field was defined in the File Section for the SD file (see Figure 3-12). It should be noted that more than one field may be specified as a control field by using the data-name-2, etc. entries. The fields specified for data-name-2, etc. are minor to the previous data-name; that is, the field specified first with data-name-1 is the major field in the sort, the field specified second with data-name-2 is the next major field in the sort, etc. Different sort programs for different machines have varying maximums concerning the number of fields which may be specified.

The entries described previously have specified the file to be sorted and the method and key on which the records are to be sorted. It remains to specify which file(s) are to be input to the sort and what file is to be output from the sort. In order to specify the input file, the name of the file must be specified following the keyword USING. In the example, the input file is the PROGRAM-MASTER-INPUT-FILE.

In order to specify the output file to be created by the sorting process, the GIVING keyword is used. In the example, it can be seen that the filename specified following the GIVING keyword is the file SORTED-PROGRAM-MASTER-FILE. Thus, when the sorting process is completed, as illustrated in Figure 3-10, the sorted data will be written on the SORTED-PROGRAM-MASTER-FILE.

It should be noted that when the Sort verb is used with the USING and GIVING keywords, the files specified cannot be opened or closed within the body of the COBOL program; that is, they are automatically opened and closed by the Sort verb. After the sorting is completed, the output file is closed by the Sort verb. After it is closed, the program can open the file as an input file and process the sorted data. This is the processing which is to take place within the sample program

SAMPLE PROGRAM

In order to illustrate the Sort verb and multiple input file processing, it will be recalled that the sample program is to read the Sorted Program Master File and the Employee Identification File and create the Application Programmer Status Report. Before beginning the design of the program to accomplish this processing, it is critical that the programmer understand the basic processing which is to occur within the program. It is not possible to properly design a program without first thoroughly understanding what is to be accomplished by the program.

As noted, information from both the Sorted Program Master File and the Employee Identification File is to be used to create the Application Programmer Status Report. There will be an entry on the report for each record which is found in the Sorted Program Master File. This is illustrated below.

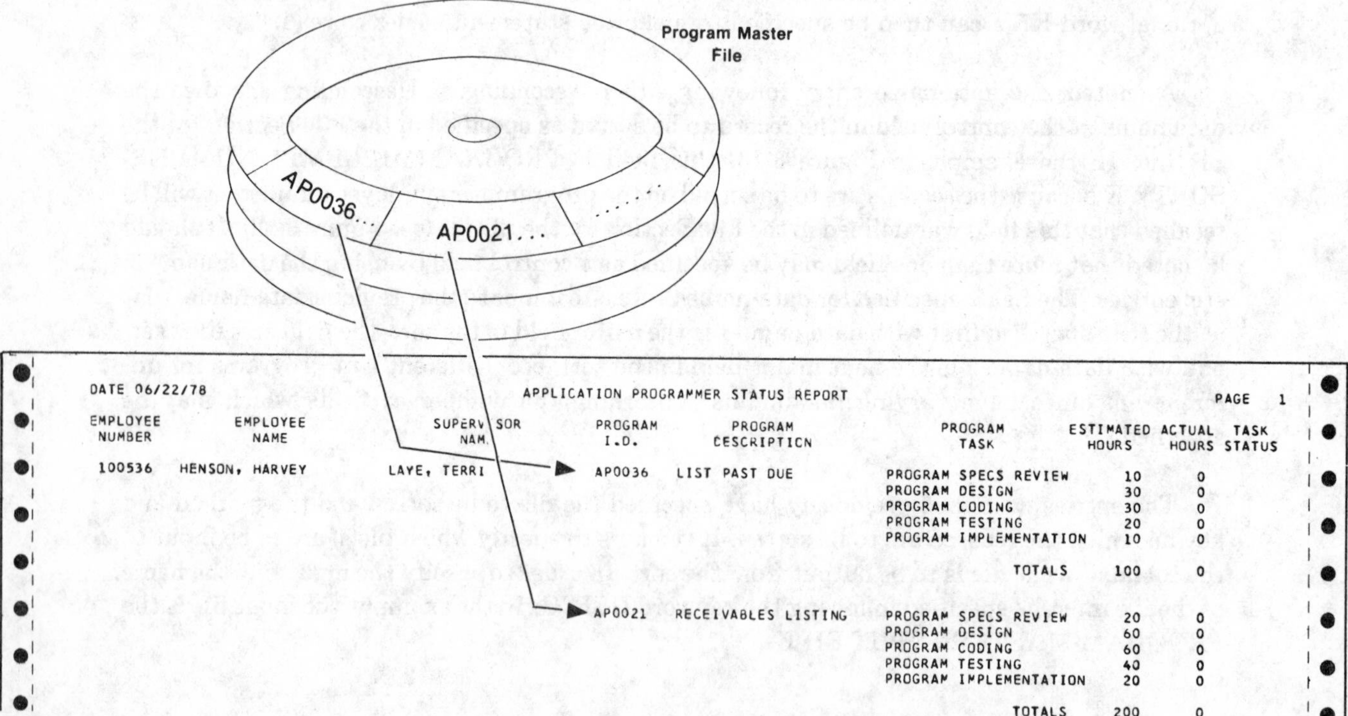

Figure 3-14 Example of Report

Note from Figure 3-14 that for each record on the Program Master File, there is an entry on the report. It is important to realize that this means that the processing required for the program utilizes two basic steps: 1) Read a record from the Program Master File; 2) Write an entry on the report. Again, each record in the Program Master File will have a corresponding entry on the report.

It will be recalled that information for the report is also being obtained from the Employee Identification File. Each record on this file, however, will not necessarily generate information for the report because it is possible that there are programmers in the Employee Identification File who are not assigned to programs. When the Employee Identification File is considered, the processing for the program becomes as follows:

1. Read a record from the Program Master File.
2. If it is the first time and a record has not been read from the Employee Identification File, then read a record from the Employee Identification File.
3. Compare the Employee Number in the record from the Program Master File with the Employee Number in the Employee Identification Record.
4. If the Employee Numbers in the two records are equal, then write the report using data from both of the records.
5. If the Employee Numbers in the two records are not equal, then read one or more records from the Employee Identification File until the Employee Numbers are equal. When the Employee Numbers are equal, then write the report using data from both records. It should be noted that there will always be a record on the Employee Identification File which contains an Employee Number equal to the Employee Number in the Program Master File, since this was specified in the programming specifications (see page 3.6).

Each time data is to be obtained for the report, the sequence specified above will be followed. Therefore, each time data is required for the report, one record from the Program Master File will be read, and it will generate an entry on the report.

The following examples illustrate the cases which can occur when matching records from the Program Master File with records from the Employee Identification File.

Case 1: A record from the Program Master File is read and its Employee Number is not equal to the Employee Number in the Employee Identification record. Therefore, a record is read from the Employee Identification File.

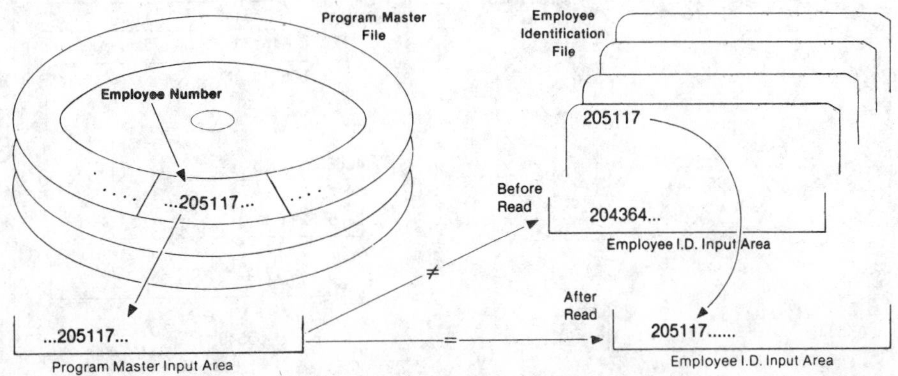

Figure 3-15 Example of Reading Records to Find Equal Employee Numbers

Note from Figure 3-15 that a record with Employee Number 205117 is read from the Program Master File. The Employee Number is then compared with the Employee Number in the record stored in the Employee Identification Input Area, which is 204364. Since they are not equal, a record must be read from the Employee Identification File. The record read contains Employee Number 205117. Thus, the Employee Numbers are equal. The report will then be written using data from both of the records.

Case 2: A record is read from the Program Master File and the Employee Number in the record is compared to the Employee Number in the record stored in the Employee Identification Input Area. The Employee Numbers are equal.

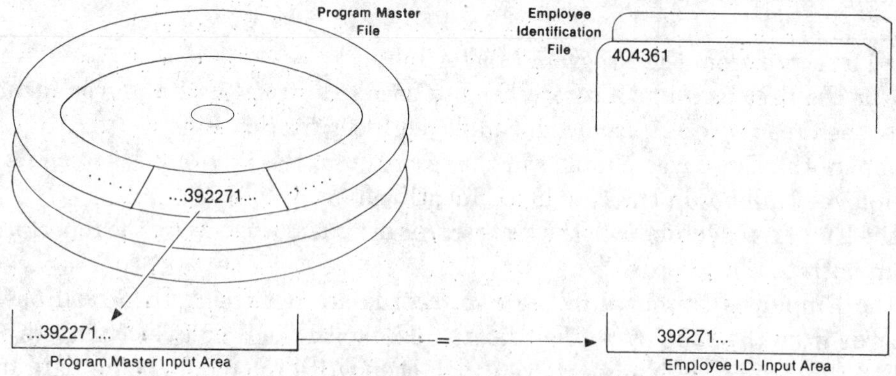

Figure 3-16 Example of Equal Record Already in Storage

Note in Figure 3-16 that when the record is read from the Program Master File, the record which is in the input area for the Employee Identification File contains an equal Employee Number. When this occurs, it is not necessary to read a record from the Employee Identification File; it is already in storage. It should be noted that this is a valid case since more than one program can be assigned to a programmer; that is, there may be more than one record on the Program Master File with the same Employee Number. When this case occurs, the report would be written using data from both of the records.

Case 3: A record is read from the Program Master File and the Employee Number in the record is compared to the Employee Number in the record stored in the Employee Identification Input Area. In order to find an equal Employee Number in the Employee Identification File, more than one record must be read from the Employee Identification File.

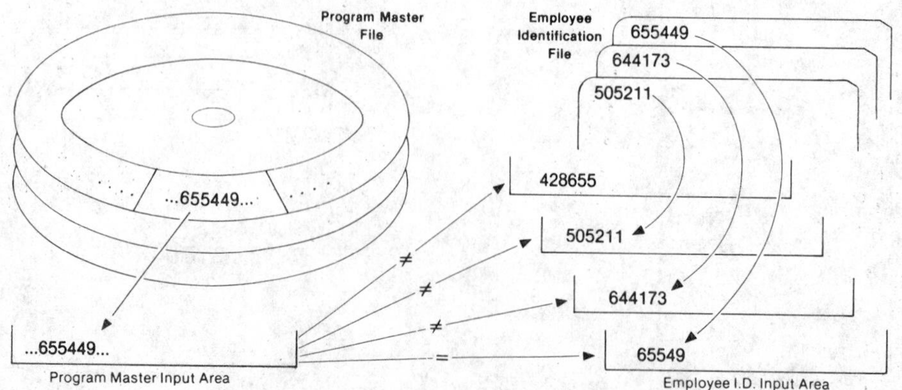

Figure 3-17 Example of Multiple Reads

From Figure 3-17 it can be seen that when a record with Employee Number 655449 is read from the Program Master File, it is compared to the Employee Number contained in the record in the Employee Identification Input Area. Since they are not equal, a record with Employee Number 505211 is read from the Employee Identification File. This Employee Number is not equal to the Employee Number in the record read from the Program Master File. Therefore, another record is read from the Employee Identification File, with Employee Number 644173. Again, these Employee Numbers are not equal, so another record is read from the Employee Identification File. The third record read contains the Employee Number 655449. Since this Employee Number is equal to the Employee Number in the record from the Program Master File, the report will be written using data from both of the equal records.

In all of the previous examples, after the report is written, another record from the Program Master File is read. It is then compared to the Employee Number in the record from the Employee Identification File and if they are not equal, records are read from the Employee Identification File until they are equal. This process of reading a record from the Program Master File, if necessary reading one or more records from the Employee Identification File until the Employee Numbers are equal, and then writing the report will continue until all of the records on the Program Master File have been processed; at which time, the program will be terminated.

PROGRAM DESIGN — IPO CHARTS AND HIERARCHY CHART

After gaining an understanding of the processing which is to occur within the program, the program must be designed. The program design begins with the development of the structure of the program using IPO Charts. The IPO Chart for the top level module in the program, whose function is to Create the Status Report, is illustrated below.

IPO CHART

PROGRAM: Application Programmer Status Report	PROGRAMMER: Shelly/Cashman	DATE: June 1
MODULE NAME: Create Status Report	REF: AØØØ	MODULE FUNCTION: Create the Status Report

INPUT	PROCESSING	REF:	OUTPUT
1. Program Master File	1. Initialize		1. Application Programmer
2. Employee Identification File	2. Obtain status report data	BØØØ	Status Report
	3. Write status report	BØ1Ø	
	4. Terminate		

Figure 3-18 IPO Chart — Create Status Report Module

As can be seen from Figure 3-18, the output from the module whose function is to create the status report is the Application Programmer Status Report. The input consists of the Program Master File and the Employee Identification File. The major processing tasks to create the output from the input are Initialize, Obtain status report data, Write status report, and Terminate.

In analyzing these tasks, it is found that the Initialize task consists merely of opening the files, so it does not justify a separate module. The task of Obtaining status report data consists of a number of major tasks since the two input files must be read and matched. Therefore, this task requires a separate module, with the reference number B000. The third major task of writing the status report also requires a separate module, while the task of termination requires merely the closing of the files and stopping the run. Therefore, it does not justify a separate module.

It should be noted that in this highest level module, the major processing tasks specified consist of merely "obtain the data" and "write the report." Thus, on this highest level, the program designer is not concerned with the actual reading of the files, the matching of the files, or the other detail processing which must take place within the program; rather, the concern is with the high level processing tasks which must take place to transform the input to the output. Only when the lower-level modules are designed is the designer concerned with the detail processing.

The hierarchy chart developed as a result of the IPO Chart in Figure 3-18 is illustrated below.

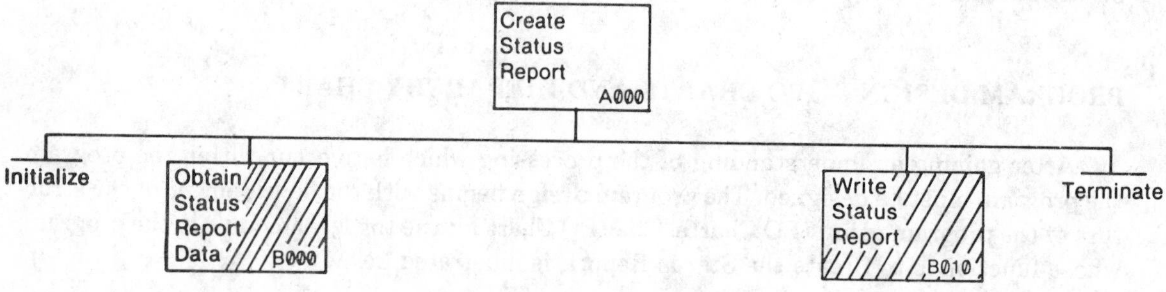

Figure 3-19 Hierarchy Chart

As can be seen in Figure 3-19, there are four major processing tasks required to Create the Status Report. The Initialize and Terminate tasks do not require separate modules, but the tasks of Obtaining Status Report Data and Writing the Status Report do require separate modules.

The next step in the program design is to design the IPO Chart for the module whose function is to obtain status report data. This IPO Chart is shown in Figure 3-20.

IPO CHART

PROGRAM: Application Programmer Status Report	PROGRAMMER: Shelly/Cashman		DATE: June 1
MODULE NAME: Obtain Status Report Data	REF: B000	MODULE FUNCTION: Obtain Data For the Status Report	

INPUT	PROCESSING	REF:	OUTPUT
1. Program Master File	1. Obtain master record	C000	1. Data for Report
2. Employee Identification File	2. Obtain employee identification record		
	3. Match master and employee records		

Figure 3-20 IPO Chart — Obtain Status Report Module

The output from the module which obtains status report data is the data for the report. The input to the module is the Program Master File and the Employee Identification File. The major processing tasks are Obtain a Master Record, Obtain Employee Identification Record, and Match Master and Employee Records. In order to obtain a master record, there are several things which must be done. Certainly the input record must be read; but, in addition, the Program Master File must be sorted prior to being read. Therefore, this processing appears to be long and complex enough to justify a separate module.

Obtaining the Employee Identification Record appears to be merely a read statement while matching the master and employee records does not seem to be a large or complex operation. As a result of this analysis, it is decided that obtaining the master record will be a separate module while the other two tasks can be contained within the module. The hierarchy chart after this analysis is illustrated below.

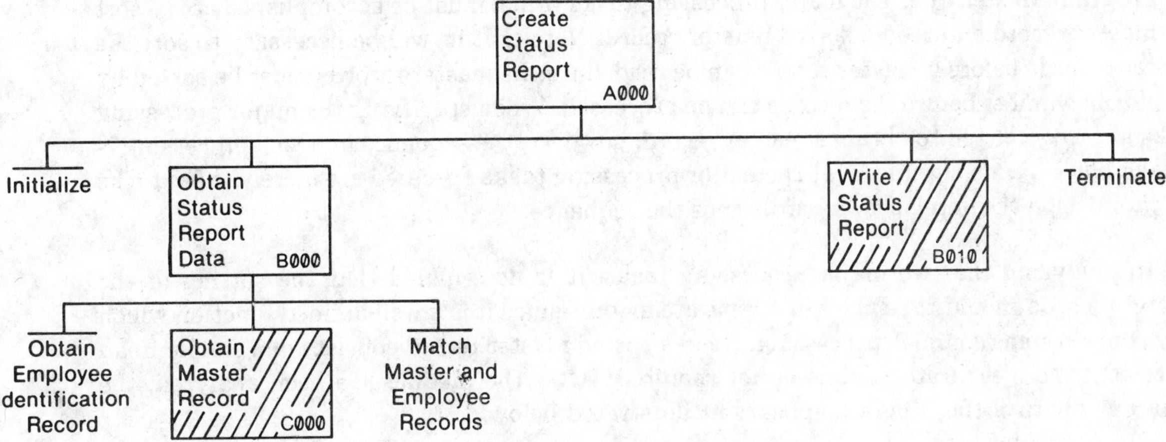

Figure 3-21 Hierarchy Chart

As can be seen, there are three major processing tasks in the module which obtains the status report data. One of these tasks, obtain master record, will be a separate module while the other two will be contained within the module.

It will be recalled that it is possible to analyze the modules in more than one sequence. In this program, the designer decided to next analyze the module which obtains the master record. The IPO Chart for this module is illustrated in Figure 3-22.

IPO CHART

PROGRAM: Application Programmer Status Report		PROGRAMMER: Shelly/Cashman		DATE: June 1
MODULE NAME: Obtain Master Record	REF: CØØØ	MODULE FUNCTION: Obtain a Master Record		
INPUT	**PROCESSING**		**REF:**	**OUTPUT**
1. Program Master File	1. Sort master records		DØØØ	1. Program Master Record
	2. Read sorted master record			

Figure 3-22 IPO Chart — Obtain Master Record Module

The output from the module illustrated above is the Program Master Record. The input is the Program Master File. The major processing tasks which must be accomplished are to sort the master record and read a sorted master record. Note that it will be necessary to sort the master records before a master record can be read since the master records must be sorted by Employee Number before the records can be processed. When specifying the major processing tasks to be completed to obtain a master record, however, the sequence in which processing is to take place has no significance. The major processing tasks specified are merely those tasks which must be accomplished, regardless of the sequence.

In analyzing the two major processing tasks, it is determined that the sorting of the master records should take place in a separate module since it is a well-defined function which may contain some complex processing. Read a sorted master record consists of a simple Read Statement, so a separate module is not required. After the module has been analyzed, the hierarchy chart of the program appears as illustrated below.

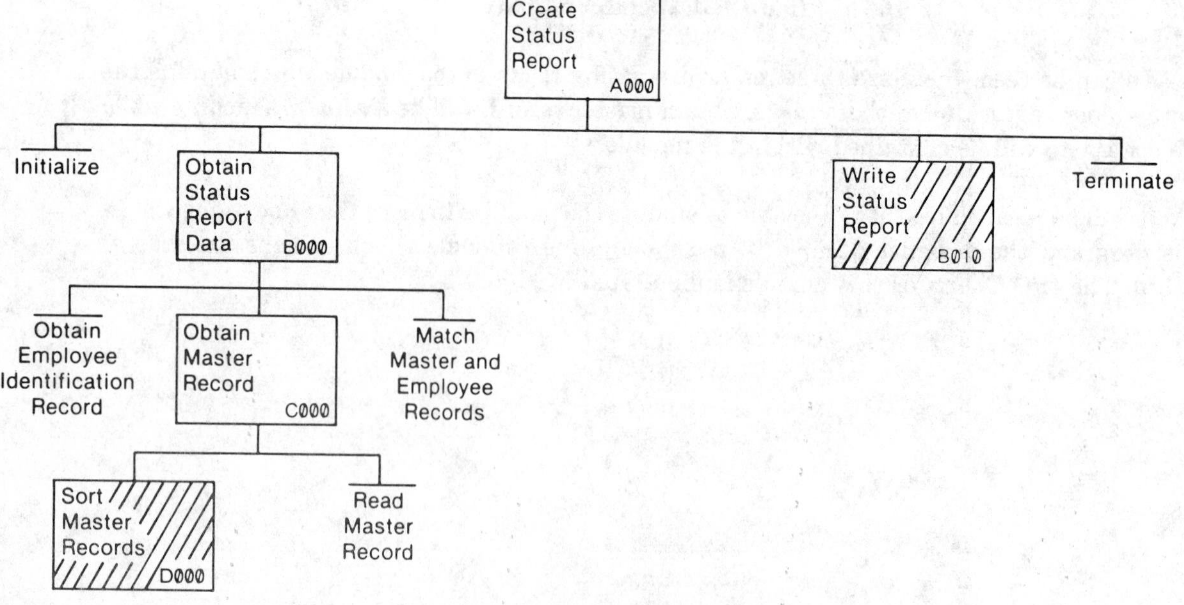

Figure 3-23 Hierarchy Chart

Continuing down the input "leg" of the program structure, the next module to analyze with an IPO Chart is the module whose function is to Sort the Master Records. The IPO Chart for this module is shown below.

IPO CHART					
PROGRAM: Application Programmer Status Report		PROGRAMMER: Shelly/Cashman			DATE: June 1
MODULE NAME: Sort Master Records	REF: DØØØ	MODULE FUNCTION: Sort the Master File			
INPUT	PROCESSING		REF:	OUTPUT	
1. Unsorted Program Master File	1. Sort program master file on			1. Sorted Program Master File	
	employee number				

Figure 3-24 IPO Chart — Sort Master Records Module

As can be seen, the output from the module is the sorted Program Master File, and the input to the module is the unsorted Program Master File. The only major processing task which must be accomplished is to sort the Program Master File on Employee Number. Since this is the only task to be accomplished by the module, a lower level module is not required. Thus, the hierarchy chart remains as was shown in Figure 3-23.

Since the structure of the input "leg" of the program has been completely designed, the programmer would turn attention to the output side of the program. The first module to analyze is the module which writes the status report. The IPO Chart for this module is shown below.

IPO CHART					
PROGRAM: Application Programmer Status Report		PROGRAMMER: Shelly/Cashman			DATE: June 1
MODULE NAME: Write Status Report	REF: BØ1Ø	MODULE FUNCTION: Write the Status Report			
INPUT	PROCESSING		REF:	OUTPUT	
1. Data For Report	1. Print headings		CØ1Ø	1. Status Report Line	
	2. Format detail line				
	3. Accumulate and reset totals				
	4. Write total line		CØ2Ø		
	5. Write detail line				

Figure 3-25 IPO Chart — Write Status Report Module

Note in Figure 3-25 that the output from the module is a Status Report Line. The input to the module is the data for the report which was obtained by the input "leg" of the program. The major processing tasks which must be accomplished in order to write the status report are Print the headings, Format the detail line, Accumulate and reset the totals, Write the total line, and Write the detail line.

In analyzing these major processing tasks, it is found that printing the headings may be somewhat lengthy (that is, greater than 8-10 statements), so it will be done in a separate module. Formatting the detail line will be a series of straightforward move statements, so there is no reason to make it a separate module. Accumulating and resetting the total required on the report is just a small task, so it is not a separate module. Writing the total line may be somewhat lengthy, so it is made a separate module. Finally, writing the detail line is a simple write statement. Thus, the module which writes the status report will have two submodules — one to print the headings (C010), and one to write the total line (C020). The hierarchy chart after this analysis is shown in Figure 3-26.

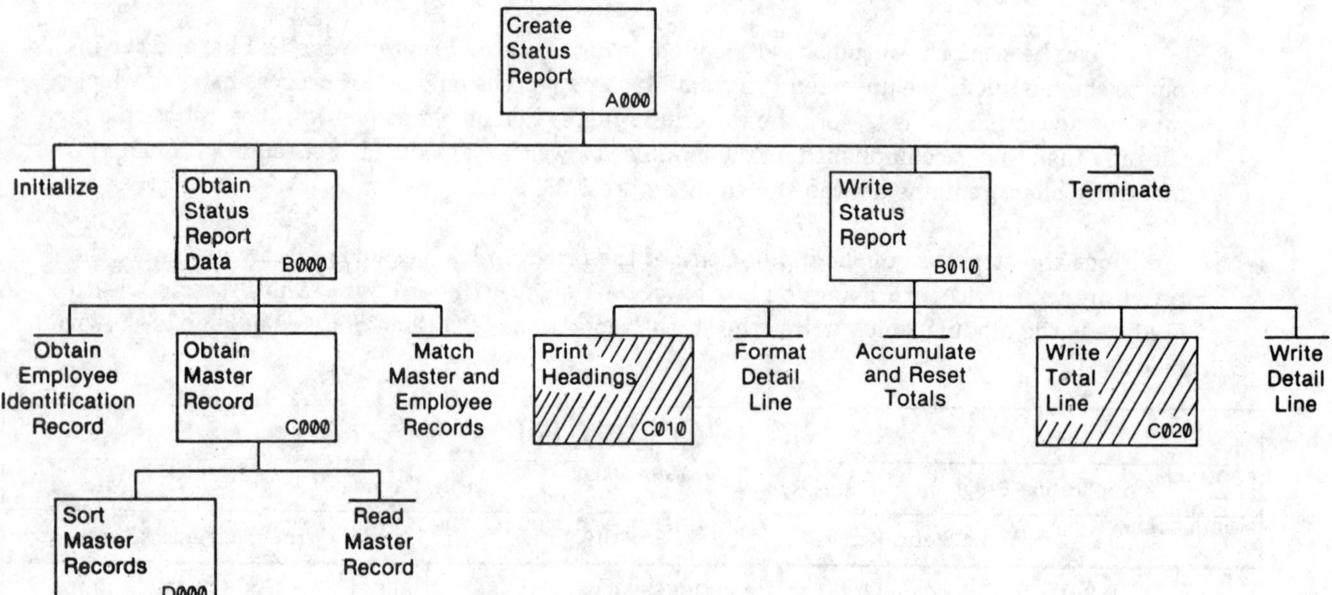

Figure 3-26 Hierarchy Chart

Note from the hierarchy chart above that the five major processing tasks involved in writing the status report have been added. There are two separate modules — printing the headings and writing the total line. The other three major processing tasks — formatting the detail line, accumulating and resetting the totals, and writing the detail line will be contained within the module which writes the status report.

The next two modules to be analyzed, one to print the headings and one to write the total line are illustrated in Figure 3-27.

IPO CHART					
PROGRAM: Application Programmer Status Report		PROGRAMMER: Shelly/Cashman		DATE: June 1	
MODULE NAME: Print Headings	REF: C010	MODULE FUNCTION: Print the Report Headings			
INPUT	PROCESSING		REF:	OUTPUT	
	1. Format heading lines			1. Report Headings	
	2. Write heading lines				

IPO CHART					
PROGRAM: Application Programmer Status Report		PROGRAMMER: Shelly/Cashman		DATE: June 1	
MODULE NAME: Write Total Line	REF: C020	MODULE FUNCTION: Write the Report Total Lines			
INPUT	PROCESSING		REF:	OUTPUT	
1. Accumulators	1. Format total line			1. Total Line	
	2. Write total line				

Figure 3-27 IPO Charts — Print Headings and Write Total Line Modules

Note from Figure 3-27 that the output of the module which prints the report headings are the heading lines. The major processing tasks to accomplish the printing of the report headings are formatting the heading lines and writing the heading lines. Neither of these tasks is so large or complex as to justify a separate module.

The output from the module which is to write the total lines is the total line which will appear on the report. The input to the module are the total accumulators. The major tasks consist of formatting the total line and writing the total line; neither of which is large or complex. Therefore, there are no lower level modules required to write the total lines.

Summary

As can be seen, the development of the structure of a program proceeds in the same manner regardless of the task to be accomplished by the program. It is important that the programmer develop the methodology in such a way that the approach to each program is the same, that is, the method used to solve the problem is the same. In this manner, well-designed programs will become a habit rather than an occasional occurrence.

PROGRAM DESIGN — PSEUDOCODE SPECIFICATIONS

Once the structure of the program has been developed, the programmer turns to developing the logic for each of the modules in the program through the use of pseudocode. The following pages contain the pseudocode for the modules in the sample program.

Pseudocode Specifications — Create Status Report

The pseudocode specifications for the module whose function is to create the status report are illustrated below.

PSEUDOCODE SPECIFICATIONS		
PROGRAM: Application Programmer Status Report	PROGRAMMER: Shelly/Cashman	DATE: June 1
MODULE NAME: Create Status Report REF: AØØØ	MODULE FUNCTION: Create the Status Report	
PSEUDOCODE	**REF:**	**FILES, RECORDS, FIELDS REQUIRED**
Open status report and employee identification files		Status report file
Obtain data for report	BØØØ	Employee identification file
PERFORM UNTIL no more sorted program master records		No more master records indicator
Write status report	BØ1Ø	
Obtain data for report	BØØØ	
ENDPERFORM		
Close status report and employee files		
Stop run		

Figure 3-28 Pseudocode Specifications — Create Status Report Module

Note from Figure 3-28 that the first statement opens the Status Report File and the Employee Identification File. It should be noted that the Program Master File is not opened at this point. This is because the file is going to be input to the sort process and, as was mentioned previously, the input, sort work, and output files should not be opened or closed in another part of the program prior to the sorting process.

After the two files are opened, the B000 module is entered to obtain data for the report. This module will control the reading of records from the Sorted Program Master File and the Employee Identification File. A loop is then entered, as indicated by the Perform Until Statement, which will cause the report to be written by the B010 module and then cause more data to be obtained by the B000 module. This processing will continue until there are no more Sorted Program Master File records, at which time the Status Report File and the Employee Identification File will be closed and the program will be terminated. It should be recalled that the files used in conjunction with the sort processing are not opened at the start of the program and, therefore, should not be closed at the conclusion of the program.

Pseudocode Specifications — Obtain Status Report Data

The next module for which to develop the logic is the module whose function is to obtain the status report data. The pseudocode for this module is shown in Figure 3-29.

PSEUDOCODE SPECIFICATIONS		
PROGRAM: Application Programmer Status Report	PROGRAMMER: Shelly/Cashman	DATE: June 1
MODULE NAME: Obtain Status Report Data	REF: BØØØ	MODULE FUNCTION: Obtain Data for the Status Report
PSEUDOCODE	**REF:**	**FILES, RECORDS, FIELDS REQUIRED**

Obtain a program master record
IF this is the first time
    Read employee identification record
    Indicate not the first time
ENDIF
PERFORM UNTIL program master record =
        employee identification record or
        there are no more program master records
    Read employee identification file
ENDPERFORM
	CØØØ	First time indicator
		Employee number from program master record
		Employee number from employee identification file
		No more program master records indicator
		Employee identification file
		Employee file record area
		    Employee number
		    Employee name
		    Supervisor name

Figure 3-29 Pseudocode Specifications — Obtain Status Report Data

The first step in obtaining data for the status report is to obtain a Program Master Record. This is accomplished by the C000 module. Then, if a record has not been read from the Employee Identification File, that is, if it is the first time, then a record is read from the Employee Identification File and an indicator is set to show that it is no longer the first time through the module.

The next step in the logic illustrated in Figure 3-29 is to enter a loop which will be performed until either the Employee Number in the Program Master Record is equal to the Employee Number in the Employee Identification File or there are no more Program Master Records. The only instruction in this loop is to read an Employee Identification File Record.

It is important to understand why this loop is sufficient to process all of the Program Master File data. It is based upon the fact that for every record in the Program Master File, there is a matching record in the Employee Identification File. When a Program Master Record is read, the Employee Identification Record will contain either an Employee Number which is equal to the Employee Number in the Program Master Record or is less than the Employee Number in the Program Master Record. This is illustrated in the examples which follow.

EXAMPLE — Processing Matching Records

Step 1: The first record from the Program Master File (which is sorted in Employee Number sequence) is read and stored in the Program Master File input area; and, since this is the first time, a record from the Employee Identification File is read and stored in the Employee Identification File input area.

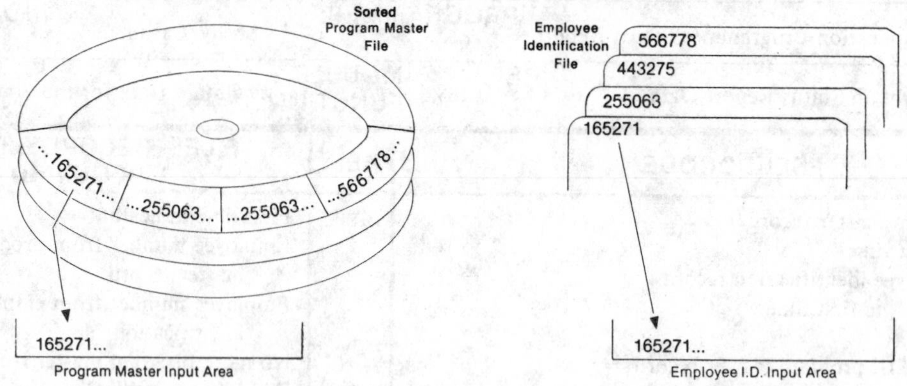

Figure 3-30 First Records are Read from Input Files

Note from Figure 3-30 that the first record in the Program Master File is read into the input area and, since it is the first time, the first record in the Employee Identification File is read into its input area. After these records are read into storage, the Employee Numbers will be compared. As can be seen from Figure 3-30, the Employee Number in the Program Master Input Area is equal to the Employee Number in the Employee Identification Input Area. Therefore, when the Perform Statement checks the conditions for entering the loop (see Figure 3-29), the loop will not be entered because the Employee Numbers are equal.

Control, therefore, will be returned to the module which called the B000 module — the Create Status Report module (see Figure 3-28) — which will in turn call the module which will print the report.

Upon return to the B000 module illustrated in Figure 3-29, another Program Master File Record will be read. The input areas after this read has taken place are illustrated in Figure 3-31.

Step 2: The next record from the Program Master File is read.

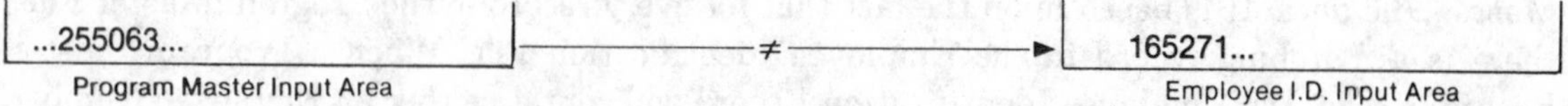

Figure 3-31 Program Master Record is Read

Note in Figure 3-31 that the next record from the Program Master File has been read. Note also that the Employee Number in the record which was just read is not equal to the Employee Number in the Employee Identification Input Area. Therefore, when the conditions on the Perform Until Statement in Figure 3-29 are checked, the loop will be entered. When the loop is entered, a record from the Employee Identification File will be read. The input areas after this read takes place are illustrated in Figure 3-32.

Step 3: The next record from the Employee Identification File is read.

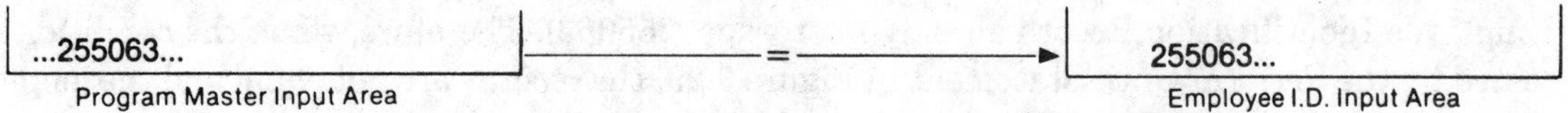

Figure 3-32 Employee Identification Record is Read

Note from Figure 3-32 that a record has been read from the Employee Identification File. When the Employee Numbers are compared by the Perform Until Statement, it is found that they are equal. Therefore, the loop is terminated and control is returned to the calling module, which will cause the information to be printed on the report.

After the information is printed on the report, control will again return to the B000 module and another record from the Program Master File will be read.

Step 4: The next record from the Program Master File is read.

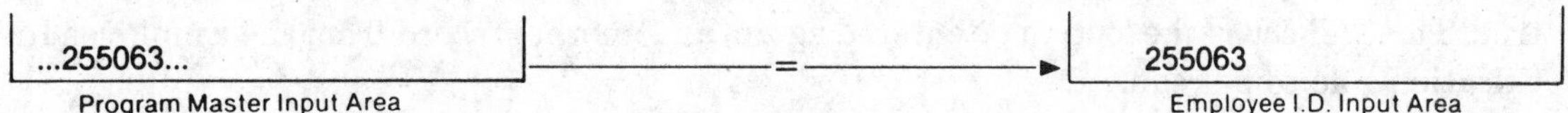

Figure 3-33 Record is Read from Program Master File

When the next (third) record is read from the Program Master File, the Employee Numbers will again be compared by the Perform Until Statement illustrated in Figure 3-29. When they are compared, it is found that they are equal. As can be seen, the second and third records in the Program Master File contain the same Employee Number. This is acceptable as it will be recalled that it is possible for one programmer to be assigned to more than one program.

Since the Employee Numbers are equal, the loop to read the Employee Identification File will never be entered. Instead, control will be passed back to the higher-level module, which will cause the report to be printed.

When control is returned to the B000 module after printing the report, another record from the Program Master File will be read, as illustrated in Figure 3-34.

Step 5: The next record from the Program Master File is read.

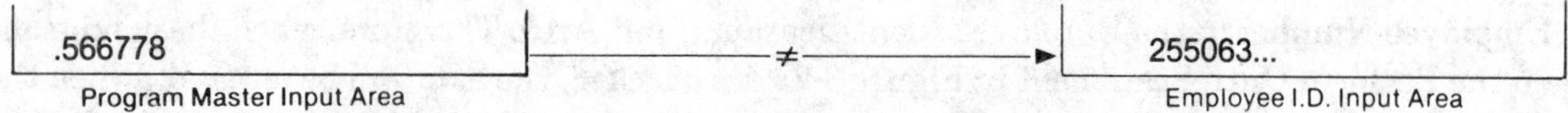

Figure 3-34 Record is Read from Program Master File

Note from Figure 3-34 that when the next record from the Program Master File is read, the Employee Number in the record (566778) is not equal to the Employee Number in the Employee Identification Record already in storage (255063). Therefore, when the condition is tested by the Perform Until Statement in Figure 3-29, the records are not equal and the loop to read a record from the Employee Identification File will be entered.

Step 6: The next record from the Employee Identification File is read.

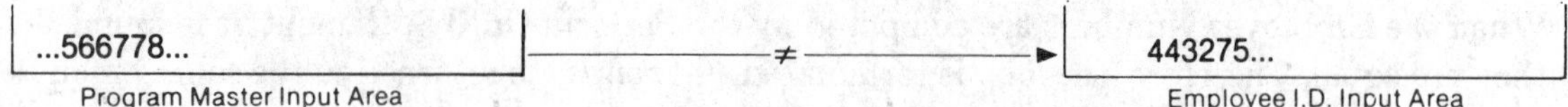

Figure 3-35 Record is Read from Employee Identification File

As can be seen from Figure 3-35, when the next record is read from the Employee Identification File, the Employee Number found is 443275. This number is not equal to the Employee Number in the Program Master Input Area (566778). Therefore, when the condition is checked in the Perform Until Statement (see Figure 3-29), the equal condition will not be true. This will cause the loop to be entered again, and another record from the Employee Identification File to be read.

Step 7: Another record from the Employee Identification File is read.

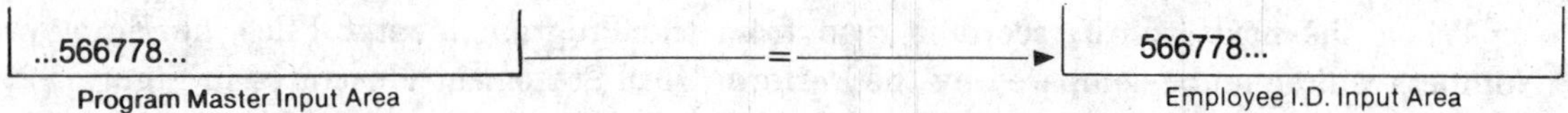

Figure 3-36 Record is Read from Employee Identification File

Note in Figure 3-36 that when the next record from the Employee Identification File is read, the Employee Numbers are equal. Therefore, the loop would be terminated and the report would be written.

Note in the example above that the Employee Number in the Employee Identification Record is always less than or equal to the Employee Number in the Program Master Record. This will always be the case because, by the definition of the problem to be solved, every record in the Program Master File has a matching record in the Employee Identification File.

The logic expressed by the pseudocode in Figure 3-29 should be well understood, since it is a basic logic which can be used when matching two input files.

Pseudocode Specifications — Obtain Master Record

The next module to be designed is the module whose function is to obtain the master record. The pseudocode for this module is illustrated below.

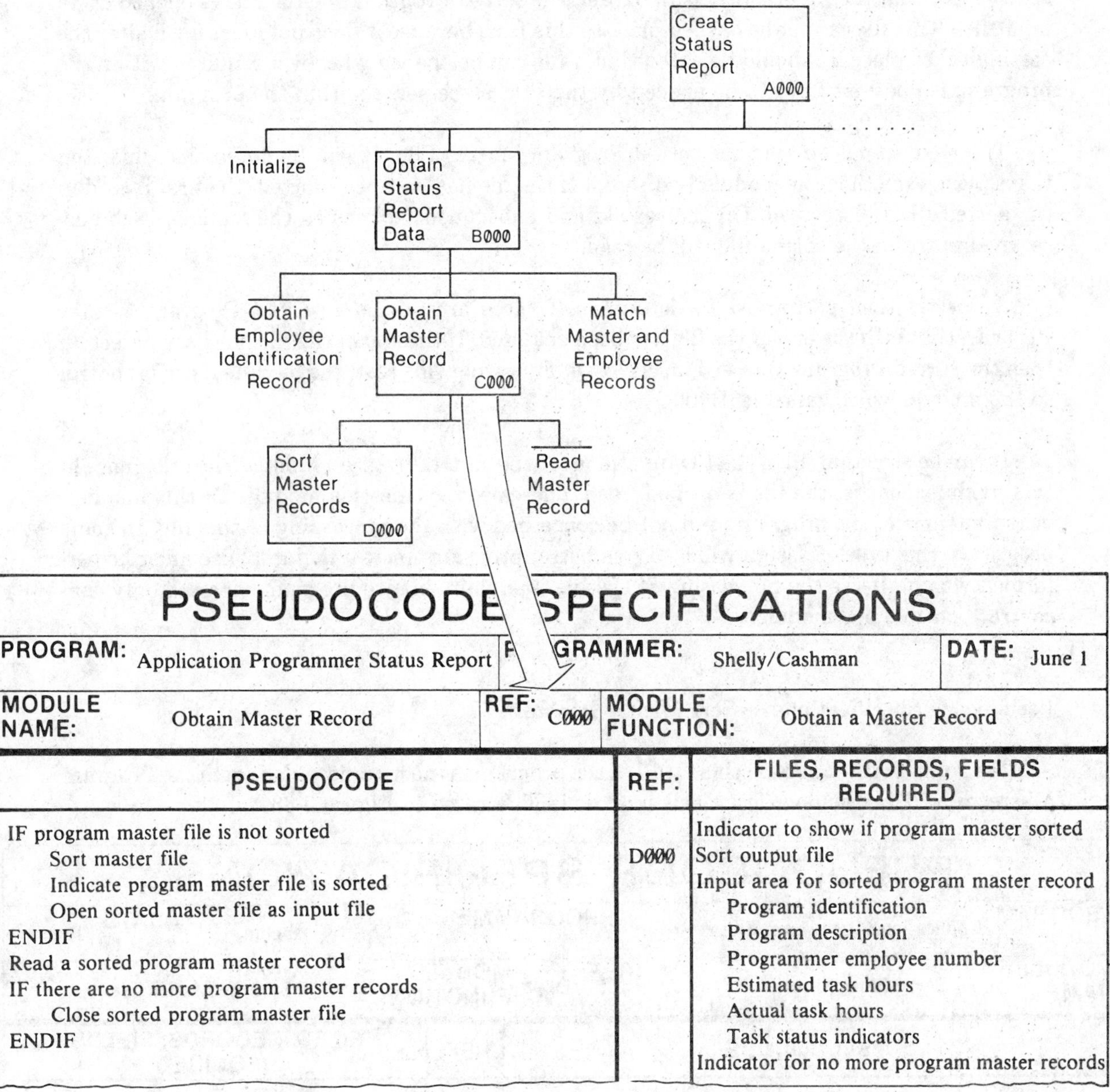

PSEUDOCODE SPECIFICATIONS

PROGRAM: Application Programmer Status Report	PROGRAMMER: Shelly/Cashman	DATE: June 1
MODULE NAME: Obtain Master Record	REF: C000	MODULE FUNCTION: Obtain a Master Record

PSEUDOCODE	REF:	FILES, RECORDS, FIELDS REQUIRED

IF program master file is not sorted
    Sort master file
    Indicate program master file is sorted
    Open sorted master file as input file
ENDIF
Read a sorted program master record
IF there are no more program master records
    Close sorted program master file
ENDIF
	
	D000
		Indicator to show if program master sorted
		Sort output file
		Input area for sorted program master record
		    Program identification
		    Program description
		    Programmer employee number
		    Estimated task hours
		    Actual task hours
		    Task status indicators
		Indicator for no more program master records

Figure 3-37 Pseudocode Specifications — Obtain Master Record

Note from Figure 3-37 that the first step in the pseudocode for the module whose function is to obtain the master record is to determine if the Program Master File has been sorted. The first time the module is entered, the file will not have been sorted. If it has not been sorted, then it is sorted in module D000, as indicated by the Reference column. The indicator is then set to show that the file has been sorted, and the sorted Program Master File is opened as an input file. This file cannot be opened prior to this time because it does not exist until after the sorting takes place. It should be noted that a file can be opened whenever required within the program; it does not have to be opened by the first statements within the program.

The next step is to read the sorted Program Master File. It will be noted that this step takes place each time the module is entered. If the file has just been sorted, the first record in the sorted file will be read. On the second and subsequent entries to the module, each successive record in the sorted file will be read.

A test is then performed to determine if there are no more sorted Program Master Records, that is, if the end of the file has been detected. If the end of the file has been detected, then the sorted Program Master File is closed. Following this test, the module returns control to the module which called it (B000).

It can be seen that all of the I/O functions for the sorted Program Master File take place in this module; that is, the file is opened, read, and closed within this module. In this manner, other portions of the program need not be concerned with the processing of this file. In some programs, this type of design will lead to a better program since, if maintenance must be performed which affects the processing of the file, the maintenance programmer need only concentrate on this one module.

Pseudocode Specifications — Sort Master Records

The remaining module on this "leg" of the program is the module which sorts the Program Master File. The pseudocode for this module is illustrated in Figure 3-38.

PSEUDOCODE SPECIFICATIONS		
PROGRAM: Application Programmer Status Report	PROGRAMMER: Shelly/Cashman	DATE: June 1
MODULE NAME: Sort Master Records	REF: DØØØ	MODULE FUNCTION: Sort the Master File
PSEUDOCODE	REF:	FILES, RECORDS, FIELDS REQUIRED
Sort the program master file (Input from master file) (Output to a separate file)		Sort output file Sort work file

Figure 3-38 Pseudocode Specifications — Sort Program Master Records Module

As can be seen from Figure 3-38, the pseudocode for the module whose function is to sort the Program Master File is straightforward — it says to sort the file. As noted, the input to the sort processing is the Program Master File in Program Identification sequence, and the output is the sorted Program Master File in Employee Number sequence.

Pseudocode Specifications — Write Status Report

The next module to consider is the module whose function is to write the status report. The pseudocode for this module is shown in Figure 3-39.

PSEUDOCODE SPECIFICATIONS

PROGRAM: Application Programmer Status Report	PROGRAMMER: Shelly/Cashman	DATE: June 1
MODULE NAME: Write Status Report	REF: BØ1Ø	MODULE FUNCTION: Write the Status Report

PSEUDOCODE	REF:	FILES, RECORDS, FIELDS REQUIRED
IF employee number not = previous employee number		Employee number-current record
Print headings	CØ1Ø	Previous employee number compare area
Move spaces to report area		Report output area
Move employee number, employee name, supervisor name to report area		Employee number Employee name
Move employee number to previous employee number area		Employee supervisor
ELSE		Program I.D.
IF first page or number of lines ≥ page size		Program description
Print headings	CØ1Ø	Program task
Move spaces to report area		Estimated hours
Move employee number, employee name, supervisor name to report area		Actual hours Task status
ENDIF		Data for report
ENDIF		Employee number
Move program I.D., description to report area		Employee name
Set loop count (i.e. the subscript) to 1		Employee supervisor
PERFORM UNTIL all tasks have been printed		Program I.D.
Move task (subscript) to report area		Program description
Move estimated hours (subscript) to report area		Program tasks
Move actual hours (subscript) to report area		"Program Specs Review"
IF task status (subscript) is complete		"Program Design"
Move "complete" to report area		"Program Coding"
ENDIF		"Program Testing"
Write detail line		"Program Implementation"
Add estimated hours (subscript) to accumulator		Estimated hours
Add actual hours (subscript) to accumulator		Actual hours
Increment lines printed		Task status
Set spacing for single spacing		"Complete" constant
Move spaces to report area		First page indicator
Add 1 to subscript		Lines printed counter
ENDPERFORM		Page size constant
Write total line	CØ2Ø	Loop count (i.e. subscript)
Reset accumulators to zero		Indicator that all tasks have been printed
Set spacing for triple spacing		Estimated hours accumulator
Move spaces to report area		Actual hours accumulator
		Space control field
		Single spacing control character
		Triple spacing control character

Figure 3-39 Pseudocode Specifications — Write Status Report Module

Prior to analyzing the pseudocode for the module which writes the status report, the format of the output report should be reviewed (see Figure 3-4). In reviewing the output report, it can be seen that the Employee Number, Employee Name, Supervisor Name, Program Identification, and Program Description are group-indicated. The Employee Number, Employee Name, and Supervisor Name are group indicated for each programmer who is processed while the Program Identification and Program Description are group-indicated for each program which is reported. This group indication is controlled by the first series of instructions in the pseudocode illustrated in Figure 3-39.

The first statement in the pseudocode in Figure 3-39 checks if the current Employee Number in the Program Master File is different from the previous Employee Number which was processed. The previous Employee Number field will be initialized when the program is coded so that an unequal condition will occur the first time a record is processed. If the Employee Numbers are not equal, it indicates that a new Employee is to be printed on the report. It will be recalled that the programming specifications state that each new employee is to begin on a separate page; therefore, if the Employee Number has changed, headings must be printed on the report.

In addition, after the headings are printed, the report area is cleared and the Employee Number, Employee Name, and Supervisor Name are moved to the report area. These are the fields which are group-indicated on the report whenever a new employee is to be processed and, therefore, must be moved when a new employee is found. After these fields are moved to the report area, the current Employee Number is moved to the Previous Employee Number field so that subsequent comparisons can take place properly.

If the current Employee Number is equal to the Previous Employee Number, then the "Else" portion of the IF Statement is executed. The page count and the first page indicator are checked to determine if report headings should be printed on the report. If so, the report headings are printed by the C010 module, the report area is cleared, and the group-indicated data is moved to the report area. It should be noted that this check for first page and page overflow will not take place if a new employee is being printed, that is, if the current Employee Number is not equal to the previous Employee Number. The reason for this is that if there is a new employee, headings will be printed on a new page. Therefore, there should not be another check to determine if headings should be printed. It is important to note also that the check for a new employee is done before the check for the first page or page overflow. If it was not, the possibility exists that a new heading could be printed because the line count had reached the page size, and then headings would be printed again because a new employee had been found. It is important, therefore, to understand the logic involved in the nested IF Statement in Figure 3-39.

After the headings are printed, the Program Identification and Description are moved to the report area. These fields are group-indicated for each program which is to be printed on the report. Therefore, they are moved at this point in the processing rather than within the loop which will print out the five lines for each program.

The next processing which is to occur is to format the remainder of the print lines with the Program Task, Estimated Hours, Actual Hours, and Task Status value. A unique characteristic of this report is that the Estimated Hours, Actual Hours, and Task Status Codes, which are stored as a series of adjacent fields in the input record, are to be printed on individual lines. In the sample program, this will be accomplished through the use of a loop which will print one line on each pass through the loop. In addition, the identification of each program task with the constants, "Program Specs Review," "Program Design," "Program Coding," "Program Testing," and "Program Implementation" will be printed in the loop.

To begin this processing, a counter or subscript is set equal to the value one in order to initialize the loop which will actually print the data on the report. The loop is then entered and will continue until all tasks have been printed on the report. The loop processing consists of moving the task constants (Review, Design, Code, Test, or Implementation) to the report area, moving the Estimated Hours and Actual Hours from the sorted Program Master File to the report area, moving the constant "complete" to the report area if a given task is indicated as complete in the Program Master Record, and writing the detail line for each task. The Estimated and Actual Hours are then added to accumulators which will be printed after the detail lines are printed, the lines printed counter is incremented, spacing is set, the report area is cleared, and the subscript is incremented for the next pass through the loop.

The processing which would take place to print data from a Program Master Record is illustrated below.

Step 1: The group-indicated data is moved to the report area.

```
723445 JONES, HANK  SMITH, VERNON  AP2654  ACCTS. PAY.
```

Report Area

Step 2: The loop is entered and the data for the program review is moved to the report area.

```
723445 JONES, HANK  SMITH, VERNON   AP2654   ACCTS. PAY.   PROGRAM SPECS REVIEW 0100 0050 COMPLETE
```

Report Area

Step 3: The line is printed on the report.

```
723445 JONES, HANK  SMITH, VERNON  AP2654  ACCTS. PAY  PROGRAM SPECS REVIEW 0100 0050 COMPLETE
```

Step 4: The printer report area is cleared; and on the next pass through the loop, the data for the program design will be printed.

```
723445 JONES, HANK  SMITH, VERNON  AP2654  ACCTS. PAY  PROGRAM SPECS REVIEW 0100 0050 COMPLETE
                                                       PROGRAM DESIGN       0500 0070
```

Step 5: The remainder of the lines for Program Coding, Program Testing, and Program Implementation would be printed in a similar manner.

After the detail lines for each program are printed through the use of the loop, the total line is printed on the report. The accumulators are then reset to zero, the spacing set for triple spacing, and the report area is cleared.

It is important to understand the looping process specified in Figure 3-39 and illustrated in the steps above as it can be a valuable technique to use.

Pseudocode Specifications — Print Headings and Write Total Line

The last two modules in the program are the modules which print the headings and write the total line. Since they are both simple and straightforward, the pseudocode for both of them is illustrated in Figure 3-40.

PSEUDOCODE SPECIFICATIONS

PROGRAM: Application Programmer Status Report	PROGRAMMER: Shelly/Cashman	DATE: June 1
MODULE NAME: Print Headings	REF: CØ1Ø	MODULE FUNCTION: Print the Report Headings

PSEUDOCODE	REF:	FILES, RECORDS, FIELDS REQUIRED
Move current date to first heading line Move page number to first heading line Write the first heading line Add 1 to the page count Write the second heading line Write the third heading line Set the spacing for double spacing Reset lines printed counter to zero		Current date First heading line Page number (count) Second heading line Third heading line Space control field Double spacing control character Lines printed counter

PSEUDOCODE SPECIFICATIONS

PROGRAM: Application Programmer Status Report	PROGRAMMER: Shelly/Cashman	DATE: June 1
MODULE NAME: Write Total Line	REF: CØ2Ø	MODULE FUNCTION: Write the Report Total Lines

PSEUDOCODE	REF:	FILES, RECORDS, FIELDS REQUIRED
Move estimated hours total to total line Move actual hours total to total line Write the total line		Estimated hours accumulator Total line Actual hours accumulator

Figure 3-40 Pseudocode Specifications — Print Headings and Write Total Line

As can be seen, the processing required to print the headings consists of the same processing as has been seen in previous programs — the date and page number are moved to the first heading line and it is printed. The page number is then incremented, the second and third lines are printed, the spacing is set, and the lines printed counter is reset to zero.

The total line processing consists of moving the accumulated totals to the total line and writing the line.

It will be noted that the module which prints the total line contains only three statements. It may be argued that this module, since it is very short and, in fact, violates the size rule as specified in Chapter 1 that a module should contain 7 - 8 statements as a minimum, should be moved up into the module which calls it. It was also mentioned in Chapter 1, however, that there can legitimately be exceptions to the general rules, and the module which prints the total line may be an exception. Writing the totals on the report is a distinct function which must be performed within the program. Therefore, the module is functionally cohesive, as mentioned in Chapter 1. In addition, the module which calls the write total module, which is the write status report module (see Figure 3-39), is a long module; and if a functionally cohesive module can be taken out of that module, then it adds to the ease of understanding of the write status report module. A third reason that justifies the module's being a separate module is that there is the possibility in the future that a change could be made to writing the totals; for example, it may be required to determine what percentage of the Estimated Hours have actually been used by the Actual Hours. If this is the change, then the module where the change should be made is the write total module. Since it is a separate module, the change would be an easy one to make. For these reasons, the function of writing the total lines is performed in a separate module.

Summary

The logic presented in this program contains several important concepts — that of matching the input records from two different files and that of printing the detail lines of the report in a loop. These two concepts should be thoroughly understood before examining the code in the program which implements this logic.

PROGRAM CODE

The coding of the program is straightforward and implements the logic expressed in the pseudocode for each module. There are, however, several coding techniques which should be understood. These are explained in the following paragraphs.

Subscripted Condition Names

In previous programs, the use of condition names has been illustrated for indicators and other types of data within the program. It is also possible to use condition names with data which is defined with the Occurs Clause. In the sample program, the Task Status Code in the Program Master Input Record is used to indicate whether a particular task within the program development cycle has been completed. If the code field contains a 'C,' then the task is completed. There are five Task Status Codes: one for Review, one for Design, one for Coding, one for Testing, and one for Implementation. The fields in the input record are defined with an Occurs Clause so that they can be referenced with a subscript. The definition of the Program Master Input Record in the sample program is illustrated in Figure 3-41.

EXAMPLE

```
006110 01  SORTED-MASTER-INPUT-RECORD.
006120     05  PROGRAM-IDENTIFICATION-SORTMST               PIC X(6).
006130     05  PROGRAM-DESCRIPTION-SORTMST                  PIC X(20).
006140     05  PROGRAMMER-EMPL-NUMBER-SORTMST               PIC X(6).
006150     05  ESTIMATED-TASK-HOURS-SORTMST OCCURS          5 TIMES
006160                                                      PIC 9(4).
006170     05  ACTUAL-TASK-HOURS-SORTMST    OCCURS          5 TIMES
006180                                                      PIC 9(4).
006190     05  TASK-STATUS-INDICATORS-SORTMST OCCURS 5 TIMES
006200                                                      PIC X.
006210         88  TASK-IS-COMPLETE                          VALUE 'C'.
```

Figure 3-41 Example of Condition Name and Occurs Clause

Note from the example in Figure 3-41 that the TASK-STATUS-INDICATORS-SORTMST field, which contains the status codes, occurs five times with a picture PIC X. Thus, the indicators in the field will be referenced with the data-name TASK-STATUS-INDICATORS-SORTMST and a subscript.

Within the logic of the program, it is necessary to determine if any of the individual tasks are complete, that is, if any of the five positions contains the value 'C.' If so, then the particular task is complete (see Figure 3-39). In order to check this condition, the condition name TASK-IS-COMPLETE is defined for the five characters. It should be noted, however, that the condition name could apply to any one of the five positions within the TASK-STATUS-INDICATORS-SORTMST field. Therefore, not only must the field be referenced with the field name and a subscript, so too must the condition name be referenced with the condition name and a subscript. The example in Figure 3-42 illustrates this use in the sample program.

EXAMPLE

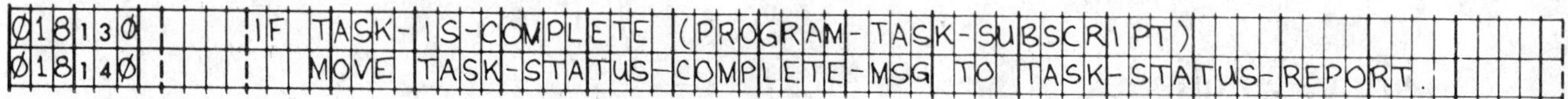

```
018130     IF TASK-IS-COMPLETE (PROGRAM-TASK-SUBSCRIPT)
018140         MOVE TASK-STATUS-COMPLETE-MSG TO TASK-STATUS-REPORT.
```

Figure 3-42 Example of Subscripted Condition Name

Note in the example above that the condition name TASK-IS-COMPLETE is specified together with the subscript PROGRAM-TASK-SUBSCRIPT. The value in the subscript (ranging from 1 to 5) will determine which of the five positions in the TASK-STATUS-INDICATORS-SORTMST field is checked for the value 'C' when testing the condition TASK-IS-COMPLETE. Condition names can be used with subscripts whenever the fields they are testing contain an Occurs Clause.

Coding for Matching Records

It will be recalled that the module whose task is to obtain status report data must determine when records from each of the input files match. The coding to perform this determination is illustrated below.

EXAMPLE

```
B000-OBTAIN-STATUS-REPORT-DATA.

    PERFORM C000-OBTAIN-MASTER-RECORD.
    IF THIS-IS-THE-FIRST-TIME
        PERFORM B001-READ-EMPLOYEE-RECORD
        MOVE 'NO ' TO IS-THIS-THE-FIRST-TIME.
    PERFORM B001-READ-EMPLOYEE-RECORD
            UNTIL PROGRAMMER-EMPL-NUMBER-SORTMST =
                        EMPLOYEE-NUMBER-EMPL-IN OR
                  THERE-ARE-NO-MORE-MSTR-RECORDS.



B001-READ-EMPLOYEE-RECORD.

    READ EMPL-IDENTIFICATION-INPUT-FILE
            AT END
                MOVE 'NO ' TO ARE-THERE-MORE-MSTR-RECORDS.
```

Figure 3-43 Example of Matching Record Processing

Note in the example above that a Payroll Master Record is first obtained by performing the C000-OBTAIN-MASTER-RECORD module. An indicator is then checked to determine if THIS-IS-THE-FIRST-TIME. If it is, then the B001-READ-EMPLOYEE-RECORD paragraph is performed to read the first Employee Identification Record. It will be recalled that this is necessary for the first record so that valid comparisons can be made when matching the records.

The loop is then entered in which the B001-READ-EMPLOYEE-RECORD paragraph will be performed until either the PROGRAMMER-EMPL-NUMBER-SORTMST field is equal to the EMPLOYEE-NUMBER-EMPL-IN field, that is, until the Employee Number in the Sorted Program Master Record is equal to the Employee Number in the Employee Identification Record, or until THERE-ARE-NO-MORE-MSTR-RECORDS. If there are no more master records, the B001-READ-EMPLOYEE-RECORD paragraph will not be performed; if there are master records, the Employee Identification File will be read until an equal Employee Number is found. If, when the conditions are checked the first time, the Employee Numbers are equal, then the B001-READ-EMPLOYEE-RECORD paragraph will not be performed.

It will be recalled that when the data is sorted properly, there is no possibility that end-of-file will occur for the Employee Identification File before it occurs for the Program Master File. It should also be recalled, however, that every Read Statement in a COBOL program requires the "At End" Clause. If it should ever happen that the Employee Identification File reached end-of-file before the master file, there would be a serious error in the data and the program should be terminated immediately. In order to solve these two requirements, the At End Clause with the statement which Reads the Employee Identification File indicates that the master file has reached end-of-file. In this manner, no more processing will take place within the program.

SOURCE LISTING

The source listing for the sample program in this chapter is illustrated on this and the following pages.

```
PP 5740-CB1 RELEASE 1.2  DEC 15, 1976              IBM OS/VS COBOL                    22.21.15  DATE JUN 22,1978

    1                         22.21.15          JUN 22,1978

001010 IDENTIFICATION DIVISION.                                                 STATREPT
001020                                                                          STATREPT
001030 PROGRAM-ID.     STATREPT.                                                STATREPT
001040 AUTHOR.         SHELLY AND CASHMAN.                                      STATREPT
001050 INSTALLATION.   ANAHEIM.                                                 STATREPT
001060 DATE-WRITTEN.   06/01/78.                                                STATREPT
001070 DATE-COMPILED.  JUN 22,1978.                                             STATREPT
001080 SECURITY.       UNCLASSIFIED.                                            STATREPT
001090                                                                          STATREPT
001100*****************************************************************         STATREPT
001110*                                                               *         STATREPT
001120*  THIS PROGRAM CREATES THE APPLICATION PROGRAMMER STATUS       *         STATREPT
001130*  REPORT. THE OUTPUT FROM THE PROGRAM IS THE REPORT. THE INPUT*          STATREPT
001140*  TO THE PROGRAM CONSISTS OF THE APPLICATIONS PROGRAM MASTER   *         STATREPT
001150*  FILE (TO BE RESORTED INTO PROGRAMMER EMPLOYEE NUMBER         *         STATREPT
001160*  SEQUENCE) AND THE EMPLOYEE IDENTIFICATION FILE (ALREADY      *         STATREPT
001170*  SORTED IN PROGRAMMER EMPLOYEE NUMBER SEQUENCE). THE TWO      *         STATREPT
001180*  FILES ARE MATCHED ON PROGRAMMER EMPLOYEE NUMBER, AND WHEN A  *         STATREPT
001190*  MATCH OCCURS, DATA FROM BOTH RECORDS IS USED FOR THE REPORT.*          STATREPT
001200*  IT IS KNOWN PRIOR TO PROCESSING THE DATA IN THIS PROGRAM     *         STATREPT
002010*  THAT EVERY RECORD IN THE APPLICATIONS PROGRAM MASTER FILE    *         STATREPT
002020*  HAS A CORRESPONDING RECORD IN THE EMPLOYEE IDENTIFICATION    *         STATREPT
002030*  FILE. HOWEVER, THERE MAY NOT BE A RECORD IN THE PROGRAM      *         STATREPT
002040*  MASTER FILE FOR EVERY RECORD IN THE EMPLOYEE IDENTIFICATION *          STATREPT
002050*  FILE (IE. SOME PROGRAMMERS MAY NOT BE ASSIGNED A PROGRAM)    *         STATREPT
002060*  OR THERE MAY BE TWO OR MORE RECORDS IN THE PROGRAM MASTER    *         STATREPT
002070*  FILE WHICH MATCH ONE RECORD IN THE EMPLOYEE IDENTIFICATION   *         STATREPT
002080*  FILE (IE. A PROGRAMMER IS ASSIGNED TWO OR MORE PROGRAMS).    *         STATREPT
002090*                                                               *         STATREPT
002100*****************************************************************         STATREPT
002110                                                                          STATREPT
002120                                                                          STATREPT
002130                                                                          STATREPT
002140 ENVIRONMENT DIVISION.                                                    STATREPT
002150                                                                          STATREPT
002160 CONFIGURATION SECTION.                                                   STATREPT
002170                                                                          STATREPT
002180 SOURCE-COMPUTER. IBM-370.                                                STATREPT
002190 OBJECT-COMPUTER. IBM-370.                                                STATREPT
002200 SPECIAL-NAMES.    C01 IS TO-THE-TOP-OF-THE-PAGE.                         STATREPT
003010                                                                          STATREPT
003020 INPUT-OUTPUT SECTION.                                                    STATREPT
003030                                                                          STATREPT
003040 FILE-CONTROL.                                                            STATREPT
003050     SELECT EMPL-IDENTIFICATION-INPUT-FILE                                STATREPT
003060             ASSIGN TO UR-S-SYSIN.                                        STATREPT
003070     SELECT PROGRAM-MASTER-INPUT-FILE                                     STATREPT
003080             ASSIGN TO DA-S-PGMSTR.                                       STATREPT
003090     SELECT PROGRAMMER-STATUS-REPORT-FILE                                 STATREPT
003100             ASSIGN TO UR-S-SYSOUT.                                       STATREPT
003110     SELECT SORTED-PROGRAM-MASTER-FILE                                    STATREPT
003120             ASSIGN TO DA-S-SORTPGM.                                      STATREPT
003130     SELECT SORT-WORK-FILE                                                STATREPT
003140             ASSIGN TO DA-S-SORTWK01.                                     STATREPT
```

Figure 3-44 Source Listing (Part 1 of 6)

```
2                22.21.15        JUN 22,1978

DATA DIVISION.                                                         STATREPT
                                                                       STATREPT
FILE SECTION.                                                          STATREPT
                                                                       STATREPT
FD  EMPL-IDENTIFICATION-INPUT-FILE                                     STATREPT
        RECORD CONTAINS 80 CHARACTERS                                  STATREPT
        LABEL RECORDS ARE OMITTED                                      STATREPT
        DATA RECORD IS EMPL-IDENTIFICATION-INPUT-REC.                  STATREPT
                                                                       STATREPT
01  EMPL-IDENTIFICATION-INPUT-REC.                                     STATREPT
    05  EMPLOYEE-NUMBER-EMPL-IN               PIC X(6).                STATREPT
    05  EMPLOYEE-NAME-EMPL-IN                 PIC X(20).               STATREPT
    05  SUPERVISOR-NAME-EMPL-IN               PIC X(20).               STATREPT
    05  FILLER                                PIC X(34).               STATREPT
                                                                       STATREPT
FD  PROGRAM-MASTER-INPUT-FILE                                          STATREPT
        BLOCK CONTAINS 20 RECORDS                                      STATREPT
        RECORD CONTAINS 77 CHARACTERS                                  STATREPT
        LABEL RECORDS ARE STANDARD                                     STATREPT
        DATA RECORD IS PROGRAM-MASTER-INPUT-RECORD.                    STATREPT
                                                                       STATREPT
01  PROGRAM-MASTER-INPUT-RECORD               PIC X(77).               STATREPT
                                                                       STATREPT
FD  PROGRAMMER-STATUS-REPORT-FILE                                      STATREPT
        RECORD CONTAINS 133 CHARACTERS                                 STATREPT
        LABEL RECORDS ARE OMITTED                                      STATREPT
        DATA RECORD IS PROGRAMMER-STATUS-REPORT-LINE.                  STATREPT
                                                                       STATREPT
01  PROGRAMMER-STATUS-REPORT-LINE.                                     STATREPT
    05  CARRIAGE-CONTROL                      PIC X.                   STATREPT
    05  FILLER                                PIC X.                   STATREPT
    05  EMPLOYEE-NUMBER-REPORT                PIC X(6).                STATREPT
    05  FILLER                                PIC X(3).                STATREPT
    05  EMPLOYEE-NAME-REPORT                  PIC X(20).               STATREPT
    05  FILLER                                PIC X(3).                STATREPT
    05  SUPERVISOR-NAME-REPORT                PIC X(20).               STATREPT
    05  FILLER                                PIC X(3).                STATREPT
    05  PROGRAM-IDENTIFICATION-REPORT         PIC X(6).                STATREPT
    05  FILLER                                PIC X(3).                STATREPT
    05  PROGRAM-DESCRIPTION-REPORT            PIC X(20).               STATREPT
    05  FILLER                                PIC X(3).                STATREPT
    05  PROGRAM-TASK-REPORT                   PIC X(22).               STATREPT
    05  FILLER                                PIC X.                   STATREPT
    05  ESTIMATED-HOURS-REPORT                PIC Z,ZZ9.               STATREPT
    05  FILLER                                PIC X(2).                STATREPT
    05  ACTUAL-HOURS-REPORT                   PIC Z,ZZ9.               STATREPT
    05  FILLER                                PIC X.                   STATREPT
    05  TASK-STATUS-REPORT                    PIC X(8).                STATREPT
                                                                       STATREPT
FD  SORTED-PROGRAM-MASTER-FILE                                         STATREPT
        BLOCK CONTAINS 20 RECORDS                                      STATREPT
        RECORD CONTAINS 77 CHARACTERS                                  STATREPT
        LABEL RECORDS ARE STANDARD                                     STATREPT
        DATA RECORD IS SORTED-MASTER-INPUT-RECORD.                     STATREPT
                                                                       STATREPT
01  SORTED-MASTER-INPUT-RECORD.                                        STATREPT
    05  PROGRAM-IDENTIFICATION-SORTMST            PIC X(6).            STATREPT
    05  PROGRAM-DESCRIPTION-SORTMST               PIC X(20).           STATREPT
    05  PROGRAMMER-EMPL-NUMBER-SORTMST            PIC X(6).            STATREPT
    05  ESTIMATED-TASK-HOURS-SORTMST OCCURS 5 TIMES                    STATREPT
                                                  PIC 9(4).            STATREPT
    05  ACTUAL-TASK-HOURS-SORTMST       OCCURS 5 TIMES                 STATREPT
                                                  PIC 9(4).            STATREPT
    05  TASK-STATUS-INDICATORS-SORTMST OCCURS 5 TIMES                  STATREPT
                                                  PIC X.               STATREPT
        88  TASK-IS-COMPLETE                        VALUE 'C'.         STATREPT
                                                                       STATREPT
SD  SORT-WORK-FILE                                                     STATREPT
        RECORD CONTAINS 77 CHARACTERS                                  STATREPT
        DATA RECORD IS SORT-WORK-RECORD.                               STATREPT
                                                                       STATREPT
01  SORT-WORK-RECORD.                                                  STATREPT
    05  FILLER                                    PIC X(26).           STATREPT
    05  PROGRAMMER-EMPL-NUMBER-SORTWK             PIC X(6).            STATREPT
    05  FILLER                                    PIC X(45).           STATREPT
                                                                       STATREPT
WORKING-STORAGE SECTION.                                               STATREPT
                                                                       STATREPT
01  PROGRAM-INDICATORS.                                                STATREPT
    05  ARE-THERE-MORE-MSTR-RECORDS PIC XXX   VALUE 'YES'.             STATREPT
        88  THERE-ARE-NO-MORE-MSTR-RECORDS    VALUE 'NO '.             STATREPT
    05  IS-PGM-MASTER-FILE-SORTED   PIC XXX   VALUE 'NO '.             STATREPT
        88  PGM-MASTER-FILE-IS-NOT-SORTED     VALUE 'NO '.             STATREPT
    05  IS-THIS-THE-FIRST-TIME      PIC XXX   VALUE 'YES'.             STATREPT
        88  THIS-IS-THE-FIRST-TIME            VALUE 'YES'.             STATREPT
                                                                       STATREPT
01  INPUT-RECORD-COMPARE-AREA.                                         STATREPT
    05  PREVIOUS-EMPLOYEE-NUMBER    PIC X(6) VALUE LOW-VALUES.         STATREPT
                                                                       STATREPT
```

Figure 3-45 Source Listing (Part 2 of 6)

```
3                     22.21.15          JUN 22,1978

008020 01  TOTAL-ACCUMULATORS                          USAGE IS COMP-3.    STATREPT
008030     05  ESTIMATED-HOURS-ACCUM     PIC S9(4)     VALUE ZERO.         STATREPT
008040     05  ACTUAL-HOURS-ACCUM        PIC S9(4)     VALUE ZERO.         STATREPT
008050                                                                     STATREPT
008060 01  PROGRAM-CONSTANTS.                                              STATREPT
008070     05  REPORT-PROGRAM-TASK-MSGS.                                   STATREPT
008080         10  FILLER                PIC X(22)     VALUE               STATREPT
008090                                     'PROGRAM SPECS REVIEW   '.STATREPT
008100         10  FILLER                PIC X(22)     VALUE               STATREPT
008110                                     'PROGRAM DESIGN         '.STATREPT
008120         10  FILLER                PIC X(22)     VALUE               STATREPT
008130                                     'PROGRAM CODING         '.STATREPT
008140         10  FILLER                PIC X(22)     VALUE               STATREPT
008150                                     'PROGRAM TESTING        '.STATREPT
008160         10  FILLER                PIC X(22)     VALUE               STATREPT
008170                                     'PROGRAM IMPLEMENTATION'.STATREPT
008180     05  ALL-REPORT-PROGRAM-TASK-MSGS REDEFINES                      STATREPT
008190           REPORT-PROGRAM-TASK-MSGS              OCCURS 5 TIMES      STATREPT
008200                                   PIC X(22).                        STATREPT
009010     05  TASK-STATUS-COMPLETE-MSG PIC X(8)       VALUE 'COMPLETE'.   STATREPT
009020                                                                     STATREPT
009030 01  PROGRAM-SUBSCRIPTS.                                             STATREPT
009040     05  PROGRAM-TASK-SUBSCRIPT    PIC S9(8)     USAGE IS COMP       STATREPT
009050                                                 SYNC.               STATREPT
009060         88  ALL-TASKS-HAVE-BEEN-PRINTED         VALUE +6.           STATREPT
009070                                                                     STATREPT
009080 01  PRINTER-CONTROL.                                                STATREPT
009090     05  PROPER-SPACING            PIC 9.                            STATREPT
009100     05  SPACE-ONE-LINE            PIC 9         VALUE 1.            STATREPT
009110     05  SPACE-TWO-LINES           PIC 9         VALUE 2.            STATREPT
009120     05  SPACE-THREE-LINES         PIC 9         VALUE 3.            STATREPT
009130     05  NUMBER-OF-LINES-PRINTED PIC S999        VALUE ZERO          STATREPT
009140                                                 USAGE IS COMP-3.    STATREPT
009150     05  PAGE-SIZE                 PIC 999       VALUE 40            STATREPT
009160                                                 USAGE IS COMP-3.    STATREPT
009170     05  PAGE-NUMBER-COUNT         PIC S999      VALUE +1            STATREPT
009180                                                 USAGE IS COMP-3.    STATREPT
009190         88  THIS-IS-THE-FIRST-PAGE              VALUE +1.           STATREPT
009200                                                                     STATREPT
010010 01  HEADING-LINES.                                                  STATREPT
010020     05  FIRST-HEADING-LINE.                                         STATREPT
010030         10  CARRIAGE-CONTROL      PIC X.                            STATREPT
010040         10  FILLER                PIC X(5)      VALUE 'DATE '.      STATREPT
010050         10  CURRENT-DATE-HDG1     PIC X(8).                         STATREPT
010060         10  FILLER                PIC X(35)     VALUE SPACES.       STATREPT
010070         10  FILLER                PIC X(12)     VALUE               STATREPT
010080                                               'APPLICATION '.       STATREPT
010090         10  FILLER                PIC X(11)     VALUE 'PROGRAMMER '.STATREPT
010100         10  FILLER                PIC X(7)      VALUE 'STATUS '.    STATREPT
010110         10  FILLER                PIC X(6)      VALUE 'REPORT'.     STATREPT
010120         10  FILLER                PIC X(40)     VALUE SPACES.       STATREPT
010130         10  FILLER                PIC X(5)      VALUE 'PAGE '.      STATREPT
010140         10  PAGE-NUMBER-HDG1      PIC ZZ9.                          STATREPT
010150     05  SECOND-HEADING-LINE.                                        STATREPT
010160         10  CARRIAGE-CONTROL      PIC X.                            STATREPT
010170         10  FILLER                PIC X(8)      VALUE 'EMPLOYEE'.   STATREPT
010180         10  FILLER                PIC X(8)      VALUE SPACES.       STATREPT
010190         10  FILLER                PIC X(8)      VALUE 'EMPLOYEE'.   STATREPT
010200         10  FILLER                PIC X(14)     VALUE SPACES.       STATREPT
011010         10  FILLER                PIC X(10)     VALUE 'SUPERVISOR'. STATREPT
011020         10  FILLER                PIC X(8)      VALUE SPACES.       STATREPT
011030         10  FILLER                PIC X(7)      VALUE 'PROGRAM'.    STATREPT
011040         10  FILLER                PIC X(8)      VALUE SPACES.       STATREPT
011050         10  FILLER                PIC X(7)      VALUE 'PROGRAM'.    STATREPT
011060         10  FILLER                PIC X(16)     VALUE SPACES.       STATREPT
011070         10  FILLER                PIC X(7)      VALUE 'PROGRAM'.    STATREPT
011080         10  FILLER                PIC X(7)      VALUE SPACES.       STATREPT
011090         10  FILLER                PIC X(9)      VALUE 'ESTIMATED'.  STATREPT
011100         10  FILLER                PIC X         VALUE SPACE.        STATREPT
011110         10  FILLER                PIC X(6)      VALUE 'ACTUAL'.     STATREPT
011120         10  FILLER                PIC XX        VALUE SPACES.       STATREPT
011130         10  FILLER                PIC X(4)      VALUE 'TASK'.       STATREPT
011140         10  FILLER                PIC XX        VALUE SPACES.       STATREPT
011150     05  THIRD-HEADING-LINE.                                         STATREPT
011160         10  CARRIAGE-CONTROL      PIC X.                            STATREPT
011170         10  FILLER                PIC X         VALUE SPACE.        STATREPT
011180         10  FILLER                PIC X(6)      VALUE 'NUMBER'.     STATREPT
011190         10  FILLER                PIC X(11)     VALUE SPACES.       STATREPT
011200         10  FILLER                PIC X(4)      VALUE 'NAME'.       STATREPT
012010         10  FILLER                PIC X(19)     VALUE SPACES.       STATREPT
012020         10  FILLER                PIC X(4)      VALUE 'NAME'.       STATREPT
012030         10  FILLER                PIC X(12)     VALUE SPACES.       STATREPT
012040         10  FILLER                PIC X(4)      VALUE 'I.D.'.       STATREPT
012050         10  FILLER                PIC X(8)      VALUE SPACES.       STATREPT
012060         10  FILLER                PIC X(11)     VALUE 'DESCRIPTION'.STATREPT
012070         10  FILLER                PIC X(16)     VALUE SPACES.       STATREPT
012080         10  FILLER                PIC X(4)      VALUE 'TASK'.       STATREPT
012090         10  FILLER                PIC X(10)     VALUE SPACES.       STATREPT
012100         10  FILLER                PIC X(5)      VALUE 'HOURS'.      STATREPT
012110         10  FILLER                PIC X(4)      VALUE SPACES.       STATREPT
012120         10  FILLER                PIC X(5)      VALUE 'HOURS'.      STATREPT
```

Figure 3-46 Source Listing (Part 3 of 6)

```
4                 22.21.15        JUN 22,1978

                10  FILLER                  PIC X          VALUE SPACE.        STATREPT
                10  FILLER                  PIC X(6)       VALUE 'STATUS'.     STATREPT
                10  FILLER                  PIC X          VALUE SPACE.        STATREPT
                                                                               STATREPT
        01  TOTAL-LINES.                                                       STATREPT
            05  PROGRAM-TOTAL-LINE.                                            STATREPT
                10  CARRIAGE-CONTROL        PIC X.                             STATREPT
                10  FILLER                  PIC X(102)     VALUE SPACES.       STATREPT
                10  FILLER                  PIC X(6)       VALUE 'TOTALS'.     STATREPT
                10  FILLER                  PIC X(3)       VALUE SPACES.       STATREPT
                10  ESTIMATED-HOURS-TOTAL-LINE PIC Z,ZZ9.                      STATREPT
                10  FILLER                  PIC XX         VALUE SPACES.       STATREPT
                10  ACTUAL-HOURS-TOTAL-LINE PIC Z,ZZ9.                         STATREPT
                10  FILLER                  PIC X(9)       VALUE SPACES.       STATREPT
```

```
5                 22.21.15        JUN 22,1978

       PROCEDURE DIVISION.                                                     STATREPT
                                                                               STATREPT
      ************************************************************************ STATREPT
      *                                                                      * STATREPT
      * THE FUNCTION OF THIS MODULE IS TO CREATE THE APPLICATION             * STATREPT
      * PROGRAMMER STATUS REPORT. IT IS ENTERED FROM AND EXITS TO             * STATREPT
      * THE OPERATING SYSTEM.                                                * STATREPT
      *                                                                      * STATREPT
      ************************************************************************ STATREPT
                                                                               STATREPT
       A000-CREATE-STATUS-REPORT.                                              STATREPT
                                                                               STATREPT
           OPEN INPUT  EMPL-IDENTIFICATION-INPUT-FILE                          STATREPT
                OUTPUT PROGRAMMER-STATUS-REPORT-FILE.                          STATREPT
           PERFORM B000-OBTAIN-STATUS-REPORT-DATA.                             STATREPT
           PERFORM A001-WRITE-AND-READ                                         STATREPT
               UNTIL THERE-ARE-NO-MORE-MSTR-RECORDS.                           STATREPT
           CLOSE EMPL-IDENTIFICATION-INPUT-FILE                                STATREPT
               PROGRAMMER-STATUS-REPORT-FILE.                                  STATREPT
           STOP RUN.                                                           STATREPT
                                                                               STATREPT
                                                                               STATREPT
                                                                               STATREPT
       A001-WRITE-AND-READ.                                                    STATREPT
                                                                               STATREPT
           PERFORM B010-WRITE-STATUS-REPORT.                                   STATREPT
           PERFORM B000-OBTAIN-STATUS-REPORT-DATA.                             STATREPT
```

```
6                 22.21.15        JUN 22,1978

      ************************************************************************ STATREPT
      *                                                                      * STATREPT
      *  THIS MODULE IS ENTERED TO OBTAIN DATA FOR THE APPLICATION           * STATREPT
      *  PROGRAMMER STATUS REPORT FROM TWO FILES - THE EMPLOYEE              * STATREPT
      *  IDENTIFICATION FILE AND THE PROGRAM MASTER FILE. IT IS              * STATREPT
      *  ENTERED FROM AND EXITS TO THE A000-CREATE-STATUS-REPORT             * STATREPT
      *  MODULE.                                                             * STATREPT
      *                                                                      * STATREPT
      ************************************************************************ STATREPT
                                                                               STATREPT
       B000-OBTAIN-STATUS-REPORT-DATA.                                         STATREPT
                                                                               STATREPT
           PERFORM C000-OBTAIN-MASTER-RECORD.                                  STATREPT
           IF THIS-IS-THE-FIRST-TIME                                           STATREPT
               PERFORM B001-READ-EMPLOYEE-RECORD                               STATREPT
               MOVE 'NO' TO IS-THIS-THE-FIRST-TIME.                            STATREPT
           PERFORM B001-READ-EMPLOYEE-RECORD                                   STATREPT
               UNTIL PROGRAMMER-EMPL-NUMBER-SORTMST =                          STATREPT
                           EMPLOYEE-NUMBER-EMPL-IN OR                          STATREPT
                     THERE-ARE-NO-MORE-MSTR-RECORDS.                           STATREPT
                                                                               STATREPT
                                                                               STATREPT
                                                                               STATREPT
       B001-READ-EMPLOYEE-RECORD.                                              STATREPT
                                                                               STATREPT
           READ EMPL-IDENTIFICATION-INPUT-FILE                                 STATREPT
               AT END                                                          STATREPT
                   MOVE 'NO ' TO ARE-THERE-MORE-MSTR-RECORDS.                  STATREPT
```

Figure 3-47 Source Listing (Part 4 of 6)

```
        7                 22.21.15        JUN 22,1978

      ***************************************************************  STATREPT
      *                                                             *  STATREPT
      *  THE FUNCTION OF THIS MODULE IS TO WRITE THE APPLICATION    *  STATREPT
      *  PROGRAMMER STATUS REPORT. IT IS ENTERED FROM AND EXITS TO  *  STATREPT
      *  THE A000-CREATE-STATUS-REPORT MODULE.                      *  STATREPT
      *                                                             *  STATREPT
      ***************************************************************  STATREPT
                                                                       STATREPT
       B010-WRITE-STATUS-REPORT.                                       STATREPT
                                                                       STATREPT
           IF PROGRAMMER-EMPL-NUMBER-SORTMST NOT =                     STATREPT
                   PREVIOUS-EMPLOYEE-NUMBER                            STATREPT
               PERFORM C010-PRINT-HEADINGS                             STATREPT
               MOVE SPACES TO PROGRAMMER-STATUS-REPORT-LINE            STATREPT
               MOVE PROGRAMMER-EMPL-NUMBER-SORTMST TO                  STATREPT
                       EMPLOYEE-NUMBER-REPORT                          STATREPT
               MOVE EMPLOYEE-NAME-EMPL-IN TO EMPLOYEE-NAME-REPORT      STATREPT
               MOVE SUPERVISOR-NAME-EMPL-IN TO SUPERVISOR-NAME-REPORT  STATREPT
               MOVE PROGRAMMER-EMPL-NUMBER-SORTMST TO                  STATREPT
                       PREVIOUS-EMPLOYEE-NUMBER                        STATREPT
           ELSE                                                        STATREPT
               IF THIS-IS-THE-FIRST-PAGE OR                            STATREPT
                       NUMBER-OF-LINES-PRINTED = PAGE-SIZE OR          STATREPT
                       IS GREATER THAN PAGE-SIZE                       STATREPT
                   PERFORM C010-PRINT-HEADINGS                         STATREPT
                   MOVE SPACES TO PROGRAMMER-STATUS-REPORT-LINE        STATREPT
                   MOVE PROGRAMMER-EMPL-NUMBER-SORTMST TO              STATREPT
                           EMPLOYEE-NUMBER-REPORT                      STATREPT
                   MOVE EMPLOYEE-NAME-EMPL-IN TO EMPLOYEE-NAME-REPORT  STATREPT
                   MOVE SUPERVISOR-NAME-EMPL-IN TO SUPERVISOR-NAME-REPORT.STATREPT
           MOVE PROGRAM-IDENTIFICATION-SORTMST TO                      STATREPT
                   PROGRAM-IDENTIFICATION-REPORT.                      STATREPT
           MOVE PROGRAM-DESCRIPTION-SORTMST TO                         STATREPT
                   PROGRAM-DESCRIPTION-REPORT.                         STATREPT
           PERFORM B011-PRINT-EACH-TASK                                STATREPT
                   VARYING PROGRAM-TASK-SUBSCRIPT FROM 1 BY 1          STATREPT
                   UNTIL ALL-TASKS-HAVE-BEEN-PRINTED.                  STATREPT
           PERFORM C020-WRITE-TOTAL-LINE.                              STATREPT
           MOVE ZEROS TO ESTIMATED-HOURS-ACCUM                         STATREPT
                         ACTUAL-HOURS-ACCUM.                           STATREPT
           MOVE SPACE-THREE-LINES TO PROPER-SPACING.                   STATREPT
           MOVE SPACES TO PROGRAMMER-STATUS-REPORT-LINE.               STATREPT
                                                                       STATREPT
                                                                       STATREPT
                                                                       STATREPT
       B011-PRINT-EACH-TASK.                                           STATREPT
                                                                       STATREPT
           MOVE ALL-REPORT-PROGRAM-TASK-MSGS (PROGRAM-TASK-SUBSCRIPT) TOSTATREPT
                   PROGRAM-TASK-REPORT.                                STATREPT
           MOVE ESTIMATED-TASK-HOURS-SORTMST (PROGRAM-TASK-SUBSCRIPT) TOSTATREPT
                   ESTIMATED-HOURS-REPORT.                             STATREPT
           MOVE ACTUAL-TASK-HOURS-SORTMST (PROGRAM-TASK-SUBSCRIPT) TO  STATREPT
                   ACTUAL-HOURS-REPORT.                                STATREPT
           IF TASK-IS-COMPLETE (PROGRAM-TASK-SUBSCRIPT)                STATREPT
               MOVE TASK-STATUS-COMPLETE-MSG TO TASK-STATUS-REPORT.    STATREPT
           WRITE PROGRAMMER-STATUS-REPORT-LINE                         STATREPT
                   AFTER PROPER-SPACING.                               STATREPT
           ADD ESTIMATED-TASK-HOURS-SORTMST (PROGRAM-TASK-SUBSCRIPT) TO STATREPT
                   ESTIMATED-HOURS-ACCUM.                              STATREPT
           ADD ACTUAL-TASK-HOURS-SORTMST (PROGRAM-TASK-SUBSCRIPT) TO   STATREPT
                   ACTUAL-HOURS-ACCUM.                                 STATREPT
           ADD PROPER-SPACING TO NUMBER-OF-LINES-PRINTED.              STATREPT
           MOVE SPACE-ONE-LINE TO PROPER-SPACING.                      STATREPT
           MOVE SPACES TO PROGRAMMER-STATUS-REPORT-LINE.               STATREPT
```

Figure 3-48 Source Listing (Part 5 of 6)

```
8                    22.21.15          JUN 22,1978

      ****************************************************************** STATREPT
      *                                                                * STATREPT
      *  THE FUNCTION OF THIS MODULE IS TO OBTAIN A RECORD FROM THE    * STATREPT
      *  PROGRAM MASTER FILE. IT IS ENTERED FROM AND EXITS TO THE      * STATREPT
      *  B000-OBTAIN-STATUS-REPORT-DATA MODULE.                        * STATREPT
      *                                                                * STATREPT
      ****************************************************************** STATREPT
                                                                         STATREPT
       C000-OBTAIN-MASTER-RECORD.                                        STATREPT
                                                                         STATREPT
           IF PGM-MASTER-FILE-IS-NOT-SORTED                              STATREPT
               PERFORM D000-SORT-MASTER-RECORDS                          STATREPT
               MOVE 'YES' TO IS-PGM-MASTER-FILE-SORTED                   STATREPT
               OPEN INPUT SORTED-PROGRAM-MASTER-FILE.                    STATREPT
           READ SORTED-PROGRAM-MASTER-FILE                               STATREPT
                   AT END                                                STATREPT
                       MOVE 'NO ' TO ARE-THERE-MORE-MSTR-RECORDS.        STATREPT
           IF THERE-ARE-NO-MORE-MSTR-RECORDS                             STATREPT
               CLOSE SORTED-PROGRAM-MASTER-FILE.                         STATREPT

9                    22.21.15          JUN 22,1978

      ****************************************************************** STATREPT
      *                                                                * STATREPT
      *  THE FUNCTION OF THIS MODULE IS TO PRINT THE HEADINGS ON THE   * STATREPT
      *  APPLICATION PROGRAMMER STATUS REPORT. IT IS ENTERED FROM AND  * STATREPT
      *  EXITS TO THE B010-WRITE-STATUS-REPORT MODULE.                 * STATREPT
      *                                                                * STATREPT
      ****************************************************************** STATREPT
                                                                         STATREPT
       C010-PRINT-HEADINGS.                                              STATREPT
                                                                         STATREPT
           MOVE CURRENT-DATE TO CURRENT-DATE-HDG1.                       STATREPT
           MOVE PAGE-NUMBER-COUNT TO PAGE-NUMBER-HDG1.                   STATREPT
           WRITE PROGRAMMER-STATUS-REPORT-LINE FROM FIRST-HEADING-LINE   STATREPT
                   AFTER ADVANCING TO-THE-TOP-OF-THE-PAGE.               STATREPT
           ADD 1 TO PAGE-NUMBER-COUNT.                                   STATREPT
           WRITE PROGRAMMER-STATUS-REPORT-LINE FROM SECOND-HEADING-LINE  STATREPT
                   AFTER ADVANCING 2 LINES.                              STATREPT
           WRITE PROGRAMMER-STATUS-REPORT-LINE FROM THIRD-HEADING-LINE   STATREPT
                   AFTER ADVANCING 1 LINES.                              STATREPT
           MOVE SPACE-TWO-LINES TO PROPER-SPACING.                       STATREPT
           MOVE ZERO TO NUMBER-OF-LINES-PRINTED.                         STATREPT

10                   22.21.15          JUN 22,1978

      ****************************************************************** STATREPT
      *                                                                * STATREPT
      *  THE FUNCTION OF THIS MODULE IS TO WRITE THE REPORT TOTAL      * STATREPT
      *  LINES. IT IS ENTERED FROM AND EXITS TO THE                    * STATREPT
      *  B010-WRITE-STATUS-REPORT MODULE.                              * STATREPT
      *                                                                * STATREPT
      ****************************************************************** STATREPT
                                                                         STATREPT
       C020-WRITE-TOTAL-LINE.                                            STATREPT
                                                                         STATREPT
           MOVE ESTIMATED-HOURS-ACCUM TO ESTIMATED-HOURS-TOTAL-LINE.     STATREPT
           MOVE ACTUAL-HOURS-ACCUM TO ACTUAL-HOURS-TOTAL-LINE.           STATREPT
           WRITE PROGRAMMER-STATUS-REPORT-LINE FROM PROGRAM-TOTAL-LINE   STATREPT
                   AFTER ADVANCING 2 LINES.                              STATREPT

11                   22.21.15          JUN 22,1978

      ****************************************************************** STATREPT
      *                                                                * STATREPT
      *  THE FUNCTION OF THIS MODULE IS TO SORT THE PROGRAM MASTER     * STATREPT
      *  FILE IN AN ASCENDING SEQUENCE BY PROGRAMMER EMPLOYEE NUMBER.  * STATREPT
      *  IT IS ENTERED FROM AND EXITS TO THE                           * STATREPT
      *  C000-OBTAIN-MASTER-RECORD MODULE.                             * STATREPT
      *                                                                * STATREPT
      ****************************************************************** STATREPT
                                                                         STATREPT
       D000-SORT-MASTER-RECORDS.                                         STATREPT
                                                                         STATREPT
           SORT SORT-WORK-FILE                                           STATREPT
                ASCENDING KEY PROGRAMMER-EMPL-NUMBER-SORTWK              STATREPT
                USING PROGRAM-MASTER-INPUT-FILE                          STATREPT
                GIVING SORTED-PROGRAM-MASTER-FILE.                       STATREPT
```

Figure 3-49 Source Listing (Part 6 of 6)

CHAPTER 3

REVIEW QUESTIONS

1. What is meant by the "key" of a record?

2. Briefly explain the processing which occurs when using the SORT Verb in COBOL.

3. What files must be defined in the Environment Division and Data Division when using the SORT Verb in COBOL?

4. When is the entry SD used in the File Section of the Data Divison?

5. Write the COBOL statements required in the Procedure Division to sort a file called PAYROLL-INPUT-FILE, storing the sorted records in SORTED-PAYROLL-FILE. The file is to be sorted in ascending sequence on the EMPLOYEE-NUMBER-SORTWK field. The name of the sort work file is PAYROLL-SORT-WORK-FILE.

6. Write the COBOL statements required in the Procedure Division to sort a file called SALESMAN-MASTER-FILE, storing the sorted records in SORTED-SALESMAN-FILE. The file is to be sorted in ascending sequence by the field ITEMS-SOLD-SORTWK within the field SALESMAN-NUMBER-SORTWK. The name of the sort work file is SALESMAN-SORT-WORK-FILE.

CHAPTER 3

PROGRAMMING ASSIGNMENT 1

OVERVIEW – PROGRAMMING ASSIGNMENTS

The programming assignments in Chapter 3 consist of two parts: 1) The design and programming of an application which creates the Decathlon Summary Report; 2) The maintenance of the program which creates the Decathlon Summary Report to increase the information contained on the report. Three approaches are possible when utilizing these programming assignments:

1. Only Programming Assignment 1 is assigned. This approach results in the design and coding of a relatively small program which illustrates the basic concepts discussed in the chapter.

2. Programming Assignment 1 may be assigned. After this program has been designed, coded, and tested, Programming Assignment 1A may be assigned. Assignment 1A involves the revision and maintenance of the program completed in Assignment 1. Upon completion of Assignment 1A, the student will have completed a program of the approximate difficulty of the program in the chapter.

3. Programming Assignment 1 and Programming Assignment 1A may be viewed as one large programming project and be written as a single assignment.

The method of assigning the program is at the option of the instructor.

INSTRUCTIONS

A program is to be written to produce a Decathlon Summary Report. Design and write the COBOL program to produce the required report. A hierarchy chart, IPO Charts, and Pseudocode Specifications should be used when designing the program.

OUTPUT

The output from the program is the Decathlon Summary Report. The format of the report is illustrated on the following page.

PRINTER SPACING CHART

```
 1
 2 XX/XX/XX             DECATHLON SUMMARY REPORT            PAGE XØX
 3
 4 COACH                                                    TOTAL
 5 NUMBER        COACH NAME                 ATHLETE NAME    SCORE
 6
 7  XØX    XXXXXXXXXXXXXXXXXXXXXXXX    XXXXXXXXXXXXXXXXXXXXX   XXXX
 8
 9                                     XXXXXXXXXXXXXXXXXXXXX   XXXX
10
11                                     XXXXXXXXXXXXXXXXXXXXX   XXXX
12
13       —NEW PAGE FOR EACH COACH—
```

Note on the printer spacing chart above that the Decathlon Summary Report contains the Coach Number, the Coach Name, the Athlete Name, and the Total Score for the athlete. The Coach Number and Coach Name are group-indicated since there is the possibility that more than one athlete may have the same coach. Each athlete line is to be double spaced. When a new coach is to be printed, a new page should be started, that is, each coach is to begin on a new page. A maximum of six athletes should be printed on one page.

INPUT

The input to the program consists of the Decathlon Master File which was created in Chapter 2 and the Coach Identification File.

The format of the Decathlon Master File depends upon whether the file was created in Chapter 2 Programming Assignment 1 or Chapter 2 Programming Assignment 1A. The two formats are illustrated below and on the next page.

Decathlon Master File — Chapter 2 Programming Assignment 1

FIELD	POSITION	NUMBER OF DIGITS	ATTRIBUTES
Athlete Number	1-3	3	Numeric
Athlete Name	4-23	20	Alphanumeric
Coach Number	24-26	3	Numeric
Total Decathlon Score	27-30	4	Numeric

Decathlon Master File — Chapter 2 Programming Assignment 1A

FIELD	POSITION	NUMBER OF DIGITS	ATTRIBUTES
School Identification	1-3	3	Alphanumeric
Athlete Number	4-6	3	Numeric
Athlete Name	7-26	20	Alphanumeric
Coach Number	27-29	3	Numeric
100 Meters Score	30-33	4	Numeric
Long Jump Score	34-37	4	Numeric
Shot Put Score	38-41	4	Numeric
High Jump Score	42-45	4	Numeric
400 Meters Score	46-49	4	Numeric
110 Meter Hurdles Score	50-53	4	Numeric
Discus Score	54-57	4	Numeric
Pole Vault Score	58-61	4	Numeric
Javelin Score	62-65	4	Numeric
1500 Meters Score	66-69	4	Numeric
Best Score-100 Meters	70-73	4	Numeric
Best Score-Long Jump	74-77	4	Numeric
Best Score-Shot Put	78-81	4	Numeric
Best Score-High Jump	82-85	4	Numeric
Best Score-400 Meters	86-89	4	Numeric
Best Score-110 Meter Hurdles	90-93	4	Numeric
Best Score-Discus	94-97	4	Numeric
Best Score-Pole Vault	98-101	4	Numeric
Best Score-Javelin	102-105	4	Numeric
Best Score-1500 Meters	106-109	4	Numeric

The only difference when using these two files to create the Decathlon Summary Report concerns where the Total Score for each athlete is obtained. If the file is used from Chapter 2 Programming Assignment 1, the Total Score is contained within the record. If the file is used from Chapter 2 Programming Assignment 1A, the Total Score will have to be calculated by adding the Individual Event Scores.

It will be noted also on the Decathlon Summary Report that the Coach Name is included on the report, but the Coach Name is not included in the Decathlon Master File. The Coach Name is to be obtained from the Coach Identification File. The format of the Coach Identification File is illustrated on the next page.

Coach Identification File

COACH NUMBER | COACH NAME

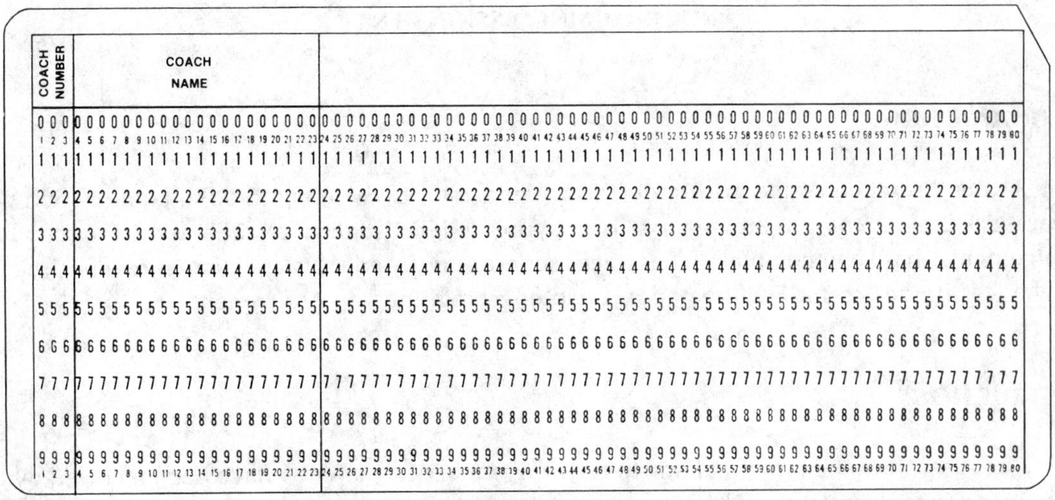

As can be seen from the card format above, the record in the Coach Identification File contains the Coach Number and the Coach Name. The file is sorted in Coach Number Sequence.

PROCESSING

To prepare the report, the following processing is necessary:

1. The Decathlon Master created in either Programming Assignment 1 in Chapter 2 or in Programming Assignment 1A in Chapter 2 must be sorted in Coach Number sequence.

2. Records from the Decathlon Master File and the Coach Identification File must be read and the Coach Numbers matched. When the Coach Numbers match, the Coach Name should be extracted from the Coach Identification File for printing on the Decathlon Summary Report. The other fields on the report will be obtained from the matching Decathlon Master Record.

3. Each record in the Decathlon Master File is to be printed. For each record in the Decathlon Master File, there will be a record in the Coach Identification File with a matching Coach Number.

4. It is possible, however, to have records in the Coach Identification File which do not match a record in the Decathlon Master File. This may occur when a coach in the Coach Identification File does not have an athlete who participates in the decathlon.

5. There may be more than one record in the Decathlon Master File with the same coach number; that is, more than one record in the Decathlon Master File may match one record from the Coach Identification File. This will occur when a coach has more than one athlete who competes in the decathlon.

6. As noted previously, if the Decathlon Master File which is being used in this program was created in Chapter 2 Programming Assignment 1A, the Total Score for the athlete will have to be calculated by adding the Individual Event Scores.

CHAPTER 3

PROGRAMMING ASSIGNMENT 1A

INTRODUCTION

At the discretion of the instructor, this assignment may be completed in combination with Chapter 3 Programming Assignment 1, or may be assigned only after Chapter 3 Programming Assignment 1 has been completely designed, coded, and tested. This assignment requires the use of the Decathlon Master File created in Chapter 2 Programming Assignment 1A.

INSTRUCTIONS

A request for some modifications to the program in Assignment 1 have been received by the data processing department. The requested changes are as follows:

1. The school which the athlete attends should be printed on the report.
2. The individual event scores for each event in the decathlon should be printed for each athlete.
3. The best score in each event in the decathlon should be printed for each athlete.

IMPLEMENTATION OF CHANGES

After considering the modifications requested, the following changes were made to the output specified for Programming Assignment 1.

Decathlon Summary Report

The format of the report was changed to correspond to the printer spacing chart illustrated below.

PRINTER SPACING CHART

```
XX/XX/XX                                             DECATHLON SUMMARY REPORT
                                                                                                                          PAGE XØX
COACH
NUMBER       COACH NAME             ATHLETE                       SCHOOL NAME                 TOTAL                   EVENT  BEST
                                                                                              SCORE    EVENT NAME     SCORES SCORES
 XØX    XXXXXXXXXXXXXXXXXXXX    XXXXXXXXXXXXXXXXXXXX    XXXXXXXXXXXXXXXXXXXXXXXXXXXXXXXXXXX
                                                                                              XXXX     1ØØ METERS      XXØX   XXØX
                                                                                                       LONG JUMP       XXØX   XXØX
                                                                                                       SHOT PUT        XXØX   XXØX
                                                                                                       HIGH JUMP       XXØX   XXØX
                                                                                                       4ØØ METERS      XXØX   XXØX
                                                                                                       11Ø M. HURDLES  XXØX   XXØX
                                                                                                       DISCUS          XXØX   XXØX
                                                                                                       POLE VAULT      XXØX   XXØX
                                                                                                       JAVELIN         XXØX   XXØX
                                                                                                       15ØØ METERS     XXØX   XXØX

                                XXXXXXXXXXXXXXXXXXXX
                                                        XXXXXXXXXXXXXXXXXXXXXXXXXXXXXXXXXXX   XXXX     XXXXXXXXXXXXXX  XXØX   XXØX
     -NEW PAGE FOR EACH COACH-
```

Note from the printer spacing chart that the School Name has been added to the report as well as the Event Name, the Event Scores which, when added, are equal to the Total Score, and the Best Scores which the athlete has obtained in each of the events.

INPUT

As noted previously, the input to this assignment requires that the Decathlon Master File was created in Programming Assignment 1A in Chapter 2. There are no changes in the Coach Identification File.

PROCESSING

The changes to the processing are specified below:

1. In order to print the School Name on the report, the School Identification in the Decathlon Master File will be used to look up the entire school name as it is to appear on the report. The School Identification and the School Names which are to appear on the report are listed below.

   STA — STANFORD UNIVERSITY
   ORS — OREGON STATE UNIVERSITY
   ORU — UNIVERSITY OF OREGON
   UCB — UNIVERSITY OF CALIFORNIA AT BERKELEY
   UCL — UNIVERSITY OF CALIFORNIA AT LOS ANGELES
   USC — UNIVERSITY OF SOUTHERN CALIFORNIA
   WAS — WASHINGTON STATE UNIVERSITY
   WAU — UNIVERSITY OF WASHINGTON

2. The report must be printed in alphabetical order by Athlete within Coach Number sequence.

3. The Coach Number, Coach Name, Athlete Name, School, and Total Score are group-indicated as shown on the printer spacing chart. When a new athlete is read, the Coach Number and Coach Name will continue to be group-indicated. Whenever a new coach is read, a new page will begin on the report.

4. A maximum of four athletes are to be printed on any one page of the report.

Sequential File Updating

> *"An hour of design is worth a day of maintenance."*[1]

INTRODUCTION

In Chapter 2, the Program Master File was created. It was mentioned there that a master file is a file which contains up-to-date data reflecting the status of the system of which the file is a part. After a master file is built, however, the data within the file will likely become obsolete relatively quickly unless there is some method with which to keep current data in the file. In order to keep current data in a master file, the master file must be UPDATED; that is, the data must be deleted, changed, added, or otherwise altered so that the master file continually reflects the most up-to-date status of the system.

This File Maintenance, or updating of information stored in files, is a critical part of the programs and systems which are found in most data processing organizations, for it is only with valid and current information that the data processing department can fulfill the needs of the user community. Since file updating is such an important part of any installation, this chapter will be devoted to examining the methods and techniques which can be used to update a master file which is processed sequentially.

MASTER FILE UPDATING

As noted, once a master file has been created, it is periodically necessary to update this file with current information so that the file always contains the most recent data. Typically, file updating procedures take three forms: Additions, Deletions, and Changes.

An ADDITION takes place when a new record is added to an already established master file. For example, in a system keeping track of programs being designed and written in a data processing installation, when a new program is assigned to a programmer, a record for the new program would be added to the master file reflecting the assignment of a new program.

A DELETION becomes necessary when data currently stored in the master file is to be removed. For example, if a program is completed or is terminated for some reason, it would be necessary to delete the corresponding master record from the file so that the program would not be considered an active program.

A CHANGE must be made to the master file whenever the data in the master file no longer contains accurate, up-to-date information. For example, if the programmer completed the program design task, a change to the master record must be made to indicate the completion of the design task.

---

1 *G. M. Weinberg, S. E. Wright, R. Kauffman, M. A. Goetz,* High Level COBOL Programming, *Winthrop Publishers, Inc., 1977.*

SEQUENTIAL FILE UPDATING

When there are numerous records in the master file which frequently require updating, that is, when there are numerous and frequent additions, deletions, and changes to the master file, sequential file organization is an efficient way in which to store and process the file. When the file is stored and processed sequentially, the records must be arranged sequentially on the basis of some control field. For example, in an application program reporting system, the records could be arranged by Program Identification. When the file updating takes place, the master file is processed against a Transaction File containing additions, deletions, and changes. This transaction file must also be arranged in sequence based upon the same key or control field.

SEQUENTIAL UPDATING thus involves the reading of a sequential master file, the reading of a sorted sequential transaction file, and the creation of a new, updated master file. Normally, an Exception Report which lists transaction errors such as invalid transaction codes is also created.

Figure 4-1 illustrates the basic concept of a file updating procedure in which a master file stored sequentially on a direct access device is updated by a sorted transaction file stored on punched cards.

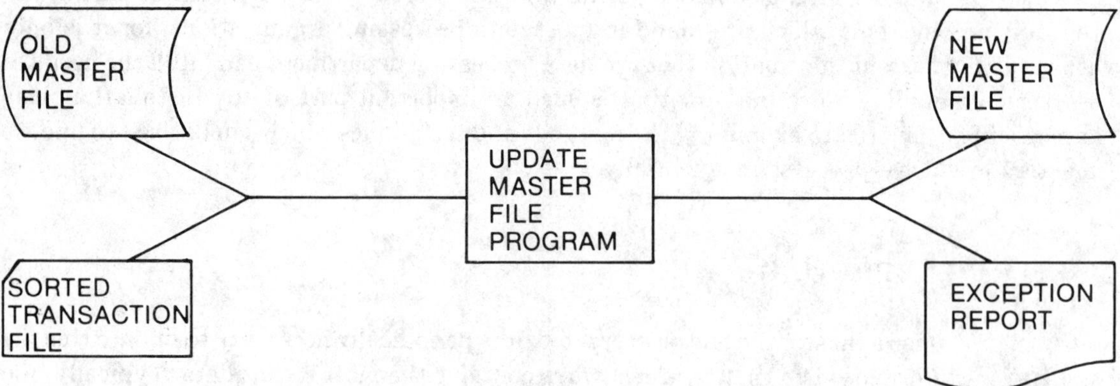

Figure 4-1 Flow Diagram of Sequential Update

Note from Figure 4-1 that after the updating process has been completed, the output consists of a new updated master file reflecting all additions, deletions, and changes to the original master file and, in addition, a printed exception report listing any transaction records in error, such as one containing an invalid code.

It should be noted that on the next file updating cycle, the newly created master file becomes the "old master file" and is input to the system. Any new transaction records are then processed against this file. The "old master file" can then be discarded, although most installations normally retain the "old master files" for at least three generations back in case difficulties are encountered, such as the current master file's being accidentally damaged or destroyed.

SAMPLE PROGRAM

In order to illustrate sequential file updating, the Program Master File created in Chapter 2 and printed in Chapter 3 will be updated by a Transaction File stored on punched cards. The format of the Program Master File is illustrated below.

Application Program Master File

FIELD	POSITION	NUMBER OF DIGITS	ATTRIBUTES
Program Identification	1 - 6	6	
Application Designation	1 - 2		Alphanumeric
Identification Number	3 - 6		Numeric
Program Description	7 - 26	20	Alphanumeric
Programmer Employee Number	27 - 32	6	Numeric
Estimated Review Hours	33 - 36	4	Numeric
Estimated Design Hours	37 - 40	4	Numeric
Estimated Code Hours	41 - 44	4	Numeric
Estimated Test Hours	45 - 48	4	Numeric
Estimated Implementation Hours	49 - 52	4	Numeric
Actual Review Hours	53 - 56	4	Numeric
Actual Design Hours	57 - 60	4	Numeric
Actual Code Hours	61 - 64	4	Numeric
Actual Test Hours	65 - 68	4	Numeric
Actual Implementation Hours	69 - 72	4	Numeric
Review Status Code	73	1	Alphanumeric
Design Status Code	74	1	Alphanumeric
Code Status Code	75	1	Alphanumeric
Test Status Code	76	1	Alphanumeric
Implementation Status Code	77	1	Alphanumeric

File Information: Record Length — 77 characters
Blocking Factor — 20 records per block
Storage Medium — Direct Access Device
Organization — Sequential
Access — Sequential

Figure 4-2 Format of Program Master File

As can be seen from Figure 4-2, the format of the Program Master File is the same as was created in Chapter 2 and used in Chapter 3. It should be noted in this program that the key to the file is the Program Identification; and the file, when created, was stored in ascending sequence by Program Identification. Therefore, there is no sorting required in order to update the Program Master File.

The Transaction File is stored on punched cards. The format of the records in the Transaction File is illustrated below.

Transaction File

PROGRAM IDENT.	PROGRAM DESCRIPTION	EMPLOYEE NUMBER	ESTIMATED HOURS					ACTUAL HOURS					STATUS CODES						CODE
			REVIEW	DESIGN	CODE	TEST	IMPLEM	REVIEW	DESIGN	CODE	TEST	IMPLEM	REV	DES	CODE	TEST	IMPL		
1–6	7–26	27–32	33–36	37–40	41–44	45–48	49–52	53–56	57–60	61–64	65–68	69–72	73	74	75	76	77	78–79	80

Figure 4-3 Format of Transaction Record

From Figure 4-3 it can be seen that the Transaction Record contains the Program Identification, Program Description, Employee Number, Estimated Hours, Actual Hours, Status Codes, and a Transaction Code. The Program Identification field is used as the field which is matched to the Master Record so that updating can take place. The Transaction Code field, in column 80, is used to specify the type of processing which is to take place by using the particular transaction record. The field can contain the value "A" to indicate that an Addition is to occur, the value "D" to indicate that a master record should be Deleted, and the value "C" to show that a Change should be made to the master record. Any other value in the Transaction Code field is invalid.

The remaining fields in the Transaction Record are used to update the Program Master File. When the Transaction Code is equal to the value "A," that is, when an Addition is to take place, the Program Description, Employee Number, and Estimated Hours are used to supply the information required for the New Master Record. When the record is to be changed, the Employee Number, Actual Hours, and Status Codes fields are used to change the record. When the record is deleted, only the Program Identification field is required in addition to the Transaction Code field.

The detailed processing which is to occur within the program is specified in the Program Specifications beginning in Figure 4-4.

PROGRAMMING SPECIFICATIONS		
SUBJECT Update Application Program Master File	DATE June 10	PAGE 1 OF 4
TO Programmer	FROM Systems Analyst	

Write a program to update the Application Program Master File. The format of the Application Program Master File, the Transaction File which will be used to update the master file, and the Exception Report to be created when there are errors found in the processing are included as a part of this narrative. The detailed processing is specified below.

1. The Program Master File is input to the program and contains the following fields: Program Identification, Program Description, Programmer Employee Number, Estimated Hours, Actual Hours, and Program Status Codes. The file is sorted in an ascending sequence by Program Identification.

2. The Transaction File contains transaction records which indicate the type of updating which should occur to the Program Master File. The record can contain the following fields: Program Identification, Program Description, Programmer Employee Number, Estimated Hours, Actual Hours, Program Status Codes, and a Transaction Code.

3. Three types of processing can take place. A record can be added to the file, a record can be deleted from the master file, or a record in the Program Master File can be changed.

   a. Additions — A record is to be added to the Program Master File if the Transaction Code contains the value "A." When a record is added to the Program Master File, the Program Identification, Program Description, Programmer Employee Number, and Estimated Hours are taken from the Transaction Record and are placed in the new Program Master Record. The Actual Hours in the new record are set to zero and the Program Status Codes fields are set to blank in the new record. An addition can only take place if there is no record on the Program Master File with the same Program Identification. If there is a record on the Program Master File with the same Program Identification as a transaction record with a Transaction "A," this is an error and the addition cannot take place. Instead, an entry must be made on the Exception Report indicating an error.

Figure 4-4 Program Specifications (Part 1 of 4)

PROGRAMMING SPECIFICATIONS

SUBJECT	DATE	
Update Applications Program Master File	June 10	PAGE 2 OF 4
TO Programmer	**FROM** Systems Analyst	

b. Deletions — A master record is to be deleted from the Program Master File if the Transaction Code in the Transaction Record contains the value "D." In order for a deletion to take place, the Program Identification in the Transaction Record must be equal to the Program Identification in the Program Master Record. When they are equal, the corresponding Master Record should not be written on the new Program Master File. The only fields required in the Transaction Record whose function is to delete a master record are the Program Identification and the Transaction Code "D." If the Program Identification in the Transaction Record is not equal to a Program Identification in a Program Master Record and the Transaction Code is equal to "D," an error has occurred; and an entry should be made on the Exception Report.

c. Changes — Fields within a Program Master Record will be changed if the Transaction Code in the Transaction Record is equal to the value "C," and the Program Identification in the Transaction Record is equal to the Program Identification in the Program Master Record. There are three fields which can be changed in the Program Master Record — the Programmer Employee Number, the Actual Hours, and the Program Status Codes. In order for a change to a Master Record to take place, the Transaction Code in the Transaction Record must be equal to the value "C," and the Program Identification in the Transaction Record must equal the Program Identification in the Program Master Record.

When these conditions are met, then the following changes may take place:

1. If the Programmer Employee Number field in the Transaction Record contains data, then the value in the field will replace the value in the Program Master Record.
2. If any of the five Actual Hours fields (Review, Design, Code, Test, or Implement) contains data, that is, is not blank, then the value in the Transaction Record should be added to the appropriate field in the Program Master Record. For example, if the Actual Hours Code field was not blank in the Transaction Record, then the value in the Transaction Record should be added to the value in the Program Master Record.

Figure 4-5 Program Specifications (Part 2 of 4)

PROGRAMMING SPECIFICATIONS		
SUBJECT Update Application Program Master File	DATE June 10	PAGE 3 OF 4
TO Programmer	FROM Systems Analyst	

3. If any of the Status Codes in the Transaction Record (Review, Design, Code, Test, or Implement) contains the value "C," then the corresponding field in the Program Master Record should also be changed to the value "C." For example, if the Review Status Code field in the Transaction Record contained the value "C," then the value "C" should also be moved to the Review Status Code field in the Program Master Record.

If a Change record ("C" in Transaction Code) is read and there is no matching Program Master Record, then an entry should be made on the Exception Report indicating this error.

4. The only valid Transaction Codes are "A," "D," and "C." If any other code is found in a Transaction Record, the record is in error and should not be used in processing against the Program Master File. Instead, an entry should be made on the Exception Report.

5. The Exception Report is to contain the following information:
   a. Program Identification of the Transaction in error;
   b. Transaction Code from the Transaction in error;
   c. The Type of Error.

   The Types of Errors which can occur are:
   a. Duplicate Master Record — This occurs when the Transaction Record indicates that an Addition is to take place, but there is already a master record in the Program Master File with a Program Identification equal to the one found in the Transaction Record.
   b. Invalid Transaction Code — This occurs whenever the Transaction Code is not equal to "A," "D," or "C."
   c. Non-Matching Master Record — This error occurs when a Transaction Code of "C" or "D" is found in the Transaction Record, but there is no Program Master Record with a Program Identification equal to the Program Identification in the Transaction Record.

Figure 4-6 Program Specifications (Part 3 of 4)

PROGRAMMING SPECIFICATIONS		
SUBJECT Update Application Program Master File	**DATE** June 10	**PAGE** 4 **OF** 4
TO Programmer	**FROM** Systems Analyst	

6. The Transaction File has been presorted in Program Identification sequence.

7. All fields in the Transaction Records which may be used to add or change data within the Program Master File have been previously edited. Therefore, there is no need to edit any input data in this program.

8. The program should be written in COBOL.

Figure 4-7 Program Specifications (Part 4 of 4)

As will be noted from the Program Specifications, an Exception Report is to be produced from the program listing those errors which occur in the Transaction File. The printer spacing chart for the Exception Report is illustrated in Figure 4-8.

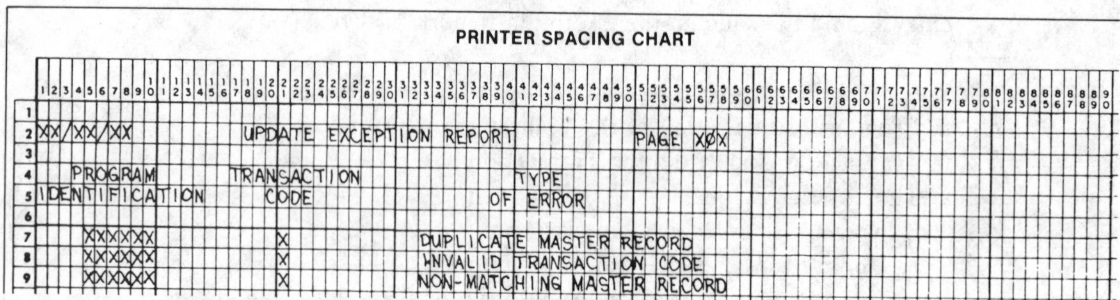

Figure 4-8 Exception Report

As can be seen from Figure 4-8, the Exception Report includes the Program Identification, the Transaction Code, and the Type of Error. One line will be written for each transaction which is in error. A maximum of 40 detail lines should be written on one page of the report.

SEQUENTIAL FILE UPDATING PROCESSING

When updating a sequential file, it is mandatory that both the file being updated (Program Master File) and the file containing the records with the update information (Transaction File) be sorted in either an ascending or descending sequence based upon the same key or control field within the records. In the sample program, the Program Master Records and the Transaction Records are sorted in an ascending sequence based upon the Program Identification. Therefore, when a record is read from one of the files, there will never be a record which is read from the same file with a lower Program Identification. This is illustrated in Figure 4-9.

EXAMPLE

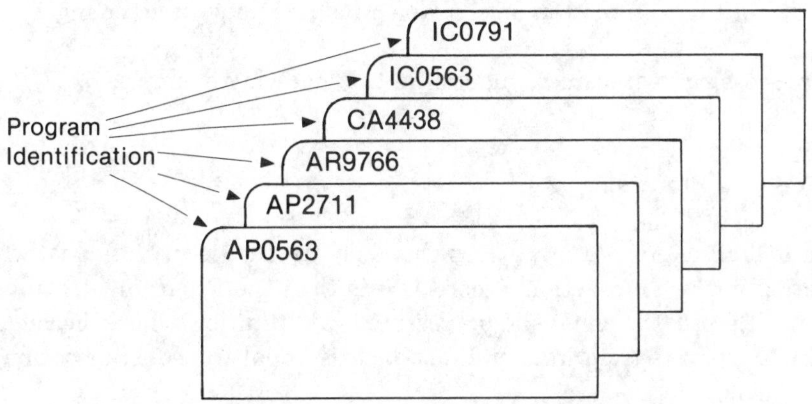

Figure 4-9 Example of Sorted Transaction File

Note in Figure 4-9 that the Transaction File is sorted on Program Identification. When the first record, with Program Identification AP0563 is read, the programmer is assured that there will never be a record in the file with a Program Identification less than AP0563, since the records are sorted in an ascending sequence. Note that this is true for each subsequent record in the Transaction File. The same holds true for the Program Master File which is sorted in an ascending sequence by Program Identification. It is extremely important that this fact be realized in order to understand the processing which takes place when updating a sequential file.

The basic processing involved when updating a sequential file is as follows:

1. A record from the master file and a record from the transaction file are read.

2. The control fields in each of the records are compared. In the sample program, this means that the Program Identification in the Program Master Record will be compared with the Program Identification in the Transaction Record.

3. Based upon the result of the comparison, the following processing will take place:

   a. If the Transaction Record is less than the Program Master Record, the only valid action is an addition to the Program Master File. Thus, the record from the Transaction File will be added to the Program Master File.

   b. If the Program Identification in the Transaction Record is equal to the Program Identification in the Program Master Record, then the Transaction Record can be used to either Change the Master Record or to Delete the Master Record.

   c. If the Master Record is less than the Transaction Record, it means that there is no Transaction which is going to be updating the Master Record. Therefore, the Master Record will be written on the New Master File with no changes.

This processing is explained in detail in the following examples.

Transaction Low Processing

When a Transaction Record is less than the Master Record, that is, when the Program Identification in the Transaction Record is less than the Program Identification in the Program Master Record, the only valid processing is an Addition. This is because there will never be a record in the Program Master File which is equal to the Transaction Record. This is illustrated below.

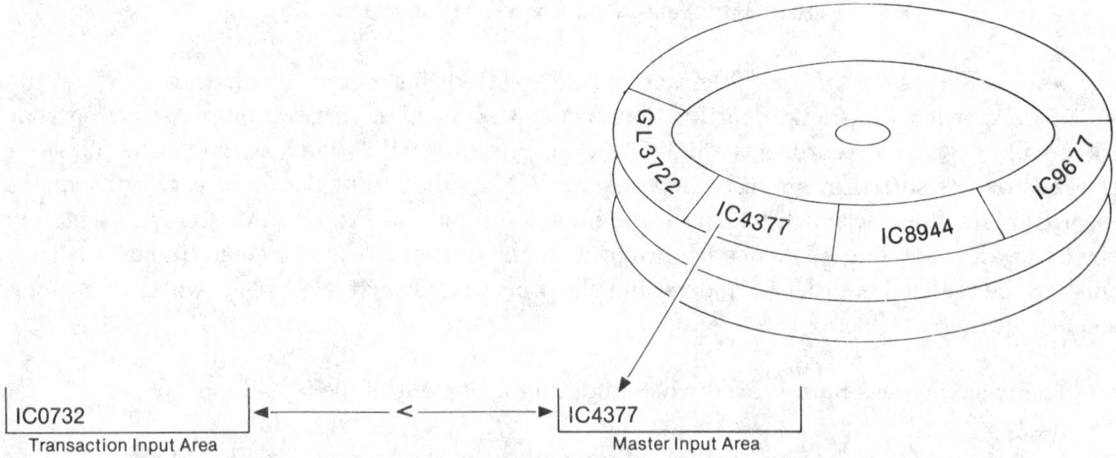

Figure 4-10 Example of Transaction Low Processing

Note from Figure 4-10 that the Program Identification for the Transaction Record is IC0732. The Program Identification for the Master Record is IC4377. Therefore, when they are compared, the Transaction Record will be less than the Master Record. Since the Program Master Records are sorted in an ascending sequence by Program Identification, each succeeding Master Record will have a Program Identification greater than IC4377. Thus, there will never be a Master Record which is equal to the Program Identification IC0732 found in the Transaction Record.

Since the Program Identification values will never be equal, the Transaction Record cannot be used to Change or Delete a Master Record since one of the requirements to Change or Delete a Master Record is that the Program Identification values be equal. Therefore, the only valid action which can occur is that the record with the Program Identification IC0732 is added to the New Program Master File. In the example in Figure 4-10, it would be placed in the New Master File between the record with Program Identification GL3722 and the record with Program Identification IC4377.

Thus, when the Transaction Record is less than the Master Record, the following processing must occur:

A. The Transaction Code is checked to ensure that it indicates that an Addition is to take place; that is, that the Transaction Code field contains the code "A."

B. If the Transaction Code contains the value "A," the following must take place:

   1. The data in the Transaction Record is moved to the output area for the new Program Master File.

   2. The New Master File record is written.

   3. The next Transaction Record is read.

This processing is illustrated in the following diagram.

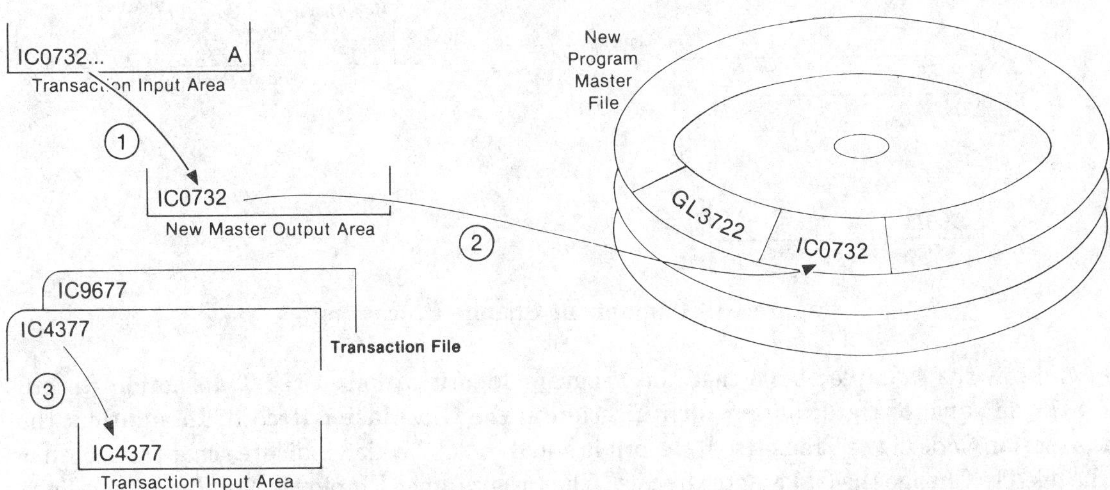

Figure 4-11 Low Transaction Record Processing

Note from Figure 4-11 that the Transaction which is contained in the Transaction Input Area is moved to the New Program Master Output Area. The record is then written on the New Master File and a Transaction Record is read from the Transaction File. This is the processing which must take place when the Transaction Record is less than the Master Record.

If the Transaction Code in the Transaction Record is not equal to "A," then an error has occurred and the appropriate error message should be written on the Exception Report.

Transaction Record Equal to Master Record

When the Transaction Record is equal to the Master Record, that is, when the Program Identification in the Transaction Record is equal to the Program Identification in the Master Record, two types of valid processing may occur: Either the Transaction Record can cause the corresponding Master Record to be Deleted from the Program Master File, or it can cause the corresponding Master Record to be Changed. The following processing should occur when the records are equal.

A. If the Transaction Code indicates that the Transaction Record is to be used to Change the Program Master Record (i.e. Transaction Code = "C"), then the following occurs:

1. The field(s) in the Transaction Record are used to change the corresponding fields in the Master Record.

2. The next Transaction Record is read.

This processing is illustrated below.

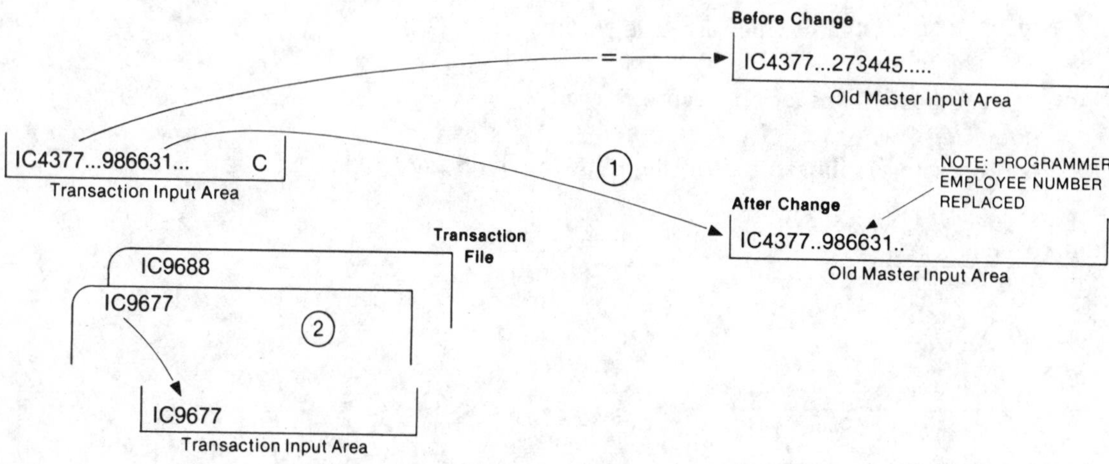

Figure 4-12 Example of Change Processing

Note in the example above that the Program Identification in the Transaction Record (IC4377) is equal to the Program Identification in the Old Master Record. In addition, the Transaction Code in the Transaction Record is equal to "C," which indicates that the record is to be used to Change the Old Master Record. The Programmer Employee Number is contained in the Transaction Record. Therefore, the Programmer Employee Number in the Transaction Record is to replace the Programmer Employee Number in the Old Master Record. As can be seen from Figure 4-12, this processing has taken place. If the Transaction Record contained other fields, such as Program Status Codes or Actual Hours values, then these changes would also take place as specified in the Programming Specifications.

After the change is made to the Master Record, the Transaction Record has been completely processed. Therefore, it is necessary to read the next Transaction Record. It should be noted that the Master Record was not written on the New Master File. This is because it is possible that more than one Transaction Record will be used to update the same Master Record. For example, a Transaction Record could be read which is used to update the Programmer Employee Number, as was seen in Figure 4-12. The next Transaction Record could contain the same Program Identification and be used to update the Actual Hours in the Program Master Record. Therefore, whenever a change is to take place to the Program Master Record, the updated or changed Program Master Record is not written on the file as a part of the change processing.

B. The second processing which can take place if the Program Identification in the Transaction Record is equal to the Program Identification in the Master Record is the Delete function. When a Master Record is deleted from the Master File, it is not written on the New Program Master File. The processing which should occur is:

   1. The next Program Master Record should be read without writing the Master Record to be deleted.

   2. The next Transaction Record is read.

This processing is illustrated below.

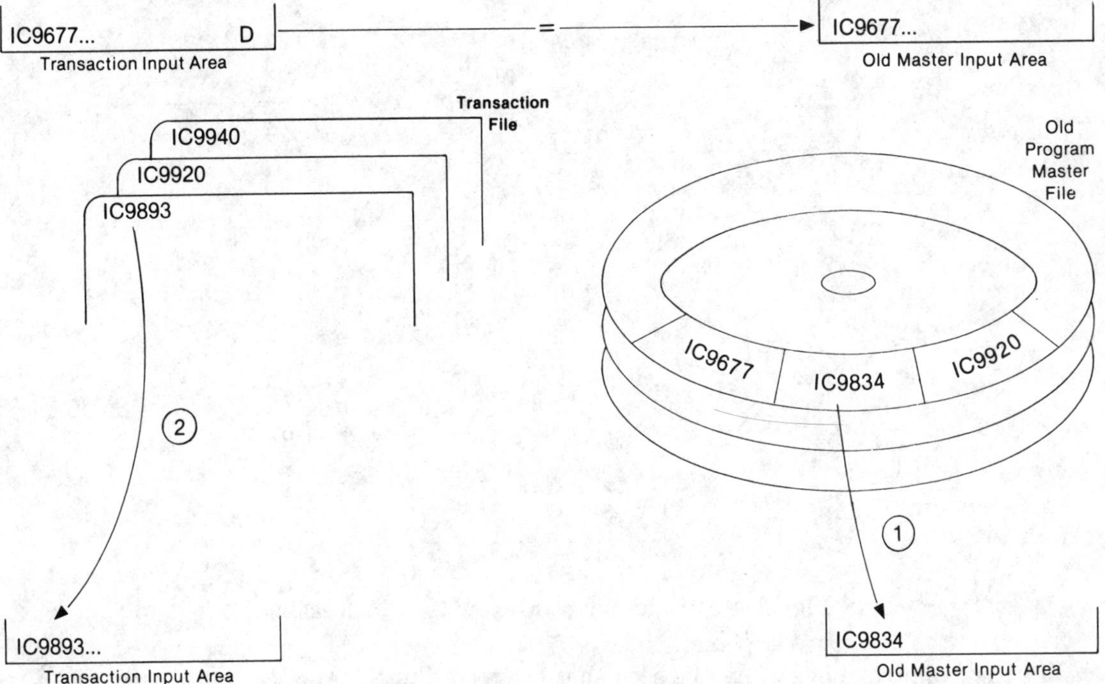

Figure 4-13 Example of Deletion Processing

Note from Figure 4-13 that the Program Identification for the Transaction File (IC9677) is equal to the Program Identification for the Program Master File and, in addition, the Transaction Code is equal to "D," indicating that the Master Record is to be deleted. In order to accomplish this, another record from the Program Master File is read and another record from the Transaction File is read. Note that no record was written on the New Master File. Therefore, since the Old Master Record was not written on the New Master File, it has been deleted from the Program Master File, which was the desired processing.

Master Record Less Than Transaction Record

The third condition which can occur is that the record from the Program Master File has a Program Identification which is less than the Program Identification in the Transaction File. When this occurs, the processing should be as follows:

A. Write the Old Master Record on the New Master File.

B. Read another record from the Old Master File.

This processing is illustrated below.

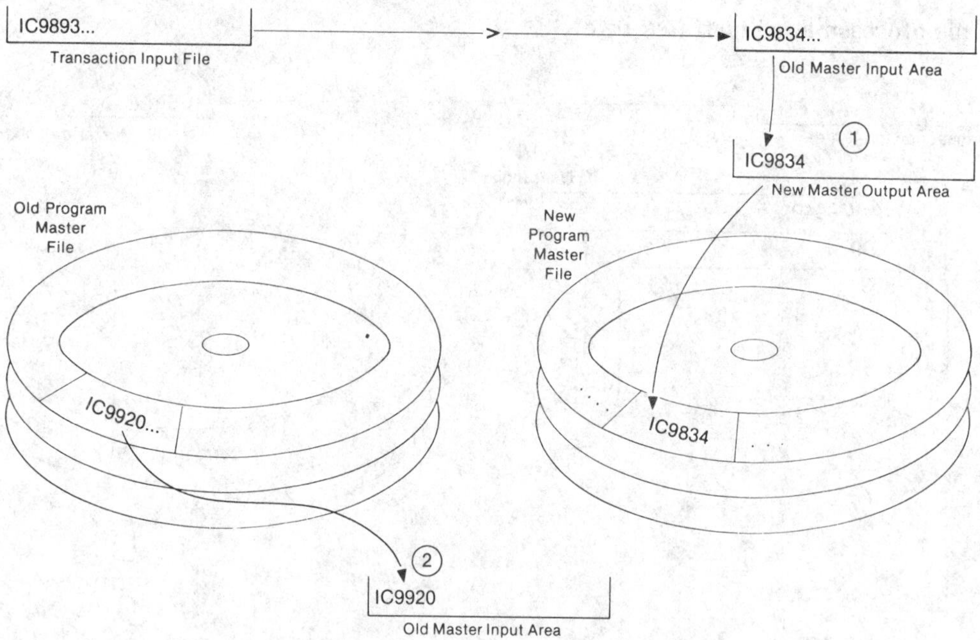

Figure 4-14 Example of Master Low Processing

In the example above, it can be seen that the record in the Master Input Area with Program Identification IC9834 is less than the record in the Transaction Input Area with Program Identification IC9893. When this occurs, there will never be a Transaction Record which will match the Master Record because, as will be recalled, the Transaction File is sorted in an ascending sequence, and each subsequent Transaction Record will have a Program Identification equal to or greater than IC9893. Since there cannot be a Transaction Record which will match the Master Record, there is no processing to be performed to the Master Record. Therefore, as illustrated above, the Master Record is written in the New Master File and another Master Record is read.

End of File Processing

As can be seen from the previous examples, two input files are being read and processed by the program, and it is possible to read a record from one file and not read a record from the other file. For example, when the Transaction Record is less than the Master Record, a Transaction Record is read after the processing is completed, but a Master Record is not. When processing two files in this manner, one of the files will reach end-of-file before the other. Therefore, the programmer must be aware of what processing should take place if the Transaction File reaches end-of-file before the Master File does, and also if the Master File reaches end-of-file before the Transaction File does.

When the Transaction File reaches end-of-file before the Master File does, it means that there are records in the Master File to be processed, but there will be no matching Transaction Records since there are no more Transaction Records. Therefore, the processing which should take place in this situation is the same as when the Master Record is less than the Transaction Record; that is, the Old Master Record should be written in the New Master File and another Old Master Record should be read. Note that the Transaction File should not be read because there are no more records in the Transaction File.

When the Master File reaches end-of-file before the Transaction File, there are records in the Transaction File to be processed but there are no matching Master Records for these Transaction Records since there are no more Master Records. When this occurs, the processing should be the same as when the Transaction Record is less than the Master Record; that is, the Transaction should be an Add record which is adding a record to the New Master File. This is because there are no Master Records which will match the Transaction Record since there are no more Master Records; and, of course, there will be no Master Records which are greater than the Transaction Record. Therefore, when the Master File reaches end-of-file before the Transaction File, all of the remaining Transaction Records should be Add records. If they are, then a valid addition to the New Master File can take place. If they are not, then an error has occurred; and an entry should be made on the Exception Report.

This end-of-file processing is as important as the processing which takes place when both files have records to be processed and should be well understood by the programmer.

Summary — Sequential File Updating Processing

As can be seen from the previous examples, the processing which takes place is dependent upon the comparison between the records from the Transaction File and the records from the Master File. This processing is summarized below.

1. If the Transaction is less than the Master, the only valid processing is adding the Transaction Record to the New Master File.

2. If the Transaction is equal to the Master, the Master Record can be changed by the Transaction Record or it can be deleted from the New Master File by the Transaction.

3. If the Master Record is less than the Transaction Record, there will never be a Transaction Record which matches the Master Record. Therefore, the Master Record is written in the New Master File with no further processing.

4. If the Transaction File reaches end-of-file before the Master File, the processing should be the same as if the Master Record is less than the Transaction File; that is, the Master Record is written in the New Master File with no further processing.

5. If the Master File reaches end-of-file before the Transaction File, the processing is the same as if the Transaction File is less than the Master File; that is, the only valid processing is adding the Transaction Record to the New Master File.

It is critical that the programmer understand not only the processing which will take place when each of the five conditions occurs, but also the reasons for the processing prior to embarking upon the design of the sequential file update program.

PROGRAM DESIGN — IPO CHARTS AND HIERARCHY CHART

Once the processing which is to be accomplished within the program is thoroughly understood, the programmer should begin designing the structure of the program. The first task is to identify the function of the top-level module in the program through the use of an IPO Chart. The IPO Chart for the top-level module in the sample program is illustrated in Figure 4-15.

IPO CHART			
PROGRAM: Program Master File Update	PROGRAMMER: Shelly/Cashman		DATE: June 16
MODULE NAME: Update Program Master	REF: AØØØ	MODULE FUNCTION: Update the Program Master File	
INPUT	**PROCESSING**	**REF:**	**OUTPUT**
1. Old Program Master File	1. Initialize		1. New Program Master File
2. Update Transaction File	2. Obtain data for new master	BØØØ	
	3. Write new master file	BØ1Ø	
	4. Terminate		

Figure 4-15 IPO Chart — Update Program Master

As can be seen from the IPO Chart in Figure 4-15, the function of the top-level module is to Update the Program Master File. The output from the module is the New Program Master File. The input to the module is the Old Program Master File and the Update Transaction File. As was mentioned in Chapter 2, the Exception Report is not considered output from the top-level module because it is produced only when errors occur. Therefore, it will be considered output from those modules which will determine that an error has occurred.

The major processing tasks which are necessary to update the Program Master File are the following: Initialize, Obtain Data for New Master, Write New Master File, and Terminate. Note from these tasks that the updating of a sequential master file can be thought of as a two-step operation. First, the data for the New Master File is obtained and then the data is used to Write the New Program Master File.

In analyzing the major processing tasks required in this high-level module, it is seen that the Initialize task involves merely opening the files and, therefore, does not require a separate module. The task of Obtaining New Master Data, on the other hand, requires matching the input files and extracting the data for the new master. This is considerable work, so the task of Obtaining New Master Data will be a separate module.

The task of Writing the New Master File also appears to be more than a few statements, so it will be a separate module. The Terminate task does not appear to be of any size or difficulty, so it will not be a separate module. After this analysis, the hierarchy chart for the program would be drawn, as illustrated in Figure 4-16.

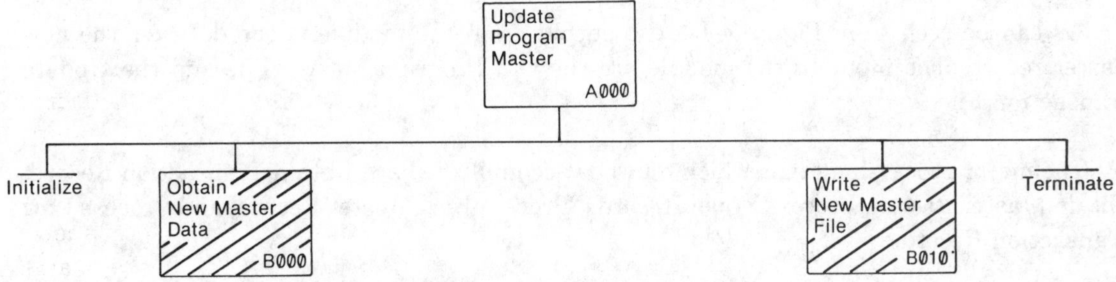

Figure 4-16 Hierarchy Chart

As can be seen from the hierarchy chart in Figure 4-16, the tasks of Initialize and Terminate will be contained within the A000 module, while the tasks of Obtain New Master Data and Write New Master will be in separate modules.

The IPO Chart for the module whose task is to Obtain New Master Data is illustrated in Figure 4-17.

IPO CHART			
PROGRAM: Program Master File Update	PROGRAMMER: Shelly/Cashman		DATE: June 16
MODULE NAME: Obtain New Master Data	REF: BØØØ	MODULE FUNCTION: Obtain Data for the New Master	
INPUT	PROCESSING	REF:	OUTPUT
1. Old Program Master File	1. Obtain transaction record		1. Data For New Master Record
2. Update Transaction File	2. Obtain master record		
	3. Process equal records	CØØØ	
	4. Process low master record	CØ1Ø	
	5. Process low transaction record	CØ2Ø	

Figure 4-17 IPO Chart — Obtain New Master Data

As can be seen from Figure 4-17, the output from the module is the data for the new master record. The input to the module are the Old Program Master File and the Update Transaction File.

The major processing tasks which must be accomplished are Obtain Transaction Record, Obtain Master Record, Process Equal Records, Process Low Master Record, and Process Low Transaction Record.

The major processing tasks of Obtaining a Transaction Record and Obtaining a Master Record are not lengthy or complex, so they do not require a separate module. The tasks of Processing Equal Records, Processing Low Master Records, and Processing Low Transaction Records, however, do require significant processing. Therefore, they will be made separate modules.

The hierarchy chart after the IPO Chart above has been analyzed is illustrated in Figure 4-18.

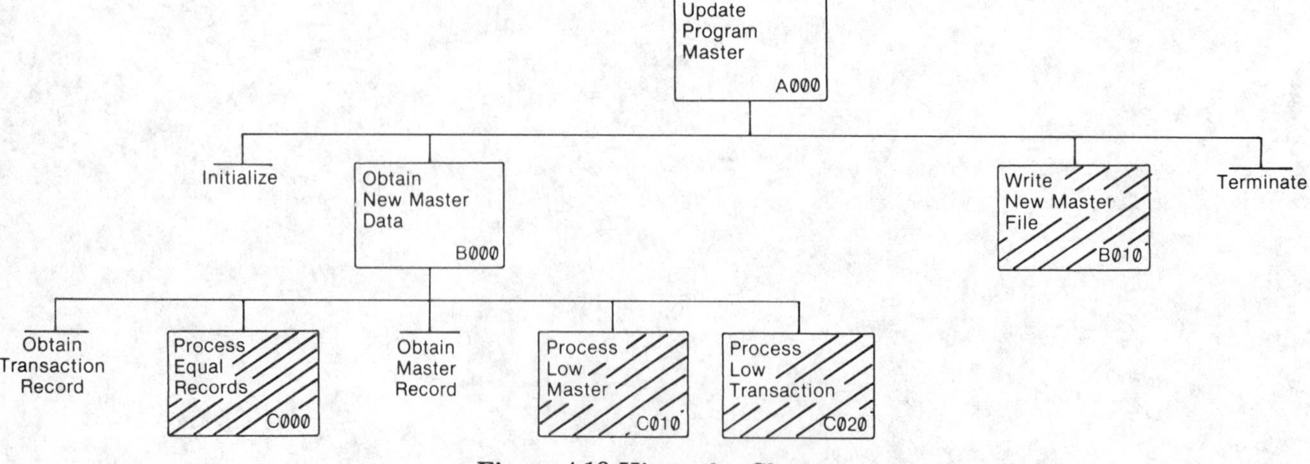

Figure 4-18 Hierarchy Chart

The next module to analyze is the module whose function is to Write the New Master File. The IPO Chart for this module is illustrated below.

IPO CHART			
PROGRAM: Program Master File Update	PROGRAMMER: Shelly/Cashman		DATE: June 16
MODULE NAME: Write New Master File	REF: BØ1Ø	MODULE FUNCTION: Write the New Master File	
INPUT	PROCESSING	REF:	OUTPUT
1. Data for New Master Record	1. Format new master record		1. New Master File
	2. Write the new master record		

Figure 4-19 IPO Chart — Write New Master File

The output from the module is the New Master File. The input to the module is the data for the new master record which is obtained elsewhere in the program. The major processing tasks are Format the New Master Record and Write the New Master Record. Neither of these tasks is lengthy or complex, so neither requires a separate module. The hierarchy chart after this analysis is shown in Figure 4-20.

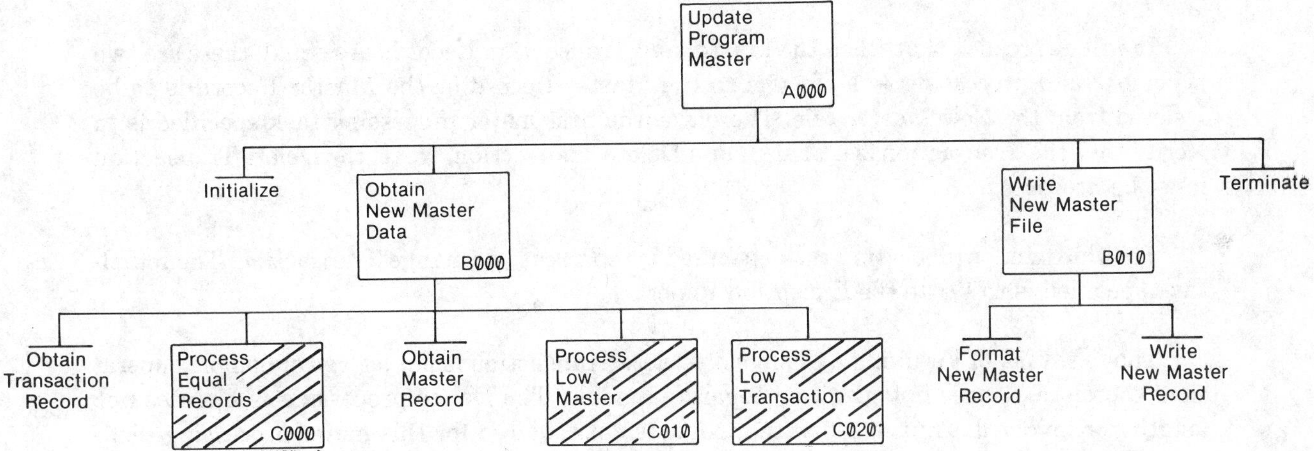

Figure 4-20 Hierarchy Chart

Note in the hierarchy chart above that the two major processing tasks required to Write the New Master File, Format the New Master Record and Write the New Master Record, are illustrated below the module whose function is to Write the New Master File, but they are not enclosed within boxes. Instead, they are specified below a horizontal line. As has been seen previously, this is the technique used to show that the major processing tasks specified will be contained within the module above them.

The module whose function is to Process Equal Records must now be analyzed. The IPO Chart for this module is illustrated in Figure 4-21.

IPO CHART			
PROGRAM: Program Master File Update	PROGRAMMER: Shelly/Cashman		DATE: June 16
MODULE NAME: Process Equal Records	REF: CØØØ	MODULE FUNCTION: Process Equal Master and Transaction Records	
INPUT	PROCESSING	REF:	OUTPUT
1. Equal Master and	1. Verify change or delete transactions		1. Data For New Master
Transaction Records	2. Process delete transaction		2. Exception Report
	3. Process change transaction	DØØØ	
	4. Write exception report	UØØØ	

Figure 4-21 IPO Chart — Process Equal Records

As can be seen from Figure 4-21, the output of the module which Processes the Equal Records is the Data for the New Master and the Exception Report. The input to the module are the equal Master and Transaction Records.

It will be recalled that when the Master and Transaction Records are equal, there are two types of valid processing — a Change to the Master Record or the Master Record is to be Deleted from the New Master File. Therefore, the first major processing task specified is to Verify that the Transaction is a Change or a Delete Transaction. Next, the Delete Transaction must be processed.

The third major processing task specified is to Process a Change Transaction. The fourth task specified is to Write the Exception Report.

The first task of Verifying a Change or Delete Transaction is not a large or complex operation; therefore, it does not require a separate module. The Delete processing is likewise not lengthy or involved. Thus, a separate module is not required for this major processing task.

The task of Processing a Change Transaction, however, could be lengthy or complex. It will be recalled that when a Change takes place to the Master Record, three different fields can be changed. Therefore, this major processing task appears as if it should be a separate module. Whenever there is the possibility that a major processing task will be lengthy or complex, it should be made a separate module.

The last task of Writing the Exception Report will be done by the utility module with Reference Number U000.

The hierarchy chart after this analysis is illustrated below.

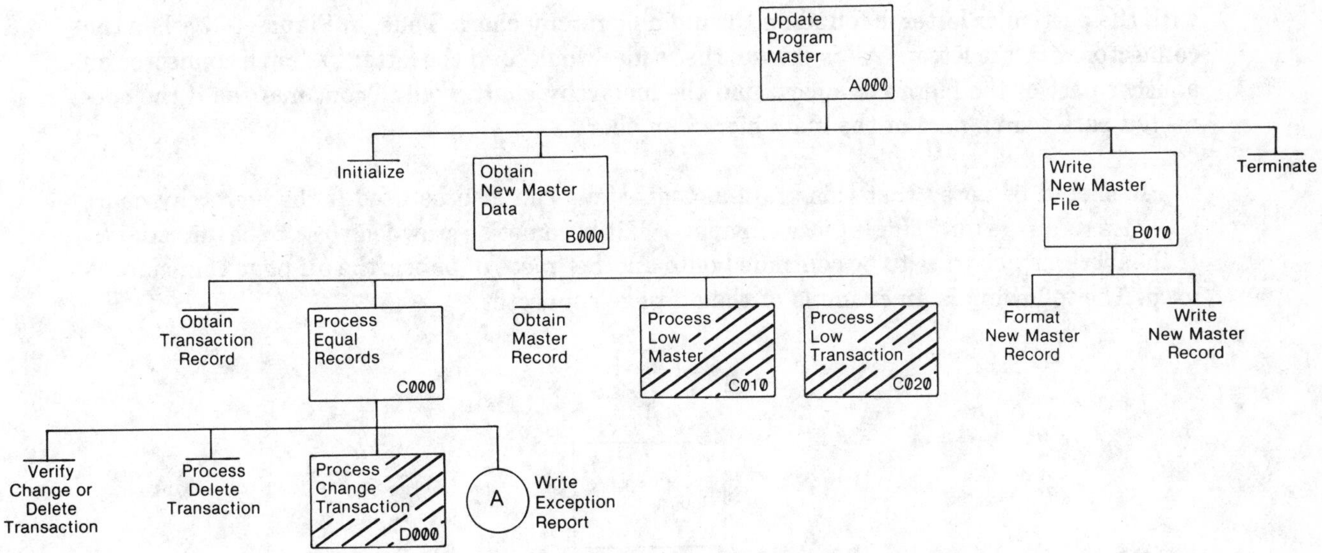

Figure 4-22 Hierarchy Chart

As can be seen from the hierarchy chart above, a separate module which Processes a Change Transaction will have the reference number D000. It should also be noted that a box is not used for the module which will Write the Exception Report. Instead, a circle "connector" is specified with the letter "A" contained in the circle. The name of the module is written alongside the circular connector. This method of indicating a module can be used when there is a module which is to be used in more than one area of the hierarchy chart. In this example, the module which Writes the Exception Report will be called from several different modules. Therefore, the connector is used to indicate that the definition of the module will occur elsewhere on the page.

The following example illustrates the Write Exception Report module defined on another part of the hierarchy chart.

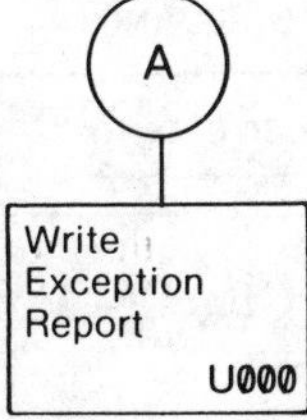

Figure 4-23 Example of Connector on Hierarchy Chart

Note in Figure 4-23 that the circular connector is drawn on a separate area of the hierarchy chart. Immediately below it is the module which is to be called when the circular connector with the particular letter is found on the main hierarchy chart. Thus, in Figure 4-22 when the connector with the letter "A" is drawn, the reader would find the letter "A" in a connector on another part of the hierarchy chart; and the hierarchy chart would "continue" as if the connected part were a part of the main hierarchy chart.

It should be noted that this graphing technique can also be used if the hierarchy chart becomes too large for a single piece of paper or if it becomes so crowded so as to be unreadable. If the hierarchy chart is to be continued onto another piece of paper, the off-page connector is used. The following is an example of the off-page connector.

Figure 4-24 Example of Off-Page Connector

The off-page connector as illustrated in Figure 4-24 is used whenever the hierarchy chart is to be continued onto another page. By using both the on-page connector (circle) and the off-page connector (pentagon), it is possible to make the hierarchy chart as large as possible in order to diagram the structure of a computer program.

The next module to be analyzed is the module which Processes a Low Master Record. The IPO Chart for this module is illustrated in Figure 4-25.

<table>
<tr><th colspan="4">IPO CHART</th></tr>
<tr><td>PROGRAM: Program Master File Update</td><td colspan="2">PROGRAMMER: Shelly/Cashman</td><td>DATE: June 16</td></tr>
<tr><td>MODULE NAME: Process Low Master</td><td>REF: CØ1Ø</td><td colspan="2">MODULE FUNCTION: Process Low Master Record</td></tr>
<tr><th>INPUT</th><th>PROCESSING</th><th>REF:</th><th>OUTPUT</th></tr>
<tr><td>1. Low Master Record</td><td>1. Format new master data</td><td></td><td>1. Data For New Master</td></tr>
</table>

Figure 4-25 IPO Chart — Process Low Master

The output from the module which Processes a Low Master Record is data for the new master record. The input to the module is the low Master Record. It will be recalled that when the Master Record is low, that is, the Program Identification in the Program Master File is less than the Program Identification in the Transaction File, there is no processing which will be performed on the Master Record (see Figure 4-14). Thus, the only processing which must be done when the Master Record is low is to move the data from the Master Record to an area which is accessible by the module which actually formats and writes the Master Record (see Figure 4-19). This is the task which is specified for the Process Low Master module in Figure 4-25. Since it is the only major processing task which must be accomplished by the module, there will be no lower-level modules out of this module; and the hierarchy chart would remain as illustrated in Figure 4-22.

The next module to consider is the module whose function is to Process a Low Transaction. The IPO Chart for this module is illustrated in Figure 4-26.

IPO CHART

PROGRAM: Program Master File Update	PROGRAMMER: Shelly/Cashman	DATE: June 16
MODULE NAME: Process Low Transaction	REF: C020	MODULE FUNCTION: Process Low Transaction Record

INPUT	PROCESSING	REF:	OUTPUT
1. Transaction Record	1. Verify valid transaction type		1. Data for New Master
	2. Format new master record data		2. Exception Report
	3. Write exception report	U000	

Figure 4-26 IPO Chart — Process Low Transaction

As will be recalled, when the Transaction Record contains a Program Identification which is less than the Program Identification in the Program Master Record, the only valid processing which can occur is to add a record to the Program Master File. Thus, the output from the module is the data for the new master record. In addition, the Exception Report is output because if an invalid transaction type is found, an entry will be made on the Exception Report.

The input to the module is the Transaction Record. Note that no Master Record is input to this module because there is no matching Master Record to process. The processing tasks are the following: Verify valid transaction type, Format new master record data, and Write the Exception Report. As noted, the transaction must be an addition. Thus, the transaction type must be verified. If it is valid, then the new master data is to be formatted for use by the module which writes the new Master File. If it is not valid, then an entry must be made on the Exception Report.

In analyzing the major processing tasks to be performed, it is found that verifying a valid transaction type is not a lengthy or complex operation; neither is the task of formatting the new master record data. Thus, neither of these major processing tasks will be a separate module. As noted previously, the Exception Report will be written by the utility module U000.

After this analysis, the hierarchy chart appears as illustrated in Figure 4-27.

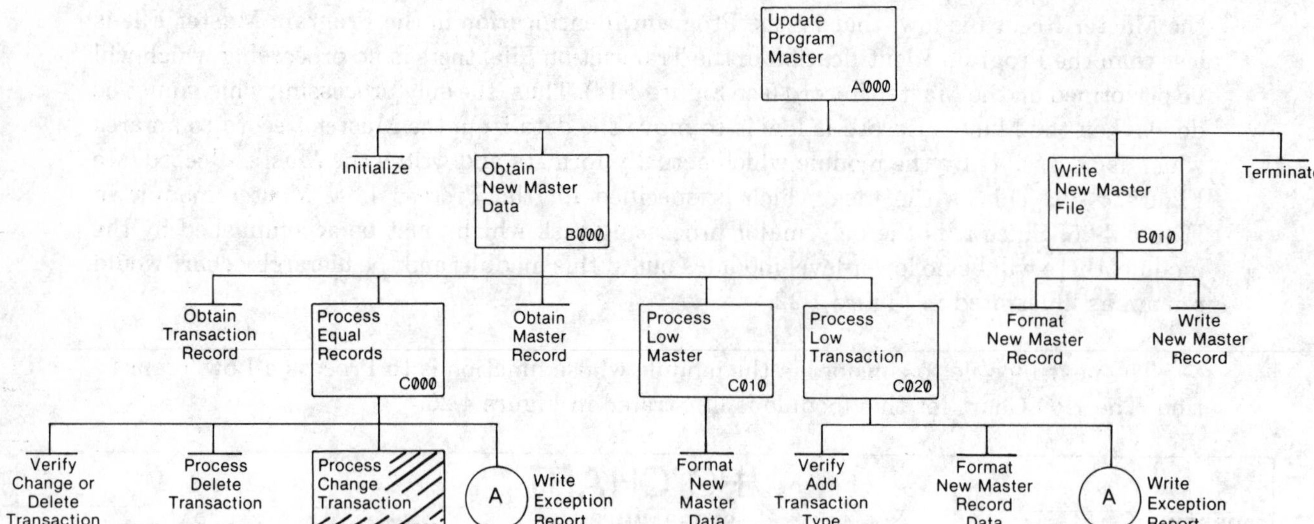

Figure 4-27 Hierarchy Chart

Note in the hierarchy chart above that the major processing tasks which were not made into separate modules are nevertheless shown on the hierarchy chart under the horizontal line so that the maintenance programmer will be able to see from looking at the hierarchy chart where the processing is taking place within the program. Note also that the reference to the module which is to write the Exception Report is through the use of the on-page connector. Again, this means that the module which is being referenced will be defined on a separate part of the page on which the connector appears.

The last module to be analyzed which appears in the main hierarchy chart is the module which Processes a Change Transaction. The IPO Chart for this module is shown in Figure 4-28.

IPO CHART			
PROGRAM: Program Master File Update	PROGRAMMER: Shelly/Cashman		DATE: June 16
MODULE NAME: Process Change Transaction	REF: D000	MODULE FUNCTION: Process a Change Transaction	
INPUT	PROCESSING	REF:	OUTPUT
1. Matched Master and	1. Determine type of change		1. Changed Master Record
Transaction Records	2. Change the master record		

Figure 4-28 IPO Chart — Process Change Transaction

Note from the IPO Chart in Figure 4-28 that the output of the module which Processes a Change Transaction is a Changed Master Record. The input to the module is the matched Master and Transaction Records. The major processing tasks in order to change the master record are: Determine the Type of Change and Change the Master Record. Determining the type of change is not a complex or lengthy operation, so it will not be made a separate module. Similarly, changing the Master Record is not long or difficult. Therefore, neither of these major processing tasks will require separate modules.

After this analysis, the hierarchy chart appears as follows:

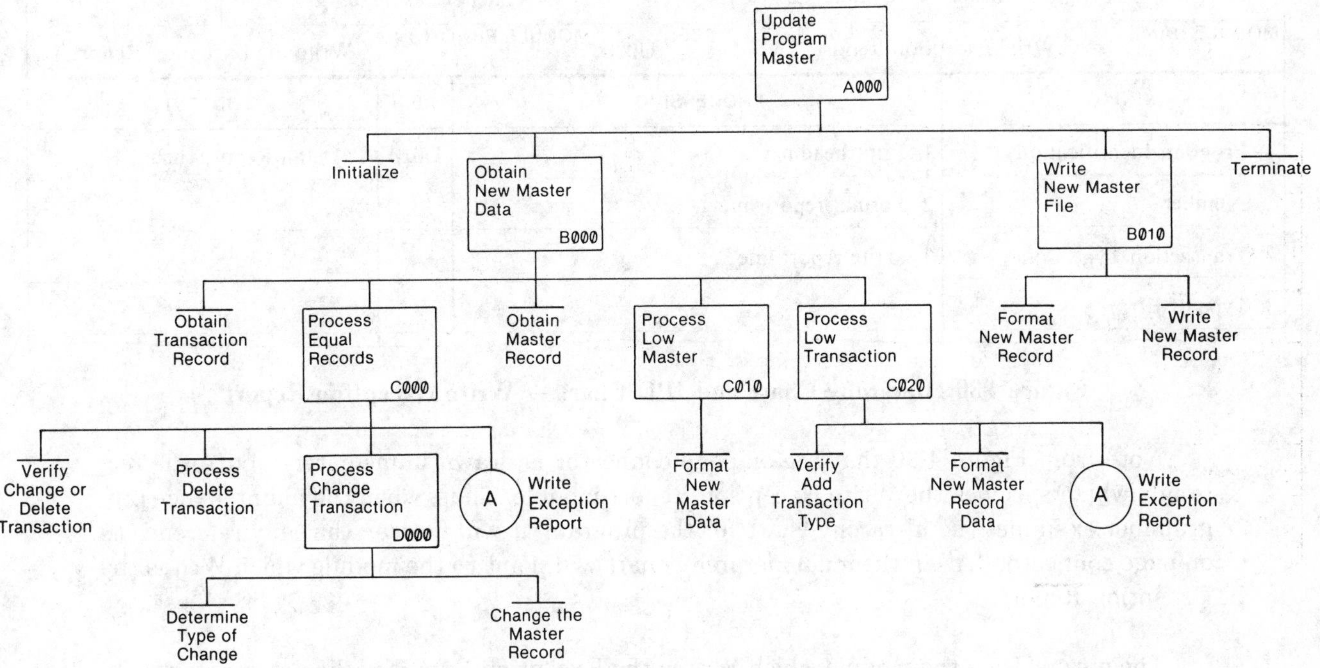

Figure 4-29 Hierarchy Chart

Note from Figure 4-29 that no modules remain to be analyzed on the main hierarchy chart. It will be recalled, however, that the module which Writes the Exception Report has been referenced in several places by an on-page connector. Therefore, this module must still be analyzed. The hierarchy chart for this module and the IPO Chart for the module which Writes the Exception Report are illustrated in Figure 4-30.

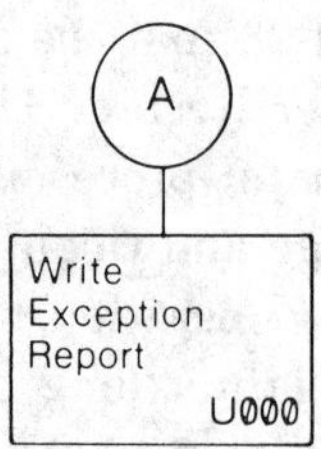

IPO CHART

PROGRAM: Program Master File Update		PROGRAMMER: Shelly/Cashman	DATE: June 16
MODULE NAME: Write Exception Report	REF: UØØØ	MODULE FUNCTION: Write the Exception Report	

INPUT	PROCESSING	REF:	OUTPUT
1. Program Identification	1. Print headings	UØ1Ø	1. Detail Report Line
Number	2. Format report line		
2. Transaction Type Code	3. Write report line		
3. Type of Error			

Figure 4-30 Hierarchy Chart and IPO Chart — Write Exception Report

Note from Figure 4-30 that the on-page connector is drawn immediately above the rectangle which specifies the Write Exception Report module. Thus, when the maintenance programmer examines the hierarchy chart for the program, it will be seen that any reference to on-page connector "A" in the main hierarchy chart will point to the module which Writes the Exception Report.

The output from the module which Writes the Exception Report is the detail report line. The input is the Program Identification Number, the Transaction Type Code, and the Type of Error. This data is necessary for the report detail (see Figure 4-8 for the format of the Exception Report).

The major processing tasks which must be accomplished are the following: Print headings, Format report line, and Write report line. Printing the headings will likely involve more than a few statements, so it will be made a separate module. Formatting the report line consists of a few Move Statements while Writing the report line will be a single Write Statement. Therefore, these two major processing tasks do not require a separate module.

The hierarchy chart after this analysis is illustrated in Figure 4-31.

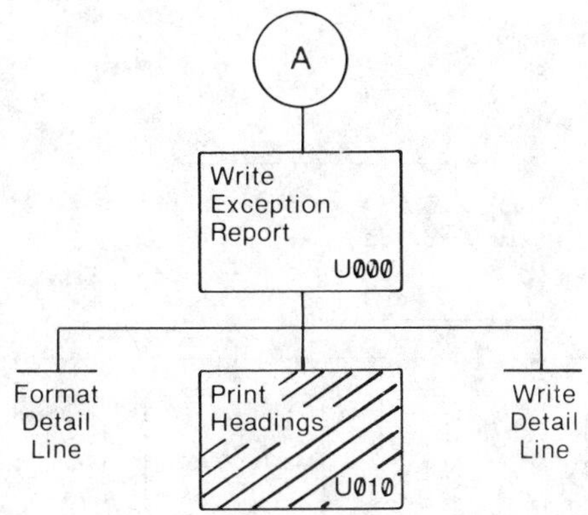

Figure 4-31 Hierarchy Chart

Note from Figure 4-31 that the module which Prints the Headings is a separate module while the other major processing tasks in the module which Writes the Exception Report will be included within the module. The IPO Chart for the module which Prints the Headings is illustrated below.

IPO CHART

PROGRAM: Program Master File Update	PROGRAMMER: Shelly/Cashman	DATE: June 16
MODULE NAME: Print Headings	REF: UØ1Ø	MODULE FUNCTION: Print Report Headings

INPUT	PROCESSING	REF:	OUTPUT
	1. Format heading lines		1. Report Headings
	2. Write heading lines		

Figure 4-32 IPO Chart — Print Headings

As can be seen, the output from the module which Prints the Headings are the Report Headings. There is no input specified because there is no data which must be passed to the Headings module in order for it to accomplish its function. The major processing tasks which must be accomplished are Format Heading Lines and Write Heading Lines. Since neither of these tasks is large or complex, they do not require separate modules.

The design of the structure of the program is now complete because there are no other modules which must be analyzed. The final hierarchy chart for the program which updates the Program Master File is illustrated in Figure 4-33.

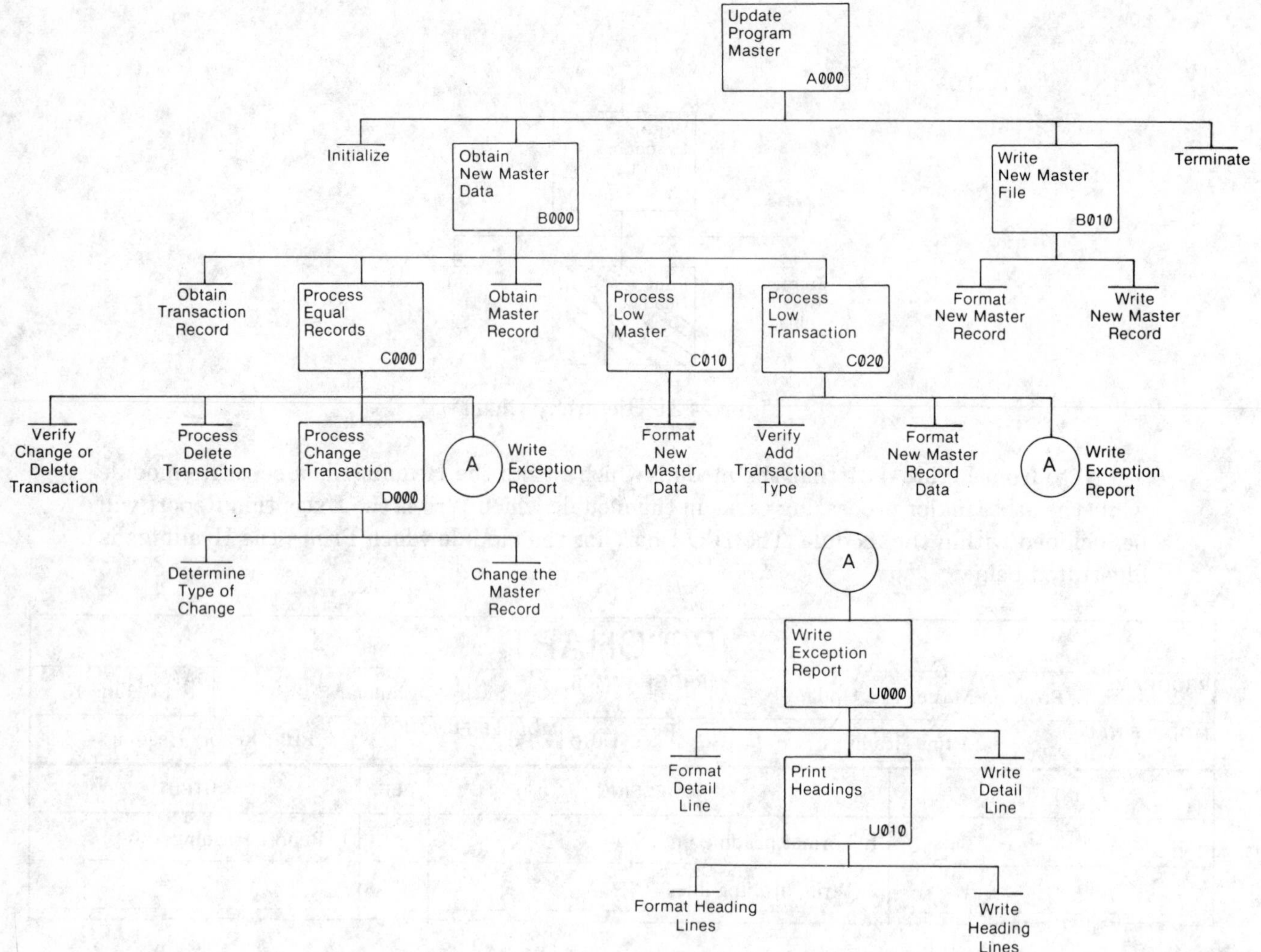

Figure 4-33 Final Hierarchy Chart

Note from Figure 4-33 that the completed hierarchy chart contains all of the modules which have been analyzed previously. Each major processing task which has been defined, whether or not it requires a separate module, is illustrated on the chart. Therefore, when a maintenance programmer examines the hierarchy chart to determine where within the program certain processing is to take place, it is an easy matter to identify the tasks accomplished and where they are accomplished. Thus, the hierarchy chart acts as a "map" to anyone who must examine the program to determine what is taking place where within the program.

PROGRAM DESIGN — PSEUDOCODE SPECIFICATIONS

After the structure of the program has been completed, the programmer should begin designing the logic for each of the modules within the program.

Pseudocode Specifications — Update Program Master

The pseudocode specifications for the module whose function is to Update the Program Master are illustrated in Figure 4-34.

PSEUDOCODE SPECIFICATIONS		
PROGRAM: Program Master File Update	PROGRAMMER: Shelly/Cashman	DATE: June 19
MODULE NAME: Update Program Master	REF: AØØØ	MODULE FUNCTION: Update the Program Master File

PSEUDOCODE	REF:	FILES, RECORDS, FIELDS REQUIRED
Open the files		Old program master file
Obtain new master data	BØØØ	New program master file
PERFORM UNTIL there are no more master records and there are no more transaction records		Update transaction file Update exception report file
Write new master file	BØ1Ø	No more master records indicator
Obtain new master data	BØØØ	No more transaction records indicator
ENDPERFORM		Data obtained indicator
IF data obtained		
Write new master file	BØ1Ø	
ENDIF		
Close the files		
Stop run		

Figure 4-34 Pseudocode Specifications — Update Program Master

The first step in the highest-level module whose function is to Update the Program Master File is to open the four required files — the Transaction File, the Old Program Master File, the New Program Master File, and the Exception Report File.

The next step is to obtain new master data, which is accomplished by the B000 module. A loop is then entered which will continue until there are no more master records and there are no more transaction records. Both conditions must be specified because it is possible to reach end-of-file on one file and still have records to process from another file. Within the loop, the New Master File is written by the B010 module and then more New Master Data is obtained by the B000 module.

When the loop is terminated, a check is performed to determine if data has been obtained from the B000 module which has not yet been written on the New Master File. If this is the case, then the last record will be written on the New Master File by the B010 module. The files are then closed and the program is stopped.

Pseudocode Specifications — Obtain New Master Data

The next module for which to design the logic is the module which Obtains the New Master Data. The pseudocode for this module is illustrated below.

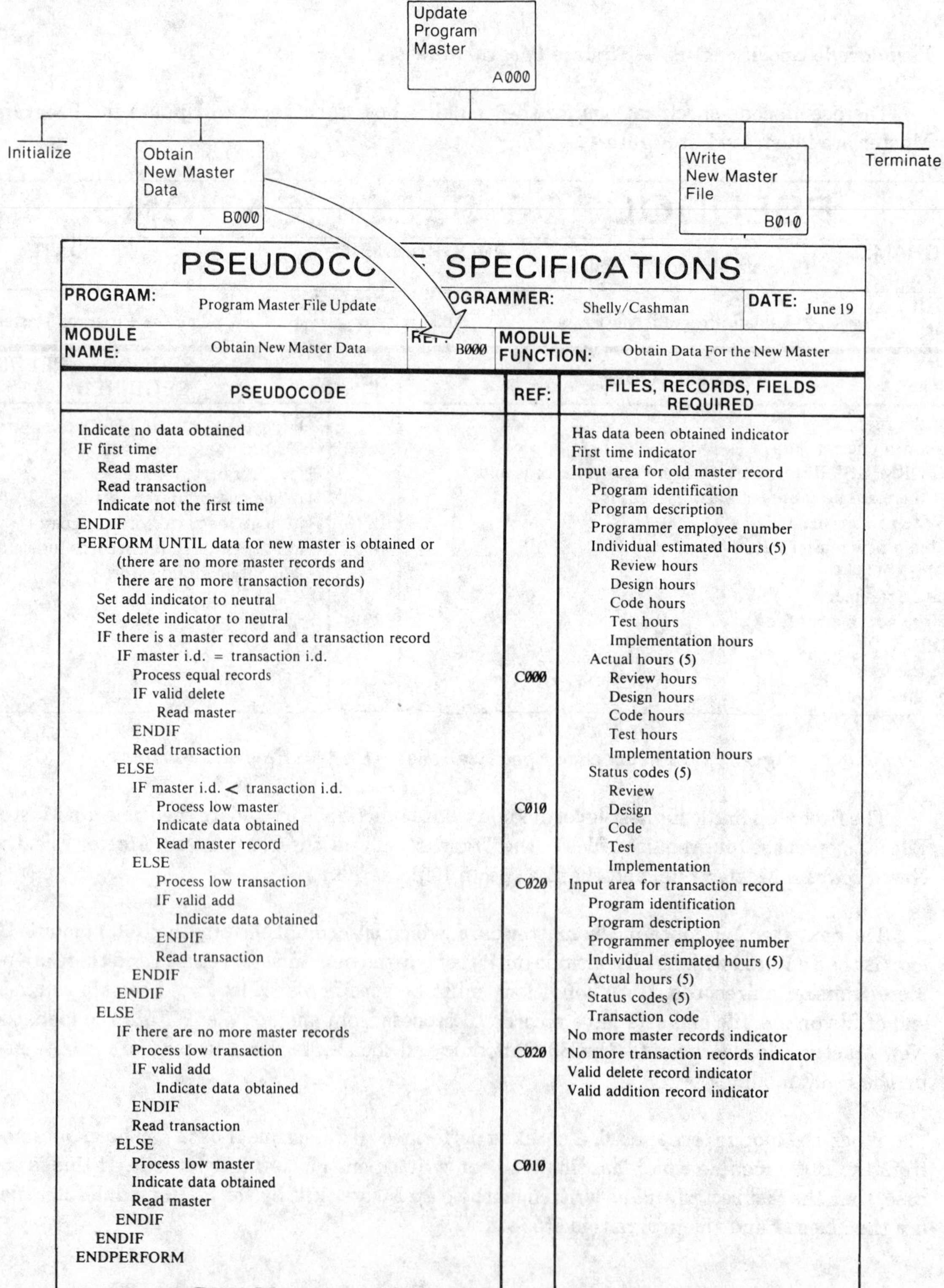

PSEUDOCODE SPECIFICATIONS

PROGRAM: Program Master File Update	PROGRAMMER: Shelly/Cashman	DATE: June 19
MODULE NAME: Obtain New Master Data REF: B000	MODULE FUNCTION: Obtain Data For the New Master	

PSEUDOCODE (REF:)

```
Indicate no data obtained
IF first time
    Read master
    Read transaction
    Indicate not the first time
ENDIF
PERFORM UNTIL data for new master is obtained or
        (there are no more master records and
        there are no more transaction records)
    Set add indicator to neutral
    Set delete indicator to neutral
    IF there is a master record and a transaction record
        IF master i.d. = transaction i.d.
            Process equal records                      C000
            IF valid delete
                Read master
            ENDIF
            Read transaction
        ELSE
            IF master i.d. < transaction i.d.
                Process low master                     C010
                Indicate data obtained
                Read master record
            ELSE
                Process low transaction                C020
                IF valid add
                    Indicate data obtained
                ENDIF
                Read transaction
            ENDIF
        ENDIF
    ELSE
        IF there are no more master records
            Process low transaction                    C020
            IF valid add
                Indicate data obtained
            ENDIF
            Read transaction
        ELSE
            Process low master                         C010
            Indicate data obtained
            Read master
        ENDIF
    ENDIF
ENDPERFORM
```

FILES, RECORDS, FIELDS REQUIRED

```
Has data been obtained indicator
First time indicator
Input area for old master record
    Program identification
    Program description
    Programmer employee number
    Individual estimated hours (5)
        Review hours
        Design hours
        Code hours
        Test hours
        Implementation hours
    Actual hours (5)
        Review hours
        Design hours
        Code hours
        Test hours
        Implementation hours
    Status codes (5)
        Review
        Design
        Code
        Test
        Implementation
Input area for transaction record
    Program identification
    Program description
    Programmer employee number
    Individual estimated hours (5)
    Actual hours (5)
    Status codes (5)
    Transaction code
No more master records indicator
No more transaction records indicator
Valid delete record indicator
Valid addition record indicator
```

Figure 4-35 Pseudocode Specifications — Obtain New Master Data

The first step in the module which Obtains New Master Data is to initialize the indicator which shows whether data has been obtained. As a general rule, if an indicator is tested within a module, the indicator should be initialized in the module which tests it prior to the test's being performed so that the tests will be performed properly and the indicators will not contain values which remain from previous testing. If the programmer is not aware of all indicators which are to be tested within a module when the design of the logic for a module begins, there is no difficulty so long as the programmer remembers to initialize the required indicators at the start of the module when it is found they are necessary.

A test is then performed to determine if this is the first time the module has been entered. If it is the first time, then records have not been read from the Old Program Master File or the Transaction File. Thus, if it is the first time, a record is read from the Old Program Master File and from the Transaction File. The indicator is then set to indicate that the module has been entered. On subsequent entries to this module, these two Read Statements will not be executed.

A loop is then entered as indicated by the Perform Until Statement. The loop will continue until one of two conditions occurs. If data for the New Program Master File is obtained, then the loop will be terminated. Also, if there are no more Old Program Master File Records and there are no more Transaction File Records, then the loop will be terminated. The "Until" clause should be carefully analyzed. Note that both an "or" and an "and" are specified. In addition, parentheses are used to indicate how the compound condition will be implemented. In the example, the conditions within the parentheses will be analyzed first. They must both be true since they are enclosed within parentheses. The first condition ("data for new master is obtained") is then analyzed. If either of these conditions is true, then the loop will be terminated. Thus, the conditions will be analyzed as follows:

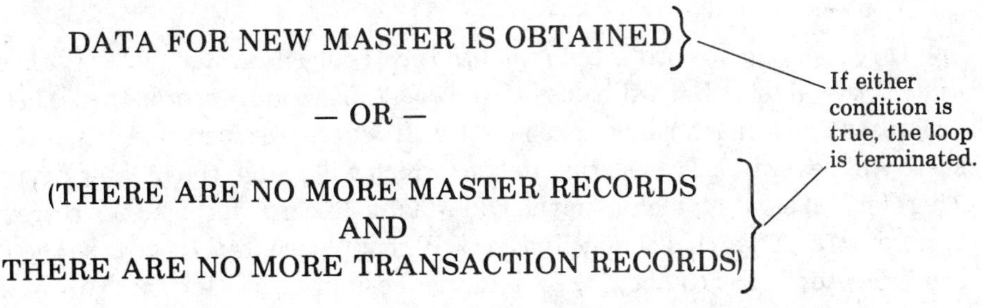

As will be recalled, the function of the module is to Obtain New Master Data. It will continue its task until either data is obtained or there is no more data to be obtained. These conditions should be well understood before continuing with the analysis of the logic within this module.

The first task within the loop is to initialize the indicators which show whether there has been a valid delete transaction and whether there has been a valid add transaction. These indicators are tested on each "pass" through the loop, so they should be initialized each time the loop is entered for processing.

In order to understand the logic within the loop, it is necessary to recall the processing which is to take place when matching the Master Records and the Transaction Records. In order to match these records, it is first necessary that there be both a Master Record and a Transaction Record. If one of these files has reached end-of-file, then they cannot be matched. Thus, the first test is to determine if there is a Master Record and a Transaction Record.

If there are, then the matching of the two records can take place. The first test is to determine if the Program Identification in the Master Record is equal to the Program Identification in the Transaction Record. If so, then the equal records will be processed by the C000 module. It should be recalled that when the Master Record is equal to the Transaction Record, either the Master Record can be changed or the Master Record can be deleted (see Figure 4-12 and Figure 4-13).

Upon return from the C000 module, a test is then performed to determine if the Transaction Record just processed was a valid deletion transaction. If it was, it means that another Master Record should be read without writing the Master Record which was to be deleted. Therefore, if a valid delete was found, another record will be read from the Program Master File. If it was not a valid delete record, then a Master Record should not be read since, as has been stated previously, more than one Transaction Record can be used to change a single Master Record. It should be noted that the indicator stating whether a valid Delete Transaction Record was processed will be set in the module which processes the equal records (C000). After this test is performed, a Transaction Record will be read because the Transaction Record which was equal to the Master Record has been completely processed.

After this processing has been completed, control will return to the Perform Until Statement, which will check the conditions described previously. Note that when the Transaction Record is equal to the Program Master Record, the indicator specifying that data has been obtained is not altered from its indication that no data has been obtained. This is because the processing of the equal Master Record is not yet complete; there may be more than one Transaction Record which is going to change the Master Record. Therefore, whenever the Transaction Record is equal to the Master Record, the loop will be entered again to process the Transaction Record which was just read. No writing will occur for the New Master File.

If the Master Record is not equal to the Transaction Record, a test is performed to determine if the Master Record is less than the Transaction Record. If so, then the module which processes a low master is invoked (C010). It will be recalled that when this condition occurs, there will never be a Transaction Record which will match the Master Record (see Figure 4-14). Therefore, the data which is in the Old Master Record will be used to create the New Master Record data. After this is done in the C010 module, control returns to the B000 module where the indicator is set to show that data has been obtained for the New Master File. The data which has been obtained is the data from the Old Master Record. Another Old Master Record is then read. This is necessary because the data from the Master Record has been processed, and the next Master Record should be processed on the next "pass" through the module. Control will then pass to the Perform Until Statement which will find that data has been obtained for the New Master File. Therefore, control will pass back to the calling module which will in turn call the module to Write the New Master File (see Figure 4-34).

It should be noted that if the Master Record is less than the Transaction Record, a Transaction Record is not read when the processing of the Master Record has been completed. This is because the Transaction Record has not yet been processed. Therefore, another Transaction Record should not be read. A Transaction Record will be read only after the Transaction Record in storage has been processed.

If the Master Record is not equal to the Transaction Record and the Master Record is not less than the Transaction Record, then the Transaction Record must be less than the Master Record; that is, the Program Identification in the Transaction Record is less than the Program Identification in the Program Master Record. The processing which will take place when this occurs is again illustrated in Figure 4-36.

Pseudocode Specifications — Obtain New Master Data

```
.
.
.
IF there is a master record and a transaction record
   IF master i.d. = transaction i.d.
      .
      .
      .
   ELSE
      IF master i.d. < transaction i.d.
         .
         .
         .
      ELSE
         Process low transaction                          C020
         IF valid add
            Indicate data obtained
         ENDIF
         Read transaction
      ENDIF
   ENDIF
   .
   .
   .
```

Figure 4-36 Pseudocode Specification — Low Transaction

When the Program Identification in the Transaction Record is less than the Program Identification in the Program Master Record, the only valid processing is an Addition to New Program Master File (see Figure 4-10 and Figure 4-11). This condition will be checked in the module which processes the low transaction (see Figure 4-26). Upon return from the C020 module, a test is then performed to determine if the Transaction Record was a valid Addition record. If it was, then data has been obtained for the New Master File and the indicator is set to indicate this. If it was not a valid Addition record, then the Transaction Record will have been recorded on the Exception Report; and data has not been obtained for the New Master File. Therefore, the indicator is not set to indicate that data has been obtained.

Regardless of whether a valid addition record was found, a Transaction Record will then be read. The record is read because the Transaction Record which was less than the Master Record has been completely processed; if it was a valid Addition record, it will be placed in the New Master File; and if it was an invalid Addition record, it will have been written on the Exception Report. In either case, a new Transaction Record is required.

After this processing is complete, the conditions in the Perform Until Statement are checked. If data was obtained through a valid addition Transaction Record, the control will be passed back to the calling module (A000) which will cause the addition record to be written on the New Program Master File. If data was not obtained, then the loop will be processed again.

The previous discussion has covered the processing which will take place when there are both Master Records and Transaction Records remaining to be processed. It will be recalled, however, that one of the files can reach end-of-file before the other and processing should continue. The logic to process this situation is again illustrated in Figure 4-37.

Pseudocode Specifications — Obtain New Master Data

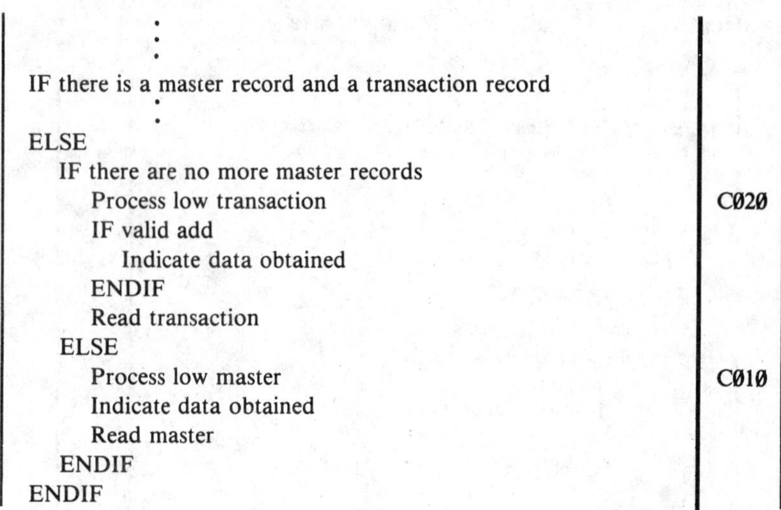

```
            .
            .
            .
IF there is a master record and a transaction record
            .
            .
ELSE
   IF there are no more master records
      Process low transaction                              C020
      IF valid add
         Indicate data obtained
      ENDIF
      Read transaction
   ELSE
      Process low master                                   C010
      Indicate data obtained
      Read master
   ENDIF
ENDIF
```

Figure 4-37 Pseudocode Specifications -- End-Of-File Processing

In the example of the pseudocode above, it can be seen that if there is not both a Master and a Transaction Record, then a check is performed to determine if there are no more Master Records. It should be recalled that if there are no more Master Records, then the only valid operation is to add Transaction Records to the New Master File. Therefore, the processing is the same as if the Transaction Record is Low; that is, the Low Transaction Record is processed by the C020 module; if the Transaction Record was a valid addition record, the indicator is set to show that data has been obtained; and a Transaction Record is read.

If there are more Master Records, then there must not be any more Transaction Records. It will be recalled that this condition is the same as if the Master Record is Low. Therefore, the Low Master Record is processed (module C010), the indicator is set to indicate that data has been obtained, and another record is read from the Old Master File. As can be seen, this is the same processing that occurs when the Master Record is Low (see Figure 4-35).

It should be noted that the logic in the module which Obtains the New Master Data is the "heart" of the sequential file update processing, and this logic should be well understood prior to examining the logic for the remaining modules within the program.

Pseudocode Specifications — Write New Master File

The next module for which the logic must be developed is the module whose function is to Write the New Master File. The pseudocode for this module is illustrated in Figure 4-38.

PSEUDOCODE SPECIFICATIONS		
PROGRAM: Program Master File Update	PROGRAMMER: Shelly/Cashman	DATE: June 19
MODULE NAME: Write New Master	REF: BØ1Ø	MODULE FUNCTION: Write the New Master File

PSEUDOCODE	REF:	FILES, RECORDS, FIELDS REQUIRED
Move program identification to new master area Move program description to new master area Move programmer employee number to new master area Move estimated hours to new master area Move actual hours to new master area Move task status indicators to new master area Write new master record		New master work area Program identification Program description Programmer employee number Individual estimated hours Actual hours Task status indicators New master output area Program identification Program description Programmer employee number Individual estimated hours Actual hours Task status indicators

Figure 4-38 Pseudocode Specifications — Write New Master

As can be seen from Figure 4-38, the steps in the module which Writes the New Master File consist of moving the fields contained in the New Master Work Area to the New Master Output Area, and then writing the New Master Record. The data which is contained within the new Master Work Area will be placed there by the modules whose function is to obtain the data for the New Master File. As has been seen in previous programs, a work area is used so that the module which Writes the New Master File need access only one area in storage and also to lower the coupling in the program.

Pseudocode Specifications — Process Equal Records

The next module to be designed is the module which processes equal records; that is, Master Records and Transaction Records which have equal Program Identifications. The pseudocode for this module is illustrated in Figure 4-39.

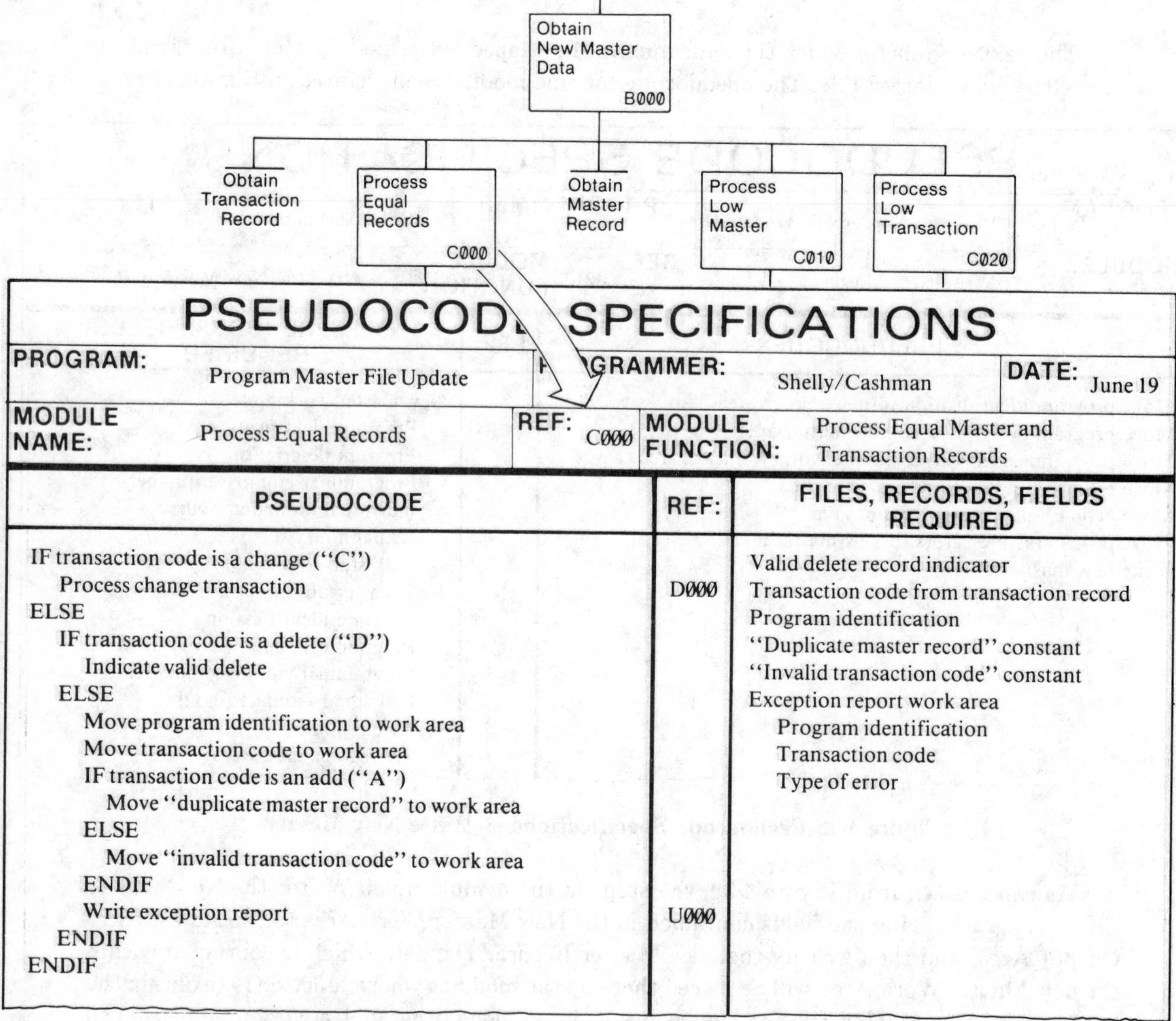

PSEUDOCODE SPECIFICATIONS

PROGRAM: Program Master File Update	PROGRAMMER: Shelly/Cashman	DATE: June 19
MODULE NAME: Process Equal Records	REF: C000	MODULE FUNCTION: Process Equal Master and Transaction Records

PSEUDOCODE	REF:	FILES, RECORDS, FIELDS REQUIRED
IF transaction code is a change ("C")		Valid delete record indicator
Process change transaction	D000	Transaction code from transaction record
ELSE		Program identification
IF transaction code is a delete ("D")		"Duplicate master record" constant
Indicate valid delete		"Invalid transaction code" constant
ELSE		Exception report work area
Move program identification to work area		Program identification
Move transaction code to work area		Transaction code
IF transaction code is an add ("A")		Type of error
Move "duplicate master record" to work area		
ELSE		
Move "invalid transaction code" to work area		
ENDIF		
Write exception report	U000	
ENDIF		
ENDIF		

Figure 4-39 Pseudocode Specifications — Process Equal Records

It will be recalled that when the Program Identification in the Program Master Record is equal to the Program Identification in the Transaction Record, two types of processing are valid — Change the Master Record, or Delete the Master Record. Therefore, this is the processing which must occur within the module illustrated in Figure 4-39.

The first test is to determine if the Transaction Record is a Change Record; that is, is the Transaction Code equal to the value "C." If so, the module which processes change transactions, D000, is entered to process the change transaction.

If the Transaction Record is not a Change Record, the next test checks if the Transaction Record is a Delete Record; that is, is the Transaction Code equal to the value "D." If so, the only processing required is to set the Delete Indicator to indicate that a valid Delete Transaction has been read. Upon return to the calling module, this indicator will be checked and the appropriate processing will occur (see Figure 4-35).

If the Transaction Code is neither "C" nor "D," then the Transaction Record is in error because the only valid processing which can occur when the Master Record is equal to the Transaction Record is to Change or Delete a Master Record. Therefore, if the Code is not equal to "C" or "D," the Program Identification is moved to the Exception Report Work Area; the Transaction Code is moved to the work area; the appropriate error message is moved to the work area; and the Exception Report is written by the U000 module.

Note that if the Transaction Code is not equal to "C" or "D," there are two possible errors which might have occurred. If the Transaction Code is equal to "A," then an attempt is being made to Add a record to the Program Master File; but there is already a record with the same Program Identification in the Program Master File. Thus, the message "Duplicate Master Record" is moved to the work area for the type of error. If the Transaction Code is not equal to "A," then an invalid Transaction Code is contained in the Transaction Record because the code is not equal to "C," "D," or "A." Therefore, the message "Invalid Transaction Code" is moved to the type of error work area.

After this processing is complete, control is returned to the B000 module.

Pseudocode Specifications — Process Low Master

The next module for which the logic must be developed is the module whose function is to Process Low Master Records. The pseudocode specifications for this module are illustrated in Figure 4-40.

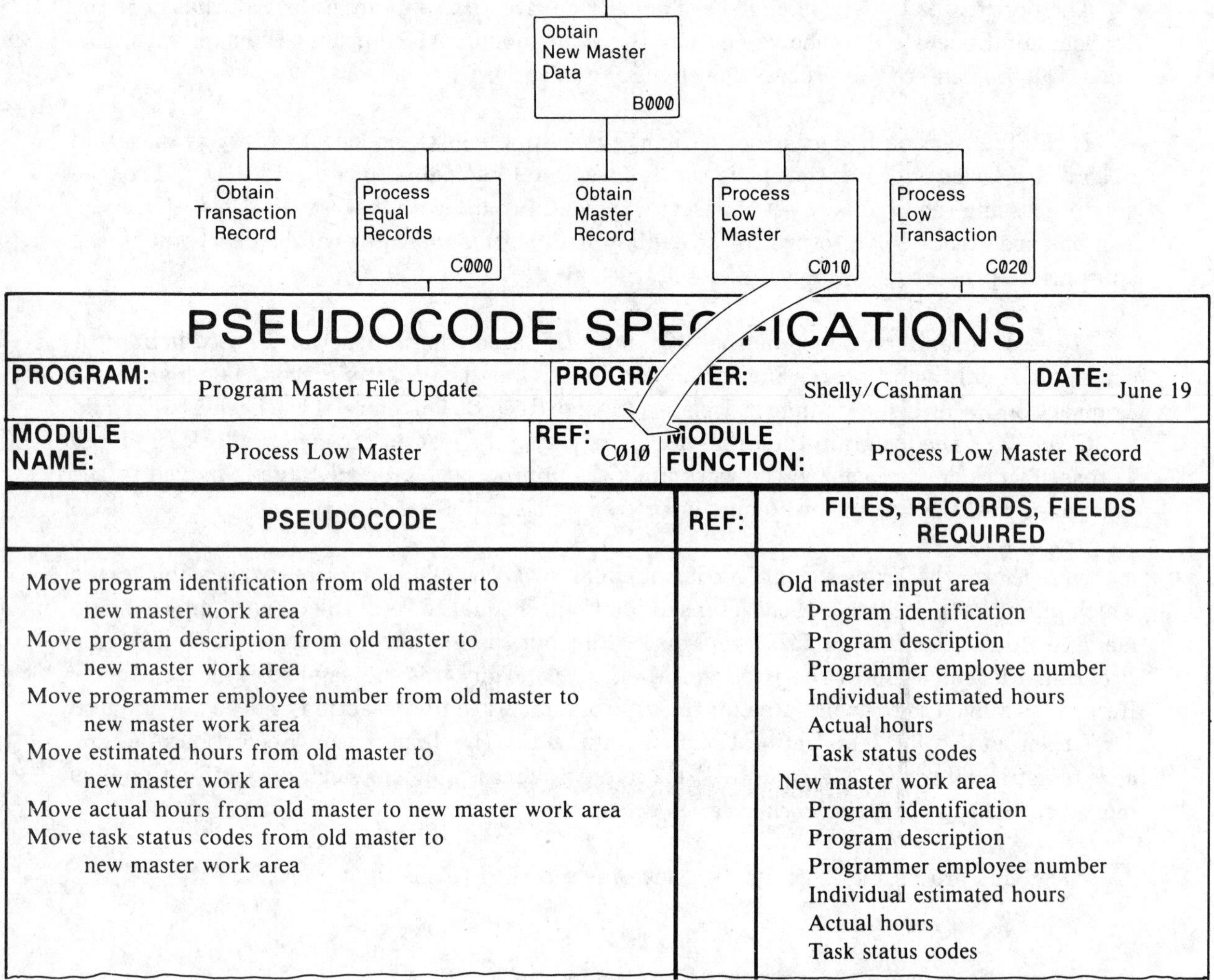

Figure 4-40 Pseudocode Specifications — Process Low Master

It will be recalled that when the Program Identification in the Program Master Record is less than the Program Identification in the Transaction Record, there will never be a Transaction Record which matches the Master Record since the Transaction Record is in an ascending sequence by Program Identification. Therefore, the only processing which can take place is to write the record from the Old Program Master File in the New Program Master File with no changes.

The module illustrated in Figure 4-40 processes the low Master Record by moving the Program Identification, Program Description, Programmer Employee Number, Estimated Hours, Actual Hours, and Task Status Codes from the Old Master Record Input Area to the New Master Work Area. Control is then returned to the B000 module which will return control to the A000 module. This module will then call the module which writes the new Master File (B010), and the record will be written on the New Master File.

Pseudocode Specifications — Process Low Transaction

The pseudocode for the module which processes the low Transaction Records is illustrated below.

PSEUDOCODE SPECIFICATIONS			
PROGRAM: Program Master File Update	PROGRAMMER: Shelly/Cashman		DATE: June 19
MODULE NAME: Process Low Transaction	REF: CØ2Ø	MODULE FUNCTION: Process Low Transaction Record	

PSEUDOCODE	REF:	FILES, RECORDS, FIELDS REQUIRED

IF transaction code is an add ("A")
  Move program identification from trans to new master work area
  Move program description from trans to new master work area
  Move programmer employee number from trans to
      new master work area
  Move estimated hours from trans to new master work area
  Move zeros to actual hours in new master work area
  Move spaces to task status codes in new master work area
  Indicate a valid add transaction
ELSE
  Move program identification to report work area
  Move transaction code to report work area
  IF transaction code is a delete ("D") or change ("C")
    Move "non-matching master record" to report work area
  ELSE
    Move "invalid transaction code" to report work area
  ENDIF
  Write exception report
ENDIF
	
	UØØØ
		Transaction input area
		  Program identification
		  Program description
		  Programmer employee number
		  Estimated hours
		  Transaction code
		New master work area
		  Program identification
		  Program description
		  Programmer employee number
		  Estimated hours
		  Actual hours
		  Task status codes
		Valid add transaction indicator
		Exception report work area
		  Program identification
		  Transaction code
		  Type of error
		"Non-matching master record" constant
		"Invalid transaction code" constant

Figure 4-41 Pseudocode Specifications — Process Low Transaction

When the Program Identification in the Transaction Record is less than the Program Identification in the Program Master Record, the only valid processing is to Add the Transaction Record to the New Master File. The module above first checks the value in the Transaction Code. If the value is equal to "A," it indicates an Add Transaction and is a valid record. If the value is not equal to "A," the Transaction is in error.

If the Transaction Code is equal to "A," it can be seen that the module moves the Program Identification, Program Description, Programmer Employee Number, and Estimated Hours from the Transaction Record to the New Master Work Area. In addition, it sets the Actual Hours in the New Master Work Area to zeros, moves spaces to the Task Status Codes in the New Master Work Area, and sets the indicator to show that a valid Add Transaction was found and processed.

If the Transaction Code is not equal to "A," the Transaction Record is in error. Therefore, the Program Identification and Transaction Code are moved to the Exception Report Work Area. A determination is then made as to the type of error which has occurred. If the Transaction Code is equal to "C" or "D," the Code is valid; but there is not a matching record to either change or delete. Therefore, the error message "Non-Matching Master Record" is moved to the report work area. If the code is not equal to "C" or "D," then the Transaction Code is invalid; and the message "Invalid Transaction Code" is moved to the Exception Report Work Area. The report is then written and control will return to the module which calls this module (B000).

Pseudocode Specifications — Process Change Transaction

The next module for which to design the logic is the module with the function, Process Change Transaction. The pseudocode for this module is illustrated in Figure 4-42.

PSEUDOCODE SPECIFICATIONS

PROGRAM: Program Master File Update	PROGRAMMER: Shelly/Cashman	DATE: June 19
MODULE NAME: Process Change Transaction	REF: DØØØ	MODULE FUNCTION: Process a Change Transaction

PSEUDOCODE

```
IF programmer employee is not blank
   Move programmer employee number in trans to
         programmer employee number in old master
ENDIF
Set subscript to 1
PERFORM UNTIL all actual hours have been added
   IF actual hours in trans (subscript) is not blank
      Add actual hours in trans (subscript) to
              actual hours in old master (subscript)
   ENDIF
   Add 1 to subscript
ENDPERFORM
Set subscript to 1
PERFORM UNTIL all task status codes have been checked
   IF task status code (subscript) in trans = "C"
      Move "C" to task status code in old master (subscript)
   ENDIF
   Add 1 to subscript
ENDPERFORM
```

REF:

FILES, RECORDS, FIELDS REQUIRED

Transaction input area
  Programmer employee number
  Actual hours (5)
  Task status codes (5)
Old master input area
  Programmer employee number
  Actual hours (5)
  Task status codes (5)
Subscript to add actual hours
All actual hours added indicator
Subscript to move task status codes
All task status codes checked indicator
"C" constant

Figure 4-42 Pseudocode Specifications — Process Change Transactions

As will be recalled, there are three types of changes which can take place in the update program. First, the Employee Number in the Master Record can be changed. Second, the Actual Hours in the Master Record can be incremented by the Actual Hours contained in a Change Transaction Record. Third, the Task Status Codes can be changed to indicate that a task is completed. In order to determine the change processing which is to occur from any one Transaction Record, the field in the Transaction Record is examined to find if it contains data. If it does, then the respective field in the Master Record is updated.

Thus, the first check which is performed in the D000 module is to determine if the Programmer Employee Number in the Transaction Record is blank. If it is not blank, then the Programmer Employee Number in the Transaction Record is moved to the Programmer Employee Number in the Old Master Record. As can be seen, the data is changed in the Old Master Record whenever a change is to take place.

The next step in the pseudocode illustrated in Figure 4-42 is to set a subscript to the value 1 and then enter a Perform Loop which will be executed until all of the Actual Hours in the Transaction Record have been added. In the loop, the Actual Hours in the Transaction Record is checked for blanks; if it does not contain blanks, then the value in the field is added to the respective Actual Hours in the Old Master Record. It will be noted that each of the individual Actual Hours fields are referenced through the use of a Subscript which is initially set to the value one and then is incremented each time the loop is processed. Thus, the first time the loop is entered, the first Actual Hours in the Transaction Record is checked. This is the Actual Hours field for the Specifications Review. On the second pass through the loop, the second Actual Hours field, which is the Design Hours, is checked for blanks. This processing continues until all of the Actual Hours fields in the Transaction Record have been checked for blanks.

After the Actual Hours have been checked, a subscript is initialized to the value 1, and the Task Status Code fields in the Transaction Record are each checked for the value "C." If the Task Status Code field in the Transaction Record contains the value "C," it indicates that the corresponding Task Status Code in the Program Master Record should be set to the value "C" to indicate that the Task is completed. As with the Actual Hours, the subscript is incremented on each pass through the loop so that all five Task Status Code fields in the Transaction Record are checked for the value "C." After the check of the Task Status Code fields is completed, the D000 module returns control to the module which called it (C000).

Pseudocode Specifications — Write Exception Report and Print Headings

The last two modules for which the logic must be designed are the modules which Write the Exception Report and Print the Headings on the Exception Report. The pseudocode specifications for these two modules are illustrated in Figure 4-43.

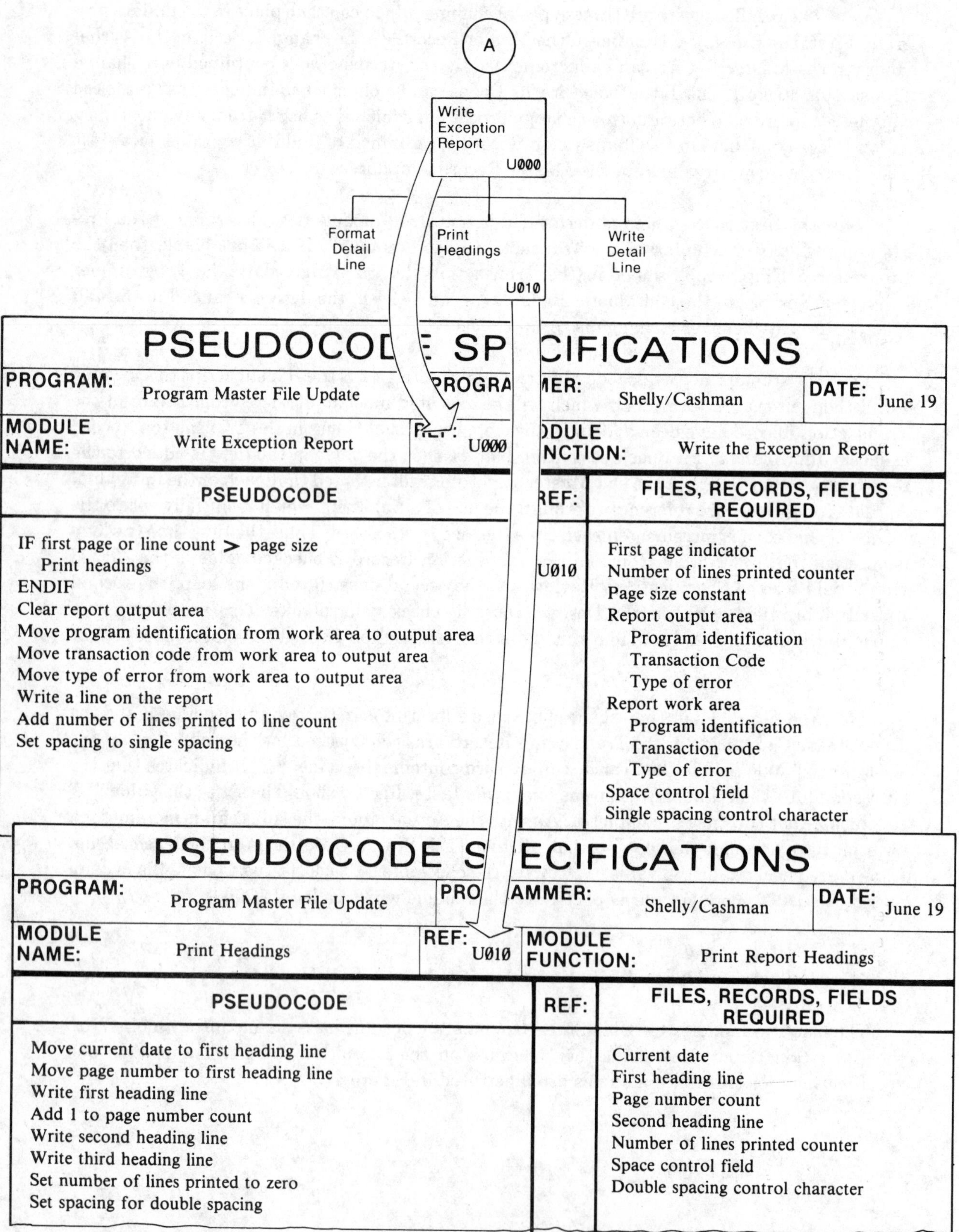

Figure 4-43 Pseudocode Specifications — Write Exception Report and Print Headings

Note in the module which Writes the Exception Report that, if necessary, the Headings are printed. Then, the data is moved from the Exception Report Work Area to the Exception Report Output Area. The data is printed, the line count is incremented, and the spacing is set for single spacing.

In the module which Prints the Headings, the Current Date and Page Number are moved to the first heading line which is then printed. The second and third heading lines are printed, the line count is set to zero, and the spacing is set for double. Both of these modules contain straight-forward processing which has been seen previously and should present no logic problems for the programmer.

Summary

The logic which has been developed for this program, particularly the logic for the module which Obtains New Master Data, is very important to understand because it is likely that this logic will be found many times in business application programming. The Sequential Update Logic, or variations of it, is one of the most frequently encountered logic requirements which the programmer will find and, therefore, should be thoroughly understood.

COBOL CODING

There are several coding points which should be reviewed prior to examining the entire source listing of the program which updates the Program Master File. This coding is explained in the following paragraphs.

Definition of the New Program Master File

Whenever sequential updating is taking place, a new Master File is being created. The new Master File will be the input to the program the next time the file must be updated. Therefore, the input and output Master Files in a sequential update program must be defined to have identical attributes, including the Record Length, the Blocking Factor, and the Record Format. The definitions of the Old Program Master File and the New Program Master File are illustrated in Figure 4-44.

Old Master File

```
005070 FD  OLD-PROGRAM-MASTER-INPUT-FILE
005080         BLOCK CONTAINS 20 RECORDS
005090         RECORD CONTAINS 77 CHARACTERS
005100         LABEL RECORDS ARE STANDARD
005110         DATA RECORD IS OLD-PROGRAM-MASTER-INPUT-REC.
005120
005130 01  OLD-PROGRAM-MASTER-INPUT-REC.
005140     05  PROGRAM-IDENTIFICATION-OLDMST           PIC X(6).
005150     05  PROGRAM-DESCRIPTION-OLDMST              PIC X(20).
005160     05  PROGRAMMER-EMPL-NUMBER-OLDMST           PIC X(6).
005170     05  ESTIMATED-TASK-HOURS-OLDMST             PIC X(20).
005180     05  ACTUAL-TASK-HOURS-OLDMST.
005190         10  SINGLE-ACTUAL-HOUR-OLDMST           PIC S9(4)
005200                                                  OCCURS 5 TIMES.
005210     05  TASK-STATUS-INDICATORS-OLDMST.
005220         10  SINGLE-STATUS-INDICATOR-OLDMST      PIC X
005230                                                  OCCURS 5 TIMES.
```

New Master File

```
006030 FD  NEW-PROGRAM-MASTER-OUTPUT-FILE
006040         BLOCK CONTAINS 20 RECORDS
006050         RECORD CONTAINS 77 CHARACTERS
006060         LABEL RECORDS ARE STANDARD
006070         DATA RECORD IS NEW-PROGRAM-MASTER-OUTPUT-REC.
006080
006090 01  NEW-PROGRAM-MASTER-OUTPUT-REC.
006100     05  PROGRAM-IDENTIFICATION-NEWMST           PIC X(6).
006110     05  PROGRAM-DESCRIPTION-NEWMST              PIC X(20).
006120     05  PROGRAMMER-EMPL-NUMBER-NEWMST           PIC X(6).
006130     05  ESTIMATED-TASK-HOURS-NEWMST             PIC X(20).
006140     05  ACTUAL-TASK-HOURS-NEWMST                PIC X(20).
006150     05  TASK-STATUS-INDICATORS-NEWMST           PIC X(5).
```

Figure 4-44 Definition of Old and New Program Master Files

Note from Figure 4-44 that the Blocking Factor and Record Length are identical for the Old Program Master File and the New Program Master File. This must be done so that when the Program Master File which is created in one run of the program is used as the input file to the next run of the program, the format of the file will be correct.

It should be noted also that although the formats of the file do not appear to be identical, they in fact are the same. The two differences involve the Actual Hours fields and the Task Status Indicator fields. In the New Master File record definition, the ACTUAL-TASK-HOURS-NEWMST field is defined as PIC X(20). In the Old Master File record definition, on the other hand, the ACTUAL-TASK-HOURS-OLDMST field is a group field, with the elementary item SINGLE-ACTUAL-HOUR-OLDMST in the group. The Single Hour field is defined as PIC S9(4), occurring 5 times. Note that this definition is considerably different than that found in the New Master Record, but that they both are twenty characters in length, that is, both the PIC X(20) and the PIC S9(4) Occurs 5 Times fields occupy 20 characters. Therefore, when the New Master File is created, the Actual Hours fields will be twenty characters in length. When they are read in the next running of the Update Program, they will be treated as a twenty character field even though defined differently. The same analysis is true for the Task Status Indicators Fields.

Field Redefinition

It will be recalled from the program specifications and the analysis of the pseudocode that one requirement in the program is to check the Actual Hours fields in the Transaction Record to determine if they contain spaces. If an Actual Hour field contains spaces, then no updating is to take place to the same Actual Hour field in the Old Master Record. If, however, the Actual Hour field does not contain spaces, then the value in the field is to be added to the Actual Hour field in the Old Master Record. See Figure 4-42 for the pseudocode and detailed explanation of this processing.

In the processing, it should be noted that the field is to both be checked for spaces and is to be added to another field. In order to check the field for spaces, it must be defined as an alphanumeric field (PIC X). However, in order to add the field, it must be defined as a numeric field (PIC 9). Thus, when defining the Actual Hours fields in the Transaction Record, it is necessary to have the Actual Hours field be defined both as alphanumeric and numeric. This is accomplished through the use of the Redefines Clause as illustrated below.

EXAMPLE

Data Division

```
       05  ACTUAL-TASK-HOURS-TRANS.
           10  SINGLE-ACTUAL-HOUR-TRANS          PIC 9(4)
                                                  OCCURS 5 TIMES.
       05  ACTUAL-TASK-HOURS-X-TRANS REDEFINES
            ACTUAL-TASK-HOURS-TRANS.
           10  SINGLE-ACTUAL-HOUR-X-TRANS        PIC X(4)
                                                  OCCURS 5 TIMES.
```

Procedure Division

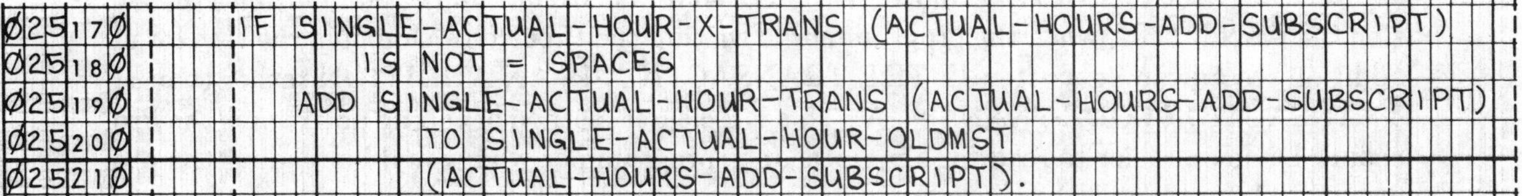

```
           IF SINGLE-ACTUAL-HOUR-X-TRANS (ACTUAL-HOURS-ADD-SUBSCRIPT)
                   IS NOT = SPACES
               ADD SINGLE-ACTUAL-HOUR-TRANS (ACTUAL-HOURS-ADD-SUBSCRIPT)
                       TO SINGLE-ACTUAL-HOUR-OLDMST
                       (ACTUAL-HOURS-ADD-SUBSCRIPT).
```

Figure 4-45 Redefinition of Actual Hours Fields

Note from Figure 4-45 that the ACTUAL-TASK-HOURS-TRANS field is defined as a group item, and the SINGLE-ACTUAL-HOUR-TRANS field is the elementary item with PIC 9(4). This field occurs 5 times because there are five separate Actual Hours in the field (Review, Design, Code, Test, Implement). The field ACTUAL-TASK-HOURS-X-TRANS then redefines the ACTUAL-TASK-HOURS-TRANS field. This means that ACTUAL-TASK-HOURS-X-TRANS can be used to reference the same area as the ACTUAL-TASK-HOURS-TRANS field. The elementary item SINGLE-ACTUAL-HOUR-X-TRANS field is then defined as PIC X(4), occuring 5 times. Therefore, any of the Actual Hours fields (Review, Design, Code, Test, or Implement) can be referenced by either the name SINGLE-ACTUAL-HOUR-TRANS or SINGLE-ACTUAL-HOUR-X-TRANS together with a subscript.

When the Actual Hours fields are checked in the Procedure Division, the test for Spaces uses the SINGLE-ACTUAL-HOUR-X-TRANS field because the test for Spaces requires an alphanumeric (Picture X) field (lines 025170-025180). When the Actual Hours field is added to the Actual Hours field in the Old Master Record, however, the SINGLE-ACTUAL-HOUR-TRANS field is used because an addition operation requires a numeric (Picture 9) field (lines 025190-025210). Thus, as can be seen, through the use of the Redefines Clause, data in storage can be referenced in different ways, depending upon the requirements of the program. This technique of redefining data so that it can be used in different ways is a common technique when programming in COBOL and should be well understood.

Condition Names — Input Codes

It will be recalled that the Transaction Record contains a Transaction Code which indicates the type of processing which should occur when using the Transaction Record. This code can be "A" (Addition), "D" (Deletion), or "C" (Change). As has been seen in previous programs, the use of Condition Names for Indicators in the program can be useful when making the program more easy to read. The same is true of Codes which are found in input records. The use of condition names for the codes which are found in the Transaction Record for the Program Master File Update are illustrated below.

```
       05  TRANSACTION-CODE-TRANS                   PIC X.
           88  THE-TRANSACTION-IS-AN-ADDITION        VALUE 'A'.
           88  THE-TRANSACTION-IS-A-DELETION         VALUE 'D'.
           88  THE-TRANSACTION-IS-A-CHANGE           VALUE 'C'.
```

Figure 4-46 Condition Names with Transaction Codes

The Transaction Code field in the Transaction Record is defined with the name TRANSACTION-CODE-TRANS. The three condition names following the definition of the Transaction Code relate to the values "A," "D," and "C" which can be found in the Transaction Code field. Thus, when the programmer is writing the Procedure Division, the test for an addition record can be written IF THE-TRANSACTION-IS-AN-ADDITION rather than IF TRANSACTION-CODE-TRANS = 'A.' This is a clearer method of coding and makes the Procedure Division easier to read for a maintenance programmer who would be reading the program at a later time. As has been noted previously, whenever the program can be made easier to read, the programmer should do so. The use of Condition Names will normally add to the readability of the program.

Nested IF Statement in COBOL

Generally, any Nested IF Statement logic which is developed in the pseudocode for a program will be able to be directly translated into COBOL. There are, however, several instances when this is not possible. The following pseudocode illustrates one of these instances.

Pseudocode

```
IF transaction code is a change ("C")
    Process change transaction                                   DØØØ
ELSE
    IF transaction code is a delete ("D")
        Indicate valid delete
    ELSE
        Move program identification to work area
        Move transaction code to work area
        IF transaction code is an add ("A")
            Move "duplicate master record" to work area
        ELSE
            Move "invalid transaction code" to work area
        ENDIF
        Write exception report                                   UØØØ
    ENDIF
ENDIF
```

Figure 4-47 Example of Nested IF Statement in Pseudocode

The pseudocode illustrated above is taken from the module which processes equal Transaction and Master Records (see Figure 4-39). Note the If Statement which is indicated; it tests the transaction code to determine if it is equal to the value "A." If so, the message "Duplicate Master Record" is moved to the Exception Report Work Area. If not, the message "Invalid Transaction Code" is moved to the work area. Regardless of whether the Transaction Code is equal to the value "A," the Exception Report is then to be written. It should be noted that the end of the effect of the If Statement is the ENDIF statement appearing immediately before the Write Exception Report Statement. Thus, regardless of the result of the If Statement, the Exception Report will be written.

Unfortunately, COBOL does not have an ENDIF Statement. Therefore, all statements following an ELSE Clause in an If Statement will be executed only when the condition tested is not true. Thus, the coding illustrated in Figure 4-48 would NOT properly implement the logic illustrated in Figure 4-47.

EXAMPLE — INCORRECT CODING

```
020010    IF THE-TRANSACTION-IS-A-CHANGE
020020       PERFORM DØØØ-PROCESS-CHANGE-TRANSACTION
020030    ELSE
020040       IF THE-TRANSACTION-IS-A-DELETION
020050          MOVE 'YES' TO WAS-IT-A-VALID-DELETE-RECORD
020060       ELSE
020070          MOVE PROGRAM-IDENTIFICATION-TRANS TO
020080                PROGRAM-IDENTIFICATION-RPTWORK
020090          MOVE TRANSACTION-CODE-TRANS TO
020100                TRANSACTION-CODE-RPTWORK
020110          IF THE-TRANSACTION-IS-AN-ADDITION
020120             MOVE DUPLICATE-RECORD-ERRMSG TO
020130                   TYPE-OF-ERROR-RPTWORK
020140          ELSE
020150             MOVE INVALID-TRANS-CODE-ERRMSG TO
020160                   TYPE-OF-ERROR-RPTWORK
020170          PERFORM UØØØ-WRITE-EXCEPTION-REPORT.
```

Figure 4-48 Example of INCORRECT NESTED IF STATEMENT

Note from Figure 4-48 that the coding directly duplicates the pseudocode in Figure 4-47. The only difference is that the ENDIF Statement which stops the effect of the Nested If Statement is not present in the COBOL code. As a result of the code in Figure 4-48, the only time the Exception Report would be written is if the Transaction was not a Change, Delete, or Addition Transaction. The reason is that the Perform Statement on pg/line 020170 will be executed only if the condition tested on pg/line 020110 is not true; that is, when the Else portion of that If Statement is executed.

In order to overcome this difficulty, there are several techniques available. Probably the most common is to Perform the If Statement which must be terminated by an ENDIF Clause. Thus, the coding which will implement the logic illustrated in Figure 4-47 and the one used in the sample program is illustrated in Figure 4-49.

EXAMPLE — CORRECT CODING

```
Ø2Ø1ØØ     IF THE-TRANSACTION-IS-A-CHANGE
Ø2Ø11Ø         PERFORM DØØØ-PROCESS-CHANGE-TRANSACTION
Ø2Ø12Ø     ELSE
Ø2Ø13Ø         IF THE-TRANSACTION-IS-A-DELETION
Ø2Ø14Ø             MOVE 'YES' TO WAS-IT-A-VALID-DELETE-RECORD
Ø2Ø15Ø         ELSE
Ø2Ø16Ø             MOVE PROGRAM-IDENTIFICATION-TRANS TO
Ø2Ø17Ø                     PROGRAM-IDENTIFICATION-RPTWORK
Ø2Ø18Ø             MOVE TRANSACTION-CODE-TRANS TO
Ø2Ø19Ø                     TRANSACTION-CODE-RPTWORK
Ø2Ø2ØØ             PERFORM CØØ1-DETERMINE-TYPE-OF-ERROR
Ø21Ø1Ø             PERFORM UØØØ-WRITE-EXCEPTION-REPORT.
Ø21Ø2Ø
Ø21Ø3Ø
Ø21Ø4Ø
Ø21Ø5Ø CØØ1-DETERMINE-TYPE-OF-ERROR.
Ø21Ø6Ø
Ø21Ø7Ø     IF THE-TRANSACTION-IS-AN-ADDITION
Ø21Ø8Ø         MOVE DUPLICATE-RECORD-ERRMSG TO TYPE-OF-ERROR-RPTWORK
Ø21Ø9Ø     ELSE
Ø211ØØ         MOVE INVALID-TRANS-CODE-ERRMSG TO TYPE-OF-ERROR-RPTWORK.
```

Figure 4-49 Example of CORRECT NESTED IF STATEMENT

In Figure 4-49 it can be seen that on pg/line 020200, the paragraph C001-DETERMINE-TYPE-OF-ERROR is performed. In this paragraph is contained the IF Statement which checks the Transaction Code. Note that regardless of the result of the IF Statement in the separate paragraph, the Exception Report will be written by the Perform Statement on pg/line 021010. Thus, by placing the IF Statement in a separate paragraph, the problem illustrated in Figure 4-48 is overcome.

It must be noted that the reason for having an extra paragraph is the result of a flaw in the COBOL language and is not an error in the logic which was developed. When developing the logic using pseudocode, the programmer should not consider the shortcomings of the COBOL language. Instead, the logic should be developed correctly using the ENDIF and any other features of pseudocode available. When it is necessary to implement the logic in a language such as COBOL, then the programmer should be concerned with the method used for implementation. Again, when developing the logic using pseudocode, the programmer should not be concerned with the shortcomings of the language which will be used to implement the logic.

SOURCE LISTING

The source listing for the sample program is contained on the following pages.

```
PP 5740-CB1 RELEASE 1.2  DEC 15, 1976              IBM OS/VS COBOL                 20.24.44  DATE AUG 17,1978

  1                    20.24.44        AUG 17,1978

IDENTIFICATION DIVISION.                                                MSTRUPDT
                                                                        MSTRUPDT
PROGRAM-ID.     MSTRUPDT.                                               MSTRUPDT
AUTHOR.         SHELLY AND CASHMAN.                                     MSTRUPDT
INSTALLATION.   ANAHEIM.                                                MSTRUPDT
DATE-WRITTEN.   06/19/78.                                               MSTRUPDT
DATE-COMPILED.  AUG 17,1978.                                            MSTRUPDT
SECURITY.       UNCLASSIFIED.                                           MSTRUPDT
                                                                        MSTRUPDT
*****************************************************************       MSTRUPDT
*                                                                *      MSTRUPDT
*  THIS PROGRAM UPDATES THE APPLICATION PROGRAM MASTER FILE.     *      MSTRUPDT
*  THE OUTPUT OF THE PROGRAM IS THE NEW, UPDATED APPLICATION     *      MSTRUPDT
*  PROGRAM MASTER FILE AND AN EXCEPTION REPORT WHICH LISTS ANY   *      MSTRUPDT
*  TRANSACTIONS WHICH CANNOT BE PROCESSED BY THE PROGRAM. THESE*        MSTRUPDT
*  TRANSACTIONS INCLUDE 1) TRANSACTIONS WITH TRANSACTION CODES   *      MSTRUPDT
*  OTHER THAN 'A' (ADD), 'D' (DELETE), OR 'C' (CHANGE);          *      MSTRUPDT
*  2) ADD TRANSACTIONS WITH A CORRESPONDING MASTER ON THE OLD    *      MSTRUPDT
*  MASTER FILE; 3) CHANGE OR DELETE TRANSACTIONS WITH NO         *      MSTRUPDT
*  CORRESPONDING OLD MASTER RECORD. THE PROCESSING IN THE        *      MSTRUPDT
*  PROGRAM CONSISTS OF THREE TYPES OF UPDATING WHICH CAN BE      *      MSTRUPDT
*  PERFORMED ON THE APPLICATION PROGRAM MASTER FILE:             *      MSTRUPDT
*       1) ADDITIONS - NEW RECORDS ARE ADDED TO THE MASTER FILE.*       MSTRUPDT
*                      THE TRANSACTION CODE IS 'A'. THE DATA IN *       MSTRUPDT
*                      THE NEW RECORD CONSISTS OF DATA IN THE   *       MSTRUPDT
*                      TRANSACTION RECORD. THE ACTUAL HOURS IN  *       MSTRUPDT
*                      THE NEW MASTER RECORD WILL BE SET TO ZERO*       MSTRUPDT
*                      AND THE TASK STATUS CODES WILL BE SET    *       MSTRUPDT
*                      EQUAL TO BLANKS.                         *       MSTRUPDT
*       2) DELETIONS - RECORDS FROM THE MASTER FILE ARE DELETED.*       MSTRUPDT
*                      THE TRANSACTION CODE IS 'D'. A DELETION  *       MSTRUPDT
*                      TRANSACTION WILL CAUSE THE CORRESPONDING *       MSTRUPDT
*                      MASTER RECORD TO NOT BE WRITTEN ON THE   *       MSTRUPDT
*                      NEW MASTER FILE.                         *       MSTRUPDT
*       3) CHANGES   - CHANGES ARE MADE TO EXISTING MASTER      *       MSTRUPDT
*                      RECORDS AND THE CHANGED RECORDS ARE      *       MSTRUPDT
*                      WRITTEN ON THE NEW MASTER FILE. THREE    *       MSTRUPDT
*                      TYPES OF CHANGES CAN BE MADE - A CHANGE  *       MSTRUPDT
*                      IN THE PROGRAMMER EMPLOYEE NUMBER,       *       MSTRUPDT
*                      ADDITIONS TO THE ACTUAL HOURS USED FOR   *       MSTRUPDT
*                      EACH PROGRAMMING TASK, AND CHANGING ANY  *       MSTRUPDT
*                      OF THE TASK STATUS CODES FROM BLANK TO   *       MSTRUPDT
*                      THE VALUE 'C' TO INDICATE THE TASK IS    *       MSTRUPDT
*                      COMPLETE. THESE CHANGES WILL BE MADE IN  *       MSTRUPDT
*                      THE MASTER RECORD WHENEVER THE           *       MSTRUPDT
*                      CORRESPONDING FIELD IN THE TRANSACTION   *       MSTRUPDT
*                      RECORD CONTAINS A NON-BLANK VALUE. ONE OR*       MSTRUPDT
*                      MORE FIELDS CAN BE CHANGED BY ONE CHANGE *       MSTRUPDT
*                      TRANSACTION RECORD AND ONE OR MORE CHANGE*       MSTRUPDT
*                      TRANSACTION RECORDS CAN BE PROCESSED     *       MSTRUPDT
*                      AGAINST A SINGLE OLD MASTER RECORD.      *       MSTRUPDT
*                                                                *      MSTRUPDT
*  ALL MASTER RECORDS AND TRANSACTION RECORDS ARE SORTED IN      *      MSTRUPDT
*  AN ASCENDING SEQUENCE BY PROGRAM IDENTIFICATION, THE CONTROL*        MSTRUPDT
*  FIELD. ALL DATA CONTAINED IN THE TRANSACTION RECORDS HAS      *      MSTRUPDT
*  BEEN PREVIOUSLY EDITED AND WILL BE CORRECT WHEN USED AS       *      MSTRUPDT
*  INPUT TO THIS PROGRAM.                                        *      MSTRUPDT
*                                                                *      MSTRUPDT
*****************************************************************       MSTRUPDT
                                                                        MSTRUPDT
                                                                        MSTRUPDT
                                                                        MSTRUPDT
ENVIRONMENT DIVISION.                                                   MSTRUPDT
                                                                        MSTRUPDT
CONFIGURATION SECTION.                                                  MSTRUPDT
                                                                        MSTRUPDT
SOURCE-COMPUTER. IBM-370.                                               MSTRUPDT
OBJECT-COMPUTER. IBM-370.                                               MSTRUPDT
SPECIAL-NAMES.    C01 IS TO-THE-TOP-OF-THE-PAGE.                        MSTRUPDT
                                                                        MSTRUPDT
INPUT-OUTPUT SECTION.                                                   MSTRUPDT
                                                                        MSTRUPDT
FILE-CONTROL.                                                           MSTRUPDT
    SELECT OLD-PROGRAM-MASTER-INPUT-FILE                                MSTRUPDT
            ASSIGN TO DA-S-OLDMSTR.                                     MSTRUPDT
    SELECT NEW-PROGRAM-MASTER-OUTPUT-FILE                               MSTRUPDT
            ASSIGN TO DA-S-NEWMSTR.                                     MSTRUPDT
    SELECT UPDATE-TRANSACTION-INPUT-FILE                                MSTRUPDT
            ASSIGN TO UR-S-SYSIN.                                       MSTRUPDT
    SELECT UPDATE-EXCEPTION-REPORT-FILE                                 MSTRUPDT
            ASSIGN TO UR-S-SYSOUT.                                      MSTRUPDT
```

Figure 4-50 Source Listing (Part 1 of 7)

```
  2                       20.24.44          AUG 17,1978

       DATA DIVISION.

       FILE SECTION.

       FD  OLD-PROGRAM-MASTER-INPUT-FILE
               BLOCK CONTAINS 20 RECORDS
               RECORD CONTAINS 77 CHARACTERS
               LABEL RECORDS ARE STANDARD
               DATA RECORD IS OLD-PROGRAM-MASTER-INPUT-REC.

       01  OLD-PROGRAM-MASTER-INPUT-REC.
           05  PROGRAM-IDENTIFICATION-OLDMST          PIC X(6).
           05  PROGRAM-DESCRIPTION-OLDMST             PIC X(20).
           05  PROGRAMMER-EMPL-NUMBER-OLDMST          PIC X(6).
           05  ESTIMATED-TASK-HOURS-OLDMST            PIC X(20).
           05  ACTUAL-TASK-HOURS-OLDMST.
               10  SINGLE-ACTUAL-HOUR-OLDMST          PIC S9(4)
                                                       OCCURS 5 TIMES.
           05  TASK-STATUS-INDICATORS-OLDMST.
               10  SINGLE-STATUS-INDICATOR-OLDMST     PIC X
                                                       OCCURS 5 TIMES.

       FD  NEW-PROGRAM-MASTER-OUTPUT-FILE
               BLOCK CONTAINS 20 RECORDS
               RECORD CONTAINS 77 CHARACTERS
               LABEL RECORDS ARE STANDARD
               DATA RECORD IS NEW-PROGRAM-MASTER-OUTPUT-REC.

       01  NEW-PROGRAM-MASTER-OUTPUT-REC.
           05  PROGRAM-IDENTIFICATION-NEWMST          PIC X(6).
           05  PROGRAM-DESCRIPTION-NEWMST             PIC X(20).
           05  PROGRAMMER-EMPL-NUMBER-NEWMST          PIC X(6).
           05  ESTIMATED-TASK-HOURS-NEWMST            PIC X(20).
           05  ACTUAL-TASK-HOURS-NEWMST               PIC X(20).
           05  TASK-STATUS-INDICATORS-NEWMST          PIC X(5).

       FD  UPDATE-TRANSACTION-INPUT-FILE
               RECORD CONTAINS 80 CHARACTERS
               LABEL RECORDS ARE OMITTED
               DATA RECORD IS UPDATE-TRANSACTION-INPUT-REC.

       01  UPDATE-TRANSACTION-INPUT-REC.
           05  PROGRAM-IDENTIFICATION-TRANS           PIC X(6).
           05  PROGRAM-DESCRIPTION-TRANS              PIC X(20).
           05  PROGRAMMER-EMPL-NUMBER-TRANS           PIC X(6).
           05  ESTIMATED-TASK-HOURS-TRANS             PIC X(20).
           05  ACTUAL-TASK-HOURS-TRANS.
               10  SINGLE-ACTUAL-HOUR-TRANS           PIC 9(4)
                                                       OCCURS 5 TIMES.
           05  ACTUAL-TASK-HOURS-X-TRANS REDEFINES
                   ACTUAL-TASK-HOURS-TRANS.
               10  SINGLE-ACTUAL-HOUR-X-TRANS         PIC X(4)
                                                       OCCURS 5 TIMES.
           05  TASK-STATUS-INDICATORS-TRANS.
               10  SINGLE-STATUS-INDICATOR-TRANS      PIC X
                                                       OCCURS 5 TIMES.
           05  FILLER                                 PIC XX.
           05  TRANSACTION-CODE-TRANS                 PIC X.
               88  THE-TRANSACTION-IS-AN-ADDITION       VALUE 'A'.
               88  THE-TRANSACTION-IS-A-DELETION        VALUE 'D'.
               88  THE-TRANSACTION-IS-A-CHANGE          VALUE 'C'.

       FD  UPDATE-EXCEPTION-REPORT-FILE
               RECORD CONTAINS 133 CHARACTERS
               LABEL RECORDS ARE OMITTED
               DATA RECORD IS UPDATE-EXCEPTION-REPORT-LINE.

       01  UPDATE-EXCEPTION-REPORT-LINE.
           05  CARRIAGE-CONTROL                       PIC X.
           05  FILLER                                 PIC X(4).
           05  PROGRAM-IDENTIFICATION-REPORT          PIC X(6).
           05  FILLER                                 PIC X(10).
           05  TRANSACTION-CODE-REPORT                PIC X.
           05  FILLER                                 PIC X(11).
           05  TYPE-OF-ERROR-REPORT                   PIC X(30).
           05  FILLER                                 PIC X(70).

       WORKING-STORAGE SECTION.

       01  PROGRAM-INDICATORS.
           05  ARE-THERE-MORE-MSTR-RECORDS     PIC XXX VALUE 'YES'.
               88  THERE-ARE-MORE-MSTR-RECORDS         VALUE 'YES'.
               88  THERE-ARE-NO-MORE-MSTR-RECORDS      VALUE 'NO '.
           05  ARE-THERE-MORE-TRAN-RECORDS     PIC XXX VALUE 'YES'.
               88  THERE-ARE-MORE-TRAN-RECORDS         VALUE 'YES'.
               88  THERE-ARE-NO-MORE-TRAN-RECORDS      VALUE 'NO '.
           05  HAS-DATA-BEEN-OBTAINED          PIC XXX VALUE 'NO '.
               88  DATA-HAS-BEEN-OBTAINED              VALUE 'YES'.
               88  DATA-HAS-NOT-BEEN-OBTAINED          VALUE 'NO '.
           05  IS-THIS-THE-FIRST-TIME          PIC XXX VALUE 'YES'.
               88  THIS-IS-THE-FIRST-TIME              VALUE 'YES'.
           05  WAS-IT-A-VALID-DELETE-RECORD    PIC XXX VALUE 'NO '.
               88 IT-WAS-A-VALID-DELETE-RECORD         VALUE 'YES'.
           05  WAS-IT-A-VALID-ADD-RECORD       PIC XXX VALUE 'NO '.
               88  IT-WAS-A-VALID-ADD-RECORD           VALUE 'YES'.
```

Figure 4-51 Source Listing (Part 2 of 7)

```
     3                   20.24.44        AUG 17,1978

     009150 01  PROGRAM-WORK-AREAS.                                        MSTRUPDT
     009160     05  NEW-MASTER-WORK-AREA.                                  MSTRUPDT
     009170         10  PROGRAM-IDENTIFICATION-MSTWORK  PIC X(6).          MSTRUPDT
     009180         10  PROGRAM-DESCRIPTION-MSTWORK     PIC X(20).         MSTRUPDT
     009190         10  PROGRAMMER-EMPL-NUMBER-MSTWORK  PIC X(6).          MSTRUPDT
     009200         10  ESTIMATED-TASK-HOURS-MSTWORK    PIC X(20).         MSTRUPDT
     010010         10  ACTUAL-TASK-HOURS-MSTWORK       PIC X(20).         MSTRUPDT
     010020         10  TASK-STATUS-INDICATORS-MSTWORK  PIC X(5).          MSTRUPDT
     010030     05  EXCEPTION-REPORT-WORK-AREA.                            MSTRUPDT
     010040         10  PROGRAM-IDENTIFICATION-RPTWORK  PIC X(6).          MSTRUPDT
     010050         10  TRANSACTION-CODE-RPTWORK        PIC X.             MSTRUPDT
     010060         10  TYPE-OF-ERROR-RPTWORK           PIC X(30).         MSTRUPDT
     010070                                                                MSTRUPDT
     010080 01  PROGRAM-CONSTANTS.                                         MSTRUPDT
     010090     05  DUPLICATE-RECORD-ERRMSG          PIC X(30) VALUE       MSTRUPDT
     010100                                 'DUPLICATE MASTER RECORD      '.MSTRUPDT
     010110     05  INVALID-TRANS-CODE-ERRMSG        PIC X(30) VALUE       MSTRUPDT
     010120                                 'INVALID TRANSACTION CODE     '.MSTRUPDT
     010130     05  NON-MATCHING-MASTER-ERRMSG       PIC X(30) VALUE       MSTRUPDT
     010140                                 'NON-MATCHING MASTER RECORD   '.MSTRUPDT
     010150     05  COMPLETED-CONSTANT               PIC X     VALUE 'C'.  MSTRUPDT
     010160                                                                MSTRUPDT
     010170 01  PROGRAM-SUBSCRIPTS.                                        MSTRUPDT
     010180     05  ACTUAL-HOURS-ADD-SUBSCRIPT       PIC S9(8) USAGE IS COMP  MSTRUPDT
     010190                                                SYNC.           MSTRUPDT
     010200         88  ALL-ACTUAL-HOURS-ARE-ADDED             VALUE +6.   MSTRUPDT
     011010     05  STATUS-CODES-SUBSCRIPT           PIC S9(8) USAGE IS COMP  MSTRUPDT
     011020                                                SYNC.           MSTRUPDT
     011030         88  ALL-STATUS-CODES-ARE-CHECKED           VALUE +6.   MSTRUPDT
     011040                                                                MSTRUPDT
     011050 01  PRINTER-CONTROL.                                           MSTRUPDT
     011060     05  PROPER-SPACING              PIC 9.                     MSTRUPDT
     011070     05  SPACE-ONE-LINE              PIC 9       VALUE 1.       MSTRUPDT
     011080     05  SPACE-TWO-LINES             PIC 9       VALUE 2.       MSTRUPDT
     011090     05  NUMBER-OF-LINES-PRINTED PIC S999        VALUE ZERO     MSTRUPDT
     011100                                                 USAGE IS COMP-3.  MSTRUPDT
     011110     05  PAGE-SIZE                   PIC 999     VALUE 40       MSTRUPDT
     011120                                                 USAGE IS COMP-3.  MSTRUPDT
     011130     05  PAGE-NUMBER-COUNT           PIC S999    VALUE +1       MSTRUPDT
     011140                                                 USAGE IS COMP-3.  MSTRUPDT
     011150         88  THIS-IS-THE-FIRST-PAGE              VALUE +1.      MSTRUPDT
     011160                                                                MSTRUPDT
     011170 01  HEADING-LINES.                                             MSTRUPDT
     011180     05  FIRST-HEADING-LINE.                                    MSTRUPDT
     011190         10  CARRIAGE-CONTROL        PIC X.                     MSTRUPDT
     011200         10  CURRENT-DATE-HDG1       PIC X(8).                  MSTRUPDT
     012010         10  FILLER                  PIC X(9)    VALUE SPACES.  MSTRUPDT
     012020         10  FILLER                  PIC X(7)    VALUE 'UPDATE '.  MSTRUPDT
     012030         10  FILLER                  PIC X(10)   VALUE 'EXCEPTION '. MSTRUPDT
     012040         10  FILLER                  PIC X(6)    VALUE 'REPORT'.   MSTRUPDT
     012050         10  FILLER                  PIC X(10)   VALUE SPACES.  MSTRUPDT
     012060         10  FILLER                  PIC X(5)    VALUE 'PAGE '. MSTRUPDT
     012070         10  PAGE-NUMBER-HDG1        PIC ZZ9.                   MSTRUPDT
     012080         10  FILLER                  PIC X(74)   VALUE SPACES.  MSTRUPDT
     012090     05  SECOND-HEADING-LINE.                                   MSTRUPDT
     012100         10  CARRIAGE-CONTROL        PIC X.                     MSTRUPDT
     012110         10  FILLER                  PIC X(3)    VALUE SPACES.  MSTRUPDT
     012120         10  FILLER                  PIC X(7)    VALUE 'PROGRAM'.  MSTRUPDT
     012130         10  FILLER                  PIC X(6)    VALUE SPACES.  MSTRUPDT
     012140         10  FILLER                  PIC X(11)   VALUE 'TRANSACTION'.MSTRUPDT
     012150         10  FILLER                  PIC X(13)   VALUE SPACES.  MSTRUPDT
     012160         10  FILLER                  PIC X(4)    VALUE 'TYPE'.  MSTRUPDT
     012170         10  FILLER                  PIC X(88)   VALUE SPACES.  MSTRUPDT
     012180     05  THIRD-HEADING-LINE.                                    MSTRUPDT
     012190         10  CARRIAGE-CONTROL        PIC X.                     MSTRUPDT
     012200         10  FILLER                  PIC X(14)   VALUE          MSTRUPDT
     013010                                    'IDENTIFICATION'.           MSTRUPDT
     013020         10  FILLER                  PIC X(5)    VALUE SPACES.  MSTRUPDT
     013030         10  FILLER                  PIC X(4)    VALUE 'CODE'.  MSTRUPDT
     013040         10  FILLER                  PIC X(15)   VALUE SPACES.  MSTRUPDT
     013050         10  FILLER                  PIC X(8)    VALUE 'OF ERROR'.  MSTRUPDT
     013060         10  FILLER                  PIC X(86)   VALUE SPACES.  MSTRUPDT
```

Figure 4-52 Source Listing (Part 3 of 7)

```
4                     20.24.44        AUG 17,1978

013080 PROCEDURE DIVISION.                                               MSTRUPDT
013090                                                                   MSTRUPDT
013100****************************************************************** MSTRUPDT
013110*                                                                * MSTRUPDT
013120*  THE FUNCTION OF THIS MODULE IS TO UPDATE THE PROGRAM MASTER   * MSTRUPDT
013130*  FILE. IT IS ENTERED FROM AND EXITS TO THE OPERATING SYSTEM.   * MSTRUPDT
013140*                                                                * MSTRUPDT
013150****************************************************************** MSTRUPDT
013160                                                                   MSTRUPDT
013170 A000-UPDATE-PROGRAM-MASTER.                                       MSTRUPDT
013180                                                                   MSTRUPDT
013190     OPEN INPUT  OLD-PROGRAM-MASTER-INPUT-FILE                     MSTRUPDT
013200                 UPDATE-TRANSACTION-INPUT-FILE                     MSTRUPDT
014010          OUTPUT NEW-PROGRAM-MASTER-OUTPUT-FILE                    MSTRUPDT
014020                 UPDATE-EXCEPTION-REPORT-FILE.                     MSTRUPDT
014030     PERFORM B000-OBTAIN-NEW-MASTER-DATA.                          MSTRUPDT
014040     PERFORM A001-WRITE-AND-READ                                   MSTRUPDT
014050         UNTIL THERE-ARE-NO-MORE-MSTR-RECORDS AND                  MSTRUPDT
014060               THERE-ARE-NO-MORE-TRAN-RECORDS.                     MSTRUPDT
014070     IF DATA-HAS-BEEN-OBTAINED                                     MSTRUPDT
014080        PERFORM B010-WRITE-NEW-MASTER.                             MSTRUPDT
014090     CLOSE OLD-PROGRAM-MASTER-INPUT-FILE                           MSTRUPDT
014100           UPDATE-TRANSACTION-INPUT-FILE                           MSTRUPDT
014110           NEW-PROGRAM-MASTER-OUTPUT-FILE                          MSTRUPDT
014120           UPDATE-EXCEPTION-REPORT-FILE.                           MSTRUPDT
014130     STOP RUN.                                                     MSTRUPDT
014140                                                                   MSTRUPDT
014150                                                                   MSTRUPDT
014160                                                                   MSTRUPDT
014170 A001-WRITE-AND-READ.                                              MSTRUPDT
014180                                                                   MSTRUPDT
014190     PERFORM B010-WRITE-NEW-MASTER.                                MSTRUPDT
014200     PERFORM B000-OBTAIN-NEW-MASTER-DATA.                          MSTRUPDT

5                     20.24.44        AUG 17,1978

014220****************************************************************** MSTRUPDT
014230*                                                                * MSTRUPDT
014240*  THE FUNCTION OF THIS MODULE IS TO OBTAIN THE DATA REQUIRED    * MSTRUPDT
015010*  FOR A NEW MASTER RECORD. IT IS ENTERED FROM AND EXITS TO THE* MSTRUPDT
015020*  A000-UPDATE-PROGRAM-MASTER MODULE.                            * MSTRUPDT
015030*                                                                * MSTRUPDT
015040****************************************************************** MSTRUPDT
015050                                                                   MSTRUPDT
015060 B000-OBTAIN-NEW-MASTER-DATA.                                      MSTRUPDT
015070                                                                   MSTRUPDT
015080     MOVE 'NO ' TO HAS-DATA-BEEN-OBTAINED.                         MSTRUPDT
015090     IF THIS-IS-THE-FIRST-TIME                                     MSTRUPDT
015100        PERFORM B002-READ-A-MASTER-RECORD                          MSTRUPDT
015110        PERFORM B003-READ-A-TRANSACTION-RECORD                     MSTRUPDT
015120        MOVE 'NO ' TO IS-THIS-THE-FIRST-TIME.                      MSTRUPDT
015130     PERFORM B001-COMPARE-INPUT-RECORDS                            MSTRUPDT
015140         UNTIL DATA-HAS-BEEN-OBTAINED OR                           MSTRUPDT
015150              (THERE-ARE-NO-MORE-MSTR-RECORDS AND                  MSTRUPDT
015160               THERE-ARE-NO-MORE-TRAN-RECORDS).                    MSTRUPDT
015170                                                                   MSTRUPDT
015180                                                                   MSTRUPDT
015190                                                                   MSTRUPDT
015200 B001-COMPARE-INPUT-RECORDS.                                       MSTRUPDT
016010                                                                   MSTRUPDT
016020     MOVE SPACES TO WAS-IT-A-VALID-DELETE-RECORD.                  MSTRUPDT
016030     MOVE SPACES TO WAS-IT-A-VALID-ADD-RECORD.                     MSTRUPDT
016040     IF THERE-ARE-MORE-MSTR-RECORDS AND                            MSTRUPDT
016050           THERE-ARE-MORE-TRAN-RECORDS                             MSTRUPDT
016060        IF PROGRAM-IDENTIFICATION-OLDMST =                         MSTRUPDT
016070              PROGRAM-IDENTIFICATION-TRANS                         MSTRUPDT
016080           PERFORM C000-PROCESS-EQUAL-RECORDS                      MSTRUPDT
016090           IF IT-WAS-A-VALID-DELETE-RECORD                         MSTRUPDT
016100              PERFORM B002-READ-A-MASTER-RECORD                    MSTRUPDT
016110              PERFORM B003-READ-A-TRANSACTION-RECORD               MSTRUPDT
016120           ELSE                                                    MSTRUPDT
016130              PERFORM B003-READ-A-TRANSACTION-RECORD               MSTRUPDT
016140        ELSE                                                       MSTRUPDT
016150           IF PROGRAM-IDENTIFICATION-OLDMST IS LESS THAN           MSTRUPDT
016160                 PROGRAM-IDENTIFICATION-TRANS                      MSTRUPDT
016170              PERFORM C010-PROCESS-LOW-MASTER                      MSTRUPDT
016180              MOVE 'YES' TO HAS-DATA-BEEN-OBTAINED                 MSTRUPDT
016190              PERFORM B002-READ-A-MASTER-RECORD                    MSTRUPDT
016200           ELSE                                                    MSTRUPDT
017010              PERFORM C020-PROCESS-LOW-TRANSACTION                 MSTRUPDT
017020              IF IT-WAS-A-VALID-ADD-RECORD                         MSTRUPDT
017030                 MOVE 'YES' TO HAS-DATA-BEEN-OBTAINED              MSTRUPDT
017040                 PERFORM B003-READ-A-TRANSACTION-RECORD            MSTRUPDT
017050              ELSE                                                 MSTRUPDT
017060                 PERFORM B003-READ-A-TRANSACTION-RECORD            MSTRUPDT
017070     ELSE                                                          MSTRUPDT
017080        IF THERE-ARE-NO-MORE-MSTR-RECORDS                          MSTRUPDT
017090           PERFORM C020-PROCESS-LOW-TRANSACTION                    MSTRUPDT
017100           IF IT-WAS-A-VALID-ADD-RECORD                            MSTRUPDT
017110              MOVE 'YES' TO HAS-DATA-BEEN-OBTAINED                 MSTRUPDT
017120              PERFORM B003-READ-A-TRANSACTION-RECORD               MSTRUPDT
017130           ELSE                                                    MSTRUPDT
017140              PERFORM B003-READ-A-TRANSACTION-RECORD               MSTRUPDT
```

Figure 4-53 Source Listing (Part 4 of 7)

```
  6                      20.24.44        AUG 17,1978

017150          ELSE                                                    MSTRUPDT
017160              PERFORM C010-PROCESS-LOW-MASTER                     MSTRUPDT
017170              MOVE 'YES' TO HAS-DATA-BEEN-OBTAINED                MSTRUPDT
017180              PERFORM B002-READ-A-MASTER-RECORD.                  MSTRUPDT
017190                                                                  MSTRUPDT
017200                                                                  MSTRUPDT
018010                                                                  MSTRUPDT
018020 B002-READ-A-MASTER-RECORD.                                       MSTRUPDT
018030                                                                  MSTRUPDT
018040     READ OLD-PROGRAM-MASTER-INPUT-FILE                           MSTRUPDT
018050         AT END                                                   MSTRUPDT
018060             MOVE 'NO ' TO ARE-THERE-MORE-MSTR-RECORDS.           MSTRUPDT
018070                                                                  MSTRUPDT
018080                                                                  MSTRUPDT
018090                                                                  MSTRUPDT
018100 B003-READ-A-TRANSACTION-RECORD.                                  MSTRUPDT
018110                                                                  MSTRUPDT
018120     READ UPDATE-TRANSACTION-INPUT-FILE                           MSTRUPDT
018130         AT END                                                   MSTRUPDT
018140             MOVE 'NO ' TO ARE-THERE-MORE-TRAN-RECORDS.           MSTRUPDT
```

```
  7                      20.24.44        AUG 17,1978

018160*****************************************************************  MSTRUPDT
018170*                                                               *  MSTRUPDT
018180*  THIS MODULE WRITES THE NEW MASTER RECORDS. IT IS ENTERED     *  MSTRUPDT
018190*  FROM AND EXITS TO THE A000-UPDATE-PROGRAM-MASTER MODULE.     *  MSTRUPDT
018200*                                                               *  MSTRUPDT
019010*****************************************************************  MSTRUPDT
019020                                                                  MSTRUPDT
019030 B010-WRITE-NEW-MASTER.                                           MSTRUPDT
019040                                                                  MSTRUPDT
019050     MOVE PROGRAM-IDENTIFICATION-MSTWORK TO                       MSTRUPDT
019060             PROGRAM-IDENTIFICATION-NEWMST.                       MSTRUPDT
019070     MOVE PROGRAM-DESCRIPTION-MSTWORK TO                          MSTRUPDT
019080             PROGRAM-DESCRIPTION-NEWMST.                          MSTRUPDT
019090     MOVE PROGRAMMER-EMPL-NUMBER-MSTWORK TO                       MSTRUPDT
019100             PROGRAMMER-EMPL-NUMBER-NEWMST.                       MSTRUPDT
019110     MOVE ESTIMATED-TASK-HOURS-MSTWORK TO                         MSTRUPDT
019120             ESTIMATED-TASK-HOURS-NEWMST.                         MSTRUPDT
019130     MOVE ACTUAL-TASK-HOURS-MSTWORK TO                            MSTRUPDT
019140             ACTUAL-TASK-HOURS-NEWMST.                            MSTRUPDT
019150     MOVE TASK-STATUS-INDICATORS-MSTWORK TO                       MSTRUPDT
019160             TASK-STATUS-INDICATORS-NEWMST.                       MSTRUPDT
019170     WRITE NEW-PROGRAM-MASTER-OUTPUT-REC.                         MSTRUPDT
```

```
  8                      20.24.44        AUG 17,1978

019190*****************************************************************  MSTRUPDT
019200*                                                               *  MSTRUPDT
020010*  THIS MODULE PROCESSES EQUAL MASTER AND TRANSACTION RECORDS.  *  MSTRUPDT
020020*  IT IS ENTERED FROM AND EXITS TO THE B000-OBTAIN-NEW-MASTER-  *  MSTRUPDT
020030*  DATA MODULE.                                                 *  MSTRUPDT
020040*                                                               *  MSTRUPDT
020050*****************************************************************  MSTRUPDT
020060                                                                  MSTRUPDT
020070 C000-PROCESS-EQUAL-RECORDS.                                      MSTRUPDT
020080                                                                  MSTRUPDT
020100     IF THE-TRANSACTION-IS-A-CHANGE                               MSTRUPDT
020110         PERFORM D000-PROCESS-CHANGE-TRANS                        MSTRUPDT
020120     ELSE                                                         MSTRUPDT
020130         IF THE-TRANSACTION-IS-A-DELETION                         MSTRUPDT
020140             MOVE 'YES' TO WAS-IT-A-VALID-DELETE-RECORD           MSTRUPDT
020150         ELSE                                                     MSTRUPDT
020160             MOVE PROGRAM-IDENTIFICATION-TRANS TO                 MSTRUPDT
020170                     PROGRAM-IDENTIFICATION-RPTWORK               MSTRUPDT
020180             MOVE TRANSACTION-CODE-TRANS TO                       MSTRUPDT
020190                     TRANSACTION-CODE-RPTWORK                     MSTRUPDT
020200             PERFORM C001-DETERMINE-TYPE-OF-ERROR                 MSTRUPDT
021010             PERFORM U000-WRITE-EXCEPTION-REPORT.                 MSTRUPDT
021020                                                                  MSTRUPDT
021030                                                                  MSTRUPDT
021040                                                                  MSTRUPDT
021050 C001-DETERMINE-TYPE-OF-ERROR.                                    MSTRUPDT
021060                                                                  MSTRUPDT
021070     IF THE-TRANSACTION-IS-AN-ADDITION                            MSTRUPDT
021080         MOVE DUPLICATE-RECORD-ERRMSG TO TYPE-OF-ERROR-RPTWORK    MSTRUPDT
021090     ELSE                                                         MSTRUPDT
021100         MOVE INVALID-TRANS-CODE-ERRMSG TO TYPE-OF-ERROR-RPTWORK. MSTRUPDT
```

Figure 4-54 Source Listing (Part 5 of 7)

```
  9                    20.24.44        AUG 17,1978

021120********************************************************************* MSTRUPDT
021130*                                                                   * MSTRUPDT
021140*  THE FUNCTION OF THIS MODULE IS TO PROCESS A LOW MASTER           * MSTRUPDT
021150*  RECORD. IT IS ENTERED FROM AND EXITS TO THE B000-OBTAIN-NEW-*      MSTRUPDT
021160*  MASTER-DATA MODULE.                                              * MSTRUPDT
021170*                                                                   * MSTRUPDT
021180********************************************************************* MSTRUPDT
021190                                                                      MSTRUPDT
021200 C010-PROCESS-LOW-MASTER.                                             MSTRUPDT
022010                                                                      MSTRUPDT
022020     MOVE PROGRAM-IDENTIFICATION-OLDMST TO                            MSTRUPDT
022030             PROGRAM-IDENTIFICATION-MSTWORK.                          MSTRUPDT
022040     MOVE PROGRAM-DESCRIPTION-OLDMST TO                               MSTRUPDT
022050             PROGRAM-DESCRIPTION-MSTWORK.                             MSTRUPDT
022060     MOVE PROGRAMMER-EMPL-NUMBER-OLDMST TO                            MSTRUPDT
022070             PROGRAMMER-EMPL-NUMBER-MSTWORK.                          MSTRUPDT
022080     MOVE ESTIMATED-TASK-HOURS-OLDMST TO                              MSTRUPDT
022090             ESTIMATED-TASK-HOURS-MSTWORK.                            MSTRUPDT
022100     MOVE ACTUAL-TASK-HOURS-OLDMST TO ACTUAL-TASK-HOURS-MSTWORK.      MSTRUPDT
022110     MOVE TASK-STATUS-INDICATORS-OLDMST TO                            MSTRUPDT
022120             TASK-STATUS-INDICATORS-MSTWORK.                          MSTRUPDT
```

```
 10                    20.24.44        AUG 17,1978

022140********************************************************************* MSTRUPDT
022150*                                                                   * MSTRUPDT
022160*  THE FUNCTION OF THIS MODULE IS TO PROCESS A LOW TRANSACTION      * MSTRUPDT
022170*  RECORD. IT IS ENTERED FROM AND EXITS TO THE                      * MSTRUPDT
022180*  B000-OBTAIN-NEW-MASTER-DATA MODULE.                              * MSTRUPDT
022190*                                                                   * MSTRUPDT
022200********************************************************************* MSTRUPDT
023010                                                                      MSTRUPDT
023020 C020-PROCESS-LOW-TRANSACTION.                                        MSTRUPDT
023030                                                                      MSTRUPDT
023050     IF THE-TRANSACTION-IS-AN-ADDITION                                MSTRUPDT
023060         MOVE PROGRAM-IDENTIFICATION-TRANS TO                         MSTRUPDT
023070                 PROGRAM-IDENTIFICATION-MSTWORK                       MSTRUPDT
023080         MOVE PROGRAM-DESCRIPTION-TRANS TO                            MSTRUPDT
023090                 PROGRAM-DESCRIPTION-MSTWORK                          MSTRUPDT
023100         MOVE PROGRAMMER-EMPL-NUMBER-TRANS TO                         MSTRUPDT
023110                 PROGRAMMER-EMPL-NUMBER-MSTWORK                       MSTRUPDT
023120         MOVE ESTIMATED-TASK-HOURS-TRANS TO                           MSTRUPDT
023130                 ESTIMATED-TASK-HOURS-MSTWORK                         MSTRUPDT
023140         MOVE ZEROS TO ACTUAL-TASK-HOURS-MSTWORK                      MSTRUPDT
023150         MOVE SPACES TO TASK-STATUS-INDICATORS-MSTWORK                MSTRUPDT
023160         MOVE 'YES' TO WAS-IT-A-VALID-ADD-RECORD                      MSTRUPDT
023170     ELSE                                                             MSTRUPDT
023180         MOVE PROGRAM-IDENTIFICATION-TRANS TO                         MSTRUPDT
023190                 PROGRAM-IDENTIFICATION-RPTWORK                       MSTRUPDT
023200         MOVE TRANSACTION-CODE-TRANS TO TRANSACTION-CODE-RPTWORK      MSTRUPDT
023210         PERFORM C021-DETERMINE-ERROR-TYPE                            MSTRUPDT
024010         PERFORM U000-WRITE-EXCEPTION-REPORT.                         MSTRUPDT
024020                                                                      MSTRUPDT
024030                                                                      MSTRUPDT
024040                                                                      MSTRUPDT
024050 C021-DETERMINE-ERROR-TYPE.                                           MSTRUPDT
024060                                                                      MSTRUPDT
024070     IF THE-TRANSACTION-IS-A-DELETION OR                              MSTRUPDT
024080             THE-TRANSACTION-IS-A-CHANGE                              MSTRUPDT
024090         MOVE NON-MATCHING-MASTER-ERRMSG TO TYPE-OF-ERROR-RPTWORK     MSTRUPDT
024100     ELSE                                                             MSTRUPDT
024110         MOVE INVALID-TRANS-CODE-ERRMSG TO TYPE-OF-ERROR-RPTWORK.     MSTRUPDT
```

Figure 4-55 Source Listing (Part 6 of 7)

```
11                    20.24.44        AUG 17,1978

024130*****************************************************************  MSTRUPDT
024140*                                                               *  MSTRUPDT
024150*  THE FUNCTION OF THIS MODULE IS TO PROCESS A CHANGE           *  MSTRUPDT
024160*  TRANSACTION. IT IS ENTERED FROM AND EXITS TO THE             *  MSTRUPDT
024170*  C000-PROCESS-EQUAL-RECORDS MODULE.                           *  MSTRUPDT
024180*                                                               *  MSTRUPDT
024190*****************************************************************  MSTRUPDT
024200                                                                   MSTRUPDT
025010 D000-PROCESS-CHANGE-TRANS.                                        MSTRUPDT
025020                                                                   MSTRUPDT
025030     IF PROGRAMMER-EMPL-NUMBER-TRANS NOT = SPACES                  MSTRUPDT
025040         MOVE PROGRAMMER-EMPL-NUMBER-TRANS TO                      MSTRUPDT
025050             PROGRAMMER-EMPL-NUMBER-OLDMST.                        MSTRUPDT
025060     PERFORM D001-CHECK-ACTUAL-HOURS                               MSTRUPDT
025070         VARYING ACTUAL-HOURS-ADD-SUBSCRIPT FROM 1 BY 1            MSTRUPDT
025080         UNTIL ALL-ACTUAL-HOURS-ARE-ADDED.                         MSTRUPDT
025090     PERFORM D002-CHECK-STATUS-CODES                               MSTRUPDT
025100         VARYING STATUS-CODES-SUBSCRIPT FROM 1 BY 1                MSTRUPDT
025110         UNTIL ALL-STATUS-CODES-ARE-CHECKED.                       MSTRUPDT
025120                                                                   MSTRUPDT
025130                                                                   MSTRUPDT
025140                                                                   MSTRUPDT
025150 D001-CHECK-ACTUAL-HOURS.                                          MSTRUPDT
025160                                                                   MSTRUPDT
025170     IF SINGLE-ACTUAL-HOUR-X-TRANS (ACTUAL-HOURS-ADD-SUBSCRIPT)    MSTRUPDT
025180         IS NOT = SPACES                                           MSTRUPDT
025190         ADD SINGLE-ACTUAL-HOUR-TRANS (ACTUAL-HOURS-ADD-SUBSCRIPT) MSTRUPDT
025200             TO SINGLE-ACTUAL-HOUR-OLDMST                          MSTRUPDT
025210             (ACTUAL-HOURS-ADD-SUBSCRIPT).                         MSTRUPDT
025220                                                                   MSTRUPDT
026010                                                                   MSTRUPDT
026020                                                                   MSTRUPDT
026030 D002-CHECK-STATUS-CODES.                                          MSTRUPDT
026040                                                                   MSTRUPDT
026050     IF SINGLE-STATUS-INDICATOR-TRANS (STATUS-CODES-SUBSCRIPT)     MSTRUPDT
026060         = COMPLETED-CONSTANT                                      MSTRUPDT
026070         MOVE COMPLETED-CONSTANT TO                                MSTRUPDT
026080             SINGLE-STATUS-INDICATOR-OLDMST                        MSTRUPDT
026090             (STATUS-CODES-SUBSCRIPT).                             MSTRUPDT
```

```
12                    20.24.44        AUG 17,1978

026110*****************************************************************  MSTRUPDT
026120*                                                               *  MSTRUPDT
026130*  THE FUNCTION OF THIS UTILITY MODULE IS TO WRITE THE          *  MSTRUPDT
026140*  EXCEPTION REPORT. IT IS ENTERED FROM AND EXITS TO SEVERAL    *  MSTRUPDT
026150*  MODULES WITHIN THE PROGRAM (SEE HIERARCHY CHART).            *  MSTRUPDT
026160*                                                               *  MSTRUPDT
026170*****************************************************************  MSTRUPDT
026180                                                                   MSTRUPDT
026190 U000-WRITE-EXCEPTION-REPORT.                                      MSTRUPDT
026200                                                                   MSTRUPDT
027010     IF THIS-IS-THE-FIRST-PAGE OR                                  MSTRUPDT
027020             NUMBER-OF-LINES-PRINTED IS GREATER THAN PAGE-SIZE     MSTRUPDT
027030         PERFORM U010-PRINT-HEADINGS.                              MSTRUPDT
027040     MOVE SPACES TO UPDATE-EXCEPTION-REPORT-LINE.                  MSTRUPDT
027050     MOVE PROGRAM-IDENTIFICATION-RPTWORK TO                        MSTRUPDT
027060         PROGRAM-IDENTIFICATION-REPORT.                            MSTRUPDT
027070     MOVE TRANSACTION-CODE-RPTWORK TO TRANSACTION-CODE-REPORT.     MSTRUPDT
027080     MOVE TYPE-OF-ERROR-RPTWORK TO TYPE-OF-ERROR-REPORT.           MSTRUPDT
027090     WRITE UPDATE-EXCEPTION-REPORT-LINE                            MSTRUPDT
027100         AFTER PROPER-SPACING.                                     MSTRUPDT
027110     ADD PROPER-SPACING TO NUMBER-OF-LINES-PRINTED.                MSTRUPDT
027120     MOVE SPACE-ONE-LINE TO PROPER-SPACING.                        MSTRUPDT
```

```
13                    20.24.44        AUG 17,1978

027140*****************************************************************  MSTRUPDT
027150*                                                               *  MSTRUPDT
027160*  THIS MODULE PRINTS THE HEADINGS ON THE EXCEPTION REPORT. IT  *  MSTRUPDT
027170*  IS ENTERED FROM AND EXITS TO THE U000-WRITE-EXCEPTION-REPORT*  MSTRUPDT
027180*  MODULE.                                                      *  MSTRUPDT
027190*                                                               *  MSTRUPDT
027200*****************************************************************  MSTRUPDT
028010                                                                   MSTRUPDT
028020 U010-PRINT-HEADINGS.                                              MSTRUPDT
028030                                                                   MSTRUPDT
028040     MOVE CURRENT-DATE TO CURRENT-DATE-HDG1.                       MSTRUPDT
028050     MOVE PAGE-NUMBER-COUNT TO PAGE-NUMBER-HDG1.                   MSTRUPDT
028060     WRITE UPDATE-EXCEPTION-REPORT-LINE FROM FIRST-HEADING-LINE    MSTRUPDT
028070         AFTER ADVANCING TO-THE-TOP-OF-THE-PAGE.                   MSTRUPDT
028080     ADD 1 TO PAGE-NUMBER-COUNT.                                   MSTRUPDT
028090     WRITE UPDATE-EXCEPTION-REPORT-LINE FROM SECOND-HEADING-LINE   MSTRUPDT
028100         AFTER ADVANCING 2 LINES.                                  MSTRUPDT
028110     WRITE UPDATE-EXCEPTION-REPORT-LINE FROM THIRD-HEADING-LINE    MSTRUPDT
028120         AFTER ADVANCING 1 LINES.                                  MSTRUPDT
028130     MOVE ZERO TO NUMBER-OF-LINES-PRINTED.                         MSTRUPDT
028140     MOVE SPACE-TWO-LINES TO PROPER-SPACING.                       MSTRUPDT
```

Figure 4-56 Source Listing (Part 7 of 7)

CHAPTER 4

REVIEW QUESTIONS

1. When updating a sequential file, what are the three procedures that are normally performed during the updating process?

2. When should sequential file updating procedures be used?

3. Draw a flow diagram illustrating sequential file updating and briefly describe the steps that occur.

4. When updating a sequential file, describe the processing that must occur when the Transaction Record is less than the Master Record.

5. When updating a sequential file, describe the processing that must occur when the Transaction Record and Master Record are equal.

6. When updating a sequential file, describe the processing that must occur when the Master Record is less than the Transaction Record.

CHAPTER 4

PROGRAMMING ASSIGNMENT 1

OVERVIEW — PROGRAMMING ASSIGNMENTS

The programming assignments in Chapter 4 consist of writing one or more programs to update the Decathlon Master File created in Chapter 2. A variety of approaches are possible when utilizing these programming assignments.

1. Only Programming Assignment 1 may be assigned utilizing the Decathlon Master File created in Chapter 2, Assignment 1. This approach results in the design and coding of a relatively small sequential file update program which illustrates the basic concepts discussed in the chapter.

2. Programming Assignment 1A may be assigned utilizing the Decathlon Master File created in Chapter 2, Assignment 1A. This results in the design and coding of a program slightly more complex than Programming Assignment 1.

3. Programming Assignment 1B may be assigned in conjunction with Programming Assignment 1A utilizing the Decathlon Master File created in Chapter 2, Assignment 1A. Upon completion of this assignment, the student will have completed a program of the approximate difficulty of the program contained in the chapter.

4. Programming Assignment 1A may be assigned. After this assignment is completely designed, coded, and tested, Programming Assignment 1B may be assigned as a maintenance program to be designed, coded, and tested after completion of Assignment 1A.

The method of assigning the program is at the option of the instructor.

INSTRUCTIONS — PROGRAMMING ASSIGNMENT 1

A program is to be written which is to update the Decathlon Master File created in Chapter 2, Programming Assignment 1. Design and write the COBOL program. Use a Hierarchy Chart, IPO Charts, and Pseudocode Specifications when designing the program.

INPUT

The input to the program is the Decathlon Master File created in Chapter 2, Programming Assignment 1 and a Master Transaction File. The format of the Decathlon Master File created in Chapter 2, Programming Assignment 1 is illustrated below.

Decathlon Master File — Chapter 2, Programming Assignment 1

FIELD	POSITION	NUMBER OF DIGITS	ATTRIBUTES
Athlete Number	1-3	3	Numeric
Athlete Name	4-23	20	Alphanumeric
Coach Number	24-26	3	Numeric
Total Decathlon Score	27-30	4	Numeric

The Decathlon Master File has a blocking factor of 20 records per block. It is stored in an ascending sequence by Athlete Number.

The format of the Master Transaction File, which is stored on punched cards, is illustrated below.

Master Transaction File

SCHOOL I.D.	ATHLETE NUMBER	ATHLETE NAME	COACH NUMBER	100 METERS	LONG JUMP	SHOT PUT	HIGH JUMP	400 METERS	110 METER HURDLES	DISCUS	POLE VAULT	JAVELIN	1500 METERS		CODE

Note from the Transaction Record format that the record contains the Athlete Number, the Athlete Name, the Coach Number, the Scores in each decathlon event, reflecting the athlete's most recent competition, and a Transaction Code. The Transaction Code should contain one of the three codes: "A" (Addition), "D" (Deletion), or "C" (Change). Thus, records in the Transaction File can be used to Add records to the Decathlon Master File, Delete records from the Decathlon Master File, or Change records in the Decathlon Master File. The Transaction File will already be sorted in an ascending sequence by Athlete Number prior to being read by the Update Program. All data in the Transaction Record has been edited; therefore, all data in the Transaction Record is valid data.

OUTPUT

The output from the Update Program consists of a New Decathlon Master File and an Exception Report listing any errors which occur in the processing of the Transaction Records against the Old Decathlon Master File.

The format of the New Decathlon Master File is the same as the record format of the Old Decathlon Master File illustrated on page 4.60.

The format of the Exception Report is illustrated below.

PRINTER SPACING CHART

```
1
2 XX/XX/XX              UPDATE EXCEPTION REPORT                PAGE XØX
3
4    ATHLETE           TRANSACTION             TYPE
5    NUMBER                CODE             OF ERROR
6
7      XXX                  X           DUPLICATE MASTER RECORD
8      XXX                  X            INVALID TRANSACTION CODE
9      XXX                  X           NON-MATCHING MASTER RECORD
```

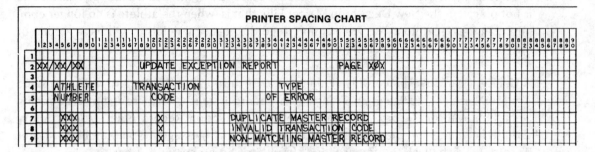

Note that the Exception Report contains the Athlete Number, the Transaction Code of the Transaction Record in error, and the Type of Error which has occurred.

PROCESSING

The processing which is to take place in the Update Program consists of three types of updating: Additions to the Decathlon Master File, Deletions from the Decathlon Master File, and Changes to the records in the Decathlon Master File. These processing tasks are explained below.

Additions

1. An addition takes place when a new record is added to the Decathlon Master File, that is, when a new athlete is added to the file. The Transaction Record to cause an addition will have a code of "A" in the Transaction Code field.

2. An addition can take place only if there is no current Decathlon Master Record with the same Athlete Number. If an Addition Transaction Record is read and there is a record on the Old Decathlon Master File with the same Athlete Number, then the Addition Transaction is in error; an entry should be made on the Exception Report with the message "Duplicate Master Record"; and the Addition Transaction should not be added to the Decathlon Master File.

3. If an Addition Transaction is read and there is no matching Decathlon Master Record, the addition should be added to the New Decathlon Master File. The Athlete Number, Athlete Name, and Coach Number will be taken directly from the Transaction Record. The Total Decathlon Score will be calculated by summing the ten Individual Event Scores in the Transaction Record and placing the total in the Total Decathlon Score of the New Decathlon Master Record.

Deletions

1. A deletion takes place when a record which is currently in the Old Decathlon Master File is not placed in the New Decathlon Master File, that is, when the athlete is no longer competing in the decathlon. The Transaction Record to cause a deletion will have a code of "D" in the Transaction Code field.

2. A deletion can take place only if there is a Decathlon Master Record with the same Athlete Number. If a Deletion Transaction Record is read and there is not a matching Decathlon Master Record, then the Deletion Transaction Record is in error; an entry should be made on the Exception Report with the message "Non-Matching Master Record," and the Deletion Transaction should not be processed further.

3. If a Deletion Transaction is read and there is a matching Decathlon Master Record, the matching Decathlon Master Record should not be written in the New Decathlon Master File. The only two fields required in the Transaction Record which causes a deletion to take place are the Athlete Number and the Deletion Transaction Code.

Changes

1. A change takes place when one or more fields in a record stored in the Old Decathlon Master File are to be changed. Changes can be made to either the Coach Number field or the Total Decathlon Score field or both. A Transaction Record to cause a change to take place must contain the Transaction Code "C."

2. A change can take place only if there is a Decathlon Master Record with the same Athlete Number as the Transaction Record. If a Change Transaction Record is read and there is not a matching Decathlon Master Record, then the Change Transaction is in error; an entry should be made on the Exception Report with the message "Non-Matching Master Record," and the Change Transaction should not be processed further.

3. A change to the Coach Number or a change to the Total Decathlon Score may take place.

   a. A change to the Coach Number field will take place when the Transaction Code in the Transaction Record is equal to "C" and the Coach Number field contains data. If the Coach Number field in the Transaction Record contains data, that is, is not equal to spaces, then the Coach Number in the Transaction Record should replace the Coach Number in the Decathlon Master Record.
   b. A change to the Total Decathlon Score field should take place if the Individual Event Fields in the Transaction Record are not blank, and the sum of the Individual Event Fields is greater than the Total Decathlon Score in the Decathlon Master Record. It should be noted that since the fields in the Transaction Record have been previously edited, there will never be a Transaction Record with non-numeric data or blanks imbedded within the Individual Event Scores. Thus, if columns 34-73 are not all blank, then the Individual Event Scores in the Transaction Record are valid numeric values.

4. A Change Transaction Record with the Transaction Code "C" may cause a change to the Coach Number in the Decathlon Master Record, a change to the Total Decathlon Score, or a change to both the Coach Number and the Total Decathlon Score. Therefore, both fields in the Transaction Record should be checked for each Change Transaction Record processed.

Invalid Transactions

1. The only valid codes in the Transaction Record are "A" (Addition), "D" (Deletion), and "C" (Change). If a Transaction Record does not contain one of the three codes, an entry should be made on the Exception Report with the message "Invalid Transaction Code."

CHAPTER 4

PROGRAMMING ASSIGNMENT 1A

INTRODUCTION

This programming assignment should be completed only if the Decathlon Master File in Chapter 2, Programming Assignment 1A was created. The Decathlon Master File created in Chapter 2, Programming Assignment 1 cannot be used for this programming assignment.

INSTRUCTIONS

A program is to be written which is to update the Decathlon Master File created in Chapter 2, Programming Assignment 1A. Design and write the COBOL program. Use a Hierarchy Chart, IPO Charts, and Pseudocode Specifications when designing the program.

INPUT

The input to the program is the Decathlon Master File created in Chapter 2, Programming Assignment 1A, and a Master Transaction File. The format of the Decathlon Master File created in Chapter 2, Programming Assignment 1A is illustrated below.

Decathlon Master File — Chapter 2, Programming Assignment 1A

FIELD	POSITION	NUMBER OF DIGITS	ATTRIBUTES
School Identification	1-3	3	Alphanumeric
Athlete Number	4-6	3	Numeric
Athlete Name	7-26	20	Alphanumeric
Coach Number	27-29	3	Numeric
100 Meters Score	30-33	4	Numeric
Long Jump Score	34-37	4	Numeric
Shot Put Score	38-41	4	Numeric
High Jump Score	42-45	4	Numeric
400 Meters Score	46-49	4	Numeric
110 Meter Hurdles Score	50-53	4	Numeric
Discus Score	54-57	4	Numeric
Pole Vault Score	58-61	4	Numeric
Javelin Score	62-65	4	Numeric
1500 Meters Score	66-69	4	Numeric
Best Score-100 Meters	70-73	4	Numeric
Best Score-Long Jump	74-77	4	Numeric
Best Score-Shot Put	78-81	4	Numeric
Best Score-High Jump	82-85	4	Numeric
Best Score-400 Meters	86-89	4	Numeric
Best Score-110 Meter Hurdles	90-93	4	Numeric
Best Score-Discus	94-97	4	Numeric
Best Score-Pole Vault	98-101	4	Numeric
Best Score-Javelin	102-105	4	Numeric
Best Score-1500 Meters	106-109	4	Numeric

The Decathlon Master File has a blocking factor of 20 records per block. It is stored in an ascending sequence by Athlete Number.

The format of the Master Transaction File, which is stored on punched cards, is illustrated below.

Master Transaction File

SCHOOL I.D.	ATHLETE NUMBER	ATHLETE NAME	COACH NUMBER		100 METERS	LONG JUMP	SHOT PUT	HIGH JUMP	400 METERS	110 METER HURDLES	DISCUS	POLE VAULT	JAVELIN	1500 METERS		CODE
1–3	4–6	7–26	27–29	30–33	34–37	38–41	42–45	46–49	50–53	54–57	58–61	62–65	66–69	70–73	74–79	80

Note from the Transaction Record format that the record contains the School Identification Code, the Athlete Number, the Athlete Name, the Coach Number, the Scores in each decathlon event reflecting the athlete's most recent competition, and a Transaction Code. The Transaction Code should contain one of three codes: "A" (Addition), "D" (Deletion), or "C" (Change). Thus, records in the Transaction File can be used to Add records to the Decathlon Master File, Delete records from the Decathlon Master File, or Change records in the Decathlon Master File. The Transaction File will already be sorted in an ascending sequence by Athlete Number prior to being read by the Update Program. All data in the Transaction Record has been edited; therefore, all data in the Transaction Record is valid data.

OUTPUT

The output from the Update Program consists of a New Decathlon Master File and an Exception Report listing any errors which occur in the processing of the Transaction Records against the Old Decathlon Master File.

The format of the New Decathlon Master File is the same as the record format for the Old Decathlon Master File illustrated on page 4.64.

The format of the Exception Report is illustrated below.

PRINTER SPACING CHART

```
XX/XX/XX         UPDATE EXCEPTION REPORT          PAGE XØX

   ATHLETE      TRANSACTION             TYPE
   NUMBER          CODE               OF ERROR

    XXX             X           DUPLICATE MASTER RECORD
    XXX             X           INVALID TRANSACTION CODE
    XXX             X           NON-MATCHING MASTER RECORD
```

Note that the Exception Report contains the Athlete Number, the Transaction Code of the Transaction Record in error, and the Type of Error which has occurred.

PROCESSING

The processing which is to take place in the Update Program consists of three types of updating: Additions to the Decathlon Master File, Deletions from the Decathlon Master File, and Changes to the records in the Decathlon Master File. These processing tasks are explained below.

Additions

1. An addition takes place when a new record is added to the Decathlon Master File, that is, when a new athlete is added to the file. The Transaction Record to cause an addition will have a code of "A" in the Transaction Code field.

2. An addition can take place only if there is no current Decathlon Master Record with the same Athlete Number. If an Addition Transaction Record is read and there is a record on the Old Decathlon Master File with the same Athlete Number, then the Addition Transaction is in error; an entry should be made on the Exception Report with the message "Duplicate Master Record"; and the Addition Transaction should not be added to the Decathlon Master File.

3. If an Addition Transaction is read and there is no matching Decathlon Master Record, the addition should be made to the New Decathlon Master File. The School Identification Code, Athlete Number, Athlete Name, Coach Number and Individual Event Scores will be taken directly from the Transaction Record. The Individual Event Scores should also be placed in the Best Scores for Each Event fields. Thus, for example, if the Individual Event Score for the 100 Meters in the Transaction Record was 800, the value 800 would be placed in both the Individual Event Score field in the Decathlon Master Record and the Best Score 100 Meters field in the Decathlon Master Record.

Deletions

1. A deletion takes place when a record which is currently in the Old Decathlon Master File is not placed in the New Decathlon Master File, that is, when the athlete is no longer competing in the decathlon. The Transaction Record to cause a deletion will have a code of "D" in the Transaction Code field.

2. A deletion can take place only if there is a Decathlon Master Record with the same Athlete Number. If a Deletion Transaction Record is read and there is not a matching Decathlon Master Record, then the Deletion Transaction Record is in error; an entry should be made on the Exception Report with the message "Non-Matching Master Record," and the Deletion Transaction should not be processed further.

3. If a Deletion Transaction is read and there is a matching Decathlon Master Record, the matching Decathlon Master Record should not be written in the New Decathlon Master File. The only two fields required in the Transaction Record which causes a deletion to take place are the Athlete Number and the Deletion Transaction Code.

Changes

1. A change takes place when one or more fields in a record stored in the Old Decathlon Master File are to be changed. Changes can be made to the School Identification Code, the Coach Number, or the Individual Event Scores. A Transaction Record to cause a change to take place must contain the Transaction Code "C."

2. A change can take place only if there is a Decathlon Master Record with the same Athlete Number as the Transaction Record. If a Change Transaction Record is read and there is not a matching Decathlon Master Record, then the Change Transaction is in error; an entry should be made on the Exception Report with the message "Non-Matching Master Record," and the Change Transaction should not be processed further.

3. A change to the School Identification Code, the Coach Number, or to the Individual Event Scores may take place.

   a. A change to the School Identification Code will take place when the Transaction Code is equal to "C" and the School Identification Code field in the Transaction Record contains data. If the School Identification Code field contains data, that is, it is not equal to spaces, then the School Identification Code in the Transaction Record should replace the School Identification Code in the Decathlon Master Record.

   b. A change to the Coach Number field will take place when the Transaction Code in the Transaction Record is equal to "C" and the Coach Number field contains data. If the Coach Number field in the Transaction Record contains data, that is, is not equal to spaces, then the Coach Number in the Transaction Record should replace the Coach Number in the Decathlon Master Record.

   c. A change to the Individual Event Scores in the Decathlon Master Record should take place when the Individual Event Fields in the Transaction Record are not blank, and the sum of the Individual Event Scores in the Transaction Record is greater than the sum of the Individual Event Scores in the Decathlon Master Record. It should be noted that since the fields in the Transaction Record have been previously edited, there will never be a Transaction Record with non-numeric data or blanks imbedded within the Individual Event Scores. Thus, if columns 34-73 are not all blank, then the Individual Event Scores in the Transaction Record are valid numeric values.

4. A Change Transaction Record with the Transaction Code "C" may cause a change to the School Identification Code, the Coach Number, or to the Individual Event Scores; or to two of these fields, or to all three of the fields with one record. Therefore, all fields in the Transaction Record should be checked for each Change Transaction Record processed.

Invalid Transactions

1. The only valid codes in the Transaction Record are "A" (Addition), "D" (Deletion), and "C" (Change). If a Transaction Record does not contain one of the three codes, an entry should be made on the Exception Report with the message "Invalid Transaction Code."

CHAPTER 4

PROGRAMMING ASSIGNMENT 1B

OVERVIEW – PROGRAMMING ASSIGNMENT 1B

This programming assignment utilizes the Decathlon Master File created in Chapter 2, Programming Assignment 1A, and may be undertaken as a single assignment together with Programming Assignment 1A in this chapter; or may be viewed as a problem in program maintenance, in which case the problem should be programmed only after Programming Assignment 1A in this chapter has been completely designed, coded, and tested.

The method of assigning the program is at the option of the instructor.

INSTRUCTIONS

A request for a modification to the program in Assignment 1A has been received by the data processing department. The requested change is:

1. The Best Scores fields in the Decathlon Master Record are to be updated. If any of the Individual Event Scores in a Change Transaction are greater than the Best Score for the respective event, then the Individual Event Score which is higher should replace the Best Score in the Master Record.

IMPLEMENTATION OF CHANGES

After considering the modification requested, it was decided to implement the change. Therefore, the clause on page 4.70 was added to the Processing Specifications from Program Assignment 1A.

Processing

3.d. A change to the Best Score field for a given event should take place if the Event Score in the Transaction Record is greater than the Best Score for the given event. For example, if the Best Score in the Decathlon Master Record for the 100 Meters was 800 and the 100 Meters Score in the Transaction Record was 900, then the Best Score for the 100 Meters in the Master Record (800) should be replaced by the score from the Transaction Record (900). All ten event scores should be compared to the corresponding Best Score in the Decathlon Master Record when the Event Scores in the Transaction Record are not blank. From zero to ten Best Scores in the Decathlon Master Record can be changed by this processing.

NOTE: The above processing is the only change to Programming Assignment 1A. If Programming Assignment 1A and 1B are given as a single programming assignment, all of the specifications in Programming Assignment 1A should be used in addition to the specification above. The input and output are the same as Programming Assignment 1A.

Indexed Sequential Access Method

"NEVER TRUST ANY DATA"[1]

INTRODUCTION

Sequential processing, as has been shown, involves processing records one after another. Due to the addressing scheme used on direct access devices, another type of processing called RANDOM PROCESSING is possible. Random processing is a means by which non-sequential records may be read, written, and processed. Devices such as card readers and tape drives cannot process records randomly because there is no way, for example, to read the fourth record in an input stream and then read the first record because the first record must be read first, followed by the second, third, fourth, etc.

Direct access devices, such as magnetic disks, offer the opportunity to read the fourth record in a file and then the first record in a file because the only thing governing which record is read is the record address.

A common type of file organization and processing used with direct access devices is the Indexed Sequential Access Method (ISAM). The Indexed Sequential Access Method, which is explained in this chapter, allows BOTH sequential and random access to a file.

FILE STRUCTURE

The records of an indexed sequential file are organized on the basis of a collating sequence determined by a specific control field or "key" within the record. An indexed sequential file exists in space allocated on the disk called PRIME data areas, OVERFLOW areas, and INDEX areas.

When an indexed sequential file is initially established on the disk, or "loaded," all data records are loaded into an area called the PRIME DATA AREA. The data in this area is available to be processed by both sequential and random access methods. Figure 5-1 illustrates this concept.

---

1 Brian W. Kernigan, P. J. Plauger, The Elements of Programming Style, Mc Graw-Hill, 1974.

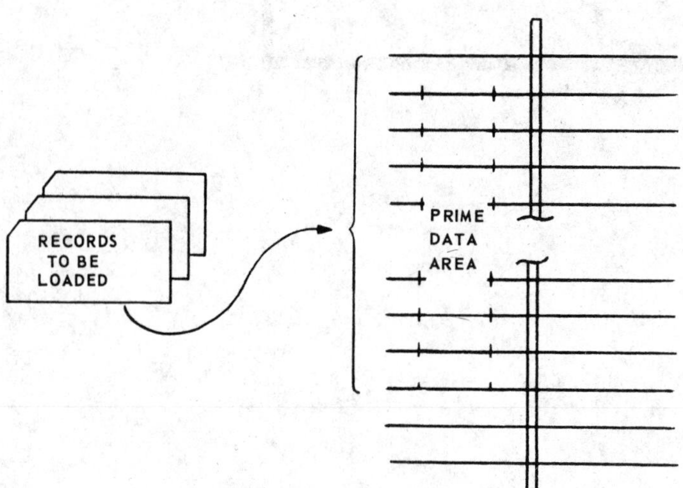

Figure 5-1 Prime Data Area

After the file is established, the user can ADD records without reorganizing the entire file as in sequential file organization. A new record added to an indexed sequential file is placed into a location on a track determined by the value of a "key" or control field in each record. To handle additions, an OVERFLOW AREA exists.

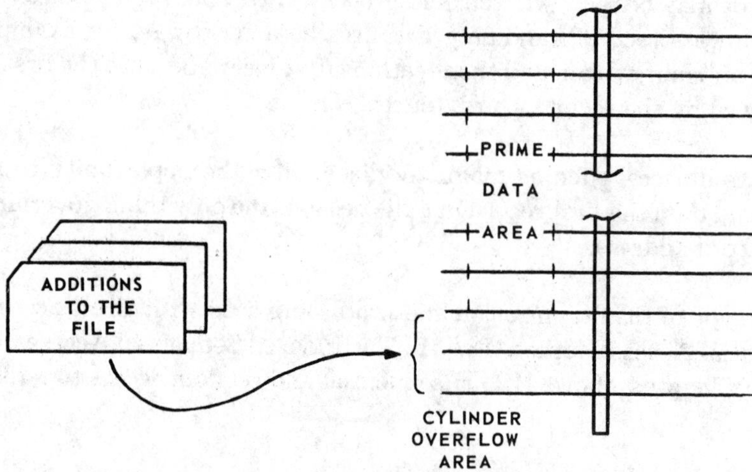

Figure 5-2 Cylinder Overflow Area

Two types of overflow areas may be used either separately or together — the cylinder overflow area and the independent overflow area. A CYLINDER OVERFLOW AREA is a track or tracks located on each cylinder within the prime data area. COBOL will allocate tracks on the device being used for the file. The INDEPENDENT OVERFLOW AREA is a separate area outside the prime area and is used strictly as an overflow area.

The following diagram illustrates the concept of the Prime Data area, the Cylinder Overflow area, and the Independent Overflow area as they appear on the disk.

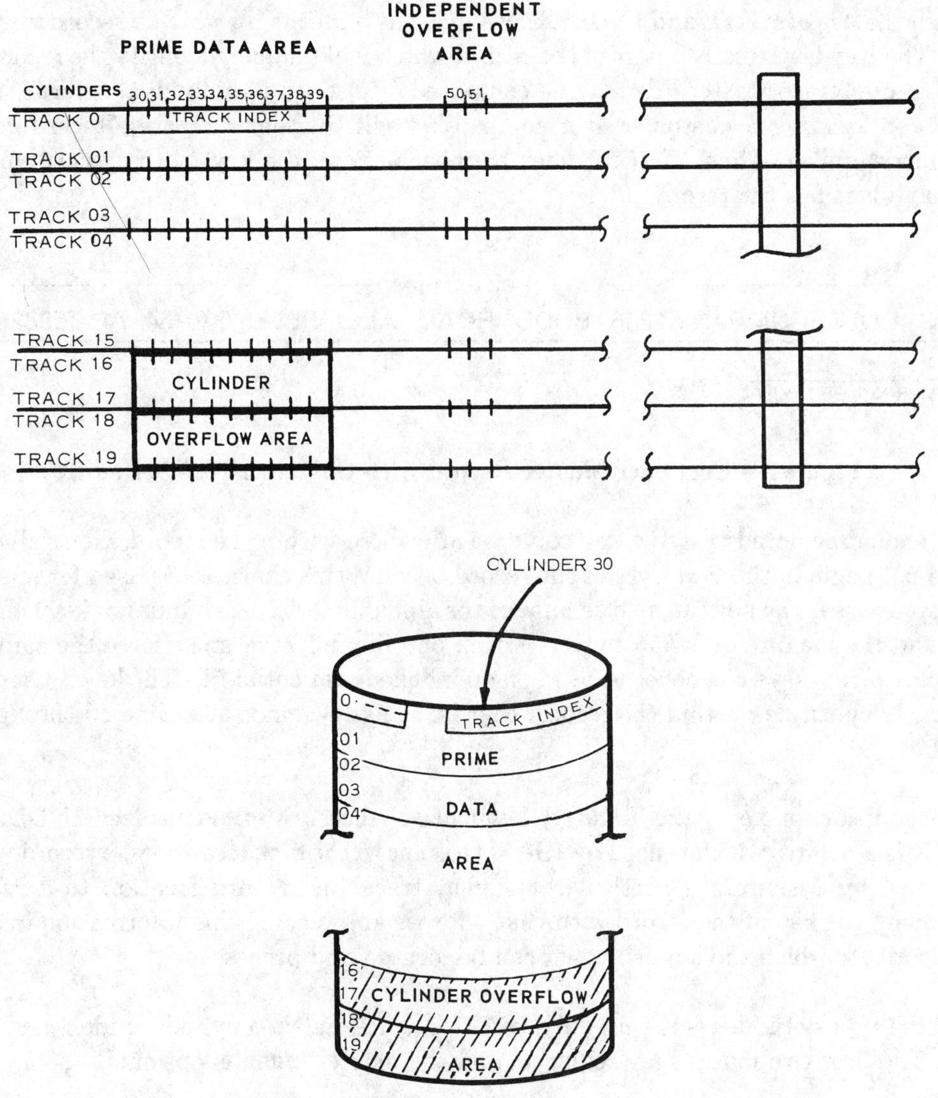

Figure 5-3 Prime Data Area and Overflow Area

In Figure 5-3, Cylinders 30-39 are assigned for the Prime Data area and the Cylinder Overflow area. Track 0 is used for the Track Index, and Tracks 0 through 15 can be used to store data when the file is loaded. Tracks 16 through 19 are assigned to the Cylinder Overflow area. Thus, on each cylinder, Tracks 16 through 19 will be used for overflow. Cylinders 50-51 are used as the Independent Overflow area. All twenty tracks (0-19) will be used for the Independent Overflow area.

KEYS AND INDEXES

The indexed sequential access method allows both sequential and random access to data through the use of KEYS and INDEXES. A KEY is a means by which a record may be identified. The Key is normally a part of the record which will uniquely identify the record. For example, a Customer Master File may be composed of a series of individual records, with each record representing a customer of a company. Each Customer Master Record contains a Customer Number. Thus, the Customer Number acts as the key to the record and always uniquely identifies the record.

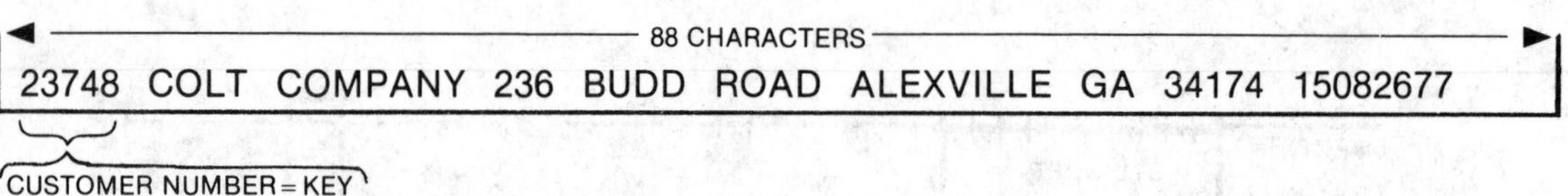

Figure 5-4 Customer Master Record with Customer Number as Key

It should be noted that the key could be anywhere within the record. Generally, the key should not begin in the first byte of the record because this character is used for special processing purposes. The key can also be numeric or alphanumeric. The minimum key length is one byte, and the maximum is 255 bytes. Within one file, all keys must have the same length. Duplicate prime keys can never be used on an indexed sequential file. The key must consist of consecutive positions within the record; that is, the key cannot be scattered throughout the record.

In addition to keys, the Indexed Sequential Access Method utilizes INDEXES. An INDEX is a pointer which is used by ISAM to point to the disk location of a record within the file. Thus, by assigning a particular cylinder, track and record location to a record and associating the key of the record with that address and placing this information in an index, any record for which the key is known can be located and processed.

Three types of indexes are used by ISAM: a track index, a cylinder index, and a master index. The first two indexes are required, and the master index is optional.

TRACK INDEX

The lowest level index used is the TRACK INDEX. A track index is built on every cylinder which is used in the indexed sequential file. Thus, if there were 10 cylinders used for the file, there would be 10 track indexes. The track index is built on the first track of each cylinder used in the file. Therefore, if the location of the prime data area of the file were Cylinder 30 Track 0 through Cylinder 39 Track 19, each cylinder (30, 31, 32, etc.) would have a track index on its Track 0. The track index is always contained on the cylinder for which it is the index, and it contains index entries for only the cylinder on which it resides (see Figure 5-1).

The format of the track index and a schematic of the data records as they are stored on disk is illustrated in Figure 5-5. Note that the track index consists of a series of entries for the prime data area and the overflow area for each track, with each of these entries containing a KEY entry and a DATA entry.

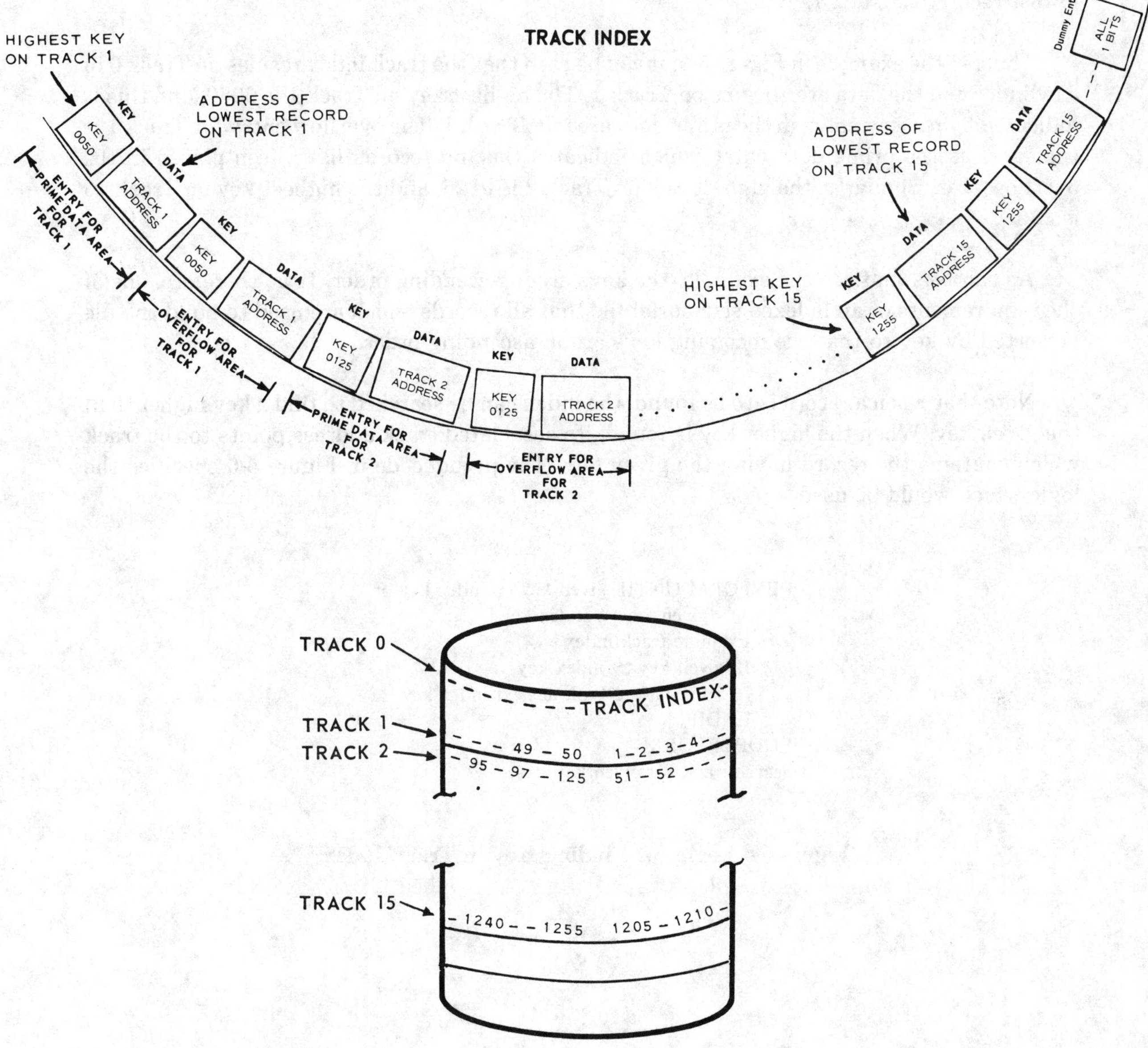

Figure 5-5 Track Index

The track index consists of two parts: (1) For the prime data area, the KEY entry in the track index specifies the HIGHEST KEY of a record on that track and the DATA entry specifies the ADDRESS of the LOWEST RECORD on that track; (2) For the overflow area, the KEY entry specifies the HIGHEST KEY associated with that track; and the DATA entry specifies the ADDRESS of the LOWEST RECORD in the overflow area. If no overflow entry has been made, the second entry is the same as the first entry.

The DATA entry labeled TRACK 1 ADDRESS uses a cylinder number and a track number to specify the address of the lowest record on a track. For example, in Figure 5-3, the basic entries in the TRACK 1 ADDRESS would include "Cylinder 30" (where Cylinder 30 is the cylinder for which the track index is used) and "Track 1." Since the first record on the track is always the lowest, this TRACK 1 ADDRESS entry would effectively "point" to the lowest record on Track 1.

Thus, in the example in Figure 5-5, it can be seen that the track index resides on Track 0 of a cylinder and the data area begins on Track 1. The highest key on Track 1 is 0050, and this is indicated by the key entry in the prime data area for Track 1. The overflow entry for Track 1 is the same as the prime data entry which indicates that no records have been placed in the overflow area. Similarly, the highest key on Track 2 is 0125, and the highest key on Track 15 is 1255.

As can be seen from the example, the keys are in ascending order. It is, therefore, one of the requirements of an indexed sequential file that all records which are used to build the file be sorted by key so that the incoming keys are in ascending order.

Note that when a record is to be found, the index can be searched to find a key higher than the given key. When the higher key is found, its associated track address points to the track which contains the record having the given key. The pseudocode in Figure 5-6 specifies the logic which would be used.

```
PERFORM UNTIL given key = index key or
        given key < index key
    Examine track index
    IF given key > index key
        Prepare to look at next index key
    ENDIF
ENDPERFORM
Search track for given key
```

Figure 5-6 Logic for Finding Key in Track Index

In the example below, the logic illustrated in Figure 5-6 is used to find a record. The record to be found has a key of 0095. Since the highest key on Track 1 is 0050, the next entry in the index is checked. It shows that the highest key on Track 2 is 0125. Therefore, the desired record resides on Track 2. The track is then read for the proper key, and the record can then be retrieved.

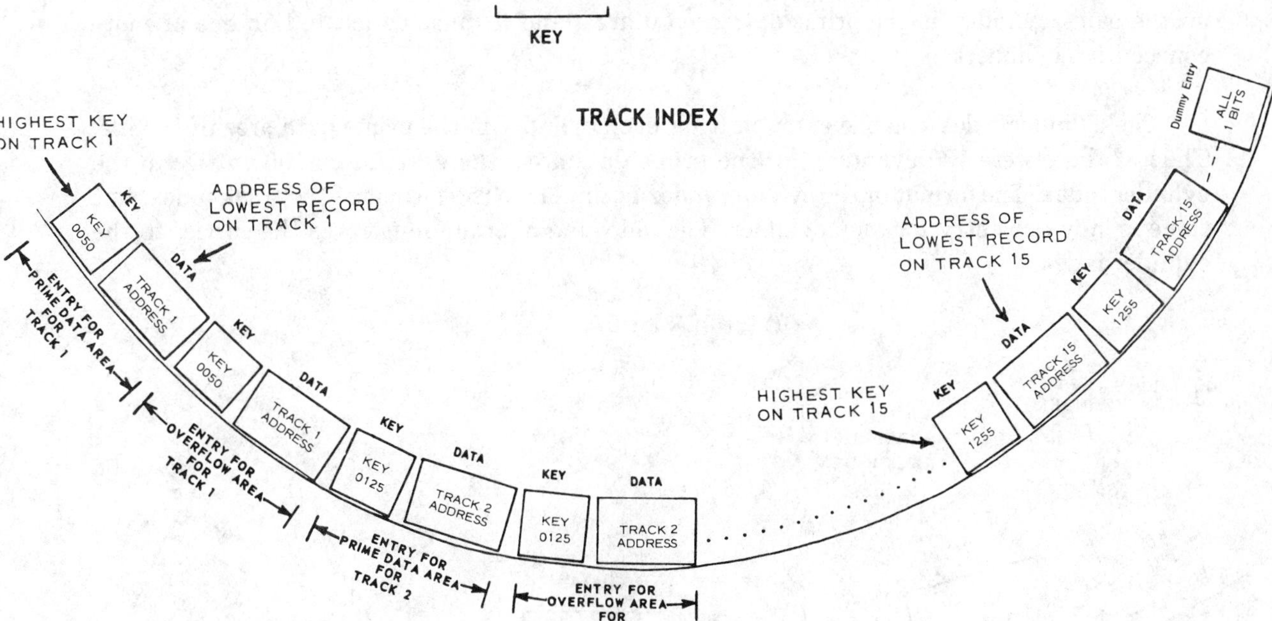

Figure 5-7 Record and Track Index

Note in the example that the last record in the track index is a dummy record which indicates the end of the track index — it is a record of all 1 bits. Therefore, to avoid any problems, a key should never be all 1 bits.

Note also that Track 15 is the last entry in the index when the file is organized — this is because of the cylinder overflow feature.

CYLINDER INDEX

The CYLINDER INDEX is the intermediate index used by the Indexed Sequential Access Method. It has a function similar to that of the track index, except that it points to the cylinders in the file rather than the tracks within the cylinder. The cylinder index is built on a separate area of the disk from the prime data and overflow areas. Job control statements are used to specify the cylinder(s) to be used for the cylinder index. The cylinder index cannot be on the same cylinder as the prime data record area, and it must be located on one or more consecutive cylinders.

The cylinder index has one entry in it for each cylinder in the prime data area of the file. Thus, if there were 100 cylinders for the prime data area, there would be 100 entries in the cylinder index. The format of the cylinder index is similar to the format of the track index, but there is only one entry for each cylinder. The following diagram illustrates the entries in the cylinder index.

CYLINDER INDEX

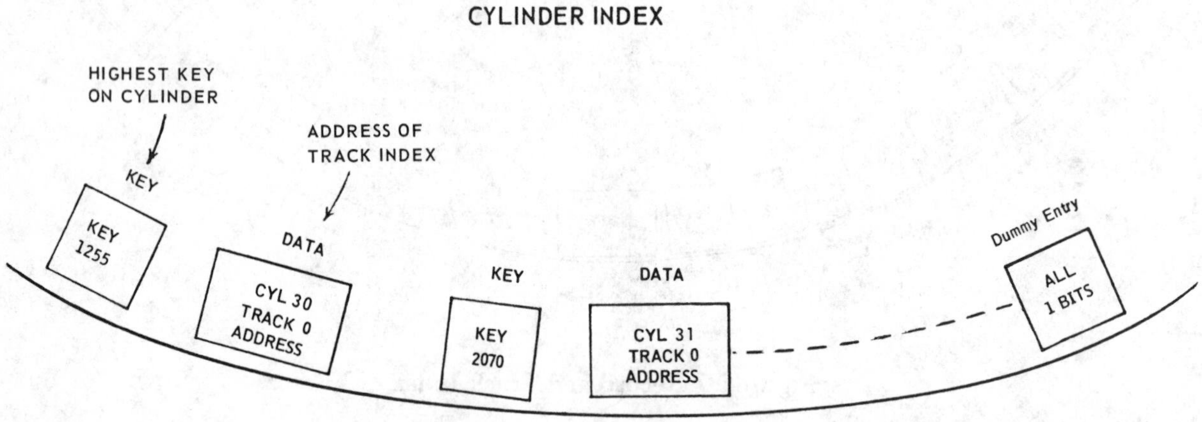

Figure 5-8 Cylinder Index

The entries in the cylinder index consist of the HIGHEST KEY OF A RECORD on the entire cylinder and the ADDRESS OF THE TRACK INDEX for that cylinder. The key area contains the highest key associated with the given cylinder. The data area contains the address of the associated track index. Thus, in the example, the highest key on Cylinder 30 is 1255 and the address of the track index is Cylinder 30 Track 0. The track index for Cylinder 30 is contained in Figure 5-5. The highest key on Cylinder 31 is 2070, and the address of the track index is Cylinder 31 Track 0. This example assumes the prime data area begins on Cylinder 30.

To retrieve Record 95, the cylinder index is searched using the same logic as illustrated in Figures 5-6 and 5-7. In the example, Record 95 would be compared to the first KEY entry in the cylinder index. Since Record 95 is less than 1255, the associated track index whose address is specified in the DATA portion of the first entry is searched in the manner shown previously. In this example, the track index would be found on Cylinder 30 Track 0.

MASTER INDEX

The master index is an optional index which can be used if desired by the programmer. It contains the track address of each track in the cylinder index and the highest key referenced by the corresponding track. Its use is not recommended unless the cylinder index is more than four tracks. This is because it is more efficient, time-wise, to search a 4-track cylinder index than it is to search a master index and then the 4-track cylinder index.

The master index is built on the device specified by job control statements. The master index must immediately precede the cylinder index on the disk volume. It may be more than one cylinder long.

MASTER INDEX

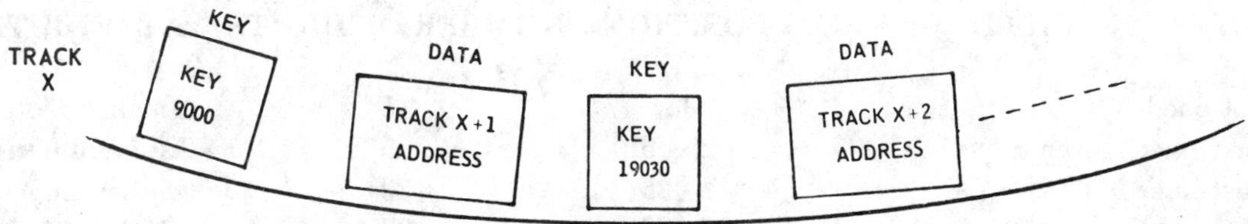

Figure 5-9 Master Index

The key portion of the master index specifies the highest key contained on a given track of the cylinder index, and the data portion of the master index contains the address of the track in the cylinder index. In the example above, the master index is located on Track X. Further, since the master index in the example is one track in length, and the cylinder index must immediately follow the master index, the first track of the cylinder index would be Track (X + 1). Thus, Track (X + 1) is specified in the data portion of the first entry in the master index.

By using these indexes, the indexed sequential access method can randomly retrieve any record for which the key is known. It can also process the records sequentially by beginning anywhere in the file (determined by key) and sequentially process the records by just reading the prime data and overflow areas. This flexibility of indexed sequential files makes it an extremely useful tool in many applications requiring diversified usage of the data on the file.

SAMPLE PROBLEM

In order to illustrate the use of Indexed Sequential Files, the sample program in this chapter is designed to load a Customer Master File which is to be stored as an indexed sequential file. After the Customer Master File is loaded, a Customer Master File List report will be printed, listing all of the records in the Customer Master File. The following chapter, Chapter 6, will then illustrate the random updating of the Customer Master File.

Output — Customer Master File

The format of the Customer Master File, which is to be stored on disk as an indexed sequential file, is illustrated below.

Customer Master File

FIELD	POSITION	NUMBER OF DIGITS	ATTRIBUTES
Not used	1	1	Blank
Customer Number	2 - 6	5	Alphanumeric
Customer Name	7 - 26	20	Alphanumeric
Customer Address	27 - 53	27	Alphanumeric
Customer City	54 - 73	20	Alphanumeric
Customer State	74 - 75	2	Alphanumeric
Customer Zip Code	76 - 80	5	Numeric
Customer Discount	81 - 82	2	Numeric
Last Activity Date	83 - 88	6	Numeric

File Information: Record Length — 88 characters
Blocking Factor — 20 records per block
Storage Medium — Disk
Organization — Indexed Sequential
Access — Sequential

Figure 5-10 Format of Customer Master File

As can be seen from Figure 5-10, the record contains 88 characters and is blocked 20 records per block. The file will be stored on disk using the Indexed Sequential organization.

The first position in the Customer Master Record is not used to store customer data. Instead, it is left blank when the master record is created. This position will be used when the Customer Master File is updated (Chapter 6) to contain a special character indicating that the master record is logically deleted from the Customer Master File. Generally, the first position in a record which is stored in an indexed sequential file should not be used for data.

The remainder of the record contains the Customer Number, Customer Name, Customer Address, Customer City, Customer State, Customer Zip Code, Customer Discount, and Last Activity Date. The Customer Discount contains a numeric percentage discount for the customer, while the Last Activity Date is the date on which the customer last purchased merchandise from the company.

Input — Customer Transaction File

The input to the program is the Customer Transaction File from which the information for the Customer Master File will be taken. In the Customer Transaction File, there are two records required for each customer which is to be loaded into the Customer Master File. The format of these two records is illustrated below.

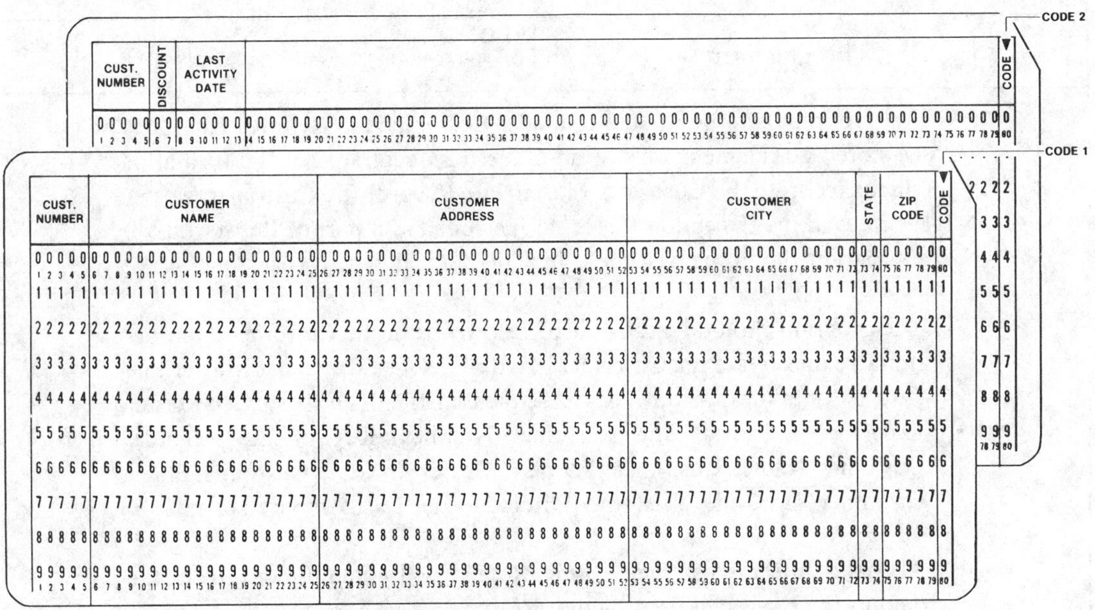

Figure 5-11 Format of Input Records

Note from Figure 5-11 that the data required to load the Customer Master File is contained in the two records illustrated. The first record contains the Customer Number, Customer Name, Customer Address, Customer City, Customer State, Customer Zip Code, and a Transaction Code of "1," indicating it is the first record of a two-record pair.

The second input record contains the Customer Number, Customer Discount, Last Activity Date, and a Transaction Code of 2, indicating the second record of the two-record pair. These two input records are both required in order to properly load a record in the Customer Master File.

Processing

The processing which is to occur within the program consists basically of reading a pair of records from the Customer Transaction File, editing these records to ensure that they contain valid data, and then formatting and writing the Customer Master Record in the Customer Master File, which is stored as an indexed sequential file. Those input records which do not pass the input edit are not to be placed in the Customer Master File; rather, they are to appear on an Exception Report. The exact processing which is to occur within the program is explained in the Programming Specifications below and on the following pages.

PROGRAMMING SPECIFICATIONS

SUBJECT	DATE	PAGE 1 OF 3
Load Customer Master File	June 2	
TO	**FROM**	
Programmer	Systems Analyst	

A program is to be written to load a Customer Master File. The file is to be stored on magnetic disk as an indexed sequential file. The format of the input records, the Customer Master File Record, the Customer Master File List, and the Exception Report are included as a part of this narrative. The program should be written to include the following processing.

1. The program should read a pair of records from the Customer Transaction File and create the Customer Master File. The Customer Master File is to be organized as an indexed sequential file. The Customer Master Record will contain the Customer Number (Key of the Record), Customer Name, Customer Address, Customer City, Customer State, Customer Zip Code, Customer Discount, and Last Activity Date.

2. All fields in the Customer Master Record will come directly from the data in the Customer Transaction Records.

3. The Customer Transaction File must be sorted by Transaction Code within Customer Number.

4. Before this information in the Transaction Records is used to build the Customer Master File, the data in the input records must be edited. If the data in the Transaction Records passes the editing criteria established in these specifications, then the data can be used to create the Customer Master Record. If any of the editing tests is not met by the data in the Transaction Records, then the input records for that Customer must not be used for the Customer Record. Instead, the records should be reported on the Exception Report.

5. The following editing should be performed on the Transaction Records:

   a. The Transaction Code in the Transaction Records must be "1" or "2." If a record contains any other Transaction Code, it should not be used.

Figure 5-12 Programming Specifications (Part 1 of 3)

PROGRAMMING SPECIFICATIONS		
SUBJECT Load Customer Master File	**DATE** June 2	**PAGE** 2 **OF** 3
TO Programmer	**FROM** Systems Analyst	

b. There must be both a Type 1 and Type 2 input record for each customer. If both records are not present for each customer, an error message is to appear on an Exception Report; and the records are not to be placed in the Customer Master File. Further editing need not be performed.

c. The Customer Number must be numeric and satisfy a Modulus 11 check.

d. The Customer Name, Address, City, and State fields must not be blank.

e. The State Code must be one of the valid 51 state codes (50 states and the District of Columbia).

f. The Zip Code must be numeric.

g. The Customer Discount field must be numeric and must not be greater than 20 %.

h. The Last Activity Date must be numeric, and the month must not be less than 01 or greater than 12. The day of the month in the Transaction Record must not exceed the maximum days in that month.

i. The Customer Transaction Records must be in ascending sequence by Customer Number. If they are not, an entry should be made on the Exception Report.

j. There can be no duplicate Master Records. Therefore, if two pairs of Transaction Records with the same Customer Number are found, only one pair should be loaded. The error should be reported on the Exception Report.

6. All fields in each pair of Transaction Records should be checked provided there is a valid pair of records.

7. If any field is found to be in error, the appropriate entry should be made on the Exception Report. The fields on the Exception Report are explained below.

Figure 5-13 Programming Specifications (Part 2 of 3)

PROGRAMMING SPECIFICATIONS		
SUBJECT Load Customer Master File	**DATE** June 2	**PAGE** 3 **OF** 3
TO Programmer	**FROM** Systems Analyst	

a. Customer Number — This field should contain the Customer Number of any record which contains one or more errors. It is to be group-indicated on the report; that is, if a single input record contains more than one error, the Customer Number should appear for the first error on the first line only.

b. Field in Error — This field should identify the field which contains the error. If the error concerns the fact that there is a Type 1 record but no Type 2 record, or a Type 2 record but no Type 1 record, the Field in Error should be specified as "Customer Records."

c. Type of Error — This field indicates the type of error which has been found in the input record.

d. Format of the Report — The report headings and other formatting should be printed as illustrated on the accompanying printer spacing chart.

e. The maximum number of detail lines on a single page of the Exception Report is forty (40) lines.

8. The Customer Master File list report should be printed after the Customer Master File has been completely created. The report should contain all of the data in the Customer Master File as illustrated on the accompanying printer spacing chart. The report format and headings should be printed as shown on the printer spacing chart. The maximum number of detail lines on a single page of the report is twenty (20) lines.

9. The program should be written in COBOL.

Figure 5-14 Programming Specifications (Part 3 of 3)

Program Reports

As noted in the Programming Specifications, there are two reports which are created in this program — the Exception Report which indicates the errors which may have occurred in the input data, and the Customer Master File List report which lists all of the records in the Customer Master File after the file has been created.

The printer spacing chart for the Exception Report is illustrated below.

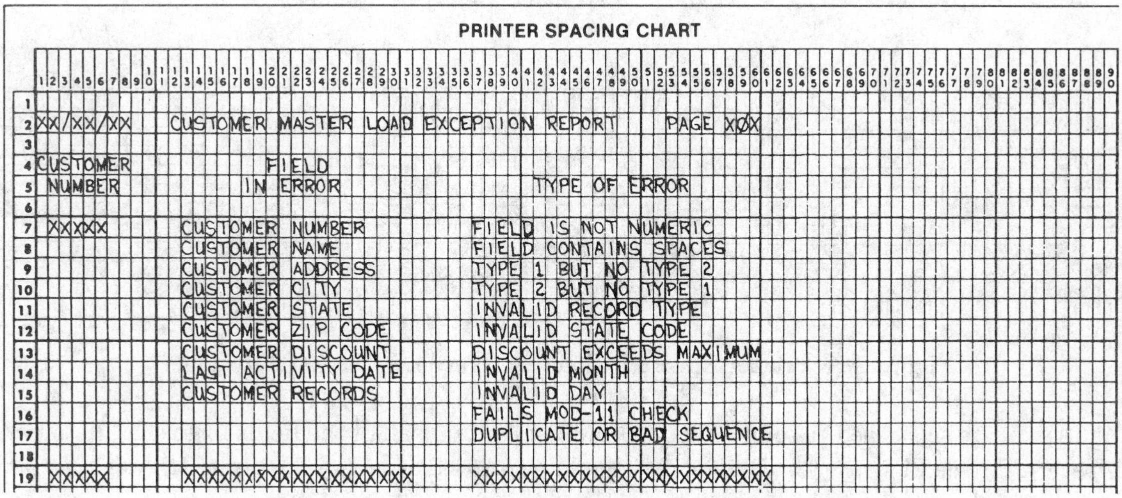

PRINTER SPACING CHART

```
 1
 2 XX/XX/XX   CUSTOMER MASTER LOAD EXCEPTION REPORT    PAGE XØX
 3
 4 CUSTOMER           FIELD
 5  NUMBER          IN ERROR                TYPE OF ERROR
 6
 7  XXXXX      CUSTOMER NUMBER         FIELD IS NOT NUMERIC
 8             CUSTOMER NAME           FIELD CONTAINS SPACES
 9             CUSTOMER ADDRESS        TYPE 1 BUT NO TYPE 2
10             CUSTOMER CITY           TYPE 2 BUT NO TYPE 1
11             CUSTOMER STATE          INVALID RECORD TYPE
12             CUSTOMER ZIP CODE       INVALID STATE CODE
13             CUSTOMER DISCOUNT       DISCOUNT EXCEEDS MAXIMUM
14             LAST ACTIVITY DATE      INVALID MONTH
15             CUSTOMER RECORDS        INVALID DAY
16                                     FAILS MOD-11 CHECK
17                                     DUPLICATE OR BAD SEQUENCE
18
19  XXXXX      XXXXXXXXXXXXXXXXXXXX    XXXXXXXXXXXXXXXXXXXXXXXX
```

Figure 5-15 Printer Spacing Chart — Exception Report

From the report format illustrated above, it can be seen that the Customer Number, the Field in Error, and the Type of Error are contained on the Exception Report. The Customer Number is group-indicated on the report.

The Field in Error contains all of the fields which can contain errors when the Customer Transaction Record is edited. The constant "Customer Records" should be used with the errors, "Type 1 But No Type 2," and "Type 2 But No Type 1."

The Type of Error field specifies the type of error which has occurred. It should be noted that in the printer spacing chart, the constants in the Type of Error field are not horizontally aligned with the Field in Error constants.

The Customer Master File List report is printed after the Customer Master File has been created. The printer spacing chart for this report is illustrated below.

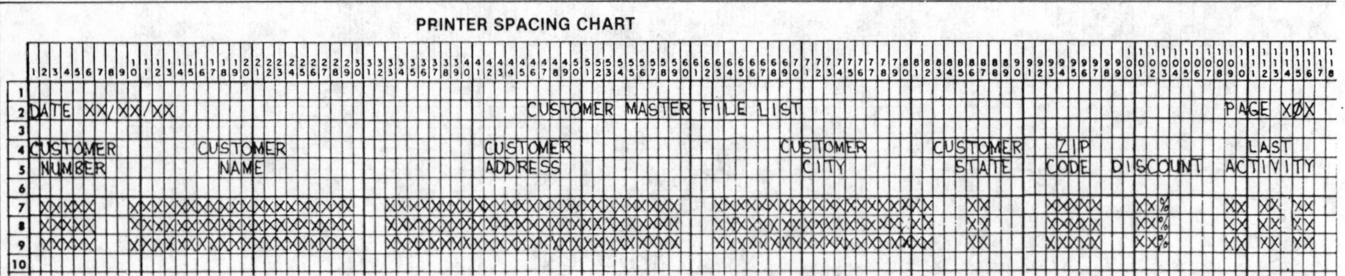

Figure 5-16 Printer Spacing Chart — Customer Master File List

As can be seen, the Customer Master File List contains all of the fields from the Customer Master File (see Figure 5-10). This report should be printed after the Customer Master File has been created.

PROCESSING MULTIPLE RECORD TYPES

As indicated by the Programming Specifications (see Figure 5-12 through Figure 5-14), the sample problem requires the processing of multiple record types; that is, the Transaction File contains records with a Transaction Code equal to "1" and records with a Transaction Code equal to "2." The basic processing required for multiple records types in the sample problem is explained below.

1. A record is read and verified as being a Type 1 record.

2. If the first record of the pair is a Type 1 record, the second record of the pair is read and verified as being a Type 2 record with a Customer Number equal to the Customer Number in the Type 1 record.

Thus, two basic conditions must be met for normal processing to take place: A Type 1 record must be the first record of a pair of records; and a Type 2 record must be the second record of a pair of records with a Customer Number equal to the Customer Number found in the Type 1 record. These two conditions are illustrated in Figure 5-17.

Example-Multiple Record Processing

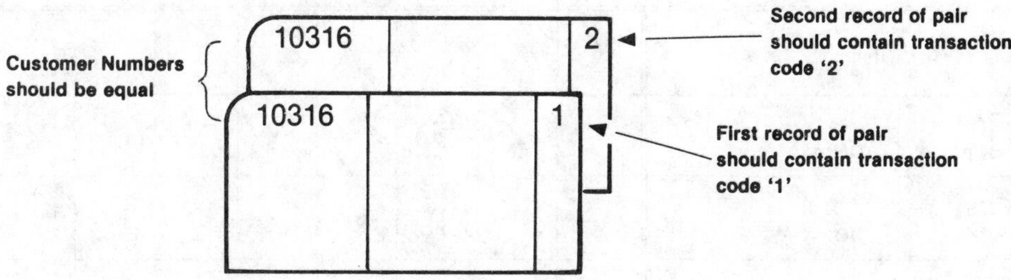

Figure 5-17 Example-Multiple Record Processing

In the example above, it can be seen that the first record of the pair contains a Transaction Code 1 and the second record of the pair contains a Transaction Code 2. In addition, the Customer Number in the first record of the pair with Transaction Code 1 is equal to the Customer Number in the second record of the pair with Transaction Code 2. Therefore, the two records illustrated above are valid; and, assuming the other data in the records passes the editing criteria, these two records would be used to build a Customer Master Record.

Whenever processing multiple record types, there are a number of error conditions which can occur and which the programmer must account for when designing the logic of the program. For example, if the second record in the pair of records contains a Transaction Code 1, an error has occurred and the proper processing must take place to handle this type of error.

When there are a number of conditions which may occur within the logical processing of data, it is many times difficult to keep in mind all of the different combinations which may occur. At the same time, it is extremely important to be able to identify and process all possible conditions that may occur so that the logic of the program may properly process all input data and reliably produce output under all circumstances. When there are a number of conditions, one tool which may be used to clarify the action which is to be taken under certain conditions is the Decision Table.

Decision Tables

A Decision Table is a graphical representation of the logical decisions which must be made concerning certain conditions which can occur within a program. In a Decision Table, both the Conditions which must be tested and the Actions which will be taken are graphically illustrated. The Conditions which may occur are placed in the upper left-hand portion of the Decision Table, while the Actions to be taken are specified in the lower left-hand portion of the Decision Table. This is illustrated in Figure 5-18 where the Decision Table for the Multiple Record Processing is shown.

		1	2	3	4	5	6	7	8	9	10
CONDITIONS	No Record From Pair	X									
	Result of First Record Check: Type = 1		X			X	X	X	X		X
	Result of First Record check: Type = 2			X							
	Result of First Record Check: Type Not = 1 or 2				X						
	Result of Second Record Check: Type = 2 Cust Numbers =					X					
	Result of Second Record Check: Type = 2 Cust Numbers ≠						X				
	Result of Second Record Check: Type = 1							X			
	Result of Second Record Check: Type Not = 1 or 2								X		
	End of File — Reading First Record									X	
	End of File — Reading Second Record										X
ACTIONS	Write "Type 1 But No Type 2"						X	X	X		X
	Write "Type 2 But No Type 1"			X			X				
	Write "Invalid Record Type"				X				X		
	Read First Record of Pair	X		X	X		X		X		
	Check First Record of Pair For Type = 1	X		X	X		X	X	X		
	Read Second Record of Pair		X								
	Check Second Record of Pair For Type = 2 and Equal Customer Numbers		X								
	Exit Module					X				X	X

Figure 5-18 Decision Table

In Figure 5-18, it can be seen that the Decision Table consists of a set of Conditions in the upper-left portion of the table and a series of Actions in the lower-left portion of the table. The numbers across the top of the Decision Table are called Rules. The Rules columns contain both the Conditions and Actions which are to be taken. For example, the Condition for Rule 2 is "Result of First Record Type: Type = 1." The Action for Rule 2 is "Read Second Pair of Records" and "Check Second Record of Pair." Note that an "X" is placed in each Condition and Action which is to occur within the rule.

Another example is Rule 8. The conditions of Rule 8, as indicated by the X's in the column, are "Result of First Record Check: Type = 1" and "Result of Second Record Check: Type Not = 1 or 2." The Actions to be taken when these conditons are found are "Write 'Type 1 But No Type 2'," "Write 'Invalid Type'," "Read First Record of Pair," and "Check First Record of Pair."

In order to develop a Decision Table, the programmer would list all of the different types of conditions which can occur in the Conditions portion of the Decision Table, and then list all of the Actions which can occur in the Actions portion of the Decision Table. The Rules are then developed by asking which Condition or Conditions can occur either singly or in combination with other conditions, and what should the Actions be when these conditions occur. It will be noted from Figure 5-18 that there are 10 rules which must have actions. Some of them (Rules 1-4) are conditions which occur by themselves, while others (Rules 5-10) are conditions which occur in combination with other conditions.

By specifying these conditions, actions, and rules in the Decision Table, the programmer is able to identify the processing which should occur under certain conditions and is more able to ensure that valid processing will take place within the program.

In order to explain the processing which must occur when multiple record types are being processed within the sample program, each of the rules is examined below with examples.

DECISION TABLE RULE 1

CONDITION: No Record from Pair
ACTION: Read First Record of Pair
Check First Record of Pair for Type 1

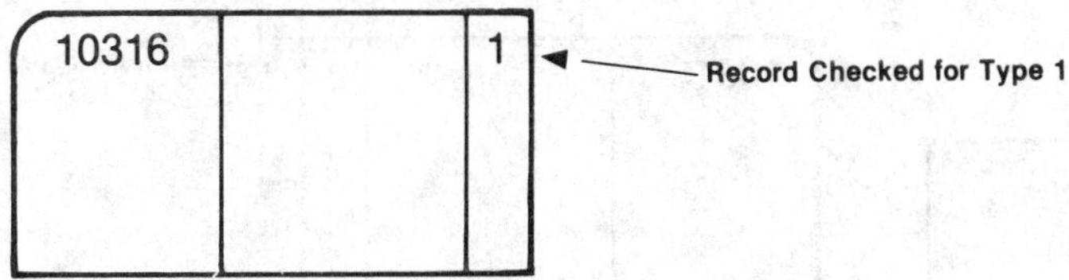

Figure 5-19 Decision Table Rule 1

The first rule in the decision table states that when no record from a pair of records has been read, the first record of the pair should be read and the record read should be checked for Type 1. This condition will occur each time the module which performs this checking is entered.

DECISION TABLE RULE 2

CONDITION: Result of First Record Check: Type = 1
ACTION: Read Second Record of Pair
Check Second Record of Pair for Type 2 and Equal Customer Numbers

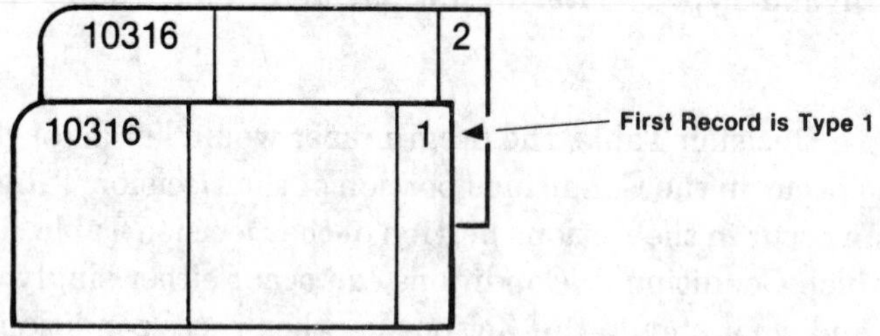

Figure 5-20 Decision Table Rule 2

In the example above for Decision Table Rule 2, the condition states that the result of the first record check is the first record is a Type 1 record. This means that the first record of the pair is a valid first record. Therefore, the action to be taken is to read the second record of the pair and determine if it is a Type 2 record and also that the Customer Number in the second record is equal to the Customer Number in the first record.

DECISION TABLE RULE 3

CONDITION: Result of First Record Check: Type = 2
ACTION: Write "Type 2 But No Type 1"
Read First Record of Pair (next pair)
Check First Record of Pair For Type 1

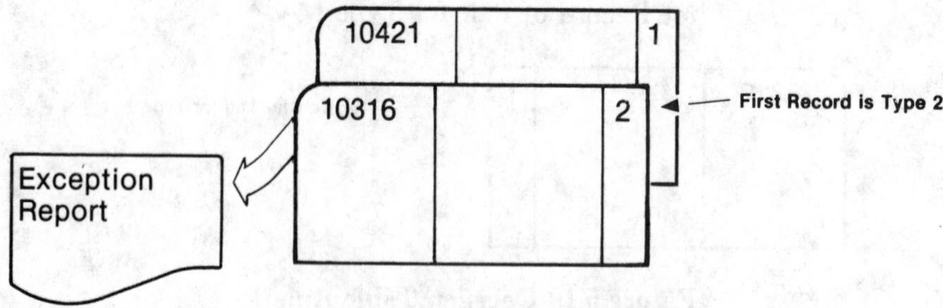

Figure 5-21 Decision Table Rule 3

When the first record of the pair contains a Record Type of 2, it indicates that there is a Type 2 record for a pair but there is no Type 1 record for the pair. Therefore, the message "Type 2 But No Type 1" is written on the Exception Report. Since no valid first record has been found, another first record must then be read and checked.

DECISION TABLE RULE 4

CONDITION: Result of First Record Check: Type Not = 1 or 2
ACTION: Write "Invalid Record Type"
Read First Record of Pair
Check First Record of Pair for Type 1

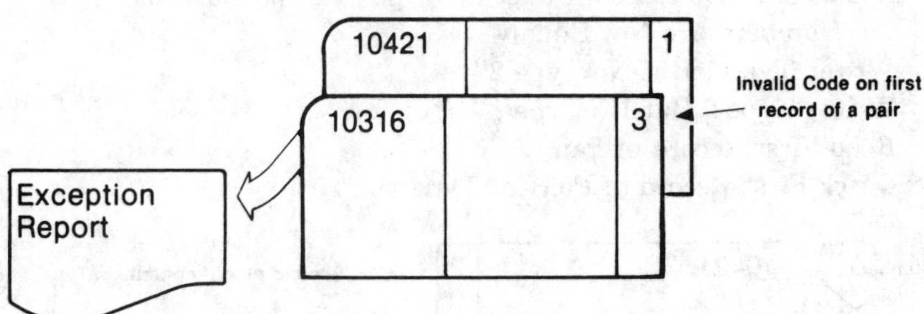

Figure 5-22 Decision Table Rule 4

When the first record is read and the Type is not equal to "1" or "2," then the first record contains an invalid record type and is not a valid first record. Therefore, the "Invalid Record Type" message is printed on the Exception Report; and another record must be read in order to find a valid first record.

DECISION TABLE RULE 5

CONDITION: Result of First Record Check: Type = 1
Result of Second Record Check: Type = 2 and
Customer Numbers are Equal
ACTION: Exit Module (Normal Processing — Master Record Will Be Written)

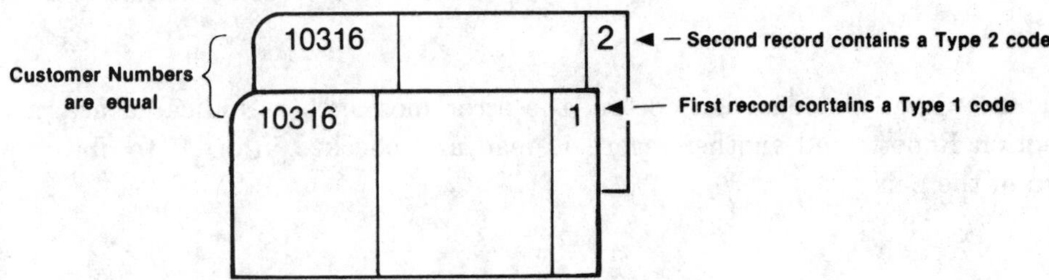

Figure 5-23 Decision Table Rule 5

In the example in Figure 5-23, it can be seen that the first record is a Type 1 record and the second record is a Type 2 record. In addition, the Customer Numbers, 10316, are equal. This is the desired sequence of the Transaction Input Records and is the "normal" way in which the records will be read. When this sequence occurs, the module which is obtaining a valid pair of records, that is, the module which processes the records according to the Decision Table in Figure 5-18, will exit back to the module which called it because a valid pair of records have been obtained.

DECISION TABLE RULE 6

CONDITION: Result of First Record Check: Type = 1
Result of Second Record Check: Type = 2 and Customer Numbers Are Not Equal

ACTION: Write "Type 1 But No Type 2"
Write "Type 2 But No Type 1"
Read First Record of Pair
Check First Record of Pair for Type 1

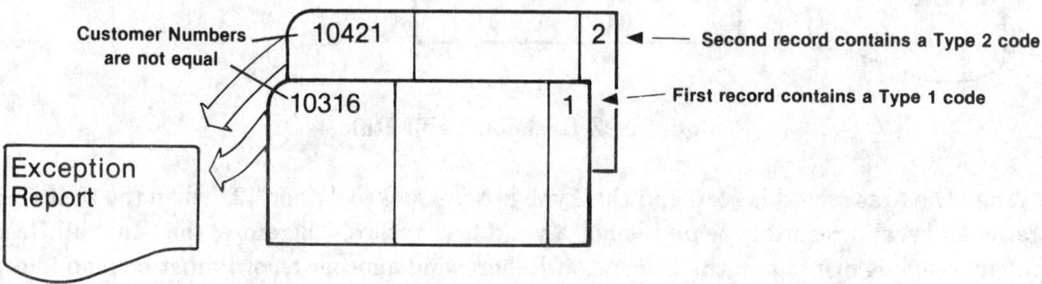

Figure 5-24 Decision Table Rule 6

When the first record is a Type 1 record and the second record is a Type 2 record but the Customer Numbers are not equal, it indicates that there is no Type 2 record for the Type 1 record (in the example, no Type 2 record for Customer Number 10316) and there is no Type 1 record for the Type 2 record (in the example, no Type 1 record for Customer Number 10421). The programmer must recognize this is true because the records are sorted in Transaction Code Sequence within Customer Number. Thus, in the example, there will not be a Type 1 record for Customer Number 10421 because if there were, it would be read before the Type 2 record.

Thus, when this condition occurs, the error messages as indicated are printed on the Exception Report; and another record is read and checked in order to obtain a valid first record of the pair.

DECISION TABLE RULE 7

CONDITION: Result of First Record Check: Type = 1
Result of Second Record Check: Type = 1
ACTION: Write "Type 1 But No Type 2"
Check First Record of Pair for Type 1

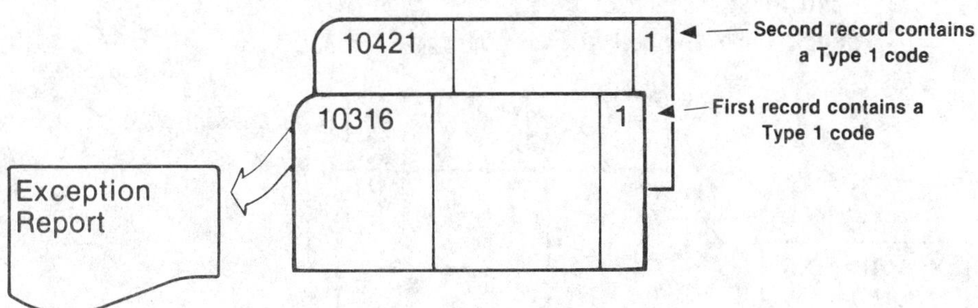

Figure 5-25 Decision Table Rule 7

Note in Figure 5-25 that the first record contains a Type 1 code, and the second record contains a Type 1 code. When this occurs, there will never be a matching Type 2 code for the first record; that is, there will never be a Type 2 record with Customer Number 10316. Therefore, the message "Type 1 But No Type 2" must be printed on the Exception Report. It should be noted that since the second record has a type = 1, there is the possibility that it is a valid "first record" of another pair. Therefore, another first record should not be read. Instead, the second record with type = 1 should be checked to determine if it is a valid first record. Again, when the second record of a pair contains a type code of 1, it may turn out that the record is a valid first record of the next pair; therefore, it should be checked to determine if it is a valid first record instead of reading another record and checking it.

DECISION TABLE RULE 8

CONDITION: Result of First Record Check: Type = 1
Result of Second Record Check: Type Not = 1 or 2
ACTION: Write "Type 1 But No Type 2"
Write "Invalid Record Type"
Read First Record of Pair
Check First Record of Pair for Type 1

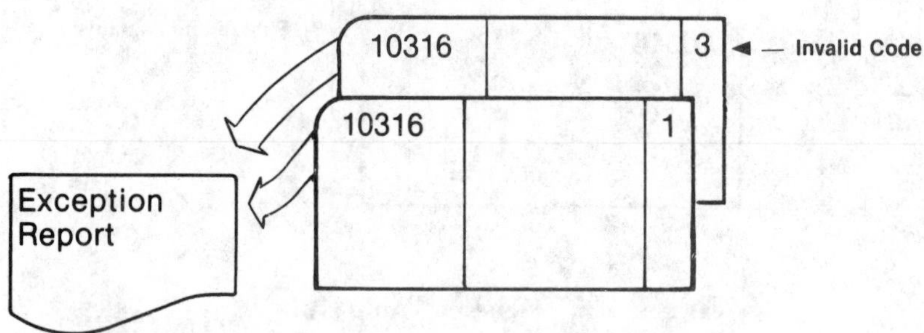

Figure 5-26 Decision Table Rule 8

Note in Figure 5-26 that the first record contains a Transaction Code of "1," but the second record contains a Transaction Code of "3." Therefore, there is a valid Type 1 Record but not a valid Type 2 Record. The messages written as a result of this condition indicate that there is a Type 1 but no Type 2 Record and that an invalid code has been found.

When this condition occurs, both of the records in Figure 5-26 have been processed. Thus, it is necessary to begin the search for a valid first record again by reading the first record of a pair and checking the first record of the pair for a Type 1 Record.

DECISION TABLE RULE 9

CONDITION: End-of-File — Reading First Record
ACTION: Exit module

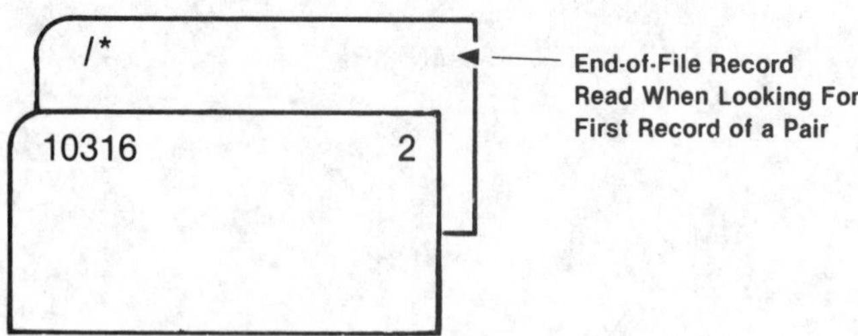

Figure 5-27 Decision Table Rule 9

In the example in Figure 5-27, the end-of-file record (/* in columns 1-2) is read when looking for the first record in a pair. When this occurs, it means that there is not a Type 1 record which has already been read and is ready to be processed because the search is for the first record. Therefore, there are no more input records to process and there are no error messages which should be printed. The module is exited, and it should not be reentered since there is no more data to be processed.

DECISION TABLE RULE 10

CONDITION: Result of First Record Check: Type = 1
End-of-File — Reading Second Record
ACTION: Write "Type 1 But No Type 2"
Exit Module

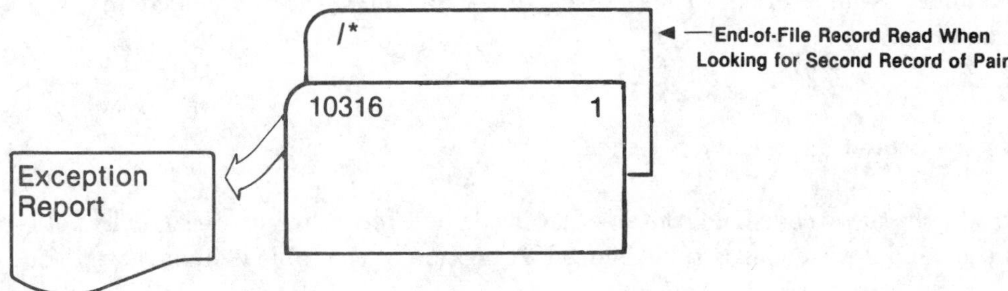

Figure 5-28 Decision Table Rule 10

In the example above, a Type 1 record was found but then the end-of-file record was read. Thus, there is a valid Type 1 record but no Type 2 record. This is the error indicated by the message which is printed. The module is exited because there are no more records to read. Control should not be returned to this module.

Summary

As can be seen from the previous examples, a decision table can be useful when numerous conditions can occur and the programmer must be able to specify an action to be taken under each of the conditions. The processing illustrated should be well-understood before continuing in the chapter because it is basic to the program design which will be presented later.

INPUT EDITING — SAMPLE PROBLEM

Three types of input editing are contained in the sample problem that have not been discussed in previous chapters. These techniques include several uses of tables in the editing process and the testing of a Check Digit on a numeric field.

It will be recalled from the programming specifications that the two character State field in the Type 1 record is to be checked to ensure that the field contains one of the 50 valid state codes (or "DC" for Washington, D. C.). In addition, the Last Activity Date field on the Type 2 record is to be checked to ensure that it contains a valid month; that is, the number of the month is not less than 01 or greater than 12, and that the day of the month in the Last Activity Date field is not greater than the number of days within the given month. Lastly, the programming specifications indicate that a Modulus 11 check-digit test should be performed on the Customer Number field. These three types of editing are explained in the following paragraphs.

Editing the State Code Field

To edit the State code field contained in the Type 1 record to ensure that the field contains one of the valid state codes, a table is used. A portion of the table is illustrated in the coding below.

EXAMPLE

```
 Ø1  PROGRAM-TABLES.
     Ø5  STATE-TABLE.
         1Ø  VALID-STATE-CONSTANTS.
             15  FILLER                PIC XX           VALUE 'AK'.
             15  FILLER                PIC XX           VALUE 'AL'.
             15  FILLER                PIC XX           VALUE 'AR'.
             15  FILLER                PIC XX           VALUE 'AZ'.
             15  FILLER                PIC XX           VALUE 'CA'.
             15  FILLER                PIC XX           VALUE 'CO'.
                       :
             15  FILLER                PIC XX           VALUE 'WV'.
             15  FILLER                PIC XX           VALUE 'WY'.
         1Ø  VALID-STATE-TABLE REDEFINES VALID-STATE-CONSTANTS
                                                        OCCURS 51 TIMES
                                                        ASCENDING KEY IS
                                                                STATE-CODE
                                                         INDEXED BY
                                                                STATE-CODE-INDEX.
             15  STATE-CODE            PIC XX.
```

Figure 5-29 Example of State Code Table

From Figure 5-29, it can be seen that each of the valid state codes is defined as a constant under the group VALID-STATE-CONSTANTS. The VALID-STATE-CONSTANTS group is then redefined with the name VALID-STATE-TABLE. VALID-STATE-TABLE occurs 51 times. The entries in the table can be referenced using the STATE-CODE elementary item plus the index STATE-CODE-INDEX. The table is written in alphabetical order by State Code, so it is in ascending sequence by STATE-CODE.

In order to determine if the State Code contained in the Transaction Record is a valid code, the VALID-STATE-TABLE must be searched using the State Code in the Transaction Record as the argument when searching. The statements in the Procedure Division to cause this searching to take place are illustrated in Figure 5-30.

EXAMPLE

```
Ø3304Ø     SEARCH ALL VALID-STATE-TABLE
Ø3305Ø         AT END
Ø3306Ø             MOVE CUSTOMER-NUMBER-TRANSORT1 TO
Ø3307Ø                         CUSTOMER-NUMBER-EXCP-WORK
Ø3308Ø             MOVE CUSTOMER-STATE-FIELD-MSG TO
Ø3309Ø                         FIELD-IN-ERROR-EXCP-WORK
Ø3310Ø             MOVE BAD-STATE-CODE-ERROR-MSG TO
Ø3311Ø                         TYPE-OF-ERROR-EXCP-WORK
Ø3312Ø             PERFORM UØØØ-WRITE-EXCEPTION-REPORT
Ø3313Ø             MOVE 'NO ' TO ARE-TRAN-RECORDS-VALID
Ø3314Ø         WHEN STATE-CODE (STATE-CODE-INDEX) =
Ø3315Ø                     CUSTOMER-STATE-TRANSORT1
Ø3316Ø             NEXT SENTENCE.
```

Figure 5-30 Example of Searching State Code Table

From the COBOL statements above, it can be seen that the VALID-STATE-TABLE is searched using the Search All Verb. It will be recalled that the Search All verb causes a "binary search" to take place on the table specified. If the Search All verb does not find a match between the STATE-CODE (STATE-CODE-INDEX) and the CUSTOMER-STATE-TRANSORT1 fields, the At End portion of the statement is executed.

As can be seen, if the At End Clause is executed, the Customer Number, Customer State Field Error Message, and Bad State Code Error Message are moved to the Exception Report Work Area; and the Exception Report is written.

If, on the other hand, a match is found, the "When" processing is executed. It merely specifies "Next Sentence" without any special processing. Thus, it can be seen that the table search is used only to determine if a given value is contained within the table, rather than extracting data as has been seen in previous programs.

It should be noted that a possible way in which the State Codes could be checked for validity would be to use Condition Names as has been done previously. The use of Condition Names, however, results in a sequential search of the State Codes. Therefore, an average search would require 25 comparisons to find the code. The binary search, though, requires a maximum of six comparisons to find the code. Thus, as the number of values which must be checked increases, the programmer should give consideration to using a table to verify valid values as opposed to condition names.

Editing the Date Field

In the Type 2 record, the Last Activity Date is recorded in the record in the form of Month, Day, and Year. Thus, an entry of 042978 would indicate the fourth month (April), the 29th day of 1978. The editing specifications require the verification of a valid Month, that is, a month number of 01 through 12; and a verification that the number of days in the month is not greater than possible for a given month (for example, 31 days in April is invalid).

Since the number of values to check is not large, the editing to determine if the Month field contains a valid Month Number (from 01 to 12) makes use of a condition name specifying the values 01 through 12. This condition name is then referenced in the Procedure Division to cause an error message to print on the Exception Report if the Month Number is not within a valid range. If the Month Number is within a valid range, normal processing would occur. A segment of the coding to edit the Month Number is illustrated below.

EXAMPLE

Data Division

```
       Ø5  LAST-ACTIVITY-DATE-TRANSORT2.
           1Ø  MONTH-LAST-ACTIVITY-TRANSORT2    PIC 99.
               88  VALID-MONTH                  VALUE Ø1 THRU 12.
           1Ø  DAY-LAST-ACTIVITY-TRANSORT2      PIC XX.
           1Ø  YEAR-LAST-ACTIVITY-TRANSORT2     PIC XX.
```

Procedure Division

```
           IF NOT VALID-MONTH
               MOVE CUSTOMER-NUMBER-TRANSORT2 TO
                           CUSTOMER-NUMBER-EXCP-WORK
               MOVE LAST-ACTIVITY-DATE-FIELD-MSG TO
                           FIELD-IN-ERROR-EXCP-WORK
               MOVE BAD-MONTH-ERROR-MSG TO TYPE-OF-ERROR-EXCP-WORK
               PERFORM UØØØ-WRITE-EXCEPTION-REPORT
               MOVE 'NO ' TO ARE-TRAN-RECORDS-VALID
           ELSE
```

Figure 5-31 Example of NOT Condition Name

From Figure 5-31, it can be seen that the field MONTH-LAST-ACTIVITY-TRANSORT2 is defined for the Month in the Last Activity Date field. The condition name VALID-MONTH is then specified for the values "01" through "12." Thus, if the MONTH-LAST-ACTIVITY-TRANSORT2 field contains the values "01" through "12," the condition will be considered true. If, however, the field does not contain these values, the condition will be considered not true.

In the Procedure Division coding, it can be seen that the statement using the condition name is "IF NOT VALID-MONTH." This statement is testing for the condition's not being true, that is, for the Month field containing a value not equal to "01" through "12." Thus, condition names can be used both to check a condition's being true and a condition's not being true.

If the condition is not true, then the Customer Number, Last Activity Field Message, and an error message are moved to the Exception Report Work Area and a line on the Exception Report is written. The indicator is then set to indicate that the record is not valid.

To edit the days in the Last Activity Date field to ensure that the days in the input record do not exceed the number of days for a given month, a table will be used which contains the number of the month and the number of days in each month. The table to check the number of days in the month is illustrated below.

EXAMPLE

```
       Ø5  MONTH-DAY-TABLE.
           1Ø  MONTH-DAY-CONSTANTS.
               15  FILLER          PIC X(4)     VALUE 'Ø131'.
               15  FILLER          PIC X(4)     VALUE 'Ø229'.
               15  FILLER          PIC X(4)     VALUE 'Ø331'.
               15  FILLER          PIC X(4)     VALUE 'Ø43Ø'.
               15  FILLER          PIC X(4)     VALUE 'Ø531'.
               15  FILLER          PIC X(4)     VALUE 'Ø63Ø'.
               15  FILLER          PIC X(4)     VALUE 'Ø731'.
               15  FILLER          PIC X(4)     VALUE 'Ø831'.
               15  FILLER          PIC X(4)     VALUE 'Ø93Ø'.
               15  FILLER          PIC X(4)     VALUE '1Ø31'.
               15  FILLER          PIC X(4)     VALUE '113Ø'.
               15  FILLER          PIC X(4)     VALUE '1231'.
           1Ø  MONTHS-AND-DAYS-TABLE REDEFINES MONTH-DAY-CONSTANTS
                                                OCCURS 12 TIMES
                                                INDEXED BY
                                                    MONTH-DAY-INDEX.
               15  MONTH-TABLE                PIC XX.
               15  NUMBER-OF-DAYS-IN-MONTH    PIC XX.
```

Figure 5-32 Example of Table for Day Check

From the table in Figure 5-32, it can be seen that the first two digits specified in the table are the number of the month (01 through 12). For each entry, the number of the month is followed by the number of days in the month. For example, for month 06 on pg/line 016170, the number of days specified is 30.

The constants are redefined using the name MONTHS-AND-DAYS-TABLE, which occurs 12 times. The number of days entries in the table can be referenced using the data-name NUMBER-OF-DAYS-IN-MONTH with the index MONTH-DAY-INDEX.

It should be noted that the number of the months specified as the first two digits in each entry within the table are merely used to document the entries in the table and will not be used in determining a valid value in the Day field in the input record. These month entries were included in the table to make it more readable for a maintenance programmer at some later time; a table with just the number of days is not nearly as clear as a table with both the number of the month and the number of days. Thus, whenever defining data in the Data Division, the programmer must constantly be aware of program clarity and readability.

The statements in the Procedure Division to perform the actual checking of the days in the transaction input record are illustrated below.

EXAMPLE

```
Ø3619Ø         SET MONTH-DAY-INDEX TO MONTH-LAST-ACTIVITY-TRANSORT2
Ø362ØØ         IF DAY-LAST-ACTIVITY-TRANSORT2 IS LESS THAN
Ø37Ø1Ø                 FIRST-DAY-OF-MONTH-NUMBER OR
Ø37Ø2Ø                 DAY-LAST-ACTIVITY-TRANSORT2 IS GREATER THAN
Ø37Ø3Ø                 NUMBER-OF-DAYS-IN-MONTH (MONTH-DAY-INDEX)
Ø37Ø4Ø             MOVE CUSTOMER-NUMBER-TRANSORT2 TO
Ø37Ø5Ø                     CUSTOMER-NUMBER-EXCP-WORK
Ø37Ø6Ø             MOVE LAST-ACTIVITY-DATE-FIELD-MSG TO
Ø37Ø7Ø                     FIELD-IN-ERROR-EXCP-WORK
Ø37Ø8Ø             MOVE BAD-DAY-ERROR-MSG TO TYPE-OF-ERROR-EXCP-WORK
Ø37Ø9Ø             PERFORM UØØØ-WRITE-EXCEPTION-REPORT
Ø371ØØ             MOVE 'NO ' TO ARE-TRAN-RECORDS-VALID.
```

Figure 5-33 Editing the Day Field

The first task when editing the day field for a proper value is to set the index so that the proper entry in the table will be examined. This is done by using the SET Verb, which sets the index MONTH-DAY-INDEX to the value in the field MONTH-LAST-ACTIVITY-TRANSORT2. Thus, the index used to examine the table illustrated in Figure 5-32 will contain the number of the month. It should be noted in Figure 5-31 that the field MONTH-LAST-ACTIVITY-TRANSORT2 must be defined as a numeric field since it is being used with the Set Verb.

After the index is set, the value in the DAY-LAST-ACTIVITY-TRANSORT2 field is compared to the FIRST-DAY-OF-MONTH-NUMBER field (with a value of "01" in the Working-Storage-Section) and to the number of days in the month as contained in the table. If the day in the Transaction Record is less than "01" or greater than the day found in the table, then it is in error and an entry will be printed on the Exception Report.

It should be noted that the Month Number is being used as the index to the table rather than "searching" the table by varying an index or subscript. This is a valid method to extract information from a table provided the value used for the index is numeric, is greater than zero, and is not greater than the number of entries in the table. Therefore, prior to using the month as the index in the example in Figure 5-33, the value in the Month field should be checked to ensure that it is numeric and that it contains a value greater than zero and equal to or less than 12.

Editing — Modulus 11 Check Digit

The previous examples of editing were primarily concerned with determining that the values contained within various fields to be checked were valid and correct in terms of content. There are also checks which may be applied to fields such as Customer Numbers or Employee Numbers to ensure, as much as possible, that no errors were made by the data entry operator when the data was transcribed from the source document to the input document. The errors by data entry operators are generally classed as transcription errors, where there is an error in copying a digit of a number; or transposition errors, where there is a "swapping" of numeric values. For example, a transcription error would occur when the number 2865 is copied on the input record as 2365. Transposition errors occur when two numbers are switched; for example, the number 2457 is copied as 2547.

The primary means used in data processing systems to find these types of errors is the use of a method known as "check digits." A check digit is a number which is appended to the normal number used for a particular function which will allow the program to test and ensure that the normal number is properly recorded. For example, assume a Customer Number consists of four digits and a check digit is to be appended to the number. The number would appear as illustrated below.

OLD CUSTOMER NUMBER = 6532

NEW CUSTOMER NUMBER = 65323 ← Customer Number With Check Digit

The fifth digit is the check digit and is used to ensure that all of the numbers in the Customer Number are properly recorded. This is quite important, for the Customer Number could act as the key for a record; and it is critical that there be no errors in the recording of the Customer Number from the source document to the input record.

There are a number of ways in which a check digit can be generated. The most accurate and widely used is known as the Modulus 11 check digit. The process of using a check digit includes the calculating of a unique digit from the original number and then placing this unique digit as the last character of the original number. In order to illustrate the use of a Modulus 11 check digit, the following example will be used.

EXAMPLE

Step 1: Assume that the old Customer Number was 6532. In order to calculate the Modulus 11 check digit and, therefore, the new Customer Number, the first step is to assign a "weight" to each of the digits in the old Customer Number. When using the Modulus 11 technique, "weights" are assigned to each of the digits of the Customer Number. The "weights" run from 2 through a possible maximum of 10, beginning with the low order position in the field. Therefore, the following weights would be assigned to the Customer Number.

CUSTOMER NUMBER: 6 5 3 2

WEIGHTS: 5 4 3 2

Note that beginning with the low-order digit, a weight — starting with 2 and increasing by 1 — is assigned from right to left. It must be noted that the weight assigned has no relationship to the value contained within the number to be checked; the weights are always the same, moving from right to left. It should also be noted that the maximum weight which can be assigned is 10. Thus, if there were more than nine digits in a number for which a check digit was to be calculated, the weights would start over with 2 being assigned the tenth digit in the number, and so on.

Step 2: After the weights have been assigned, each value within the number to be checked is multiplied by its weight.

CUSTOMER NUMBER:	6	5	3	2
WEIGHT:	x5	x4	x3	x2
RESULT:	30	20	9	4

Note from the example that each of the digits within the number to be check is multiplied by its respective weight.

Step 3: The results of the multiplication are added together.

$$30 + 20 + 9 + 4 = 63$$

Note that the sum 63 is derived by adding together the products of the multiplication of the values in`the number by their respective weights.

Step 4: The sum of the products of the multiplication is divided by the modulus number, in this case the number 11.

$$63 \div 11 = 5 \text{ with a remainder } 8$$

Step 5: The remainder is then subtracted from the modulus number, giving the check digit.

$$11 - 8 = 3$$

Therefore, the Modulus 11 check digit for Customer Number 6532 is 3. The new Customer Number to be used would then be 65323.

Check Digit "X"

With some numbers, the character "X" is appended to a number as the check digit. This occurs when the value calculated for the check digit is 10. As only a single digit can be appended to a number, an "X" is used as the check digit when using the Modulus 11 check. This is illustrated in the example on page 5.34

EXAMPLE

Step 1: Weights are assigned to a number.

CUSTOMER NUMBER:	6	5	2	0
WEIGHT:	5	4	3	2

Step 2: Each value within the number to be checked is multiplied by its weight.

CUSTOMER NUMBER:	6	5	2	0
WEIGHT:	x5	x4	x3	x2
RESULT:	30	20	6	0

Step 3: The results of the multiplication are added together.

$$30 + 20 + 6 + 0 = 56$$

Step 4: The sum of the products of the multiplication is divided by the modulus number, in this case, the number 11.

$$56 \div 11 = 5, \text{ with a remainder } 1$$

Step 5: The remainder is then subtracted from the modulus number.

$$11 - 1 = 10$$

Note in this example, the check digit is 10. When 10 is the check digit, an "X" is appended to the number as the check digit. The Customer Number becomes 6520X in this example.

Because a number of calculations must be performed to generate a check digit, a computer program will normally be written which will convert a given control field without a check digit into a field with a check digit. This program would then list all of the numbers which have been generated with check digits, and these numbers would be used when the new system was implemented.

Editing Fields Containing Check Digits

When a number which has a check digit is read as input to an edit program, the program will check the number to be sure that none of the data entry errors mentioned previously has taken place. The process which the edit program would perform to check the digit is illustrated in the following example.

EXAMPLE

Step 1: All digits in the number except the check digit are multiplied by the same weights as when the check digit was determined.

CUSTOMER NUMBER:	6	5	3	2	3
WEIGHTS:	x5	x4	x3	x2	
	30	20	9	4	

Step 2: The products of the multiplication are added together.

$$30 + 20 + 9 + 4 = 63$$

Step 3: The check digit is added to the sum of the products of the multiplication.

$$63 + 3 = 66$$

Step 4: The sum is divided by 11. If the remainder is equal to zero, the number is correct. If the remainder is not equal to zero, the number is incorrect.

$$66 \div 6 = 6, \text{ remainder is } 0$$

Note in the example above that the remainder after the division by 11 is zero. Therefore, the number which was checked is correct. If the remainder was not zero, then it would indicate that some type of error had occurred in the preparation of the input value. If an error is found, then the input record would normally not be processed, and the record would be listed on an Exception Report.

If a check digit of "X" is found, then the value 10 is added to the sum of the products in Step 3, instead of the check digit. This will result in a remainder of zero if the number has been properly recorded.

It can be seen that the use of the check digit can lead to verification of the proper number being used and this can be quite important, especially when the value being checked is used as a key to a file. The Modulus 11 check digit method will normally catch all transcription and transposition errors and about 95 percent of the other random errors which occur in the preparation of data.

Pseudocode — Modulus 11 Check

It is important to understand the logic for implementing the Modulus 11 check. The following pseudocode illustrates the detail steps in checking an input field to assure that the field contains the proper modulus 11 check digit in the low order position.

PSEUDOCODE SPECIFICATIONS

PROGRAM: Load Customer Master File	PROGRAMMER: Shelly	DATE: May 2
MODULE NAME: MOD11CHK	REF:	MODULE FUNCTION: Check Module 11 Check Digit

PSEUDOCODE	REF:	FILES, RECORDS, FIELDS REQUIRED

```
Set subscript to 1
PERFORM UNTIL character in field containing number
        to be checked = blank or subscript > 20
    Add 1 to subscript
ENDPERFORM
Calculate number of digits in field = subscript - 1
IF number of digits in field = 0
    Indicate invalid check digit
ELSE
    Move number of digits in field to check digit subscript
    Move check digit (check digit subscript) to work area
    Set total digit value to zero
    Calculate number of digits to process subscript =
              number of digits in field - 1
    Set weight factor to 2
    PERFORM UNTIL all digits are processed
        Calculate digit value = digit to be checked (digits
                  to process subscript) x weight factor
        Add digit value to total digit value
        IF weight factor = 10
            Set weight factor to 2
        ELSE
            Add 1 to weight factor
        ENDIF
        Subtract 1 from digits to process subscript
    ENDPERFORM
    IF check digit = "X"
        Add 10 to total digit value
    ELSE
        Add check digit to total digit value
    ENDIF
    Divide total digit value by 11
    IF remainder = 0
        Indicate valid check digit
    ELSE
        Indicate invalid check digit
    ENDIF
ENDIF
Return
```

Figure 5-34 Pseudocode — Modulus 11 Check

The pseudocode in Figure 5-34 will check the Modulus 11 check digit on any field up to 20 characters in length. Therefore, the first requirement is to determine the number of characters to be checked. This is done by searching the field for blanks. As soon as a blank is found, the end of the data to be checked has been reached. This is illustrated in Figure 5-35.

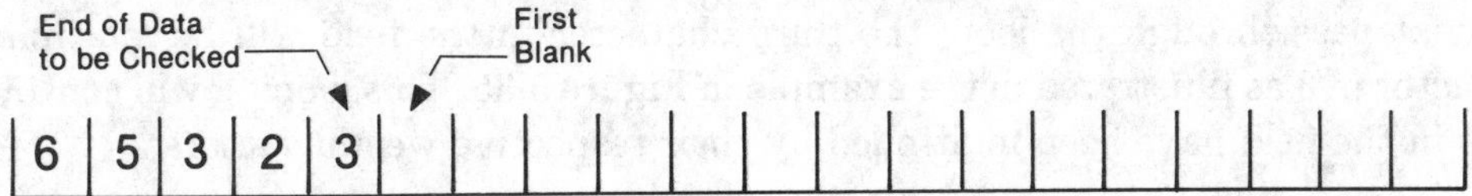

Figure 5-35 Illustration of Field to Be Checked for Modulus 11

Note from Figure 5-35 that there is a twenty character field in which the data to be checked has been placed. The data would be placed in this field prior to entering the module illustrated in Figure 5-34.

The first blank in the field indicates the end of the data to be checked. Thus, the number to be checked is 65323.

The number of digits to be checked is determined in Figure 5-34 by subtracting the value 1 from the value in the subscript used to search the field. Thus, in Figure 5-35, the value in the subscript would be 6 because the sixth position contains the first blank. By subtracting 1, the value 5 is obtained which is the number of digits to be checked in the field.

A check is then performed in the pseudocode in Figure 5-34 to determine if the number of characters to be checked is zero. If so, the check digit is indicated invalid.

If not, then the number of digits in the field is moved to a subscript, and the check digit itself is moved from the number to a work area. In Figure 5-35, the check digit for the number is 3. This is referenced by using the subscript which contains the number of digits in the field. The check digit 3 is moved to a work area so that it can be referenced later in the processing.

The total digit value field where the sum of the products will be stored is set to zero. The number of digits which should be multiplied by weight factors is then determined by subtracting 1 from the number of digits in the field. Thus, in Figure 5-35, this calculation would determine that there are four digits which should be multiplied by weight factors. The weight factor is then set to the value 2.

The loop is then entered which will multiply each of the values in the field to be checked by their respective weight factors. The first step in the loop is to calculate the digit value by multiplying the digit by the weight factor. For the first time through the loop, the fourth digit would be multiplied by a weight factor of 2. Thus, in the example in Figure 5-35, the fourth digit (2) would be multiplied by a weight factor of 2, giving a product of 4. This product is then added to the total digit value field, which accumulates the sum of the digit multiplication.

A check is then made to determine if the weight factor is equal to the value 10. If so, it is reset to a value of 2 for the next pass through the loop. This is done because, as will be recalled, the maximum value for the weight factor when calculating the Modulus 11 check digit is 10. If the check digit is not equal to 10, then it is incremented by 1 for the next pass through the loop. The value in the process subscript is then decremented by one, and the loop is repeated. On the next pass through the loop, the third character in the field will be multiplied by a weight factor of 3 as illustrated in the example in Figure 5-35. This looping will continue until all digits in the field have been multiplied by their respective weight factors.

After the loop is complete, the check digit, which was saved in a work area earlier, is compared to the value "X." If it is equal to "X," then the value 10 is added to the total digit value which has been accumulated. Otherwise, the check digit is added to the total digit value. The total digit value is then divided by 11. If the remainder is equal to zero, the check digit is valid and the indicator is set to show that the check digit is valid. If the remainder is not zero, then the indicator is set to show an invalid check digit. The module then returns control to the module which called it.

Summary

The editing techniques which have been demonstrated illustrate three ways in which input data can be edited prior to being loaded into a master file or otherwise being processed. These techniques, together with techniques explained previously, form an important part of the types of processing which take place in business application programming and should be well understood by the business applications programmer.

PROGRAM DESIGN — IPO CHARTS AND HIERARCHY CHART

After the programming specifications have been reviewed and the processing which is to be accomplished within the program is thoroughly understood, the programmer should begin designing the structure of the program. If there are any questions concerning the processing to be accomplished in the program, the programming specifications contained in Figure 5-12 through Figure 5-14 should be reviewed. The first step in the design of the program is to identify the function of the top-level module in the program through the use of an IPO Chart.

The IPO Chart for the top-level module in the program is illustrated below.

IPO CHART			
PROGRAM: Load Customer Master File	PROGRAMMER: Shelly/Cashman		DATE: May 2
MODULE NAME: Load Customer Master File	REF: AØØØ	MODULE FUNCTION: Load the Customer Master File	

INPUT	PROCESSING	REF:	OUTPUT
1. Customer Transaction File	1. Initialize		1. Customer Master File
	2. Obtain valid data to load master file	BØØØ	2. Customer Master File List
	3. Write customer master file	BØ1Ø	
	4. List customer master file	BØ2Ø	
	5. Terminate		

Figure 5-36 IPO Chart — Load Customer Master File

From the IPO Chart in Figure 5-36, it can be seen that the function of the top-level module is to Load the Customer Master File. The output of the module is the Customer Master File, which is to be stored on disk as an indexed sequential file, and the Customer Master File List, which will be a listing of the Customer Master File. It should be noted that the Exception Report as specified in the Programming Specifications is not considered output from the top-level module because it is produced only when errors occur; therefore, it will be considered output from those modules which will determine that an error has occurred.

The major processing tasks which are necessary to Load the Customer Master File are similar to those in previous problems. In analyzing the major processing tasks required in this high-level module, it can be seen that the Initialize task involves merely opening the files and, therefore, does not require a separate module. The tasks of Obtaining Valid Data to Load Master File, Write Customer Master File, and List Customer Master File are each tasks that appear to require a significant amount of processing; thus, each will require a separate module. The Terminate task does not require a large amount of processing, so it will not be a separate module. After this analysis, the hierarchy chart for the program would be as illustrated in Figure 5-37.

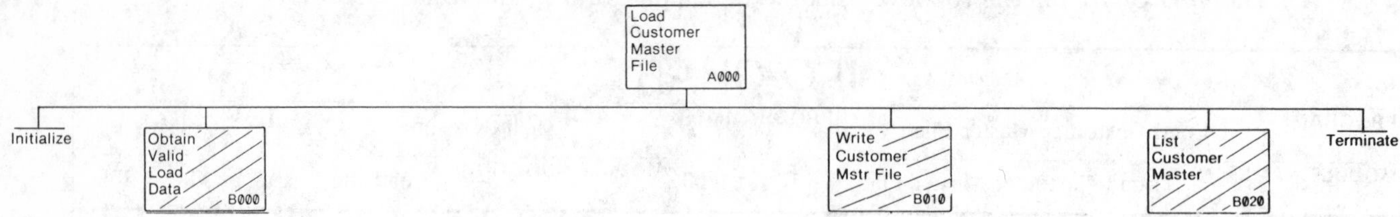

Figure 5-37 Hierarchy Chart

As can be seen from the hierarchy chart above, the Initialize and Terminate tasks will be contained within the A000 module, while the tasks of Obtain Valid Load Data, Write Customer Master File, and List Customer Master will be in separate modules.

The IPO Chart for the module whose task is to Obtain Valid Load Data is illustrated in Figure 5-38.

IPO CHART			
PROGRAM: Load Customer Master File	PROGRAMMER: Shelly/Cashman		DATE: May 2
MODULE NAME: Obtain Valid Load Data	REF: BØØØ	MODULE FUNCTION: Obtain Valid Data to Load Master File	
INPUT	**PROCESSING**	**REF:**	**OUTPUT**
1. Customer Transaction File	1. Obtain pair of records	CØØØ	1. Valid Load Data
	2. Edit type 1 record	CØ1Ø	
	3. Edit type 2 record	CØ2Ø	

Figure 5-38 IPO Chart — Obtain Valid Load Data

As can be seen from the IPO Chart, the output from this module is to be the Valid Load Data, and the input to the module is the Customer Transaction File.

The major processing tasks include the following: Obtain Pair of Records, Edit Type 1 Record, and Edit Type 2 Record. As each task appears to require a significant amount of processing, each will become a separate module in the program.

The hierarchy chart after the IPO Chart for Obtain Valid Load Data module has been analyzed is illustrated below.

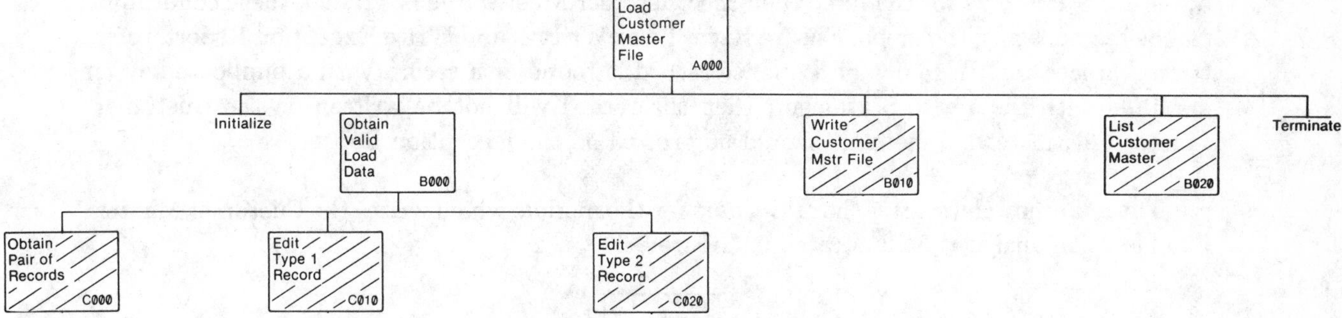

Figure 5-39 Hierarchy Chart

The next module to analyze is the module whose function is to Write the Customer Master File. The IPO Chart is illustrated below.

IPO CHART

PROGRAM: Load Customer Master File	PROGRAMMER: Shelly/Cashman		DATE: May 2
MODULE NAME: Write Customer Mstr File	REF: BØ1Ø	MODULE FUNCTION: Write the Customer Master File	

INPUT	PROCESSING	REF:	OUTPUT
1. Valid Data to Load	1. Format master output record		1. Customer Master File
Master File	2. Write master record		2. Exception Report
	3. Ensure record was written		
	4. Write exception report	UØØØ	

Figure 5-40 IPO Chart — Write Customer Master

From the IPO Chart illustrated in Figure 5-40, it can be seen that the output of the module is the Customer Master File and the Exception Report. The input is the data to load the Customer Master File. The processing includes formatting the master output record, writing the master output record, ensuring that the record was written, and writing the Exception Report. The Exception Report will be written by the U000 utility module.

It will be recalled from a previous discussion that when loading an Indexed Sequential File, it is invalid to have the records written out of sequence; and also there must not be any duplicate prime keys for the file. When the Customer Master File is written, these conditions can be tested. Thus, the steps, Ensure Record was Written and Write Exception Report, refer to this processing. If an out of sequence record is found or a record with a duplicate key is specified with the Write Statement, then the record will not be written on the Customer Master File; instead, a message should be printed on the Exception Report.

The hierarchy chart after the IPO Chart for the module which writes the Customer Master File has been analyzed is illustrated in Figure 5-41.

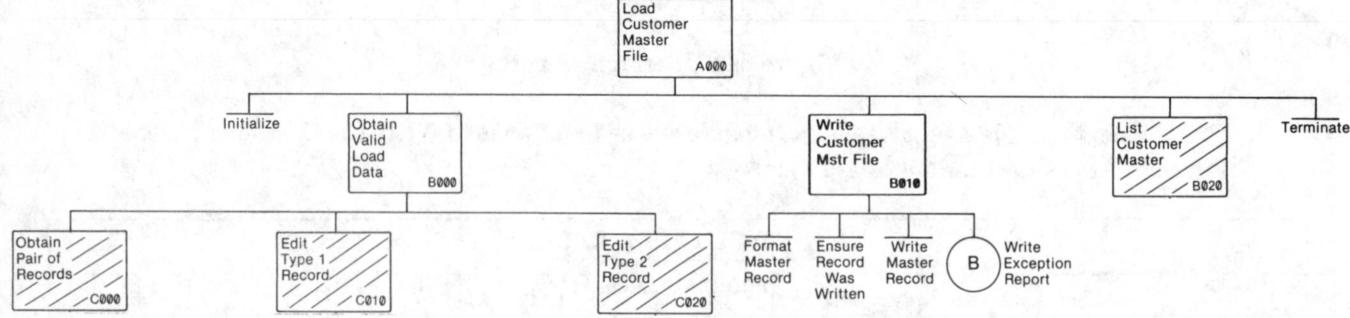

Figure 5-41 Hierarchy Chart

The next module to analyze is the module whose function is to List the Customer Master. This is the module which prints the Customer Master File after it has been created. The IPO Chart is illustrated below.

IPO CHART			
PROGRAM: Load Customer Master File	PROGRAMMER: Shelly/Cashman		DATE: May 2
MODULE NAME: List Customer Master	REF: BØ2Ø	MODULE FUNCTION: List the Customer Master File	
INPUT	PROCESSING	REF:	OUTPUT
1. Customer Master File	1. Obtain customer master record		1. Customer Master File
	2. Write list report	CØ3Ø	Listing

Figure 5-42 IPO Chart — List Customer Master

Note from Figure 5-42 that the output of the module which Lists the Customer Master File is the Customer Master File Listing. The input to the module is the Customer Master File. The major processing tasks include Obtaining the Customer Master Record and Writing the List Report. Obtaining the Customer Master Record is merely a Read Statement and does not require significant processing. Hence, it is not a separate module. Writing the List Report, on the other hand, does require some significant processing; therefore, it will be a separate module, as indicated by the entry C030 in the REF column on the IPO Chart.

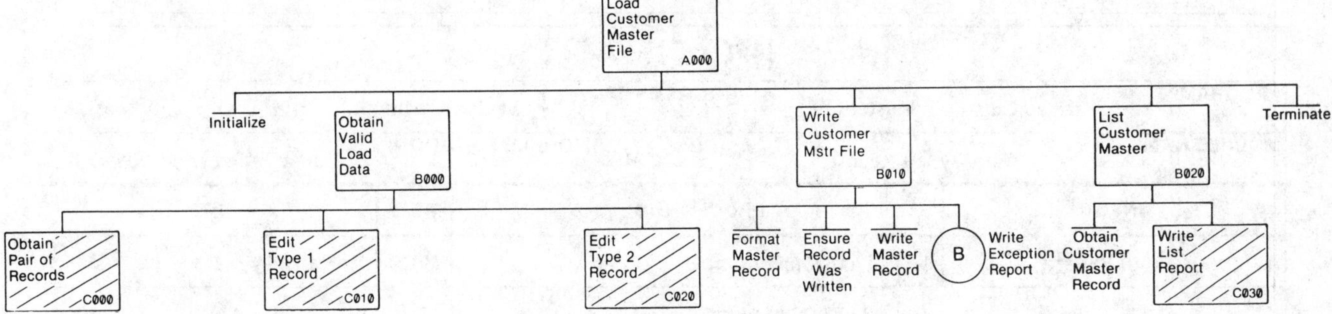

Figure 5-43 Hierarchy Chart

As can be seen from the Hierarchy Chart in Figure 5-43, the major processing tasks in all of the modules on the second level ("B" modules) have been defined. The next step is to define the major processing tasks for each of the lower level modules.

From the Hierarchy Chart, it should be noted that module B000 Obtain Valid Load Data controls the third-level ("C") modules, Obtain Pair of Records, Edit Type 1 Record, and Edit Type 2 Record. The IPO Charts for these three modules are illustrated on the following page.

IPO CHART

PROGRAM: Load Customer Master File	PROGRAMMER: Shelly/Cashman	DATE: May 2
MODULE NAME: Obtain Pair of Records	REF: CØØØ	MODULE FUNCTION: Obtain Valid Pair of Records

INPUT	PROCESSING	REF:	OUTPUT
1. Customer Transaction File	1. Sort input records	DØØØ	1. Valid Type 1 and Type 2
	2. Get valid pair of records	DØ1Ø	Records

IPO CHART

PROGRAM: Load Customer Master File	PROGRAMMER: Shelly/Cashman	DATE: May 2
MODULE NAME: Edit Type 1 Record	REF: CØ1Ø	MODULE FUNCTION: Edit a Type 1 Input Record

INPUT	PROCESSING	REF:	OUTPUT
1. Type 1 Input Record	1. Edit customer number	UØ2Ø	1. Valid Type 1
	2. Edit customer name		Input Record
	3. Edit customer address		2. Exception Report
	4. Edit customer city		
	5. Edit customer state		
	6. Edit customer zip code		
	7. Write exception report	UØØØ	

IPO CHART

PROGRAM: Load Customer Master File	PROGRAMMER: Shelly/Cashman	DATE: May 2
MODULE NAME: Edit Type 2 Record	REF: CØ2Ø	MODULE FUNCTION: Edit a Type 2 Record

INPUT	PROCESSING	REF:	OUTPUT
1. Type 2 Input Record	1. Edit customer number	UØ2Ø	1. Valid Type 2 Input
	2. Edit customer discount		Record
	3. Edit last activity date		2. Exception Report
	4. Write exception report	UØØØ	

Figure 5-44 IPO Charts — Obtain Pair of Records, Edit Type 1 Record, Edit Type 2 Record

From Figure 5-44, it can be seen that the output of the C000 Obtain Pair of Records module is a valid Type 1 record and a valid Type 2 record; that is, a valid pair of records. The input to the module is the Customer Transaction File. The major processing tasks consist of Sorting the input records and Getting a valid pair of records. Both of these major processing tasks require significant processing, so both will be separate modules within the program.

The IPO Chart for the C010 Edit Type 1 Record module specifies that the output from the module will be a valid Type 1 record and the Exception Report. An entry on the Exception Report will be written if there are errors found in the input record. The input to the module is a Type 1 input record.

The major processing tasks include the editing of each field found in the Type 1 Transaction Record. The task of editing the Customer Number requires significant processing, so it will be a separate module. The other editing tasks are not large or complex, so they will be included within the module. Writing the Exception Report will be done by the U000 module.

It should be noted that the Reference Number for the module which Edits the Customer Number is U020. This module is assigned this reference number because editing the Customer Number is required by more than one module within the program; thus, editing the Customer Number is a Utility Module.

The IPO Chart for the module which Edits a Type 2 Record is also illustrated in Figure 5-44. The output from this module is a valid Type 2 record and the Exception Report. As with the Type 1 editing, if errors are found in the input record, entries will be written on the Exception Report. The input to the module is the Type 2 Input Record.

The major processing tasks are the following: Edit Customer Number, Edit Customer Discount, Edit Last Activity Date, and Write Exception Report. Editing the Customer Number will be done by the U020 utility module; this is the same module used in the editing of the Type 1 input record. The Customer Discount and the Last Activity Date editing will take place within the module, while the Exception Report will be written by the U000 module.

After this analysis, the Hierarchy Chart for the portion of the program which obtains valid load data appears as illustrated below.

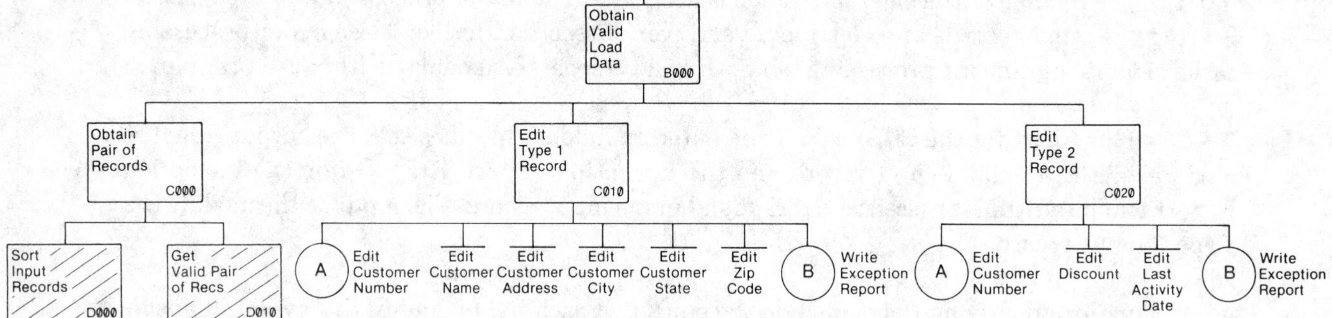

Figure 5-45 Hierarchy Chart

Note from the Hierarchy Chart in Figure 5-45 that all of the major processing tasks which are specified on the IPO Chart are included in the Hierarchy Chart. Note also that the modules which Edit the Customer Number and Write the Exception Report are to be included on a separate area of the page, since they are indicated through the use of the on-page connector (circle).

The remaining module on the third level which must be analyzed through the use of an IPO Chart is the module whose function is to Write the Master List Report. The Master List Report is created from the Customer Master File after the Customer Master File has been loaded by other parts of the program. A related module which will be developed from this module is the module which will write the headings on the report. The IPO Charts for these two modules are illustrated in Figure 5-46.

IPO CHART					
PROGRAM: Load Customer Master File		PROGRAMMER: Shelly/Cashman		DATE: May 2	
MODULE NAME: Write List Report	REF: CØ3Ø	MODULE FUNCTION: Write List Report			

INPUT	PROCESSING	REF:	OUTPUT
1. Customer Master Record	1. Print headings	DØ2Ø	1. Report Line
	2. Format report		
	3. Write a detail line		

IPO CHART					
PROGRAM: Load Customer Master File		PROGRAMMER: Shelly/Cashman		DATE: May 2	
MODULE NAME: Print List Headings	REF: DØ2Ø	MODULE FUNCTION: Print Headings on List Report			

INPUT	PROCESSING	REF:	OUTPUT
	1. Format headings		1. Report Headings
	2. Write headings		

Figure 5-46 IPO Charts — Write List Report and Print List Headings

As can be seen in Figure 5-46, the output from the module which Writes the List Report is the Report Line. The input to the module is the Customer Master Record. The major processing tasks which must be accomplished are Print headings, Format report, and Write a detail line. The headings will be printed by a separate module (D020) while the formatting of the report and writing of the detail line will take place within the module.

The D020 module, whose function is to Print the Headings on the List Report has an output of the report headings. The major processing tasks are Format the headings and Write the headings, neither of which requires a separate module.

After this analysis, the portion of the Hierarchy Chart concerning the Master List Report appears as illustrated in Figure 5-47.

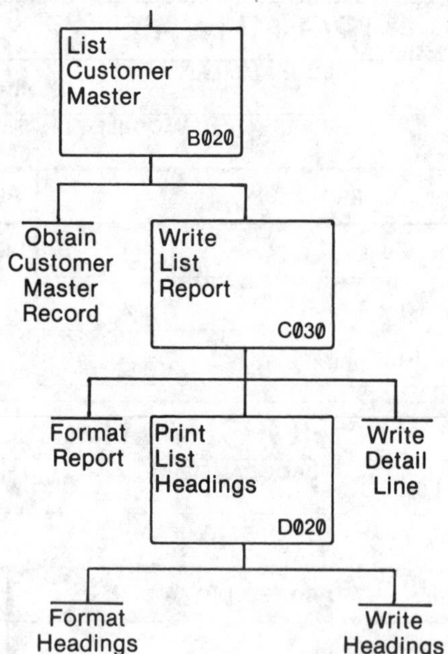

Figure 5-47 Hierarchy Chart

As can be seen from the Hierarchy Chart in Figure 5-47, the "leg" of the program concerned with printing the Customer Master File is now complete since there are no further modules to be analyzed.

It should be recalled that the module C000 Obtain Pair of Records was composed of the major processing tasks of Sorting the input records and Getting a valid pair of records. A segment of the Hierarchy Chart illustrating these modules is illustrated below.

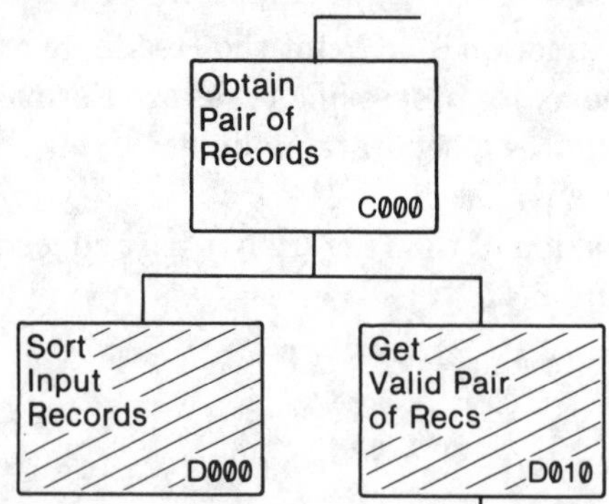

Figure 5-48 Hierarchy Chart

The IPO Charts for the modules which Sort the Input Records and Get a Valid Pair of Records are illustrated in Figure 5-49.

IPO CHART					
PROGRAM: Load Customer Master File		PROGRAMMER: Shelly/Cashman		DATE: May 2	
MODULE NAME: Sort Input Records	REF: DØØØ	MODULE FUNCTION: Sort Transaction Input Records			
INPUT	**PROCESSING**	**REF:**	**OUTPUT**		
1. Customer Transaction File	1. Sort transaction records		1. Sorted Transaction Records		
	(Customer number-major;				
	Transaction type-minor)				

IPO CHART					
PROGRAM: Load Customer Master File		PROGRAMMER: Shelly/Cashman		DATE: May 2	
MODULE NAME: Get Valid Pair of Recs	REF: DØ1Ø	MODULE FUNCTION: Get a Valid Pair of Records			
INPUT	**PROCESSING**	**REF:**	**OUTPUT**		
1. Sorted Customer	1. Read records		1. Valid Pair of Records		
Transaction File	2. Verify valid first record	EØØØ	2. Exception Report		
	3. Verify valid second record	EØ1Ø			
	4. Write exception report	UØØØ			

Figure 5-49 IPO Charts — Sort Input Records and Get Valid Pair of Records

The output of the module which sorts the input records are the Sorted Transaction Records. The input to the module is the Customer Transaction File, which is not sorted. The only task which must be accomplished is sorting the Transaction Records in Transaction Type sequence within Customer Number sequence. There will be no separate modules out of the Sort module.

The module which Gets a Valid Pair of Records has as its output a valid pair of records. The input to the module is the Sorted Customer Transaction File. The major processing tasks which must be done are the following: Read records, Verify a valid first record, Verify a valid second record, and Write the Exception Report. The verification of the records and writing the Exception Report will be accomplished by separate modules because they involve significant processing. Reading the input records will be done in the D010 module.

The Hierarchy Chart of this portion of the program after the analysis is illustrated in Figure 5-50.

Hierarchy Chart

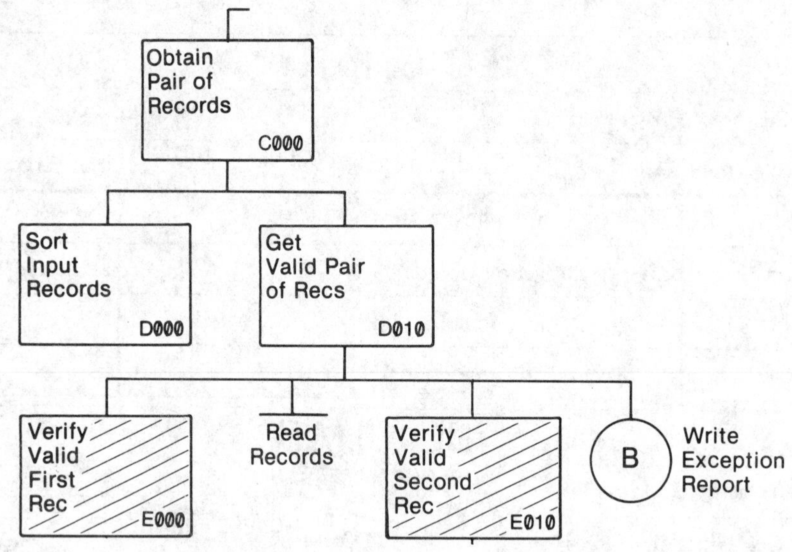

Figure 5-50 Hierarchy Chart

Note from Figure 5-50 that the task of Reading the Records will be performed within the D010 module while the tasks of Verifying a valid first record, Verifying a valid second record, and Writing the Exception Report will be done in separate modules.

The IPO Chart for the module which will Verify a Valid First Record is illustrated in Figure 5-51.

IPO CHART			
PROGRAM: Load Customer Master File	PROGRAMMER: Shelly/Cashman		DATE: May 2
MODULE NAME: Verify Valid First Rec	REF: EØØØ	MODULE FUNCTION: Verify a Valid First Record	
INPUT	**PROCESSING**	**REF:**	**OUTPUT**
1. Record Type	1. Verify record type = 1		1. Indication of Valid
2. Customer Number	2. Write exception report	UØØØ	First Record
			2. Exception Report

Figure 5-51 IPO Chart — Verify Valid First Record

The output from the module is an indicator which indicates that the first record of a pair is valid and also the Exception Report if there is an error found. The input to the module must consist of the Record Type and the Customer Number. The Record Type is checked in the module for the value "1;" and the Customer Number is required in the event an error occurs, in which case it must be passed to the module which writes the Exception Report.

The two major processing tasks are to verify that the Record Type is equal to "1" and to write the Exception Report. The writing of the Exception Report will be done in module U000.

The IPO Chart for the module whose function is to Verify a Valid Second Record is shown below.

IPO CHART			
PROGRAM: Load Customer Master File	PROGRAMMER: Shelly/Cashman		DATE: May 2
MODULE NAME: Verify Valid Second Rec	REF: EØ1Ø	MODULE FUNCTION: Verify a Valid Second Record	
INPUT	**PROCESSING**	**REF:**	**OUTPUT**
1. Record Type	1. Verify type 2 record		1. Indication of Valid
2. Customer Number from	2. Verify customer numbers equal		Second Record
Type 1 Record	3. Write exception report	UØØØ	2. Exception Report
3. Customer Number from			
Record to be Checked			

Figure 5-52 IPO Chart — Verify Valid Second Record

The output of the module above is quite similar to the previous module which verified the validity of the first record of the pair. The output consists of an indicator for the validity of the second record and the Exception Report.

Input consists of the Record Type, the Customer Number from the Type 1 record, and the Customer Number from the Record to be Checked. The major processing tasks include the following: Verify type 2 record, Verify customer numbers are equal, and Write the Exception Report. It should be noted that the Customer Number from the Type 1 record is required in this module so that the module can verify that the Customer Number in the Type 2 record is equal to the Customer Number in the Type 1 record. These are the two requirements for a valid Type 2 record.

Since there are no lower-level modules required in either the E000 or the E010 modules, except for the utility module which Writes the Exception Report (U000), the majority of the structure of the program has been designed. The Hierarchy Chart for the program which has been designed thus far is illustrated in Figure 5-53.

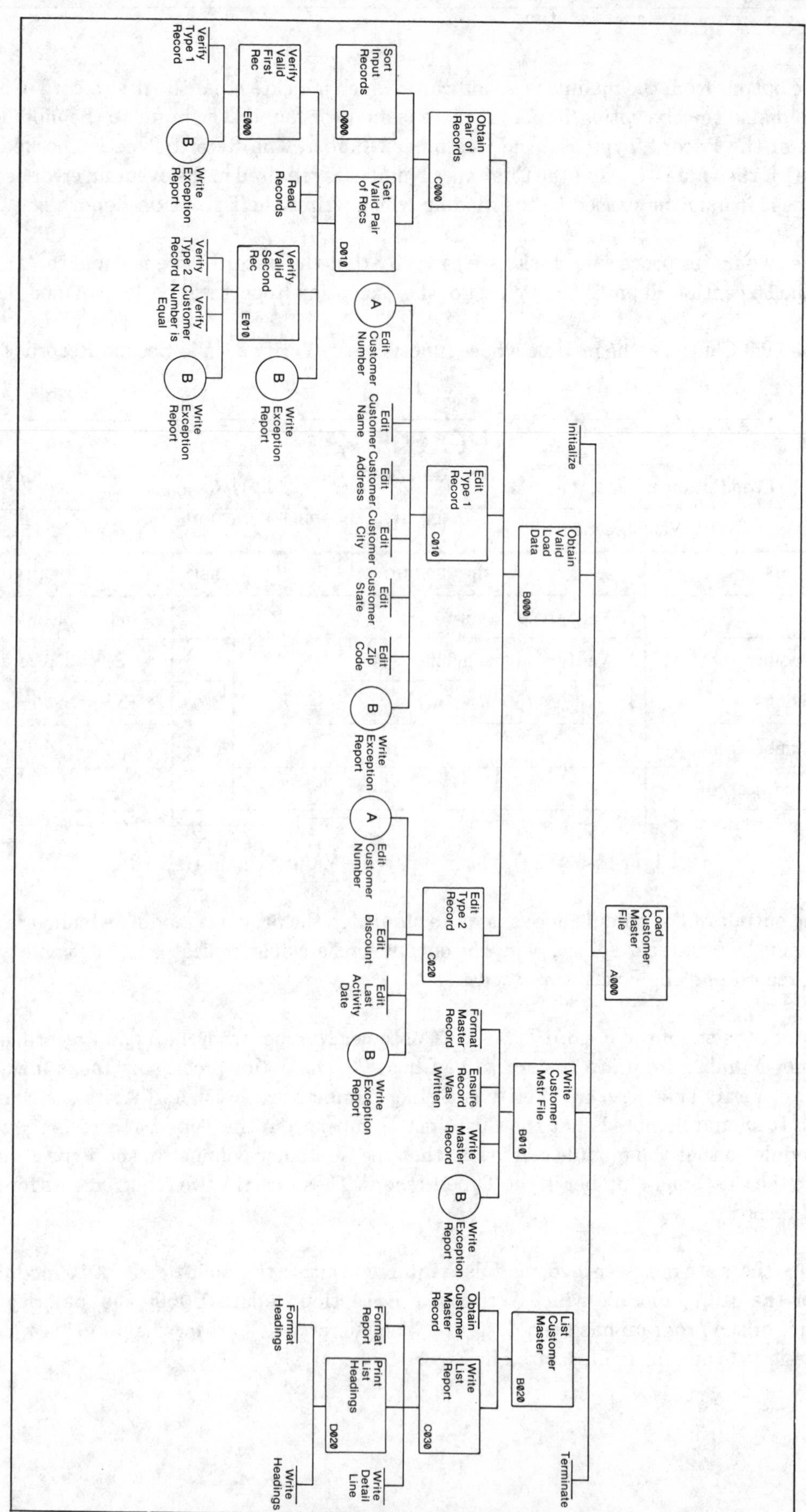

Figure 5-53 Hierarchy Chart

As can be seen from Figure 5-53, there are no further modules which must be analyzed in the main Hierarchy Chart, but the two utility modules (Edit Customer Number and Write Exception Report), which are specified through the use of on-page connectors in the Hierarchy Chart in Figure 5-53, must still be defined.

The IPO Chart for the module whose function is to Edit the Customer Number is illustrated in Figure 5-54.

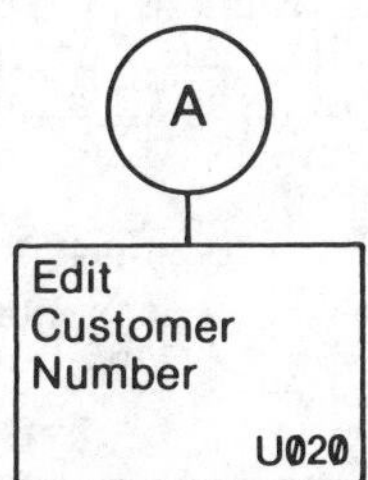

IPO CHART

PROGRAM: Load Customer Master File		PROGRAMMER: Shelly/Cashman	DATE: May 2
MODULE NAME: Edit Customer Number		REF: U020	MODULE FUNCTION: Edit the Customer Number

INPUT	PROCESSING	REF:	OUTPUT
1. Customer Number	1. Verify customer number numeric		1. Edited Customer Number
	2. Verify valid mod-11 check digit	EXT.	2. Exception Report
	3. Write exception report	U000	

Figure 5-54 IPO Chart — Edit Customer Number

The output from the module is the Edited Customer Number and, if necessary, an entry on the Exception Report. The input to the module is the Customer Number. It should be noted that this Customer Number may be from a Type 1 Transaction Record or a Type 2 Transaction Record. The major processing tasks consist of Verify customer number numeric, Verify valid mod-11 check digit, and Write Exception Report. The verification of a numeric Customer Number will take place within the module since it does not involve extensive or complex processing. The Exception Report will be written by the U000 utility module.

The verification of a valid mod-11 check digit will also be done by a separate module, but note that the REF. column contains the abbreviation EXT. rather than a module reference number. This is because the module which checks the modulus-11 check digit is an EXTernal module; that is, the module is external to the program which is being designed. It has been previously designed, coded, and tested and is available to any program which wishes to use it. Since the program which Loads the Customer Master File requires a Mod-11 check, it will use the module which is available. The method of including the module in the program will be explained later in this chapter.

The Hierarchy Chart for the "A" on-page connector after this analysis is illustrated in Figure 5-55.

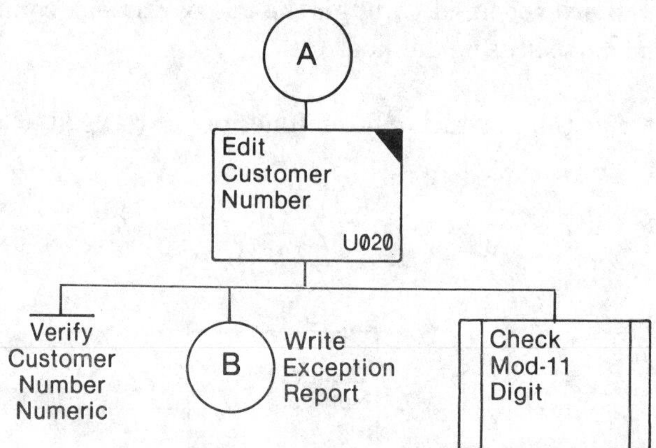

Figure 5-55 Hierarchy Chart

In the Hierarchy Chart above, it can be seen that there are three major processing tasks in the module U020. The task of verifying the Customer Number is numeric will be done within the module. As noted, the other two tasks will be done in separate modules. The module which checks the Modulus-11 check digit is an external module. This is indicated by the vertical lines inside the rectangle. Whenever a module which is external to the program is to be used within the program, the vertical lines should be included in the rectangle to indicate this. Note also that since the module which Edits the Customer Number is called from more than one module within the program, it is shaded in the upper-right corner.

The last set of modules which must be analyzed are those which Write the Exception Report. These modules are indicated as on-page connector "B" in the main Hierarchy Chart (see Figure 5-53). The IPO Chart for the module which writes the Exception Report and the associated module which prints the headings on the Exception Report are illustrated in Figure 5-56.

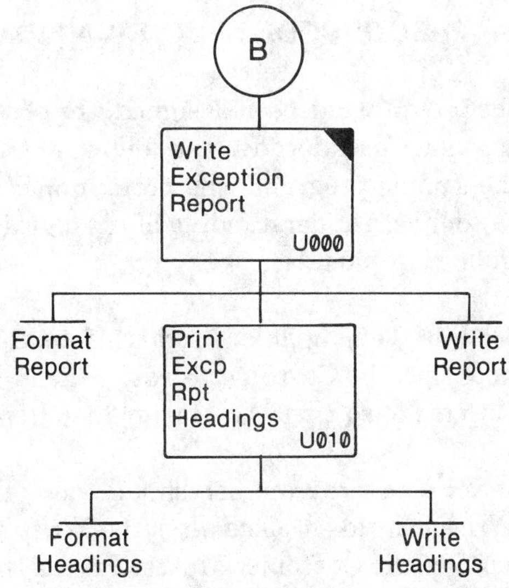

IPO CHART

PROGRAM: Load Customer Master File	PROGRAMMER: Shelly/Cashman		DATE: May 2
MODULE NAME: Write Exception Report	REF: UØØØ	MODULE FUNCTION: Write the Exception Report	

INPUT	PROCESSING	REF:	OUTPUT
1. Customer Number	1. Print headings	UØ1Ø	1. Exception Report Line
2. Field in Error	2. Format report		
3. Type of Error	3. Write report		

IPO CHART

PROGRAM: Load Customer Master File	PROGRAMMER: Shelly/Cashman		DATE: May 2
MODULE NAME: Print Excp Rpt Headings	REF: UØ1Ø	MODULE FUNCTION: Print Exception Report Headings	

INPUT	PROCESSING	REF:	OUTPUT
	1. Format headings		1. Headings on Report
	2. Write headings		

Figure 5-56 IPO Charts — Write Exception Report and Print Headings

Note from Figure 5-56 that the output, input, and major processing tasks specified correspond to those found in previous programs for the modules which write the Exception Report.

This completes the design of the structure of the program which loads the Customer Master File.

PROGRAM DESIGN – PSEUDOCODE SPECIFICATIONS

After the structure of the program has been designed, the programmer should develop the logic for each of the modules using pseudocode. The following pages contain the pseudocode for the modules found in the sample program. The programmer should examine the logic in each module to ensure that a complete understanding of the logic is obtained. Particular attention should be paid to the following modules.

A000 Load Customer Master File: This module is straightforward in its logic except that the programmer should note that the Customer Master File is closed after it is created and then is opened as an input file so that the Master List Report can be created.

B010 Write Customer Master: The programmer should note that this module checks to determine if a valid Write has taken place after the Write Statement which writes the Customer Master Record in the Customer Master File. If the Write was not successful, it indicates that either the input records were out of sequence, or there were duplicate keys for records to be written. In either case, an error message is written on the Exception Report, and the record will not appear in the Customer Master File.

D010 Get Valid Pair of Records: This module contains the logic to implement the rules specified in the Decision Table in Figure 5-18. The Decision Table, together with the examples of the rules in Figures 5-19 through 5-28, should be reviewed when examining the pseudocode in this module to ensure that the methods of implementation are clearly understood.

The pseudocode for the sample program is contained on the following pages.

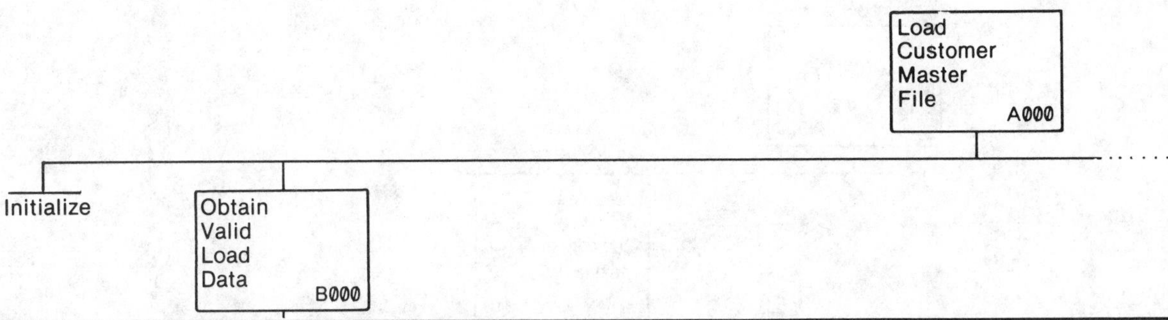

PSEUDOCODE SPECIFICATIONS

PROGRAM: Load Customer Master File	PROGRAMMER: Shelly/Cashman	DATE: May 2
MODULE NAME: Load Customer Master File	REF: AØØØ	MODULE FUNCTION: Load the Customer Master File

PSEUDOCODE	REF:	FILES, RECORDS, FIELDS REQUIRED
Open the files		New customer master file
Obtain valid load data	BØØØ	Exception report and customer list file
PERFORM UNTIL there are no more transaction records		No more transaction records indicator
Write the customer master file	BØ1Ø	Old customer master file
Obtain valid load data	BØØØ	
ENDPERFORM		
Close new customer master output file		
Open old customer master input file		
List the master file	BØ2Ø	
Close the files		
Stop run		

PSEUDOCODE SPECIFICATIONS

PROGRAM: Load Customer Master File	PROGRAMMER: Shelly/Cashman	DATE: May 2
MODULE NAME: Obtain Valid Load Data	REF: BØØØ	MODULE FUNCTION: Obtain Valid Data to Load Customer Master File

PSEUDOCODE	REF:	FILES, RECORDS, FIELDS REQUIRED
Set valid record indicator to neutral status		Valid record indicator
Obtain pair of records	CØØØ	No more trans records indicator
PERFORM UNTIL there are no more transaction records or records are valid		
Edit type 1 record	CØ1Ø	
Edit type 2 record	CØ2Ø	
IF records are not valid		
Obtain pair of records	CØØØ	
Set valid record indicator to neutral status		
ELSE		
Indicate valid records		
ENDIF		
ENDPERFORM		

Figure 5-57 Pseudocode Specifications

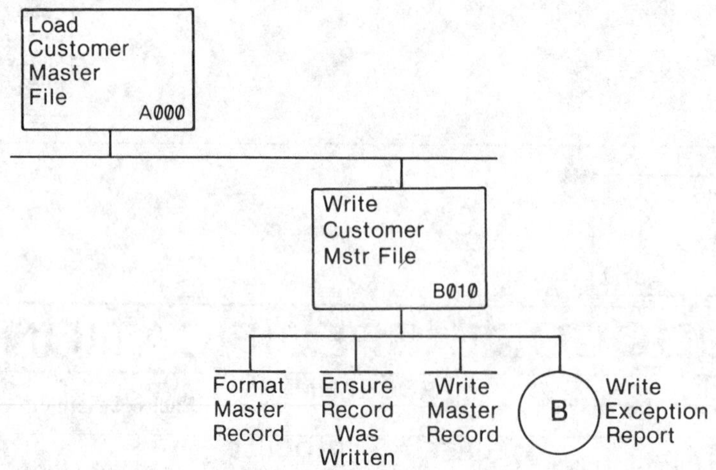

PSEUDOCODE SPECIFICATIONS

PROGRAM: Load Customer Master File **PROGRAMMER:** Shelly/Cashman **DATE:** May 2

MODULE NAME: Write Customer Mstr File **REF:** B010 **MODULE FUNCTION:** Write the Customer Master File

PSEUDOCODE	REF:	FILES, RECORDS, FIELDS REQUIRED
Move customer number to master area		New customer master output area
Move customer name to master area		Customer number
Move customer address to master area		Customer name
Move customer city to master area		Customer address
Move customer state to master area		Customer city
Move customer zip code to master area		Customer state
Move customer discount to master area		Customer zip code
Move last activity date to master area		Customer discount
Write the customer master record		Last activity date
IF write was unsuccessful		Transaction records data
Move customer number to report work area		Customer number
Move "customer number" to report work area		Customer name
Move "duplicate or bad sequence" to report work area		Customer address
Write exception report	U000	Customer city
ENDIF		Customer state
		Customer zip code
		Customer discount
		Last activity date
		Report work area
		Customer number
		Field in error
		Type of error
		"Customer number" constant
		"Duplicate or bad sequence" constant

Figure 5-58 Pseudocode Specifications

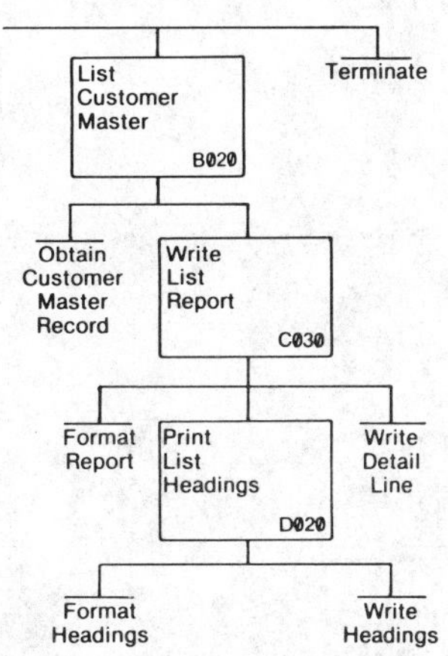

PSEUDOCODE SPECIFICATIONS

PROGRAM: Load Customer Master File | PROGRAMMER: Shelly/Cashman | DATE: May 2

MODULE NAME: List Customer Master | REF: B020 | MODULE FUNCTION: List the Customer Master File

PSEUDOCODE	REF:	FILES, RECORDS, FIELDS REQUIRED
Read customer master file		Customer master input area
PERFORM UNTIL no more master records		Customer number
Write list report	C030	Customer name
Read customer master file		Customer address
ENDPERFORM		Customer city
		Customer state
		Customer zip code
		Customer discount
		Last activity date
		No more master records indicator

PSEUDOCODE SPECIFICATIONS

PROGRAM: Load Customer Master File | PROGRAMMER: Shelly/Cashman | DATE: May 2

MODULE NAME: Write List Report | REF: C030 | MODULE FUNCTION: Write List Report

PSEUDOCODE	REF:	FILES, RECORDS, FIELDS REQUIRED
IF first page or lines printed > page size		First page indicator-list
Print headings	D020	Lines printed counter-list
ENDIF		Page size-list
Clear report area		Old master data
Move customer number to output area		Customer number
Move customer name to output area		Customer name
Move customer address to output area		Customer address
Move customer city to output area		Customer city
Move customer state to output area		Customer state
Move customer zip code to output area		Customer zip code
Move customer discount to output area		Customer discount
Move customer last activity date to output area		Last activity date
Write a line on the report		List report output area
Add spacing to line count		Customer number
Set spacing for single spacing		Customer name
		Customer address
		Customer city
		Customer state
		Customer zip code
		Customer discount
		Last activity date
		Space control field
		Single space control character

PSEUDOCODE SPECIFICATIONS

PROGRAM: Load Customer Master File | PROGRAMMER: Shelly/Cashman | DATE: May 2

MODULE NAME: Print List Headings | REF: D020 | MODULE FUNCTION: Print Headings on List Report

PSEUDOCODE	REF:	FILES, RECORDS, FIELDS REQUIRED
Move date to first heading line		Current date
Move page number to first heading line		First heading line
Write first heading line		Current date
Add 1 to page number		Page number
Write second heading line		Page number
Write third heading line		Second heading line
Set spacing for double spacing		Third heading line
Set line count to zero		Space control field
		Double space control character
		Line count

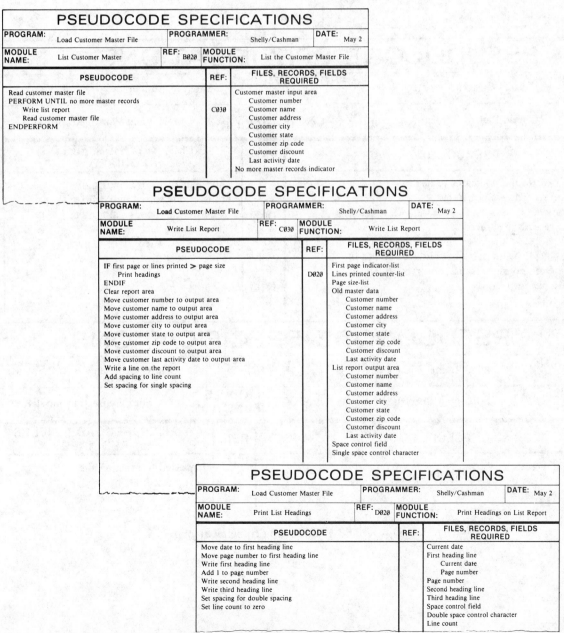

Figure 5-59 Pseudocode Specifications

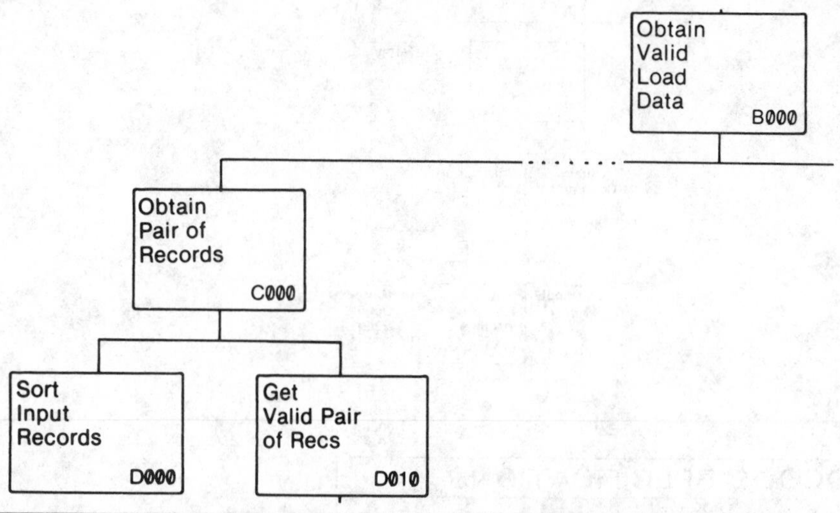

PSEUDOCODE SPECIFICATIONS

PROGRAM: Load Customer Master File	PROGRAMMER: Shelly/Cashman	DATE: May 2
MODULE NAME: Obtain Pair of Records	REF: C000	MODULE FUNCTION: Obtain Valid Pair of Records

PSEUDOCODE	REF:	FILES, RECORDS, FIELDS REQUIRED
Set valid pair of records indicator to neutral		Valid pair of records indicator
IF transaction records are not sorted		Transactions sorted indicator
Sort transaction records	D000	No more transactions indicator
Indicate records are sorted		
ENDIF		
PERFORM UNTIL valid pair of records are found or there are no more transaction records		
Get valid pair of records	D010	
ENDPERFORM		

PSEUDOCODE SPECIFICATIONS

PROGRAM: Load Customer Master File	PROGRAMMER: Shelly/Cashman	DATE: May 2
MODULE NAME: Sort Input Records	REF: D000	MODULE FUNCTION: Sort Transaction Input Records

PSEUDOCODE	REF:	FILES, RECORDS, FIELDS REQUIRED
Sort the records		Unsorted transaction file
		Sort work file

Figure 5-60 Pseudocode Specifications

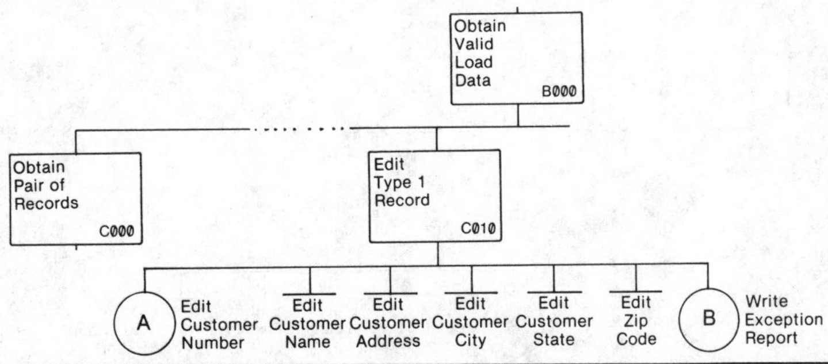

PSEUDOCODE SPECIFICATIONS

PROGRAM: Load Customer Master File	PROGRAMMER: Shelly/Cashman	DATE: May 2
MODULE NAME: Edit Type 1 Record	REF: CØ1Ø	MODULE FUNCTION: Edit a Type 1 Input Record

PSEUDOCODE	REF:	FILES, RECORDS, FIELDS REQUIRED
Move customer number to work area		Customer number work area
Edit customer number	UØ2Ø	Customer name —transaction
IF customer name = spaces		Customer number — transaction
Move customer number to report work area		Exception report work area
Move "customer name" to report work area		Customer number
Move "field contains spaces" to report work area		Field in error
Write exception report	UØØØ	Type of error
Indicate invalid records		"Customer name" constant
ENDIF		"Field contains spaces" constant
IF customer address = spaces		Invalid records indicator
Move customer number to report work area		Customer address — transaction
Move "customer address" to report work area		"Customer address" constant
Move "field contains spaces" to report work area		Customer city — transaction
Write exception report	UØØØ	"Customer city" constant
Indicate invalid records		Valid state table
ENDIF		State — transaction
IF customer city = spaces		"Customer state" constant
Move customer number to report work area		"Invalid state code" constant
Move "customer city" to report work area		Zip code — transaction
Move "field contains spaces" to report work area		"Customer zip code" constant
Write exception report	UØØØ	"Field is not numeric" constant
Indicate invalid records		
ENDIF		
Search table for valid state code		
IF state not in valid state table		
Move customer number to report work area		
Move "customer state" to report work area		
Move "invalid state code" to report work area		
Write exception report	UØØØ	
Indicate invalid records		
ENDIF		
IF zip code is not numeric		
Move customer number to report work area		
Move "customer zip code" to report work area		
Move "field is not numeric" to report work area		
Write exception report	UØØØ	
Indicate invalid records		
ENDIF		

Figure 5-61 Pseudocode Specifications

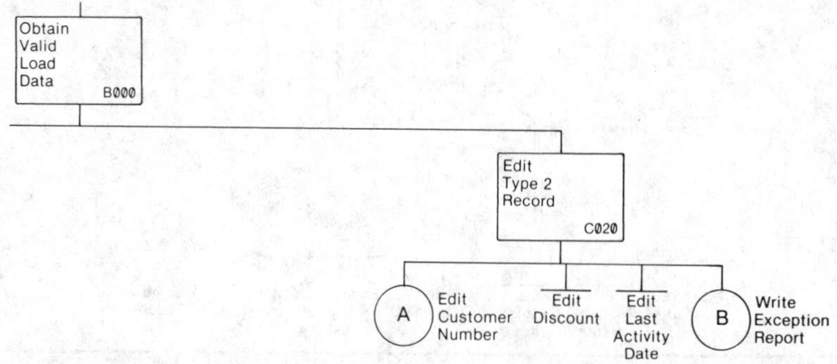

PSEUDOCODE SPECIFICATIONS

PROGRAM: Load Customer Master File	PROGRAMMER: Shelly/Cashman	DATE: May 2
MODULE NAME: Edit Type 2 Record	REF: CØ2Ø	MODULE FUNCTION: Edit a Type 2 Input Record

PSEUDOCODE / **REF:**

```
Move customer number to work area
Edit customer number                                        UØ20
IF discount is not numeric
    Move customer number to report work area
    Move "customer discount" to report work area
    Move "field is not numeric" to report work area
    Write exception report                                  UØØØ
    Indicate invalid records
ELSE
    IF discount > 20
        Move customer number to report work area
        Move "customer discount" to report work area
        Move "discount exceeds maximum" to report work area
        Write exception report                              UØØØ
        Indicate invalid record
    ENDIF
ENDIF
IF last activity date is not numeric
    Move customer number to report work area
    Move "last activity date" to report work area
    Move "field is not numeric" to report work area
    Write exception report                                  UØØØ
    Indicate invalid record
ELSE
    IF month is < 01 or > 12
        Move customer number to report work area
        Move "last activity date" to report work area
        Move "invalid month" to report work area
        Write exception report                              UØØØ
        Indicate invalid record
    ELSE
        Search month table
        IF day is < 01 or greater than day in table
            Move customer number to report work area
            Move "last activity date" to report work area
            Move "invalid day" to report work area
            Write exception report                          UØØØ
            Indicate invalid record
        ENDIF
    ENDIF
ENDIF
```

FILES, RECORDS, FIELDS REQUIRED

Customer number work area
Customer number — transaction
Discount — transaction
Report work area
    Customer number
    Field in error
    Type of error
"Customer discount" constant
"Field is not numeric" constant
Invalid records indicator
"20" constant (maximum discount)
"Discount exceeds maximum" constant
Last activity date — transaction
    Month
    Day
"Last activity date" constant
"01" constant — month
"12" constant — month
"Invalid month" constant
Valid month table
    Month
    Days in month
"01" constant — days
"Invalid day" constant

Figure 5-62 Pseudocode Specifications

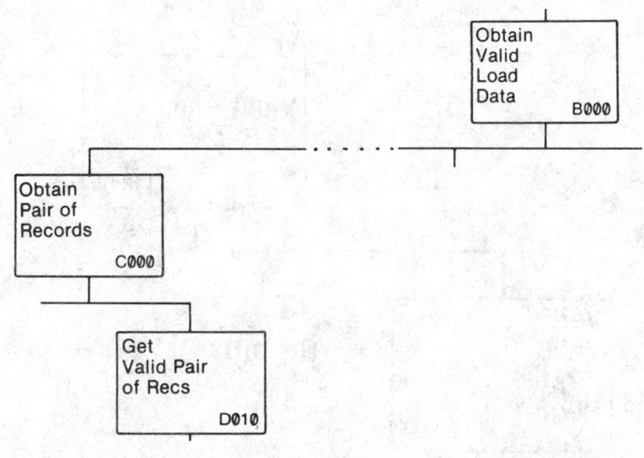

PSEUDOCODE SPECIFICATIONS

PROGRAM: Load Customer Master File		PROGRAMMER: Shelly/Cashman	DATE: May 2
MODULE NAME: Get Valid Pair of Recs	REF: DØ1Ø	MODULE FUNCTION: Verify a Valid Pair of Records	

PSEUDOCODE | **REF:**

```
Set valid pair of records indicator to neutral
Read a record
IF there is a record
   Move record to first record work area
ENDIF
PERFORM UNTIL there is a valid pair of records or
      there are no more records
   Set valid first record indicator to neutral
   Set valid second record indicator to neutral
   Move record type to record 1 work area
   Move customer number to record 1 work area
   Verify valid first record                              EØØØ
   IF the first record is valid
      Read a record
      IF there is a record
         Move record to second record work area
         Move record type to record 2 work area
         Move customer number to record 2 work area
         Verify valid second record                       EØ1Ø
         IF second record valid
            Indicate valid pair of records
         ELSE
            IF record type not = 1
               Read a record
               IF there is a record
                  Move record to first record work area
               ENDIF
            ELSE
               Move record from second record work area
                     to first record work area
            ENDIF
         ENDIF
      ELSE
         Move record 1 customer number to report work area
         Move "customer records" to report work area
         Move "type 1 but no type 2" to report work area
         Write exception report                           UØØØ
      ENDIF
   ELSE
      Read a  record
      IF there is a record
         Move the record to the first record work area
      ENDIF
   ENDIF
ENDPERFORM
```

FILES, RECORDS, FIELDS REQUIRED

Input record area
Valid pair of records indicator
Valid first record indicator
Valid second record indicator
Work area — transaction 1
  Customer number
  Customer name
  Customer address
  Customer city
  Customer state
  Customer zip code
  Transaction code
Work area — transaction 2
  Customer number
  Customer discount
  Last activity date
  Transaction code
No more records indicator
Work area to record type 1
  Record type (trans code)
  Customer number
There is a record indicator
Work area for record type 2
  Record type (trans code)
  Customer number
Exception report work area
  Customer number
  Field in error
  Type of error
"Customer records" constant
"Type 1 but no type 2" constant

Figure 5-63 Pseudocode Specifications

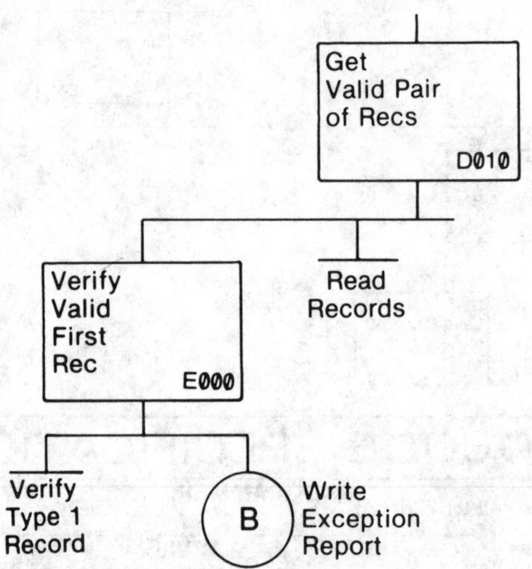

PSEUDOCODE SPECIFICATIONS

PROGRAM: Load Customer Master File	PROGRAMMER: Shelly/Cashman	DATE: May 2
MODULE NAME: Verify Valid First Record	REF: E000	MODULE FUNCTION: Verify a Valid First Record

PSEUDOCODE	REF:	FILES, RECORDS, FIELDS REQUIRED
IF record type = 1		Record type (trans code)
Indicate valid first record		Valid first record indicator
ELSE		Customer number from trans
Indicate first record not valid		Exception report work area
Move customer number to report work area		Customer number
Move "customer records" to report work area		Field in error
IF record type = 2		Type of error
Move "type 2 but no type 1" to report work area		"Customer records" constant
ELSE		"Type 2 but no type 1" constant
Move "invalid record type" to report work area		"Invalid record type" constant
ENDIF		Invalid first record indicator
Write exception report	U000	
ENDIF		

Figure 5-64 Pseudocode Specifications

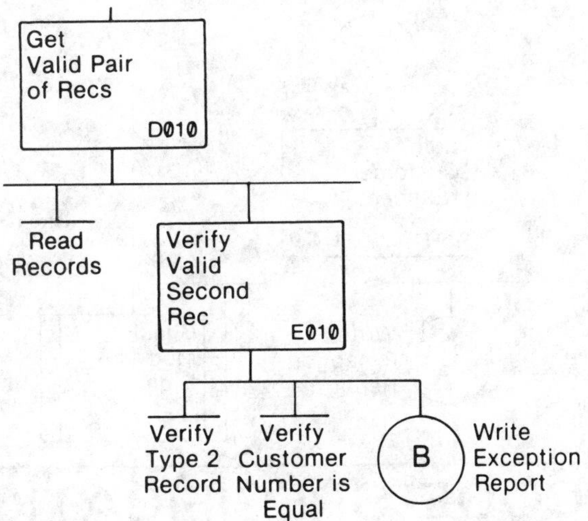

PSEUDOCODE SPECIFICATIONS

PROGRAM: Load Customer Master File	PROGRAMMER: Shelly/Cashman	DATE: May 2

MODULE NAME: Verify Valid Second Record	REF: EØ1Ø	MODULE FUNCTION: Verify a Valid Second Record

PSEUDOCODE	REF:	FILES, RECORDS, FIELDS REQUIRED
IF record type = 2		Record type
IF customer number in type 2 = customer number in type 1		Customer number in type 2 record
Indicate second record valid		Customer number in type 1 record
ELSE		Second record valid indicator
Move type 1 customer number to report work area		Exception report work area
Move "customer records" to report work area		Customer number
Move "type 1 but no type 2" to report work area		Field in error
Write exception report	UØØØ	Type of error
Move type 2 customer number to report work area		"Customer records" constant
Move "customer records" to report work area		"Type 1 but no type 2" constant
Move "type 2 but no type 1" to report work area		"Type 2 but no type 1" constant
Write exception report	UØØØ	Second record invalid indicator
Indicate second record invalid		"Invalid record type" constant
ENDIF		
ELSE		
Move type 1 customer number to report work area		
Move "customer records" to report work area		
Move "type 1 but no type 2" to report work area		
Write exception report	UØØØ	
Indicate second record invalid		
IF type not = 1		
Move customer number of second record to report work area		
Move "customer records" to report work area		
Move "invalid record type" to report work area		
Write exception report	UØØØ	
ENDIF		
ENDIF		

Figure 5-65 Pseudocode Specifications

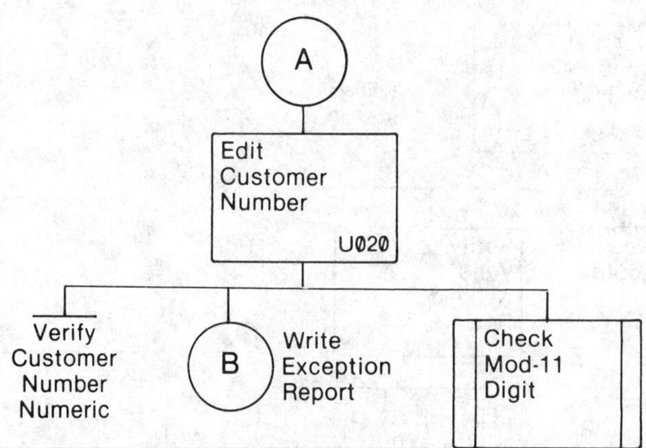

PSEUDOCODE SPECIFICATIONS

PROGRAM: Load Customer Master File	PROGRAMMER: Shelly/Cashman	DATE: May 2
MODULE NAME: Edit Customer Number	REF: UØ2Ø	MODULE FUNCTION: Edit the Customer Number

PSEUDOCODE	REF:	FILES, RECORDS, FIELDS REQUIRED
IF (first four characters of customer number not numeric) or		Customer number — work area
(fifth character not numeric and not = "X")		Report work area
Move customer number to report work area		Customer number
Move "customer number" to report work area		Field in error
Move "field is not numeric" to report work area		Type of error
Write exception report	UØØØ	"Customer number" constant
Indicate invalid records		"Field is not numeric" constant
ELSE		Invalid records indicator
Move customer number to pass area		Pass data for mod-11 module
Check mod-11 digit	EXT	Customer number in 20 char field
IF check digit is invalid		3 character indicator — valid or invalid
Move customer number to report work area		"Fails mod-11 check" constant
Move "customer number" to report work area		"X" constant
Move "fails mod-11 check" to report work area		
Write exception report	UØØØ	
Indicate invalid record		
ENDIF		
ENDIF		

Figure 5-66 Pseudocode Specifications

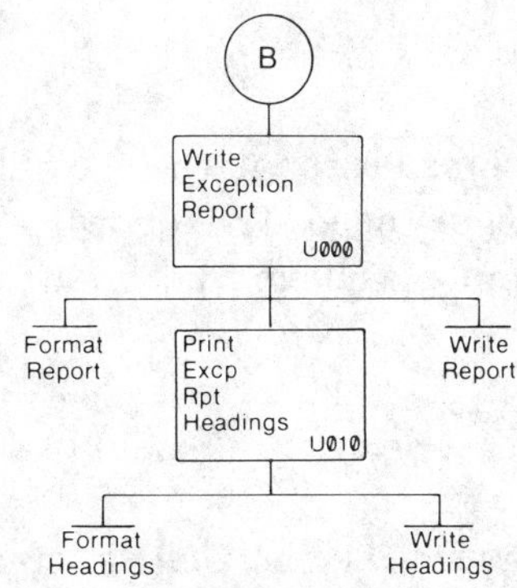

PSEUDOCODE SPECIFICATIONS

PROGRAM: Load Customer Master File	PROGRAMMER: Shelly/Cashman	DATE: May 2
MODULE NAME: Write Exception Report	REF: U000	MODULE FUNCTION: Write the Exception Report

PSEUDOCODE	REF:	FILES, RECORDS, FIELDS REQUIRED

IF first page or line count > page size
  Print headings
  Clear report area
  Move customer number to report area
ENDIF
IF current customer number not = previous customer number
  Move customer number to report area
  Move customer number to compare area
  Set for double spacing
ENDIF
Move field in error to report area
Move type of error to report area
Write a line on the report
Add spacing to number of lines printed
Set spacing for single spacing
Clear report area
	
	U010
		First page indicator — exception report
		Line count — exception report
		Page size — exception report
		Report area
		  Customer number
		  Field in error
		  Type of error
		Exception report work area (passed)
		  Customer number
		  Field in error
		  Type of error
		Previous customer number compare area
		Space control field
		Double spacing constant
		Single spacing constant

PSEUDOCODE SPECIFICATIONS

PROGRAM: Load Customer Master File	PROGRAMMER: Shelly/Cashman	DATE: May 2
MODULE NAME: Print Exception Report Headings	REF: U010	MODULE FUNCTION: Print Exception Report Headings

PSEUDOCODE	REF:	FILES, RECORDS, FIELDS REQUIRED

Move current date to first heading line
Move page number to first heading line
Write first heading line
Add 1 to page number
Write second heading line
Write third heading line
Set spacing for double spacing
Set line count to zero
		Current date
		First heading line — exception report
		  Date
		  Page number
		Page number
		Second heading line
		Third heading line
		Space control field
		Double space control character
		Line count

Figure 5-67 Pseudocode Specifications

COBOL CODING — SAMPLE PROBLEM

After the program has been designed through the use of the IPO Charts and Pseudocode Specifications, the program can then be coded. The following pages illustrate segments of the COBOL coding required for the sample problem that are unique to this application.

Loading an Indexed Sequential File — Select Statement

In order to load an indexed sequential file, that is, create the file, the System Name, ACCESS IS SEQUENTIAL, and RECORD KEY IS entries must be made in the File-Control paragraph of the Input-Output Section in the Environment Division. The required entries are illustrated below.

EXAMPLE

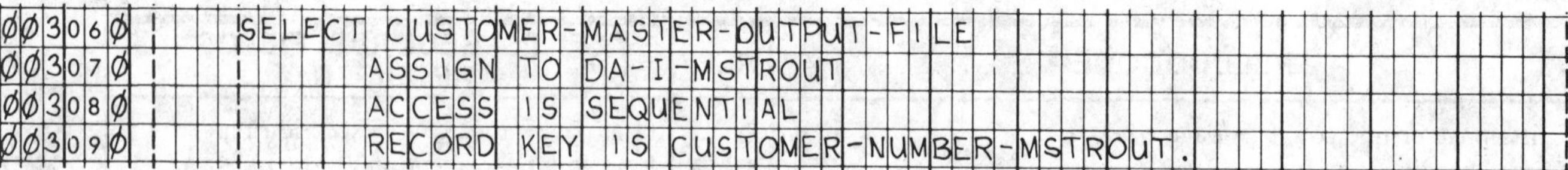

```
ØØ306Ø     SELECT CUSTOMER-MASTER-OUTPUT-FILE
ØØ307Ø         ASSIGN TO DA-I-MSTROUT
ØØ308Ø         ACCESS IS SEQUENTIAL
ØØ309Ø         RECORD KEY IS CUSTOMER-NUMBER-MSTROUT.
```

Figure 5-68 Select Sentence — Indexed Sequential File

In the example above, the filename CUSTOMER-MASTER-OUTPUT-FILE immediately follows the word SELECT in the same manner as has been used with previous file definitions. The Assign Clause indicates the type of device and organization of the file. Thus, the file is to be stored on a direct-access device (DA), and the organization is to be indexed (I). Whenever an indexed file is being defined, the type of device must be specified as a direct-access device since indexed sequential files cannot be stored on any other type of device. The organization of the file must always be specified when an indexed sequential file is being defined, regardless of whether the file is being created or being accessed in some other manner. The system-name MSTROUT is the name which will be used on job control statements to relate the file defined in the COBOL program with the file defined on the job control statements.

The ACCESS IS SEQUENTIAL clause is always used as shown when an indexed sequential file is being created. As noted previously, the Indexed Sequential Access Method utilizes keys and indexes as a means of locating records within the file. The RECORD KEY IS clause is used to identify the data field within the record in the indexed sequential file which is to be used as the key of the record. Thus, in the sample program, the data-name CUSTOMER-NUMBER-MSTROUT is to be used as the key of each record in the indexed sequential Customer Master File. The field to be used as the key can be in any data format desired by the user. Thus, it can be alphabetic, alphnumeric, or numeric.

Data Division

As with all other data files which are defined in COBOL, the indexed sequential file must be defined in the File Section of the Data Division as well as in the Environment Division. The definition of the file and the record to be stored in the file are illustrated in Figure 5-69.

```
ØØ41ØØ FD  CUSTOMER-MASTER-OUTPUT-FILE
ØØ411Ø         BLOCK CONTAINS 2Ø RECORDS
ØØ412Ø         RECORD CONTAINS 88 CHARACTERS
ØØ413Ø         LABEL RECORDS ARE STANDARD
ØØ414Ø         DATA RECORD IS CUSTOMER-MASTER-OUTPUT-RECORD.
ØØ415Ø
ØØ416Ø Ø1  CUSTOMER-MASTER-OUTPUT-RECORD.
ØØ417Ø     Ø5  FILLER                          PIC X.
ØØ418Ø     Ø5  CUSTOMER-NUMBER-MSTROUT         PIC X(5).
ØØ419Ø     Ø5  CUSTOMER-NAME-MSTROUT           PIC X(2Ø).
ØØ42ØØ     Ø5  CUSTOMER-ADDRESS-MSTROUT        PIC X(27).
ØØ5Ø1Ø     Ø5  CUSTOMER-CITY-MSTROUT           PIC X(2Ø).
ØØ5Ø2Ø     Ø5  CUSTOMER-STATE-MSTROUT          PIC XX.
ØØ5Ø3Ø     Ø5  CUSTOMER-ZIP-CODE-MSTROUT       PIC X(5).
ØØ5Ø4Ø     Ø5  CUSTOMER-DISCOUNT-MSTROUT       PIC XX.
ØØ5Ø5Ø     Ø5  LAST-ACTIVITY-DATE-MSTROUT      PIC X(6).
```

Figure 5-69 File Definition of Customer Master File

Note in Figure 5-69 that the File Section entries for an indexed sequential file do not differ from the definitions of other blocked files defined in previous chapters. Each block will contain 20 records, and each record will contain 88 characters. It should also be noted that standard labels will be used for the file. All indexed sequential files must use standard labels.

The field which is used for the Record Key CUSTOMER-NUMBER-MSTROUT, as specified in the Select sentence in Figure 5-68, is defined in the Data Division above on Line 004180. Each record in the file will be identifiable by the value contained in this field.

Open Statement

An Open Statement must be issued for the indexed sequential output file before any other processing is done with the file. The Open Statement used in the sample program is illustrated in Figure 5-70.

```
023090      OPEN OUTPUT PROGRAM-REPORT-FILE
023100                  CUSTOMER-MASTER-OUTPUT-FILE.
```

Figure 5-70 Open Statement for Indexed Sequential Output File

Note in the example above that the PROGRAM-REPORT-FILE is opened as an output file, and the Indexed Sequential File CUSTOMER-MASTER-OUTPUT-FILE is opened as an output file. The Open Statement checks the standard labels for the indexed sequential file and ensures that the indexes are readied to allow the file to be loaded. It should be noted that the Transaction File containing the Transaction Input Records is not opened at this time; the opening of the Transaction File occurs when the SORT verb with the USING option is executed, as will be done in the sample program.

Write Statement

In order to write the records on the new indexed sequential file, the Write Statement is used. The Write Statement used in the sample program is illustrated in Figure 5-71.

EXAMPLE

```
Ø2716Ø     WRITE CUSTOMER-MASTER-OUTPUT-RECORD
Ø2717Ø               INVALID KEY
Ø2718Ø                   MOVE CUSTOMER-NUMBER-TRANSORT1 TO
Ø2719Ø                           CUSTOMER-NUMBER-EXCP-WORK
Ø2720Ø                   MOVE CUSTOMER-NUMBER-FIELD-MSG TO
Ø2721Ø                           FIELD-IN-ERROR-EXCP-WORK
Ø2722Ø                   MOVE INVALID-WRITE-MSG TO TYPE-OF-ERROR-EXCP-WORK
Ø2723Ø                   PERFORM UØØØ-WRITE-EXCEPTION-REPORT.
```

Figure 5-71 Write Statement to Load an Indexed Sequential File

The record-name following the Write Statement is the name of the disk output area defined in the File Section of the Data Division (see Figure 5-69). This is the same as Write Statements used for other types of files. The Invalid Key Clause is used with Indexed Sequential Files to indicate the action to be taken if the record being written is out of sequence, that is, the key in the record being written is not greater than the previous keys which have been written; or if the record being written has the same key as a record which has already been written on the file, that is, it is a duplicate record.

As mentioned previously, the input records which are loaded into an indexed sequential file must be in ascending sequence by key and there cannot be duplicates. Thus, the Invalid Key Clause checks for these two conditions within the Write Statement.

In the sample program as illustrated in Figure 5-71, if either of these conditions occurs, the Customer Number and appropriate messages are moved to the Exception Report work area and an entry is written on the Exception Report. If the Invalid Key Clause is executed, the record will not be written in the Customer Master File because the record to be written was in error.

Sequential Retrieval — Indexed Sequential Files

It will be recalled that in the sample program after the Customer Master File is loaded, the Customer Master File List report is to be created. This report is to list the contents of the Customer Master File which was just created. In order to create the report, the Customer Master File must be retrieved sequentially.

As with all files in COBOL, the Indexed Sequential File which is to be retrieved sequentially must be defined in the Environment Division and the Data Division. The clauses, Access is Sequential and Record Key Is, are used together with the other clauses required for indexed sequential files. The following is the definition of the Customer Master File which is retrieved sequentially in the sample program.

EXAMPLE

Environment Division

```
           SELECT CUSTOMER-MASTER-INPUT-FILE
               ASSIGN TO DA-I-MSTROUT
               ACCESS IS SEQUENTIAL
               RECORD KEY IS CUSTOMER-NUMBER-MSTRIN.
```

Data Division

```
       FD  CUSTOMER-MASTER-INPUT-FILE
             BLOCK CONTAINS 2Ø RECORDS
             RECORD CONTAINS 88 CHARACTERS
             LABEL RECORDS ARE STANDARD
             DATA RECORD IS CUSTOMER-MASTER-INPUT-RECORD.

       Ø1  CUSTOMER-MASTER-INPUT-RECORD.
           Ø5  FILLER                      PIC X.
           Ø5  CUSTOMER-NUMBER-MSTRIN      PIC X(5).
           Ø5  CUSTOMER-NAME-MSTRIN        PIC X(2Ø).
           Ø5  CUSTOMER-ADDRESS-MSTRIN     PIC X(27).
           Ø5  CUSTOMER-CITY-MSTRIN        PIC X(2Ø).
           Ø5  CUSTOMER-STATE-MSTRIN       PIC XX.
           Ø5  CUSTOMER-ZIP-CODE-MSTRIN    PIC X(5).
           Ø5  CUSTOMER-DISCOUNT-MSTRIN    PIC XX.
           Ø5  LAST-ACTIVITY-DATE-MSTRIN   PIC X(6).
```

Figure 5-72 Environment and Data Division Entries for Sequential Retrieval

As can be seen from the example above, the Select Statement is similar to the one shown for creating the Indexed Sequential File. The name of the file is CUSTOMER-MASTER-INPUT-FILE. The file is contained on a direct access device as indicated by the entry "DA" in the Assign Clause. The "I" entry identifies the file as an indexed sequential file.

It is important to note that the system-name used for the file, MSTROUT, is the same system-name that was used for the Customer Master File when it was defined as an output file (see Figure 5-68). This is done because even though the file is being used first as an output file and then as an input file in the program, it is still only one file on the disk; and, therefore, only one file should be defined on the job control statements which are used for the file. In order to relate the two file definitions in the program to the single file definition on the job control statements, the same system name must be used; thus, MSTROUT is used for both the output file and the input file.

The Access Is Sequential Clause indicates that the file is to be retrieved sequentially. The Record Key Is Clause is used to identify the field within the Customer Master File record which is used as the key of the file. In the sample program, the key is the Customer Number, so the field CUSTOMER-NUMBER-MSTRIN is specified as the Record Key. The Record Key Clause is required when an indexed sequential file is being retrieved sequentially.

The entries in the Data Division describe the characteristics of the file, records, and fields being processed and should be the same as the definition of the file when it was created. As noted in Chapter 4, when a file is created and then used as input, the blocking factors and record lengths must be the same.

Opening the Indexed Sequential File

As noted previously, the Customer Master File is created as an output file and then is sequentially retrieved as an input file in order to print the Customer Master File List report. After the Customer Master File is created, it must be closed prior to opening it as an input file. The statements used in the sample program to accomplish this are illustrated in Figure 5-73.

EXAMPLE

```
023160     CLOSE CUSTOMER-MASTER-OUTPUT-FILE.
023170     OPEN INPUT CUSTOMER-MASTER-INPUT-FILE.
```

Figure 5-73 Example of Closing and Opening Same File

Note from Figure 5-73 that the CUSTOMER-MASTER-OUTPUT-FILE is closed, and then the CUSTOMER-MASTER-INPUT-FILE is opened as an input file. The file must be closed using the Close Statement prior to being opened as an input file when the file is to be sequentially retrieved in the same program that creates it. If the Customer Master File had been created in another program, then only the Open Statement would be required in order to prepare the file to be read.

After the file has been opened, it is ready for processing. The records in an indexed sequential file are read through the use of the Read Statement in much the same manner as sequential input files are read. The Read Statement used in the sample program is illustrated below.

EXAMPLE

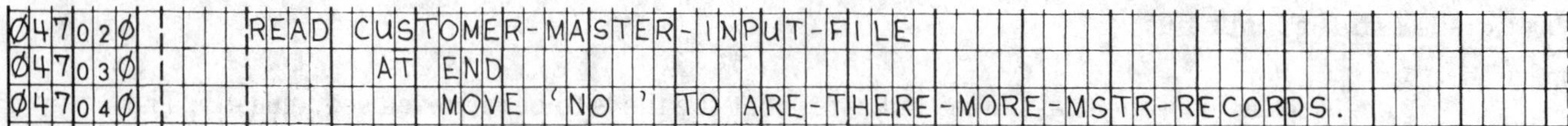

```
047020     READ CUSTOMER-MASTER-INPUT-FILE
047030         AT END
047040             MOVE 'NO ' TO ARE-THERE-MORE-MSTR-RECORDS.
```

Figure 5-74 Example of Read Statement

As can be seen from Figure 5-74, the Read Statement to sequentially retrieve records in an indexed sequential file is the same as has been used to retrieve records from a sequential file. When the last record in the file is read, the At End processing will take place as indicated.

Sequential Retrieval — Beginning With Key

Unlike sequential processing when using sequential files, sequential processing when using indexed sequential files can begin at any point in the file. This is because, using the indexes, any record in the file can be located. Thus, when programming in COBOL, the user has the option of beginning sequential retrieval at the beginning of the file or with a record within the file which has a particular key.

In addition, in some applications it is desirable to start the sequential retrieval with a "generic key," that is, a portion of the key in the indexed sequential record. For example, it may be required to begin retrieval of a record with the value 435 in the first three positions of the Customer Number, regardless of the value in the last three positions.

In order to cause this to happen, the Start Statement is used. The format of the Start Statement and an example are illustrated in Figure 5-75.

EXAMPLE

```
           START CUSTOMER-MASTER-FILE
                KEY = STARTING-KEY-VALUE
                 INVALID KEY
                   PERFORM U320-WRITE-ERROR-REPORT
                   MOVE 'NO ' TO WAS-STARTING-KEY-FOUND.
```

Format 1 — IBM

```
                                            { EQUAL TO }
START  file-name  USING KEY data-name       {          } identifier
                                            {    =     }

        [INVALID KEY  imperative-statement]
```

Format 2 — 1974 ANSI Standard

```
                              [     { IS EQUAL TO     }           ]
                              [     { IS =            }           ]
                              [     { IS GREATER THAN }           ]
START file-name               [ KEY { IS >            } data-name ]
                              [     { IS NOT LESS THAN}           ]
                              [     { IS NOT <        }           ]

        [; INVALID KEY imperative-statement]
```

Figure 5-75 Example of Start Statement

As can be seen from the example above, there are two formats which may be used with the Start Statement. Format 1 is the format found on compilers from IBM and some others while Format 2 is the format found in the 1974 ANSI Standard COBOL Compiler. The coding example uses Format 2, the 1974 ANSI Standard. Although the formats are slightly different, the Start Statement works basically the same in both instances.

The verb START must be specified for the Start Statement. It is followed by the file-name of the file to be sequentially retrieved. In the example in Figure 5-75, the name of the file is CUSTOMER-MASTER-FILE. In Format 1, the file-name is followed by the keywords USING KEY, while in Format 2, the word KEY is specified.

Following these required keywords, Format 1 requires a data-name. This data-name must be the field in the record to be processed which is specified as the Record Key in the Select Statement. Thus, if this were being used for the Customer Master File, the data-name specified would be CUSTOMER-NUMBER-MSTRIN (see Figure 5-72). Format 2 does not require the Record Key data-name to be specified.

The next entry is the conditional statement which will specify at what point sequential retrieval is to begin. Note in Format 1 that only the condition Equal can be specified, while in Format 2, six conditions can be specified.

Following the condition is the field which will contain the value specifying the key where sequential retrieval is to begin. In the example in Figure 5-75, the data-name (or identifier in Format 1) is STARTING-KEY-VALUE.

If the key specified in the data-name is not found in the file being searched, the Invalid Key processing would occur. In the example, an error message would be printed, and an indicator set to show that the starting key was not found.

The Start Statement will cause the index of the Indexed Sequential file to be searched for a value satisfying the condition specified in the Start Statement. When that condition is satisfied, a pointer will be set so that when a Read Statement is executed, the record pointed to will be the first record read. Subsequent reads of the file will cause the records following the starting record to be read.

The sequence of operations which must occur when using the Start Statement is as follows:

1. The file is opened as an input file or an input-output file.
2. The starting key is generated or otherwise obtained.
3. The starting key is moved to the data-name (identifier) specified in the Start Statement.
4. The Start Statement is executed.
5. A Read Statement is used to read the first record satisfying the conditions specified in the Start Statement.
6. Subsequent Read Statements will read the records following the record read in #5

In order to illustrate the use of the Start Statement, the following examples are presented.

Example 1: Begin With a Given Key

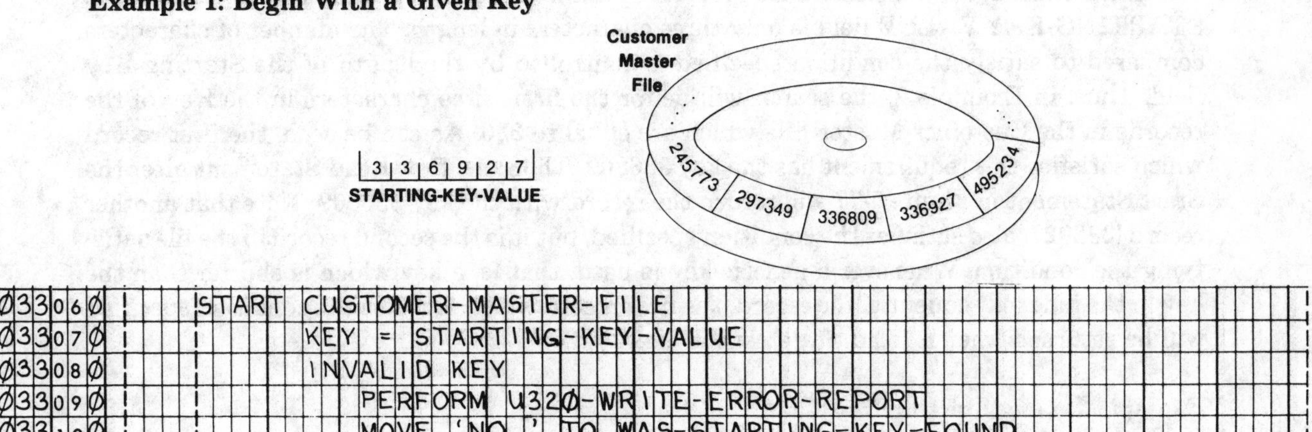
Customer
Master
File
3 3 6 9 2 7
STARTING-KEY-VALUE
245773
297349
336809
336927
495234
Ø33Ø6Ø START CUSTOMER-MASTER-FILE
Ø33Ø7Ø KEY = STARTING-KEY-VALUE
Ø33Ø8Ø INVALID KEY
Ø33Ø9Ø PERFORM U32Ø-WRITE-ERROR-REPORT
Ø331ØØ MOVE 'NO ' TO WAS-STARTING-KEY-FOUND.

Figure 5-76 Example 1 of Start Statement

Note in the example above that the file-name CUSTOMER-MASTER-FILE is specified with the Start Statement. The field containing the starting key value is STARTING-KEY-VALUE, and the condition specified is equal. Therefore, when the Start Statement is executed, the index of the file will be searched for a key equal to the value 336927. Note that this is the fourth record on the Customer Master File. Thus, the first Read Statement after the Start Statement is executed will read the record with the key 336927. The second Read Statement after the Start Statement would read the record with the key 495234.

Example 2: Begin with Part of Key

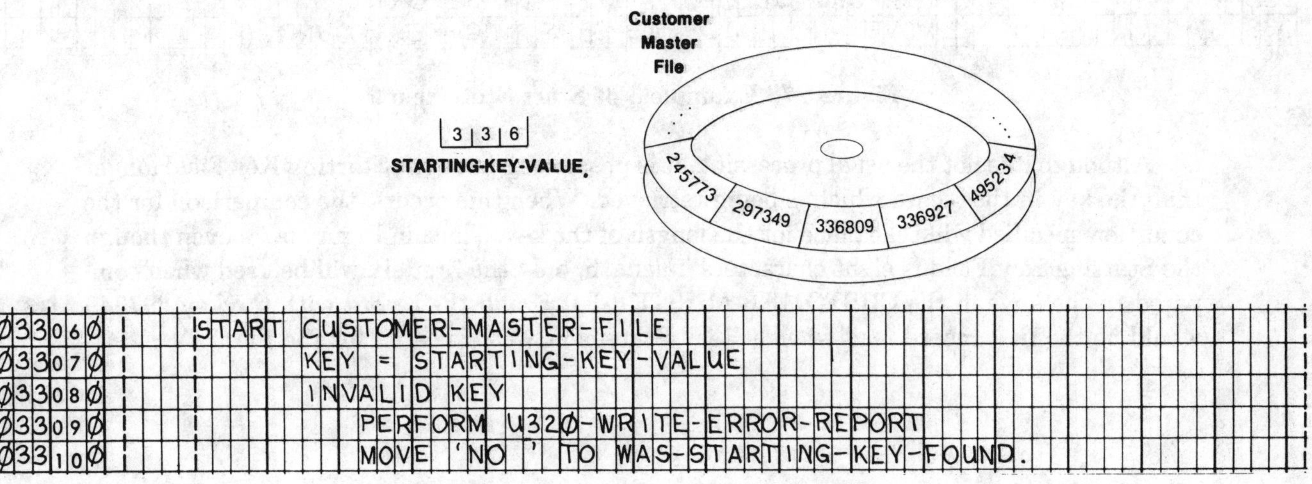
Customer
Master
File
3 3 6
STARTING-KEY-VALUE
245773
297349
336809
336927
495234
Ø33Ø6Ø START CUSTOMER-MASTER-FILE
Ø33Ø7Ø KEY = STARTING-KEY-VALUE
Ø33Ø8Ø INVALID KEY
Ø33Ø9Ø PERFORM U32Ø-WRITE-ERROR-REPORT
Ø331ØØ MOVE 'NO ' TO WAS-STARTING-KEY-FOUND.

Figure 5-77 Example 2 of Start Statement

In Example 2, it can be seen that everything is the same as in Example 1 except that the STARTING-KEY-VALUE field is only three characters in length. The number of characters compared to satisfy the condition specified is controlled by the length of the Starting Key field. Thus, in Example 2, the search will be for the first three characters in the Key of the records in the Customer Master File which are equal to 336. As can be seen, the first record which satisfies this requirement has the key 336809. Thus, the first Read Statement after the Start Statement in Figure 5-77 will return the record with the key 336809. Note that another record (336927) also satisfies the condition specified, but it is the second record in the file satisfying the condition. Whenever a generic key is used, that is, a key which is shorter than the key in the indexed sequential file record, the first record which satisfies the condition specified will be returned when a Read Statement is executed.

Example 3: Long Starting Key Value

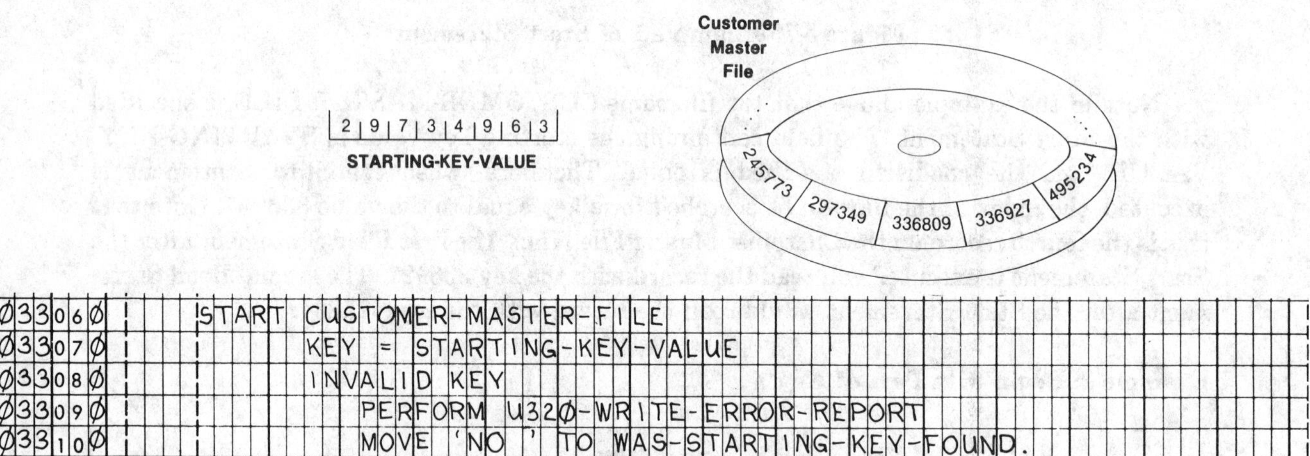
Customer
Master
File
2 9 7 3 4 9 6 3
STARTING-KEY-VALUE
245773
297349
336809
336927
495234
Ø33Ø6Ø START CUSTOMER-MASTER-FILE
Ø33Ø7Ø KEY = STARTING-KEY-VALUE
Ø33Ø8Ø INVALID KEY
Ø33Ø9Ø PERFORM U32Ø-WRITE-ERROR-REPORT
Ø331ØØ MOVE 'NO ' TO WAS-STARTING-KEY-FOUND.

Figure 5-78 Example 3 of Start Statement

Although it is not the usual processing, it is possible to have the Starting Key Field longer than the key in the record which is being retrieved. When this occurs, the comparison for the condition specified will take place for the length of the key. Thus, in Figure 5-78, even though the Starting Key Field is eight characters in length, only the first six will be used when compared to the keys in the CUSTOMER-MASTER-FILE and the record with the key 297349 would be the first record read when a Read Statement was executed for the file.

Example 4: Key Is Not In The Indexed Sequential File

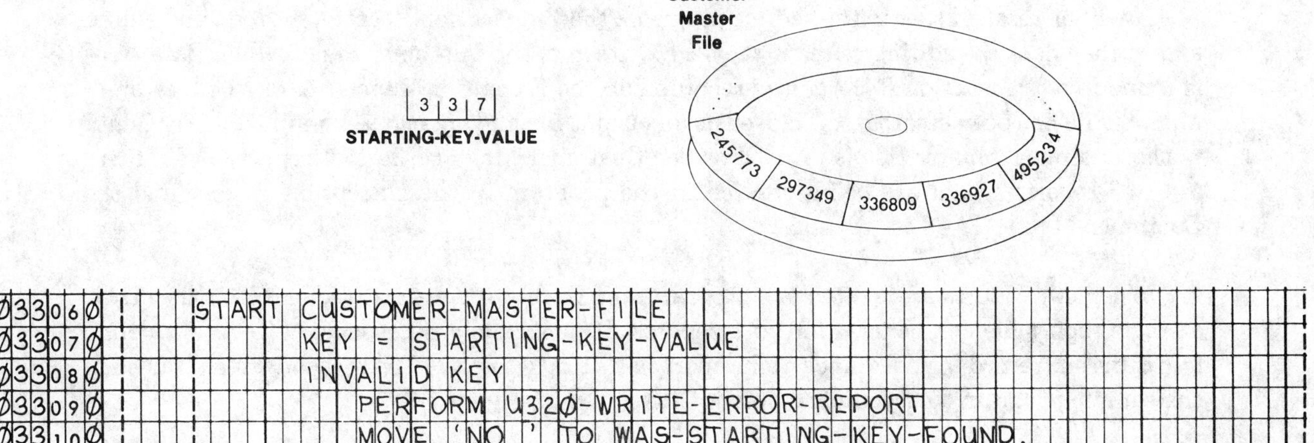

Figure 5-79 Example 4 of Start Statement

Note in the example above that the Starting Key Field is three characters in length and contains the value 337. Thus, the "generic key" 337 is being searched for by the Start Statement. It will be noted, however, that there is no record in the Customer Master File with a key containing 337 in the first three characters. Therefore, the Start processing will be unsuccessful, and the imperative statements following the Invalid Key Clause will be executed. In the example, an entry will be written on the Exception Report, and the value "NO " will be moved to the indicator WAS-STARTING-KEY-FOUND.

In all cases, the comparison made by the Start Statement to determine if the condition stated is true is a non-algebraic comparison; therefore, the keys should normally be in the Display format.

Also, it should be noted that the file must be opened prior to specifying the Start Statement. More than one Start Statement may be specified for a file after it has been opened. Whenever a Start Statement is specified, the pointer to the file will be set so that the next Read Statement will return the record with the key requested; or, if the key is not found in the file, the Invalid Key processing will take place.

Multiple Reports

It will be recalled that in the sample program, the Transaction Records are read and edited and, if they pass the editing criteria, they are written in the Customer Master File. If an error is found in a Transaction Record, it is recorded on the Exception Report. After the Customer Master File has been created, it is closed as an output file and opened as an input file. The data in the Customer Master File is printed on the Customer Master File List report. Thus, there are two reports which are being created in the program — the Exception Report and the Customer Master File List report.

When two reports are created in a program, and the reports are created one after the other, a single report file can be used for both reports. It is normally necessary, however, to define two different record formats since each report has its own format. The method which is used in the sample program to accomplish this is illustrated in Figure 5-80.

EXAMPLE

```
 FD  PROGRAM-REPORT-FILE
         RECORD CONTAINS 133 CHARACTERS
         LABEL RECORDS ARE OMITTED
         DATA RECORDS ARE EXCEPTION-REPORT-LINE,
                              MASTER-FILE-LIST-LINE.

 Ø1  EXCEPTION-REPORT-LINE.
     Ø5  CARRIAGE-CONTROL                PIC X.
     Ø5  FILLER                          PIC X.
     Ø5  CUSTOMER-NUMBER-EXCPRPT         PIC X(5).
     Ø5  FILLER                          PIC X(6).
     Ø5  FIELD-IN-ERROR-EXCPRPT          PIC X(2Ø).
     Ø5  FILLER                          PIC X(4).
     Ø5  TYPE-OF-ERROR-EXCPRPT           PIC X(25).
     Ø5  FILLER                          PIC X(71).

 Ø1  MASTER-FILE-LIST-LINE.
     Ø5  CARRIAGE-CONTROL                PIC X.
     Ø5  FILLER                          PIC X.
     Ø5  CUSTOMER-NUMBER-MSTRLIST        PIC X(5).
     Ø5  FILLER                          PIC X(3).
     Ø5  CUSTOMER-NAME-MSTRLIST          PIC X(2Ø).
     Ø5  FILLER                          PIC X(3).
     Ø5  CUSTOMER-ADDRESS-MSTRLIST       PIC X(27).
     Ø5  FILLER                          PIC X(3).
     Ø5  CUSTOMER-CITY-MSTRLIST          PIC X(2Ø).
     Ø5  FILLER                          PIC X(3).
     Ø5  CUSTOMER-STATE-MSTRLIST         PIC XX.
     Ø5  FILLER                          PIC X(5).
     Ø5  CUSTOMER-ZIP-CODE-MSTRLIST      PIC X(5).
     Ø5  FILLER                          PIC X(3).
     Ø5  CUSTOMER-DISCOUNT-MSTRLIST      PIC XX.
     Ø5  PERCENT-SIGN-MSTRLIST           PIC X.
     Ø5  FILLER                          PIC X(5).
     Ø5  LAST-ACTIVITY-DATE-MSTRLIST     PIC XXBXXBXX.
     Ø5  FILLER                          PIC X(16).
```

Figure 5-80 Example of Multiple Output Areas

Note in Figure 5-80 that a single file, PROGRAM-REPORT-FILE, is defined for both reports which will be produced. The Data Records Clause specifies that there are two records: the EXCEPTION-REPORT-LINE record and the MASTER-FILE-LIST-LINE record. Both of these records are defined using level-01 entries followed by the format of the record. Thus, there are two separate records defined which will be used for the PROGRAM-REPORT-FILE. It should be noted, however, that even though there are two records defined, there will be only one record area established for the file. When level-01 records are used in the File Section of the Data Division following the definition of a file, such as in the example, the level-01 records have an implicit Redefines Clause. Thus, in the example, the I/O area MASTER-FILE-LIST-LINE redefines the EXCEPTION-REPORT-LINE even though a Redefines Clause is not present.

When the Exception Report is written, the Write Statement would reference the EXCEPTION-REPORT-LINE. When the Master File List report is written, the Write Statement would reference the MASTER-FILE-LIST-LINE. Even though they are in fact the same output area, they are referenced with these different names so that the formatting and writing of the report lines will be correct.

Nested IF Statements

In Chapter 4 it was noted that in some instances, a Nested IF Statement can be designed in pseudocode which cannot be directly implemented in COBOL because COBOL does not contain an ENDIF Statement. In that chapter, a method was explained for handling this problem by Performing the Nested IF Statement (see Figures 4-47 through 4-49). Although that method is satisfactory, there is another method which can be used which is usually equally satisfactory. This involves repeating the code which follows the ENDIF Statement in pseudocode and is illustrated in Figure 5-81.

EXAMPLE

Pseudocode

```
IF
   :
   IF record type = 2
      Move "type 2 but no type 1" to report work area
   ELSE
      Move "invalid record type" to report work area
   ENDIF
   Write exception report
ENDIF
```

COBOL Code

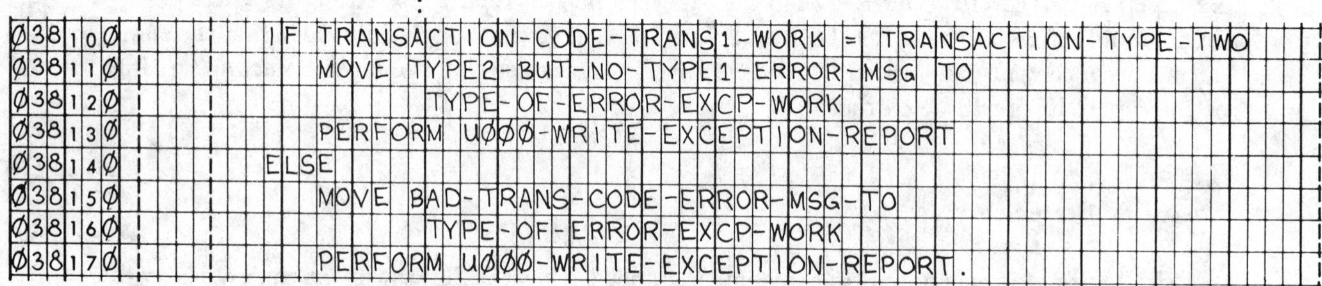

```
                    :
    IF TRANSACTION-CODE-TRANS1-WORK = TRANSACTION-TYPE-TWO
        MOVE TYPE2-BUT-NO-TYPE1-ERROR-MSG TO
                TYPE-OF-ERROR-EXCP-WORK
        PERFORM UØØØ-WRITE-EXCEPTION-REPORT
    ELSE
        MOVE BAD-TRANS-CODE-ERROR-MSG TO
                TYPE-OF-ERROR-EXCP-WORK
        PERFORM UØØØ-WRITE-EXCEPTION-REPORT.
```

Figure 5-81 Example of Nested IF Statement

Note in the example above that the "inner" IF Statment in the pseudocode determines if the Record Type is equal to 2. If it is, one message is moved to the report work area; and if it is not, another message is moved to the report work area. Regardless of whether the Record Type is equal to 2 or not, the Exception Report is then to be written.

In the COBOL coding illustrated, the test is made for Transaction Type 2. If it is a Type 2, then the error message is moved to the Exception Report Work Area; and the U000-WRITE-EXCEPTION-REPORT module is performed. If it is not a Type 2, another error message is moved to the Exception Report Work Area; and the U000-WRITE-EXCEPTION-REPORT module is again performed. Thus, as can be seen, the Perform Statement invoking the Write Exception Report module is repeated both when the Type is equal to 2 and when it is not. This is the second way in which the "ENDIF problem" can be solved in COBOL and is perfectly acceptable so long as the number of statements which must be repeated is not more than three or four statements. If it is, then the Nested IF Statement should probably be performed as illustrated in Chapter 4.

COBOL Called Programs

In many data processing installations, there are program functions which must be performed in many different applications. For example, the Modulus 11 Check Digit requirement, which is a part of the programming specifications for the sample program, is commonly required processing in many different applications. When this type of function is identified, it will usually be recognized that it is a waste of time for each programmer within the installation to have to design, code, and test his own module to perform a function which is being done by other modules within the same installation. Therefore, a module which performs a commonly required function within an installation will many times be made into a "called program," that is, a program which can be called by other programs in order to perform its function. Generally, this module will be placed in a system library so that whenever it is called, it will be available for use.

When writing in COBOL, the calling program, that is, the program which requires a function to be performed, and the called program, that is, the program which performs the function, will be compiled separately. They will then be linked together to form a single program by the Linkage Editor. This is illustrated below.

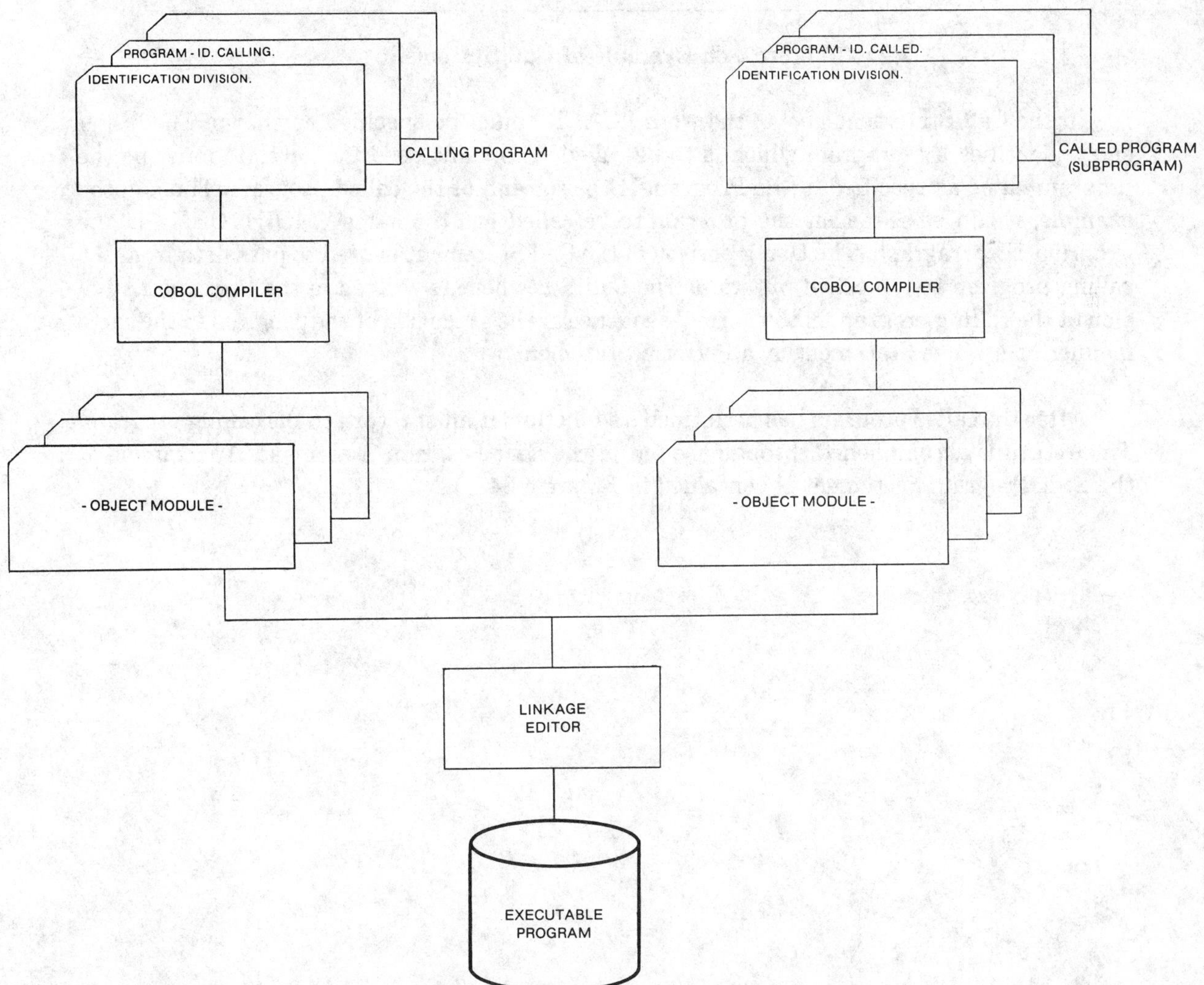

Figure 5-82 Example of Called Programs

Note in Figure 5-82 that the calling program ("CALLING") and the called program ("CALLED") are compiled as separate programs. Separate object modules are produced as a result of the separate compilations, and then these separate object modules are linked together by the Linkage Editor to form a single program which can then be executed. It should be noted that the compilations do not have to take place at the same time; in fact, as mentioned, the called program will normally be compiled one time and stored in a "library" for use by other programs. It will be extracted from the library and inserted in the calling program by the Linkage Editor when the program is link-edited.

To call a COBOL program, the Call Statement is used in the calling program. An example of a Call Statement and the general format of the Statement is illustrated below.

EXAMPLE

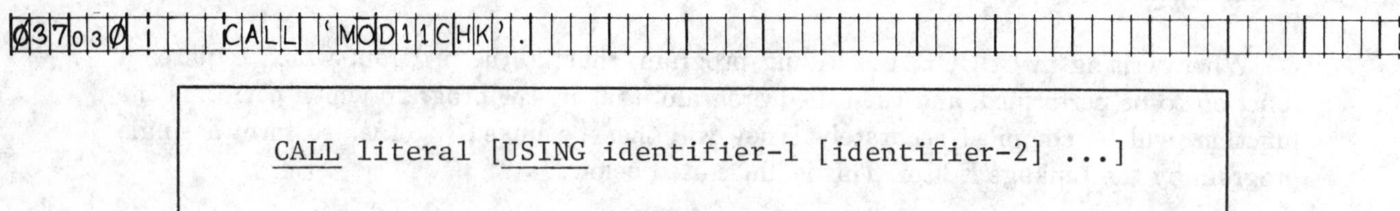


```
CALL literal [USING identifier-1 [identifier-2] ...]
```

Figure 5-83 Example of Call Statement

In the Call Statement above, the word "CALL" must be specified as shown. The literal entry identifies the program which is to be called. The value used for "literal" must be the program-name as specified in the Program-ID paragraph of the called program. Thus, in the example, it can be seen that the program to be called has the name "MOD11CHK" in the Program-ID paragraph. The Using portion of the Call Statement is used to pass data from the calling program to the called program. The Call Statement is written in the Procedure Division of the calling program in the normal sequence of the execution of the program in the same manner as a Move Statement or a Perform Statement.

After the called program has performed its function, it must return to the calling program. This return is accomplished through the use of the Exit Program Statement. An example of the Exit Program Statement is contained in Figure 5-84.

EXAMPLE

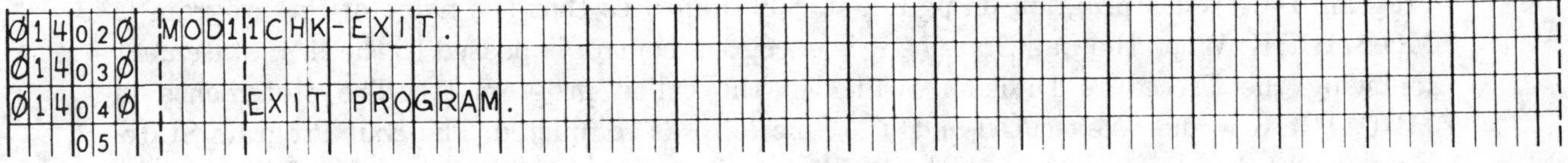
```
014020 MOD11CHK-EXIT.
014030
014040     EXIT PROGRAM.
    05
```

```
paragraph-name.  EXIT PROGRAM.
```

Figure 5-84 Example of Exit Program Statement

The Exit Program Statement must be immediately preceded by a paragraph-name and must be the only statement in the paragraph. Thus, in the example, the Exit Program Statement is the only statement in the MOD11CHK-EXIT paragraph. When this statement is encountered in the called program, control is returned to the calling program immediately following the Call Statement which called the program.

The following example illustrates the processing which takes place when the Call Statement is executed.

EXAMPLE

Calling Program

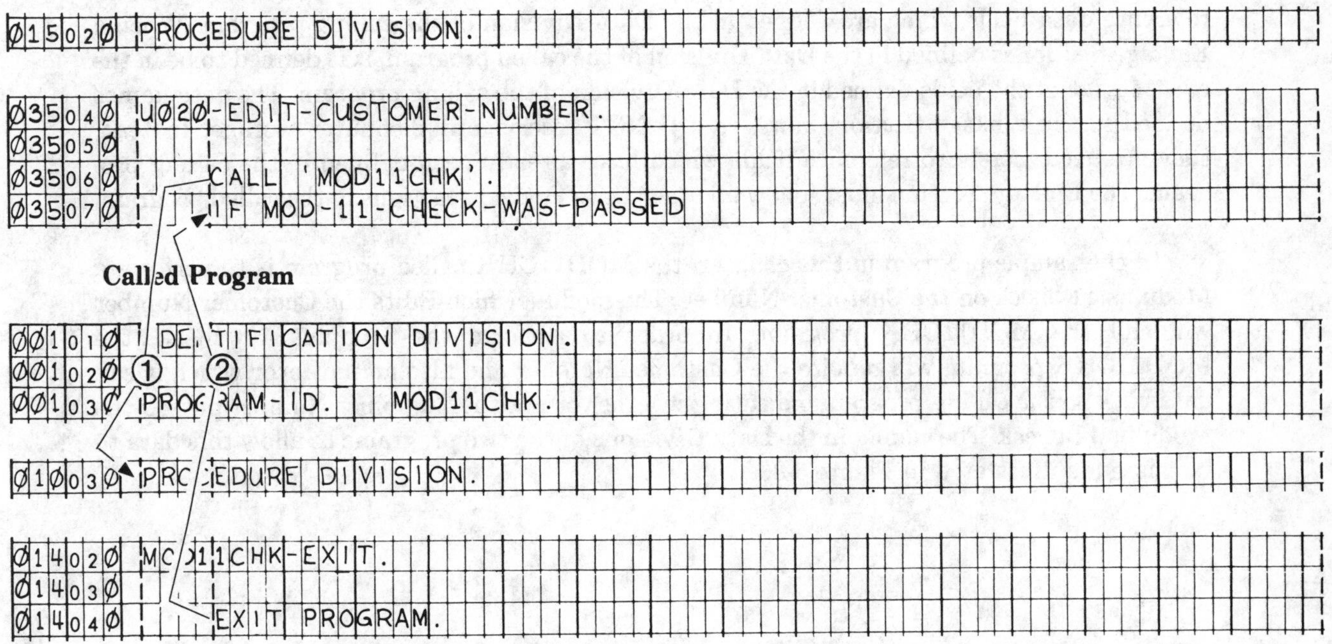
```
015020 PROCEDURE DIVISION.

035040 U020-EDIT-CUSTOMER-NUMBER.
035050
035060     CALL 'MOD11CHK'.
035070     IF MOD-11-CHECK-WAS-PASSED
```

Called Program

```
001010 IDENTIFICATION DIVISION.
001020
001030 PROGRAM-ID.     MOD11CHK.

010030 PROCEDURE DIVISION.

014020 MOD11CHK-EXIT.
014030
014040     EXIT PROGRAM.
```


Figure 5-85 Example of Call Statement Execution

Note in Figure 5-85 that the Call Statement on pg/line 035060 in the U020-EDIT-CUSTOMER-NUMBER module calls the program with the name MOD11CHK. Note that the Program-ID for this program on pg/line 001030 indicates that the name of the program is MOD11CHK. When the Call Statement is executed, control is passed to the first statement following the Procedure Division header in the called program (1). The statements in MOD11CHK would be executed until the function was completed. The Exit Program Statement would then be executed, which would pass control back to the statement following the Call Statement in the Calling Program (2). Thus, it can be seen that the Call Statement acts in a manner similar to a Perform Statement without the Until or Varying Clauses. The major difference is that the called program is compiled separately from the calling program.

Linkage Section

Another difference between the Call Statement and the Perform Statement is that since the called program is compiled separately, it has no access to the data which is stored in the calling program, whereas a paragraph which is Performed would. In most cases, however, the called program must reference some data or storage areas within the calling program in order to receive data on which to operate or to pass back data or indicators to the calling program. In order to pass information back and forth between the calling program and the called program, the Using Statement is used both in the Call Statement which calls the program and the Procedure Division header in the called program, together with a special section in the Data Division of the called program named the Linkage Section.

A Linkage Section, which is defined in the Data Division of the called program, is used to reference data fields which are defined in the Data Division of the calling program. When a Linkage Section is defined in the Data Division of the called program, it is defined to be in the exact image of the fields defined in the Data Division of the calling program. The data-names defined in the Linkage Section, however, DO NOT reserve any computer storage. Instead, they are used merely to reference fields which have already been defined in the calling program. The Linkage Section must follow all other Data Division sections in the called program.

In the sample program in this chapter, the MOD11CHK called program is to perform a Modulus 11 check on the Customer Number. The module which Edits the Customer Number will call the MOD11CHK program. In order to perform the Modulus 11 check, the MOD11CHK program will require the Customer Number and also an indicator which it can pass back to the calling program indicating whether or not the Customer Number passed the Modulus 11 check. The coding in the Data Divisions of the two programs to allow this data to be passed is illustrated in Figure 5-86.

EXAMPLE

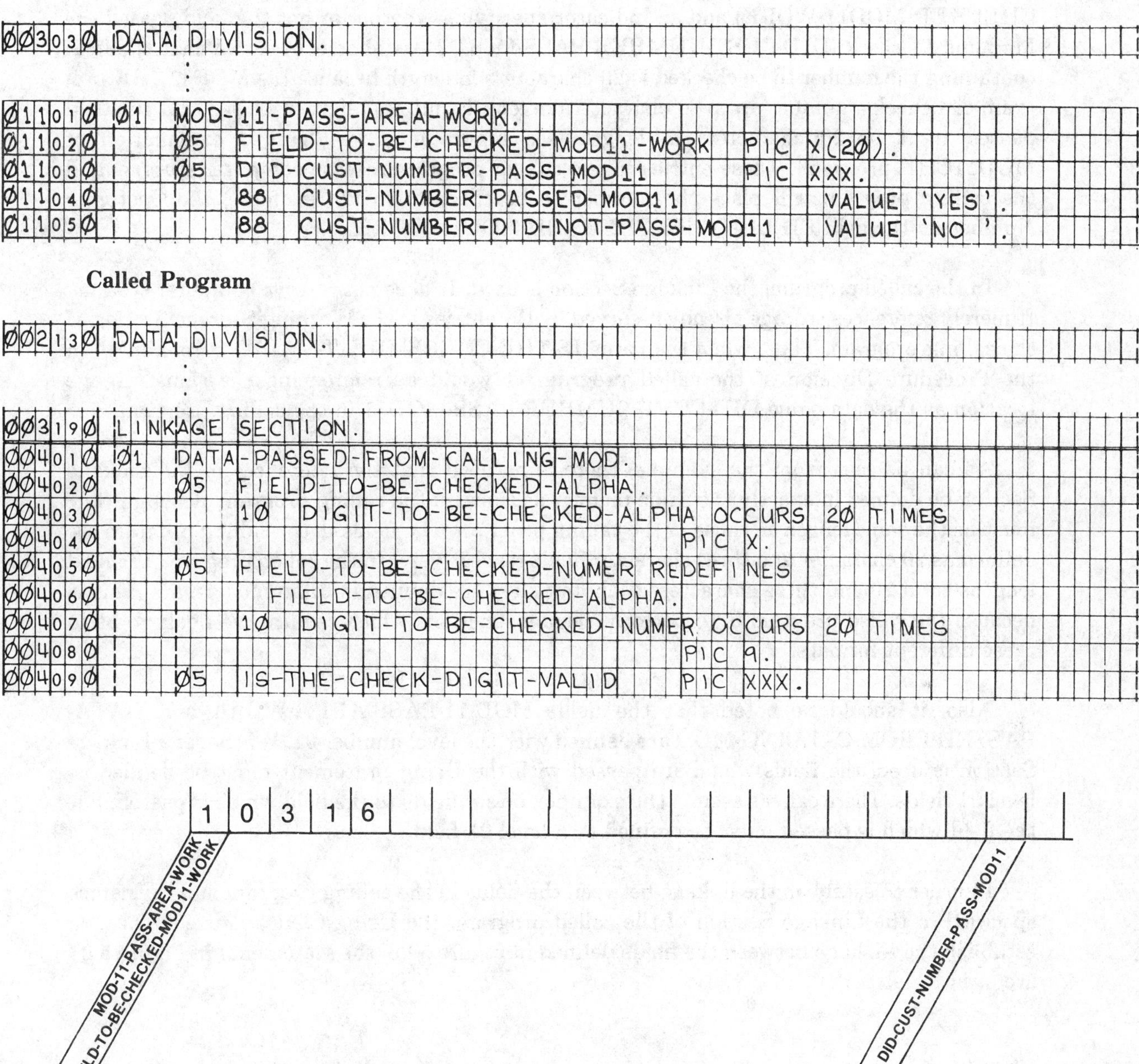

Calling Program

```
003030 DATA DIVISION.
         :
011010 01  MOD-11-PASS-AREA-WORK.
011020     05  FIELD-TO-BE-CHECKED-MOD11-WORK  PIC X(20).
011030     05  DID-CUST-NUMBER-PASS-MOD11      PIC XXX.
011040         88  CUST-NUMBER-PASSED-MOD11           VALUE 'YES'.
011050         88  CUST-NUMBER-DID-NOT-PASS-MOD11     VALUE 'NO'.
```

Called Program

```
002130 DATA DIVISION.
         :
003190 LINKAGE SECTION.
004010 01  DATA-PASSED-FROM-CALLING-MOD.
004020     05  FIELD-TO-BE-CHECKED-ALPHA.
004030         10  DIGIT-TO-BE-CHECKED-ALPHA OCCURS 20 TIMES
004040                                    PIC X.
004050     05  FIELD-TO-BE-CHECKED-NUMER REDEFINES
004060              FIELD-TO-BE-CHECKED-ALPHA.
004070         10  DIGIT-TO-BE-CHECKED-NUMER OCCURS 20 TIMES
004080                                    PIC 9.
004090     05  IS-THE-CHECK-DIGIT-VALID   PIC XXX.
```


Figure 5-86 Example of Linkage Section

The entries in the Working-Storage Section of the calling program define an area which is to be referenced in the called program — the field named MOD-11-PASS-AREA-WORK. Within this field is a field which will contain the number to be checked (FIELD-TO-BE-CHECKED-MOD11-WORK) and an indicator specifying whether or not the field passed the Modulus 11 check (DID-CUST-NUMBER-PASS-MOD11). It should be noted that the field containing the number to be checked is 20 characters in length because the MOD11CHK program can check a number up to 20 characters in length and, therefore, requires that the field passed to it be 20 characters in length (see Figure 5-34 for detailed explanation of MOD11CHK program). These entries in the calling program reserve computer storage, and the calling program will place the number to be checked (in the example, the Customer Number) in the field FIELD-TO-BE-CHECKED-MOD11-WORK.

In the called program, the Linkage Section is used. It does not reserve computer storage. It merely references storage already reserved by the entries in the Working-Storage Section of the calling program. Thus, when the name IS-THE-CHECK-DIGIT-VALID is referenced in the Procedure Division of the called program, it would be referencing the same storage location as the data-name DID-CUST-NUMBER-PASS-MOD11 in the calling program.

As can be seen from the example, there is no need that the references in the Linkage Section be defined in exactly the same manner as those in the calling program although they must be the same length as those in the calling program. The fields in the calling program are defined as 20 character and three character fields respectively. In the called program, the field lengths total 20 and three characters each, but they are defined in different formats. This is because the called program is to perform certain functions which require the fields to be in these different formats.

Also, it should be noted that the fields MOD-11-PASS-AREA-WORK and DATA-PASSED-FROM-CALLING-MOD are defined with the level number 01. Whenever a Linkage Section is used, the fields which are passed with the Using Statement must be defined as level 01 fields. There can, as seen in the example, be subfields to the field which is passed, but the field which is passed must be defined as a level 01 field.

In order to establish the linkage between the fields in the calling program and the names specified in the Linkage Section of the called program, the Using Clause is used. Thus, to establish the Linkage between the fields defined in Figure 5-86, the statements in Figure 5-87 are used.

EXAMPLE

Calling Program

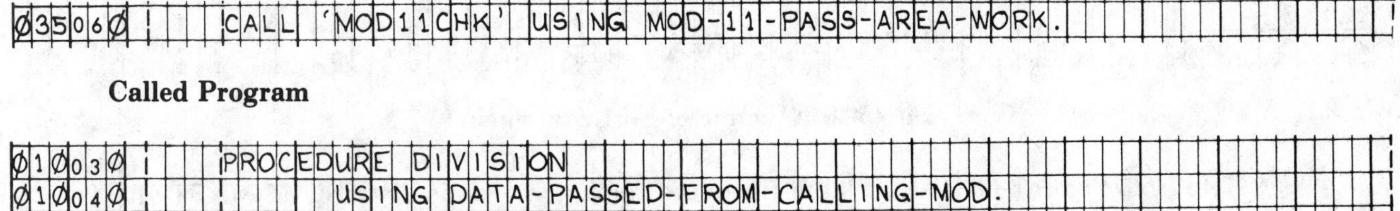

```
035060     CALL 'MOD11CHK' USING MOD-11-PASS-AREA-WORK.
```

Called Program

```
010030     PROCEDURE DIVISION
010040             USING DATA-PASSED-FROM-CALLING-MOD.
```

Figure 5-87 Example of Using Clause

In Figure 5-87, the called program will be entered at the first statement following the Procedure Division header. The linkage to the called program is established by the Call Statement in the calling program. The Using Clause in the Call Statement on pg/line 035060 indicates that the address of the field MOD-11-PASS-AREA-WORK is to be passed to the called program so that it may reference the data in the calling program. The Using Clause in the called program, as specified with the Procedure Division Header statement, identifies the Linkage Section entries in the called program which will be used to reference the data in the calling program.

When the Call Statement is executed, the called program will reference those fields which are indicated by the Call Statement in the calling program. Therefore, the entries in the Linkage Section, as illustrated in Figure 5-86, must be specified in the same sequence as those in the calling program.

The Call Statement is a poweful tool when programming in COBOL because it can be used to diminish the design and coding which must be done by the programmer by allowing modules which have already been designed, coded, and tested to be incorporated into a program. It is important to note, however, that effective use of called programs can only take place when the program is designed properly, that is, when the functions to be performed within a program are identified through the use of Structured Design.

Sort Statement — Procedures

In Chapter 3, the Sort Verb was used to sort the Program Master File. In that program, the input file to the sort was specified using the "Using" Clause in the Sort Statement, and the output file was created through the use of the "Giving" Clause in the Sort Statement. The Sort Statement which was used in Chapter 3 is again illustrated in Figure 5-88.

EXAMPLE

```
Ø2214Ø     SORT SORT-WORK-FILE
Ø2215Ø          ASCENDING KEY PROGRAMMER-EMPL-NUMBER-SORTWK
Ø2216Ø          USING PROGRAM-MASTER-INPUT-FILE
Ø2217Ø          GIVING SORTED-PROGRAM-MASTER-FILE.
```

Figure 5-88 Example of Sort Statement

Note from Figure 5-88 that the input file to the Sorting process is PROGRAM-MASTER-INPUT-FILE and the output file is SORTED-PROGRAM-MASTER-FILE. In many applications, the Sort Verb can be used quite satisfactorily in the manner illustrated above. In some applications, however, it is desirable that the program be able to either access the input records prior to their entering the sorting process or to obtain the sorted output records without creating an output file.

In order to cause these two types of processing to occur, Sort Procedures can be used. The following is the general format of the Sort Verb when Procedures are included.

```
SORT file-name-1 ON {ASCENDING | DESCENDING} KEY data-name-1 [, data-name-2] ...

{ INPUT PROCEDURE IS section-name-1 [{THROUGH | THRU} section-name-2] }
{ USING file-name-2 [, file-name-3] ...                              }

{ OUTPUT PROCEDURE IS section-name-3 [{THROUGH | THRU} section-name-4] }
{ GIVING file-name-4                                                  }
```

Figure 5-89 General Format of Sort Statement

Note from Figure 5-89 that in order to have input to the sort, one of two methods can be used: Either the Using Clause is specified, which will cause the Sort Statement to read the input records directly from the input file specified; or an Input Procedure can be specified which will be written by the programmer and will release the records to be sorted to the sorting process.

Similarly, the output from the sorting processing can be written directly in an output file when the Giving Clause is used; or the records which have been sorted can be made directly available to the program by specifying an Output Procedure.

In the sample program in this chapter, it will be recalled that the Transaction Records used to create the Customer Master File must be sorted in an ascending sequence by Transaction Code within Customer Number prior to being edited and loaded into the file. Thus, the Sort Verb is required in the sample program. In this program, however, it was determined that a Sort Output Procedure should be used instead of writing a Sort Output File through the use of the Giving Option in the Sort Statement. In most applications, this determination will be made for one of two reasons: Either there is not enough room on direct-access storage devices to write the output file; or, more likely, the time required to write the output file and then turn around and read it by the program is wasted time. Thus, by using the Output Procedure, the COBOL program can have access to the sorted data directly from the sort work area on the disk rather than from a sort output file created by the Sort Statement.

There is little editing which can be done prior to sorting the records. Therefore, an input procedure will not be used in the sample program. The Sort Statement used in the sample program to sort the Transaction File and make the sorted records available to the program is illustrated in Figure 5-90.

EXAMPLE

Data Division

```
       SD  TRANSACTION-SORT-WORK-FILE
               RECORD CONTAINS 80 CHARACTERS
               DATA RECORD IS TRANSACTION-SORT-WORK-RECORD.

       01  TRANSACTION-SORT-WORK-RECORD.
           05  CUSTOMER-NUMBER-SORTREC         PIC X(5).
           05  FILLER                          PIC X(74).
           05  TRANSACTION-CODE-SORTREC        PIC X.
```

Procedure Division

```
           SORT TRANSACTION-SORT-WORK-FILE
                    ON ASCENDING KEY CUSTOMER-NUMBER-SORTREC
                                     TRANSACTION-CODE-SORTREC
                    USING CUSTOMER-TRANS-INPUT-FILE
                    OUTPUT PROCEDURE A001-SORT-OUTPUT-PROCEDURE.
```

Figure 5-90 Example of Sort Statement

Note from Figure 5-90 that the TRANSACTION-SORT-WORK-FILE is defined in the Data Division in a manner similar to that used in Chapter 3. Since the two fields which are to be the keys for sorting are the Customer Number and the Transaction Code, these fields are defined in the TRANSACTION-SORT-WORK-RECORD.

The Sort Statement is specified using the Sort Work File as the file-name in the statement. The input data is to be sorted using the Customer Number and the Transaction Code. The Customer Number will be the major field in the sort, and the Transaction Code will be the minor field in the sort because the Customer Number is specified first and the Transaction Code is specified second in the Ascending Key Clause. The input data from the sort will be provided from the CUSTOMER-TRANS-INPUT-FILE as indicated by the Using Clause.

The output data from the sort will be processed in the A001-SORT-OUTPUT-PROCEDURE Section as specified by the Output Procedure Clause. A Section in a COBOL program is defined by a Section Header statement. The Section Header for the sort output procedure is illustrated below.

```
024120 A001-SORT-OUTPUT-PROCEDURE SECTION.
```

Figure 5-91 Example of Section Header Statement

Note in Figure 5-91 that the section is defined by stating the name of the section followed by the word SECTION. The name must be separated from the word SECTION by one or more blank characters. The section name must follow the same formation rules as a paragraph name. A section is nothing more than a portion of the Procedure Division which contains one or more paragraphs. Thus, a section can be thought of as a portion of the program which contains paragraphs, while a paragraph can be thought of as a portion of the COBOL program which contains sentences. This is illustrated in Figure 5-92.

EXAMPLE

```
SECTION—A.
PARAGRAPH—1.
    SENTENCE—1.
    SENTENCE—2.
PARAGRAPH—2.
    SENTENCE—3.
    SENTENCE—4.
    SENTENCE—5.
SECTION—B.
PARAGRAPH—3.
    SENTENCE—6.
    SENTENCE—7.
```

Figure 5-92 Illustration of Sections, Paragraphs, and Sentences

Note in Figure 5-92 that Section-A contains Paragraph-1 and Paragraph-2. Each of the paragraphs contains one or more sentences which specify processing to be executed. Section-B contains Paragraph-3 as well as perhaps more paragraphs. The notion of a Section in the Procedure Division of the COBOL program is quite important when dealing with Procedures in the Sort Statement because the Procedures must be sections in the Procedure Division.

When the Sort Statement is executed, if a procedure is specified, control is given to the section which is specified. The instructions in the section must then perform all of the processing which must be accomplished for the procedure. This is illustrated below.

EXAMPLE

```
    Sort . . . .
       USING . . . .
       OUTPUT PROCEDURE SORT-OUTPUT-PROCEDURE.
                                  :
SORT-OUTPUT-PROCEDURE SECTION.
           — Sort output processing —
SORT-OUTPUT-PROCEDURE-EXIT.
    EXIT.
```

Figure 5-93 Example of Sort Output Procedure Processing

Note in the example above that a Sort Output Procedure is specified in the Sort Statement. When the Sort Statement is executed, the data in the file specified by the using Clause will be read and sorted. After the data is sorted, control will be passed to the SORT-OUTPUT-PROCEDURE Section. So long as there is more sorted data to be processed, control MUST remain WITHIN the SORT-OUTPUT-PROCEDURE Section. There can be no statements outside of the section defining the Sort Output Procedure which are executed. This is a very important rule which must be understood when using procedures with the Sort verb: Control cannot be passed to any instructions outside the Section defined as the Sort Output Procedure when the sorted data is being processed. A violation of this rule will cause unpredictable results.

When the processing of the sorted data is completed, control should be passed to the SORT-OUTPUT-PROCEDURE-EXIT paragraph containing an Exit Statement. This will cause control to return to the statement following the Sort Statement, and the rest of the program can be executed. Again, it is important to understand that while the sorted data is being retrieved from the sort work file, control must remain within the section defined as the sort output procedure.

The coding in the sample program which implements this is illustrated below.

EXAMPLE

```
Ø2216Ø PROCEDURE DIVISION.

Ø2305Ø BEGINNING-SECTION SECTION.
Ø2306Ø
Ø2307Ø A ØØØ-LOAD-CUSTOMER-MASTER-FILE.
Ø2308Ø
Ø2309Ø         OPEN OUTPUT PROGRAM-REPORT-FILE
Ø2310Ø                     CUSTOMER-MASTER-OUTPUT-FILE.
Ø2311Ø         SORT TRANSACTION-SORT-WORK-FILE
Ø2312Ø                 ON ASCENDING KEY CUSTOMER-NUMBER-SORTREC
Ø2313Ø                                  TRANSACTION-CODE-SORTREC
Ø2314Ø                 USING CUSTOMER-TRANS-INPUT-FILE
Ø2315Ø                 OUTPUT PROCEDURE AØØ1-SORT-OUTPUT-PROCEDURE.
Ø2316Ø         CLOSE CUSTOMER-MASTER-OUTPUT-FILE.
                 .
                 .
                 .
Ø2412Ø AØØ1-SORT-OUTPUT-PROCEDURE SECTION.
Ø2413Ø
Ø2414Ø AØØ1-PROCESS-RECORDS.
Ø2415Ø
Ø2416Ø         PERFORM BØØØ-OBTAIN-VALID-LOAD-DATA.
Ø2417Ø         PERFORM AØØ2-WRITE-AND-READ
Ø2418Ø                 UNTIL THERE-ARE-NO-MORE-TRAN-RECORDS.
Ø2419Ø         GO TO VØØ1-SORT-PROCEDURE-EXIT.
Ø242ØØ
Ø25Ø1Ø
Ø25Ø2Ø
Ø25Ø3Ø AØØ2-WRITE-AND-READ.
Ø25Ø4Ø
Ø25Ø5Ø         PERFORM BØ1Ø-WRITE-CUSTOMER-MSTR-FILE.
Ø25Ø6Ø         PERFORM BØØØ-OBTAIN-VALID-LOAD-DATA.
                 .
                 .
                 .
Ø4515Ø VØØ1-SORT-PROCEDURE-EXIT.
Ø4516Ø
Ø4517Ø         EXIT.
Ø4518Ø
Ø4519Ø REST-OF-PROGRAM SECTION.
```

Figure 5-94 Example of Output Procedure Coding

In the coding in Figure 5-94, it can be seen that the BEGINNING-SECTION Section is placed at the start of the Procedure Division in order to define a section. Whenever Sort procedures are used, the entire program will normally be divided into sections. The processing in the A000-LOAD-CUSTOMER-MASTER-FILE module begins by opening the two output files and then executes the Sort Statement.

When the Sort Statement begins execution, it will first read the data from the CUSTOMER-TRANS-INPUT-FILE. This data will then be sorted. After the sort is completed, an output file from the sort will not be written; instead, control will be given to the output procedure (A001-SORT-OUTPUT-PROCEDURE SECTION) which will process the records until they have all been processed. Note in the A001-PROCESS-RECORDS paragraph that valid data is obtained, and then the loop is entered which will write the master file and obtain more data. This looping will continue until all of the sorted data has been retrieved and processed.

When the loop is terminated, control will pass to the GO TO Statement on pg/line 024190. This statement will then pass control to the V001-SORT-PROCEDURE-EXIT paragraph, which contains an Exit Statement. When the Exit Statement is executed, it signals the end of the sort output procedure processing, so control will return to the statement following the Sort Statement which initiated this processing. Thus, control will be passed to the Close Statement on pg/line 023160. The remainder of the program can then be executed. In the sample program, this means that the Customer Master File would then be printed.

It should be noted that the Exit Statement which exits from the Sort Procedure Section must be at the end of the section and should be followed by another Section Name if there are more statements in the program. Thus, the section REST-OF-PROGRAM SECTION follows the Exit Statement.

Again, it must be understood that all of the processing which will take place so long as the sorted output data is being processed MUST take place within the section designated as the output procedure. In addition, statements which are not within the sort output procedure section may not reference any modules or paragraphs which are within the sort output procedure section.

Return Statement

In the previous discussion, no mention was made of the method in which the sorted records are obtained from the sort work file by the program. In order to obtain the records from the sort work file, the Return Statement must be used. An example of the Return Statement is illustrated in Figure 5-95.

EXAMPLE

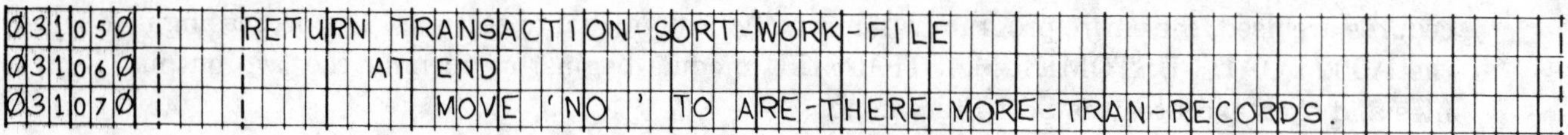

Ø31Ø5Ø RETURN TRANSACTION-SORT-WORK-FILE
Ø31Ø6Ø AT END
Ø31Ø7Ø MOVE 'NO ' TO ARE-THERE-MORE-TRAN-RECORDS.


```
RETURN file-name RECORD [INTO identifier] ; AT END imperative-statement
```

Figure 5-95 Example of Return Statement

As can be seen from Figure 5-95, the verb RETURN is specified with the file-name of the Sort Work File. Thus, in the example above, the file-name specified is TRANSACTION-SORT-WORK-FILE, which is the sort work file (see Figure 5-90). The Return Statement works in the identical manner as a Read Statement, with the only difference being that the Return Statement is making records available from the Sort Work File. Thus, when the Return Statement is executed, a single record from the Sort Work File is placed in the record area defined for the Sort Work File in the File Section of the Data Division. If the optional "Into" Clause is included, the record will also be moved to the field specified as "identifier."

When there are no more records to be processed, that is, when end-of-file is reached on the Sort Work File, the AT END processing will occur. In the example in Figure 5-95, the value "NO " will be moved to the indicator field ARE-THERE-MORE-TRAN-RECORDS.

Whenever a sort output procedure is used, the records must be obtained from the sort work file. The Return Statement is the only statement which can be used to obtain the data from the sort work file.

Release Statement

When a sort input procedure is utilized, the program must read the data from the input file or files which contain the data to be sorted. It can then process the data in any way required. After it has been processed, for example, after the data has been edited, it will be sorted. In order to make the data available to the sort, the Release Statement is used. An example of the Release Statement is illustrated in Figure 5-96.

EXAMPLE

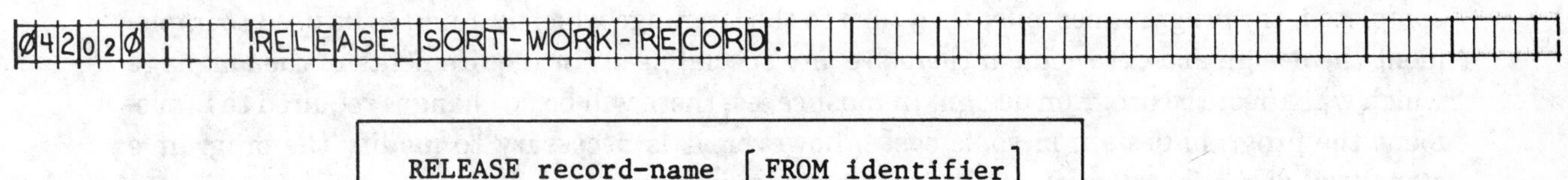


```
RELEASE record-name [FROM identifier]
```

Figure 5-96 Example of Release Statement

In the example in Figure 5-96, it can be seen that the RELEASE Verb is specified followed by the record-name for the Sort Work File. In the example, this record-name is SORT-WORK-RECORD. When the Release Statement is executed, the record contained in the record-name field will be placed in the sort work file on a direct-access device so that it is ready for sorting. When all of the records have been "released" to the sort, then the records will be sorted. The indication that all records have been released to the sort is that the Section which contains the Input Procedure will be completed; that is, an exit from the Section will take place. The rules for an input procedure are the same as for the output procedure; that is, all of the processing for the records which are going to be sorted must take place in a Section, and the instructions within the section cannot transfer control out of the section. In addition, no instructions in the program which are outside the section can reference any paragraphs which are found in the section.

The optional From Clause can be included with the Release Statement, and it works in the same manner as the From Clause in a Write Statement. If the From Clause is not used, then the record to be released to the sort will have to be moved to the record-name area by the program prior to executing the Release Statement.

Physical Packaging of COBOL Program

As has been mentioned many times, when designing a program the program designer is interested in identifying those functions and tasks which must be accomplished in order to satisfy the requirements of the program. The Hierarchy Chart is derived through the use of IPO Charts and the analysis of those tasks which must be accomplished. When the Hierarchy Chart is designed, no consideration should be given to the way in which the particular program is to be implemented or, as much as possible, to the language which will be used to implement the program. Thus, a design which is derived should be able to be implemented equally well in COBOL, FORTRAN, PL/I, or any other language.

When the design of the structure of the program and the logic for each of the modules is completed, the programmer must then turn to the language which is going to be used to implement the design and determine if there are any special needs or requirements of the language which will affect the program design. In most cases, there will be no changes required to implement the program design; in some cases, however, it is necessary to modify the program's structural design because of unique language requirements.

In the sample program, a modification to the program hierarchy is required because of the requirement in COBOL that output procedures be included in sections. It will be recalled in the program hierarchy chart that the sorting of the transaction records is specified in module D000 on the fourth level of the hierarchy (see Figure 5-53). Although this is where the sorting belongs in the structured design of the program, it cannot physically be contained there in the program because of the Section requirement of the sort output procedure. Instead, it must be moved to the top-level module since most of the processing within the program must be in the sort output procedure section. Thus, one modification to the structure chart will be moving the sort processing into the top level module. A portion of the resultant hierarchy chart is illustrated below.

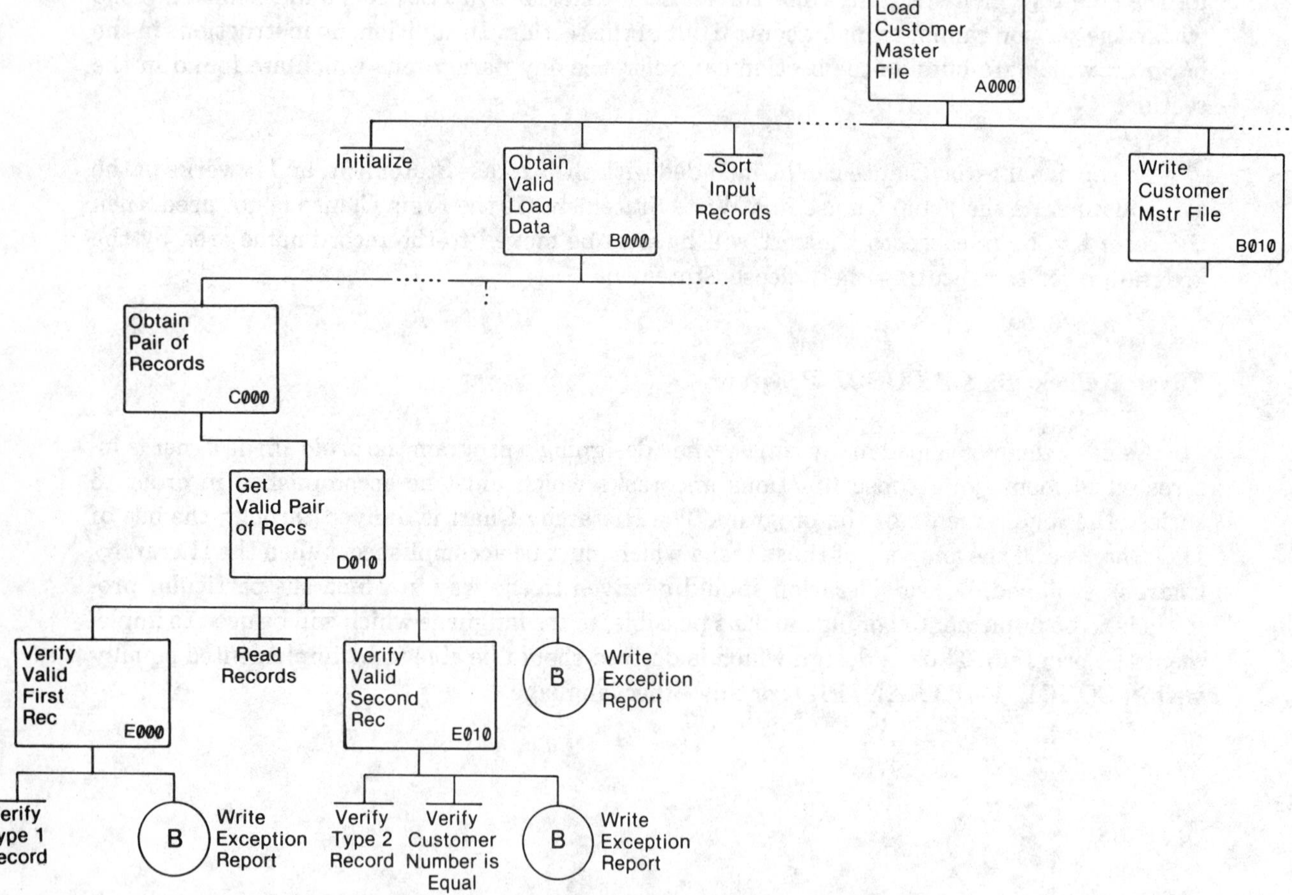

Figure 5-97 Example of Hierarchy Chart Modification

Note from Figure 5-97 that the function of Sorting the Input Records has been removed as a submodule to the C000 module and instead has been made a part of the high-level module A000. As noted, this is necessary because of the section requirement in the COBOL Sort verb.

When the sorting function is moved to the high-level module A000, it leaves but one major processing task for the C000 module. As was noted in Chapter 1, whenever the span of control is equal to 1, it is generally a good idea to examine the module to determine if the lower level module can be "married" into the higher level module. Upon examination of the processing to be performed in module C000 (see Figure 5-60), it is found that the Perform Statement required is duplicated in the module which is called — D010 (see Figure 5-63). Therefore, there is no difficulty in marrying the two modules. A portion of the resultant hierarchy chart is illustrated below.

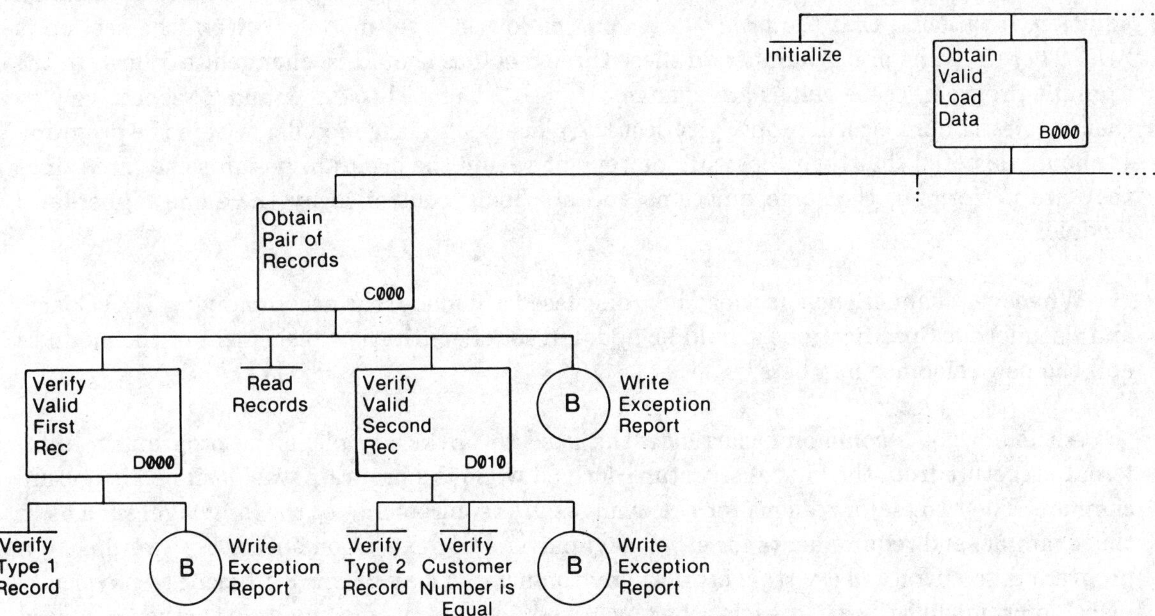

Figure 5-98 Example of "Marrying" a Module to Higher-Level Module

Note from Figure 5-98 that the module with the function Get Valid Pair of Recs, as illustrated in Figure 5-97, has been eliminated and has been moved up into the module whose function is to Obtain a Pair of Records. In addition, the module reference numbers for the modules which Verify Valid First Record and Verify Valid Second Record have been changed to reflect the fact they are now one level higher in the hierarchy of the program (i.e. moved from level "E" to level "D").

The third change to consider because of the section requirements of the output procedure on the Sort Verb concerns the physical placement of the modules which List the Customer Master. In the hierarchy chart in Figure 5-53, it can be seen that these modules have the reference numbers B020, C030, and D020. Thus, they would be physically included in the program where these reference numbers indicate. It should be noted, however, that these modules have no relationship to the processing which will take place in the section used for the sort output procedure. Therefore, they should not be included within that section. They should be physically placed behind those modules which are a part of the section. Upon examination, it is found that all modules except these three will be in the sort output procedure section. In addition, it is found that the prefix letter on the lowest level modules within the section is "U." Therefore, the prefix number on these three modules should be changed to follow. In the example program, these values are changed from B, C, and D to X, Y, and Z respectively so that the prefix number will properly reflect the placement of the modules within the program. It should be noted that their "logical" placement within the program remains the same since they are performing the same functions and are being controlled by the same higher-level modules.

Whenever changes such as those just discussed are made, the accompanying IPO Charts and Pseudocode Specifications should be updated to reflect the new placement of the modules and the new reference numbers.

Although not a common occurrence, the need to physically place the program in a different structure from the logical structure derived when the program was designed is not uncommon. The two major reasons for the changes are requirements of the language, such as in this example, and requirements for efficiency, particularly execution speed. For example, if a program is to operate in a virtual storage environment, it may be more efficient to physically place some modules next to each other even though they would not be together if placed according to the hierarchy chart when the program was designed. There is no problem doing this so long as the logical structure of the program, that is, the structure developed when the program was designed, remains the same. It will be noted that the task of physically placing modules in a different sequence within the program from that on the hierarchy chart is made a simple process because the program has been properly designed in the first place, using functionally cohesive modules.

PROGRAM TESTING

As discussed in Chapter One, an important problem that has plagued the data processing industry for many years has been the production of unreliable software. The cause of unreliable software may be attributed not only to poor program design, but also to the failure of the programmer or programmers assigned to a project to properly test the program prior to placing the program into production. Although, historically, testing has occupied over 50% of the time in the development of typical software projects, little attention has been paid, in many installations, to the necessity of developing a "scientific" approach to program testing.

Philosophy of Program Testing

After many years of testing programs, it is generally recognized that the correct philosophy in program testing is to develop test data which is designed to find errors within a program. Although it has been conclusively shown that testing, no matter how extensive, cannot be used to show that a program is entirely error free, it has also been found that by designing test data to find errors and showing that the program does not contain those errors tested for, it can be asserted with more confidence that "there is a very high probability that this program does what it is supposed to do within all constraints placed upon it."

Testing, however, should not be used as the primary tool to derive a correct program. As has been said by many authorities, the best solution to unreliable programs is to leave out the errors initially. Thus, a well-designed program is the primary tool to produce reliable software. In fact, no amount of testing can make a poorly designed program reliable.

Developing the Test Data

In addition to the designing and coding of the program, the development of test data to properly test a program is an important responsibility of the programmer. In the past, development of test data has, many times, been viewed as a necessary evil to programming; that is, the programmer knew that test data must be developed for the program, but it was put off until the program coding had been completed; and then it was thrown together as quickly and easily as possible in order to show that the program worked properly.

Today, informed opinion recognizes that the development of adequate test data is, together with good program design and coding, one of the most important tasks which must be accomplished by a programmer; for without test data which is properly designed to find any existing errors in a program, it is not possible to make any statement regarding the reliabililty of the program.

The development of test data, therefore, is viewed with the same seriousness as the design of the program. One important aspect of the development of test data is the person who develops it. As a general statement, it is recognized that no programmer should attempt to test his or her program. The reason is that when testing a program, the goal is to find any errors which remain in the program; and most persons do not like to find errors in the work which they do. Therefore, there is a psychological reluctance to find errors in a program which was developed by the tester. Instead, test data should be done by someone, either another programmer or a user or both, who has a high interest in detecting errors, rather than someone who may be biased toward not finding errors.

Another aspect which is true about testing is that testing is probably the most creative work that programmers must do; indeed it has been said that test data design demands more creativity than software design. Therefore, highly motivated, creative people are required to develop test data. The skill to develop good test data is a skill which should be practiced by all programmers, for it is a skill which is quite demanding.

Test cases must be developed with the attitude that a good test case is one which has a high probability of detecting a program error. For example, if a program contained an If Statement which checked if a field contained a value greater than 5000, good test data would have a case in which the value in the field was equal to 5000 and a case in which the value in the field was equal to 5001. In this way, the "boundary" of the data is tested. These cases are much superior to test cases where the value in the field was equal to 2500 or 7500.

Another important task of the person designing program test data is to document the expected results of each piece of test data which is used. It does no good to develop test data and then examine the results with an attitude of "that looks pretty good." There should be a reason for each piece of test data that is developed and, therefore, there should be a result which is known before the test is ever run which indicates whether or not an error was found. These results must be specified before the test is run, not afterward.

When results are obtained from a test, the results must be thoroughly examined. The results should be meticulously compared to the expected results in order to determine the conclusions which can be drawn from the test. In addition to determining whether the expected results were obtained, many times it is found that closely examining the test results will result in errors being found that were not originally being tested for.

When the test data is prepared, it should be designed to test both invalid and valid input conditions. The creativity of the person designing the test data is especially important here, since the confidence in the reliability of the program will increase with each test case which is properly handled by the program. Therefore, the designer of the test data should place great emphasis on those conditions which, however unlikely, can occur when the program is in operation.

As the testing progresses on a program, the person testing the program would do well to remember that as the number of errors found in a program increases, the probability of undetected errors increases also. Thus, when many errors are found in a piece of software, it suggests that the piece of software should be more thoroughly tested with new test data since it is likely that more errors exist. If, on the other hand, no errors are found in a piece of software after adequate testing, the likelihood of undetected errors is small.

In addition to the care taken by a programmer to develop test data, the effectiveness of the data will be increased if, after it is developed, it is subjected to a walkthrough and review by peer programmers and, in some cases, the user of the computer program. As with program design and program code, the chance exists that the test data will not be as thorough or complete as intended by the person who developed it. Thus, both the data and the documentation of the expected results should be reviewed prior to the data's being used in an actual test.

When the test is complete, many times it is advantageous to conduct a walkthrough of the test results so that more than one person can verify that the testing went according to plan. Again, the more often the phases within the program development are reviewed, the more confidence is generated that the program is operating the way it was intended.

Establishing a Test Plan

It is generally recognized that testing is an intricate part of the programming process and, therefore, should be planned within the program development cycle. There are three phases which should be included in the testing of the program. These are as follows:

1. Develop test data

2. Establish a test plan

3. Test the program

As noted previously, the development of the test data is an exacting task which must be accomplished properly in order to aid in the development of a reliable program. Although there may be variances, in general the test data for a program should be developed prior to or in conjunction with design of a program. As noted previously, the test data should be designed by someone other than the programmer who is designing and writing the program. The test data which is developed should normally be based upon the program specifications from which the design of the program is being developed. In this manner, the test data will not reflect the logic and coding which is developed by the programmer, but will rather be used to test that the program does what is required based upon the requirements of the program. Although there may be certain circumstances where data should be prepared after the program is coded, as when numerous errors are found in a given portion of the program and it is desired to further test that portion of the program, it is generally agreed that test data should be prepared prior to entering the coding stage of the program development cycle.

A test plan is normally developed after the program design is completed but before coding is begun. This test plan should specify the following items:

1. Whether top-down testing will be used;

2. Whether incremental testing, that is, testing portions of the program, will be used; or will the entire program be tested at one time;

3. If incremental testing is to be used, which modules will be tested and in what sequence;

4. What stubs, drivers, or other special coding are required in order to test the program;

5. What files, data, programs, or other things such as hardware are required in order to test the program;

6. What criteria will be established to allow testing to continue on other parts of the program. For example, it may be decided that if a single module has only one discovered error remaining, testing can proceed to other modules within the program which are used by the module; whereas, if more than one error exists, further testing will not take place until the errors are corrected.

The test plan is an important planning step in the successful implementation of a program because the progress in testing the program can be monitored. If a test plan and testing criteria are not established, the result is often the "one more bug" syndrome where testing continues forever with no apparent results. Thus, a key to successful implementation of a program, particularly a large program, is a test plan which will allow ordered testing and implementation of the program.

The testing of the program can take place only after all or a portion of the program is actually coded. The determination as to when testing can begin will normally be made when the test plan is designed. In most cases, it is wise to have a programmer other than the programmer who designed and wrote the program actually test the program. This should occur for the same reasons cited for the development of the test data. In many cases, a programmer who designed and coded the program will not be able to objectively view testing results. In addition, as mentioned previously, it is many times advantageous to have a walkthrough of the test results to ensure that the expected results have been obtained and to look for other errors which may have occurred but which were not expected.

Summary

Testing is an important part of the programming process and should be approached with the same care and precision given to the program design and the program coding. With a good program design, readable and reliable source coding, and conscientious testing, there is every likelihood that reliable programs will be developed.

SOURCE LISTING

The source listing of the sample program is contained on this and the following pages.

```
PP 5740-CB1 RELEASE 1.2  DEC 15, 1976        IBM OS/VS COBOL        20.19.30  DATE AUG 17,1978

  1                20.19.30        AUG 17,1978

001010 IDENTIFICATION DIVISION.                                       LOADCUST
001020                                                                LOADCUST
001030 PROGRAM-ID.     LOADCUST.                                      LOADCUST
001040 AUTHOR.         SHELLY AND CASHMAN.                            LOADCUST
001050 INSTALLATION.   ANAHEIM.                                       LOADCUST
001060 DATE-WRITTEN.   07/11/78.                                      LOADCUST
001070 DATE-COMPILED.  AUG 17,1978.                                   LOADCUST
001080 SECURITY.       UNCLASSIFIED.                                  LOADCUST
001090                                                                LOADCUST
001100*********************************************************************LOADCUST
001110*                                                             * LOADCUST
001120*  THIS PROGRAM LOADS THE CUSTOMER MASTER FILE, WHICH IS AN   * LOADCUST
001130*  INDEXED SEQUENTIAL FILE. THE DATA FOR EACH CUSTOMER MASTER * LOADCUST
001140*  RECORD IS STORED ON TWO TRANSACTION RECORDS WITH TRANSACTION* LOADCUST
001150*  CODE 1 AND 2. PRIOR TO BEING USED TO LOAD THE CUSTOMER     * LOADCUST
001160*  MASTER FILE THE TRANSACTION RECORDS MUST BE SORTED ON      * LOADCUST
001170*  TRANSACTION CODE WITHIN CUSTOMER NUMBER. AFTER BEING SORTED,* LOADCUST
001180*  THE TRANSACTION RECORDS ARE READ AND EDITED. THERE MUST BE * LOADCUST
001190*  A VALID TYPE 1 AND VALID TYPE 2 TRANSACTION RECORD FOR EACH * LOADCUST
001200*  MASTER RECORD WHICH IS LOADED. IF A TYPE 1 TRANSACTION IS  * LOADCUST
002010*  FOUND WITHOUT A TYPE 2, OR IF A TYPE 2 IS FOUND WITHOUT A  * LOADCUST
002020*  TYPE 1, OR IF ANY OTHER ERROR OCCURS, THE TRANSACTION      * LOADCUST
002030*  RECORDS ARE NOT USED FOR A MASTER RECORD. INSTEAD, THE     * LOADCUST
002040*  CUSTOMER NUMBER OF THE TRANSACTION IN ERROR, THE FIELD IN  * LOADCUST
002050*  ERROR AND THE TYPE OF ERROR ARE RECORDED ON AN EXCEPTION   * LOADCUST
002060*  REPORT. AFTER THE MASTER FILE IS CREATED, IT IS LISTED.    * LOADCUST
002070*                                                             * LOADCUST
002080*********************************************************************LOADCUST
002090                                                                LOADCUST
002100                                                                LOADCUST
002110                                                                LOADCUST
002120 ENVIRONMENT DIVISION.                                          LOADCUST
002130                                                                LOADCUST
002140 CONFIGURATION SECTION.                                         LOADCUST
002150                                                                LOADCUST
002160 SOURCE-COMPUTER. IBM-370.                                      LOADCUST
002170 OBJECT-COMPUTER. IBM-370.                                      LOADCUST
002180 SPECIAL-NAMES.    C01 IS TO-THE-TOP-OF-THE-PAGE.               LOADCUST
002190                                                                LOADCUST
002200 INPUT-OUTPUT SECTION.                                          LOADCUST
003010                                                                LOADCUST
003020 FILE-CONTROL.                                                  LOADCUST
003040     SELECT CUSTOMER-TRANS-INPUT-FILE                           LOADCUST
003050         ASSIGN TO UR-S-SYSIN.                                  LOADCUST
003060     SELECT CUSTOMER-MASTER-OUTPUT-FILE                         LOADCUST
003070         ASSIGN TO DA-I-MSTROUT                                 LOADCUST
003080         ACCESS IS SEQUENTIAL                                   LOADCUST
003090         RECORD KEY IS CUSTOMER-NUMBER-MSTROUT.                 LOADCUST
003100     SELECT PROGRAM-REPORT-FILE                                 LOADCUST
003110         ASSIGN TO UR-S-SYSOUT.                                 LOADCUST
003120     SELECT CUSTOMER-MASTER-INPUT-FILE                          LOADCUST
003130         ASSIGN TO DA-I-MSTROUT                                 LOADCUST
003140         ACCESS IS SEQUENTIAL                                   LOADCUST
003150         RECORD KEY IS CUSTOMER-NUMBER-MSTRIN.                  LOADCUST
003160     SELECT TRANSACTION-SORT-WORK-FILE                          LOADCUST
003170         ASSIGN TO DA-S-SORTWK01.                               LOADCUST

  2                20.19.30        AUG 17,1978

003190 DATA DIVISION.                                                 LOADCUST
003200                                                                LOADCUST
004010 FILE SECTION.                                                  LOADCUST
004020                                                                LOADCUST
004030 FD  CUSTOMER-TRANS-INPUT-FILE                                  LOADCUST
004040         RECORD CONTAINS 80 CHARACTERS                          LOADCUST
004050         LABEL RECORDS ARE OMITTED                              LOADCUST
004060         DATA RECORD IS TRANSACTION-INPUT-RECORD.               LOADCUST
004070                                                                LOADCUST
004080 01  TRANSACTION-INPUT-RECORD          PIC X(80).               LOADCUST
004090                                                                LOADCUST
004100 FD  CUSTOMER-MASTER-OUTPUT-FILE                                LOADCUST
004110         BLOCK CONTAINS 20 RECORDS                              LOADCUST
004120         RECORD CONTAINS 88 CHARACTERS                          LOADCUST
004130         LABEL RECORDS ARE STANDARD                             LOADCUST
004140         DATA RECORD IS CUSTOMER-MASTER-OUTPUT-RECORD.          LOADCUST
004150                                                                LOADCUST
```

Figure 5-99 Source Listing (Part 1 of 13)

```
3                     20.19.30        AUG 17,1978

01  CUSTOMER-MASTER-OUTPUT-RECORD.                                   LOADCUS
    05  FILLER                           PIC X.                      LOADCUST
    05  CUSTOMER-NUMBER-MSTROUT          PIC X(5).                   LOADCUST
    05  CUSTOMER-NAME-MSTROUT            PIC X(20).                  LOADCUST
    05  CUSTOMER-ADDRESS-MSTROUT         PIC X(27).                  LOADCUST
    05  CUSTOMER-CITY-MSTROUT            PIC X(20).                  LOADCUST
    05  CUSTOMER-STATE-MSTROUT           PIC XX.                     LOADCUST
    05  CUSTOMER-ZIP-CODE-MSTROUT        PIC X(5).                   LOADCUST
    05  CUSTOMER-DISCOUNT-MSTROUT        PIC XX.                     LOADCUST
    05  LAST-ACTIVITY-DATE-MSTROUT       PIC X(6).                   LOADCUST
                                                                     LOADCUST
FD  PROGRAM-REPORT-FILE                                              LOADCUST
      RECORD CONTAINS 133 CHARACTERS                                 LOADCUST
      LABEL RECORDS ARE OMITTED                                      LOADCUST
      DATA RECORDS ARE EXCEPTION-REPORT-LINE,                        LOADCUST
                       MASTER-FILE-LIST-LINE.                        LOADCUST
                                                                     LOADCUST
01  EXCEPTION-REPORT-LINE.                                           LOADCUST
    05  CARRIAGE-CONTROL                 PIC X.                      LOADCUST
    05  FILLER                           PIC X.                      LOADCUST
    05  CUSTOMER-NUMBER-EXCPRPT          PIC X(5).                   LOADCUST
    05  FILLER                           PIC X(6).                   LOADCUST
    05  FIELD-IN-ERROR-EXCPRPT           PIC X(20).                  LOADCUST
    05  FILLER                           PIC X(4).                   LOADCUST
    05  TYPE-OF-ERROR-EXCPRPT            PIC X(25).                  LOADCUST
    05  FILLER                           PIC X(71).                  LOADCUST
                                                                     LOADCUST
01  MASTER-FILE-LIST-LINE.                                           LOADCUST
    05  CARRIAGE-CONTROL                 PIC X.                      LOADCUST
    05  FILLER                           PIC X.                      LOADCUST
    05  CUSTOMER-NUMBER-MSTRLIST         PIC X(5).                   LOADCUST
    05  FILLER                           PIC X(3).                   LOADCUST
    05  CUSTOMER-NAME-MSTRLIST           PIC X(20).                  LOADCUST
    05  FILLER                           PIC X(3).                   LOADCUST
    05  CUSTOMER-ADDRESS-MSTRLIST        PIC X(27).                  LOADCUST
    05  FILLER                           PIC X(3).                   LOADCUST
    05  CUSTOMER-CITY-MSTRLIST           PIC X(20).                  LOADCUST
    05  FILLER                           PIC X(3).                   LOADCUST
    05  CUSTOMER-STATE-MSTRLIST          PIC XX.                     LOADCUST
    05  FILLER                           PIC X(5).                   LOADCUST
    05  CUSTOMER-ZIP-CODE-MSTRLIST       PIC X(5).                   LOADCUST
    05  FILLER                           PIC X(3).                   LOADCUST
    05  CUSTOMER-DISCOUNT-MSTRLIST       PIC XX.                     LOADCUST
    05  PERCENT-SIGN-MSTRLIST            PIC X.                      LOADCUST
    05  FILLER                           PIC X(5).                   LOADCUST
    05  LAST-ACTIVITY-DATE-MSTRLIST      PIC XXBXXBXX.               LOADCUST
    05  FILLER                           PIC X(16).                  LOADCUST
                                                                     LOADCUST
FD  CUSTOMER-MASTER-INPUT-FILE                                       LOADCUST
      BLOCK CONTAINS 20 RECORDS                                      LOADCUST
      RECORD CONTAINS 88 CHARACTERS                                  LOADCUST
      LABEL RECORDS ARE STANDARD                                     LOADCUST
      DATA RECORD IS CUSTOMER-MASTER-INPUT-RECORD.                   LOADCUST
                                                                     LOADCUST
01  CUSTOMER-MASTER-INPUT-RECORD.                                    LOADCUST
    05  FILLER                           PIC X.                      LOADCUST
    05  CUSTOMER-NUMBER-MSTRIN           PIC X(5).                   LOADCUST
    05  CUSTOMER-NAME-MSTRIN             PIC X(20).                  LOADCUST
    05  CUSTOMER-ADDRESS-MSTRIN          PIC X(27).                  LOADCUST
    05  CUSTOMER-CITY-MSTRIN             PIC X(20).                  LOADCUST
    05  CUSTOMER-STATE-MSTRIN            PIC XX.                     LOADCUST
    05  CUSTOMER-ZIP-CODE-MSTRIN         PIC X(5).                   LOADCUST
    05  CUSTOMER-DISCOUNT-MSTRIN         PIC XX.                     LOADCUST
    05  LAST-ACTIVITY-DATE-MSTRIN        PIC X(6).                   LOADCUST
                                                                     LOADCUST
SD  TRANSACTION-SORT-WORK-FILE                                       LOADCUST
      RECORD CONTAINS 80 CHARACTERS                                  LOADCUST
      DATA RECORD IS TRANSACTION-SORT-WORK-RECORD.                   LOADCUST
                                                                     LOADCUST
01  TRANSACTION-SORT-WORK-RECORD.                                    LOADCUST
    05  CUSTOMER-NUMBER-SORTREC          PIC X(5).                   LOADCUST
    05 FILLER                            PIC X(74).                  LOADCUST
    05  TRANSACTION-CODE-SORTREC         PIC X.                      LOADCUST
                                                                     LOADCUST
```

Figure 5-100 Source Listing (Part 2 of 13)

```
4                   20.19.30        AUG 17,1978

009050 WORKING-STORAGE SECTION.                                          LOADCUST
009060                                                                   LOADCUST
009070 01  PROGRAM-INDICATORS.                                           LOADCUST
009080     05  ARE-THERE-MORE-TRAN-RECORDS      PIC XXX VALUE 'YES'.     LOADCUST
009090         88  THERE-ARE-MORE-TRAN-RECORDS          VALUE 'YES'.     LOADCUST
009100         88  THERE-ARE-NO-MORE-TRAN-RECORDS       VALUE 'NO '.     LOADCUST
009110     05  ARE-TRAN-RECORDS-VALID           PIC XXX.                 LOADCUST
009120         88  TRAN-RECORDS-ARE-VALID               VALUE 'YES'.     LOADCUST
009130         88  TRAN-RECORDS-ARE-NOT-VALID           VALUE 'NO '.     LOADCUST
009140     05  ARE-THERE-MORE-MSTR-RECORDS      PIC XXX VALUE 'YES'.     LOADCUST
009150         88  THERE-ARE-MORE-MSTR-RECORDS          VALUE 'YES'.     LOADCUST
009160         88  THERE-ARE-NO-MORE-MSTR-RECORDS       VALUE 'NO '.     LOADCUST
009170     05  ARE-THE-PAIR-OF-RECORDS-VALID    PIC XXX.                 LOADCUST
009180         88  THE-PAIR-OF-RECORDS-ARE-VALID        VALUE 'YES'.     LOADCUST
009190     05  IS-THE-FIRST-RECORD-VALID        PIC XXX.                 LOADCUST
009200         88  THE-FIRST-RECORD-IS-VALID            VALUE 'YES'.     LOADCUST
010010         88  THE-FIRST-RECORD-IS-NOT-VALID        VALUE 'NO '.     LOADCUST
010020     05  IS-THE-SECOND-RECORD-VALID       PIC XXX.                 LOADCUST
010030         88  THE-SECOND-RECORD-IS-VALID           VALUE 'YES'.     LOADCUST
010040         88  THE-SECOND-RECORD-IS-NOT-VALID       VALUE 'NO '.     LOADCUST
010050                                                                   LOADCUST
010060 01  PROGRAM-COMPARE-AREAS.                                        LOADCUST
010070     05  PREVIOUS-CUSTOMER-NUMBER     PIC X(5)    VALUE LOW-VALUES.LOADCUST
010080                                                                   LOADCUST
010090 01  PROGRAM-WORK-AREAS.                                           LOADCUST
010100     05  EXCEPTION-REPORT-WORK-AREA.                               LOADCUST
010110         10  CUSTOMER-NUMBER-EXCP-WORK        PIC X(5).            LOADCUST
010120         10  FIELD-IN-ERROR-EXCP-WORK         PIC X(20).           LOADCUST
010130         10  TYPE-OF-ERROR-EXCP-WORK          PIC X(25).           LOADCUST
010140     05  TYPE-1-TRANS-WORK-AREA.                                   LOADCUST
010150         10  TRANSACTION-CODE-TRANS1-WORK     PIC X.               LOADCUST
010160         10  CUSTOMER-NUMBER-TRANS1-WORK      PIC X(5).            LOADCUST
010170     05  TYPE-2-TRANS-WORK-AREA.                                   LOADCUST
010180         10  TRANSACTION-CODE-TRANS2-WORK     PIC X.               LOADCUST
010190         10  CUSTOMER-NUMBER-TRANS2-WORK      PIC X(5).            LOADCUST
010200     05  CUSTOMER-NUMBER-WORK.                                     LOADCUST
010210         10  FIRST-FOUR-CHAR-CUST-NUMB-WORK   PIC X(4).            LOADCUST
010220         10  FIFTH-CHAR-CUST-NUMB-WORK        PIC X.               LOADCUST
010230             88  VALID-CHECK-DIGIT-FOR-TEN    VALUE 'X'.           LOADCUST
010240                                                                   LOADCUST
010250 01  MOD-11-PASS-AREA-WORK.                                        LOADCUST
011010         10  FIELD-TO-BE-CHECKED-MOD11-WORK   PIC X(20).           LOADCUST
011020         10  DID-CUST-NUMBER-PASS-MOD11       PIC XXX.             LOADCUST
011030             88  CUST-NUMBER-PASSED-MOD11         VALUE 'YES'.     LOADCUST
011040             88  CUST-NUMBER-DID-NOT-PASS-MOD11   VALUE 'NO '.     LOADCUST
011050                                                                   LOADCUST
011060 01  PROGRAM-CONSTANTS.                                            LOADCUST
011070     05  CUSTOMER-NAME-FIELD-MSG             PIC X(20) VALUE       LOADCUST
011080                                            'CUSTOMER NAME       '.LOADCUST
011090     05  BLANK-FIELD-ERROR-MSG               PIC X(25) VALUE       LOADCUST
011100                                       'FIELD CONTAINS SPACES    '.LOADCUST
011110     05  CUSTOMER-ADDRESS-FIELD-MSG          PIC X(20) VALUE       LOADCUST
011120                                            'CUSTOMER ADDRESS    '.LOADCUST
011130     05  CUSTOMER-CITY-FIELD-MSG             PIC X(20) VALUE       LOADCUST
011140                                            'CUSTOMER CITY       '.LOADCUST
011150     05  CUSTOMER-STATE-FIELD-MSG            PIC X(20) VALUE       LOADCUST
011160                                            'CUSTOMER STATE      '.LOADCUST
011170     05  BAD-STATE-CODE-ERROR-MSG            PIC X(25) VALUE       LOADCUST
011180                                       'INVALID STATE CODE       '.LOADCUST
011190     05  CUSTOMER-ZIP-CODE-FIELD-MSG         PIC X(20) VALUE       LOADCUST
011200                                            'CUSTOMER ZIP CODE   '.LOADCUST
012010     05  FIELD-NOT-NUMERIC-ERROR-MSG         PIC X(25) VALUE       LOADCUST
012020                                       'FIELD IS NOT NUMERIC     '.LOADCUST
012030     05  CUSTOMER-DISCOUNT-FIELD-MSG         PIC X(20) VALUE       LOADCUST
012040                                            'CUSTOMER DISCOUNT   '.LOADCUST
012050     05  MAXIMUM-DISCOUNT-PERCENT            PIC XX    VALUE '20'.LOADCUST
012060     05  BAD-DISCOUNT-ERROR-MSG              PIC X(25) VALUE       LOADCUST
012070                                       'DISCOUNT EXCEEDS MAXIMUM '.LOADCUST
012080     05  LAST-ACTIVITY-DATE-FIELD-MSG        PIC X(20) VALUE       LOADCUST
012090                                            'LAST ACTIVITY DATE  '.LOADCUST
012120     05  BAD-MONTH-ERROR-MSG                 PIC X(25) VALUE       LOADCUST
012130                                       'INVALID MONTH            '.LOADCUST
012140     05  FIRST-DAY-OF-MONTH-NUMBER           PIC XX    VALUE '01'.LOADCUST
012150     05  BAD-DAY-ERROR-MSG                   PIC X(25) VALUE       LOADCUST
012160                                       'INVALID DAY              '.LOADCUST
012170     05  CUSTOMER-RECORDS-FIELD-MSG          PIC X(20) VALUE       LOADCUST
012180                                            'CUSTOMER RECORDS    '.LOADCUST
012190     05  TYPE1-BUT-NO-TYPE2-ERROR-MSG        PIC X(25) VALUE       LOADCUST
012200                                       'TYPE 1 BUT NO TYPE 2     '.LOADCUST
012210     05  TRANSACTION-TYPE-ONE                PIC X     VALUE '1'. LOADCUST
012220     05  TRANSACTION-TYPE-TWO                PIC X     VALUE '2'. LOADCUST
013010     05  TYPE2-BUT-NO-TYPE1-ERROR-MSG        PIC X(25) VALUE       LOADCUST
013020                                       'TYPE 2 BUT NO TYPE 1     '.LOADCUST
013030     05  BAD-TRANS-CODE-ERROR-MSG            PIC X(25) VALUE       LOADCUST
013040                                       'INVALID RECORD TYPE      '.LOADCUST
013050     05  CUSTOMER-NUMBER-FIELD-MSG           PIC X(20) VALUE       LOADCUST
013060                                            'CUSTOMER NUMBER     '.LOADCUST
013070     05  FAILS-MOD11-ERROR-MSG               PIC X(25) VALUE       LOADCUST
013080                                       'FAILS MOD-11 CHECK       '.LOADCUST
013090     05  INVALID-WRITE-MSG                   PIC X(25) VALUE       LOADCUST
013100                                       'DUPLICATE OR BAD SEQUENCE'.LOADCUST
013110                                                                   LOADCUST
```

Figure 5-101 Source Listing (Part 3 of 13)

```
   5                   20.19.30        AUG 17,1976

013120 01  PROGRAM-TABLES.                                          LOADCUST
013130     05  STATE-TABLE.                                         LOADCUST
013140         10  VALID-STATE-CONSTANTS.                           LOADCUST
013150             15  FILLER          PIC XX      VALUE 'AK'.      LOADCUST
013160             15  FILLER          PIC XX      VALUE 'AL'.      LOADCUST
013170             15  FILLER          PIC XX      VALUE 'AR'.      LOADCUST
013180             15  FILLER          PIC XX      VALUE 'AZ'.      LOADCUST
013190             15  FILLER          PIC XX      VALUE 'CA'.      LOADCUST
013200             15  FILLER          PIC XX      VALUE 'CO'.      LOADCUST
013210             15  FILLER          PIC XX      VALUE 'CT'.      LOADCUST
013220             15  FILLER          PIC XX      VALUE 'DC'.      LOADCUST
013230             15  FILLER          PIC XX      VALUE 'DE'.      LOADCUST
014010             15  FILLER          PIC XX      VALUE 'FL'.      LOADCUST
014020             15  FILLER          PIC XX      VALUE 'GA'.      LOADCUST
014030             15  FILLER          PIC XX      VALUE 'HI'.      LOADCUST
014040             15  FILLER          PIC XX      VALUE 'IA'.      LOADCUST
014050             15  FILLER          PIC XX      VALUE 'ID'.      LOADCUST
014060             15  FILLER          PIC XX      VALUE 'IL'.      LOADCUST
014070             15  FILLER          PIC XX      VALUE 'IN'.      LOADCUST
014080             15  FILLER          PIC XX      VALUE 'KS'.      LOADCUST
014090             15  FILLER          PIC XX      VALUE 'KY'.      LOADCUST
014100             15  FILLER          PIC XX      VALUE 'LA'.      LOADCUST
014110             15  FILLER          PIC XX      VALUE 'MA'.      LOADCUST
014120             15  FILLER          PIC XX      VALUE 'MD'.      LOADCUST
014130             15  FILLER          PIC XX      VALUE 'ME'.      LOADCUST
014140             15  FILLER          PIC XX      VALUE 'MI'.      LOADCUST
014150             15  FILLER          PIC XX      VALUE 'MN'.      LOADCUST
014160             15  FILLER          PIC XX      VALUE 'MO'.      LOADCUST
014170             15  FILLER          PIC XX      VALUE 'MS'.      LOADCUST
014180             15  FILLER          PIC XX      VALUE 'MT'.      LOADCUST
014190             15  FILLER          PIC XX      VALUE 'NB'.      LOADCUST
014200             15  FILLER          PIC XX      VALUE 'NC'.      LOADCUST
015010             15  FILLER          PIC XX      VALUE 'ND'.      LOADCUST
015020             15  FILLER          PIC XX      VALUE 'NH'.      LOADCUST
015030             15  FILLER          PIC XX      VALUE 'NJ'.      LOADCUST
015040             15  FILLER          PIC XX      VALUE 'NM'.      LOADCUST
015050             15  FILLER          PIC XX      VALUE 'NV'.      LOADCUST
015060             15  FILLER          PIC XX      VALUE 'NY'.      LOADCUST
015070             15  FILLER          PIC XX      VALUE 'OH'.      LOADCUST
015080             15  FILLER          PIC XX      VALUE 'OK'.      LOADCUST
015090             15  FILLER          PIC XX      VALUE 'OR'.      LOADCUST
015100             15  FILLER          PIC XX      VALUE 'PA'.      LOADCUST
015110             15  FILLER          PIC XX      VALUE 'RI'.      LOADCUST
015120             15  FILLER          PIC XX      VALUE 'SC'.      LOADCUST
015130             15  FILLER          PIC XX      VALUE 'SD'.      LOADCUST
015140             15  FILLER          PIC XX      VALUE 'TN'.      LOADCUST
015150             15  FILLER          PIC XX      VALUE 'TX'.      LOADCUST
015160             15  FILLER          PIC XX      VALUE 'UT'.      LOADCUST
015170             15  FILLER          PIC XX      VALUE 'VA'.      LOADCUST
015180             15  FILLER          PIC XX      VALUE 'VT'.      LOADCUST
015190             15  FILLER          PIC XX      VALUE 'WA'.      LOADCUST
015200             15  FILLER          PIC XX      VALUE 'WI'.      LOADCUST
016010             15  FILLER          PIC XX      VALUE 'WV'.      LOADCUST
016020             15  FILLER          PIC XX      VALUE 'WY'.      LOADCUST
016030         10  VALID-STATE-TABLE REDEFINES VALID-STATE-CONSTANTS    LOADCUST
016040                                     OCCURS 51 TIMES          LOADCUST
016050                                     ASCENDING KEY IS         LOADCUST
016060                                         STATE-CODE           LOADCUST
016070                                     INDEXED BY               LOADCUST
016080                                         STATE-CODE-INDEX.    LOADCUST
016090             15  STATE-CODE      PIC XX.                      LOADCUST
016100     05  MONTH-DAY-TABLE.                                     LOADCUST
016110         10  MONTH-DAY-CONSTANTS.                             LOADCUST
016120             15  FILLER          PIC X(4)    VALUE '0131'.    LOADCUST
016130             15  FILLER          PIC X(4)    VALUE '0229'.    LOADCUST
016140             15  FILLER          PIC X(4)    VALUE '0331'.    LOADCUST
016150             15  FILLER          PIC X(4)    VALUE '0430'.    LOADCUST
016160             15  FILLER          PIC X(4)    VALUE '0531'.    LOADCUST
016170             15  FILLER          PIC X(4)    VALUE '0630'.    LOADCUST
016180             15  FILLER          PIC X(4)    VALUE '0731'.    LOADCUST
016190             15  FILLER          PIC X(4)    VALUE '0831'.    LOADCUST
016200             15  FILLER          PIC X(4)    VALUE '0930'.    LOADCUST
017010             15  FILLER          PIC X(4)    VALUE '1031'.    LOADCUST
017020             15  FILLER          PIC X(4)    VALUE '1130'.    LOADCUST
017030             15  FILLER          PIC X(4)    VALUE '1231'.    LOADCUST
017040         10  MONTHS-AND-DAYS-TABLE REDEFINES MONTH-DAY-CONSTANTS  LOADCUST
017050                                     OCCURS 12 TIMES          LOADCUST
017060                                     INDEXED BY               LOADCUST
017070                                         MONTH-DAY-INDEX.     LOADCUST
017080             15  MONTH-TABLE      PIC XX.                     LOADCUST
017090             15  NUMBER-OF-DAYS-IN-MONTH PIC XX.              LOADCUST
017100                                                              LOADCUST
017110 01  INPUT-RECORD-WORK-AREAS.                                 LOADCUST
017120     05  SORTED-TRANS-RECORD-TYPE-1.                          LOADCUST
017130         10  CUSTOMER-NUMBER-TRANSORT1           PIC X(5).    LOADCUST
017140         10  CUSTOMER-NAME-TRANSORT1             PIC X(20).   LOADCUST
017150         10  CUSTOMER-ADDRESS-TRANSORT1          PIC X(27).   LOADCUST
017160         10  CUSTOMER-CITY-TRANSORT1             PIC X(20).   LOADCUST
017170         10 CUSTOMER-STATE-TRANSORT1             PIC XX.      LOADCUST
017180         10 CUSTOMER-ZIP-CODE-TRANSORT1          PIC X(5).    LOADCUST
017190         10  TRANSACTION-CODE-TRANSORT1          PIC X.       LOADCUST
017200     05  SORTED-TRANS-RECORD-TYPE-2.                          LOADCUST
017210         10  CUSTOMER-NUMBER-TRANSORT2           PIC X(5).    LOADCUST
017220         10  CUSTOMER-DISCOUNT-TRANSORT2         PIC XX.      LOADCUST
017230         10  LAST-ACTIVITY-DATE-TRANSORT2.                    LOADCUST
017240             15  MONTH-LAST-ACTIVITY-TRANSORT2   PIC 99.      LOADCUST
017250                 88  VALID-MONTH                 VALUE 01 THRU 12.LOADCUST
017260             15  DAY-LAST-ACTIVITY-TRANSORT2     PIC XX.      LOADCUST
017270             15  YEAR-LAST-ACTIVITY-TRANSORT2    PIC XX.      LOADCUST
017280         10  FILLER                              PIC X(66).   LOADCUST
017290         10  TRANSACTION-CODE-TRANSORT2          PIC X.       LOADCUST
017300                                                              LOADCUST
```

Figure 5-102 Source Listing (Part 4 of 13)

```
   6                 20.19.30         AUG 17,1978

 017310 01  PRINTER-CONTROL-EXCEPTION-RPT.                            LOADCUST
 017320     05  PROPER-SPACING-EXCP-RPT     PIC 9.                    LOADCUST
 017330     05  SPACE-ONE-LINE-EXCP-RPT     PIC 9    VALUE 1.         LOADCUST
 017340     05  SPACE-TWO-LINES-EXCP-RPT    PIC 9    VALUE 2.         LOADCUST
 017350     05  LINES-PRINTED-EXCP-RPT      PIC S999 VALUE ZERO       LOADCUST
 017360                                          USAGE IS COMP-3.     LOADCUST
 017370     05  PAGE-SIZE-EXCP-RPT          PIC 999  VALUE 40         LOADCUST
 017380                                          USAGE IS COMP-3.     LOADCUST
 017390     05  PAGE-NUMBER-EXCP-RPT        PIC S999 VALUE +1         LOADCUST
 017400                                          USAGE IS COMP-3.     LOADCUST
 018010         88  FIRST-PAGE-EXCP-RPT              VALUE +1.        LOADCUST
 018020                                                               LOADCUST
 018030 01  PRINTER-CONTROL-MASTER-LIST.                              LOADCUST
 018040     05  PROPER-SPACING-MSTR-LIST    PIC 9.                    LOADCUST
 018050     05  SPACE-ONE-LINE-MSTR-LIST    PIC 9    VALUE 1.         LOADCUST
 018060     05  SPACE-TWO-LINES-MSTR-LIST   PIC 9    VALUE 2.         LOADCUST
 018070     05  LINES-PRINTED-MSTR-LIST     PIC S999 VALUE ZERO       LOADCUST
 018080                                          USAGE IS COMP-3.     LOADCUST
 018090     05  PAGE-SIZE-MSTR-LIST         PIC 999  VALUE 20         LOADCUST
 018100                                          USAGE IS COMP-3.     LOADCUST
 018110     05  PAGE-NUMBER-MSTR-LIST       PIC S999 VALUE +1         LOADCUST
 018120                                          USAGE IS COMP-3.     LOADCUST
 018130         88  FIRST-PAGE-MSTR-LIST             VALUE +1.        LOADCUST
 018140                                                               LOADCUST
 018150 01  EXCEPTION-REPORT-HEADINGS.                                LOADCUST
 018160     05  FIRST-HEADING-LINE-EXCP-RPT.                          LOADCUST
 018170         10  CARRIAGE-CONTROL    PIC X.                        LOADCUST
 018180         10  DATE-HDG1-EXCP-RPT  PIC X(8).                     LOADCUST
 018190         10  FILLER              PIC X(3)   VALUE SPACES.      LOADCUST
 018200         10  FILLER              PIC X(9)   VALUE 'CUSTOMER '. LOADCUST
 019010         10  FILLER              PIC X(7)   VALUE 'MASTER '.   LOADCUST
 019020         10  FILLER              PIC X(5)   VALUE 'LOAD '.     LOADCUST
 019030         10  FILLER              PIC X(10)  VALUE 'EXCEPTION '. LOADCUST
 019040         10  FILLER              PIC X(6)   VALUE 'REPORT'.    LOADCUST
 019050         10  FILLER              PIC X(4)   VALUE SPACES.      LOADCUST
 019060         10  FILLER              PIC X(5)   VALUE 'PAGE '.     LOADCUST
 019070         10  PAGE-NUMBER-HDG1-EXCP-RPT PIC ZZ9.                LOADCUST
 019080         10  FILLER              PIC X(72).                    LOADCUST
 019090     05  SECOND-HEADING-LINE-EXCP-RPT.                         LOADCUST
 019100         10  CARRIAGE-CONTROL    PIC X.                        LOADCUST
 019110         10  FILLER              PIC X(8)   VALUE 'CUSTOMER'.  LOADCUST
 019120         10  FILLER              PIC X(11)  VALUE SPACES.      LOADCUST
 019130         10  FILLER              PIC X(5)   VALUE 'FIELD'.     LOADCUST
 019140         10  FILLER              PIC X(108) VALUE SPACES.      LOADCUST
 019150     05  THIRD-HEADING-LINE-EXCP-RPT.                          LOADCUST
 019160         10  CARRIAGE-CONTROL    PIC X.                        LOADCUST
 019170         10  FILLER              PIC X      VALUE SPACE.       LOADCUST
 019180         10  FILLER              PIC X(6)   VALUE 'NUMBER'.    LOADCUST
 019190         10  FILLER              PIC X(10)  VALUE SPACES.      LOADCUST
 019200         10  FILLER              PIC X(8)   VALUE 'IN ERROR'.  LOADCUST
 020010         10  FILLER              PIC X(16)  VALUE SPACES.      LOADCUST
 020020         10  FILLER              PIC X(13)  VALUE              LOADCUST
 020030                                           'TYPE OF ERROR'.    LOADCUST
 020040         10  FILLER              PIC X(78)  VALUE SPACES.      LOADCUST
 020050                                                               LOADCUST
 020060 01  MASTER-LIST-REPORT-HEADINGS.                              LOADCUST
 020070     05  FIRST-HEADING-LINE-MSTR-LIST.                         LOADCUST
 020080         10  CARRIAGE-CONTROL    PIC X.                        LOADCUST
 020090         10  FILLER              PIC X(5)   VALUE 'DATE '.     LOADCUST
 020100         10  DATE-HDG1-MSTR-LIST PIC X(8).                     LOADCUST
 020110         10  FILLER              PIC X(32)  VALUE SPACES.      LOADCUST
 020120         10  FILLER              PIC X(9)   VALUE 'CUSTOMER '. LOADCUST
 020130         10  FILLER              PIC X(7)   VALUE 'MASTER '.   LOADCUST
 020140         10  FILLER              PIC X(5)   VALUE 'FILE'.      LOADCUST
 020150         10  FILLER              PIC X(4)   VALUE 'LIST'.      LOADCUST
 020160         10  FILLER              PIC X(38)  VALUE SPACES.      LOADCUST
 020170         10  FILLER              PIC X(5)   VALUE 'PAGE '.     LOADCUST
 020180         10  PAGE-NUMBER-HDG1-MSTR-LIST PIC ZZ9.               LOADCUST
 020190         10  FILLER              PIC X(16)  VALUE SPACES.      LOADCUST
 020200     05  SECOND-HEADING-LINE-MSTR-LIST.                        LOADCUST
 021010         10  CARRIAGE-CONTROL    PIC X.                        LOADCUST
 021020         10  FILLER              PIC X(8)   VALUE 'CUSTOMER'.  LOADCUST
 021030         10  FILLER              PIC X(7)   VALUE SPACES.      LOADCUST
 021040         10  FILLER              PIC X(8)   VALUE 'CUSTOMER'.  LOADCUST
 021050         10  FILLER              PIC X(18)  VALUE SPACES.      LOADCUST
 021060         10  FILLER              PIC X(8)   VALUE 'CUSTOMER'.  LOADCUST
 021070         10  FILLER              PIC X(19)  VALUE SPACES.      LOADCUST
 021080         10  FILLER              PIC X(8)   VALUE 'CUSTOMER'.  LOADCUST
 021090         10  FILLER              PIC X(6)   VALUE SPACES.      LOADCUST
 021100         10  FILLER              PIC X(8)   VALUE 'CUSTOMER'.  LOADCUST
 021110         10  FILLER              PIC X(3)   VALUE SPACES.      LOADCUST
 021120         10  FILLER              PIC X(3)   VALUE 'ZIP'.       LOADCUST
 021130         10  FILLER              PIC X(14)  VALUE SPACES.      LOADCUST
 021140         10  FILLER              PIC X(4)   VALUE 'LAST'.      LOADCUST
 021150         10  FILLER              PIC X(18)  VALUE SPACES.      LOADCUST
```

Figure 5-103 Source Listing (Part 5 of 13)

```
7                      20.19.30        AUG 17,1978

021160     05  THIRD-HEADING-LINE-MSTR-LIST.                                   LOADCUST
021170         10  CARRIAGE-CONTROL     PIC X.                                 LOADCUST
021180         10  FILLER               PIC X          VALUE SPACE.            LOADCUST
021190         10  FILLER               PIC X(6)       VALUE 'NUMBER'.         LOADCUST
021200         10  FILLER               PIC X(10)      VALUE SPACES.           LOADCUST
022010         10  FILLER               PIC X(4)       VALUE 'NAME'.           LOADCUST
022020         10  FILLER               PIC X(20)      VALUE SPACES.           LOADCUST
022030         10  FILLER               PIC X(7)       VALUE 'ADDRESS'.        LOADCUST
022040         10  FILLER               PIC X(22)      VALUE SPACES.           LOADCUST
022050         10  FILLER               PIC X(4)       VALUE 'CITY'.           LOADCUST
022060         10  FILLER               PIC X(10)      VALUE SPACES.           LOADCUST
022070         10  FILLER               PIC X(5)       VALUE 'STATE'.          LOADCUST
022080         10  FILLER               PIC X(3)       VALUE SPACES.           LOADCUST
022090         10  FILLER               PIC X(4)       VALUE 'CODE'.           LOADCUST
022100         10  FILLER               PIC XX         VALUE SPACES.           LOADCUST
022110         10  FILLER               PIC X(8)       VALUE 'DISCOUNT'.       LOADCUST
022120         10  FILLER               PIC X(2)       VALUE SPACES.           LOADCUST
022130         10  FILLER               PIC X(8)       VALUE 'ACTIVITY'.       LOADCUST
022140         10  FILLER               PIC X(16)      VALUE SPACES.           LOADCUST

8                      20.19.30        AUG 17,1978

022160 PROCEDURE DIVISION.                                                     LOADCUST
022170                                                                         LOADCUST
022180*****************************************************************        LOADCUST
022190*                                                               *        LOADCUST
022200*  THE FUNCTION OF THIS MODULE IS TO LOAD THE CUSTOMER MASTER   *        LOADCUST
023010*  FILE. IT IS ENTERED FROM AND EXITS TO THE OPERATING SYSTEM.  *        LOADCUST
023020*                                                               *        LOADCUST
023030*****************************************************************        LOADCUST
023040                                                                         LOADCUST
023050 BEGINNING-SECTION SECTION.                                              LOADCUST
023060                                                                         LOADCUST
023070 A000-LOAD-CUSTOMER-MASTER-FILE.                                         LOADCUST
023080                                                                         LOADCUST
023090     OPEN OUTPUT PROGRAM-REPORT-FILE                                     LOADCUST
023100                 CUSTOMER-MASTER-OUTPUT-FILE.                            LOADCUST
023110     SORT TRANSACTION-SORT-WORK-FILE                                     LOADCUST
023120         ON ASCENDING KEY CUSTOMER-NUMBER-SORTREC                        LOADCUST
023130                          TRANSACTION-CODE-SORTREC                       LOADCUST
023140         USING CUSTOMER-TRANS-INPUT-FILE                                 LOADCUST
023150         OUTPUT PROCEDURE A001-SORT-OUTPUT-PROCEDURE.                    LOADCUST
023160     CLOSE CUSTOMER-MASTER-OUTPUT-FILE.                                  LOADCUST
023170     OPEN INPUT  CUSTOMER-MASTER-INPUT-FILE.                             LOADCUST
023180     PERFORM X000-LIST-CUSTOMER-MASTER.                                  LOADCUST
023190     CLOSE PROGRAM-REPORT-FILE                                           LOADCUST
023200           CUSTOMER-MASTER-INPUT-FILE.                                   LOADCUST
023210     STOP RUN.                                                           LOADCUST
023220                                                                         LOADCUST
023230                                                                         LOADCUST
023240                                                                         LOADCUST
024010*****************************************************************        LOADCUST
024020*                                                               *        LOADCUST
024030*  THIS SECTION IS ENTERED TO PROCESS THE SORTED TRANSACTION    *        LOADCUST
024040*  RECORDS. IT IS ENTERED FROM THE SORT STATEMENT IN THE        *        LOADCUST
024050*  A000-LOAD-CUSTOMER-MASTER-FILE MODULE AND EXITS BACK TO THE *        LOADCUST
024060*  STATEMENT FOLLOWING THE SORT VERB THROUGH THE USE OF A       *        LOADCUST
024070*  GO TO STATEMENT WHICH TRANSFERS CONTROL TO THE END OF THIS   *        LOADCUST
024080*  SECTION.                                                     *        LOADCUST
024090*                                                               *        LOADCUST
024100*****************************************************************        LOADCUST
024110                                                                         LOADCUST
024120 A001-SORT-OUTPUT-PROCEDURE SECTION.                                     LOADCUST
024130                                                                         LOADCUST
024140 A001-PROCESS-RECORDS.                                                   LOADCUST
024150                                                                         LOADCUST
024160     PERFORM B000-OBTAIN-VALID-LOAD-DATA.                                LOADCUST
024170     PERFORM A002-WRITE-AND-READ                                         LOADCUST
024180         UNTIL THERE-ARE-NO-MORE-TRAN-RECORDS.                           LOADCUST
024190     GO TO V001-SORT-PROCEDURE-EXIT.                                     LOADCUST
024200                                                                         LOADCUST
025010                                                                         LOADCUST
025020                                                                         LOADCUST
025030 A002-WRITE-AND-READ.                                                    LOADCUST
025040                                                                         LOADCUST
025050     PERFORM B010-WRITE-CUSTOMER-MSTR-FILE.                              LOADCUST
025060     PERFORM B000-OBTAIN-VALID-LOAD-DATA.                                LOADCUST
```

Figure 5-104 Source Listing (Part 6 of 13)

```
   9                    20.19.30        AUG 17,1978

025080*****************************************************************  LOADCUST
025090*                                                                *  LOADCUST
025100*  THIS MODULE IS ENTERED TO OBTAIN VALID MASTER LOAD DATA.      *  LOADCUST
025110*  IT IS ENTERED FROM AND EXITS TO THE A000-LOAD-CUSTOMER-       *  LOADCUST
025120*  MASTER-FILE MODULE.                                           *  LOADCUST
025130*                                                                *  LOADCUST
025140*****************************************************************  LOADCUST
025150                                                                    LOADCUST
025160 B000-OBTAIN-VALID-LOAD-DATA.                                       LOADCUST
025170                                                                    LOADCUST
025180     MOVE SPACES TO ARE-TRAN-RECORDS-VALID.                         LOADCUST
025190     PERFORM C000-OBTAIN-PAIR-OF-RECORDS.                           LOADCUST
025200     PERFORM B001-EDIT-AND-READ                                     LOADCUST
026010         UNTIL TRAN-RECORDS-ARE-VALID OR                            LOADCUST
026020             THERE-ARE-NO-MORE-TRAN-RECORDS.                        LOADCUST
026030                                                                    LOADCUST
026040                                                                    LOADCUST
026050                                                                    LOADCUST
026060 B001-EDIT-AND-READ.                                                LOADCUST
026070                                                                    LOADCUST
026080     PERFORM C010-EDIT-TYPE-1-RECORD.                               LOADCUST
026090     PERFORM C020-EDIT-TYPE-2-RECORD.                               LOADCUST
026100     IF TRAN-RECORDS-ARE-NOT-VALID                                  LOADCUST
026110        PERFORM C000-OBTAIN-PAIR-OF-RECORDS                         LOADCUST
026120        MOVE SPACES TO ARE-TRAN-RECORDS-VALID                       LOADCUST
026130     ELSE                                                           LOADCUST
026140        MOVE 'YES' TO ARE-TRAN-RECORDS-VALID.                       LOADCUST

  10                    20.19.30        AUG 17,1978

026160*****************************************************************  LOADCUST
026170*                                                                *  LOADCUST
026180*  THIS MODULE WRITES THE CUSTOMER MASTER FILE. IT IS ENTERED    *  LOADCUST
026190*  FROM AND EXITS TO THE A000-LOAD-CUSTOMER-MASTER-FILE MODULE.*    LOADCUST
026200*                                                                *  LOADCUST
027010*****************************************************************  LOADCUST
027020                                                                    LOADCUST
027030 B010-WRITE-CUSTOMER-MSTR-FILE.                                     LOADCUST
027040                                                                    LOADCUST
027050     MOVE CUSTOMER-NUMBER-TRANSORT1 TO CUSTOMER-NUMBER-MSTROUT.     LOADCUST
027060     MOVE CUSTOMER-NAME-TRANSORT1 TO CUSTOMER-NAME-MSTROUT.         LOADCUST
027070     MOVE CUSTOMER-ADDRESS-TRANSORT1 TO CUSTOMER-ADDRESS-MSTROUT.   LOADCUST
027080     MOVE CUSTOMER-CITY-TRANSORT1 TO CUSTOMER-CITY-MSTROUT.         LOADCUST
027090     MOVE CUSTOMER-STATE-TRANSORT1 TO CUSTOMER-STATE-MSTROUT.       LOADCUST
027100     MOVE CUSTOMER-ZIP-CODE-TRANSORT1 TO                            LOADCUST
027110         CUSTOMER-ZIP-CODE-MSTROUT.                                 LOADCUST
027120     MOVE CUSTOMER-DISCOUNT-TRANSORT2 TO                            LOADCUST
027130         CUSTOMER-DISCOUNT-MSTROUT.                                 LOADCUST
027140     MOVE LAST-ACTIVITY-DATE-TRANSORT2 TO                           LOADCUST
027150         LAST-ACTIVITY-DATE-MSTROUT.                                LOADCUST
027160     WRITE CUSTOMER-MASTER-OUTPUT-RECORD                            LOADCUST
027170         INVALID KEY                                                LOADCUST
027180             MOVE CUSTOMER-NUMBER-TRANSORT1 TO                      LOADCUST
027190                 CUSTOMER-NUMBER-EXCP-WORK                          LOADCUST
027200             MOVE CUSTOMER-NUMBER-FIELD-MSG TO                      LOADCUST
027210                 CUSTOMER-NUMBER-EXCP-WORK                          LOADCUST
027220             MOVE INVALID-WRITE-MSG TO TYPE-OF-ERROR-EXCP-WORK      LOADCUST
027230             PERFORM U000-WRITE-EXCEPTION-REPORT.                   LOADCUST
```

Figure 5-105 Source Listing (Part 7 of 13)

```
11                          20.19.30          AUG 17,1978

027250*****************************************************************  LOADCUST
027260*                                                               *  LOADCUST
027270*  THIS MODULE OBTAINS A VALID PAIR OF RECORDS. IT IS ENTERED   *  LOADCUST
028010*  FROM AND EXITS TO THE B000-OBTAIN-VALID-LOAD-DATA MODULE.    *  LOADCUST
028020*                                                               *  LOADCUST
028030*****************************************************************  LOADCUST
028040                                                                   LOADCUST
028050 C000-OBTAIN-PAIR-OF-RECORDS.                                      LOADCUST
028060                                                                   LOADCUST
028070     MOVE SPACES TO ARE-THE-PAIR-OF-RECORDS-VALID.                 LOADCUST
028080     PERFORM C002-READ-A-RECORD.                                   LOADCUST
028090     IF THERE-ARE-MORE-TRAN-RECORDS                                LOADCUST
028100         MOVE TRANSACTION-SORT-WORK-RECORD TO                      LOADCUST
028110                 SORTED-TRANS-RECORD-TYPE-1.                       LOADCUST
028130     PERFORM C001-FIND-VALID-PAIR                                  LOADCUST
028140             UNTIL THE-PAIR-OF-RECORDS-ARE-VALID OR                LOADCUST
028150                 THERE-ARE-NO-MORE-TRAN-RECORDS.                   LOADCUST
028160                                                                   LOADCUST
028170                                                                   LOADCUST
028180                                                                   LOADCUST
028190 C001-FIND-VALID-PAIR.                                             LOADCUST
028200                                                                   LOADCUST
028210     MOVE SPACES TO IS-THE-FIRST-RECORD-VALID.                     LOADCUST
028220     MOVE SPACES TO IS-THE-SECOND-RECORD-VALID.                    LOADCUST
028230     MOVE TRANSACTION-CODE-TRANSORT1 TO                            LOADCUST
028240             TRANSACTION-CODE-TRANS1-WORK.                         LOADCUST
028250     MOVE CUSTOMER-NUMBER-TRANSORT1 TO                             LOADCUST
028260             CUSTOMER-NUMBER-TRANS1-WORK.                          LOADCUST
029010     PERFORM D000-VERIFY-VALID-FIRST-REC.                          LOADCUST
029020     IF THE-FIRST-RECORD-IS-VALID                                  LOADCUST
029030         PERFORM C002-READ-A-RECORD                                LOADCUST
029040         IF THERE-ARE-MORE-TRAN-RECORDS                            LOADCUST
029050             MOVE TRANSACTION-SORT-WORK-RECORD TO                  LOADCUST
029060                     SORTED-TRANS-RECORD-TYPE-2                    LOADCUST
029070             MOVE TRANSACTION-CODE-TRANSORT2 TO                    LOADCUST
029080                     TRANSACTION-CODE-TRANS2-WORK                  LOADCUST
029090             MOVE CUSTOMER-NUMBER-TRANSORT2 TO                     LOADCUST
029100                     CUSTOMER-NUMBER-TRANS2-WORK                   LOADCUST
029110             PERFORM D010-VERIFY-VALID-SECOND-REC                  LOADCUST
029120             IF THE-SECOND-RECORD-IS-VALID                         LOADCUST
029130                 MOVE 'YES' TO ARE-THE-PAIR-OF-RECORDS-VALID       LOADCUST
029140             ELSE                                                  LOADCUST
029150                 IF TRANSACTION-CODE-TRANSORT2 NOT =               LOADCUST
029160                         TRANSACTION-TYPE-ONE                      LOADCUST
029170                     PERFORM C002-READ-A-RECORD                    LOADCUST
029180                     IF THERE-ARE-MORE-TRAN-RECORDS                LOADCUST
029190                         MOVE TRANSACTION-SORT-WORK-RECORD TO      LOADCUST
029200                                 SORTED-TRANS-RECORD-TYPE-1        LOADCUST
030010                     ELSE                                          LOADCUST
030020                         NEXT SENTENCE                             LOADCUST
030070                 ELSE                                              LOADCUST
030080                     MOVE SORTED-TRANS-RECORD-TYPE-2 TO            LOADCUST
030090                             SORTED-TRANS-RECORD-TYPE-1            LOADCUST
030100         ELSE                                                      LOADCUST
030110             MOVE CUSTOMER-NUMBER-TRANS1-WORK TO                   LOADCUST
030120                     CUSTOMER-NUMBER-EXCP-WORK                     LOADCUST
030130             MOVE CUSTOMER-RECORDS-FIELD-MSG TO                    LOADCUST
030140                     FIELD-IN-ERROR-EXCP-WORK                      LOADCUST
030150             MOVE TYPE1-BUT-NO-TYPE2-ERROR-MSG TO                  LOADCUST
030160                     TYPE-OF-ERROR-EXCP-WORK                       LOADCUST
030170             PERFORM U000-WRITE-EXCEPTION-REPORT                   LOADCUST
030180     ELSE                                                          LOADCUST
030190         PERFORM C002-READ-A-RECORD                                LOADCUST
030200         IF THERE-ARE-MORE-TRAN-RECORDS                            LOADCUST
030210             MOVE TRANSACTION-SORT-WORK-RECORD TO                  LOADCUST
030220                     SORTED-TRANS-RECORD-TYPE-1.                   LOADCUST
030230                                                                   LOADCUST
031010                                                                   LOADCUST
031020                                                                   LOADCUST
031030 C002-READ-A-RECORD.                                               LOADCUST
031040                                                                   LOADCUST
031050     RETURN TRANSACTION-SORT-WORK-FILE                             LOADCUST
031060         AT END                                                    LOADCUST
031070             MOVE 'NO ' TO ARE-THERE-MORE-TRAN-RECORDS.            LOADCUST
```

Figure 5-106 Source Listing (Part 8 of 13)

```
12                 20.19.30        AUG 17,1976

      ***************************************************************** LOADCUST
      *                                                               * LOADCUST
      *  THE FUNCTION OF THIS MODULE IS TO EDIT A TYPE 1 TRANSACTION  * LOADCUST
      *  RECORD. IT IS ENTERED FROM AND EXITS TO THE                  * LOADCUST
      *  B000-OBTAIN-VALID-LOAD-DATA MODULE.                          * LOADCUST
      *                                                               * LOADCUST
      ***************************************************************** LOADCUST
                                                                        LOADCUST
       C010-EDIT-TYPE-1-RECORD.                                         LOADCUST
                                                                        LOADCUST
           MOVE CUSTOMER-NUMBER-TRANSORT1 TO CUSTOMER-NUMBER-WORK.      LOADCUST
           PERFORM U020-EDIT-CUSTOMER-NUMBER.                           LOADCUST
           IF CUSTOMER-NAME-TRANSORT1 = SPACES                          LOADCUST
               MOVE CUSTOMER-NUMBER-TRANSORT1 TO                        LOADCUST
                       CUSTOMER-NUMBER-EXCP-WORK                        LOADCUST
               MOVE CUSTOMER-NAME-FIELD-MSG TO                          LOADCUST
                       FIELD-IN-ERROR-EXCP-WORK                         LOADCUST
               MOVE BLANK-FIELD-ERROR-MSG TO TYPE-OF-ERROR-EXCP-WORK    LOADCUST
               PERFORM U000-WRITE-EXCEPTION-REPORT                      LOADCUST
               MOVE 'NO ' TO ARE-TRAN-RECORDS-VALID.                    LOADCUST
           IF CUSTOMER-ADDRESS-TRANSORT1 = SPACES                       LOADCUST
               MOVE CUSTOMER-NUMBER-TRANSORT1 TO                        LOADCUST
                       CUSTOMER-NUMBER-EXCP-WORK                        LOADCUST
               MOVE CUSTOMER-ADDRESS-FIELD-MSG TO                       LOADCUST
                       FIELD-IN-ERROR-EXCP-WORK                         LOADCUST
               MOVE BLANK-FIELD-ERROR-MSG TO TYPE-OF-ERROR-EXCP-WORK    LOADCUST
               PERFORM U000-WRITE-EXCEPTION-REPORT                      LOADCUST
               MOVE 'NO ' TO ARE-TRAN-RECORDS-VALID.                    LOADCUST
           IF CUSTOMER-CITY-TRANSORT1 = SPACES                          LOADCUST
               MOVE CUSTOMER-NUMBER-TRANSORT1 TO                        LOADCUST
                       CUSTOMER-NUMBER-EXCP-WORK                        LOADCUST
               MOVE CUSTOMER-CITY-FIELD-MSG TO                          LOADCUST
                       FIELD-IN-ERROR-EXCP-WORK                         LOADCUST
               MOVE BLANK-FIELD-ERROR-MSG TO TYPE-OF-ERROR-EXCP-WORK    LOADCUST
               PERFORM U000-WRITE-EXCEPTION-REPORT                      LOADCUST
               MOVE 'NO ' TO ARE-TRAN-RECORDS-VALID.                    LOADCUST
           SEARCH ALL VALID-STATE-TABLE                                 LOADCUST
                AT END                                                  LOADCUST
                   MOVE CUSTOMER-NUMBER-TRANSORT1 TO                    LOADCUST
                           CUSTOMER-NUMBER-EXCP-WORK                    LOADCUST
                   MOVE CUSTOMER-STATE-FIELD-MSG TO                     LOADCUST
                           FIELD-IN-ERROR-EXCP-WORK                     LOADCUST
                   MOVE BAD-STATE-CODE-ERROR-MSG TO                     LOADCUST
                           TYPE-OF-ERROR-EXCP-WORK                      LOADCUST
                   PERFORM U000-WRITE-EXCEPTION-REPORT                  LOADCUST
                   MOVE 'NO ' TO ARE-TRAN-RECORDS-VALID                 LOADCUST
                WHEN STATE-CODE (STATE-CODE-INDEX) =                    LOADCUST
                        CUSTOMER-STATE-TRANSORT1                        LOADCUST
                   NEXT SENTENCE.                                       LOADCUST
           IF CUSTOMER-ZIP-CODE-TRANSORT1 IS NOT NUMERIC                LOADCUST
               MOVE CUSTOMER-NUMBER-TRANSORT1 TO                        LOADCUST
                       CUSTOMER-NUMBER-EXCP-WORK                        LOADCUST
               MOVE CUSTOMER-ZIP-CODE-FIELD-MSG TO                      LOADCUST
                       FIELD-IN-ERROR-EXCP-WORK                         LOADCUST
               MOVE FIELD-NOT-NUMERIC-ERROR-MSG TO                      LOADCUST
                       TYPE-OF-ERROR-EXCP-WORK                          LOADCUST
               PERFORM U000-WRITE-EXCEPTION-REPORT                      LOADCUST
               MOVE 'NO ' TO ARE-TRAN-RECORDS-VALID.                    LOADCUST
```

Figure 5-107 Source Listing (Part 9 of 13)

```
13                   20.19.30        AUG 17,1978

034070*****************************************************************   LOADCUST
034080*                                                               *   LOADCUST
034090*  THE FUNCTION OF THIS MODULE IS TO EDIT A TYPE 2 TRANSACTION.*   LOADCUST
034100*  IT IS ENTERED FROM AND EXITS TO THE B000-OBTAIN-VALID-LOAD-  *   LOADCUST
034110*  DATA MODULE.                                                 *   LOADCUST
034120*                                                               *   LOADCUST
034130*****************************************************************   LOADCUST
034140                                                                    LOADCUST
034150 C020-EDIT-TYPE-2-RECORD.                                           LOADCUST
034160                                                                    LOADCUST
034170     MOVE CUSTOMER-NUMBER-TRANSORT2 TO CUSTOMER-NUMBER-WORK.        LOADCUST
034180     PERFORM U020-EDIT-CUSTOMER-NUMBER.                             LOADCUST
034190     IF CUSTOMER-DISCOUNT-TRANSORT2 IS NOT NUMERIC                  LOADCUST
034200         MOVE CUSTOMER-NUMBER-TRANSORT2 TO                          LOADCUST
034210                 CUSTOMER-NUMBER-EXCP-WORK                          LOADCUST
035010         MOVE CUSTOMER-DISCOUNT-FIELD-MSG TO                        LOADCUST
035020                 FIELD-IN-ERROR-EXCP-WORK                           LOADCUST
035030         MOVE FIELD-NOT-NUMERIC-ERROR-MSG TO                        LOADCUST
035040                 TYPE-OF-ERROR-EXCP-WORK                            LOADCUST
035050         PERFORM U000-WRITE-EXCEPTION-REPORT                        LOADCUST
035060         MOVE 'NO ' TO ARE-TRAN-RECORDS-VALID                       LOADCUST
035070     ELSE                                                           LOADCUST
035080         IF CUSTOMER-DISCOUNT-TRANSORT2 IS GREATER THAN             LOADCUST
035090                 MAXIMUM-DISCOUNT-PERCENT                           LOADCUST
035100             MOVE CUSTOMER-NUMBER-TRANSORT2 TO                      LOADCUST
035110                     CUSTOMER-NUMBER-EXCP-WORK                      LOADCUST
035120             MOVE CUSTOMER-DISCOUNT-FIELD-MSG TO                    LOADCUST
035130                     FIELD-IN-ERROR-EXCP-WORK                       LOADCUST
035140             MOVE BAD-DISCOUNT-ERROR-MSG TO                         LOADCUST
035150                     TYPE-OF-ERROR-EXCP-WORK                        LOADCUST
035160             PERFORM U000-WRITE-EXCEPTION-REPORT                    LOADCUST
035170             MOVE 'NO ' TO ARE-TRAN-RECORDS-VALID.                  LOADCUST
035180     IF LAST-ACTIVITY-DATE-TRANSORT2 IS NOT NUMERIC                 LOADCUST
035190         MOVE CUSTOMER-NUMBER-TRANSORT2 TO                          LOADCUST
035200                 CUSTOMER-NUMBER-EXCP-WORK                          LOADCUST
036010         MOVE LAST-ACTIVITY-DATE-FIELD-MSG TO                       LOADCUST
036020                 FIELD-IN-ERROR-EXCP-WORK                           LOADCUST
036030         MOVE FIELD-NOT-NUMERIC-ERROR-MSG TO                        LOADCUST
036040                 TYPE-OF-ERROR-EXCP-WORK                            LOADCUST
036050         PERFORM U000-WRITE-EXCEPTION-REPORT                        LOADCUST
036060         MOVE 'NO ' TO ARE-TRAN-RECORDS-VALID                       LOADCUST
036070     ELSE                                                           LOADCUST
036080         IF NOT VALID-MONTH                                         LOADCUST
036110             MOVE CUSTOMER-NUMBER-TRANSORT2 TO                      LOADCUST
036120                     CUSTOMER-NUMBER-EXCP-WORK                      LOADCUST
036130             MOVE LAST-ACTIVITY-DATE-FIELD-MSG TO                   LOADCUST
036140                     FIELD-IN-ERROR-EXCP-WORK                       LOADCUST
036150             MOVE BAD-MONTH-ERROR-MSG TO TYPE-OF-ERROR-EXCP-WORK    LOADCUST
036160             PERFORM U000-WRITE-EXCEPTION-REPORT                    LOADCUST
036170             MOVE 'NO ' TO ARE-TRAN-RECORDS-VALID                   LOADCUST
036180         ELSE                                                       LOADCUST
036190             SET MONTH-DAY-INDEX TO MONTH-LAST-ACTIVITY-TRANSORT2   LOADCUST
036200             IF DAY-LAST-ACTIVITY-TRANSORT2 IS LESS THAN            LOADCUST
037010                     FIRST-DAY-OF-MONTH-NUMBER OR                   LOADCUST
037020                     DAY-LAST-ACTIVITY-TRANSORT2 IS GREATER THAN    LOADCUST
037030                     NUMBER-OF-DAYS-IN-MONTH (MONTH-DAY-INDEX)      LOADCUST
037040                 MOVE CUSTOMER-NUMBER-TRANSORT2 TO                  LOADCUST
037050                         CUSTOMER-NUMBER-EXCP-WORK                  LOADCUST
037060                 MOVE LAST-ACTIVITY-DATE-FIELD-MSG TO               LOADCUST
037070                         FIELD-IN-ERROR-EXCP-WORK                   LOADCUST
037080                 MOVE BAD-DAY-ERROR-MSG TO TYPE-OF-ERROR-EXCP-WORK  LOADCUST
037090                 PERFORM U000-WRITE-EXCEPTION-REPORT                LOADCUST
037100                 MOVE 'NO ' TO ARE-TRAN-RECORDS-VALID.              LOADCUST

14                   20.19.30        AUG 17,1978

037120*****************************************************************   LOADCUST
037130*                                                               *   LOADCUST
037140*  THIS MODULE IS ENTERED TO VERIFY A VALID FIRST RECORD IN     *   LOADCUST
037150*  THE PAIR OF RECORDS. IT IS ENTERED FROM AND EXITS TO THE     *   LOADCUST
037160*  C000-OBTAIN-PAIR-OF-RECORDS MODULE.                          *   LOADCUST
037170*                                                               *   LOADCUST
037180*****************************************************************   LOADCUST
037190                                                                    LOADCUST
037200 D000-VERIFY-VALID-FIRST-REC.                                       LOADCUST
038010                                                                    LOADCUST
038020     IF TRANSACTION-CODE-TRANS1-WORK = TRANSACTION-TYPE-ONE         LOADCUST
038030         MOVE 'YES' TO IS-THE-FIRST-RECORD-VALID                    LOADCUST
038040     ELSE                                                           LOADCUST
038050         MOVE 'NO ' TO IS-THE-FIRST-RECORD-VALID                    LOADCUST
038060         MOVE CUSTOMER-NUMBER-TRANS1-WORK TO                        LOADCUST
038070                 CUSTOMER-NUMBER-EXCP-WORK                          LOADCUST
038080         MOVE CUSTOMER-RECORDS-FIELD-MSG TO                         LOADCUST
038090                 FIELD-IN-ERROR-EXCP-WORK                           LOADCUST
038100         IF TRANSACTION-CODE-TRANS1-WORK = TRANSACTION-TYPE-TWO     LOADCUST
038110             MOVE TYPE2-BUT-NO-TYPE1-ERROR-MSG TO                   LOADCUST
038120                     TYPE-OF-ERROR-EXCP-WORK                        LOADCUST
038130             PERFORM U000-WRITE-EXCEPTION-REPORT                    LOADCUST
038140         ELSE                                                       LOADCUST
038150             MOVE BAD-TRANS-CODE-ERROR-MSG TO                       LOADCUST
038160                     TYPE-OF-ERROR-EXCP-WORK                        LOADCUST
038170             PERFORM U000-WRITE-EXCEPTION-REPORT.                   LOADCUST
```

Figure 5-108 Source Listing (Part 10 of 13)

```
15                20.24.44        AUG 17,1978

*****************************************************************   LOADCUST
*                                                               *   LOADCUST
*  THIS MODULE IS ENTERED TO VERIFY A VALID SECOND RECORD. IT   *   LOADCUST
*  IS ENTERED FROM AND EXITS TO THE C000-OBTAIN-PAIR-OF-RECORDS*   LOADCUST
*  MODULE.                                                      *   LOADCUST
*                                                               *   LOADCUST
*****************************************************************   LOADCUST
                                                                    LOADCUST
 D010-VERIFY-VALID-SECOND-REC.                                      LOADCUST
                                                                    LOADCUST
     IF TRANSACTION-CODE-TRANS2-WORK = TRANSACTION-TYPE-TWO         LOADCUST
         IF CUSTOMER-NUMBER-TRANS2-WORK =                           LOADCUST
                 CUSTOMER-NUMBER-TRANS1-WORK                        LOADCUST
             MOVE 'YES' TO IS-THE-SECOND-RECORD-VALID               LOADCUST
         ELSE                                                       LOADCUST
             MOVE CUSTOMER-NUMBER-TRANS1-WORK TO                    LOADCUST
                     CUSTOMER-NUMBER-EXCP-WORK                      LOADCUST
             MOVE CUSTOMER-RECORDS-FIELD-MSG TO                     LOADCUST
                     FIELD-IN-ERROR-EXCP-WORK                       LOADCUST
             MOVE TYPE1-BUT-NO-TYPE2-ERROR-MSG TO                   LOADCUST
                     TYPE-OF-ERROR-EXCP-WORK                        LOADCUST
             PERFORM U000-WRITE-EXCEPTION-REPORT                    LOADCUST
             MOVE CUSTOMER-NUMBER-TRANS2-WORK TO                    LOADCUST
                     CUSTOMER-NUMBER-EXCP-WORK                      LOADCUST
             MOVE CUSTOMER-RECORDS-FIELD-MSG TO                     LOADCUST
                     FIELD-IN-ERROR-EXCP-WORK                       LOADCUST
             MOVE TYPE2-BUT-NO-TYPE1-ERROR-MSG TO                   LOADCUST
                     TYPE-OF-ERROR-EXCP-WORK                        LOADCUST
             PERFORM U000-WRITE-EXCEPTION-REPORT                    LOADCUST
             MOVE 'NO ' TO ARE-THE-PAIR-OF-RECORDS-VALID            LOADCUST
     ELSE                                                           LOADCUST
         MOVE CUSTOMER-NUMBER-TRANS1-WORK TO                        LOADCUST
                 CUSTOMER-NUMBER-EXCP-WORK                          LOADCUST
         MOVE CUSTOMER-RECORDS-FIELD-MSG TO                         LOADCUST
                 FIELD-IN-ERROR-EXCP-WORK                           LOADCUST
         MOVE TYPE1-BUT-NO-TYPE2-ERROR-MSG TO                       LOADCUST
                 TYPE-OF-ERROR-EXCP-WORK                            LOADCUST
         PERFORM U000-WRITE-EXCEPTION-REPORT                        LOADCUST
         MOVE 'NO ' TO ARE-THE-PAIR-OF-RECORDS-VALID                LOADCUST
         IF TRANSACTION-CODE-TRANS2-WORK NOT = TRANSACTION-TYPE-ONELOADCUST
             MOVE CUSTOMER-NUMBER-TRANS2-WORK TO                    LOADCUST
                     CUSTOMER-NUMBER-EXCP-WORK                      LOADCUST
             MOVE CUSTOMER-RECORDS-FIELD-MSG TO                     LOADCUST
                     FIELD-IN-ERROR-EXCP-WORK                       LOADCUST
             MOVE BAD-TRANS-CODE-ERROR-MSG TO                       LOADCUST
                     TYPE-OF-ERROR-EXCP-WORK                        LOADCUST
             PERFORM U000-WRITE-EXCEPTION-REPORT.                   LOADCUST

16                20.19.30        AUG 17,1978

*****************************************************************   LOADCUST
*                                                               *   LOADCUST
*  THIS MODULE WRITES THE EXCEPTION REPORT. IT IS ENTERED FROM *   LOADCUST
*  AND EXITS TO SEVERAL MODULES WITHIN THE PROGRAM (SEE         *   LOADCUST
*  HIERARCHY CHART).                                            *   LOADCUST
*                                                               *   LOADCUST
*****************************************************************   LOADCUST
                                                                    LOADCUST
 U000-WRITE-EXCEPTION-REPORT.                                       LOADCUST
                                                                    LOADCUST
     IF FIRST-PAGE-EXCP-RPT OR                                      LOADCUST
             LINES-PRINTED-EXCP-RPT IS GREATER THAN                 LOADCUST
             PAGE-SIZE-EXCP-RPT                                     LOADCUST
         PERFORM U010-PRINT-EXCP-RPT-HEADINGS                       LOADCUST
         MOVE SPACES TO EXCEPTION-REPORT-LINE                       LOADCUST
         MOVE CUSTOMER-NUMBER-EXCP-WORK TO CUSTOMER-NUMBER-EXCPRPT.LOADCUST
     IF CUSTOMER-NUMBER-EXCP-WORK NOT = PREVIOUS-CUSTOMER-NUMBER    LOADCUST
         MOVE CUSTOMER-NUMBER-EXCP-WORK TO CUSTOMER-NUMBER-EXCPRPT  LOADCUST
         MOVE CUSTOMER-NUMBER-EXCP-WORK TO PREVIOUS-CUSTOMER-NUMBERLOADCUST
         MOVE SPACE-TWO-LINES-EXCP-RPT TO PROPER-SPACING-EXCP-RPT.  LOADCUST
     MOVE FIELD-IN-ERROR-EXCP-WORK TO FIELD-IN-ERROR-EXCPRPT.       LOADCUST
     MOVE TYPE-OF-ERROR-EXCP-WORK TO TYPE-OF-ERROR-EXCPRPT.         LOADCUST
     WRITE EXCEPTION-REPORT-LINE                                    LOADCUST
             AFTER PROPER-SPACING-EXCP-RPT.                         LOADCUST
     ADD PROPER-SPACING-EXCP-RPT TO LINES-PRINTED-EXCP-RPT.         LOADCUST
     MOVE SPACE-ONE-LINE-EXCP-RPT TO PROPER-SPACING-EXCP-RPT.       LOADCUST
     MOVE SPACES TO EXCEPTION-REPORT-LINE.                          LOADCUST
```

Figure 5-109 Source Listing (Part 11 of 13)

```
 17                    20.19.30        AUG 17,1978

042150*****************************************************************  LOADCUST
042160*                                                               *  LOADCUST
042170*  THIS MODULE PRINTS THE HEADINGS ON THE EXCEPTION REPORT.     *  LOADCUST
042180*  IT IS ENTERED FROM AND EXITS TO THE U000-WRITE-EXCEPTION-    *  LOADCUST
042190*  REPORT MODULE.                                               *  LOADCUST
042200*                                                               *  LOADCUST
043010*****************************************************************  LOADCUST
043020                                                                   LOADCUST
043030 U010-PRINT-EXCP-RPT-HEADINGS.                                     LOADCUST
043040                                                                   LOADCUST
043050     MOVE CURRENT-DATE TO DATE-HDG1-EXCP-RPT.                      LOADCUST
043060     MOVE PAGE-NUMBER-EXCP-RPT TO PAGE-NUMBER-HDG1-EXCP-RPT.       LOADCUST
043070     WRITE EXCEPTION-REPORT-LINE FROM FIRST-HEADING-LINE-EXCP-RPT  LOADCUST
043080             AFTER ADVANCING TO-THE-TOP-OF-THE-PAGE.               LOADCUST
043090     ADD 1 TO PAGE-NUMBER-EXCP-RPT.                                LOADCUST
043100     WRITE EXCEPTION-REPORT-LINE FROM                              LOADCUST
043110             SECOND-HEADING-LINE-EXCP-RPT                          LOADCUST
043120             AFTER ADVANCING 2 LINES.                              LOADCUST
043130     WRITE EXCEPTION-REPORT-LINE FROM THIRD-HEADING-LINE-EXCP-RPT  LOADCUST
043140             AFTER ADVANCING 1 LINES.                              LOADCUST
043150     MOVE SPACE-TWO-LINES-EXCP-RPT TO PROPER-SPACING-EXCP-RPT.     LOADCUST
043160     MOVE ZEROS TO LINES-PRINTED-EXCP-RPT.                         LOADCUST

 18                    20.19.30        AUG 17,1978

043180*****************************************************************  LOADCUST
043190*                                                               *  LOADCUST
043200*  THIS MODULE EDITS THE CUSTOMER NUMBER IN THE TRANSACTION     *  LOADCUST
043210*  RECORDS. IT IS ENTERED FROM AND EXITS TO SEVERAL MODULES IN  *  LOADCUST
043220*  THE PROGRAM (SEE HIERARCHY CHART).                           *  LOADCUST
043230*                                                               *  LOADCUST
044010*****************************************************************  LOADCUST
044020                                                                   LOADCUST
044030 U020-EDIT-CUSTOMER-NUMBER.                                        LOADCUST
044040                                                                   LOADCUST
044050     IF (FIRST-FOUR-CHAR-CUST-NUMB-WORK IS NOT NUMERIC) OR         LOADCUST
044060             (FIFTH-CHAR-CUST-NUMB-WORK IS NOT NUMERIC AND         LOADCUST
044070             NOT VALID-CHECK-DIGIT-FOR-TEN)                        LOADCUST
044080         MOVE CUSTOMER-NUMBER-WORK TO CUSTOMER-NUMBER-EXCP-WORK    LOADCUST
044090         MOVE CUSTOMER-NUMBER-FIELD-MSG TO                         LOADCUST
044100                 FIELD-IN-ERROR-EXCP-WORK                          LOADCUST
044110         MOVE FIELD-NOT-NUMERIC-ERROR-MSG TO                       LOADCUST
044120                 TYPE-OF-ERROR-EXCP-WORK                           LOADCUST
044130         PERFORM U000-WRITE-EXCEPTION-REPORT                       LOADCUST
044140         MOVE 'NO ' TO ARE-TRAN-RECORDS-VALID                      LOADCUST
044150     ELSE                                                          LOADCUST
044160         MOVE CUSTOMER-NUMBER-WORK TO                              LOADCUST
044170                 FIELD-TO-BE-CHECKED-MOD11-WORK                    LOADCUST
044180         CALL 'MOD11CHK' USING MOD-11-PASS-AREA-WORK               LOADCUST
044190         IF CUST-NUMBER-DID-NOT-PASS-MOD11                         LOADCUST
044200             MOVE CUSTOMER-NUMBER-WORK TO CUSTOMER-NUMBER-EXCP-WORK LOADCUST
044210             MOVE CUSTOMER-NUMBER-FIELD-MSG TO                     LOADCUST
044220                     FIELD-IN-ERROR-EXCP-WORK                      LOADCUST
045010             MOVE FAILS-MOD11-ERROR-MSG TO                         LOADCUST
045020                     TYPE-OF-ERROR-EXCP-WORK                       LOADCUST
045030             PERFORM U000-WRITE-EXCEPTION-REPORT                   LOADCUST
045040             MOVE 'NO ' TO ARE-TRAN-RECORDS-VALID.                 LOADCUST

 19                    20.19.30        AUG 17,1978

045060*****************************************************************  LOADCUST
045070*                                                               *  LOADCUST
045080*  THIS PARAGRAPH CONTAINS THE EXIT STATEMENT WHICH MARKS THE   *  LOADCUST
045090*  END OF THE SORT OUTPUT PROCEDURE. IT IS BRANCHED TO BY A     *  LOADCUST
045100*  GO TO STATEMENT IN THE A000-LOAD-CUSTOMER-MASTER-FILE        *  LOADCUST
045110*  MODULE.                                                      *  LOADCUST
045120*                                                               *  LOADCUST
045130*****************************************************************  LOADCUST
045140                                                                   LOADCUST
045150 V001-SORT-PROCEDURE-EXIT.                                         LOADCUST
045160                                                                   LOADCUST
045170     EXIT.                                                         LOADCUST
```

Figure 5-110 Source Listing (Part 12 of 13)

```
  20                    20.19.30        AUG 17,1978

045190 REST-OF-PROGRAM SECTION.                                         LOADCUST
045200                                                                  LOADCUST
046010****************************************************************** LOADCUST
046020*                                                                * LOADCUST
046030*  THIS MODULE IS ENTERED TO LIST THE CUSTOMER MASTER FILE. IT   * LOADCUST
046040*  IS ENTERED FROM AND EXITS TO THE A000-LOAD-CUSTOMER-MASTER-   * LOADCUST
046050*  FILE MODULE.                                                  * LOADCUST
046060*                                                                * LOADCUST
046070****************************************************************** LOADCUST
046080                                                                  LOADCUST
046090 X000-LIST-CUSTOMER-MASTER.                                       LOADCUST
046100                                                                  LOADCUST
046110     READ CUSTOMER-MASTER-INPUT-FILE                              LOADCUST
046120         AT END                                                   LOADCUST
046130             MOVE 'NO ' TO ARE-THERE-MORE-MSTR-RECORDS.           LOADCUST
046140     PERFORM X001-WRITE-AND-READ                                  LOADCUST
046150         UNTIL THERE-ARE-NO-MORE-MSTR-RECORDS.                    LOADCUST
046160                                                                  LOADCUST
046170                                                                  LOADCUST
046180                                                                  LOADCUST
046190 X001-WRITE-AND-READ.                                             LOADCUST
046200                                                                  LOADCUST
047010     PERFORM Y000-WRITE-LIST-REPORT.                              LOADCUST
047020     READ CUSTOMER-MASTER-INPUT-FILE                              LOADCUST
047030         AT END                                                   LOADCUST
047040             MOVE 'NO ' TO ARE-THERE-MORE-MSTR-RECORDS.           LOADCUST

  21                    20.19.30        AUG 17,1978

047060****************************************************************** LOADCUST
047070*                                                                * LOADCUST
047080*  THIS MODULE IS ENTERED TO WRITE THE MASTER LIST REPORT. IT    * LOADCUST
047090*  IS ENTERED FROM AND EXITS TO THE X000-LIST-CUSTOMER-MASTER    * LOADCUST
047100*  MODULE.                                                       * LOADCUST
047110*                                                                * LOADCUST
047120****************************************************************** LOADCUST
047130                                                                  LOADCUST
047140 Y000-WRITE-LIST-REPORT.                                          LOADCUST
047150                                                                  LOADCUST
047160     IF FIRST-PAGE-MSTR-LIST OR                                   LOADCUST
047170             LINES-PRINTED-MSTR-LIST IS GREATER THAN              LOADCUST
047180             PAGE-SIZE-MSTR-LIST                                  LOADCUST
047190         PERFORM Z000-PRINT-LIST-HEADINGS.                        LOADCUST
047200     MOVE SPACES TO MASTER-FILE-LIST-LINE.                        LOADCUST
048010     MOVE CUSTOMER-NUMBER-MSTRIN TO CUSTOMER-NUMBER-MSTRLIST.     LOADCUST
048020     MOVE CUSTOMER-NAME-MSTRIN TO CUSTOMER-NAME-MSTRLIST.         LOADCUST
048030     MOVE CUSTOMER-ADDRESS-MSTRIN TO CUSTOMER-ADDRESS-MSTRLIST.   LOADCUST
048040     MOVE CUSTOMER-CITY-MSTRIN TO CUSTOMER-CITY-MSTRLIST.         LOADCUST
048050     MOVE CUSTOMER-STATE-MSTRIN TO CUSTOMER-STATE-MSTRLIST.       LOADCUST
048060     MOVE CUSTOMER-ZIP-CODE-MSTRIN TO CUSTOMER-ZIP-CODE-MSTRLIST. LOADCUST
048070     MOVE CUSTOMER-DISCOUNT-MSTRIN TO CUSTOMER-DISCOUNT-MSTRLIST. LOADCUST
048080     MOVE '%' TO PERCENT-SIGN-MSTRLIST.                           LOADCUST
048090     MOVE LAST-ACTIVITY-DATE-MSTRIN TO                            LOADCUST
048100             LAST-ACTIVITY-DATE-MSTRLIST.                         LOADCUST
048110     WRITE MASTER-FILE-LIST-LINE                                  LOADCUST
048120             AFTER PROPER-SPACING-MSTR-LIST.                      LOADCUST
048130     ADD PROPER-SPACING-MSTR-LIST TO LINES-PRINTED-MSTR-LIST.     LOADCUST
048140     MOVE SPACE-ONE-LINE-MSTR-LIST TO PROPER-SPACING-MSTR-LIST.   LOADCUST

  22                    20.19.30        AUG 17,1978

048160****************************************************************** LOADCUST
048170*                                                                * LOADCUST
048180*  THIS MODULE PRINTS THE HEADINGS ON THE MASTER LIST REPORT.    * LOADCUST
048190*  IT IS ENTERED FROM AND EXITS TO THE Y000-WRITE-LIST-REPORT    * LOADCUST
048200*  MODULE.                                                       * LOADCUST
049010*                                                                * LOADCUST
049020****************************************************************** LOADCUST
049030                                                                  LOADCUST
049040 Z000-PRINT-LIST-HEADINGS.                                        LOADCUST
049050                                                                  LOADCUST
049060     MOVE CURRENT-DATE TO DATE-HDG1-MSTR-LIST.                    LOADCUST
049070     MOVE PAGE-NUMBER-MSTR-LIST TO PAGE-NUMBER-HDG1-MSTR-LIST.    LOADCUST
049080     WRITE MASTER-FILE-LIST-LINE FROM                             LOADCUST
049090             FIRST-HEADING-LINE-MSTR-LIST                         LOADCUST
049100             AFTER ADVANCING TO-THE-TOP-OF-THE-PAGE.              LOADCUST
049110     ADD 1 TO PAGE-NUMBER-MSTR-LIST.                              LOADCUST
049120     WRITE MASTER-FILE-LIST-LINE FROM                             LOADCUST
049130             SECOND-HEADING-LINE-MSTR-LIST                        LOADCUST
049140             AFTER ADVANCING 2 LINES.                             LOADCUST
049150     WRITE MASTER-FILE-LIST-LINE FROM                             LOADCUST
049160             THIRD-HEADING-LINE-MSTR-LIST                         LOADCUST
049170             AFTER ADVANCING 1 LINES.                             LOADCUST
049180     MOVE SPACE-TWO-LINES-MSTR-LIST TO PROPER-SPACING-MSTR-LIST.  LOADCUST
049190     MOVE ZEROS TO LINES-PRINTED-MSTR-LIST.                       LOADCUST
```

Figure 5-111 Source Listing (Part 13 of 13)

```
PP 5740-CB1 RELEASE 1.2  DEC 15, 1976              IBM OS/VS COBOL                    19.41.54  DATE JUL 26,1978

   1                  19.41.54        JUL 26,1978

001010 IDENTIFICATION DIVISION.                                          CHKDIGIT
001020                                                                   CHKDIGIT
001030 PROGRAM-ID.     MOD11CHK.                                         CHKDIGIT
001040 AUTHOR.         SHELLY.                                           CHKDIGIT
001050 INSTALLATION.   ANAHEIM.                                          CHKDIGIT
001060 DATE-WRITTEN.   02/02/78.                                         CHKDIGIT
001070 DATE-COMPILED.  JUL 26,1978.                                      CHKDIGIT
001080 SECURITY.       UNCLASSIFIED.                                     CHKDIGIT
001090                                                                   CHKDIGIT
001100*********************************************************************CHKDIGIT
001110*                                                                * CHKDIGIT
001120*  THE FUNCTION OF THIS SEPARATELY COMPILED MODULE IS TO         * CHKDIGIT
001130*  DETERMINE IF A CHECK DIGIT ON A NUMBER SATISFIES THE          * CHKDIGIT
001140*  MODULUS-11 CRITERIA. IT IS CALLED WHENEVER THE MODULUS-11     * CHKDIGIT
001150*  CHECK DIGIT MUST BE VERIFIED. THE CALLING PROGRAM MUST PASS   * CHKDIGIT
001160*  A 20-CHARACTER FIELD WHICH CONTAINS THE NUMBER TO BE          * CHKDIGIT
001170*  CHECKED. IF THE NUMBER IS LESS THAN 20 DIGITS, THE NUMBER     * CHKDIGIT
001180*  MUST BE FOLLOWED BY SPACES IN THE UNUSED POSITIONS. THE       * CHKDIGIT
001190*  MAXIMUM SIZE NUMBER WHICH CAN BE CHECKED IS 20 DIGITS,        * CHKDIGIT
001200*  INCLUDING THE CHECK DIGIT.                                    * CHKDIGIT
002010*                                                                * CHKDIGIT
002020*********************************************************************CHKDIGIT
002030                                                                   CHKDIGIT
002040                                                                   CHKDIGIT
002050                                                                   CHKDIGIT
002060 ENVIRONMENT DIVISION.                                             CHKDIGIT
002070                                                                   CHKDIGIT
002080 CONFIGURATION SECTION.                                            CHKDIGIT
002090                                                                   CHKDIGIT
002100 SOURCE-COMPUTER. IBM-370.                                         CHKDIGIT
002110 OBJECT-COMPUTER. IBM-370.                                         CHKDIGIT

   2                  19.41.54        JUL 26,1978

002130 DATA DIVISION.                                                    CHKDIGIT
002140                                                                   CHKDIGIT
002150 WORKING-STORAGE SECTION.                                          CHKDIGIT
002160                                                                   CHKDIGIT
002170 01  MODULE-WORK-AREAS.                                            CHKDIGIT
002180     05  NUMBER-OF-DIGITS-IN-FIELD-WORK PIC S999  USAGE IS COMP-3.CHKDIGIT
002190     05  TOTAL-DIGIT-VALUE-WORK       PIC S9(5) USAGE IS COMP-3.CHKDIGIT
002200     05  WEIGHT-FACTOR-WORK           PIC S9(3) USAGE IS COMP-3.CHKDIGIT
003010     05  DIGIT-VALUE-WORK             PIC S9(3) USAGE IS COMP-3.CHKDIGIT
003020     05  CHECK-DIGIT-ALPHABETIC-WORK  PIC X.                       CHKDIGIT
003030     05  CHECK-DIGIT-NUMERIC-WORK REDEFINES                        CHKDIGIT
003040           CHECK-DIGIT-ALPHABETIC-WORK  PIC 9.                     CHKDIGIT
003050     05  DIVISION-RESULT-WORK         PIC S9(5) USAGE IS COMP-3.CHKDIGIT
003060     05  REMAINDER-WORK               PIC S9(3) USAGE IS COMP-3.CHKDIGIT
003070                                                                   CHKDIGIT
003080 01  MODULE-SUBSCRIPTS.                                            CHKDIGIT
003090     05  SEARCH-SUBSCRIPT             PIC S9(8) USAGE IS COMP      CHKDIGIT
003100                                                SYNC.              CHKDIGIT
003110     05  DIGITS-TO-PROCESS-SUBSCRIPT  PIC S9(8) USAGE IS COMP      CHKDIGIT
003120                                                SYNC.              CHKDIGIT
003122         88  ALL-DIGITS-ARE-PROCESSED           VALUE ZERO.        CHKDIGIT
003124     05  CHECK-DIGIT-SUBSCRIPT        PIC S9(8) USAGE IS COMP      CHKDIGIT
003126                                                SYNC.              CHKDIGIT
003128                                                                   CHKDIGIT
003130 01  MODULE-CONSTANTS.                                             CHKDIGIT
003140     05  MAXIMUM-NUMBER-OF-CHARACTERS  PIC 9(3)  VALUE 20          CHKDIGIT
003150                                                USAGE IS COMP-3.CHKDIGIT
003160                                                                   CHKDIGIT
003170                                                                   CHKDIGIT
003180                                                                   CHKDIGIT
003190 LINKAGE SECTION.                                                  CHKDIGIT
003200                                                                   CHKDIGIT
004010 01  DATA-PASSED-FROM-CALLING-MOD.                                 CHKDIGIT
004020     05  FIELD-TO-BE-CHECKED-ALPHA.                                CHKDIGIT
004030         10  DIGIT-TO-BE-CHECKED-ALPHA OCCURS 20 TIMES             CHKDIGIT
004040                                    PIC X.                         CHKDIGIT
004050     05  FIELD-TO-BE-CHECKED-NUMER REDEFINES                       CHKDIGIT
004060           FIELD-TO-BE-CHECKED-ALPHA.                              CHKDIGIT
004070         10  DIGIT-TO-BE-CHECKED-NUMER OCCURS 20 TIMES             CHKDIGIT
004080                                    PIC 9.                         CHKDIGIT
004090     05  IS-THE-CHECK-DIGIT-VALID   PIC XXX.                       CHKDIGIT
```

Figure 5-112 Source Listing — Modulus 11 Module (Part 1 of 2)

```
    3                    19.41.54        JUL 26,1978

 PROCEDURE DIVISION                                                    CHKDIGIT
            USING DATA-PASSED-FROM-CALLING-MOD.                        CHKDIGIT
                                                                       CHKDIGIT
***************************************************************** CHKDIGIT
*                                                               * CHKDIGIT
*  THIS CALLED MODULE DETERMINES IF THE MODULUS-11 CHECK DIGIT  * CHKDIGIT
*  IS VALID. IT FIRST DETERMINES THE NUMBER OF DIGITS TO        * CHKDIGIT
*  BE CHECKED AND THEN CHECKS THE NUMBER. IT IS ENTERED FROM    * CHKDIGIT
*  AND EXITS TO THE CALLING PROGRAMS.                           * CHKDIGIT
*                                                               * CHKDIGIT
***************************************************************** CHKDIGIT
                                                                       CHKDIGIT
 A000-CHECK-MODULUS-11.                                                CHKDIGIT
                                                                       CHKDIGIT
     PERFORM A002-DUMMY-PARAGRAPH                                      CHKDIGIT
         VARYING SEARCH-SUBSCRIPT FROM 1 BY 1                          CHKDIGIT
         UNTIL SEARCH-SUBSCRIPT IS GREATER THAN                        CHKDIGIT
             MAXIMUM-NUMBER-OF-CHARACTERS OR                           CHKDIGIT
             DIGIT-TO-BE-CHECKED-ALPHA (SEARCH-SUBSCRIPT) = ' '.       CHKDIGIT
     COMPUTE NUMBER-OF-DIGITS-IN-FIELD-WORK =                          CHKDIGIT
         SEARCH-SUBSCRIPT - 1.                                         CHKDIGIT
     IF NUMBER-OF-DIGITS-IN-FIELD-WORK = ZERO                          CHKDIGIT
         MOVE 'NO ' TO IS-THE-CHECK-DIGIT-VALID                        CHKDIGIT
     ELSE                                                              CHKDIGIT
         MOVE NUMBER-OF-DIGITS-IN-FIELD-WORK TO                        CHKDIGIT
             CHECK-DIGIT-SUBSCRIPT                                     CHKDIGIT
         MOVE DIGIT-TO-BE-CHECKED-ALPHA (CHECK-DIGIT-SUBSCRIPT)        CHKDIGIT
             TO CHECK-DIGIT-ALPHABETIC-WORK                            CHKDIGIT
         MOVE ZERO TO TOTAL-DIGIT-VALUE-WORK                           CHKDIGIT
         COMPUTE DIGITS-TO-PROCESS-SUBSCRIPT =                         CHKDIGIT
             NUMBER-OF-DIGITS-IN-FIELD-WORK - 1                        CHKDIGIT
         MOVE 2 TO WEIGHT-FACTOR-WORK                                  CHKDIGIT
         PERFORM A003-CALCULATE-DIGIT-VALUES                           CHKDIGIT
             UNTIL ALL-DIGITS-ARE-PROCESSED                            CHKDIGIT
         PERFORM A004-ADD-CHECK-DIGIT                                  CHKDIGIT
         DIVIDE TOTAL-DIGIT-VALUE-WORK BY 11                           CHKDIGIT
             GIVING DIVISION-RESULT-WORK                               CHKDIGIT
             REMAINDER REMAINDER-WORK                                  CHKDIGIT
         IF REMAINDER-WORK = ZERO                                      CHKDIGIT
             MOVE 'YES' TO IS-THE-CHECK-DIGIT-VALID                    CHKDIGIT
         ELSE                                                          CHKDIGIT
             MOVE 'NO ' TO IS-THE-CHECK-DIGIT-VALID.                   CHKDIGIT
                                                                       CHKDIGIT
                                                                       CHKDIGIT
                                                                       CHKDIGIT
 A001-EXIT-PARAGRAPH.                                                  CHKDIGIT
                                                                       CHKDIGIT
     EXIT PROGRAM.                                                     CHKDIGIT
                                                                       CHKDIGIT
                                                                       CHKDIGIT
                                                                       CHKDIGIT
 A002-DUMMY-PARAGRAPH.                                                 CHKDIGIT
                                                                       CHKDIGIT
     EXIT.                                                             CHKDIGIT
                                                                       CHKDIGIT
                                                                       CHKDIGIT
                                                                       CHKDIGIT
 A003-CALCULATE-DIGIT-VALUES.                                          CHKDIGIT
                                                                       CHKDIGIT
     COMPUTE DIGIT-VALUE-WORK =                                        CHKDIGIT
         DIGIT-TO-BE-CHECKED-NUMER (DIGITS-TO-PROCESS-SUBSCRIPT)CHKDIGIT
         * WEIGHT-FACTOR-WORK.                                         CHKDIGIT
     ADD DIGIT-VALUE-WORK TO TOTAL-DIGIT-VALUE-WORK.                   CHKDIGIT
     IF WEIGHT-FACTOR-WORK = 10                                        CHKDIGIT
         MOVE 2 TO WEIGHT-FACTOR-WORK                                  CHKDIGIT
     ELSE                                                              CHKDIGIT
         ADD 1 TO WEIGHT-FACTOR-WORK.                                  CHKDIGIT
     SUBTRACT 1 FROM DIGITS-TO-PROCESS-SUBSCRIPT.                      CHKDIGIT
                                                                       CHKDIGIT
                                                                       CHKDIGIT
                                                                       CHKDIGIT
 A004-ADD-CHECK-DIGIT.                                                 CHKDIGIT
                                                                       CHKDIGIT
     IF CHECK-DIGIT-ALPHABETIC-WORK = 'X'                              CHKDIGIT
         ADD 10 TO TOTAL-DIGIT-VALUE-WORK                              CHKDIGIT
     ELSE                                                              CHKDIGIT
         ADD CHECK-DIGIT-NUMERIC-WORK TO TOTAL-DIGIT-VALUE-WORK.       CHKDIGIT
```

Figure 5-113 Source Listing — Modulus 11 Module (Part 2 of 2)

CHAPTER 5

REVIEW QUESTIONS

1. List two advantages of the indexed sequential file organization as compared to the sequential file organization.

2. What is the purpose of the Prime Data Area in an indexed sequential file?

3. What is the purpose of the Overflow Area in an indexed sequential file?

4. Briefly explain how records are referenced either sequentially or randomly when using an indexed sequential file.

5. Explain where the Track Index is located when using an indexed sequential file. What is the function of the Track Index?

6. Explain the KEY entry and the DATA entry on a track index.

7. What is the function of the Cylinder Index? Master Index?

8. What is the purpose of a Decision Table?

9. Manually calculate a Modulus 11 Check Digit for Employee Number 83215.

10. The Employee Number with the Modulus 11 Check Digit appended is 844529. Is this a valid Employee Number?

11. Explain the INVALID KEY entry used with the Write Statement when creating an indexed sequential file.

CHAPTER 5

PROGRAMMING ASSIGNMENT 1

OVERVIEW — PROGRAMMING ASSIGNMENTS

The programming assignments in this chapter are designed to illustrate the loading of an indexed sequential file and are based upon the sorting and editing of a series of Real Estate Transaction Records. Three programming assignments are explained: Programming Assignments 1, 1A, and 1B. A variety of approaches are possible when utilizing these programming assignments.

1. Only Programming Assignment 1 may be assigned. This approach results in the design and coding of a relatively small program that sorts and edits a series of Real Estate Transaction Records and creates an indexed sequential file. This assignment illustrates most of the basic concepts discussed in this chapter.

2. Programming Assignment 1A may be assigned as a maintenance program, in which case the assignment is undertaken only after Programming Assignment 1 has been designed, coded, and tested.

3. Programming Assignments 1 and 1A may be viewed as a single assignment and approached as one programming project. Utilizing both Programming Assignments 1 and 1A results in completing a program of the approximate difficulty of the sample program contained within the text.

4. Programming Assignment 1B may be assigned as a maintenance program, in which case the assignment is undertaken only after the Programming Assignments 1 and 1A have been completely designed, coded, and tested.

5. Programming Assignments 1, 1A, and 1B may be viewed as a single large programming assignment.

The method of assigning the program is at the option of the instructor.

INSTRUCTIONS — PROGRAMMING ASSIGNMENT 1

A program is to be written to sort and edit a series of Real Estate Transaction Records and create the Multiple Listing Master File. The Multiple Listing Master File is to be stored on disk and is to be organized as an indexed sequential file. Design and write the COBOL program to produce the Multiple Listing Master File. Use IPO Charts, a Hierarchy Chart, and Pseudocode Specifications when designing the program.

INPUT

The input to the program consists of a Real Estate Transaction File. The format of the records in the file is illustrated below.

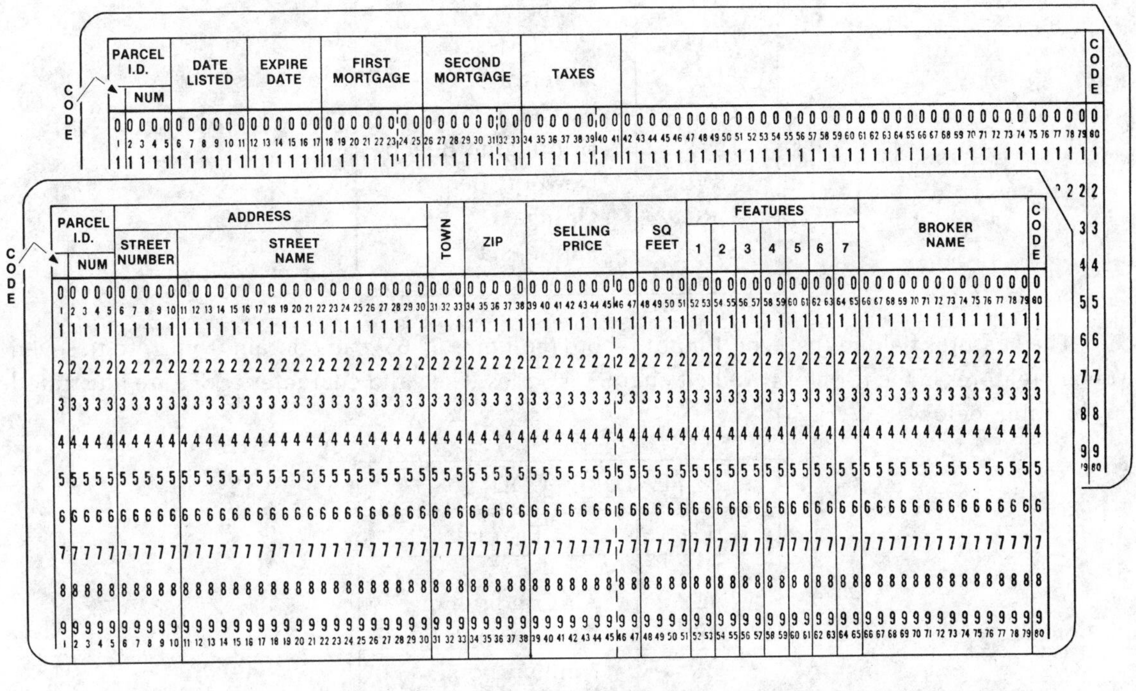

CODE	PARCEL I.D. NUM	DATE LISTED	EXPIRE DATE	FIRST MORTGAGE	SECOND MORTGAGE	TAXES		CODE
1	2–5	6–11	12–17	18–25	26–33	34–41	42–79	80

CODE	PARCEL I.D. NUM	ADDRESS: STREET NUMBER	ADDRESS: STREET NAME	TOWN	ZIP	SELLING PRICE	SQ FEET	FEATURES 1	2	3	4	5	6	7	BROKER NAME	CODE
1	2–5	6–10	11–30	31–33	34–38	39–47	48–51	52–53	54–55	56–57	58–59	60–61	62–63	64–65	66–79	80

The Real Estate Transaction Records contain data concerning real estate that is being placed on the market for sale. The input data for each piece of real estate being placed on the market is stored in two input records.

The first record contains the Parcel I.D., which contains a Parcel Code and Parcel Number, the Address of the piece of property consisting of the Street Number and the Street Name, the Town (in the form of a three-character code), the Zip Code, the Selling Price of the property, the number of Square Feet, a series of seven fields containing special features of the property, the Broker's Name, and the Type Code "1" which identifies the record as the first record in a pair of records.

The second record contains the Parcel I.D., the Date the Property was Listed, the Expiration Date of the Listing, the Amount of the First Mortgage, the Amount of the Second Mortgage, and the Yearly Property Taxes.

The Parcel I.D. consists of the Parcel Code and the Parcel Number. The Parcel Code will be either "C" (Condominium), "S" (Single Family Residence) or "M" (Multiple Family Residence).

The Town field will contain a three-digit Town Code which identifies the Town in which the property is located. The valid Town Codes are illustrated in the table below.

TOWN CODES	
Code	Town
ANA	Anaheim
CMS	Costa Mesa
FUL	Fullerton
GRD	Garden Grove
HNT	Huntington Beach
NWB	Newport Beach
ORG	Orange
STA	Santa Ana

The Features field in the Type 1 input record (columns 52-65) can contain from zero to seven special features in the form of two-digit character codes. The valid character codes are illustrated in the table below.

FEATURES CODES	
Code	Feature
AC	Air Conditioning
DR	Dining Room
FR	Family Room
HR	Horse Property
OF	Office
PT	Patio
SW	Swimming Pool

The codes illustrated above can be contained in the features columns in the Type 1 Real Estate Transaction Record. For example, if a home had air conditioning, a dining room, and a swimming pool, the entries AC, DR, and SW could be recorded in columns 52-57 of the input record. If a home had only air conditioning and a swimming pool, the entries AC and SW could appear in columns 52-55. If the property contained all seven features, there would be entries in all seven Feature Code fields while if the property contained no special features, columns 52-65 would be blank. It should be noted, however, that the codes need not be contiguous within the Features field. For example, property with an office and a patio could have the code OF in columns 52-53 and the code PT in columns 64-65.

OUTPUT

The output from the program is the Multiple Listing Master File, which is stored as an indexed sequential file, and the Real Estate Listings Report which contains selected fields from the Multiple Listing Master File.

The format of the Multiple Listing Master File is illustrated below.

FIELD	POSITION	NUMBER OF CHARACTERS	ATTRIBUTES
Not used	1	1	Alphanumeric
Parcel Code	2	1	Alphanumeric
Parcel Number	3-6	4	Numeric
Street Number	7-11	5	Numeric
Address	12-31	20	Alphanumeric
Town	32-34	3	Alphanumeric
Zip Code	35-39	5	Numeric
Selling Price	40-48	9	Numeric
Square Feet	49-52	4	Numeric
Features	53-66	14	Alphanumeric
Broker's Name	67-80	14	Alphanumeric
Date Listed	81-86	6	Numeric
Expiration Date	87-92	6	Numeric
First Mortgage	93-100	8	Numeric
Second Mortgage	101-108	8	Numeric
Yearly Taxes	109-116	8	Numeric

The blocking factor for the Multiple Listing Master File is 20 records per block. The file is to be stored as an indexed sequential file with the Parcel Code and Parcel Number (Parcel I.D.) acting as the key to the records.

After the Multiple Listing Master File is created, the Real Estate Listings Report is to be created. The format of the report is shown below.

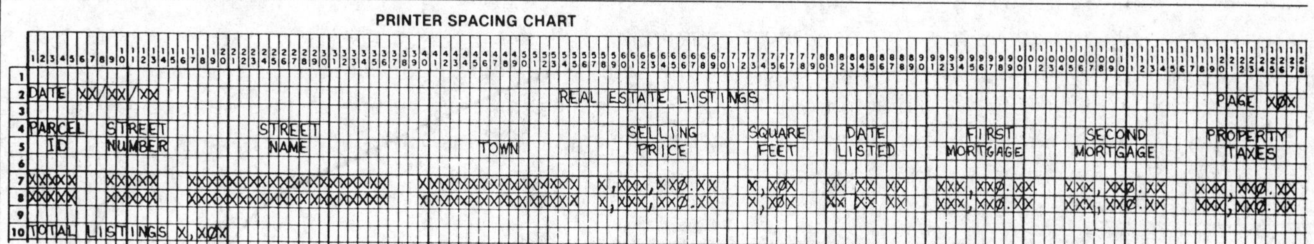

Note from the printer spacing chart for the Real Estate Listings that some of the fields contained in the Multiple Listing Master File are contained on the report. Note also that the Town field on the report contains the full-name of the town, not the abbreviation which is stored in the master file.

PROCESSING

The following processing should take place within the program.

1. The Real Estate Transaction Records should be sorted by Transaction Code (column 80) within Parcel I.D. (columns 1 -5).

2. There can be no Real Estate Transaction Records with a duplicate Parcel I.D., that is, no pairs with duplicate Parcel I.D.'s loaded into the Multiple Listing Master File. Any duplicates should be listed on the Exception Report.

3. In order to have a valid record to load in the Multiple Listing Master File, there must be a Type 1 record and a Type 2 record with the same Parcel I.D.

4. If a Type 1 and Type 2 pair of records with the same Parcel I.D. are found, the following editing should take place on the fields in the records. All fields should be checked in the records.

   a. Parcel Code — This field must contain a "C," "M," or "S."
   b. Parcel Number — This field must be numeric and pass a modulus 11 check digit test.
   c. Street Number — There must be a numeric address for each input record. However, the entire field need not contain numeric data. For example, the address 36003 is valid and so is the address blank-blank-360. As can be seen, the data is right-justified in the Street Number field. The data which is specified for the address must be numeric.
   d. Street Address — This field must contain data. If it contains blanks, it is in error.
   e. Town — This field must contain one of the valid Town Codes listed in the accompanying chart.
   f. Zip Code — This field must contain numeric data.
   g. Selling Price — This field must contain numeric data.
   h. Square Feet — This field must contain numeric data.
   i. Features Fields — Each of the seven fields may contain alphabetic data or may be blank. If the field contains alphabetic data, the data must be one of the seven special feature codes contained in the accompanying table. In addition, feature codes cannot be duplicated for a given parcel of property. For example, AC cannot appear more than one time in the features fields.
   j. Broker's Name — This field must contain data. If the field contains blanks, it is in error.
   k. Date Listed — This field must contain numeric data.
   l. Expiration Date — This field must contain numeric data.
   m. First Mortgage — This field may be blank, or it may contain data. If it contains data, the data must be numeric.
   n. Second Mortgage — This field may be blank or it may contain data. If it contains data, the data must be numeric.
   o. Property Taxes — This field must contain numeric data.

5. If either record of the pair does not pass the editing criteria, then the pair of records should not be written on the Multiple Listing Master File. Instead, it should be listed on the Exception Report.

6. The programmer should develop the test data to thoroughly test the program.

EXCEPTION REPORT

Records which do not pass the editing criteria or records which are invalid because of the lack of a pair of Type 1 and Type 2 records should be listed on the Exception Report. The Exception Report should contain the Parcel I.D., the Field in Error, and the Type of Error. The format of the Exception Report is illustrated below.

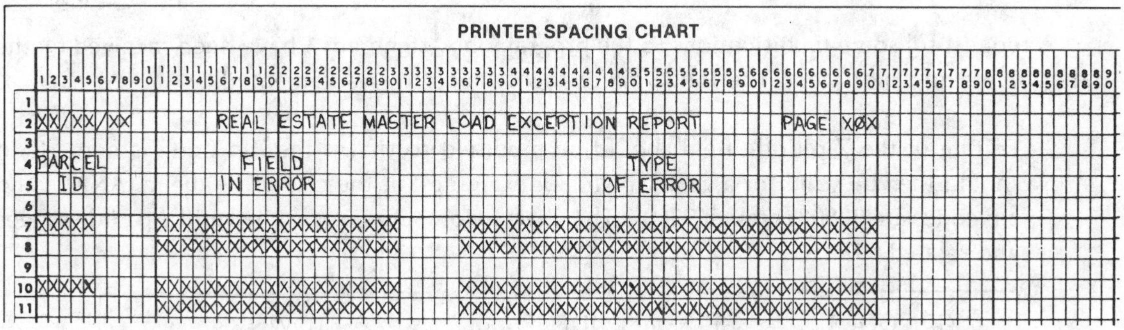

PRINTER SPACING CHART

```
 1
 2 XX/XX/XX       REAL ESTATE MASTER LOAD EXCEPTION REPORT               PAGE XØX
 3
 4 PARCEL           FIELD                           TYPE
 5  ID             IN ERROR                      OF ERROR
 6
 7 XXXXX     XXXXXXXXXXXXXXXXXXXX     XXXXXXXXXXXXXXXXXXXXXXXXXXXXXXXXXXX
 8           XXXXXXXXXXXXXXXXXXXX     XXXXXXXXXXXXXXXXXXXXXXXXXXXXXXXXXXX
 9
10 XXXXX     XXXXXXXXXXXXXXXXXXXX     XXXXXXXXXXXXXXXXXXXXXXXXXXXXXXXXXXX
11           XXXXXXXXXXXXXXXXXXXX     XXXXXXXXXXXXXXXXXXXXXXXXXXXXXXXXXXX
```

Note from the printer spacing chart above that the Exception Report contains the Parcel I.D., the Field in Error, and the Type of Error. The Field in Error messages should be descriptive of the field. The Error Messages which should appear in the Type of Error field are listed below.

<u>Error Messages</u>

INVALID PARCEL I-D
FIELD CONTAINS NON-NUMERIC DATA
NO ADDRESS PRESENT
INVALID TOWN CODE
INVALID FEATURES CODE
NO BROKER NAME PRESENT
TYPE 1 BUT NO TYPE 2
TYPE 2 BUT NO TYPE 1
DUPLICATE OR OUT OF SEQUENCE
FAILS MOD-11 CHECK

If the input record has more than one field in error for a given Parcel I.D., the Parcel I.D. should be group-indicated.

NOTE: After the Multiple Listing Master File has been created, a utility program should be used to dump the file. This program should be saved for use in Chapter 6. Also, the Modulus-11 check digit module used in the sample program can be reproduced and used for the student programming assignments.

CHAPTER 5

PROGRAMMING ASSIGNMENT 1A

INTRODUCTION

At the discretion of the instructor, this assignment may be completed in combination with Programming Assignment 1 or may be assigned only after Assignment 1 has been completely designed, coded, and tested.

INSTRUCTIONS

A request for some modifications to the program in Assignment 1 have been received by the data processing department. The following changes should be implemented:

1. Editing of the Zip Code field should be modified so that if the Zip Code is numeric, it should then be valid for a given town. For example, for the city of Anaheim (ANA), valid zip codes are 92801 through 92807. The chart below summarizes the valid zip code ranges and related towns.

ZIP CODES	CODE	TOWN
92801 - 92807	ANA	Anaheim
92626 - 92627	CMS	Costa Mesa
92631 - 92638	FUL	Fullerton
92640 - 92645	GRD	Garden Grove
92646 - 92649	HNT	Huntington Beach
92660 - 92663	NWB	Newport Beach
92665 - 92669	ORG	Orange
92701 - 92708	STA	Santa Ana

If the Zip Code is not valid for a Town, the record should not be placed in the Multiple Listing Master File. Instead, the error should be recorded on the Exception Report.

2. The Listing Date and the Expiration Date must contain valid month values, that is, the month specified must be 01 - 12. In addition, the day specified must not be greater than the number of days in the given month, nor should it be less than 01. For example, the date 043178 is invalid. If the date fields fail this editing, the record should not be written in the Multiple Listing Master File. Instead, an error message should be written on the Exception Report.

3. The Listing Date should not be later than the Expiration Date. For example, a Listing Date of 01/23/78 and an Expiration Date of 12/30/77 is invalid. If the date fields fail this editing, the record should not be written in the Multiple Listing Master File. Instead, an error message should be written on the Exception Report.

4. The maximum Square Footage for a condominium or single family residence should normally not exceed 6,000 square feet. If it does, the record can still be written in the Multiple Listing Master File, but a WARNING message should be written on the Exception Report.

5. The Selling Price for a piece of property should not exceed $90.00 per square foot. If it does, the record can still be written on the Multiple Listing Master File, but a WARNING message should be written on the Exception Report.

Additional error messages should be defined by the programmer to handle the additional editing specified in these changes. Additional test data should be developed to adequately test these changes.

Upon completion of this assignment, the program should be retained for use in Chapter 6.

CHAPTER 5

PROGRAMMING ASSIGNMENT 1B

INTRODUCTION

At the discretion of the instructor, this assignment may be completed in combination with Programming Assignment 1 and 1A, or may be assigned only after Programming Assignments 1 and 1A have been completely designed, coded, and tested.

INSTRUCTIONS

A request for additional modifications to the program defined in Programming Assignments 1 and 1A have been received by the data processing department. The following changes should be implemented.

1. The Expiration Date should not be more than three months past the Listing Date. If it is, the record can be written in the Multiple Listing Master File, but a WARNING message should appear on the Exception Report.

2. Property taxes should not be greater than 3% of the selling price or less than 1% of the selling price. If they are, the record can still be written in the Multiple Listing Master File, but a WARNING message should be written on the Exception Report.

3. The sum of the First Mortgage and the Second Mortgage should not be greater than the Selling Price. If they are, the record can be written on the Multiple Listing Master File, but a WARNING message should be written on the Exception Report.

4. An additional report should be printed. After the Multiple Listing Master File has been created and the Real Estate Listings Report has been printed, a report listing only Single family residences, as identified by the value "S" in the first position of the Parcel I.D., should be printed. The report format is illustrated in the following printer spacing chart.

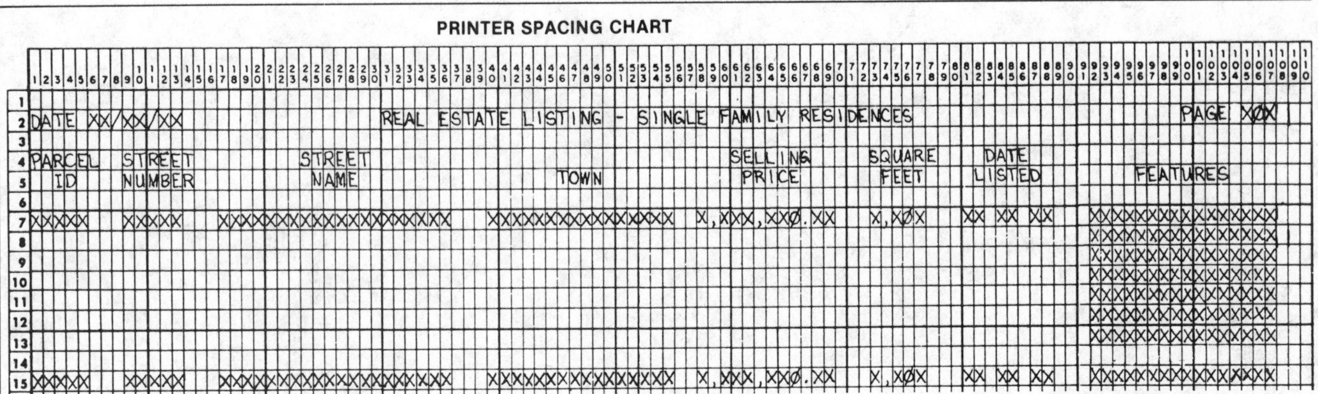

PRINTER SPACING CHART
DATE XX/XX/XX
REAL ESTATE LISTING - SINGLE FAMILY RESIDENCES
PAGE XØX
PARCEL ID
STREET NUMBER
STREET NAME
TOWN
SELLING PRICE
SQUARE FEET
DATE LISTED
FEATURES
XXXXX
XXXXX
XXXXXXXXXXXXXXXXXXXXXXX
XXXXXXXXXXXXXXXXXXX
X,XXX,XXØ.XX
X,XØX
XX XX XX
XXXXXXXXXXXXXXXXXXX

The Features field which is contained on the report is to contain the special features which are indicated for the property in the master record. The report should contain the full-name of the feature, not the feature code contained in the master record. The full-name can be determined by examining the table contained on page 5.126. If there are no special features, the field should be blank for the record.

Additional error messages should be defined by the programmer to handle the additional editing specified in these changes. Additional test data should be developed to adequately test these changes.

Upon completion of this assignment, the program should be retained for use in Chapter 6.

Indexed Sequential Access Method – Random Updating

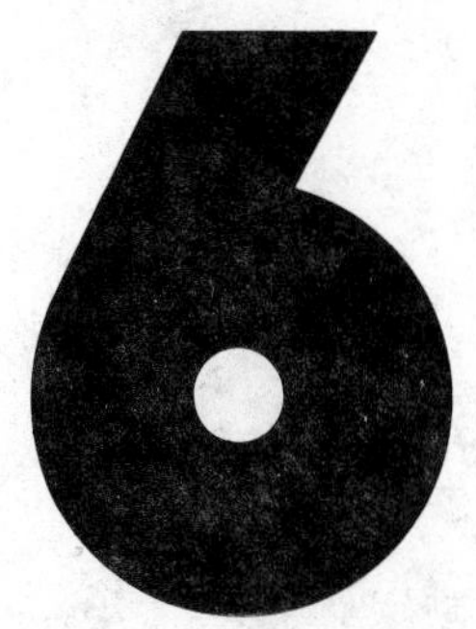

> *"The professional programmer of tomorrow will remember, more or less vividly, every error in his career."*[1]

INTRODUCTION

As discussed in Chapter 4, when a master file is created, it is normally necessary to update the file so that the master contains accurate, up-to-date information. The Indexed Sequential Access Method allows both sequential and random access to a file. Therefore, when using an indexed sequential master file, updating can take place both sequentially and randomly.

RANDOM FILE UPDATING

RANDOM updating takes place when a transaction is read, and the corresponding master record for that transaction is randomly retrieved from the master file. When a random update is used, it must be possible to randomly retrieve any record on the master file. Random updating can only be performed on a direct access storage device.

A new master file is not created when random updating is used. Thus, a deletion does not eliminate the record from the file as with a sequential update (see Chapter 4). Instead, when random updating, the record to be deleted is "flagged" to indicate that the record is to be considered deleted upon subsequent processing runs. A deletion is flagged by recording some type of code in the master record. The most commonly used code is the value HIGH-VALUE (Hex 'FF' on System/360 and System/370) placed in the first position of the master record. This is the method used in the sample program in this chapter to delete a record from the Customer Master File. This code thus indicates that the record is considered deleted even though it is still physically part of the Customer Master File. The use of the High-Value Code in the first position of the record stored in the indexed sequential file has the added advantage that when a record is sequentially retrieved from the indexed sequential file, the Indexed Sequential Access Method software which controls the retrieval of the record will treat the record as if it were not stored on the file; which is, of course, the intent when the record is deleted.

Records can also be added to files which are being randomly updated. The method of processing additions to an indexed sequential file which is being randomly updated will be explained in this chapter.

---

1 Harlan Mills, How to Write Correct Programs and Know It, IBM Federal Systems Division, IBM, February 1973.

It is important to have an overall understanding of the basic logic of the random updating of an indexed sequential file. This basic logic is explained below.

Step 1: The update transaction record is read.

Step 2: The key of the record is determined in order to control the random reading of the master record.

Step 3: Using the key from the transaction record, an attempt is made to read a record from the indexed sequential master file.

Step 4: If a record from the indexed sequential master file is read, it indicates that there is a record in the master file with the same key as the transaction record. Therefore, the transaction can be used to delete the master record or to change the master record.

a. The transaction code in the transaction record is checked. If the code indicates a delete transaction, the delete code is placed in the master record and the record is rewritten on the master file.

b. If the code in the transaction record indicates a change should occur, the fields in the master record are changed and the record is rewritten in the master file.

c. Any other code is invalid when there is a matching record in the indexed sequential master file, and a message is written on the exception report.

Step 5: If a record from the indexed sequential master file was not found in Step 3, it indicates that there is no master record which contains the same key as the transaction record. The only valid action which can be taken is to add the transaction record to the indexed sequential master file.

a. The transaction code in the transaction record is checked. If the code indicates an addition transaction, the new master record is formatted and the record is written in the master file.

b. If the transaction code does not indicate an addition, it is in error and a message is written on the exception report.

Step 6: Step 1 is then begun again.

Note that the method of random updating differs somewhat from sequential updating, but the update processing which must occur is the same; that is, master records are changed, master records are deleted, and new master records are added to the master file.

The choice of sequential or random updating is normally made by determining the type of file in use (sequential or indexed sequential) and the amount of update activity which will be done against the master file. A sequential file cannot be conveniently updated by any method except the sequential method. An indexed sequential file, however, can be easily updated using a sequential or random technique because records can be processed either sequentially or randomly. Therefore, when using an indexed sequential file, the decision to update randomly or sequentially is normally determined by how much update activity there will be against the master file.

Although sequential updating is, when compared on a record to record basis, faster than random updating, it takes a high volume of update activity to make the sequential method faster on an overall run basis. This is because when the sequential method is used, all of the records on the master file must be read and compared to the update transactions. Thus, if the master file consists of 10,000 records, 10,000 Read Statements must be issued to read the master records. If only 100 update transactions are being processed against a master file containing 10,000 records, random processing would be faster because, even though random retrieval is slower than sequential retrieval, only 100 master records would have to be retrieved as opposed to 10,000 with sequential updating. It should be noted that when using a sequential update with an indexed sequential file, a new master is NOT created. Instead, the record to be updated is rewritten on the file after being changed.

ADDITION OF RECORDS TO INDEXED SEQUENTIAL FILES

As stated previously, one of the functions to be performed by an update program is the addition of records to the master file. Records to be added to the master file have keys which normally place them somewhere between the first and last record on the master file; however, the additions may fall behind the last record on the master file (that is, the key of the record to be added is greater than any key on the master file).

When making additions to the file, the Add Function of the Indexed Sequential Access Method is utilized. This allows records to be added anywhere in the file.

The method of adding records to an existing indexed sequential file is illustrated in the following examples. These examples illustrate the contents of the cylinder index, the track index, the prime data area and the overflow area when the file is initially loaded and after records have been added to the file.

STEP 1: The file is loaded as shown in the examples in Chapter 5. Cylinder 1 Track 1 contains records 6 - 20; Cylinder 1 Track 2 contains records 24 - 45. The highest record on Cylinder 1 is record 150, which is stored on Track 15.

CYLINDER INDEX

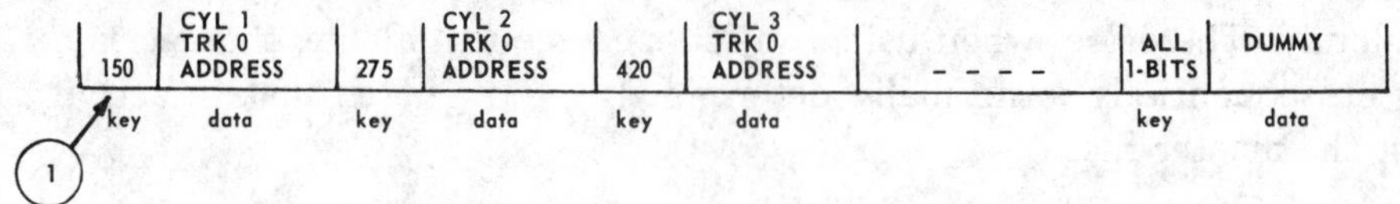

TRACK INDEX

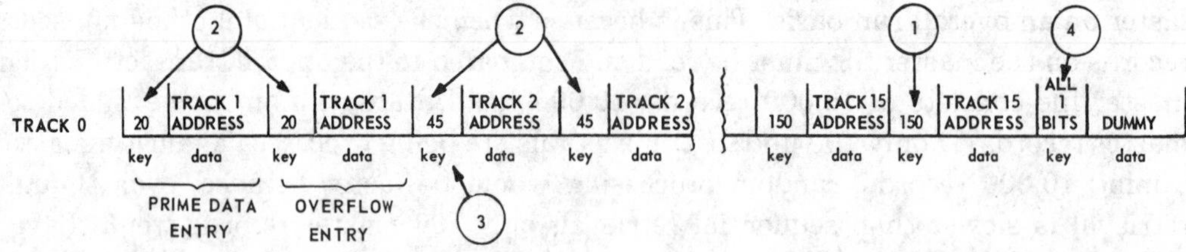

PRIME DATA AREA

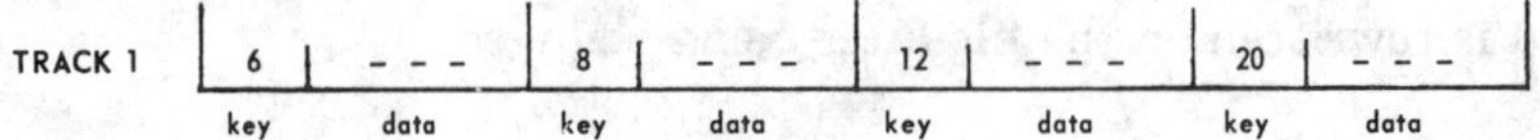

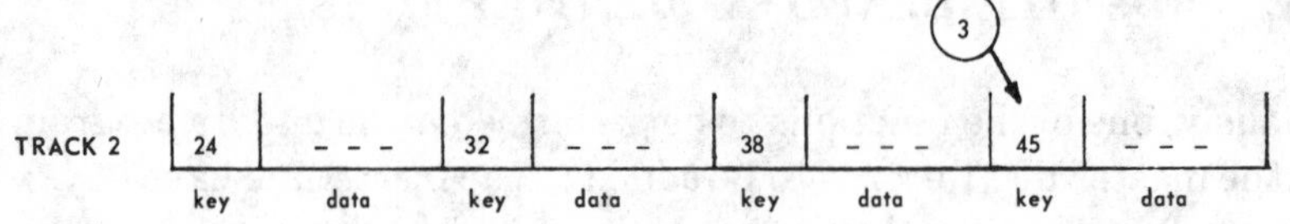

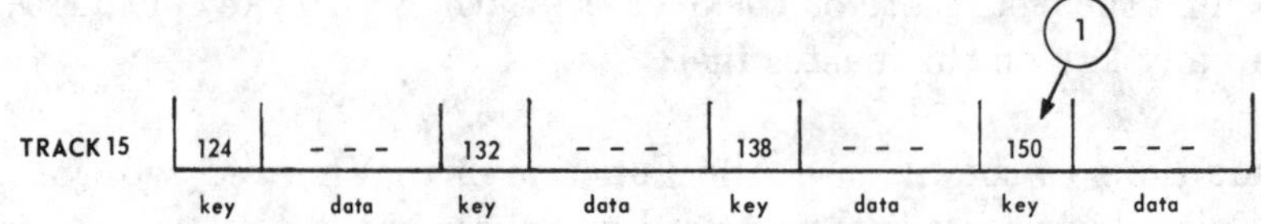

CYLINDER OVERFLOW AREA

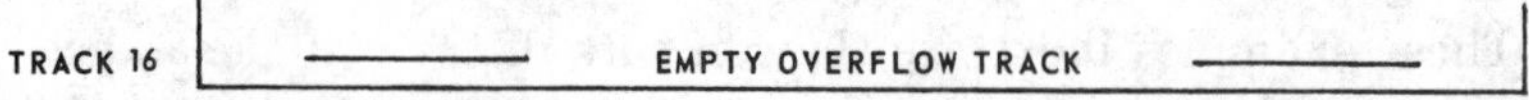

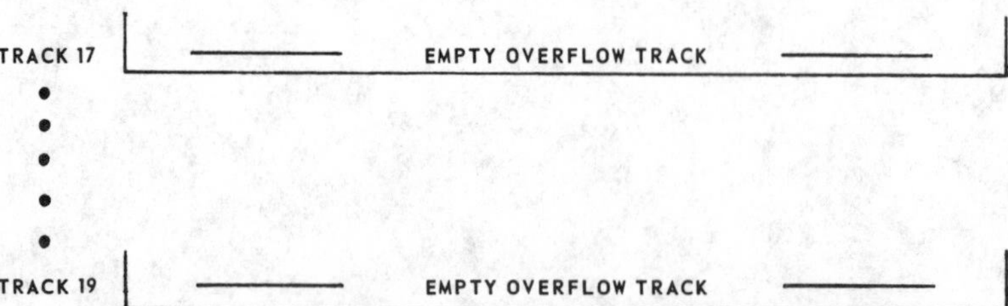

Figure 6-1 Indexes and Data Area — File is Loaded

Note in the example that Tracks 16, 17, 18, and 19 are the overflow tracks for each cylinder in the prime data area. Note also that only the first two tracks of the prime data area and the cylinder overflow area are shown. This is for illustration purposes, and the complete file would be processed in the same manner as shown for these two tracks.

Important features of the file as it is organized are:

1. The highest key contained in the cylinder index for Cylinder 1 corresponds to the highest key in the track index for Track 15, the last track used for prime data. It is always true that the cylinder index contains the highest key which is on the corresponding cylinder. In the example, the highest key on Cylinder 1 is 150. Note the entries in the cylinder index and the track index.

2. There are always two entries in the track index for each track on the cylinder. The first entry is used for the prime data area, and the second entry is used for the overflow area when records are added to the file, as will be shown. When no records are contained in the overflow area, such as in the example in Figure 6-1, the entries both contain the same value indicating the highest key on the track. In the example, the highest key on Track 1 is 20, the highest key on Track 2 is 45, etc.

3. The key specified in the track index is always the highest key which is on the associated track.

4. The end of the track index is specified by a key of all 1-bits. It is possible to have data following the track index on Track 0 if there is room on the track to write a block of data. When this is done, Track 0 is called a Shared Track. In the example, there was not enough room on Track 0 to write a record, so the data begins on Track 1.

It should be noted that if the records being used for the file are blocked, the key used for the block and in the indexes is the highest key in the block. Thus, if the block of records appeared as illustrated below, the key for the block would be 125.

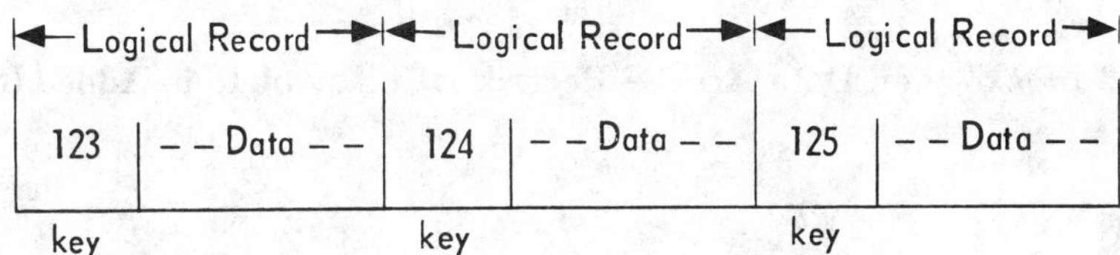

Figure 6-2 Block of Records With Keys

STEP 2: A record with a key of 18 is added to the file.

CYLINDER INDEX

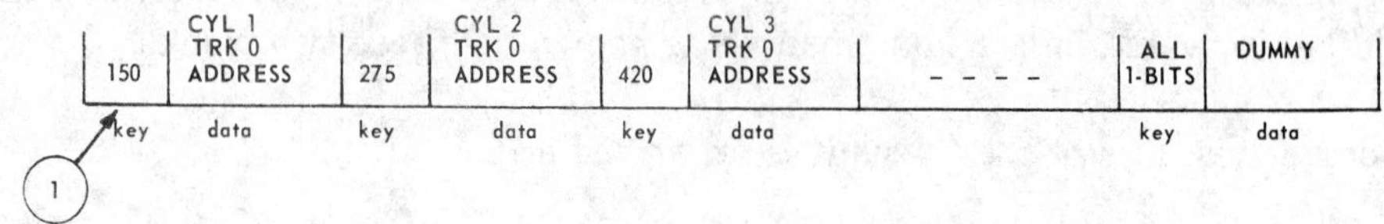

TRACK INDEX

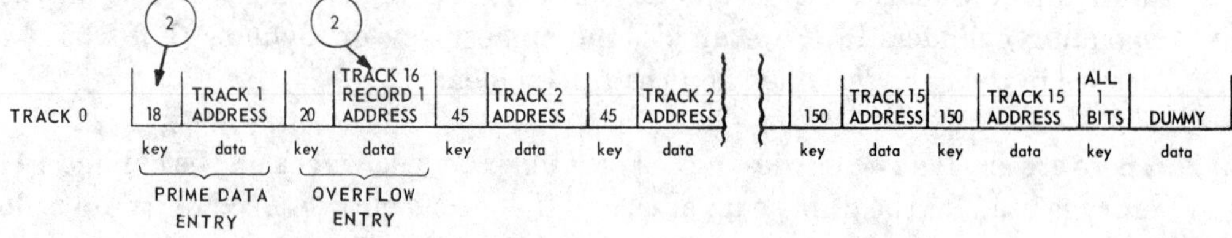

PRIME DATA AREA

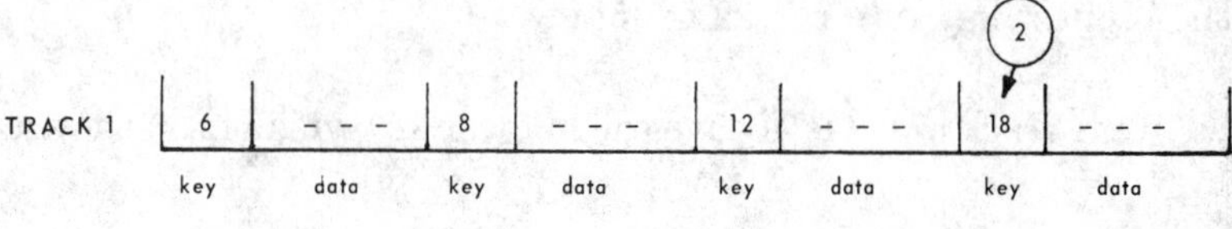

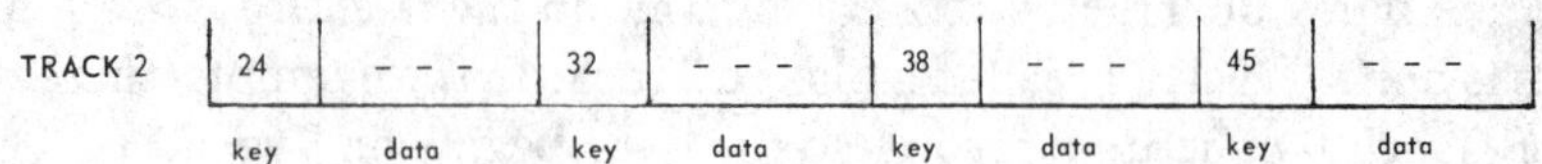

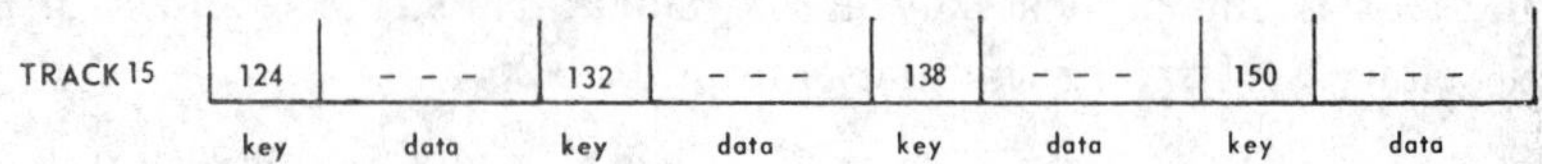

Figure 6-3 Indexes and Data Area — Record with Key of 18 is Added (Part 1 of 2)

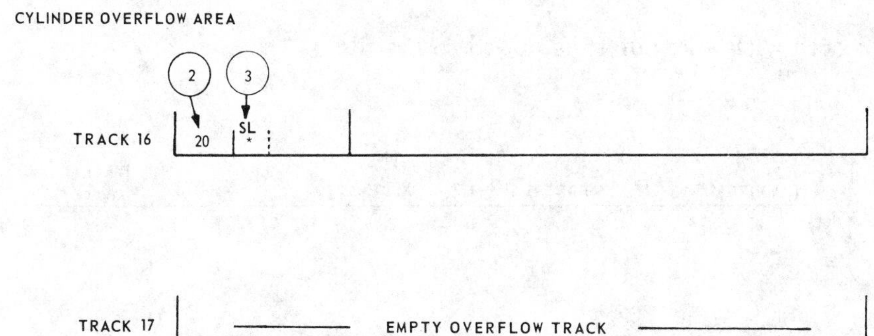

Figure 6-4 Indexes and Data Area — Record With Key of 18 is Added (Part 2 of 2)

After a record with a key = 18 has been added to the file, note the following:

1. The entries in the cylinder index have not been altered because the highest key on the cylinder has not been altered.

2. Record 18* was inserted between Record 12 and Record 20. A new record is always inserted where it belongs on the prime data area to keep the keys in an ascending sequence. When Record 18 was inserted, no room remained on the track for Record 20, so it was moved to the overflow area. The track index reflects this move by altering its entries as shown. The first entry in the track index for Track 1 contains the highest key physically stored on the track. This is Key 18 because it became the highest key on the track. The second entry contains the highest key from Track 1 which is in the overflow area. In the example, the key is 20. The data portion of the second entry for Track 1 contains the track and record address of the record which would immediately follow the highest key physically stored on the track. In the example, this is Record 20.

3. The sequence link field (S.L.) is established for every record which goes into the overflow area. The sequence link field is used to link the records in the overflow area. The * indicates that there are no other records in the overflow area from Track 1.

* When referencing the records in this example, a record with a key = 18 will be called Record 18, etc.

STEP 3: A record with a key of 15 is added to the file.

CYLINDER INDEX

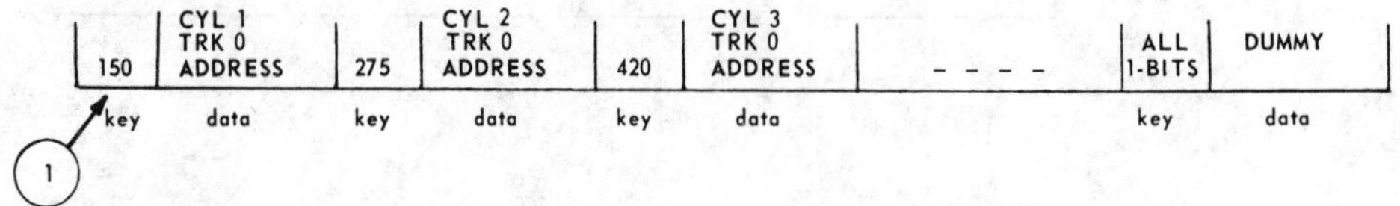

TRACK INDEX

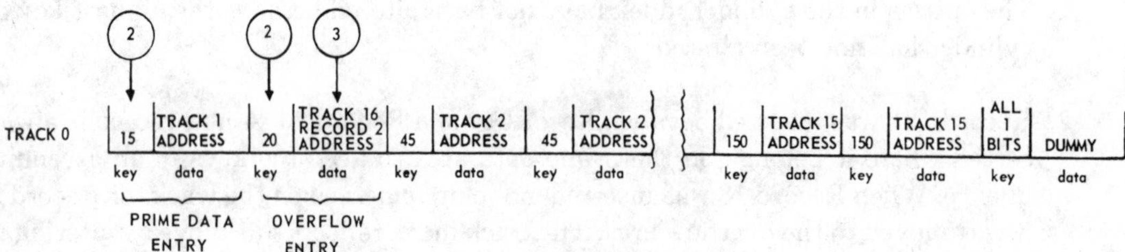

PRIME DATA AREA

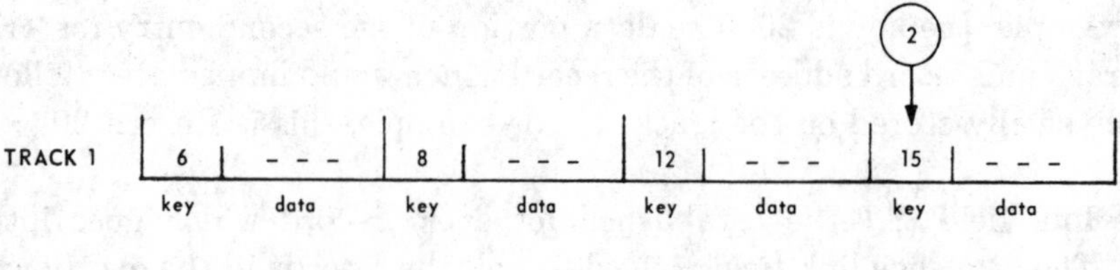

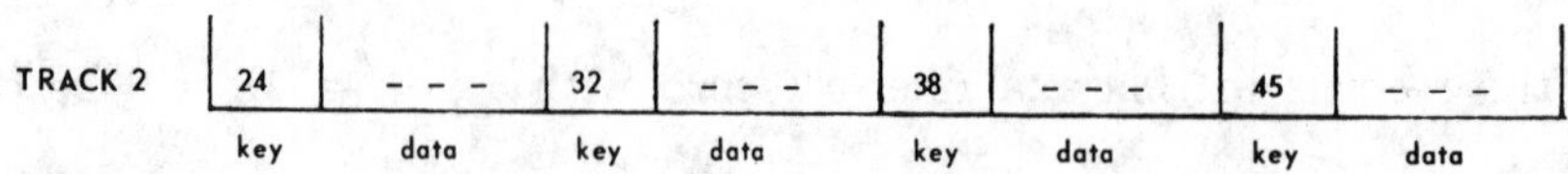

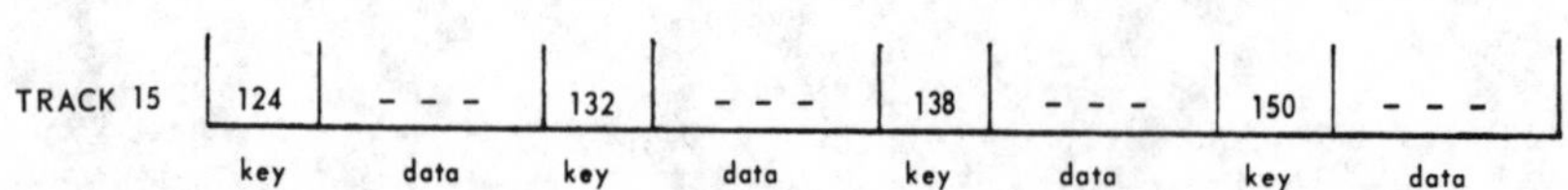

Figure 6-5 Indexes and Data Area — Record With Key of 15 is Added (Part 1 of 2)

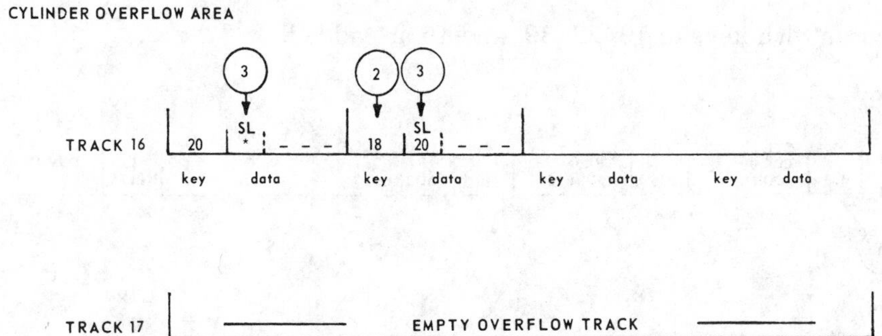

Figure 6-6 Indexes and Data Area — Record With Key of 15 is Added (Part 2 of 2)

After a record with a key of 15 has been added, note the following:

1. The cylinder index has not changed because the highest key on the cylinder has not been altered.

2. The first entry in the track index reflects the highest key stored on the track. Therefore, 15 is the key specified because the record was inserted in its proper place on the track to keep the records in an ascending sequence by key. Therefore, Record 18 was moved to the overflow area. Note, however, that the key value in the second entry of the track index still shows 20. This is because 20 is still the highest key value from Track 1 in the overflow area.

3. The sequence link field is now used because there are two records from Track 1 in the overflow area. The data in the second entry for Track 1 in the track index now points to Track 16, Record 2. This is because Record 18 is the next sequentially ascending record after the last record on Track 1 (key = 15). The sequence link field in Record 18 points to Record 20 because it is the next sequentially ascending record from Track 1. The sequence link field in Record 20 indicates no more records are in the overflow area from Track 1.

STEP 4: Records with keys of 19, 22, 39, and 16 are added.

CYLINDER INDEX

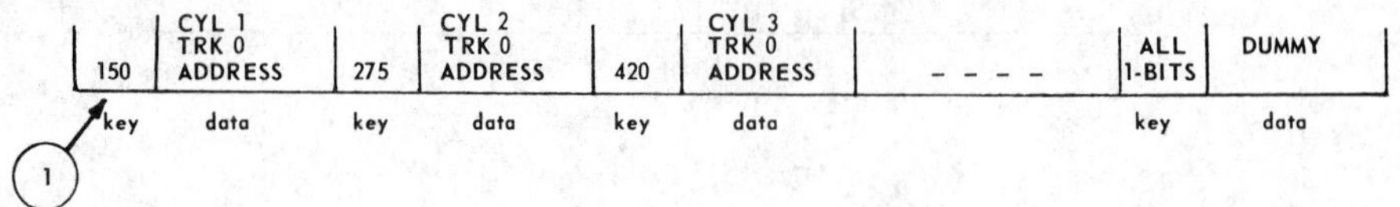

TRACK INDEX

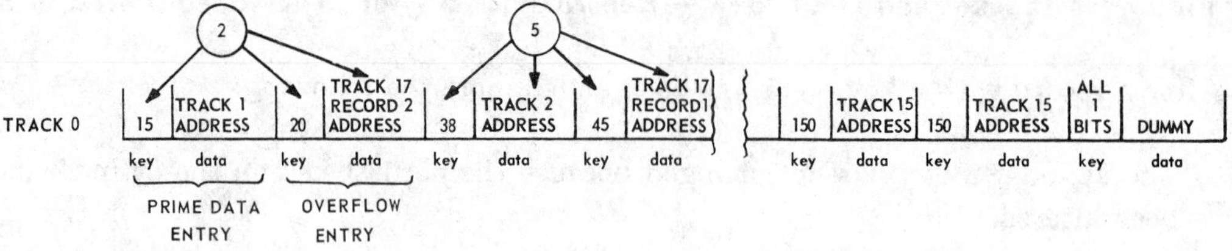

PRIME DATA AREA

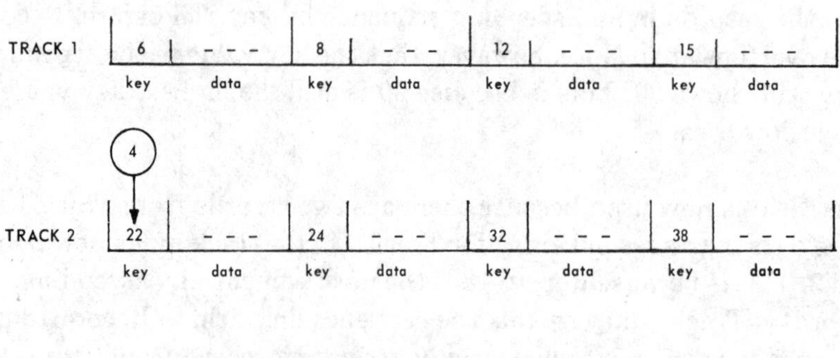

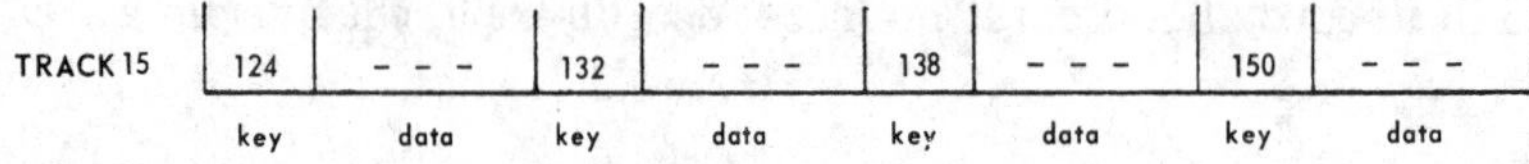

CYLINDER OVERFLOW AREA

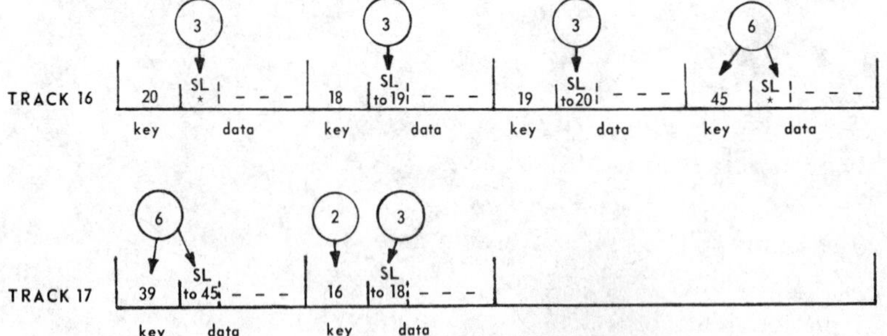

Figure 6-7 Indexes and Data Area — Records With Keys of 19, 22, 39 and 16 are Added

When Record 19 was added to the file, it was placed in the overflow area on Track 16. Record 22 was placed as the first record on Track 2 and Record 45, which was originally on Track 2 (see Figure 6-5), was placed in the overflow area on Track 16. Record 39 was placed directly in the overflow area on Track 17, as there was no room on Track 16 in the overflow area. When Record 16 was added, it was placed in the overflow area on Track 17.

After the above records have been added, note the following:

1. The cylinder index has not been altered.

2. The key entries for Track 1 in the track index are still the same. The highest key stored on the track is 15, and the highest key in the overflow area from Track 1 is 20. Note, however, that the address in the second data entry for Track 1 in the track index has changed. It now points to Record 16. Record 16 was added directly to the overflow area because its key was higher than the highest key located on Track 1 (15).

3. The sequence link fields in the overflow records for Track 1 all point to the next sequentially ascending record from Track 1. Thus, 16 points to 18, 18 points to 19, and 19 points to 20. Note that the sequence link field in Record 18 was altered to point to Record 19 when Record 19 was added. Record 20 indicates no more linkages. Even though there are higher keys in the overflow area (39 and 45), they are not from Track 1 in the prime data area and thus are not linked with Record 20.

4. Record 22 was added to Track 2. It was added to Track 2 even though its key was lower than the previous low key (24) because it was higher than the highest key on Track 1. Records are always added in this manner. The highest key on a track when a file is loaded remains the highest key when other processing is done against the file.

5. The entries in the track index have been modified to reflect the addition of records to Track 2. The first entry for Track 2 indicates that the highest key stored on Track 2 is 38. This is because Record 22 was added. The second key entry for Track 2 indicates that 45 is the highest key associated with the track. The data for the second entry points to Record 39 which is the next sequentially ascending record in the overflow area after the last record on Track 2 (38).

6. Record 45 was moved to the overflow area when Record 22 was added. Record 39 was added directly to overflow area because its key was greater than the highest key in the prime data area. Its sequence link field points to Record 45 because Record 45 is the next sequentially ascending record from Track 2.

More additions could be made to the file, and processing would continue until the overflow areas were full. At that point, it would be necessary to reorganize the file to eliminate records in the overflow areas. It should be noted that after the cylinder overflow areas are full, an independent overflow area can be used to hold additional records. All records in both the cylinder and independent overflow areas are unblocked even though the file may be blocked in the prime data areas.

RANDOM RETRIEVAL

Random retrieval and updating normally involve the retrieving of a master record from a file (based on a given key from the corresponding transaction record), updating the master record and rewriting the updated master record on the master file. When an indexed sequential file is randomly retrieved, a search of the indexes precedes the actual retrieval of the desired record. The search of the indexes locates the exact disk location of the record, and the record is then read into computer storage. If it were desired to retrieve the record with a key of 19 from the previous example, the following routine would be followed (this assumes no master index):

1. The cylinder index is read and it is determined Record 19 resides on Cylinder 1. This is because the highest key on Cylinder 1 is 150.

2. The track index is read and searched to find what track Record 19 is on. It is found that the highest key associated with Track 1 is 20, but that the highest key on Track 1 in the prime data area is 15. Therefore, Record 19, if it is on the file, must be in the overflow area.

3. The address of the first sequentially ascending record in the overflow area is obtained from the second data entry in the track index for Track 1. This address is Track 17, Record 2.

4. The record at Track 17, Record 2 is read and the key is 16. However, the sequence link field points to another record, so that record is read. The key for the record is 18, but the sequence link field points to the next record from Track 1. This record is Record 19, so it is returned to computer storage in the I/O area or work area for random retrieval. The program can then process the record.

It should be noted that, had Record 19 not been on the file, the next record would have been Record 20. Since 20 is greater than 19 and the records are in ascending order, the Invalid Key routine would have been entered, indicating that the record was not on the file.

SAMPLE PROBLEM

In order to illustrate randomly updating an indexed sequential file and adding records to an indexed sequential file, the program in this chapter will update the Customer Master File which was created in Chapter 5. In addition, prior to any changes being made to master records or records being added to the Customer Master File, each transaction input record will be completely edited to ensure that the record contains valid data.

INPUT

The input to the program consists of the Customer Master File and the Customer Transaction Input File. The format of the Customer Master File, which was created in Chapter 5, is illustrated below.

Customer Master File

FIELD	POSITION	NUMBER OF DIGITS	ATTRIBUTES
Deletion Code	1	1	Alphanumeric
Customer Number (Key)	2 - 6	5	Alphanumeric
Customer Name	7 - 26	20	Alphanumeric
Customer Address	27 - 53	27	Alphanumeric
Customer City	54 - 73	20	Alphanumeric
Customer State	74 - 75	2	Alphanumeric
Customer Zip Code	76 - 80	5	Numeric
Customer Discount	81 - 82	2	Numeric
Last Activity Date	83 - 88	6	Numeric

File Information:

File Information:	Record Length	—	88 characters
	Blocking Factor	—	20 records per block
	Storage Medium	—	Disk
	Organization	—	Indexed Sequential
	Access	—	Random

Figure 6-8 Format of Customer Master File

Note from the format illustrated in Figure 6-8 that the first position of the record, which was unused in Chapter 5, is used for the Deletion Code when the record is updated. As noted previously, if the first position of the record contains the value hex 'FF' on the System/360 and System/370, the record will be considered deleted even though it is physically still part of the indexed sequential file.

The remaining fields in the Customer Master Record are the same as those illustrated and explained in Chapter 5. The Key to the Indexed Sequential File is the Customer Number. Note that the access is specified as Random for the Customer Master File in this program.

The format of the records contained in the Customer Transaction Input File is illustrated below.

Customer Transaction Input File

CUST. NUMBER | DISCOUNT | LAST ACTIVITY DATE | CODE

CUST. NUMBER | CUSTOMER NAME | CUSTOMER ADDRESS | CUSTOMER CITY | STATE | ZIP CODE | CODE

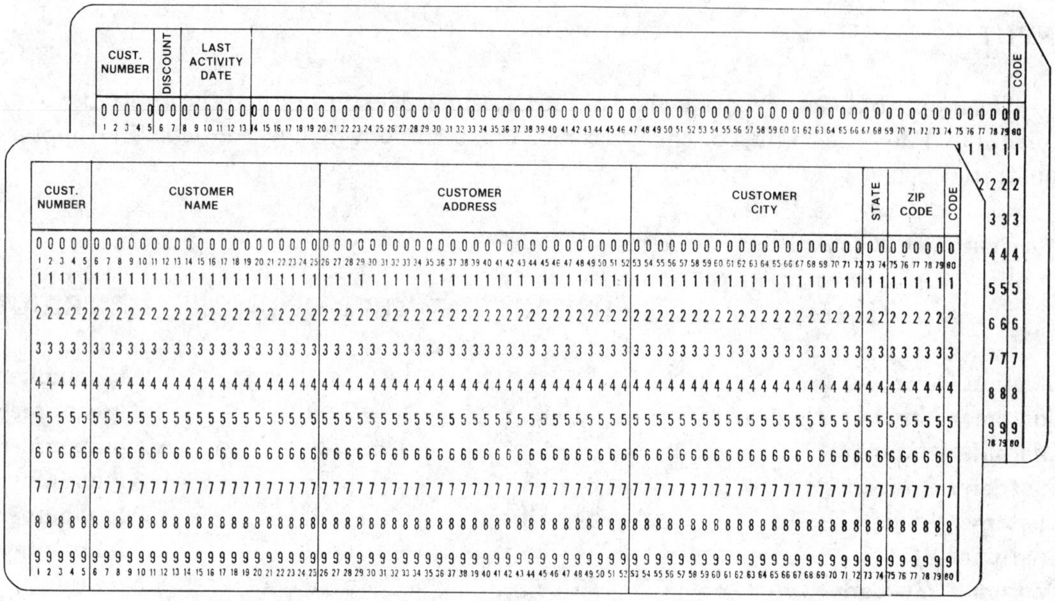

Figure 6-9 Format of Customer Transaction Input File

As can be seen from Figure 6-9, there are two different record formats the same as in Chapter 5. The first record contains the Customer Number, Customer Name, Customer Address, Customer City, State, Zip Code, and a Record Code. The code may be the value "1" which indicates that it is the first record of a pair of records which will be added to the Customer Master File; or it may be the value "3" which indicates that it will be used to change fields in a currently-existing Customer Master Record, or it may be the value "5" which indicates that the Customer Master Record with the corresponding Customer Number is to be deleted.

The second record illustrated in Figure 6-9 may have a code with the value "2," which indicates it is the second record of a pair required to add a record to the Customer Master File; or it may contain the code value "4" which indicates that the record will be used to change fields in the currently existing Customer Master Record.

OUTPUT

The output from the program consists of the updated Customer Master File and an Update Transaction Report. The format of the updated Customer Master File will be the same as the format illustrated in Figure 6-8 since a new file is not actually written; rather, as has been explained, the records will be changed and then rewritten in the same file, and additions will be added to the same file in the overflow areas.

The format of the Update Transaction Report is illustrated in Figure 6-10.

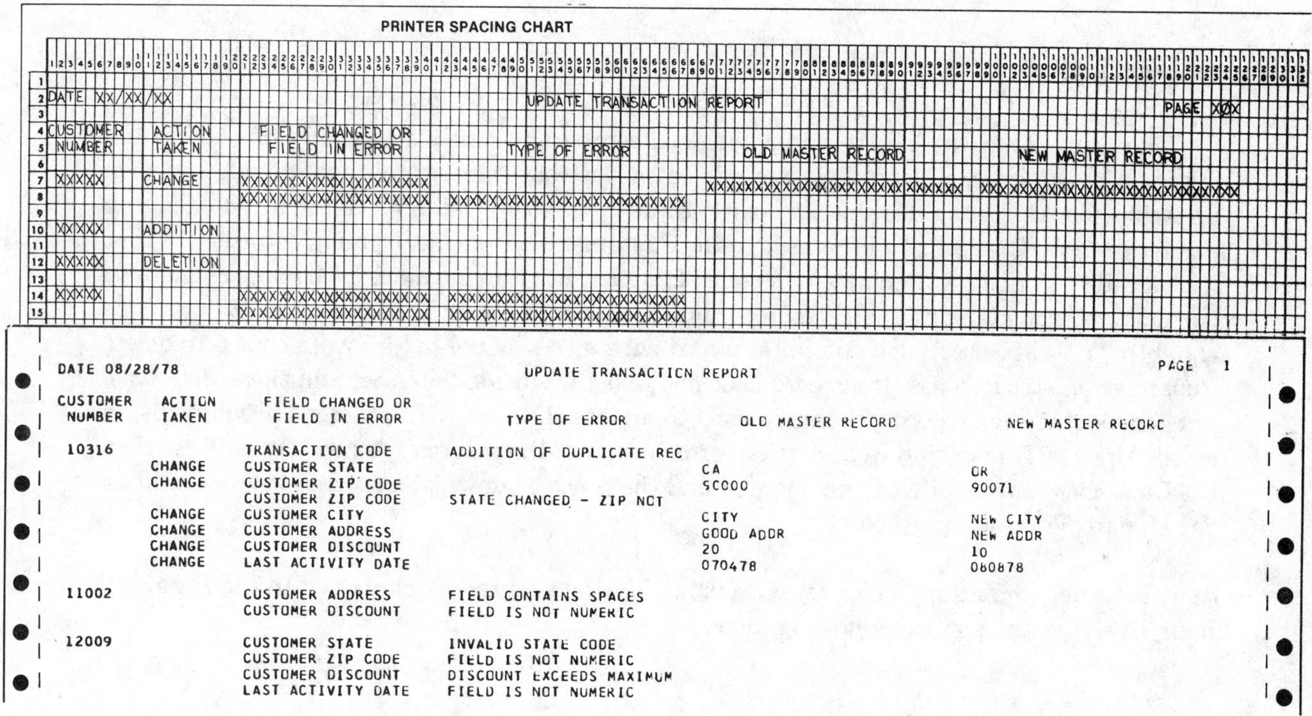

DATE 08/28/78 UPDATE TRANSACTICN REPORT PAGE 1

CUSTOMER NUMBER	ACTION TAKEN	FIELD CHANGED OR FIELD IN ERROR	TYPE OF ERROR	OLD MASTER RECORD	NEW MASTER RECORC
10316		TRANSACTION CODE	ADDITION OF DUPLICATE REC		
	CHANGE	CUSTOMER STATE		CA	OR
	CHANGE	CUSTOMER ZIP CODE		9C000	90071
		CUSTOMER ZIP CODE	STATE CHANGED - ZIP NOT		
	CHANGE	CUSTOMER CITY		CITY	NEW CITY
	CHANGE	CUSTOMER ADDRESS		GOOD ADDR	NEW ADDR
	CHANGE	CUSTOMER DISCOUNT		20	10
	CHANGE	LAST ACTIVITY DATE		070478	080878
11002		CUSTOMER ADDRESS	FIELD CONTAINS SPACES		
		CUSTOMER DISCOUNT	FIELD IS NOT NUMERIC		
12009		CUSTOMER STATE	INVALID STATE CODE		
		CUSTOMER ZIP CODE	FIELD IS NOT NUMERIC		
		CUSTOMER DISCOUNT	DISCOUNT EXCEEDS MAXIMUM		
		LAST ACTIVITY DATE	FIELD IS NOT NUMERIC		

Figure 6-10 Update Transaction Report

Note from Figure 6-10 that the report contains the Customer Number, the Action Taken, the Field Changed or Field in Error, the Type of Error, the contents of the Old Master Record, and the contents of the New Master Record. The Customer Number identifies the record being reported. The Action Taken can be either Change, Addition, or Deletion, depending upon the processing performed. The Field Changed or Field in Error will contain a description (for example, CUSTOMER ADDRESS) which identifies the field which either was changed or was in error. The Type of Error field will contain a description of the error (for example, FIELD CONTAINS SPACES) if an error is found in the field.

The Old Master Record field contains the contents of the Customer Master Record before the field is changed, and the New Master Record field contains the contents of the Customer Master Record after the field is changed.

Thus, as can be seen, the Update Transaction Report not only contains any errors which are found in the transaction input data but also contains a report of the update processing which takes place within the program. This is done so that a permanent record is kept of all changes, additions, and deletions which have been done to the file. This type of report is quite common when master files are updated.

PROCESSING

The processing which is to occur within the program consists basically of reading the Transaction Records, editing these records to ensure that they contain valid data, and then updating the Customer Master File with these records by adding, deleting, or changing master records. In order to add records to the Customer Master File, a pair of records (the first with a code "1" and the second with a code "2") must be read and edited. To make changes to currently existing Customer Master Records, a record with either a code equal to "3" or a code equal to "4" will be read and edited. A record with a code equal to "5" will be used to delete Customer Master Records. If a record does not pass the editing for either additions, deletions, or changes, then the record will not be used to update the master file; instead it will be listed on the Update Transaction Report as an error record. If the record does pass the editing, then the Customer Master File will be updated and the processing which occurred will be listed on the Update Transaction Report.

The exact processing which is to occur within the program is explained in the Programming Specifications on the following pages.

PROGRAMMING SPECIFICATIONS		
SUBJECT Customer Master File Update	DATE July 2	PAGE 1 OF 8
TO Programmer	FROM Systems Analyst	

A program is to be written to update the Customer Master File. The file is stored on magnetic disk as an indexed sequential file. The format of the Transaction Records, the Customer Master File, and the Update Transaction Report are included as a part of this narrative. The program should be written to include the following processing.

1. The program should read transaction records from the Customer Transaction Input File and use these records to update the Customer Master File. The updating is to be done randomly.

2. The Customer Master Record contains the Customer Number, the Customer Name, the Customer Address, the Customer City, the Customer State, the Customer Zip Code, the Customer Discount, and the Last Activity Date. See the accompanying file format for the exact record format.

3. The Customer Transaction Input Records are in two different formats. The first format contains the Customer Number, the Customer Name, the Customer Address, the Customer City, the Customer State, the Customer Zip Code, and a Code. The Code must be equal to "1," "3," or "5." The exact format is contained in the accompanying documentation.

   The second format includes the Customer Number, the Customer Discount, the Last Activity Date, and the Code. The Code must be equal to "2" or "4." The exact format is contained in the accompanying documentation.

   The Customer Transaction Input Records must be sorted into an ascending sequence by Transaction Code within Customer Number.

4. Three types of processing can take place. A record can be added to the Customer Master File, a record can be deleted from the Customer Master File, and a record in the Customer Master File can be changed.

Figure 6-11 Programming Specifications (Part 1 of 8)

PROGRAMMING SPECIFICATIONS

SUBJECT Customer Master File Update	DATE July 2	PAGE 2 OF 8
TO Programmer	FROM Systems Analyst	

a. Additions — Records can be added to the Customer Master File provided there is not a record with the same Customer Number already in the file. When a record is added to the Customer Master File, the Customer Number, Customer Name, Customer Address, Customer City, Customer State, Customer Zip Code, Customer Discount, and Last Activity Date will be taken from a Type "1" Transaction Record and a Type "2" Transaction Record and placed in the new Customer Master Record. Therefore, in order for a valid addition to take place, there must be both a Type 1 transaction and a Type 2 transaction with the same Customer Number. If there is a Type 1 transaction without a Type 2 transaction with the same Customer Number, or if there is a Type 2 transaction without a corresponding Type 1 transaction record, then an addition cannot take place; instead, a message should be written on the Update Transaction Report indicating a Type 1 record without a Type 2, or a Type 2 without a Type 1.

If there is a Type 1 record followed by a Type 2 record with the same Customer Number, then the data in those records can be used to add a new record to the Customer Master File provided the data within the records passes the editing specified later in these specifications.

b. Deletions — A record can be deleted from the Customer Master File if the Transaction Code in the transaction record is equal to the value "5" and there is a corresponding record in the Customer Master File; that is, a record with the same Customer Number as that found in the transaction record. In order to cause a record to be deleted, the COBOL figurative constant High-Values, which is hexadecimal "FF," should be moved to the first position of the record to be deleted. The record should then be rewritten on the Customer Master File.

Figure 6-12 Programming Specifications (Part 2 of 8)

PROGRAMMING SPECIFICATIONS		
SUBJECT Customer Master File Update	DATE July 2	PAGE 3 OF 8
TO Programmer	FROM Systems Analyst	

c. Changes — Fields within a Customer Master Record contained in the Customer Master File can be changed if the Transaction Code in the Transaction Record is equal to "3" or "4." A Transaction Record with a code equal to "3" can be used to change the Customer Address, Customer City, Customer State, and Customer Zip Code. A Transaction Record with a code equal to "4" can be used to change the Customer Discount and the Last Activity Date. In order for a change to occur, the Transaction Code must be equal to "3" or "4" and a matching Customer Master Record must be found in the Customer Master File. If a matching Customer Master Record is not found in the Customer Master File when the Transaction Code is equal to "3" or "4," then an error has occurred and an entry should be made on the Update Transaction Report.

If a Customer Master Record is found with a Customer Number equal to the Customer Number in the Transaction Record and the Transaction Record has a code of "3" or "4," then, provided the data in the Transaction Record passes the editing criteria specified later in these specifications, the following changes can be made.

Code "3" Transaction:

1) If the Customer Address in the Transaction Record is not blank, then the Customer Address in the Customer Master Record should be replaced by the Customer Address in the Transaction Record.

2) If the Customer City in the Transaction Record is not blank, then the Customer City in the Customer Master Record should be replaced by the Customer City in the Transaction Record.

3) If the Customer State in the Transaction Record is not blank, then the Customer State in the Customer Master Record should be replaced by the Customer State in the Transaction Record.

Figure 6-13 Programming Specifications (Part 3 of 8)

PROGRAMMING SPECIFICATIONS			
SUBJECT Customer Master File Update	**DATE** July 2		**PAGE** 4 **OF** 8
TO Programmer	**FROM** Systems Analyst		

4) If the Customer Zip Code in the Transaction Record is not blank, then the Customer Zip Code in the Customer Master Record should be replaced by the Customer Zip Code in the Transaction Record.

Code "4" Transaction:

1) If the Customer Discount in the Transaction Record is not blank, then the Customer Discount in the Customer Master Record should be replaced by the Customer Discount in the Transaction Record.

2) If the Last Activity Date in the Transaction Record is not blank, then the Last Activity Date in the Customer Master Record should be replaced by the Last Activity Date in the Transaction Record.

5. Before any Transaction Records can be used for additions, deletions, or changes, they must be edited to ensure that they contain valid data. The editing which must be performed is specified below.

Additions:

a. Customer Number — The Customer Number must be numeric and satisfy a Modulus 11 check.

b. Customer Address, Customer City, Customer State — The Customer Address, Customer City, and Customer State fields must not be blank.

c. Customer State — The State Code must be one of the valid 51 state codes (50 states and the District of Columbia).

d. Zip Code — The Zip Code must be numeric.

e. Customer Discount — The Customer Discount field must be numeric and must not be greater than 20%.

Figure 6-14 Programming Specifications (Part 4 of 8)

PROGRAMMING SPECIFICATIONS

SUBJECT Customer Master File Update	DATE July 2	PAGE 5 OF 8
TO Programmer	FROM Systems Analyst	

f. Last Activity Date — The Last Activity Date must be numeric and the month must not be less than 01 or greater than 12. The day of the month in the Transaction Record must not exceed the maximum number of days in that month.

Deletions:

a. Customer Number — The Customer Number must be numeric and satisfy a Modulus 11 check.

Changes:

a. Customer Number — The Customer Number must be numeric and satisfy a Modulus 11 check.

b. Customer State — The State Code must be one of the valid 51 state codes (50 states and the District of Columbia).

c. Zip Code — The Zip Code must be numeric.

d. Customer Discount — The Customer Discount field must be numeric and must not be greater than 20%.

e. Last Activity Date — The Last Activity Date must be numeric and the month must not be less than 01 or greater than 12. The day of the month in the Transaction Record must not exceed the maximum number of days in that month.

f. If a change is made to the State Code in the Master Record, then a change must also be made to the Zip Code. Thus, a Transaction Record with a State Code present but a Zip Code absent is in error.

6. For Addition Records, all fields must be checked and be valid before the record is added to the Customer Master File. The Addition Records must have both a Type 1 record and a Type 2 record with the same Customer Number before the editing takes place.

Figure 6-15 Programming Specifications (Part 5 of 8)

PROGRAMMING SPECIFICATIONS		
SUBJECT Customer Master File Update	DATE July 2	PAGE 6 OF 8
TO Programmer	FROM Systems Analyst	

7. For Change Records, a Type 3 record will be checked for Customer Number, Customer State, and Customer Zip Code provided the field in the record contains data. For example, it is valid to have a Type 3 record contain only the Customer Zip Code. In that event, only the Zip Code would be edited. The other fields would not be edited because there is no data to edit. Thus, if a field contains data which is going to be used to update the Customer Master Record, the data should be edited according to the Editing Rules set forth in #5 above. The Customer Number will always be checked.

   A Type 4 record will be checked for Customer Discount and Last Activity Date, again provided that there is data in the field. For example, if only the Last Activity Date is to be changed by a Type 4 record, then only the Last Activity Date field should be edited because the Customer Discount field will be blank. The Customer Number must be edited for each Type 4 record.

   If any field within a Change Record is found to be in error, then the entire record is considered invalid and none of the fields can be used to change the Master Record.

8. The Update Transaction Report contains a record of each Transaction Record which is processed, whether it causes a Change, Deletion, or Addition to take place or whether it contains an error. The fields on the Update Transaction are explained below:

   a. Customer Number — The Customer Number will be printed for each Transaction Record which is processed. It should be group-indicated since more than one error or more than one type of transaction can occur for the same Customer.

   b. Action Taken — This field indicates the type of updating which took place to the Master Record. The constant "CHANGE" should be printed when the Master Record is changed; the constant "ADDITION" should be printed when a record is added to the Customer Master File; the constant "DELETION" is printed when the Customer Master Record is deleted. The field should be left blank when a Transaction Record contains an error.

Figure 6-16 Programming Specifications (Part 6 of 8)

PROGRAMMING SPECIFICATIONS

SUBJECT Customer Master File Update	DATE July 2	PAGE 7 OF 8
TO Programmer	FROM Systems Analyst	

c. Field Changed or Field in Error — This field contains the name of the field which was changed by a Change Transaction or which contained an error when the Transaction Record was edited. It is left blank for Additions and Deletions. The following are the constants which should be used to identify the fields:

CUSTOMER NUMBER — Customer Number field
CUSTOMER NAME — Customer Name field
CUSTOMER ADDRESS — Customer Address field
CUSTOMER CITY — Customer City field
CUSTOMER STATE — Customer State field
CUSTOMER ZIP CODE — Customer Zip Code field
CUSTOMER DISCOUNT — Customer Discount field
LAST ACTIVITY DATE — Last Activity Date field
CUSTOMER RECORDS — Used when have Type 1 but No Type 2 Record, or Type 2 but No Type 1 Record when adding records
TRANSACTION CODE — Used when a change or delete record does not have a matching master record; when an addition of a currently existing Master Record is attempted; or when the Transaction Code is invalid (not 1 - 5)

d. Type of Error — This field is used to identify the type of error which was found in the editing processing. It is blank for Additions, Deletions, and Changes. The allowable error messages are listed below:

FIELD CONTAINS SPACES — This message is printed whenever a field which is supposed to contain data does not.
INVALID STATE CODE — This message is printed when the State Code in the Transaction Record does not contain one of the valid 51 codes.
FIELD IS NOT NUMERIC — This message is printed when a field which is supposed to contain numeric data does not.
DISCOUNT EXCEEDS MAXIMUM — This message is printed when the Customer Discount in a Transaction Record is greater than the maximum customer discount allowed.
INVALID MONTH — This message is printed when the month in the Last Activity Date is not 01 - 12.

Figure 6-17 Programming Specifications (Part 7 of 8)

PROGRAMMING SPECIFICATIONS

SUBJECT	Customer Master File Update	DATE	July 2	PAGE 8 OF 8
TO	Programmer	FROM	Systems Analyst	

INVALID DAY — This message is printed when the day in the Last Activity Date is less than 01 or greater than the number of days in the month specified in the Last Activity Date.

TYPE 1 BUT NO TYPE 2 — This message is printed when a Type 1 record is read but there is no Type 2 record with the same Customer Number.

TYPE 2 BUT NO TYPE 1 — This message is printed when a Type 2 record is read but there is no Type 1 record with the same Customer Number.

INVALID RECORD TYPE — This message is printed when the Transaction Code in the Transaction Record is not equal to 1, 2, 3, 4, or 5.

FAILS MOD-11 CHECK — This message is printed when the Customer Number does not pass the Modulus 11 test.

ADDITION OF DUPLICATE REC — This message is printed when an attempt is made to add a record with a Customer Number equal to a Customer Number already stored in the Customer Master File.

STATE CHANGED—ZIP NOT — This message is printed when a Type 3 change record contains a State Code, indicating that the State Code in the Customer Master Record is to be changed, but does not contain data in the Zip Code field to indicate that the Zip Code is to be changed also.

NO MASTER RECORD — This message is printed when a Change record or a Delete record contains a Customer Number for which there is not a record in the Customer Master File.

e. Old Master Record — This field will contain the contents of the field in the master record before a change is made to the Master Record. It will be blank for errors, additions, and deletions.

f. New Master Record — This field will contain the contents of a changed field after the change takes place. It will be blank for errors, additions, and deletions.

9. The Update Transaction Report should be formatted as illustrated in the accompanying printer spacing chart. The maximum number of detail lines for a single page should be 40 lines.

10. The program should be written in COBOL.

Figure 6-18 Programming Specifications (Part 8 of 8)

DEFINITION OF RANDOMLY-ACCESSED INDEXED SEQUENTIAL FILE

As noted, the Customer Master File, which is stored as an indexed sequential file, is to be randomly accessed in the sample program in order to add records to it and to change records in it. As with files seen previously, the Customer Master File must be defined in both the Environment Division and the Data Division.

Environment Division

The definition of the Customer Master File in the Input-Output Section of the Environment Division is illustrated in Figure 6-19.

EXAMPLE

```
003040     SELECT CUSTOMER-MASTER-I-O-FILE
003050         ASSIGN TO DA-I-CUSTMAST
003060         ACCESS IS RANDOM
003070         RECORD KEY IS CUSTOMER-NUMBER-MSTRIO
003080         NOMINAL KEY IS KEY-OF-THE-RECORD-TO-RETRIEVE.
```

Figure 6-19 Example of Select Statement for Random Indexed Sequential File

As can be seen from Figure 6-19, the Select Clause and the Assign Clause are similar to those seen previously. In order to define a file which is going to be accessed randomly, however, the compiler must be informed that this is to occur. The ACCESS IS RANDOM Clause is specified to indicate that the file is to be accessed randomly. As with the indexed sequential file when it is loaded (Chapter 5), the Record Key Is Clause must be used to identify the field within the Customer Master Record which acts as the key of the record. As has been noted, the Customer Number is the key for the Customer Master Record; therefore, the field CUSTOMER-NUMBER-MSTRIO is specified as the Record Key.

When a record is to be randomly retrieved from the Customer Master File, the key of the record must be known before it can be retrieved. As noted in the Program Specifications, the key of the record to be retrieved in order for the record to be changed or deleted will be obtained from the transaction record. When the Customer Number, which is the key of the records, is known, it must be placed in the field defined by the Nominal Key Clause prior to a Read Statement being issued to retrieve the record. The field specified must be the same size and have the same attributes as the field used as the key of the record. In the example in Figure 6-19, it can be seen that the name of the field used as the Nominal Key field is KEY-OF-THE-RECORD-TO-RETRIEVE. The definition of this field in the Data Division is illustrated in Figure 6-20.

EXAMPLE

```
007190 01  NOMINAL-KEY-FIELD.
007200         05  KEY-OF-THE-RECORD-TO-RETRIEVE    PIC X(5).
```

Figure 6-20 Example of Nominal Key Field

Note in Figure 6-20 that the name of the nominal key field is KEY-OF-THE-RECORD-TO-RETRIEVE, which was specified in the Select Statement for the file (see Figure 6-19). The field is defined as PIC X(5), since this is the size and attributes of the Customer Number field in the Customer Master Record. The nominal key field must always be the same size and have the same attributes as the field which is the key of the record in the indexed sequential file.

Data Division

The Customer Master File must also be defined in the Data Division. The definition of the file and the input-output area in the Data Division are illustrated below.

EXAMPLE

```
004130 FD  CUSTOMER-MASTER-I-O-FILE
004140         BLOCK CONTAINS 20 RECORDS
004150         RECORD CONTAINS 88 CHARACTERS
004160         LABEL RECORDS ARE STANDARD
004170         DATA RECORD IS CUSTOMER-MASTER-I-O-RECORD.
004180
004190 01  CUSTOMER-MASTER-I-O-RECORD.
004200     05  FILLER                                PIC X.
004210     05  CUSTOMER-NUMBER-MSTRIO                PIC X(5).
004220     05  FILLER                                PIC X(82).
```

Figure 6-21 Example of File Definition in Data Division

Note from Figure 6-21 that the file is defined in the same manner as illustrated in Chapter 5. The data record is given the name CUSTOMER-MASTER-I-O-RECORD. The only field defined for the record is the Customer Number, which must be defined in order to satisfy the requirements for the Record Key Clause in Select Statement. The reason that other fields are not defined is that the input and output master records will be processed in the Working-Storage Section of the program.

PROCEDURE DIVISION

In order to randomly process an indexed sequential file, the file must first be opened as an I-O file. Records are retrieved from the file using the Read Statement, and they are written on the file through the use of the Write Statement and the Rewrite Statement. These instructions are illustrated in the following sections.

Open Statement

As with other files, an indexed sequential file which is being randomly processed must be opened before other instructions are issued for the file. The Open Statement used in the sample program is illustrated in Figure 6-22.

EXAMPLE

```
015060     OPEN I-O     CUSTOMER-MASTER-I-O-FILE
015070          OUTPUT  UPDATE-TRANSACTION-REPORT-FILE.
```

Figure 6-22 Example of Open Statement

Note in Figure 6-22 that the verb OPEN is specified as in previous Open Statements. When a file is to be used to both retrieve records from a file and to rewrite records back into the file, then the file is used as both an input file and an output file. Therefore, the identification of the usage of the file must be the value "I-O" rather than INPUT or OUTPUT. The filename is specified as in any other Open Statement. Thus, from the example in Figure 6-22 it can be seen that the CUSTOMER-MASTER-I-O-FILE will be used both for retrieving records and for writing records in the file, while the UPDATE-TRANSACTION-REPORT-FILE is strictly an output file.

Reading a Randomly-Accessed Master Record

In order to randomly retrieve a record from an indexed sequential file, the Read Statement is used. The Read Statement used in the sample program is illustrated in Figure 6-23.

EXAMPLE

```
Ø1706Ø        MOVE CUSTOMER-NUMBER-CURRENT-REC TO
Ø1707Ø                KEY-OF-THE-RECORD-TO-RETRIEVE.
Ø1708Ø        READ CUSTOMER-MASTER-I-O-FILE INTO MASTER-INPUT-WORK-AREA
Ø1709Ø                INVALID KEY
Ø1710Ø                    MOVE 'NO ' TO WAS-A-MASTER-RECORD-FOUND.
```

Figure 6-23 Example of Read Statement

In the example above, the Move Statement on line 017060 moves the Customer Number from the current transaction record to the field KEY-OF-THE-RECORD-TO-RETRIEVE. It will be recalled that this is the Nominal Key field as defined previously (see Figure 6-19 and Figure 6-20). Whenever a record is going to be retrieved randomly, the key of the record to be retrieved must be moved to the Nominal Key area prior to issuing the Read Statement which will retrieve the record. Thus, in the example, the Customer Number from the Transaction Record is moved to the Nominal Key field.

In order to retrieve the record, the Read Statement is used. The filename of the file to be read is specified following the Read Verb in the same manner as has been seen for reading sequential files. In the example in Figure 6-23, the optional "Into" Clause is used so that the input record will be placed in the MASTER-INPUT-WORK-AREA, which is defined in Working-Storage. The "Into" Clause need not be used; if it is not, then the record should be processed in the file record area defined in the File Section of the Data Division.

The "Invalid Key" Clause is used to specify the processing which is to occur if a record with a key equal to that contained in the Nominal Key field is not found in the file being read. Thus, in the example, if a record in the Customer Master File does not contain a Customer Number which is equal to the Customer Number stored in the KEY-OF-THE-RECORD-TO-RETRIEVE field, the value "NO" will be moved to the indicator WAS-A-MASTER-RECORD-FOUND. The Invalid Key Clause may have any imperative statements required.

It should be noted that, unlike sequential reading, there is no "At End" clause required. This is because the records are read at random rather than one following another sequentially; thus, the "end-of-file" will never be reached since each record which is to be read will either be in the file or not in the file. If the record is not in the file, the Invalid Key processing will take place.

Rewrite Statement

After a record has been retrieved from the indexed sequential file and updated, it should be rewritten back into the file so that the file contains the updated record. The Rewrite Statement is used to rewrite a record which has been retrieved back into the file. The Rewrite Statement used in the sample program is illustrated in Figure 6-24.

EXAMPLE

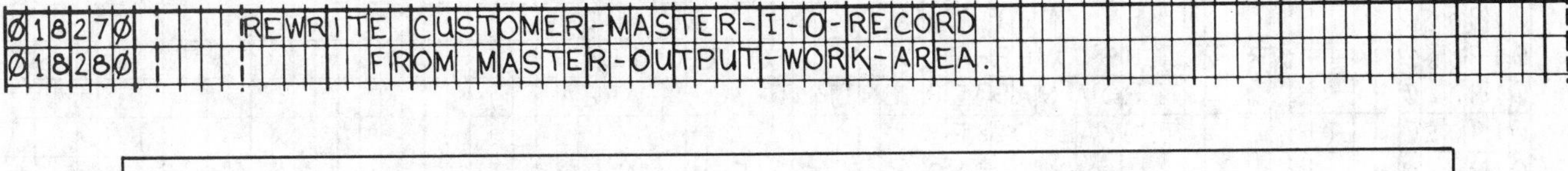

```
Ø1827Ø     REWRITE CUSTOMER-MASTER-I-O-RECORD
Ø1828Ø         FROM MASTER-OUTPUT-WORK-AREA.
```

```
REWRITE record-name [FROM identifier] [; INVALID KEY imperative-statement]
```

Figure 6-24 Example of Rewrite Statement

Note in Figure 6-24 that the verb REWRITE must be specified first followed by the record-name, that is, the name of the record as specified in the File Section of the Data Division. In the example, the name CUSTOMER-MASTER-I-O-RECORD is used, since this is the name defined in the File Section (see Figure 6-21).

The optional FROM entry is used in the example because the data to be written on the file is contained in the field MASTER-OUTPUT-WORK-AREA rather than in the I/O area itself. The effect of the From entry is to move the data from MASTER-OUTPUT-WORK-AREA to CUSTOMER-MASTER-I-O-RECORD and then to rewrite the record in the Customer Master File.

There are several requirements which must be followed when using the Rewrite Statement. First, the Rewrite Statement should not be issued unless a record has been successfully retrieved from the indexed sequential file prior to issuing the Rewrite Statement; that is, the sequence must be to first randomly retrieve a record and then rewrite that same record. If a record was not successfully retrieved from the file, then a Rewrite Statement should not be executed.

Secondly, the Nominal Key field should not be altered from the time the record is retrieved to the time the record is rewritten. This field is used by the indexed sequential access method to determine the key of the record to be rewritten. Therefore, once a record has been retrieved, which requires the key of the record to be stored in the Nominal Key area (see Figure 6-23), the Nominal Key field should not be disturbed prior to rewriting the record in the file.

Write Statement

The Write Statement is used to add a record to the indexed sequential file. The Write Statement used in the sample program to add a record to the Customer Master File is illustrated in Figure 6-25.

EXAMPLE

```
019010     MOVE CUSTOMER-NUMBER-CURRENT-REC TO
019020         KEY-OF-THE-RECORD-TO-RETRIEVE.
019030     WRITE CUSTOMER-MASTER-I-O-RECORD
019040         FROM MASTER-OUTPUT-WORK-AREA
019050         INVALID KEY
019060             MOVE 'NO ' TO DID-A-VALID-WRITE-OCCUR.
```

```
WRITE record-name [FROM identifier] [; INVALID KEY imperative-statement]
```

Figure 6-25 Example of Write Statement to Add Records

Before a Write Statement can be executed to add a record to the Customer Master File, the Customer Number of the record to be added to the file must be moved to the Nominal Key area. Thus, in the example above, the value in the field CUSTOMER-NUMBER-CURRENT-REC is moved to the Nominal Key field KEY-OF-THE-RECORD-TO-RETRIEVE. Whenever a record is to be added to an indexed sequential file, the key of the record must be placed in the Nominal Key field as illustrated.

The Write Statement includes the Write verb followed by the name of the I/O area as specified for the file in the File Section of the Data Division. In the sample program, the name of this I/O area is CUSTOMER-MASTER-I-O-RECORD. The optional From Clause is used because the record to be written is stored in the MASTER-OUTPUT-WORK-AREA.

The Invalid Key Clause must be included with the Write Statement when a record is being added to an indexed sequential file. The imperative statements following the Invalid Key words will be executed when an attempt is made to add a record with a key which already exists in the indexed sequential file. In the sample program, this will not occur because a comparison is made to determine if a record has been retrieved. If it has, the Rewrite Statement will be used, not the Write Statement. Only if a record has not been retrieved from the Customer Master File will the Write Statement be executed. Even though the Invalid Key condition will not occur, however, the Invalid Key Statement is required.

Testing for a Deleted Record

It will be recalled that a record which is stored in the Customer Master File can be a logically deleted record if high-values (Hex "FF") are stored in the first position of the record. If this is the case, then it is valid to "add" the record to the file even though it is still physically a part of the file. It must be recognized, however, that the Write Statement cannot be used to add the record to the file because the record already exists within the file, albeit as a deleted record. Thus, if a deleted record is read from the file, an Add Transaction Record is valid and should be processed; however, the Rewrite Statement should be used for the record, not the Write Statement.

Because of this processing, it is necessary when the record is read to determine if it is a deleted record. This determination can be done through the use of a Condition Name, as shown below.

EXAMPLE

```
Ø1Ø14Ø Ø1  MASTER-INPUT-WORK-AREA.
Ø1Ø15Ø     Ø5  DELETE-CODE-MSTRIN-WORK              PIC X.
Ø1Ø16Ø         88  CUSTOMER-RECORD-IS-DELETED           VALUE HIGH-VALUES.
Ø1Ø17Ø     Ø5  CUSTOMER-NUMBER-MSTRIN-WORK          PIC X(5).
Ø1Ø18Ø     Ø5  CUSTOMER-NAME-MSTRIN-WORK            PIC X(2Ø).
Ø1Ø19Ø     Ø5  CUSTOMER-ADDRESS-MSTRIN-WORK         PIC X(27).
Ø1Ø2ØØ     Ø5  CUSTOMER-CITY-MSTRIN-WORK            PIC X(2Ø).
Ø11Ø1Ø     Ø5  CUSTOMER-STATE-MSTRIN-WORK           PIC XX.
Ø11Ø2Ø     Ø5  CUSTOMER-ZIP-CODE-MSTRIN-WORK        PIC X(5).
Ø11Ø3Ø     Ø5  CUSTOMER-DISCOUNT-MSTRIN-WORK        PIC XX.
Ø11Ø4Ø     Ø5  LAST-ACTIVITY-MSTRIN-WORK            PIC X(6).
```

```
Ø17Ø8Ø     READ CUSTOMER-MASTER-I-O-FILE INTO MASTER-INPUT-WORK-AREA
Ø17Ø9Ø             INVALID KEY
Ø171ØØ                 MOVE 'NO ' TO WAS-A-MASTER-RECORD-FOUND.
```

Figure 6-26 Example of Checking for Deleted Record

As can be seen in Figure 6-26, the MASTER-INPUT-WORK-AREA is defined in Working-Storage as the area into which the Customer Master Record will be read. The Read Statement on pg/line 017080 will read the record into this area.

It will be noted that the first position in the area in Working-Storage is named DELETE-CODE-MSTRIN-WORK. This is because the first position in the record contains the code which indicates if the record is logically deleted. By testing the condition name CUSTOMER-RECORD-IS-DELETED, the program can determine if the record is logically deleted even though it is physically part of the file.

COPY STATEMENT

It will be noted from the program specifications that much of the same editing required in Chapter 5 is required in Chapter 6. When writing programs which require the same or similar processing, it is many times possible to extract modules or parts of modules from one program and include them in another program. The most practical method to include source statements from other programs into a program being written is through the use of libraries and the Copy Statement.

The Copy Statement can be used in the Environment Division, the Data Division, and the Procedure Division to include source statements which are stored in an Operating System Library in the program in which the Copy Statement appears. This operation is illustrated below.

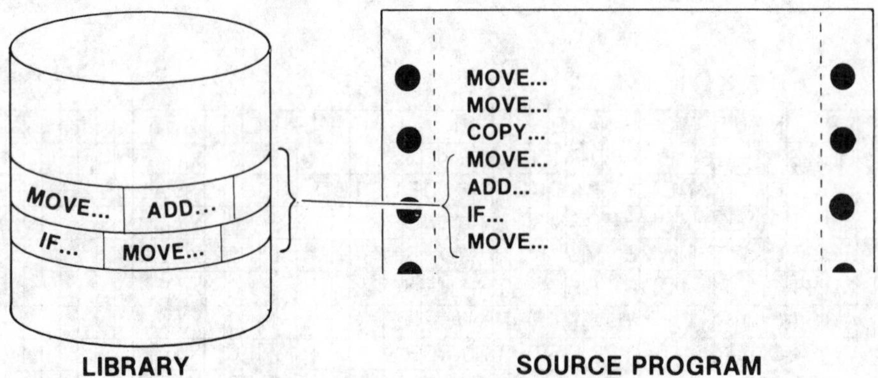

Figure 6-27 Example of Results of Copy Statement

Note in the example above that source statements are stored on the disk in a Library. The programmer would write the word Copy together with a library-name in the source program. When the program is compiled, the COBOL compiler will extract the source statements contained in the library and place them in the source program the same as if the source statements in the library had been written in the source program.

As noted, the Copy Statement can be used in the Environment Division, the Data Division, and the Procedure Division. The example in Figure 6-28 illustrates the use of the Copy Statement in the File Section of the Data Division to copy the definition of the Sort Work File which was used in Chapter 5.

EXAMPLE

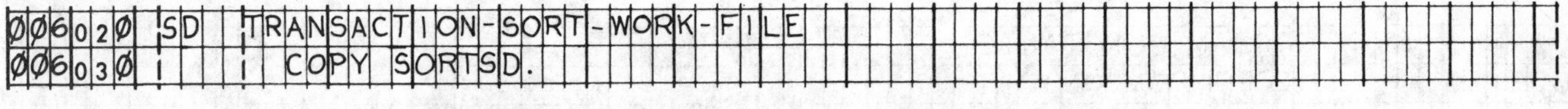
006020 SD TRANSACTION-SORT-WORK-FILE
006030 COPY SORTSD.

```
FD file-name COPY statement.
SD sort-file-name COPY statement.
```

Result of Copy Statement

```
00105      006020 SD   TRANSACTION-SORT-WORK-FILE                                       CUSTUPDT
00106      006030         COPY SORTSD.                                                  CUSTUPDT
00107 C    008020         RECORD CONTAINS 80 CHARACTERS                                 LOADCUST
00108 C    008030         DATA RECORD IS TRANSACTION-SORT-WORK-RECORD.                  LOADCUST
00109 C    008040                                                                       LOADCUST
00110 C    008050 01   TRANSACTION-SORT-WORK-RECORD.                                    LOADCUST
00111 C    009010      05  CUSTOMER-NUMBER-SORTREC       PIC X(5).                      LOADCUST
00112 C    009020      05  FILLER                        PIC X(74).                     LOADCUST
00113 C    009030      05  TRANSACTION-CODE-SORTREC      PIC X.                         LOADCUST
```

Figure 6-28 Example of Copy Statement in File Section

In the example above, it can be seen that the SD is specified in the same manner as if the Copy Statement were not going to be used. The filename TRANSACTION-SORT-WORK-FILE must also be specified by the programmer. The Copy Statement is then used to include within the source program the source coding contained in the library element SORTSD. The source statements in SORTSD must be catalogued in a library under the name SORTSD prior to compiling the program with the Copy Statement.

When the program is compiled, the statements in SORTSD are placed in the program the same as if the programmer had written them. In addition, the letter "C" is included on the source listing to indicate that the statements were included as a result of the Copy Statement.

The Copy Statement can also be used in the Working-Storage Section of the Data Division, as illustrated in Figure 6-29.

EXAMPLE

```
ØØ913Ø  Ø1  PROGRAM-CONSTANTS
ØØ914Ø          COPY PGMCON.
```

```
01  data-name COPY statement.
```

Result of Copy Statement

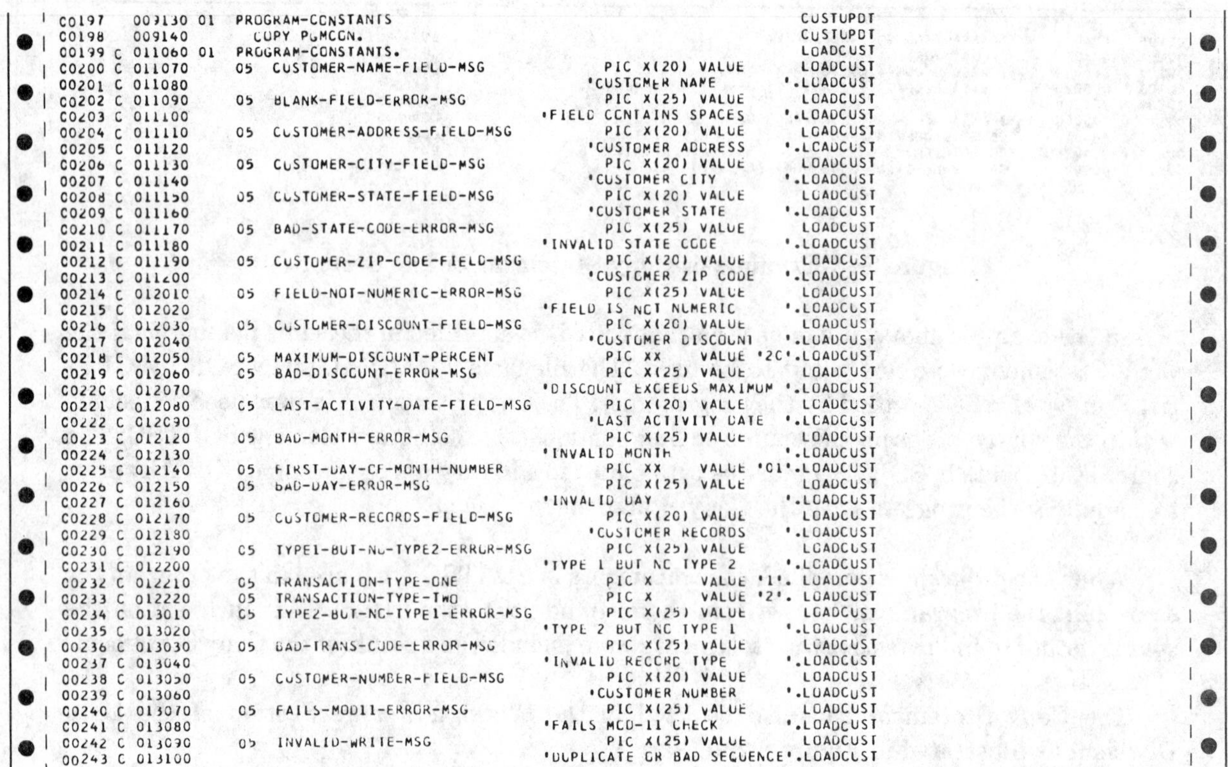

```
00197     009130 01  PROGRAM-CONSTANTS                                          CUSTUPDT
00198     009140       COPY PGMCON.                                             CUSTUPDT
00199 C   011060 01  PROGRAM-CONSTANTS.                                         LOADCUST
00200 C   011070     05  CUSTOMER-NAME-FIELD-MSG           PIC X(20) VALUE      LOADCUST
00201 C   011080                                          'CUSTOMER NAME       '.LOADCUST
00202 C   011090     05  BLANK-FIELD-ERROR-MSG             PIC X(25) VALUE      LOADCUST
00203 C   011100                                      'FIELD CONTAINS SPACES    '.LOADCUST
00204 C   011110     05  CUSTOMER-ADDRESS-FIELD-MSG        PIC X(20) VALUE      LOADCUST
00205 C   011120                                          'CUSTOMER ADDRESS    '.LOADCUST
00206 C   011130     05  CUSTOMER-CITY-FIELD-MSG           PIC X(20) VALUE      LOADCUST
00207 C   011140                                          'CUSTOMER CITY       '.LOADCUST
00208 C   011150     05  CUSTOMER-STATE-FIELD-MSG          PIC X(20) VALUE      LOADCUST
00209 C   011160                                          'CUSTOMER STATE      '.LOADCUST
00210 C   011170     05  BAD-STATE-CODE-ERROR-MSG          PIC X(25) VALUE      LOADCUST
00211 C   011180                                      'INVALID STATE CODE       '.LOADCUST
00212 C   011190     05  CUSTOMER-ZIP-CODE-FIELD-MSG       PIC X(20) VALUE      LOADCUST
00213 C   011200                                          'CUSTOMER ZIP CODE   '.LOADCUST
00214 C   012010     05  FIELD-NOT-NUMERIC-ERROR-MSG       PIC X(25) VALUE      LOADCUST
00215 C   012020                                      'FIELD IS NOT NUMERIC     '.LOADCUST
00216 C   012030     05  CUSTOMER-DISCOUNT-FIELD-MSG       PIC X(20) VALUE      LOADCUST
00217 C   012040                                          'CUSTOMER DISCOUNT   '.LOADCUST
00218 C   012050     05  MAXIMUM-DISCOUNT-PERCENT          PIC XX    VALUE '20'.LOADCUST
00219 C   012060     05  BAD-DISCOUNT-ERROR-MSG            PIC X(25) VALUE      LOADCUST
00220 C   012070                                      'DISCOUNT EXCEEDS MAXIMUM '.LOADCUST
00221 C   012080     05  LAST-ACTIVITY-DATE-FIELD-MSG      PIC X(20) VALUE      LOADCUST
00222 C   012090                                          'LAST ACTIVITY DATE  '.LOADCUST
00223 C   012120     05  BAD-MONTH-ERROR-MSG               PIC X(25) VALUE      LOADCUST
00224 C   012130                                      'INVALID MONTH            '.LOADCUST
00225 C   012140     05  FIRST-DAY-OF-MONTH-NUMBER         PIC XX    VALUE '01'.LOADCUST
00226 C   012150     05  BAD-DAY-ERROR-MSG                 PIC X(25) VALUE      LOADCUST
00227 C   012160                                      'INVALID DAY              '.LOADCUST
00228 C   012170     05  CUSTOMER-RECORDS-FIELD-MSG        PIC X(20) VALUE      LOADCUST
00229 C   012180                                          'CUSTOMER RECORDS    '.LOADCUST
00230 C   012190     05  TYPE1-BUT-NO-TYPE2-ERROR-MSG      PIC X(25) VALUE      LOADCUST
00231 C   012200                                      'TYPE 1 BUT NO TYPE 2     '.LOADCUST
00232 C   012210     05  TRANSACTION-TYPE-ONE              PIC X     VALUE '1'. LOADCUST
00233 C   012220     05  TRANSACTION-TYPE-TWO              PIC X     VALUE '2'. LOADCUST
00234 C   013010     05  TYPE2-BUT-NO-TYPE1-ERROR-MSG      PIC X(25) VALUE      LOADCUST
00235 C   013020                                      'TYPE 2 BUT NO TYPE 1     '.LOADCUST
00236 C   013030     05  BAD-TRANS-CODE-ERROR-MSG          PIC X(25) VALUE      LOADCUST
00237 C   013040                                      'INVALID RECORD TYPE      '.LOADCUST
00238 C   013050     05  CUSTOMER-NUMBER-FIELD-MSG         PIC X(20) VALUE      LOADCUST
00239 C   013060                                          'CUSTOMER NUMBER     '.LOADCUST
00240 C   013070     05  FAILS-MOD11-ERROR-MSG             PIC X(25) VALUE      LOADCUST
00241 C   013080                                      'FAILS MOD-11 CHECK       '.LOADCUST
00242 C   013090     05  INVALID-WRITE-MSG                 PIC X(25) VALUE      LOADCUST
00243 C   013100                                      'DUPLICATE OR BAD SEQUENCE'.LOADCUST
```

Figure 6-29 Example of Copy Statement in Working-Storage Section

In Figure 6-29, it can be seen from the format of the Copy Statement that the level number 01 must be specified followed by a data-name. In the example, the data-name specified is PROGRAM-CONSTANTS. Following the data-name, with no period, is the Copy Statement which will copy the element PGMCON from the library. As can be seen from the source listing illustrated, PGMCON consists of many of the constants which are required for the editing of the input data. These constants are the same ones which were used in Chapter 5.

It will be noted also that the first statement in PGMCON is a level 01 data-name (PROGRAM-CONSTANTS). A level 01 data-name is optional in the data which is to be copied into the program; regardless of whether it is there or not, the name which is used to reference the group-item is the data-name which is written by the programmer; that is, in the example, the data-name specified on pg/line 009130.

The remaining fields within the source coding which is copied into the source program can be referenced by their names in the same manner as if the coding were included in the source program as normal coding.

The Copy Statement can also be used for Procedure Division paragraphs. The examples in Figure 6-30 and Figure 6-31 illustrate the use of the Copy Statement in the Procedure Division.

EXAMPLE

```
029060 D010-EDIT-TYPE-1-RECORD.
029070
029080     COPY EDTYP1
029090         REPLACING CUSTOMER-NUMBER-EXCP-WORK BY
029100                        CUSTOMER-NUMBER-RPTWORK
029110                   FIELD-IN-ERROR-EXCP-WORK BY
029120                        FIELD-CHANGED-ERROR-RPTWORK
029130                   TYPE-OF-ERROR-EXCP-WORK BY
029140                        TYPE-OF-ERROR-RPTWORK
029150                   U000-WRITE-EXCEPTION-REPORT BY
029160                        U000-WRITE-TRANSACTION-REPORT.
```

```
    section-name SECTION [priority-number].  COPY statement.
    paragraph-name.  COPY statement.

COPY library-name

                                      word-2
   [REPLACING word-1  BY              literal-1
                                      identifier-1

                     word-4
   [word-3 BY        literal-2
                     identifier-2       ]...].
```

Figure 6-30 Example of Copy Statement in Procedure Division (Part 1 of 2)

Result of Copy Statement

```
00787     029060 0010-EDIT-TYPE-1-RECORD.                                   CUSTUPDT
00788     029070                                                            CUSTUPDT
00789     029080     COPY EDTYP1                                            CUSTUPDT
00790     029090         REPLACING CUSTOMER-NUMBER-EXCP-WORK BY             CUSTUPDT
00791     029100                   CUSTOMER-NUMBER-RPTWORK                  CUSTUPDT
00792     029110               FIELD-IN-ERROR-EXCP-WORK BY                  CUSTUPDT
00793     029120                   FIELD-CHANGED-ERROR-RPTWORK              CUSTUPDT
00794     029130               TYPE-OF-ERROR-EXCP-WORK BY                   CUSTUPDT
00795     029140                   TYPE-OF-ERROR-RPTWORK                    CUSTUPDT
00796     029150               U000-WRITE-EXCEPTION-REPORT BY               CUSTUPDT
00797     029160                   U000-WRITE-TRANSACTION-REPORT.           CUSTUPDT
00798 C   031180                                                            LOADCUST
00799 C   031190     MOVE CUSTOMER-NUMBER-TRANSORT1 TO CUSTOMER-NUMBER-WORK. LOADCUST
00800 C   031200     PERFORM U020-EDIT-CUSTOMER-NUMBER.                     LOADCUST
00801 C   031210     IF CUSTOMER-NAME-TRANSORT1 = SPACES                    LOADCUST
00802 C   032010         MOVE CUSTOMER-NUMBER-TRANSORT1 TO                  LOADCUST
00803 C   032020             CUSTOMER-NUMBER-RPTWORK                        LOADCUST
00804 C   032030         MOVE CUSTOMER-NAME-FIELD-MSG TO                    LOADCUST
00805 C   032040             FIELD-CHANGED-ERROR-RPTWORK                    LOADCUST
00806 C   032050         MOVE BLANK-FIELD-ERROR-MSG TO TYPE-OF-ERROR-RPTWORK LOADCUST
00807 C   032060         PERFORM U000-WRITE-TRANSACTION-REPORT              LOADCUST
00808 C   032070         MOVE 'NO ' TO ARE-TRAN-RECORDS-VALID.              LOADCUST
00809 C   032080     IF CUSTOMER-ADDRESS-TRANSORT1 = SPACES                 LOADCUST
00810 C   032090         MOVE CUSTOMER-NUMBER-TRANSORT1 TO                  LOADCUST
00811 C   032100             CUSTOMER-NUMBER-RPTWORK                        LOADCUST
00812 C   032110         MOVE CUSTOMER-ADDRESS-FIELD-MSG TO                 LOADCUST
00813 C   032120             FIELD-CHANGED-ERROR-RPTWORK                    LOADCUST
00814 C   032130         MOVE BLANK-FIELD-ERROR-MSG TO TYPE-OF-ERROR-RPTWORK LOADCUST
00815 C   032140         PERFORM U000-WRITE-TRANSACTION-REPORT              LOADCUST
00816 C   032150         MOVE 'NO ' TO ARE-TRAN-RECORDS-VALID.              LOADCUST
00817 C   032160     IF CUSTOMER-CITY-TRANSORT1 = SPACES                    LOADCUST
00818 C   032170         MOVE CUSTOMER-NUMBER-TRANSORT1 TO                  LOADCUST
00819 C   032180             CUSTOMER-NUMBER-RPTWORK                        LOADCUST
00820 C   032190         MOVE CUSTOMER-CITY-FIELD-MSG TO                    LOADCUST
00821 C   032200             FIELD-CHANGED-ERROR-RPTWORK                    LOADCUST
00822 C   033010         MOVE BLANK-FIELD-ERROR-MSG TO TYPE-OF-ERROR-RPTWORK LOADCUST
00823 C   033020         PERFORM U000-WRITE-TRANSACTION-REPORT              LOADCUST
00824 C   033030         MOVE 'NO ' TO ARE-TRAN-RECORDS-VALID.              LOADCUST
00825 C   033040     SEARCH ALL VALID-STATE-TABLE                           LOADCUST
00826 C   033050         AT END                                             LOADCUST
00827 C   033060             MOVE CUSTOMER-NUMBER-TRANSORT1 TO              LOADCUST
00828 C   033070                 CUSTOMER-NUMBER-RPTWORK                    LOADCUST
00829 C   033080             MOVE CUSTOMER-STATE-FIELD-MSG TO               LOADCUST
00830 C   033090                 FIELD-CHANGED-ERROR-RPTWORK                LOADCUST
00831 C   033100             MOVE BAD-STATE-CODE-ERROR-MSG TO               LOADCUST
00832 C   033110                 TYPE-OF-ERROR-RPTWORK                      LOADCUST
00833 C   033120             PERFORM U000-WRITE-TRANSACTION-REPORT          LOADCUST
00834 C   033130             MOVE 'NO ' TO ARE-TRAN-RECORDS-VALID           LOADCUST
00835 C   033140         WHEN STATE-CODE (STATE-CODE-INDEX) =               LOADCUST
00836 C   033150                 CUSTOMER-STATE-TRANSORT1                   LOADCUST
00837 C   033160             NEXT SENTENCE.                                 LOADCUST
00838 C   033170     IF CUSTOMER-ZIP-CODE-TRANSORT1 IS NOT NUMERIC          LOADCUST
00839 C   033180         MOVE CUSTOMER-NUMBER-TRANSORT1 TO                  LOADCUST
00840 C   033190             CUSTOMER-NUMBER-RPTWORK                        LOADCUST
00841 C   033200         MOVE CUSTOMER-ZIP-CODE-FIELD-MSG TO                LOADCUST
00842 C   034010             FIELD-CHANGED-ERROR-RPTWORK                    LOADCUST
00843 C   034020         MOVE FIELD-NOT-NUMERIC-ERROR-MSG TO                LOADCUST
00844 C   034030             TYPE-OF-ERROR-RPTWORK                          LOADCUST
00845 C   034040         PERFORM U000-WRITE-TRANSACTION-REPORT              LOADCUST
00846 C   034050         MOVE 'NO ' TO ARE-TRAN-RECORDS-VALID.              LOADCUST
```

Figure 6-31 Example of Copy Statement in Procedure Division (Part 2 of 2)

Note from the examples in Figure 6-30 and Figure 6-31 that the paragraph name is specified, followed by a period. The Copy Statement is then written. In the example, the paragraph name D010-EDIT-TYPE-1-RECORD is followed by the Copy Statement which copies the element named EDTYP1 into the source program. As can be seen from Figure 6-31, this coding is the same as the coding in Chapter 5 which edited a Type 1 transaction record.

The Copy Statement in Figure 6-30 utilizes another feature of the statement — the Replacing By Clause. Whenever instructions in the Procedure Division are to be copied in using the Copy Statement, the data-names in these instructions must agree with the data-names used in the program. In some cases, these data-names can be made to agree when the data-names are defined, but in other cases, the data-names used in the program are unique to that program. Therefore, it is necessary to change some of the data-names used in the instructions which are copied into the Procedure Division. This can be accomplished using the Replacing Clause.

The Replacing Clause in the Copy Statement causes the data-name specified as word-1 to be replaced by the data-name specified as identifier-2 each time word-1 appears in the information which is copied into the Procedure Division. Thus, in the example, when the name CUSTOMER-NUMBER-EXCP-WORK appears in the instructions which are copied into the Procedure Division, it will be replaced by the name CUSTOMER-NUMBER-RPTWORK. Similarly, each appearance of the name FIELD-IN-ERROR-EXCP-WORK will be replaced by the name FIELD-CHANGED-ERROR-RPTWORK, and so on. Thus, as can be seen from the listing in Figure 6-31, the names specified in the Replacing Clause are contained within the COBOL statements rather than the names which were actually stored in the statements copied into the program (for the names used in the statements copied into the program, see the source listing in Chapter 5). The Replacing By Clause can be used wherever the Copy Statement is used; it is not limited to use in the Procedure Division.

The Copy Statement can also be used in Configuration Section, Input-Output Section, and File-Control paragraph in the Environment Division. The formats for these three uses are illustrated in Figure 6-32.

```
                 Configuration Section

SOURCE-COMPUTER.  COPY statement.
OBJECT-COMPUTER.  COPY statement.
SPECIAL-NAMES.  COPY statement.
```

```
                 Input-Output Section

FILE-CONTROL.  COPY statement.
I-O-CONTROL.  COPY statement.
```

```
                 FILE-CONTROL Paragraph

SELECT file-name COPY statement.
```

Figure 6-32 Formats of Copy Statement

Use of the Copy Statement

The Copy Statement can be a very useful tool for the COBOL programmer when good Structured Design methodologies are used because the various functions which must be performed within the program are easily identified. When these functions must be performed in other programs, the source coding developed to accomplish the major processing task can be Copied into the program which requires the major processing task to be accomplished. In this manner, the programmer saves considerable coding time and considerable testing time because the coding which is incorporated into the program using the Copy Statement has already been written and debugged. Therefore, provided the same function is to be performed, there should be little testing and debugging required in order to incorporate the function into the program.

The same holds true for data which is required within a program; that is, if similar data is required for different programs, then the source coding to define this data can be catalogued in the library and included in the program via the Copy Statement when required.

It should be noted that in the Procedure Division, the Copy Statement can be used to copy entire modules from another program and can also be used to copy the coding for major processing tasks which are contained within a module. Thus, in the program in this chapter, the coding for Editing a Type 1 Record is included in the program by copying the entire module from the Chapter 5 program. In addition, it is required in this program to edit the Last Activity Date. Thus, the coding which edits the Last Activity Date is included within the source program via the Copy Statement by extracting that coding in the Chapter 5 program. This is easy to do because the major processing task of editing the Last Activity Date is identified on the hierarchy chart for the program.

The Copy Statement should always be considered whenever similar functions must be performed within the program. With the use of the Replacing By Clause, the statements within a module can be modified to process the data-names defined within the program.

PROGRAM DESIGN

The following pages contain the Hierarchy Chart, IPO Charts, and Pseudocode Specifications for the program in this chapter. It should be noted that those modules included in the source program through the use of the Copy Statement will not have pseudocode developed for them because the logic for the modules has already been designed, coded, and tested.

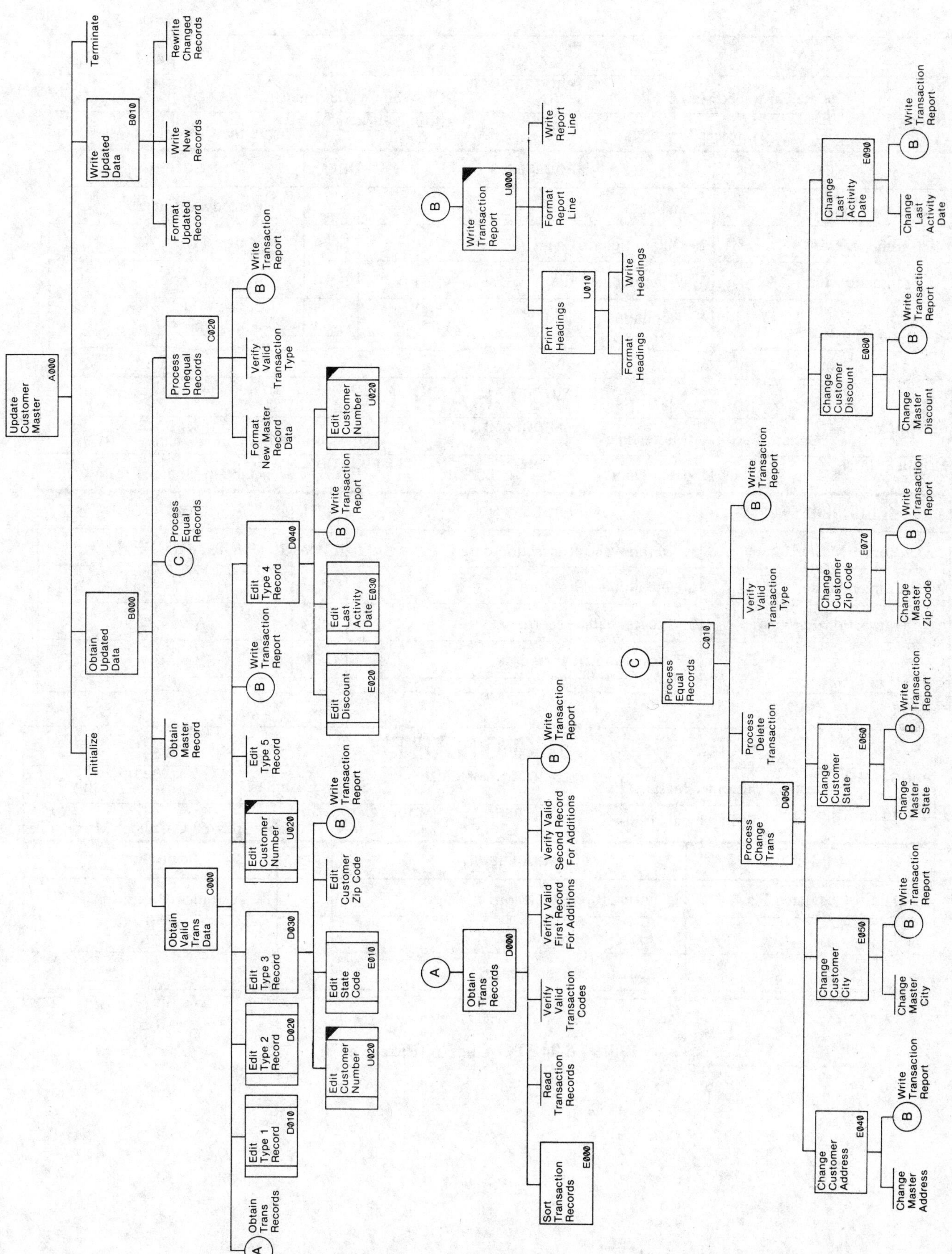

Figure 6-33 Hierarchy Chart

IPO CHART

PROGRAM: Update Customer Master File		PROGRAMMER: Shelly/Cashman	DATE: July 25
MODULE NAME: Update Customer Master	REF: AØØØ	MODULE FUNCTION: Update the Customer Master File	

INPUT	PROCESSING	REF:	OUTPUT
1. Customer Master File	1. Initialize		1. Updated Customer
2. Customer Master	2. Obtain updated data	BØØØ	Master File
Transaction File	3. Write updated file	BØ1Ø	
	4. Terminate		

IPO CHART

PROGRAM: Update Customer Master File		PROGRAMMER: Shelly/Cashman	DATE: July 25
MODULE NAME: Obtain Updated Data	REF: BØØØ	MODULE FUNCTION: Obtain Updated Data	

INPUT	PROCESSING	REF:	OUTPUT
1. Customer Master File	1. Obtain valid transaction data	CØØØ	1. Updated data
2. Customer Master	2. Obtain master record		
Transaction File	3. Process equal records	CØ1Ø	
	4. Process unequal records	CØ2Ø	

IPO CHART

PROGRAM: Update Customer Master File		PROGRAMMER: Shelly/Cashman	DATE: July 25
MODULE NAME: Write Updated File	REF: BØ1Ø	MODULE FUNCTION: Write Updated Customer Master File	

INPUT	PROCESSING	REF:	OUTPUT
1. Data for Updated File	1. Format updated record		1. Customer Master File
	2. Write new records		
	3. Rewrite changed records		

Figure 6-34 IPO Charts (Part 1 of 8)

IPO CHART

PROGRAM: Update Customer Master File		PROGRAMMER: Shelly/Cashman		DATE: July 25
MODULE NAME: Obtain Valid Trans Data	REF: CØØØ	MODULE FUNCTION: Obtain Valid Transaction Data		

INPUT	PROCESSING	REF:	OUTPUT
1. Customer Master	1. Obtain transaction records	DØØØ	1. Valid Transaction Data
Transaction File	2. Edit type 1 transaction	DØ1Ø	2. Transaction Report
	3. Edit type 2 transaction	DØ2Ø	
	4. Edit type 3 transaction	DØ3Ø	
	5. Edit type 4 transaction	DØ4Ø	
	6. Edit type 5 transaction		
	7. Write transaction report	UØØØ	
	8. Edit customer number	UØ2Ø	

IPO CHART

PROGRAM: Update Customer Master File		PROGRAMMER: Shelly/Cashman		DATE: July 25
MODULE NAME: Process Equal Records	REF: CØ1Ø	MODULE FUNCTION: Process Equal Master and Transaction Records		

INPUT	PROCESSING	REF:	OUTPUT
1. Valid Transaction Record	1. Process change transaction	DØ5Ø	1. Data for Updated Master
2. Master Record	2. Process delete transaction		2. Transaction Report
	3. Write transaction report	UØØØ	
	4. Verify valid transaction type		

IPO CHART

PROGRAM: Update Customer Master File		PROGRAMMER: Shelly/Cashman		DATE: July 25
MODULE NAME: Process Unequal Record	REF: CØ2Ø	MODULE FUNCTION: Process Unequal Transaction Record		

INPUT	PROCESSING	REF:	OUTPUT
1. Transaction Record	1. Format new master record data		1. Data for Updated Master
	2. Write transaction report	UØØØ	
	3. Verify valid transaction type		

Figure 6-35 IPO Charts (Part 2 of 8)

IPO CHART

PROGRAM: Update Customer Master File	PROGRAMMER: Shelly/Cashman	DATE: July 25
MODULE NAME: Obtain Trans Records	REF: DØØØ	MODULE FUNCTION: Obtain Valid Transaction Records

INPUT	PROCESSING	REF:	OUTPUT
1. Customer Master	1. Sort transaction records	EØØØ	1. Valid Transaction Records
Transaction File	2. Read transaction records		2. Transaction Report
	3. Verify valid transaction codes		
	4. Verify valid first record for additions		
	5. Verify valid second record for additions		
	6. Write transaction report	UØØØ	

IPO CHART

PROGRAM: Update Customer Master File	PROGRAMMER: Shelly/Cashman	DATE: July 25
MODULE NAME: Edit Type 1 Transaction	REF: DØ1Ø	MODULE FUNCTION: Edit Type 1 Transaction

INPUT	PROCESSING	REF:	OUTPUT
1. Type 1 Record	1. Edit type 1 transaction	COPY	1. Edited Type 1 Record
			2. Transaction Report

IPO CHART

PROGRAM: Update Customer Master File	PROGRAMMER: Shelly/Cashman	DATE: July 25
MODULE NAME: Edit Type 2 Transaction	REF: DØ2Ø	MODULE FUNCTION: Edit a Type 2 Transaction

INPUT	PROCESSING	REF:	OUTPUT
1. Type 2 Record	1. Edit type 2 transaction	COPY	1. Edited Type 2 Record
			2. Transaction Record

Figure 6-36 IPO Charts (Part 3 of 8)

IPO CHART

PROGRAM: Update Customer Master File		PROGRAMMER: Shelly/Cashman	DATE: July 25
MODULE NAME: Edit Type 3 Transaction	REF: DØ3Ø	MODULE FUNCTION: Edit a Type 3 Transaction	

INPUT	PROCESSING	REF:	OUTPUT
1. Type 3 Record	1. Edit state code	EØ1Ø	1. Edited Type 3 Transaction
	2. Edit customer zip code		2. Transaction Report
	3. Write transaction report	UØØØ	
	4. Edit customer number	UØ2Ø	

IPO CHART

PROGRAM: Update Customer Master File		PROGRAMMER: Shelly/Cashman	DATE: July 25
MODULE NAME: Edit Type 4 Transaction	REF: DØ4Ø	MODULE FUNCTION: Edit a Type 4 Transaction	

INPUT	PROCESSING	REF:	OUTPUT
1. Type 4 Transaction Record	1. Edit customer discount	EØ2Ø	1. Edited Type 4 Transaction
	2. Edit last activity date	EØ3Ø	2. Transaction Report
	3. Write transaction report	UØØØ	
	4. Edit customer number	UØ2Ø	

IPO CHART

PROGRAM: Update Customer Master File		PROGRAMMER: Shelly/Cashman	DATE: July 25
MODULE NAME: Process Change Transaction	REF: DØ5Ø	MODULE FUNCTION: Process a Change Transaction	

INPUT	PROCESSING	REF:	OUTPUT
1. Type 3 Transaction Record	1. Change customer address	EØ4Ø	1. Changed Master Record
2. Type 4 Transaction Record	2. Change customer city	EØ5Ø	
3. Master Record with	3. Change customer state	EØ6Ø	
Matching Customer Number	4. Change customer zip code	EØ7Ø	
	5. Change customer discount	EØ8Ø	
	6. Change last activity date	EØ9Ø	

Figure 6-37 IPO Charts (Part 4 of 8)

IPO CHART

PROGRAM: Update Customer Master File	PROGRAMMER: Shelly/Cashman	DATE: July 25
MODULE NAME: Sort Transaction Records	REF: EØØØ	MODULE FUNCTION: Sort the Transaction Records

INPUT	PROCESSING	REF:	OUTPUT
1. Unsorted Transaction File	1. Sort transaction records		1. Sorted Transaction Records
	(Customer number — major;		
	Transaction code — minor)		

IPO CHART

PROGRAM: Update Customer Master File	PROGRAMMER: Shelly/Cashman	DATE: July 25
MODULE NAME: Edit State Code	REF: EØ1Ø	MODULE FUNCTION: Edit the State Code

INPUT	PROCESSING	REF:	OUTPUT
1. State Code	1. Edit state code	COPY	1. Valid State Code
2. State Code Table			2. Transaction Report

IPO CHART

PROGRAM: Update Customer Master File	PROGRAMMER: Shelly/Cashman	DATE: July 25
MODULE NAME: Edit Discount	REF: EØ2Ø	MODULE FUNCTION: Edit the Discount

INPUT	PROCESSING	REF:	OUTPUT
1. Discount	1. Edit discount	COPY	1. Edited Discount
2. Maximum Discount			2. Transaction Report
Percentage			

IPO CHART

PROGRAM: Update Customer Master File	PROGRAMMER: Shelly/Cashman	DATE: July 25
MODULE NAME: Edit Last Activity Date	REF: EØ3Ø	MODULE FUNCTION: Edit the Last Activity Date

INPUT	PROCESSING	REF:	OUTPUT
1. Last Activity Date	1. Edit last activity date	COPY	1. Edited Last Activity Date
2. Days in Months Table			2. Transaction Report

Figure 6-38 IPO Charts (Part 5 of 8)

IPO CHART

PROGRAM: Update Customer Master File		PROGRAMMER: Shelly/Cashman	DATE: July 25
MODULE NAME: Change Customer Address	REF: EØ4Ø	MODULE FUNCTION: Change the Customer Address	

INPUT	PROCESSING	REF:	OUTPUT
1. Master Record	1. Change master address		1. Changed Master Record
2. Transaction Address	2. Write transaction report	UØØØ	2. Transaction Report

IPO CHART

PROGRAM: Update Customer Master File		PROGRAMMER: Shelly/Cashman	DATE: July 25
MODULE NAME: Change Customer City	REF: EØ5Ø	MODULE FUNCTION: Change the Customer City	

INPUT	PROCESSING	REF:	OUTPUT
1. Master Record	1. Change master city		1. Changed Master Record
2. Transaction City	2. Write transaction report	UØØØ	2. Transaction Report

IPO CHART

PROGRAM: Update Customer Master File		PROGRAMMER: Shelly/Cashman	DATE: July 25
MODULE NAME: Change Customer State	REF: EØ6Ø	MODULE FUNCTION: Change the Customer State	

INPUT	PROCESSING	REF:	OUTPUT
1. Master Record	1. Change master state		1. Changed Master Record
2. Transaction State	2. Write transaction report	UØØØ	2. Transaction Report

IPO CHART

PROGRAM: Update Customer Master File		PROGRAMMER: Shelly/Cashman	DATE: July 25
MODULE NAME: Change Customer Zip Code	REF: EØ7Ø	MODULE FUNCTION: Change the Customer Zip Code	

INPUT	PROCESSING	REF:	OUTPUT
1. Master Record	1. Change master zip code		1. Changed Master Record
2. Transaction Zip Code	2. Write transaction report	UØØØ	2. Transaction Report

Figure 6-39 IPO Charts (Part 6 of 8)

IPO CHART

PROGRAM: Update Customer Master File	PROGRAMMER: Shelly/Cashman	DATE: July 25
MODULE NAME: Change Customer Discount	REF: EØ8Ø	MODULE FUNCTION: Change the Customer Discount

INPUT	PROCESSING	REF:	OUTPUT
1. Master Record	1. Change master discount		1. Changed Master Record
2. Transaction Discount	2. Write transaction report	UØØØ	2. Transaction Report

IPO CHART

PROGRAM: Update Customer Master File	PROGRAMMER: Shelly/Cashman	DATE: July 25
MODULE NAME: Change Last Activity Date	REF: EØ9Ø	MODULE FUNCTION: Change the Last Activity Date

INPUT	PROCESSING	REF:	OUTPUT
1. Master Record	1. Change last activity date		1. Changed Master Record
2. Transaction Last Activity Date	2. Write transaction report	UØØØ	2. Transaction Report

IPO CHART

PROGRAM: Update Customer Master File	PROGRAMMER: Shelly/Cashman	DATE: July 25
MODULE NAME: Write Transaction Report	REF: UØØØ	MODULE FUNCTION: Write the Transaction Report

INPUT	PROCESSING	REF:	OUTPUT
1. Customer Number	1. Print headings	UØ1Ø	1. Detail Report Line
2. Action Taken	2. Format report line		
3. Field Changed or Field in Error	3. Write report line		
4. Type of Error			
5. Old Master Changed Field			
6. New Master Changed Field			

Figure 6-40 IPO Charts (Part 7 of 8)

IPO CHART

PROGRAM: Update Customer Master File		PROGRAMMER: Shelly/Cashman	DATE: July 25
MODULE NAME: Print Headings	REF: UØ1Ø	MODULE FUNCTION: Print Transaction Report Headings	

INPUT	PROCESSING	REF:	OUTPUT
	1. Format headings		1. Transaction Report Headings
	2. Write headings		

IPO CHART

PROGRAM: Update Customer Master File		PROGRAMMER: Shelly/Cashman	DATE: July 25
MODULE NAME: Edit Customer Number	REF: UØ2Ø	MODULE FUNCTION: Edit the Customer Number	

INPUT	PROCESSING	REF:	OUTPUT
1. Customer Number	1. Edit customer number	COPY	1. Edited Customer Number
			2. Transaction Report

Figure 6-41 IPO Charts (Part 8 of 8)

PSEUDOCODE SPECIFICATIONS

PSEUDOCODE SPECIFICATIONS

PROGRAM: Update Customer Master File		PROGRAMMER: Shelly/Cashman	DATE: July 25
MODULE NAME: Update Customer Master	REF: AØØØ	MODULE FUNCTION: Update Customer Master File	

PSEUDOCODE	REF:	FILES, RECORDS, FIELDS REQUIRED
Open the files		Customer master file (I—O file)
Obtain updated data	BØØØ	Transaction report file
PERFORM UNTIL there are no more transaction records		No more tran records indicator
Write updated master file	BØ1Ø	
Obtain updated data	BØØØ	
ENDPERFORM		
Close files		
Stop run		

Figure 6-42 Pseudocode Specifications (Part 1 of 12)

PSEUDOCODE SPECIFICATIONS

PROGRAM: Update Customer Master File	PROGRAMMER: Shelly/Cashman	DATE: July 25

MODULE NAME: Obtain Updated Data	REF: B000	MODULE FUNCTION: Obtain Updated Data

PSEUDOCODE	REF:	FILES, RECORDS, FIELDS REQUIRED
Set updated data obtained indicator to no data obtained		Updated data obtained indicator
Obtain valid transaction data	C000	No more tran records indicator
PERFORM UNTIL updated data has been obtained or		Transaction customer number
there are no more transaction records		Master key area (nominal key)
Set add indicator to neutral		Master file input area
Set delete indicator to neutral		Delete code field
Set change indicator to neutral		Customer number
Set master found indicator to "yes"		Customer name
Move customer number to master key area		Customer address
Read the master file		Customer city
IF a record was found		Customer state
Move master record customer number to		Customer zip code
master record being processed work area		Customer discount
ELSE		Last activity date
Move spaces to master record being processed work area		Valid add indicator
ENDIF		Valid delete indicator
IF a master record was not found or		Valid change indicator
a master record was found and it is deleted		Record is found indicator
Process unequal records	C020	Master record being processed work area
IF valid add record		
Indicate updated data obtained		
ELSE		
Obtain valid transaction data	C000	
ENDIF		
ELSE		
Process equal records	C010	
IF valid change record or valid delete record		
Indicate updated data obtained		
ELSE		
Obtain valid transaction data	C000	
ENDIF		
ENDIF		
ENDPERFORM		

Figure 6-43 Pseudocode Specifications (Part 2 of 12)

PSEUDOCODE SPECIFICATIONS

PROGRAM: Update Customer Master File		PROGRAMMER: Shelly/Cashman	DATE: July 25
MODULE NAME: Write Updated File	REF: BØ1Ø	MODULE FUNCTION: Write Updated Customer Master File	

PSEUDOCODE	REF:	FILES, RECORDS, FIELDS REQUIRED

Set valid write indicator to neutral
Move entire master work area to master output area
IF the master record being processed =
        key of the record which was retrieved
    Rewrite master record
ELSE
    Write master record
    IF write not successful
        Indicate a valid write did not occur
    ENDIF
ENDIF
		Valid write indicator
		New master work area
		    Delete code
		    Customer number
		    Customer name
		    Customer address
		    Customer city
		    Customer state
		    Customer zip code
		    Customer discount
		    Last activity date
		Updated master output area
		    Delete code
		    Customer number
		    Customer name
		    Customer address
		    Customer city
		    Customer state
		    Customer zip code
		    Customer discount
		    Last activity date
		Master record being processed work area
		Key of record which was retrieved

Figure 6-44 Pseudocode Specifications (Part 3 of 12)

PSEUDOCODE SPECIFICATIONS

PROGRAM: Update Customer Master File	PROGRAMMER: Shelly/Cashman	DATE: July 25

MODULE NAME: Obtain Valid Trans Data	REF: CØØØ	MODULE FUNCTION: Obtain Valid Transaction Data

PSEUDOCODE	REF:	FILES, RECORDS, FIELDS REQUIRED
Set valid record indicator to neutral		Valid record indicator
Obtain transaction record	DØØØ	No more tran records indicator
PERFORM UNTIL no more transaction records or		Transaction code
valid record(s) are obtained		"1" constant
IF transaction type 1		"3" constant
Edit type 1 transaction	DØ1Ø	"4" constant
Edit type 2 transaction	DØ2Ø	"5" constant
ELSE IF transaction type 3		Transaction customer number
Edit type 3 transaction	DØ3Ø	Customer number work area
ELSE IF transaction type 4		First 4 digits
Edit type 4 transaction	DØ4Ø	Check digit
ELSE IF transaction type 5		
Move customer number to work area		
Edit customer number	UØ2Ø	
ENDIF		
IF invalid record(s)		
Set valid record indicator to neutral		
Obtain transaction record(s)	DØØØ	
ELSE		
Indicate valid record		
ENDIF		
ENDPERFORM		

Figure 6-45 Pseudocode Specifications (Part 4 of 12)

PSEUDOCODE SPECIFICATIONS

PROGRAM: Update Customer Master File		PROGRAMMER: Shelly/Cashman	DATE: July 25
MODULE NAME: Process Equal Records	REF: CØ1Ø	MODULE FUNCTION: Process Equal Master and Transaction Records	

PSEUDOCODE	REF:	FILES, RECORDS, FIELDS REQUIRED
IF record type is a change ("3" or "4")		Transaction code
Process change transaction	DØ5Ø	"3" constant
Move old master record to new master work area		"4" constant
Indicate valid change		Old master record
ELSE IF record type is a deletion ("5")		— all fields —
Move delete code ("FF") to master record		New master work area
Move old master record to new master work area		— all fields —
Indicate valid delete		Valid change indicator
Move customer number to report work area		"5" constant
Move "deletion" to report work area		Delete code ("FF")
Write transaction report	UØØØ	Valid delete indicator
ELSE		Report work area
Move customer number to report work area		Customer number
Move "transaction code" to report work area		Action taken
Move "addition of duplicate record" to report work area		Field in error
Write transaction report	UØØØ	Type of error
Indicate no valid change		"Deletion" constant
Indicate no valid delete		Customer number-transaction
ENDIF		"Transaction code" constant
		"Addition of duplicate rec" constant

PSEUDOCODE SPECIFICATIONS

PROGRAM: Update Customer Master File		PROGRAMMER: Shelly/Cashman	DATE: July 25
MODULE NAME: Process Unequal Records	REF: CØ2Ø	MODULE FUNCTION: Process Unequal Transaction Records	

PSEUDOCODE	REF:	FILES, RECORDS, FIELDS REQUIRED
IF record type is an addition ("1" and "2")		Transaction Records (1 and 2)
Move customer number from trans to new master work area		— all fields —
Move customer name from trans to new master work area		New master work area
Move customer address from trans to new master work area		— all fields —
Move customer city from trans to new master work area		"Addition" constant
Move customer state from trans to new master work area		Report work area
Move customer zip code from trans to new master work area		Customer number
Move customer discount from trans to new master work area		Action taken
Move last activity date from trans to new master work area		Field in error
Move spaces to delete code		Type of error
Move customer number to report work area		Valid addition indicator
Move "addition" to report work area		
Write transaction report	UØØØ	
Indicate valid addition		
ELSE		
Move customer number to report work area		
Move "transaction code" to report work area		
Move "unmatched master record" to report work area		
Write transaction report	UØØØ	
Indicate no valid addition		
ENDIF		

Figure 6-46 Pseudocode Specifications (Part 5 of 12)

PSEUDOCODE SPECIFICATIONS

PROGRAM: Update Customer Master File	PROGRAMMER: Shelly/Cashman	DATE: July 25
MODULE NAME: Obtain Trans Records	REF: DØØØ	MODULE FUNCTION: Obtain Valid Transaction Records

PSEUDOCODE	REF:	FILES, RECORDS, FIELDS REQUIRED
Set valid transaction code indicator to neutral		Valid trans code indicator
IF transaction file is not sorted		Transaction file sorted indicator
Sort transaction file	EØØØ	Sorted transaction file
Open sorted transaction file		Transaction input area
Indicate file is sorted		First record area
ENDIF		Customer number
Read a transaction record into first record area		Customer name
PERFORM UNTIL valid codes or no more trans records		Customer address
IF trans code = 3 or 4 or 5		Customer city
Move code to current code work area		Customer state
Move customer number to current customer		Customer zip code
number work area		Transaction code
Indicate valid trans code		Second record area
IF trans code = 4		Customer number
Move record to type 2 work area		Customer discount
ENDIF		Last activity date
ELSE IF trans code = 1		Transaction code
Read a record into second record area		No more tran records indicator
IF a record was read		Record was read indicator
IF trans code = 2 and customer number in first		Report work area
record = customer number		Customer number
in second record		Field in error
Indicate valid trans code		Type of error
Move code to work area		"Customer records" constant
Move customer number to work area		"Type 1 but no type 2" constant
ELSE		"Type 2 but no type 1" constant
Move customer number of type 1 to		"Transaction code" constant
report work area		"Invalid record type" constant
Move "customer records" to report work area		
Move "type 1 but no type 2" to		
report work area		
Write transaction report	UØØØ	
Move second record to first record area		
ENDIF		
ELSE		
Move customer number of type 1 to report work area		
Move "customer records" to report work area		
Move "type 1 but no type 2" to report work area		
Write transaction report	UØØØ	
ENDIF		
ELSE IF trans code = 2		
Move customer number to report work area		
Move "customer records" to report work area		
Move "type 2 but no type 1" to report work area		
Write transaction report	UØØØ	
Read a record into first record area		
ELSE		
Move customer number to report work area		
Move "transaction code" to report work area		
Move "invalid record type" to report work area		
Write transaction report	UØØØ	
Read a transaction record into first record area		
ENDIF		
ENDPERFORM		
IF there are no more tran records		
Close sorted transaction file		
ENDIF		

Figure 6-47 Pseudocode Specifications (Part 6 of 12)

PSEUDOCODE SPECIFICATIONS

PROGRAM: Update Customer Master File	PROGRAMMER: Shelly/Cashman	DATE: July 25

MODULE NAME: Edit Type 3 Transaction	REF: DØ3Ø	MODULE FUNCTION: Edit a Type 3 Transaction

PSEUDOCODE	REF:	FILES, RECORDS, FIELDS REQUIRED
Move customer number to work area		Customer number work area
Edit customer number	UØ2Ø	First four characters
IF state is not = spaces		Check digit
Move customer number to work area for state code edit		State code — transaction
Move state code to work area		State code work area
Edit state code	EØ1Ø	Customer number — transaction
IF zip codes = spaces		Report work area
Move customer number to report work area		Customer number
Move "zip code" to report work area		Field in error
Move "state changed—zip not" to report work area		Type of error
Write transaction report	UØØØ	"Zip code" constant
Indicate invalid record		"State changed — zip not" constant
ENDIF		"Field not numeric" constant
ENDIF		Invalid record indicator
IF zip code not = spaces and zip code not numeric		Customer number work area for state code edit
Move customer number to report work area		
Move "zip code" to report work area		
Move "field is not numeric" to report work area		
Write transaction report	UØØØ	
Indicate invalid record		
ENDIF		

PSEUDOCODE SPECIFICATIONS

PROGRAM: Update Customer Master File	PROGRAMMER: Shelly/Cashman	DATE: July 25

MODULE NAME: Edit Type 4 Transaction	REF: DØ4Ø	MODULE FUNCTION: Edit a Type 4 Transaction

PSEUDOCODE	REF:	FILES, RECORDS, FIELDS REQUIRED
Move customer number to work area		Customer number work area
Edit customer number	UØ2Ø	First four digits
IF discount not = spaces		Check digit
Move customer number to work area for discount edit		Customer number — transaction
Move discount to work area		Discount — transaction
Edit discount	EØ2Ø	Discount work area
ENDIF		Last activity date — transaction
IF last activity date not = spaces		Last activity date work area
Move customer number to work area for date edit		Customer number work area for discount edit
Move last activity date to work area		
Edit last activity date	EØ3Ø	Customer number work area for last activity date edit
ENDIF		

Figure 6-48 Pseudocode Specifications (Part 7 of 12)

PSEUDOCODE SPECIFICATIONS

PROGRAM: Update Customer Master File		PROGRAMMER: Shelly/Cashman	DATE: July 25
MODULE NAME: Process Change Transaction	REF: D050	MODULE FUNCTION: Process a Change Transaction	

PSEUDOCODE	REF:	FILES, RECORDS, FIELDS REQUIRED
IF transaction code = 3		Transaction code
Move customer number to type 3 change work area		"3" constant
IF address is not = spaces		Address — transaction
Move transaction address to work area		Address work area
Change customer address	E040	City — transaction
ENDIF		City work area
IF city is not = spaces		State — transaction
Move transaction city to work area		State work area
Change customer city	E050	Zip code — transaction
ENDIF		Zip code work area
IF state is not = spaces		Discount — transaction
Move transaction state to work area		Discount work area
Change customer state	E060	Last activity date — transaction
ENDIF		Last activity date work area
IF zip code is not = spaces		Customer number — current record
Move transaction zip code to work area		Type 3 change work area for
Change customer zip code	E070	customer number
ENDIF		Type 4 change work area for
ELSE		customer number
Move customer number to type 4 change work area		
IF discount is not = spaces		
Move transaction discount to work area		
Change customer discount	E080	
ENDIF		
IF last activity date is not = spaces		
Move transaction last activity date to work area		
Change customer last activity date	E090	
ENDIF		
ENDIF		

PSEUDOCODE SPECIFICATIONS

PROGRAM: Update Customer Master File		PROGRAMMER: Shelly/Cashman	DATE: July 25
MODULE NAME: Sort Transaction Records	REF: E000	MODULE FUNCTION: Sort the Transaction Records	

PSEUDOCODE	REF:	FILES, RECORDS, FIELDS REQUIRED
Sort records		Sort work file
Using unsorted transaction file		Unsorted transaction file
Giving sorted transaction file		Sorted transaction file

Figure 6-49 Pseudocode Specifications (Part 8 of 12)

PSEUDOCODE SPECIFICATIONS

PROGRAM: Update Customer Master File		PROGRAMMER: Shelly/Cashman	DATE: July 25
MODULE NAME: Change Customer Address	REF: EØ4Ø	MODULE FUNCTION: Change the Customer Address	

PSEUDOCODE	REF:	FILES, RECORDS, FIELDS REQUIRED
Move master address to report work area		Address — old master
Move transaction address to report work area		Address — new master
Move customer number to report work area		Address — transaction-work
Move "customer address" to report work area		Customer number
Move "change" to report work area		Report work area
Write transaction report	UØØØ	Customer number
Move transaction address to master address		Action taken
		Field changed
		Old master
		New master
		"Customer address" constant
		"Change" constant

PSEUDOCODE SPECIFICATIONS

PROGRAM: Update Customer Master File		PROGRAMMER: Shelly/Cashman	DATE: July 25
MODULE NAME: Change Customer City	REF: EØ5Ø	MODULE FUNCTION: Change the Customer City	

PSEUDOCODE	REF:	FILES, RECORDS, FIELDS REQUIRED
Move master city to report work area		City — old master
Move transaction city to report work area		City — new master
Move customer number to report work area		City — transaction-work
Move "customer city" to report work area		Customer number
Move "change" to report work area		Report work area
Write transaction report	UØØØ	Customer number
Move transaction address to master address		Action taken
		Field changed
		Old master
		New master
		"Customer city" constant
		"Change" constant

Figure 6-50 Pseudocode Specifications (Part 9 of 12)

PSEUDOCODE SPECIFICATIONS

PROGRAM: Update Customer Master File		PROGRAMMER: Shelly/Cashman	DATE: July 25
MODULE NAME: Change Customer State	REF: EØ6Ø	MODULE FUNCTION: Change the Customer State	

PSEUDOCODE	REF:	FILES, RECORDS, FIELDS REQUIRED
Move master state to report work area		State — old master
Move transaction state to report work area		State — new master
Move customer number to report work area		State — transaction-work
Move "customer state" to report work area		Customer number
Move "change" to report work area		Report work area
Write transaction report	UØØØ	Customer number
Move transaction state to master state		Action taken
		Field changed
		Old master
		New master
		"Customer state" constant
		"Change" constant

PSEUDOCODE SPECIFICATIONS

PROGRAM: Update Customer Master File		PROGRAMMER: Shelly/Cashman	DATE: July 25
MODULE NAME: Change Customer Zip Code	REF: EØ7Ø	MODULE FUNCTION: Change the Customer Zip Code	

PSEUDOCODE	REF:	FILES, RECORDS, FIELDS REQUIRED
Move master zip code to report work area		Zip code — old master
Move transaction zip code to report work area		Zip code — new master
Move customer number to report work area		Zip code — transaction-work
Move "customer zip code" to report work area		Customer number
Move "change" to report work area		Report work area
Write transaction report	UØØØ	Customer number
Move transaction zip code to master zip code		Action taken
		Field changed
		Old master
		New master
		"Customer zip code" constant
		"Change" constant

Figure 6-51 Pseudocode Specifications (Part 10 of 12)

PSEUDOCODE SPECIFICATIONS

PROGRAM: Update Customer Master File		PROGRAMMER: Shelly/Cashman	DATE: July 25
MODULE NAME: Change Customer Discount	REF: EØ8Ø	MODULE FUNCTION: Change the Customer Discount	

PSEUDOCODE	REF:	FILES, RECORDS, FIELDS REQUIRED
Move master discount to report work area		Discount — old master
Move transaction discount to report work area		Discount — new master
Move customer number to report work area		Discount — transaction-work
Move "customer discount" to report work area		Customer number
Move "change" to report work area		Report work area
Write transaction report	UØØØ	Customer number
Move transaction discount to master discount		Action taken
		Field changed
		Old master
		New master
		"Customer discount" constant
		"Change" constant

PSEUDOCODE SPECIFICATIONS

PROGRAM: Update Customer Master File		PROGRAMMER: Shelly/Cashman	DATE: July 25
MODULE NAME: Change Last Activity Date	REF: EØ9Ø	MODULE FUNCTION: Change the Last Activity Date	

PSEUDOCODE	REF:	FILES, RECORDS, FIELDS REQUIRED
Move master last activity date to report work area		Last activity date — old master
Move transaction last activity date to report work area		Last activity date — new master
Move customer number to report work area		Last activity date — transaction-work
Move "last activity date" to report work area		Customer number
Move "change" to report work area		Report work area
Write transaction report	UØØØ	Customer number
Move transaction last activity date to		Action taken
master last activity date		Field changed
		Old master
		New master
		"Last activity date" constant
		"Change" constant

Figure 6-52 Pseudocode Specifications (Part 11 of 12)

PSEUDOCODE SPECIFICATIONS

PROGRAM: Update Customer Master File	PROGRAMMER: Shelly/Cashman	DATE: July 25
MODULE NAME: Write Transaction Report	REF: UØØØ	MODULE FUNCTION: Write the Transaction Report

PSEUDOCODE	REF:	FILES, RECORDS, FIELDS REQUIRED
IF first page or line count > page size		First page indicator
Print headings	UØ1Ø	Line count
Clear report area		Page size
Move customer number to report area		Report output area
ENDIF		Customer number
IF current customer number not = previous customer number		Action taken
Move customer number to report area		Field changed or in error
Move customer number to compare area		Type of error
Set spacing for double spacing		Old master record
ENDIF		New master record
Move action taken to report area		Report work area
Move field to report area		Customer number
Move type of error to report area		Action taken
Move old master data to report area		Field changed or in error
Move new master data to report area		Type of error
Write a line on the report		Old master record
Add spacing to number of lines printed		New master record
Set spacing for single spacing		Previous customer compare area
Clear report area		Spacing control field
Clear report work area		Double spacing control character
		Single spacing control character

PSEUDOCODE SPECIFICATIONS

PROGRAM: Update Customer Master File	PROGRAMMER: Shelly/Cashman	DATE: July 25
MODULE NAME: Print Headings	REF: UØ1Ø	MODULE FUNCTION: Print Transaction Report Headings

PSEUDOCODE	REF:	FILES, RECORDS, FIELDS REQUIRED
Move current date to first heading line		Current date
Move page number to first heading line		First heading line
Write first heading line		Current date
Add 1 to page number		Page number
Write second heading line		Page number
Write third heading line		Second heading line
Set spacing for double spacing		Third heading line
Set line count to zero		Spacing control field
		Double spacing control character
		Line count

Figure 6-53 Pseudocode Specifications (Part 12 of 12)

SOURCE LISTING

The source listing for the sample program is contained on this and the following pages.

```
PP 5740-CB1 RELEASE 1.2  DEC 15, 1976            IBM OS/VS COBOL                          19.16.07  DATE SEP  5,1978

  1                    19.16.07        SEP  5,1978

001010 IDENTIFICATION DIVISION.                                         CUSTUPDT
001020                                                                  CUSTUPDT
001030 PROGRAM-ID.    CUSTUPDT.                                         CUSTUPDT
001040 AUTHOR.        SHELLY AND CASHMAN.                               CUSTUPDT
001050 INSTALLATION.  ANAHEIM.                                          CUSTUPDT
001060 DATE-WRITTEN.  07/27/78.                                         CUSTUPDT
001070 DATE-COMPILED. SEP  5,1978.                                      CUSTUPDT
001080 SECURITY.      UNCLASSIFIED.                                     CUSTUPDT
001090                                                                  CUSTUPDT
001100***************************************************************** CUSTUPDT
001110*                                                               * CUSTUPDT
001120*  THIS PROGRAM UPDATES THE CUSTOMER MASTER FILE, AN INDEXED    * CUSTUPDT
001130*  SEQUENTIAL FILE. RECORDS CAN BE ADDED TO THE FILE, RECORDS   * CUSTUPDT
001140*  CAN BE DELETED FROM THE FILE, AND FIELDS WITHIN A MASTER     * CUSTUPDT
001150*  RECORD CAN BE CHANGED. THE TRANSACTION FILE RECORDS MUST BE * CUSTUPDT
001160*  SORTED IN THE PROGRAM BECAUSE AN ADDITION TO THE MASTER FILE* CUSTUPDT
001170*  REQUIRES A TYPE 1 AND TYPE 2 TRANSACTION IN SEQUENCE         * CUSTUPDT
001180*  WITHIN CUSTOMER NUMBER. EACH TRANSACTION WHICH IS READ       * CUSTUPDT
001190*  WILL BE COMPLETELY EDITED BEFORE BEING USED TO UPDATE THE    * CUSTUPDT
001200*  CUSTOMER MASTER FILE. A TRANSACTION REPORT IS PRINTED WHICH * CUSTUPDT
002010*  CONTAINS ANY ERRORS FOUND IN EDITING AND ALSO A LIST OF ALL * CUSTUPDT
002020*  ADDITIONS, CHANGES, OR DELETIONS WHICH ARE PERFORMED ON      * CUSTUPDT
002030*  THE CUSTOMER MASTER FILE.                                    * CUSTUPDT
002040*                                                               * CUSTUPDT
002050***************************************************************** CUSTUPDT
002060                                                                  CUSTUPDT
002070                                                                  CUSTUPDT
002080                                                                  CUSTUPDT
002090 ENVIRONMENT DIVISION.                                            CUSTUPDT
002100                                                                  CUSTUPDT
002110 CONFIGURATION SECTION.                                           CUSTUPDT
002120                                                                  CUSTUPDT
002130 SOURCE-COMPUTER. IBM-370.                                        CUSTUPDT
002140 OBJECT-COMPUTER. IBM-370.                                        CUSTUPDT
002150 SPECIAL-NAMES.    C01 IS TO-THE-TOP-OF-THE-PAGE.                 CUSTUPDT
002160                                                                  CUSTUPDT
002170 INPUT-OUTPUT SECTION.                                            CUSTUPDT
002180                                                                  CUSTUPDT
002190 FILE-CONTROL.                                                    CUSTUPDT
002200     SELECT CUSTOMER-TRANS-INPUT-FILE                             CUSTUPDT
003010            ASSIGN TO UR-S-SYSIN.                                 CUSTUPDT
003020     SELECT SORTED-CUST-TRANS-INPUT-FILE                          CUSTUPDT
003030            ASSIGN TO DA-S-SORTRANS.                              CUSTUPDT
003040     SELECT CUSTOMER-MASTER-I-O-FILE                              CUSTUPDT
003050            ASSIGN TO DA-I-CUSTMAST                               CUSTUPDT
003060            ACCESS IS RANDOM                                      CUSTUPDT
003070            RECORD KEY IS CUSTOMER-NUMBER-MSTRIO                  CUSTUPDT
003080            NOMINAL KEY IS KEY-OF-THE-RECORD-TO-RETRIEVE.         CUSTUPDT
003090     SELECT UPDATE-TRANSACTION-REPORT-FILE                        CUSTUPDT
003100            ASSIGN TO UR-S-SYSOUT.                                CUSTUPDT
003110     SELECT TRANSACTION-SORT-WORK-FILE                            CUSTUPDT
003120            ASSIGN TO DA-S-SORTWK01.                              CUSTUPDT
```

```
  2                    19.16.07        SEP  5,1978

003140 DATA DIVISION.                                                   CUSTUPDT
003150                                                                  CUSTUPDT
003160 FILE SECTION.                                                    CUSTUPDT
003170                                                                  CUSTUPDT
003180 FD  CUSTOMER-TRANS-INPUT-FILE                                    CUSTUPDT
003190         RECORD CONTAINS 80 CHARACTERS                            CUSTUPDT
003200         LABEL RECORDS ARE OMITTED                                CUSTUPDT
004010         DATA RECORD IS TRANSACTION-INPUT-RECORD.                 CUSTUPDT
004020                                                                  CUSTUPDT
004030 01  TRANSACTION-INPUT-RECORD          PIC X(80).                 CUSTUPDT
004040                                                                  CUSTUPDT
004050 FD  SORTED-CUST-TRANS-INPUT-FILE                                 CUSTUPDT
004060         BLOCK CONTAINS 20 RECORDS                                CUSTUPDT
004070         RECORD CONTAINS 80 CHARACTERS                            CUSTUPDT
004080         LABEL RECORDS ARE STANDARD                               CUSTUPDT
004090         DATA RECORD IS SORTED-CUST-TRANS-INPUT-RECORD.           CUSTUPDT
004100                                                                  CUSTUPDT
004110 01  SORTED-CUST-TRANS-INPUT-RECORD  PIC X(80).                   CUSTUPDT
004120                                                                  CUSTUPDT
004130 FD  CUSTOMER-MASTER-I-O-FILE                                     CUSTUPDT
004140         BLOCK CONTAINS 20 RECORDS                                CUSTUPDT
004150         RECORD CONTAINS 88 CHARACTERS                            CUSTUPDT
004160         LABEL RECORDS ARE STANDARD                               CUSTUPDT
004170         DATA RECORD IS CUSTOMER-MASTER-I-O-RECORD.               CUSTUPDT
004180                                                                  CUSTUPDT
```

Figure 6-54 Source Listing (Part 1 of 19)

```
3                       19.16.07        SEP  5,1978

01  CUSTOMER-MASTER-I-O-RECORD.                                          CUSTUPDT
    05  FILLER                          PIC X.                           CUSTUPDT
    05  CUSTOMER-NUMBER-MSTRIO          PIC X(5).                        CUSTUPDT
    05  FILLER                          PIC X(82).                       CUSTUPDT
                                                                         CUSTUPDT
FD  UPDATE-TRANSACTION-REPORT-FILE                                       CUSTUPDT
    RECORD CONTAINS 133 CHARACTERS                                       CUSTUPDT
    LABEL RECORDS ARE OMITTED                                            CUSTUPDT
    DATA RECORD IS UPDATE-TRANSACTION-REPORT-LINE.                       CUSTUPDT
                                                                         CUSTUPDT
01  UPDATE-TRANSACTION-REPORT-LINE.                                      CUSTUPDT
    05  CARRIAGE-CONTROL                PIC X.                           CUSTUPDT
    05  FILLER                          PIC X.                           CUSTUPDT
    05  CUSTOMER-NUMBER-REPORT          PIC X(5).                        CUSTUPDT
    05  FILLER                          PIC X(4).                        CUSTUPDT
    05  ACTION-TAKEN-REPORT             PIC X(8).                        CUSTUPDT
    05  FILLER                          PIC XX.                          CUSTUPDT
    05  FIELD-CHANGED-ERROR-REPORT      PIC X(20).                       CUSTUPDT
    05  FILLER                          PIC XX.                          CUSTUPDT
    05  TYPE-OF-ERROR-REPORT            PIC X(25).                       CUSTUPDT
    05  FILLER                          PIC XX.                          CUSTUPDT
    05  OLD-MASTER-RECORD-REPORT        PIC X(27).                       CUSTUPDT
    05  FILLER                          PIC XX.                          CUSTUPDT
    05  NEW-MASTER-RECORD-REPORT        PIC X(27).                       CUSTUPDT
    05  FILLER                          PIC X(7).                        CUSTUPDT
                                                                         CUSTUPDT
SD  TRANSACTION-SORT-WORK-FILE                                           CUSTUPDT
    COPY SORTSD.                                                         CUSTUPDT
  C RECORD CONTAINS 80 CHARACTERS                                        LOADCUST
  C DATA RECORD IS TRANSACTION-SORT-WORK-RECORD.                         LOADCUST
  C                                                                      LOADCUST
  C 01  TRANSACTION-SORT-WORK-RECORD.                                     LOADCUST
  C     05  CUSTOMER-NUMBER-SORTREC     PIC X(5).                        LOADCUST
  C     05  FILLER                      PIC X(74).                       LOADCUST
  C     05  TRANSACTION-CODE-SORTREC    PIC X.                           LOADCUST
 **                                                                      CUSTUPDT
WORKING-STORAGE SECTION.                                                 CUSTUPDT
                                                                         CUSTUPDT
01  PROGRAM-INDICATORS.                                                  CUSTUPDT
    05  ARE-THERE-MORE-TRAN-RECORDS          PIC XXX VALUE 'YES'.        CUSTUPDT
        88  THERE-ARE-MORE-TRAN-RECORDS              VALUE 'YES'.        CUSTUPDT
        88  A-TRAN-RECORD-WAS-READ                   VALUE 'YES'.        CUSTUPDT
        88  THERE-ARE-NO-MORE-TRAN-RECORDS           VALUE 'NO '.        CUSTUPDT
    05  ARE-TRAN-RECORDS-VALID               PIC XXX.                    CUSTUPDT
        88  TRAN-RECORDS-ARE-VALID                   VALUE 'YES'.        CUSTUPDT
        88  TRAN-RECORDS-ARE-NOT-VALID               VALUE 'NO '.        CUSTUPDT
    05  HAS-UPDATED-DATA-BEEN-OBTAINED       PIC XXX.                    CUSTUPDT
        88  UPDATED-DATA-HAS-BEEN-OBTAINED           VALUE 'YES'.        CUSTUPDT
        88  DATA-HAS-NOT-BEEN-OBTAINED               VALUE 'NO '.        CUSTUPDT
    05  WAS-IT-A-VALID-ADD-RECORD            PIC XXX.                    CUSTUPDT
        88  IT-WAS-A-VALID-ADD-RECORD                VALUE 'YES'.        CUSTUPDT
    05  WAS-IT-A-VALID-DELETE-RECORD         PIC XXX.                    CUSTUPDT
        88  IT-WAS-A-VALID-DELETE-RECORD             VALUE 'YES'.        CUSTUPDT
    05  WAS-IT-A-VALID-CHANGE-RECORD         PIC XXX.                    CUSTUPDT
        88  IT-WAS-A-VALID-CHANGE-RECORD             VALUE 'YES'.        CUSTUPDT
    05  WAS-A-MASTER-RECORD-FOUND            PIC XXX.                    CUSTUPDT
        88  A-MASTER-RECORD-WAS-FOUND                VALUE 'YES'.        CUSTUPDT
        88  A-MASTER-RECORD-WAS-NOT-FOUND            VALUE 'NO '.        CUSTUPDT
    05  DID-A-VALID-WRITE-OCCUR              PIC XXX.                    CUSTUPDT
        88  A-VALID-WRITE-DID-NOT-OCCUR              VALUE 'NO '.        CUSTUPDT
    05  IS-TRANSACTION-CODE-VALID            PIC XXX.                    CUSTUPDT
        88  TRANSACTION-CODE-IS-VALID                VALUE 'YES'.        CUSTUPDT
        88  TRANSACTION-CODE-IS-NOT-VALID            VALUE 'NO '.        CUSTUPDT
    05  IS-TRANSACTION-FILE-SORTED           PIC XXX VALUE 'NO '.        CUSTUPDT
        88  TRANSACTION-FILE-IS-NOT-SORTED           VALUE 'NO '.        CUSTUPDT
                                                                         CUSTUPDT
01  PROGRAM-COMPARE-AREAS.                                               CUSTUPDT
    05  PREVIOUS-CUSTOMER-NUMBER      PIC X(5) VALUE LOW-VALUES.         CUSTUPDT
                                                                         CUSTUPDT
01  NOMINAL-KEY-FIELD.                                                   CUSTUPDT
    05  KEY-OF-THE-RECORD-TO-RETRIEVE        PIC X(5).                   CUSTUPDT
                                                                         CUSTUPDT
01  PROGRAM-WORK-AREAS.                                                  CUSTUPDT
    05  TRANSACTION-REPORT-WORK-AREA.                                    CUSTUPDT
        10  CUSTOMER-NUMBER-RPTWORK           PIC X(5)  VALUE            CUSTUPDT
                                                        SPACES.          CUSTUPDT
        10  ACTION-TAKEN-RPTWORK              PIC X(8)  VALUE            CUSTUPDT
                                                        SPACES.          CUSTUPDT
        10  FIELD-CHANGED-ERROR-RPTWORK       PIC X(20) VALUE            CUSTUPDT
                                                        SPACES.          CUSTUPDT
        10  TYPE-OF-ERROR-RPTWORK             PIC X(25) VALUE            CUSTUPDT
                                                        SPACES.          CUSTUPDT
        10  OLD-MASTER-RECORD-RPTWORK         PIC X(27) VALUE            CUSTUPDT
                                                        SPACES.          CUSTUPDT
        10  NEW-MASTER-RECORD-RPTWORK         PIC X(27) VALUE            CUSTUPDT
                                                        SPACES.          CUSTUPDT
    05  CUSTOMER-NUMBER-WORK.                                            CUSTUPDT
        10  FIRST-FOUR-CHAR-CUST-NUMB-WORK    PIC X(4).                  CUSTUPDT
        10  FIFTH-CHAR-CUST-NUMB-WORK         PIC X.                     CUSTUPDT
            88  VALID-CHECK-DIGIT-FOR-TEN    VALUE 'X'.                  CUSTUPDT
```

Figure 6-55 Source Listing (Part 2 of 19)

```
 4                        19.16.07        SEP  5,1978

  008200    05  STATE-EDIT-WORK                       PIC XX.              CUSTUPDT
  008210    05  DISCOUNT-EDIT-WORK                    PIC XX.              CUSTUPDT
  008220    05  LAST-ACTIVITY-EDIT-WORK.                                   CUSTUPDT
                10  MONTH-LAST-ACTIVITY-WORK          PIC 99.              CUSTUPDT
  008230
  008240            88  VALID-MONTH-WORK               VALUE 01 THRU 12.   CUSTUPDT
  008250        10  DAY-LAST-ACTIVITY-WORK            PIC XX.              CUSTUPDT
  008260        10  YEAR-LAST-ACTIVITY-WORK           PIC XX.              CUSTUPDT
  008270    05  ADDRESS-CHANGE-WORK                   PIC X(27).           CUSTUPDT
  008280    05  CITY-CHANGE-WORK                      PIC X(20).           CUSTUPDT
  008290    05  STATE-CHANGE-WORK                     PIC XX.              CUSTUPDT
  008300    05  ZIP-CODE-CHANGE-WORK                  PIC X(5).            CUSTUPDT
  008310    05  DISCOUNT-CHANGE-WORK                  PIC XX.              CUSTUPDT
  008320    05  LAST-ACTIVITY-CHANGE-WORK             PIC X(6).            CUSTUPDT
  008330    05  CUSTOMER-NUMBER-STATEDIT-WORK         PIC X(5).            CUSTUPDT
  008340    05  CUSTOMER-NUMBER-DISCEDIT-WORK         PIC X(5).            CUSTUPDT
  008350    05  CUSTOMER-NUMBER-DATEDIT-WORK          PIC X(5).            CUSTUPDT
  009010    05  CUSTOMER-NUMBER-TYPE-3-CHANGE         PIC X(5).            CUSTUPDT
  009020    05  CUSTOMER-NUMBER-TYPE-4-CHANGE         PIC X(5).            CUSTUPDT
  009030    05  TRANSACTION-CODE-CURRENT-REC          PIC X.               CUSTUPDT
  009040    05  CUSTOMER-NUMBER-CURRENT-REC           PIC X(5).            CUSTUPDT
  009050    05  MASTER-RECORD-BEING-PROCESSED         PIC X(5).            CUSTUPDT
  009060                                                                   CUSTUPDT
  009070 01  MOD-11-PASS-AREA-WORK.                                        CUSTUPDT
  009080    05  FIELD-TO-BE-CHECKED-MOD11-WORK        PIC X(20).           CUSTUPDT
  009090    05  DID-CUST-NUMBER-PASS-MOD11            PIC XXX.             CUSTUPDT
  009100        88  CUST-NUMBER-PASSED-MOD11           VALUE 'YES'.        CUSTUPDT
  009110        88  CUST-NUMBER-DID-NOT-PASS-MOD11     VALUE 'NO '.        CUSTUPDT
  009120                                                                   CUSTUPDT
  009130 01  PROGRAM-CONSTANTS                                             CUSTUPDT
              COPY PGMCON.                                                 CUSTUPDT
  009140
C 011060 01  PROGRAM-CONSTANTS.                                            LOADCUST
C 011070    05  CUSTOMER-NAME-FIELD-MSG              PIC X(20) VALUE      LOADCUST
C 011080                                       'CUSTOMER NAME        '.LOADCUST
C 011090    05  BLANK-FIELD-ERROR-MSG                PIC X(25) VALUE      LOADCUST
C 011100                                  'FIELD CONTAINS SPACES     '.LOADCUST
C 011110    05  CUSTOMER-ADDRESS-FIELD-MSG           PIC X(20) VALUE      LOADCUST
C 011120                                       'CUSTOMER ADDRESS     '.LOADCUST
C 011130    05  CUSTOMER-CITY-FIELD-MSG              PIC X(20) VALUE      LOADCUST
C 011140                                       'CUSTOMER CITY        '.LOADCUST
C 011150    05  CUSTOMER-STATE-FIELD-MSG             PIC X(20) VALUE      LOADCUST
C 011160                                       'CUSTOMER STATE       '.LOADCUST
C 011170    05  BAD-STATE-CODE-ERROR-MSG             PIC X(25) VALUE      LOADCUST
C 011180                                  'INVALID STATE CODE        '.LOADCUST
C 011190    05  CUSTOMER-ZIP-CODE-FIELD-MSG          PIC X(20) VALUE      LOADCUST
C 011200                                       'CUSTOMER ZIP CODE    '.LOADCUST
C 012010    05  FIELD-NOT-NUMERIC-ERROR-MSG          PIC X(25) VALUE      LOADCUST
C 012020                                  'FIELD IS NOT NUMERIC      '.LOADCUST
C 012030    05  CUSTOMER-DISCOUNT-FIELD-MSG          PIC X(20) VALUE      LOADCUST
C 012040                                       'CUSTOMER DISCOUNT    '.LOADCUST
C 012050    05  MAXIMUM-DISCOUNT-PERCENT             PIC XX    VALUE '20'.LOADCUST
C 012060    05  BAD-DISCOUNT-ERROR-MSG               PIC X(25) VALUE      LOADCUST
C 012070                                  'DISCOUNT EXCEEDS MAXIMUM  '.LOADCUST
C 012080    05  LAST-ACTIVITY-DATE-FIELD-MSG         PIC X(20) VALUE      LOADCUST
C 012090                                       'LAST ACTIVITY DATE   '.LOADCUST
C 012120    05  BAD-MONTH-ERROR-MSG                  PIC X(25) VALUE      LOADCUST
C 012130                                  'INVALID MONTH             '.LOADCUST
C 012140    05  FIRST-DAY-OF-MONTH-NUMBER            PIC XX    VALUE '01'.LOADCUST
C 012150    05  BAD-DAY-ERROR-MSG                    PIC X(25) VALUE      LOADCUST
C 012160                                  'INVALID DAY               '.LOADCUST
C 012170    05  CUSTOMER-RECORDS-FIELD-MSG           PIC X(20) VALUE      LOADCUST
C 012180                                       'CUSTOMER RECORDS     '.LOADCUST
C 012190    05  TYPE1-BUT-NO-TYPE2-ERROR-MSG         PIC X(25) VALUE      LOADCUST
C 012200                                  'TYPE 1 BUT NO TYPE 2      '.LOADCUST
C 012210    05  TRANSACTION-TYPE-ONE                 PIC X     VALUE '1'. LOADCUST
C 012220    05  TRANSACTION-TYPE-TWO                 PIC X     VALUE '2'. LOADCUST
C 013010    05  TYPE2-BUT-NO-TYPE1-ERROR-MSG         PIC X(25) VALUE      LOADCUST
C 013020                                  'TYPE 2 BUT NO TYPE 1      '.LOADCUST
C 013030    05  BAD-TRANS-CODE-ERROR-MSG             PIC X(25) VALUE      LOADCUST
C 013040                                  'INVALID RECORD TYPE       '.LOADCUST
C 013050    05  CUSTOMER-NUMBER-FIELD-MSG            PIC X(20) VALUE      LOADCUST
C 013060                                       'CUSTOMER NUMBER      '.LOADCUST
C 013070    05  FAILS-MOD11-ERROR-MSG                PIC X(25) VALUE      LOADCUST
C 013080                                  'FAILS MOD-11 CHECK        '.LOADCUST
C 013090    05  INVALID-WRITE-MSG                    PIC X(25) VALUE      LOADCUST
C 013100                                  'DUPLICATE OR BAD SEQUENCE'.LOADCUST
**009150    05  DELETE-CODE-CONSTANT                 PIC X     VALUE      CUSTUPDT
  009160                                            HIGH-VALUES.          CUSTUPDT
  009170    05  TRANSACTION-TYPE-THREE               PIC X     VALUE '3'. CUSTUPDT
  009180    05  TRANSACTION-TYPE-FOUR                PIC X     VALUE '4'. CUSTUPDT
  009190    05  TRANSACTION-TYPE-FIVE                PIC X     VALUE '5'. CUSTUPDT
  009200    05  DELETION-MSG                         PIC X(8)  VALUE      CUSTUPDT
  009210                                                 'DELETION'. CUSTUPDT
  009220    05  TRANSACTION-CODE-FIELD-MSG           PIC X(20) VALUE      CUSTUPDT
  009230                                       'TRANSACTION CODE     '.CUSTUPDT
  009240    05  ADD-OF-DUPLICATE-ERROR-MSG           PIC X(25) VALUE      CUSTUPDT
  009250                                  'ADDITION OF DUPLICATE REC'.CUSTUPDT
  009260    05  ADDITION-MSG                         PIC X(8)  VALUE      CUSTUPDT
  009270                                                 'ADDITION'. CUSTUPDT
  009280    05  STATE-BUT-NO-ZIP-ERROR-MSG           PIC X(25) VALUE      CUSTUPDT
  009290                                  'STATE CHANGED - ZIP NOT   '.CUSTUPDT
  009300    05  CHANGE-MSG                           PIC X(8)  VALUE      CUSTUPDT
  009310                                                 'CHANGE  '. CUSTUPDT
  010010    05  NO-MASTER-RECORD-MSG                 PIC X(25) VALUE      CUSTUPDT
  010020                                  'NO MASTER RECORD          '.CUSTUPDT
  010070                                                                  CUSTUPDT
```

Figure 6-56 Source Listing (Part 3 of 19)

```
  5                               19.16.07        SEP  5,1978

       010080 01  PROGRAM-TABLES                                              CUSTUPDT
       010090       COPY PGMTBLS.                                             CUSTUPDT
     C 013120 01  PROGRAM-TABLES.                                             LOADCUST
     C 013130     05  STATE-TABLE.                                            LOADCUST
     C 013140         10  VALID-STATE-CONSTANTS.                              LOADCUST
     C 013150             15  FILLER           PIC XX       VALUE 'AK'.       LOADCUST
     C 013160             15  FILLER           PIC XX       VALUE 'AL'.       LOADCUST
     C 013170             15  FILLER           PIC XX       VALUE 'AR'.       LOADCUST
     C 013180             15  FILLER           PIC XX       VALUE 'AZ'.       LOADCUST
     C 013190             15  FILLER           PIC XX       VALUE 'CA'.       LOADCUST
     C 013200             15  FILLER           PIC XX       VALUE 'CO'.       LOADCUST
     C 013210             15  FILLER           PIC XX       VALUE 'CT'.       LOADCUST
     C 013220             15  FILLER           PIC XX       VALUE 'DC'.       LOADCUST
     C 013230             15  FILLER           PIC XX       VALUE 'DE'.       LOADCUST
     C 014010             15  FILLER           PIC XX       VALUE 'FL'.       LOADCUST
     C 014020             15  FILLER           PIC XX       VALUE 'GA'.       LOADCUST
     C 014030             15  FILLER           PIC XX       VALUE 'HI'.       LOADCUST
     C 014040             15  FILLER           PIC XX       VALUE 'IA'.       LOADCUST
     C 014050             15  FILLER           PIC XX       VALUE 'ID'.       LOADCUST
     C 014060             15  FILLER           PIC XX       VALUE 'IL'.       LOADCUST
     C 014070             15  FILLER           PIC XX       VALUE 'IN'.       LOADCUST
     C 014080             15  FILLER           PIC XX       VALUE 'KS'.       LOADCUST
     C 014090             15  FILLER           PIC XX       VALUE 'KY'.       LOADCUST
     C 014100             15  FILLER           PIC XX       VALUE 'LA'.       LOADCUST
     C 014110             15  FILLER           PIC XX       VALUE 'MA'.       LOADCUST
     C 014120             15  FILLER           PIC XX       VALUE 'MD'.       LOADCUST
     C 014130             15  FILLER           PIC XX       VALUE 'ME'.       LOADCUST
     C 014140             15  FILLER           PIC XX       VALUE 'MI'.       LOADCUST
     C 014150             15  FILLER           PIC XX       VALUE 'MN'.       LOADCUST
     C 014160             15  FILLER           PIC XX       VALUE 'MO'.       LOADCUST
     C 014170             15  FILLER           PIC XX       VALUE 'MS'.       LOADCUST
     C 014180             15  FILLER           PIC XX       VALUE 'MT'.       LOADCUST
     C 014190             15  FILLER           PIC XX       VALUE 'NB'.       LOADCUST
     C 014200             15  FILLER           PIC XX       VALUE 'NC'.       LOADCUST
     C 015010             15  FILLER           PIC XX       VALUE 'ND'.       LOADCUST
     C 015020             15  FILLER           PIC XX       VALUE 'NH'.       LOADCUST
     C 015030             15  FILLER           PIC XX       VALUE 'NJ'.       LOADCUST
     C 015040             15  FILLER           PIC XX       VALUE 'NM'.       LOADCUST
     C 015050             15  FILLER           PIC XX       VALUE 'NV'.       LOADCUST
     C 015060             15  FILLER           PIC XX       VALUE 'NY'.       LOADCUST
     C 015070             15  FILLER           PIC XX       VALUE 'OH'.       LOADCUST
     C 015080             15  FILLER           PIC XX       VALUE 'OK'.       LOADCUST
     C 015090             15  FILLER           PIC XX       VALUE 'OR'.       LOADCUST
     C 015100             15  FILLER           PIC XX       VALUE 'PA'.       LOADCUST
     C 015110             15  FILLER           PIC XX       VALUE 'RI'.       LOADCUST
     C 015120             15  FILLER           PIC XX       VALUE 'SC'.       LOADCUST
     C 015130             15  FILLER           PIC XX       VALUE 'SD'.       LOADCUST
     C 015140             15  FILLER           PIC XX       VALUE 'TN'.       LOADCUST
     C 015150             15  FILLER           PIC XX       VALUE 'TX'.       LOADCUST
     C 015160             15  FILLER           PIC XX       VALUE 'UT'.       LOADCUST
     C 015170             15  FILLER           PIC XX       VALUE 'VA'.       LOADCUST
     C 015180             15  FILLER           PIC XX       VALUE 'VT'.       LOADCUST
     C 015190             15  FILLER           PIC XX       VALUE 'WA'.       LOADCUST
     C 015200             15  FILLER           PIC XX       VALUE 'WI'.       LOADCUST
     C 016010             15  FILLER           PIC XX       VALUE 'WV'.       LOADCUST
     C 016020             15  FILLER           PIC XX       VALUE 'WY'.       LOADCUST
     C 016030         10  VALID-STATE-TABLE REDEFINES VALID-STATE-CONSTANTS   LOADCUST
     C 016040                                   OCCURS 51 TIMES               LOADCUST
     C 016050                                   ASCENDING KEY IS              LOADCUST
     C 016060                                       STATE-CODE                LOADCUST
     C 016070                                   INDEXED BY                    LOADCUST
     C 016080                                       STATE-CODE-INDEX.LOADCUST
     C 016090             15  STATE-CODE       PIC XX.                        LOADCUST
     C 016100     05  MONTH-DAY-TABLE.                                        LOADCUST
     C 016110         10  MONTH-DAY-CONSTANTS.                                LOADCUST
     C 016120             15  FILLER           PIC X(4)     VALUE '0131'.     LOADCUST
     C 016130             15  FILLER           PIC X(4)     VALUE '0229'.     LOADCUST
     C 016140             15  FILLER           PIC X(4)     VALUE '0331'.     LOADCUST
     C 016150             15  FILLER           PIC X(4)     VALUE '0430'.     LOADCUST
     C 016160             15  FILLER           PIC X(4)     VALUE '0531'.     LOADCUST
     C 016170             15  FILLER           PIC X(4)     VALUE '0630'.     LOADCUST
     C 016180             15  FILLER           PIC X(4)     VALUE '0731'.     LOADCUST
     C 016190             15  FILLER           PIC X(4)     VALUE '0831'.     LOADCUST
     C 016200             15  FILLER           PIC X(4)     VALUE '0930'.     LOADCUST
     C 017010             15  FILLER           PIC X(4)     VALUE '1031'.     LOADCUST
     C 017020             15  FILLER           PIC X(4)     VALUE '1130'.     LOADCUST
     C 017030             15  FILLER           PIC X(4)     VALUE '1231'.     LOADCUST
     C 017040         10  MONTHS-AND-DAYS-TABLE REDEFINES MONTH-DAY-CONSTANTS LOADCUST
     C 017050                                   OCCURS 12 TIMES               LOADCUST
     C 017060                                   INDEXED BY                    LOADCUST
     C 017070                                       MONTH-DAY-INDEX.  LOADCUST
     C 017080             15  MONTH-TABLE      PIC XX.                        LOADCUST
     C 017090             15  NUMBER-OF-DAYS-IN-MONTH PIC XX.                 LOADCUST
     **010100                                                                 CUSTUPDT
```

Figure 6-57 Source Listing (Part 4 of 19)

```
6                    19.16.07        SEP  5,1978

  010110 01  TRANSACTION-RECORDS-WORK-AREA                                       CUSTUPDT
  010120       COPY INPRECS.                                                     CUSTUPDT
C 017110 01  TRANSACTION-RECORDS-WORK-AREA.                                      LOADCUST
C 017120     05  SORTED-TRANS-RECORD-TYPE-1.                                     LOADCUST
C 017130         10  CUSTOMER-NUMBER-TRANSORT1           PIC X(5).               LOADCUST
C 017140         10  CUSTOMER-NAME-TRANSORT1             PIC X(20).              LOADCUST
C 017150         10  CUSTOMER-ADDRESS-TRANSORT1          PIC X(27).              LOADCUST
C 017160         10  CUSTOMER-CITY-TRANSORT1             PIC X(20).              LOADCUST
C 017170         10 CUSTOMER-STATE-TRANSORT1             PIC XX.                 LOADCUST
C 017180         10 CUSTOMER-ZIP-CODE-TRANSORT1          PIC X(5).               LOADCUST
C 017190         10  TRANSACTION-CODE-TRANSORT1          PIC X.                  LOADCUST
C 017200     05  SORTED-TRANS-RECORD-TYPE-2.                                     LOADCUST
C 017210         10  CUSTOMER-NUMBER-TRANSORT2           PIC X(5).               LOADCUST
C 017220         10  CUSTOMER-DISCOUNT-TRANSORT2         PIC XX.                 LOADCUST
C 017230         10  LAST-ACTIVITY-DATE-TRANSORT2.                               LOADCUST
C 017240             15  MONTH-LAST-ACTIVITY-TRANSORT2   PIC 99.                 LOADCUST
C 017250                 88  VALID-MONTH                 VALUE 01 THRU 12.LOADCUST
C 017260             15  DAY-LAST-ACTIVITY-TRANSORT2     PIC XX.                 LOADCUST
C 017270             15  YEAR-LAST-ACTIVITY-TRANSORT2    PIC XX.                 LOADCUST
C 017280         10  FILLER                              PIC X(66).              LOADCUST
C 017290         10  TRANSACTION-CODE-TRANSORT2          PIC X.                  LOADCUST
**010130                                                                         CUSTUPDT
  010140 01  MASTER-INPUT-WORK-AREA.                                             CUSTUPDT
  010150     05  DELETE-CODE-MSTRIN-WORK         PIC X.                          CUSTUPDT
  010160         88  CUSTOMER-RECORD-IS-DELETED          VALUE HIGH-VALUES.      CUSTUPDT
  010170     05  CUSTOMER-NUMBER-MSTRIN-WORK     PIC X(5).                       CUSTUPDT
  010180     05  CUSTOMER-NAME-MSTRIN-WORK       PIC X(20).                      CUSTUPDT
  010190     05  CUSTOMER-ADDRESS-MSTRIN-WORK    PIC X(27).                      CUSTUPDT
  010200     05  CUSTOMER-CITY-MSTRIN-WORK       PIC X(20).                      CUSTUPDT
  011010     05  CUSTOMER-STATE-MSTRIN-WORK      PIC XX.                         CUSTUPDT
  011020     05  CUSTOMER-ZIP-CODE-MSTRIN-WORK   PIC X(5).                       CUSTUPDT
  011030     05  CUSTOMER-DISCOUNT-MSTRIN-WORK   PIC XX.                         CUSTUPDT
  011040     05  LAST-ACTIVITY-MSTRIN-WORK       PIC X(6).                       CUSTUPDT
  011050                                                                         CUSTUPDT
  011060 01  MASTER-OUTPUT-WORK-AREA.                                            CUSTUPDT
  011070     05  DELETE-CODE-MSTROUT-WORK        PIC X.                          CUSTUPDT
  011080     05  CUSTOMER-NUMBER-MSTROUT-WORK    PIC X(5).                       CUSTUPDT
  011090     05  CUSTOMER-NAME-MSTROUT-WORK      PIC X(20).                      CUSTUPDT
  011100     05  CUSTOMER-ADDRESS-MSTROUT-WORK   PIC X(27).                      CUSTUPDT
  011110     05  CUSTOMER-CITY-MSTROUT-WORK      PIC X(20).                      CUSTUPDT
  011120     05  CUSTOMER-STATE-MSTROUT-WORK     PIC XX.                         CUSTUPDT
  011130     05  CUSTOMER-ZIP-CODE-MSTROUT-WORK  PIC X(5).                       CUSTUPDT
  011140     05  CUSTOMER-DISCOUNT-MSTROUT-WORK  PIC XX.                         CUSTUPDT
  011150     05  LAST-ACTIVITY-MSTROUT-WORK      PIC X(6).                       CUSTUPDT
  011160                                                                         CUSTUPDT
  011170 01  PRINTER-CONTROL.                                                    CUSTUPDT
  011180     05  PROPER-SPACING              PIC 9.                              CUSTUPDT
  011190     05  SPACE-ONE-LINE              PIC 9    VALUE 1.                   CUSTUPDT
  011200     05  SPACE-TWO-LINES             PIC 9    VALUE 2.                   CUSTUPDT
  012010     05  NUMBER-OF-LINES-PRINTED     PIC S999 VALUE ZERO                 CUSTUPDT
  012020                                              USAGE IS COMP-3.           CUSTUPDT
  012030     05  PAGE-SIZE                   PIC 999  VALUE 40                   CUSTUPDT
  012040                                              USAGE IS COMP-3.           CUSTUPDT
  012050     05  PAGE-NUMBER-COUNT           PIC S999 VALUE +1                   CUSTUPDT
  012060                                              USAGE IS COMP-3.           CUSTUPDT
  012070         88  THIS-IS-THE-FIRST-PAGE           VALUE +1.                  CUSTUPDT
  012080                                                                         CUSTUPDT
  012090 01  HEADING-LINES.                                                      CUSTUPDT
  012100     05  FIRST-HEADING-LINE.                                             CUSTUPDT
  012110         10  CARRIAGE-CONTROL    PIC X.                                  CUSTUPDT
  012120         10  FILLER              PIC X(5)     VALUE 'DATE '.             CUSTUPDT
  012130         10  DATE-HDG1           PIC X(8).                               CUSTUPDT
  012140         10  FILLER              PIC X(37)    VALUE SPACES.              CUSTUPDT
  012150         10  FILLER              PIC X(7)     VALUE 'UPDATE '.           CUSTUPDT
  012160         10  FILLER              PIC X(12)    VALUE                      CUSTUPDT
  012170                                             'TRANSACTION '.             CUSTUPDT
  012180         10  FILLER              PIC X(6)     VALUE 'REPORT'.            CUSTUPDT
  012190         10  FILLER              PIC X(42)    VALUE SPACES.              CUSTUPDT
  012200         10  FILLER              PIC X(5)     VALUE 'PAGE '.             CUSTUPDT
  013010         10  PAGE-NUMBER-HDG1    PIC ZZ9.                                CUSTUPDT
  013020         10  FILLER              PIC X(7)     VALUE SPACES.              CUSTUPDT
  013030                                                                         CUSTUPDT
  013040     05  SECOND-HEADING-LINE.                                            CUSTUPDT
  013050         10  CARRIAGE-CONTROL    PIC X.                                  CUSTUPDT
  013060         10  FILLER              PIC X(8)     VALUE 'CUSTOMER'.          CUSTUPDT
  013070         10  FILLER              PIC XXX      VALUE SPACES.              CUSTUPDT
  013080         10  FILLER              PIC X(6)     VALUE 'ACTION'.            CUSTUPDT
  013090         10  FILLER              PIC X(5)     VALUE SPACES.              CUSTUPDT
  013100         10  FILLER              PIC X(6)     VALUE 'FIELD '.            CUSTUPDT
  013110         10  FILLER              PIC X(10)    VALUE 'CHANGED OR'.        CUSTUPDT
  013120         10  FILLER              PIC X(94)    VALUE SPACES.              CUSTUPDT
  013130                                                                         CUSTUPDT
  013140     05  THIRD-HEADING-LINE.                                             CUSTUPDT
  013150         10  CARRIAGE-CONTROL    PIC X.                                  CUSTUPDT
  013160         10  FILLER              PIC X        VALUE SPACE.               CUSTUPDT
  013170         10  FILLER              PIC X(6)     VALUE 'NUMBER'.            CUSTUPDT
  013180         10  FILLER              PIC X(4)     VALUE SPACES.              CUSTUPDT
  013190         10  FILLER              PIC X(5)     VALUE 'TAKEN'.             CUSTUPDT
  013200         10  FILLER              PIC X(7)     VALUE SPACES.              CUSTUPDT
  014010         10  FILLER              PIC X(6)     VALUE 'FIELD '.            CUSTUPDT
  014020         10  FILLER              PIC X(8)     VALUE 'IN ERROR'.          CUSTUPDT
  014030         10  FILLER              PIC X(11)    VALUE SPACES.              CUSTUPDT
  014040         10  FILLER              PIC X(5)     VALUE 'TYPE '.             CUSTUPDT
  014050         10  FILLER              PIC X(8)     VALUE 'OF ERROR'.          CUSTUPDT
  014060         10  FILLER              PIC X(12)    VALUE SPACES.              CUSTUPDT
  014070         10  FILLER              PIC X(11)    VALUE 'OLD MASTER '.CUSTUPDT
  014080         10  FILLER              PIC X(6)     VALUE 'RECORD'.            CUSTUPDT
  014090         10  FILLER              PIC X(12)    VALUE SPACES.              CUSTUPDT
  014100         10  FILLER              PIC X(11)    VALUE 'NEW MASTER '.CUSTUPDT
  014110         10  FILLER              PIC X(6)     VALUE 'RECORD'.            CUSTUPDT
  014120         10  FILLER              PIC X(13)    VALUE SPACES.              CUSTUPDT
```

Figure 6-58 Source Listing (Part 5 of 19)

```
  7                   19.16.07        SEP  5,1978

014140 PROCEDURE DIVISION.                                               CUSTUPDT
014150                                                                   CUSTUPDT
014160*************************************************************     CUSTUPDT
014170*                                                            *     CUSTUPDT
014180*  THE FUNCTION OF THIS MODULE IS TO UPDATE THE CUSTOMER     *     CUSTUPDT
014190*  MASTER FILE. IT IS ENTERED FROM AND EXITS TO THE OPERATING *    CUSTUPDT
014200*  SYSTEM.                                                   *     CUSTUPDT
015010*                                                            *     CUSTUPDT
015020*************************************************************     CUSTUPDT
015030                                                                   CUSTUPDT
015040 A000-UPDATE-CUSTOMER-MASTER.                                      CUSTUPDT
015050                                                                   CUSTUPDT
015060     OPEN I-O    CUSTOMER-MASTER-I-O-FILE                          CUSTUPDT
015070          OUTPUT UPDATE-TRANSACTION-REPORT-FILE.                   CUSTUPDT
015080     PERFORM B000-OBTAIN-UPDATED-DATA.                             CUSTUPDT
015090     PERFORM A001-WRITE-AND-READ                                   CUSTUPDT
015100             UNTIL THERE-ARE-NO-MORE-TRAN-RECORDS.                 CUSTUPDT
015110     CLOSE CUSTOMER-MASTER-I-O-FILE                                CUSTUPDT
015120           UPDATE-TRANSACTION-REPORT-FILE.                         CUSTUPDT
015130     STOP RUN.                                                     CUSTUPDT
015140                                                                   CUSTUPDT
015150                                                                   CUSTUPDT
015160                                                                   CUSTUPDT
015170 A001-WRITE-AND-READ.                                              CUSTUPDT
015180                                                                   CUSTUPDT
015190     PERFORM B010-WRITE-UPDATED-FILE.                              CUSTUPDT
015200     PERFORM B000-OBTAIN-UPDATED-DATA.                             CUSTUPDT
```

```
  8                   19.16.07        SEP  5,1978

016020*************************************************************     CUSTUPDT
016030*                                                            *     CUSTUPDT
016040*  THIS MODULE OBTAINS UPDATED DATA FOR THE CUSTOMER MASTER  *     CUSTUPDT
016050*  FILE UPDATE. IT IS ENTERED FROM AND EXITS TO THE          *     CUSTUPDT
016060*  A000-UPDATE-CUSTOMER-MASTER MODULE.                       *     CUSTUPDT
016070*                                                            *     CUSTUPDT
016080*************************************************************     CUSTUPDT
016090                                                                   CUSTUPDT
016100 B000-OBTAIN-UPDATED-DATA.                                         CUSTUPDT
016110                                                                   CUSTUPDT
016160     MOVE 'NO ' TO HAS-UPDATED-DATA-BEEN-OBTAINED.                 CUSTUPDT
016170     PERFORM C000-OBTAIN-VALID-TRANS-DATA.                         CUSTUPDT
016180     PERFORM B001-SEARCH-FOR-VALID-DATA                            CUSTUPDT
016190             UNTIL UPDATED-DATA-HAS-BEEN-OBTAINED OR               CUSTUPDT
016200                   THERE-ARE-NO-MORE-TRAN-RECORDS.                 CUSTUPDT
016210                                                                   CUSTUPDT
016220                                                                   CUSTUPDT
016230                                                                   CUSTUPDT
016240 B001-SEARCH-FOR-VALID-DATA.                                       CUSTUPDT
017010                                                                   CUSTUPDT
017020     MOVE SPACES TO WAS-IT-A-VALID-ADD-RECORD.                     CUSTUPDT
017030     MOVE SPACES TO WAS-IT-A-VALID-DELETE-RECORD.                  CUSTUPDT
017040     MOVE SPACES TO WAS-IT-A-VALID-CHANGE-RECORD.                  CUSTUPDT
017050     MOVE 'YES' TO WAS-A-MASTER-RECORD-FOUND.                      CUSTUPDT
017060     MOVE CUSTOMER-NUMBER-CURRENT-REC TO                           CUSTUPDT
017070            KEY-OF-THE-RECORD-TO-RETRIEVE.                         CUSTUPDT
017080     READ CUSTOMER-MASTER-I-O-FILE INTO MASTER-INPUT-WORK-AREA     CUSTUPDT
017090            INVALID KEY                                            CUSTUPDT
017100                MOVE 'NO ' TO WAS-A-MASTER-RECORD-FOUND.           CUSTUPDT
017110     IF A-MASTER-RECORD-WAS-FOUND                                  CUSTUPDT
017120         MOVE CUSTOMER-NUMBER-MSTRIN-WORK TO                       CUSTUPDT
017130                MASTER-RECORD-BEING-PROCESSED                      CUSTUPDT
017140     ELSE                                                          CUSTUPDT
017150         MOVE SPACES TO MASTER-RECORD-BEING-PROCESSED.             CUSTUPDT
017160     IF (A-MASTER-RECORD-WAS-NOT-FOUND) OR                         CUSTUPDT
017170            (A-MASTER-RECORD-WAS-FOUND AND                         CUSTUPDT
017180            CUSTOMER-RECORD-IS-DELETED)                            CUSTUPDT
017190         PERFORM C020-PROCESS-UNEQUAL-RECORDS                      CUSTUPDT
017200         IF IT-WAS-A-VALID-ADD-RECORD                              CUSTUPDT
017210             MOVE 'YES' TO HAS-UPDATED-DATA-BEEN-OBTAINED          CUSTUPDT
017220         ELSE                                                      CUSTUPDT
017230             PERFORM C000-OBTAIN-VALID-TRANS-DATA                  CUSTUPDT
017240     ELSE                                                          CUSTUPDT
017250         PERFORM C010-PROCESS-EQUAL-RECORDS                        CUSTUPDT
017260         IF IT-WAS-A-VALID-CHANGE-RECORD OR                        CUSTUPDT
018010                IT-WAS-A-VALID-DELETE-RECORD                       CUSTUPDT
018020             MOVE 'YES' TO HAS-UPDATED-DATA-BEEN-OBTAINED          CUSTUPDT
018030         ELSE                                                      CUSTUPDT
018040             PERFORM C000-OBTAIN-VALID-TRANS-DATA.                 CUSTUPDT
```

Figure 6-59 Source Listing (Part 6 of 19)

```
9                    19.16.07        SEP  5,1978

018060****************************************************************** CUSTUPDT
018070*                                                                * CUSTUPDT
018080*  THE FUNCTION OF THIS MODULE IS TO WRITE THE UPDATED FILE.     * CUSTUPDT
018090*  IT IS ENTERED FROM AND EXITS TO THE A000-UPDATE-CUSTOMER-     * CUSTUPDT
018100*  MASTER MODULE.                                                * CUSTUPDT
018110*                                                                * CUSTUPDT
018120****************************************************************** CUSTUPDT
018130                                                                   CUSTUPDT
018140 B010-WRITE-UPDATED-FILE.                                          CUSTUPDT
018150                                                                   CUSTUPDT
018160     MOVE SPACES TO DID-A-VALID-WRITE-OCCUR.                       CUSTUPDT
018170     IF MASTER-RECORD-BEING-PROCESSED =                            CUSTUPDT
018180             KEY-OF-THE-RECORD-TO-RETRIEVE                         CUSTUPDT
018190         PERFORM B011-REWRITE-THE-MASTER-RECORD                    CUSTUPDT
018200     ELSE                                                          CUSTUPDT
018210         PERFORM B012-WRITE-A-NEW-MASTER-RECORD.                   CUSTUPDT
018220                                                                   CUSTUPDT
018230                                                                   CUSTUPDT
018240                                                                   CUSTUPDT
018250 B011-REWRITE-THE-MASTER-RECORD.                                   CUSTUPDT
018260                                                                   CUSTUPDT
018270     REWRITE CUSTOMER-MASTER-I-O-RECORD                            CUSTUPDT
018280             FROM MASTER-OUTPUT-WORK-AREA.                         CUSTUPDT
018290                                                                   CUSTUPDT
018300                                                                   CUSTUPDT
018310                                                                   CUSTUPDT
018320 B012-WRITE-A-NEW-MASTER-RECORD.                                   CUSTUPDT
018330                                                                   CUSTUPDT
018340     MOVE CUSTOMER-NUMBER-CURRENT-REC TO                           CUSTUPDT
019010             KEY-OF-THE-RECORD-TO-RETRIEVE.                        CUSTUPDT
019020     WRITE CUSTOMER-MASTER-I-O-RECORD                              CUSTUPDT
019030             FROM MASTER-OUTPUT-WORK-AREA                          CUSTUPDT
019040             INVALID KEY                                           CUSTUPDT
019050                 MOVE 'NO ' TO DID-A-VALID-WRITE-OCCUR.            CUSTUPDT
```

```
10                   19.16.07        SEP  5,1978

019070****************************************************************** CUSTUPDT
019080*                                                                * CUSTUPDT
019090*  THE FUNCTION OF THIS MODULE IS TO OBTAIN VALID TRANSACTION    * CUSTUPDT
019100*  DATA. IT IS ENTERED FROM AND EXITS TO THE                     * CUSTUPDT
019110*  B000-OBTAIN-UPDATED-DATA MODULE.                              * CUSTUPDT
019120*                                                                * CUSTUPDT
019130****************************************************************** CUSTUPDT
019140                                                                   CUSTUPDT
019150 C000-OBTAIN-VALID-TRANS-DATA.                                     CUSTUPDT
019160                                                                   CUSTUPDT
019170     MOVE SPACES TO ARE-TRAN-RECORDS-VALID.                        CUSTUPDT
019180     PERFORM D000-OBTAIN-TRANS-RECORDS.                            CUSTUPDT
019190     PERFORM C001-READ-AND-EDIT                                    CUSTUPDT
019200             UNTIL TRAN-RECORDS-ARE-VALID OR                       CUSTUPDT
020010                 THERE-ARE-NO-MORE-TRAN-RECORDS.                   CUSTUPDT
020020                                                                   CUSTUPDT
020030                                                                   CUSTUPDT
020040                                                                   CUSTUPDT
020050 C001-READ-AND-EDIT.                                               CUSTUPDT
020060                                                                   CUSTUPDT
020070     IF TRANSACTION-CODE-CURRENT-REC = TRANSACTION-TYPE-ONE        CUSTUPDT
020080         PERFORM D010-EDIT-TYPE-1-RECORD                           CUSTUPDT
020090         PERFORM D020-EDIT-TYPE-2-RECORD                           CUSTUPDT
020100     ELSE IF TRANSACTION-CODE-CURRENT-REC = TRANSACTION-TYPE-THREECUSTUPDT
020110         PERFORM D030-EDIT-TYPE-3-RECORD                           CUSTUPDT
020120     ELSE IF TRANSACTION-CODE-CURRENT-REC = TRANSACTION-TYPE-FOUR  CUSTUPDT
020150         PERFORM D040-EDIT-TYPE-4-RECORD                           CUSTUPDT
020160     ELSE                                                          CUSTUPDT
020170         MOVE CUSTOMER-NUMBER-CURRENT-REC TO CUSTOMER-NUMBER-WORK  CUSTUPDT
020180         PERFORM U020-EDIT-CUSTOMER-NUMBER.                        CUSTUPDT
020190     IF TRAN-RECORDS-ARE-NOT-VALID                                 CUSTUPDT
020200         MOVE SPACES TO ARE-TRAN-RECORDS-VALID                     CUSTUPDT
020210         PERFORM D000-OBTAIN-TRANS-RECORDS                         CUSTUPDT
020220     ELSE                                                          CUSTUPDT
021010         MOVE 'YES' TO ARE-TRAN-RECORDS-VALID.                     CUSTUPDT
```

Figure 6-60 Source Listing (Part 7 of 19)

```
11                    19.16.07        SEP  5,1978

      ******************************************************************* CUSTUPDT
      *                                                                 * CUSTUPDT
      *  THE FUNCTION OF THIS MODULE IS TO PROCESS EQUAL MASTER AND     * CUSTUPDT
      *  TRANSACTION RECORDS. IT IS ENTERED FROM AND EXITS TO THE       * CUSTUPDT
      *  B000-OBTAIN-UPDATED-DATA MODULE.                               * CUSTUPDT
      *                                                                 * CUSTUPDT
      ******************************************************************* CUSTUPDT
                                                                          CUSTUPDT
       C010-PROCESS-EQUAL-RECORDS.                                        CUSTUPDT
                                                                          CUSTUPDT
           IF TRANSACTION-CODE-CURRENT-REC = TRANSACTION-TYPE-THREE OR    CUSTUPDT
                   TRANSACTION-CODE-CURRENT-REC = TRANSACTION-TYPE-FOUR   CUSTUPDT
               PERFORM D050-PROCESS-CHANGE-TRANS                          CUSTUPDT
               MOVE MASTER-INPUT-WORK-AREA TO MASTER-OUTPUT-WORK-AREA     CUSTUPDT
               MOVE 'YES' TO WAS-IT-A-VALID-CHANGE-RECORD                 CUSTUPDT
           ELSE                                                           CUSTUPDT
               IF TRANSACTION-CODE-CURRENT-REC = TRANSACTION-TYPE-FIVE    CUSTUPDT
                   MOVE DELETE-CODE-CONSTANT TO DELETE-CODE-MSTRIN-WORK   CUSTUPDT
                   MOVE MASTER-INPUT-WORK-AREA TO MASTER-OUTPUT-WORK-AREA CUSTUPDT
                   MOVE 'YES' TO WAS-IT-A-VALID-DELETE-RECORD             CUSTUPDT
                   MOVE CUSTOMER-NUMBER-CURRENT-REC TO                    CUSTUPDT
                           CUSTOMER-NUMBER-RPTWORK                        CUSTUPDT
                   MOVE DELETION-MSG TO ACTION-TAKEN-RPTWORK              CUSTUPDT
                   PERFORM U000-WRITE-TRANSACTION-REPORT                  CUSTUPDT
               ELSE                                                       CUSTUPDT
                   MOVE CUSTOMER-NUMBER-CURRENT-REC TO                    CUSTUPDT
                           CUSTOMER-NUMBER-RPTWORK                        CUSTUPDT
                   MOVE TRANSACTION-CODE-FIELD-MSG TO                     CUSTUPDT
                           FIELD-CHANGED-ERROR-RPTWORK                    CUSTUPDT
                   MOVE ADD-OF-DUPLICATE-ERROR-MSG TO                     CUSTUPDT
                           TYPE-OF-ERROR-RPTWORK                          CUSTUPDT
                   PERFORM U000-WRITE-TRANSACTION-REPORT                  CUSTUPDT
                   MOVE 'NO ' TO WAS-IT-A-VALID-CHANGE-RECORD             CUSTUPDT
                   MOVE 'NO ' TO WAS-IT-A-VALID-DELETE-RECORD.            CUSTUPDT

12                    19.16.07        SEP  5,1978

      ******************************************************************* CUSTUPDT
      *                                                                 * CUSTUPDT
      *  THE FUNCTION OF THIS MODULE IS TO PROCESS AN UNEQUAL           * CUSTUPDT
      *  TRANSACTION RECORD. IT IS ENTERED FROM AND EXITS TO THE        * CUSTUPDT
      *  B000-OBTAIN-UPDATED-DATA MODULE.                               * CUSTUPDT
      *                                                                 * CUSTUPDT
      ******************************************************************* CUSTUPDT
                                                                          CUSTUPDT
       C020-PROCESS-UNEQUAL-RECORDS.                                      CUSTUPDT
                                                                          CUSTUPDT
           IF TRANSACTION-CODE-CURRENT-REC = TRANSACTION-TYPE-ONE         CUSTUPDT
               MOVE CUSTOMER-NUMBER-TRANSORT1 TO                          CUSTUPDT
                       CUSTOMER-NUMBER-MSTROUT-WORK                       CUSTUPDT
               MOVE CUSTOMER-NAME-TRANSORT1 TO CUSTOMER-NAME-MSTROUT-WORKCUSTUPDT
               MOVE CUSTOMER-ADDRESS-TRANSORT1 TO                         CUSTUPDT
                       CUSTOMER-ADDRESS-MSTROUT-WORK                      CUSTUPDT
               MOVE CUSTOMER-CITY-TRANSORT1 TO CUSTOMER-CITY-MSTROUT-WORKCUSTUPDT
               MOVE CUSTOMER-STATE-TRANSORT1 TO                           CUSTUPDT
                       CUSTOMER-STATE-MSTROUT-WORK                        CUSTUPDT
               MOVE CUSTOMER-ZIP-CODE-TRANSORT1 TO                        CUSTUPDT
                       CUSTOMER-ZIP-CODE-MSTROUT-WORK                     CUSTUPDT
               MOVE CUSTOMER-DISCOUNT-TRANSORT2 TO                        CUSTUPDT
                       CUSTOMER-DISCOUNT-MSTROUT-WORK                     CUSTUPDT
               MOVE LAST-ACTIVITY-DATE-TRANSORT2 TO                       CUSTUPDT
                       LAST-ACTIVITY-MSTROUT-WORK                         CUSTUPDT
               MOVE SPACES TO DELETE-CODE-MSTROUT-WORK                    CUSTUPDT
               MOVE CUSTOMER-NUMBER-TRANSORT1 TO                          CUSTUPDT
                       CUSTOMER-NUMBER-RPTWORK                            CUSTUPDT
               MOVE ADDITION-MSG TO ACTION-TAKEN-RPTWORK                  CUSTUPDT
               PERFORM U000-WRITE-TRANSACTION-REPORT                      CUSTUPDT
               MOVE 'YES' TO WAS-IT-A-VALID-ADD-RECORD                    CUSTUPDT
           ELSE                                                           CUSTUPDT
               MOVE CUSTOMER-NUMBER-CURRENT-REC TO                        CUSTUPDT
                       CUSTOMER-NUMBER-RPTWORK                            CUSTUPDT
               MOVE TRANSACTION-CODE-FIELD-MSG TO                         CUSTUPDT
                       FIELD-CHANGED-ERROR-RPTWORK                        CUSTUPDT
               MOVE NO-MASTER-RECORD-MSG TO TYPE-OF-ERROR-RPTWORK         CUSTUPDT
               PERFORM U000-WRITE-TRANSACTION-REPORT                      CUSTUPDT
               MOVE 'NO ' TO WAS-IT-A-VALID-ADD-RECORD.                   CUSTUPDT
```

Figure 6-61 Source Listing (Part 8 of 19)

```
 13                    19.16.07        SEP  5,1978

**********************************************************************  CUSTUPDT
*                                                                    *  CUSTUPDT
*  THIS MODULE OBTAINS A TRANSACTION RECORD(S) WITH VALID            *  CUSTUPDT
*  TRANSACTION CODES. IT IS ENTERED FROM AND EXITS TO THE            *  CUSTUPDT
*  C000-OBTAIN-VALID-TRANS-DATA MODULE.                              *  CUSTUPDT
*                                                                    *  CUSTUPDT
**********************************************************************  CUSTUPDT
                                                                        CUSTUPDT
D000-OBTAIN-TRANS-RECORDS.                                              CUSTUPDT
                                                                        CUSTUPDT
    MOVE SPACES TO IS-TRANSACTION-CODE-VALID.                           CUSTUPDT
    IF TRANSACTION-FILE-IS-NOT-SORTED                                   CUSTUPDT
        PERFORM E000-SORT-TRANSACTION-RECORDS                           CUSTUPDT
        OPEN INPUT SORTED-CUST-TRANS-INPUT-FILE                         CUSTUPDT
        MOVE 'YES' TO IS-TRANSACTION-FILE-SORTED.                       CUSTUPDT
    PERFORM D002-READ-FIRST-RECORD                                      CUSTUPDT
    PERFORM D001-CHECK-FOR-VALID-CODES                                  CUSTUPDT
            UNTIL TRANSACTION-CODE-IS-VALID OR                          CUSTUPDT
                    THERE-ARE-NO-MORE-TRAN-RECORDS.                     CUSTUPDT
    IF THERE-ARE-NO-MORE-TRAN-RECORDS                                   CUSTUPDT
        CLOSE SORTED-CUST-TRANS-INPUT-FILE.                             CUSTUPDT
                                                                        CUSTUPDT
                                                                        CUSTUPDT
                                                                        CUSTUPDT
D001-CHECK-FOR-VALID-CODES.                                             CUSTUPDT
                                                                        CUSTUPDT
    IF TRANSACTION-CODE-TRANSORT1 = TRANSACTION-TYPE-THREE OR           CUSTUPDT
                                  = TRANSACTION-TYPE-FOUR  OR           CUSTUPDT
                                  = TRANSACTION-TYPE-FIVE               CUSTUPDT
        MOVE TRANSACTION-CODE-TRANSORT1 TO                              CUSTUPDT
                TRANSACTION-CODE-CURRENT-REC                            CUSTUPDT
        MOVE CUSTOMER-NUMBER-TRANSORT1 TO                               CUSTUPDT
                CUSTOMER-NUMBER-CURRENT-REC                             CUSTUPDT
        MOVE 'YES' TO IS-TRANSACTION-CODE-VALID                         CUSTUPDT
        IF TRANSACTION-CODE-CURRENT-REC = TRANSACTION-TYPE-FOUR         CUSTUPDT
            MOVE SORTED-TRANS-RECORD-TYPE-1 TO                          CUSTUPDT
                    SORTED-TRANS-RECORD-TYPE-2                          CUSTUPDT
        ELSE                                                            CUSTUPDT
            NEXT SENTENCE                                               CUSTUPDT
    ELSE IF TRANSACTION-CODE-TRANSORT1 = TRANSACTION-TYPE-ONE           CUSTUPDT
        PERFORM D003-READ-SECOND-RECORD                                 CUSTUPDT
        IF A-TRAN-RECORD-WAS-READ                                       CUSTUPDT
            IF TRANSACTION-CODE-TRANSORT2 = TRANSACTION-TYPE-TWO        CUSTUPDT
                    AND CUSTOMER-NUMBER-TRANSORT1 =                     CUSTUPDT
                    CUSTOMER-NUMBER-TRANSORT2                           CUSTUPDT
                MOVE 'YES' TO IS-TRANSACTION-CODE-VALID                 CUSTUPDT
                MOVE TRANSACTION-CODE-TRANSORT1 TO                      CUSTUPDT
                        TRANSACTION-CODE-CURRENT-REC                    CUSTUPDT
                MOVE CUSTOMER-NUMBER-TRANSORT1 TO                       CUSTUPDT
                        CUSTOMER-NUMBER-CURRENT-REC                     CUSTUPDT
            ELSE                                                        CUSTUPDT
                MOVE CUSTOMER-NUMBER-TRANSORT1 TO                       CUSTUPDT
                        CUSTOMER-NUMBER-RPTWORK                         CUSTUPDT
                MOVE CUSTOMER-RECORDS-FIELD-MSG TO                      CUSTUPDT
                        FIELD-CHANGED-ERROR-RPTWORK                     CUSTUPDT
                MOVE TYPE1-BUT-NO-TYPE2-ERROR-MSG TO                    CUSTUPDT
                        TYPE-OF-ERROR-RPTWORK                           CUSTUPDT
```

Figure 6-62 Source Listing (Part 9 of 19)

```
14                  19.16.07        SEP  5,1978

                    PERFORM U000-WRITE-TRANSACTION-REPORT              CUSTUPDT
                    MOVE SORTED-TRANS-RECORD-TYPE-2 TO                 CUSTUPDT
                         SORTED-TRANS-RECORD-TYPE-1                    CUSTUPDT
               ELSE                                                    CUSTUPDT
                   MOVE CUSTOMER-NUMBER-TRANSORT1 TO                   CUSTUPDT
                        CUSTOMER-NUMBER-RPTWORK                        CUSTUPDT
                   MOVE CUSTOMER-RECORDS-FIELD-MSG TO                  CUSTUPDT
                        FIELD-CHANGED-ERROR-RPTWORK                    CUSTUPDT
                   MOVE TYPE1-BUT-NO-TYPE2-ERROR-MSG TO                CUSTUPDT
                        TYPE-OF-ERROR-RPTWORK                          CUSTUPDT
                   PERFORM U000-WRITE-TRANSACTION-REPORT               CUSTUPDT
           ELSE IF TRANSACTION-CODE-TRANSORT1 = TRANSACTION-TYPE-TWO   CUSTUPDT
               MOVE CUSTOMER-NUMBER-TRANSORT1 TO                       CUSTUPDT
                    CUSTOMER-NUMBER-RPTWORK                            CUSTUPDT
               MOVE CUSTOMER-RECORDS-FIELD-MSG TO                      CUSTUPDT
                    FIELD-CHANGED-ERROR-RPTWORK                        CUSTUPDT
               MOVE TYPE2-BUT-NO-TYPE1-ERROR-MSG TO                    CUSTUPDT
                    TYPE-OF-ERROR-RPTWORK                              CUSTUPDT
               PERFORM U000-WRITE-TRANSACTION-REPORT                   CUSTUPDT
               PERFORM D002-READ-FIRST-RECORD                          CUSTUPDT
           ELSE                                                        CUSTUPDT
               MOVE CUSTOMER-NUMBER-TRANSORT1 TO                       CUSTUPDT
                    CUSTOMER-NUMBER-RPTWORK                            CUSTUPDT
               MOVE TRANSACTION-CODE-FIELD-MSG TO                      CUSTUPDT
                    FIELD-CHANGED-ERROR-RPTWORK                        CUSTUPDT
               MOVE BAD-TRANS-CODE-ERROR-MSG TO                        CUSTUPDT
                    TYPE-OF-ERROR-RPTWORK                              CUSTUPDT
               PERFORM U000-WRITE-TRANSACTION-REPORT                   CUSTUPDT
               PERFORM D002-READ-FIRST-RECORD.                         CUSTUPDT
                                                                       CUSTUPDT
                                                                       CUSTUPDT
                                                                       CUSTUPDT
       D002-READ-FIRST-RECORD.                                         CUSTUPDT
                                                                       CUSTUPDT
           READ SORTED-CUST-TRANS-INPUT-FILE                           CUSTUPDT
                INTO SORTED-TRANS-RECORD-TYPE-1                        CUSTUPDT
                AT END                                                 CUSTUPDT
                    MOVE 'NO ' TO ARE-THERE-MORE-TRAN-RECORDS.         CUSTUPDT
                                                                       CUSTUPDT
                                                                       CUSTUPDT
                                                                       CUSTUPDT
       D003-READ-SECOND-RECORD.                                        CUSTUPDT
                                                                       CUSTUPDT
           READ SORTED-CUST-TRANS-INPUT-FILE                           CUSTUPDT
                INTO SORTED-TRANS-RECORD-TYPE-2                        CUSTUPDT
                AT END                                                 CUSTUPDT
                    MOVE 'NO ' TO ARE-THERE-MORE-TRAN-RECORDS.         CUSTUPDT
```

Figure 6-63 Source Listing (Part 10 of 19)

```
15                        19.16.07        SEP  5,1978

      ***************************************************************** CUSTUPDT
      *                                                               * CUSTUPDT
      *  THE FUNCTION OF THIS MODULE IS TO EDIT A TYPE 1 TRANSACTION. * CUSTUPDT
      *  IT IS ENTERED FROM AND EXITS TO THE C000-OBTAIN-VALID-TRANS- * CUSTUPDT
      *  DATA MODULE.                                                 * CUSTUPDT
      *                                                               * CUSTUPDT
      ***************************************************************** CUSTUPDT
                                                                        CUSTUPDT
       D010-EDIT-TYPE-1-RECORD.                                         CUSTUPDT
                                                                        CUSTUPDT
           COPY EDTYP1                                                  CUSTUPDT
                REPLACING CUSTOMER-NUMBER-EXCP-WORK BY                  CUSTUPDT
                                CUSTOMER-NUMBER-RPTWORK                 CUSTUPDT
                          FIELD-IN-ERROR-EXCP-WORK BY                   CUSTUPDT
                                FIELD-CHANGED-ERROR-RPTWORK             CUSTUPDT
                          TYPE-OF-ERROR-EXCP-WORK BY                    CUSTUPDT
                                TYPE-OF-ERROR-RPTWORK                   CUSTUPDT
                          U000-WRITE-EXCEPTION-REPORT BY                CUSTUPDT
                                U000-WRITE-TRANSACTION-REPORT.          CUSTUPDT
C                                                                       LOADCUST
C          MOVE CUSTOMER-NUMBER-TRANSORT1 TO CUSTOMER-NUMBER-WORK.      LOADCUST
C          PERFORM U020-EDIT-CUSTOMER-NUMBER.                           LOADCUST
C          IF CUSTOMER-NAME-TRANSORT1 = SPACES                          LOADCUST
C              MOVE CUSTOMER-NUMBER-TRANSORT1 TO                        LOADCUST
C                      CUSTOMER-NUMBER-RPTWORK                          LOADCUST
C              MOVE CUSTOMER-NAME-FIELD-MSG TO                          LOADCUST
C                      FIELD-CHANGED-ERROR-RPTWORK                      LOADCUST
C              MOVE BLANK-FIELD-ERROR-MSG TO TYPE-OF-ERROR-RPTWORK      LOADCUST
C              PERFORM U000-WRITE-TRANSACTION-REPORT                    LOADCUST
C              MOVE 'NO ' TO ARE-TRAN-RECORDS-VALID.                    LOADCUST
C          IF CUSTOMER-ADDRESS-TRANSORT1 = SPACES                       LOADCUST
C              MOVE CUSTOMER-NUMBER-TRANSORT1 TO                        LOADCUST
C                      CUSTOMER-NUMBER-RPTWORK                          LOADCUST
C              MOVE CUSTOMER-ADDRESS-FIELD-MSG TO                       LOADCUST
C                      FIELD-CHANGED-ERROR-RPTWORK                      LOADCUST
C              MOVE BLANK-FIELD-ERROR-MSG TO TYPE-OF-ERROR-RPTWORK      LOADCUST
C              PERFORM U000-WRITE-TRANSACTION-REPORT                    LOADCUST
C              MOVE 'NO ' TO ARE-TRAN-RECORDS-VALID.                    LOADCUST
C          IF CUSTOMER-CITY-TRANSORT1 = SPACES                          LOADCUST
C              MOVE CUSTOMER-NUMBER-TRANSORT1 TO                        LOADCUST
C                      CUSTOMER-NUMBER-RPTWORK                          LOADCUST
C              MOVE CUSTOMER-CITY-FIELD-MSG TO                          LOADCUST
C                      FIELD-CHANGED-ERROR-RPTWORK                      LOADCUST
C              MOVE BLANK-FIELD-ERROR-MSG TO TYPE-OF-ERROR-RPTWORK      LOADCUST
C              PERFORM U000-WRITE-TRANSACTION-REPORT                    LOADCUST
C              MOVE 'NO ' TO ARE-TRAN-RECORDS-VALID.                    LOADCUST
C          SEARCH ALL VALID-STATE-TABLE                                 LOADCUST
C                AT END                                                 LOADCUST
C                    MOVE CUSTOMER-NUMBER-TRANSORT1 TO                  LOADCUST
C                            CUSTOMER-NUMBER-RPTWORK                    LOADCUST
C                    MOVE CUSTOMER-STATE-FIELD-MSG TO                   LOADCUST
C                            FIELD-CHANGED-ERROR-RPTWORK                LOADCUST
C                    MOVE BAD-STATE-CODE-ERROR-MSG TO                   LOADCUST
C                            TYPE-OF-ERROR-RPTWORK                      LOADCUST
C                    PERFORM U000-WRITE-TRANSACTION-REPORT              LOADCUST
C                    MOVE 'NO ' TO ARE-TRAN-RECORDS-VALID               LOADCUST
C                WHEN STATE-CODE (STATE-CODE-INDEX) =                   LOADCUST
C                        CUSTOMER-STATE-TRANSORT1                       LOADCUST
C                    NEXT SENTENCE.                                     LOADCUST
C          IF CUSTOMER-ZIP-CODE-TRANSORT1 IS NOT NUMERIC                LOADCUST
C              MOVE CUSTOMER-NUMBER-TRANSORT1 TO                        LOADCUST
C                      CUSTOMER-NUMBER-RPTWORK                          LOADCUST
C              MOVE CUSTOMER-ZIP-CODE-FIELD-MSG TO                      LOADCUST
C                      FIELD-CHANGED-ERROR-RPTWORK                      LOADCUST
C              MOVE FIELD-NOT-NUMERIC-ERROR-MSG TO                      LOADCUST
C                      TYPE-OF-ERROR-RPTWORK                            LOADCUST
C              PERFORM U000-WRITE-TRANSACTION-REPORT                    LOADCUST
C              MOVE 'NO ' TO ARE-TRAN-RECORDS-VALID.
```

Figure 6-64 Source Listing (Part 11 of 19)

```
16                        19.16.07          SEP  5,1978

  034070***************************************************************** CUSTUPDT
  034080*                                                               * CUSTUPDT
  034090*  THE FUNCTION OF THIS MODULE IS TO EDIT A TYPE 2 TRANSACTION.* CUSTUPDT
  034100*  IT IS ENTERED FROM AND EXITS TO THE C000-OBTAIN-VALID-TRANS-* CUSTUPDT
  034110*  DATA MODULE.                                                 * CUSTUPDT
  034120*                                                               * CUSTUPDT
  034130***************************************************************** CUSTUPDT
  034140                                                                  CUSTUPDT
  034150 D020-EDIT-TYPE-2-RECORD.                                         CUSTUPDT
  034160                                                                  CUSTUPDT
  034170     COPY EDTYP2                                                  CUSTUPDT
  034180            REPLACING CUSTOMER-NUMBER-EXCP-WORK BY                CUSTUPDT
  034190                          CUSTOMER-NUMBER-RPTWORK                 CUSTUPDT
  034200                     FIELD-IN-ERROR-EXCP-WORK BY                  CUSTUPDT
  035010                          FIELD-CHANGED-ERROR-RPTWORK             CUSTUPDT
  035020                     TYPE-OF-ERROR-EXCP-WORK BY                   CUSTUPDT
  035030                          TYPE-OF-ERROR-RPTWORK                   CUSTUPDT
  035040                     U000-WRITE-EXCEPTION-REPORT BY               CUSTUPDT
  035050                          U000-WRITE-TRANSACTION-REPORT.          CUSTUPDT
C*034160                                                                  LOADCUST
C 034170     MOVE CUSTOMER-NUMBER-TRANSORT2 TO CUSTOMER-NUMBER-WORK.      LOADCUST
C 034180     PERFORM U020-EDIT-CUSTOMER-NUMBER.                           LOADCUST
C 034190     IF CUSTOMER-DISCOUNT-TRANSORT2 IS NOT NUMERIC                LOADCUST
C 034200         MOVE CUSTOMER-NUMBER-TRANSORT2 TO                        LOADCUST
C 034210                 CUSTOMER-NUMBER-RPTWORK                          LOADCUST
C 035010         MOVE CUSTOMER-DISCOUNT-FIELD-MSG TO                      LOADCUST
C 035020                 FIELD-CHANGED-ERROR-RPTWORK                      LOADCUST
C 035030         MOVE FIELD-NOT-NUMERIC-ERROR-MSG TO                      LOADCUST
C 035040                 TYPE-OF-ERROR-RPTWORK                            LOADCUST
C 035050         PERFORM U000-WRITE-TRANSACTION-REPORT                    LOADCUST
C 035060         MOVE 'NO ' TO ARE-TRAN-RECORDS-VALID                     LOADCUST
C 035070     ELSE                                                         LOADCUST
C 035080         IF CUSTOMER-DISCOUNT-TRANSORT2 IS GREATER THAN           LOADCUST
C 035090                 MAXIMUM-DISCOUNT-PERCENT                         LOADCUST
C 035100             MOVE CUSTOMER-NUMBER-TRANSORT2 TO                    LOADCUST
C 035110                     CUSTOMER-NUMBER-RPTWORK                      LOADCUST
C 035120             MOVE CUSTOMER-DISCOUNT-FIELD-MSG TO                  LOADCUST
C 035130                     FIELD-CHANGED-ERROR-RPTWORK                  LOADCUST
C 035140             MOVE BAD-DISCOUNT-ERROR-MSG TO                       LOADCUST
C 035150                     TYPE-OF-ERROR-RPTWORK                        LOADCUST
C 035160             PERFORM U000-WRITE-TRANSACTION-REPORT                LOADCUST
C 035170             MOVE 'NO ' TO ARE-TRAN-RECORDS-VALID.                LOADCUST
C 035180     IF LAST-ACTIVITY-DATE-TRANSORT2 IS NOT NUMERIC               LOADCUST
C 035190         MOVE CUSTOMER-NUMBER-TRANSORT2 TO                        LOADCUST
C 035200                 CUSTOMER-NUMBER-RPTWORK                          LOADCUST
C 036010         MOVE LAST-ACTIVITY-DATE-FIELD-MSG TO                     LOADCUST
C 036020                 FIELD-CHANGED-ERROR-RPTWORK                      LOADCUST
C 036030         MOVE FIELD-NOT-NUMERIC-ERROR-MSG TO                      LOADCUST
C 036040                 TYPE-OF-ERROR-RPTWORK                            LOADCUST
C 036050         PERFORM U000-WRITE-TRANSACTION-REPORT                    LOADCUST
C 036060         MOVE 'NO ' TO ARE-TRAN-RECORDS-VALID                     LOADCUST
C 036070     ELSE                                                         LOADCUST
C 036080         IF NOT VALID-MONTH                                       LOADCUST
C 036110             MOVE CUSTOMER-NUMBER-TRANSORT2 TO                    LOADCUST
C 036120                     CUSTOMER-NUMBER-RPTWORK                      LOADCUST
C 036130             MOVE LAST-ACTIVITY-DATE-FIELD-MSG TO                 LOADCUST
C 036140                     FIELD-CHANGED-ERROR-RPTWORK                  LOADCUST
C 036150             MOVE BAD-MONTH-ERROR-MSG TO TYPE-OF-ERROR-RPTWORK    LOADCUST
C 036160             PERFORM U000-WRITE-TRANSACTION-REPORT                LOADCUST
C 036170             MOVE 'NO ' TO ARE-TRAN-RECORDS-VALID                 LOADCUST
C 036180         ELSE                                                     LOADCUST
C 036190             SET MONTH-DAY-INDEX TO MONTH-LAST-ACTIVITY-TRANSORT2 LOADCUST
C 036200             IF DAY-LAST-ACTIVITY-TRANSORT2 IS LESS THAN          LOADCUST
C 037010                     FIRST-DAY-OF-MONTH-NUMBER OR                 LOADCUST
C 037020                     DAY-LAST-ACTIVITY-TRANSORT2 IS GREATER THAN  LOADCUST
C 037030                     NUMBER-OF-DAYS-IN-MONTH (MONTH-DAY-INDEX)    LOADCUST
C 037040                 MOVE CUSTOMER-NUMBER-TRANSORT2 TO                LOADCUST
C 037050                         CUSTOMER-NUMBER-RPTWORK                  LOADCUST
C 037060                 MOVE LAST-ACTIVITY-DATE-FIELD-MSG TO             LOADCUST
C 037070                         FIELD-CHANGED-ERROR-RPTWORK              LOADCUST
C 037080                 MOVE BAD-DAY-ERROR-MSG TO TYPE-OF-ERROR-RPTWORK  LOADCUST
C 037090                 PERFORM U000-WRITE-TRANSACTION-REPORT            LOADCUST
C 037100                 MOVE 'NO ' TO ARE-TRAN-RECORDS-VALID.            LOADCUST
```

Figure 6-65 Source Listing (Part 12 of 19)

```
17                    19.16.07         SEP  5,1978

035070*****************************************************************  CUSTUPDT
035080*                                                               *  CUSTUPDT
035090*   THIS MODULE EDITS A TYPE 3 TRANSACTION RECORD. IT IS         *  CUSTUPDT
035100*   ENTERED FROM AND EXITS TO THE C000-OBTAIN-VALID-TRANS-DATA   *  CUSTUPDT
035110*   MODULE.                                                      *  CUSTUPDT
035120*                                                               *  CUSTUPDT
035130*****************************************************************  CUSTUPDT
035140                                                                    CUSTUPDT
035150 D030-EDIT-TYPE-3-RECORD.                                          CUSTUPDT
035160                                                                    CUSTUPDT
035170     MOVE CUSTOMER-NUMBER-TRANSORT1 TO CUSTOMER-NUMBER-WORK.        CUSTUPDT
035180     PERFORM U020-EDIT-CUSTOMER-NUMBER.                             CUSTUPDT
035190     IF CUSTOMER-STATE-TRANSORT1 NOT = SPACES                       CUSTUPDT
035200         MOVE CUSTOMER-NUMBER-TRANSORT1 TO                          CUSTUPDT
035210             CUSTOMER-NUMBER-STATEDIT-WORK                          CUSTUPDT
035220         MOVE CUSTOMER-STATE-TRANSORT1 TO                           CUSTUPDT
035230             STATE-EDIT-WORK                                        CUSTUPDT
035240         PERFORM E010-EDIT-STATE-CODE                               CUSTUPDT
036010         IF CUSTOMER-ZIP-CODE-TRANSORT1 = SPACES                    CUSTUPDT
036020             MOVE CUSTOMER-NUMBER-TRANSORT1 TO                      CUSTUPDT
036030                 CUSTOMER-NUMBER-RPTWORK                            CUSTUPDT
036040             MOVE CUSTOMER-ZIP-CODE-FIELD-MSG TO                    CUSTUPDT
036050                 FIELD-CHANGED-ERROR-RPTWORK                        CUSTUPDT
036060             MOVE STATE-BUT-NO-ZIP-ERROR-MSG TO                     CUSTUPDT
036070                 TYPE-OF-ERROR-RPTWORK                              CUSTUPDT
036080             PERFORM U000-WRITE-TRANSACTION-REPORT                  CUSTUPDT
036090             MOVE 'NO ' TO ARE-TRAN-RECORDS-VALID.                  CUSTUPDT
036100     IF CUSTOMER-ZIP-CODE-TRANSORT1 NOT = SPACES AND                CUSTUPDT
036110             CUSTOMER-ZIP-CODE-TRANSORT1 IS NOT NUMERIC             CUSTUPDT
036120         MOVE CUSTOMER-NUMBER-TRANSORT1 TO                          CUSTUPDT
036130             CUSTOMER-NUMBER-RPTWORK                                CUSTUPDT
036140         MOVE CUSTOMER-ZIP-CODE-FIELD-MSG TO                        CUSTUPDT
036150             FIELD-CHANGED-ERROR-RPTWORK                            CUSTUPDT
036160         MOVE FIELD-NOT-NUMERIC-ERROR-MSG TO                        CUSTUPDT
036170             TYPE-OF-ERROR-RPTWORK                                  CUSTUPDT
036180         PERFORM U000-WRITE-TRANSACTION-REPORT                      CUSTUPDT
036190         MOVE 'NO ' TO ARE-TRAN-RECORDS-VALID.                      CUSTUPDT
```

```
18                    19.16.07         SEP  5,1978

037010*****************************************************************  CUSTUPDT
037020*                                                               *  CUSTUPDT
037030*   THIS MODULE EDITS A TYPE 4 TRANSACTION RECORD. IT IS ENTERED*  CUSTUPDT
037040*   FROM AND EXITS TO THE C000-OBTAIN-VALID-TRANS-DATA MODULE.  *  CUSTUPDT
037050*                                                               *  CUSTUPDT
037060*****************************************************************  CUSTUPDT
037070                                                                    CUSTUPDT
037080 D040-EDIT-TYPE-4-RECORD.                                          CUSTUPDT
037090                                                                    CUSTUPDT
037100     MOVE CUSTOMER-NUMBER-TRANSORT2 TO CUSTOMER-NUMBER-WORK.        CUSTUPDT
037110     PERFORM U020-EDIT-CUSTOMER-NUMBER.                             CUSTUPDT
037120     IF CUSTOMER-DISCOUNT-TRANSORT2 NOT = SPACES                    CUSTUPDT
037130         MOVE CUSTOMER-NUMBER-TRANSORT2 TO                          CUSTUPDT
037140             CUSTOMER-NUMBER-DISCEDIT-WORK                          CUSTUPDT
037150         MOVE CUSTOMER-DISCOUNT-TRANSORT2 TO                        CUSTUPDT
037160             DISCOUNT-EDIT-WORK                                     CUSTUPDT
037170         PERFORM E020-EDIT-DISCOUNT.                                CUSTUPDT
037180     IF LAST-ACTIVITY-DATE-TRANSORT2 NOT = SPACES                   CUSTUPDT
037190         MOVE CUSTOMER-NUMBER-TRANSORT2 TO                          CUSTUPDT
037200             CUSTOMER-NUMBER-DATEDIT-WORK                           CUSTUPDT
038010         MOVE LAST-ACTIVITY-DATE-TRANSORT2 TO                       CUSTUPDT
038020             LAST-ACTIVITY-EDIT-WORK                                CUSTUPDT
038030         PERFORM E030-EDIT-LAST-ACTIVITY-DATE.                      CUSTUPDT
```

Figure 6-66 Source Listing (Part 13 of 19)

```
19                   19.16.07        SEP  5,1978

038050*****************************************************************    CUSTUPDT
038060*                                                               *    CUSTUPDT
038070*  THIS MODULE PROCESSES CHANGE TRANSACTIONS. IT IS ENTERED     *    CUSTUPDT
038080*  FROM AND EXITS TO THE C010-PROCESS-EQUAL-RECORDS MODULE.     *    CUSTUPDT
038090*                                                               *    CUSTUPDT
038100*****************************************************************    CUSTUPDT
038110                                                                     CUSTUPDT
038120 D050-PROCESS-CHANGE-TRANS.                                          CUSTUPDT
038130                                                                     CUSTUPDT
038140     IF TRANSACTION-CODE-CURRENT-REC = TRANSACTION-TYPE-THREE        CUSTUPDT
038150         PERFORM D051-CHECK-TYPE-THREE-TRANS                         CUSTUPDT
038160     ELSE                                                            CUSTUPDT
038170         PERFORM D052-CHECK-TYPE-FOUR-TRANS.                         CUSTUPDT
038180                                                                     CUSTUPDT
038190                                                                     CUSTUPDT
038200                                                                     CUSTUPDT
039010 D051-CHECK-TYPE-THREE-TRANS.                                        CUSTUPDT
039020                                                                     CUSTUPDT
039030     MOVE CUSTOMER-NUMBER-CURRENT-REC TO                             CUSTUPDT
039040             CUSTOMER-NUMBER-TYPE-3-CHANGE.                          CUSTUPDT
039050     IF CUSTOMER-ADDRESS-TRANSORT1 NOT = SPACES                      CUSTUPDT
039060         MOVE CUSTOMER-ADDRESS-TRANSORT1 TO ADDRESS-CHANGE-WORK      CUSTUPDT
039070         PERFORM E040-CHANGE-CUSTOMER-ADDRESS.                       CUSTUPDT
039080     IF CUSTOMER-CITY-TRANSORT1 NOT = SPACES                         CUSTUPDT
039090         MOVE CUSTOMER-CITY-TRANSORT1 TO CITY-CHANGE-WORK            CUSTUPDT
039100         PERFORM E050-CHANGE-CUSTOMER-CITY.                          CUSTUPDT
039110     IF CUSTOMER-STATE-TRANSORT1 NOT = SPACES                        CUSTUPDT
039120         MOVE CUSTOMER-STATE-TRANSORT1 TO STATE-CHANGE-WORK          CUSTUPDT
039130         PERFORM E060-CHANGE-CUSTOMER-STATE.                         CUSTUPDT
039140     IF CUSTOMER-ZIP-CODE-TRANSORT1 NOT = SPACES                     CUSTUPDT
039150         MOVE CUSTOMER-ZIP-CODE-TRANSORT1 TO ZIP-CODE-CHANGE-WORK    CUSTUPDT
039160         PERFORM E070-CHANGE-CUSTOMER-ZIP-CODE.                      CUSTUPDT
039170                                                                     CUSTUPDT
039180                                                                     CUSTUPDT
039190                                                                     CUSTUPDT
039200 D052-CHECK-TYPE-FOUR-TRANS.                                         CUSTUPDT
040010                                                                     CUSTUPDT
040020     MOVE CUSTOMER-NUMBER-CURRENT-REC TO                             CUSTUPDT
040030             CUSTOMER-NUMBER-TYPE-4-CHANGE.                          CUSTUPDT
040040     IF CUSTOMER-DISCOUNT-TRANSORT2 NOT = SPACES                     CUSTUPDT
040050         MOVE CUSTOMER-DISCOUNT-TRANSORT2 TO DISCOUNT-CHANGE-WORK    CUSTUPDT
040060         PERFORM E080-CHANGE-CUSTOMER-DISCOUNT.                      CUSTUPDT
040070     IF LAST-ACTIVITY-DATE-TRANSORT2 NOT = SPACES                    CUSTUPDT
040080         MOVE LAST-ACTIVITY-DATE-TRANSORT2 TO                        CUSTUPDT
040090                 LAST-ACTIVITY-CHANGE-WORK                           CUSTUPDT
040100         PERFORM E090-CHANGE-LAST-ACTIVITY-DATE.                     CUSTUPDT
```

```
20                   19.16.07        SEP  5,1978

040120*****************************************************************    CUSTUPDT
040130*                                                               *    CUSTUPDT
040140*  THIS MODULE SORTS THE TRANSACTION INPUT FILE INTO            *    CUSTUPDT
040150*  TRANSACTION CODE WITHIN CUSTOMER NUMBER SEQUENCE. IT IS      *    CUSTUPDT
040160*  ENTERED FROM AND EXITS TO THE D000-OBTAIN-TRANS-RECORDS      *    CUSTUPDT
040170*  MODULE.                                                      *    CUSTUPDT
040180*                                                               *    CUSTUPDT
040190*****************************************************************    CUSTUPDT
040200                                                                     CUSTUPDT
040210 E000-SORT-TRANSACTION-RECORDS.                                      CUSTUPDT
041010                                                                     CUSTUPDT
041020     SORT TRANSACTION-SORT-WORK-FILE                                 CUSTUPDT
041030             ON ASCENDING KEY CUSTOMER-NUMBER-SORTREC                CUSTUPDT
041040                              TRANSACTION-CODE-SORTREC               CUSTUPDT
041050             USING  CUSTOMER-TRANS-INPUT-FILE                        CUSTUPDT
041060             GIVING SORTED-CUST-TRANS-INPUT-FILE.                    CUSTUPDT
```

Figure 6-67 Source Listing (Part 14 of 19)

```
  21                    19.16.07        SEP  5,1978

  041080************************************************************** CUSTUPDT
  041090*                                                            * CUSTUPDT
  041100*  THIS MODULE IS ENTERED TO EDIT THE STATE CODE. IT IS      * CUSTUPDT
  041110*  ENTERED FROM AND EXITS TO THE D030-EDIT-TYPE-3-RECORD     * CUSTUPDT
  041120*  MODULE.                                                   * CUSTUPDT
  041130*                                                            * CUSTUPDT
  041140************************************************************** CUSTUPDT
  041150                                                               CUSTUPDT
  041160 E010-EDIT-STATE-CODE.                                         CUSTUPDT
  041170                                                               CUSTUPDT
  041180     COPY EDSTCODE                                             CUSTUPDT
  041190          REPLACING CUSTOMER-NUMBER-TRANSORT1 BY               CUSTUPDT
  041200                        CUSTOMER-NUMBER-STATEDIT-WORK          CUSTUPDT
  042010                 CUSTOMER-NUMBER-EXCP-WORK BY                  CUSTUPDT
  042020                        CUSTOMER-NUMBER-RPTWORK                CUSTUPDT
  042030                 FIELD-IN-ERROR-EXCP-WORK BY                   CUSTUPDT
  042040                        FIELD-CHANGED-ERROR-RPTWORK            CUSTUPDT
  042050                 TYPE-OF-ERROR-EXCP-WORK BY                    CUSTUPDT
  042060                        TYPE-OF-ERROR-RPTWORK                  CUSTUPDT
  042070                 U000-WRITE-EXCEPTION-REPORT BY                CUSTUPDT
  042080                        U000-WRITE-TRANSACTION-REPORT          CUSTUPDT
  042090                 CUSTOMER-STATE-TRANSORT1 BY                   CUSTUPDT
  042100                        STATE-EDIT-WORK.                       CUSTUPDT
C*033040     SEARCH ALL VALID-STATE-TABLE                              LOADCUST
C 033050          AT END                                               LOADCUST
C 033060              MOVE CUSTOMER-NUMBER-STATEDIT-WORK TO            LOADCUST
C 033070                      CUSTOMER-NUMBER-RPTWORK                  LOADCUST
C 033080              MOVE CUSTOMER-STATE-FIELD-MSG TO                 LOADCUST
C 033090                      FIELD-CHANGED-ERROR-RPTWORK              LOADCUST
C 033100              MOVE BAD-STATE-CODE-ERROR-MSG TO                 LOADCUST
C 033110                      TYPE-OF-ERROR-RPTWORK                    LOADCUST
C 033120              PERFORM U000-WRITE-TRANSACTION-REPORT            LOADCUST
C 033130              MOVE 'NO ' TO ARE-TRAN-RECORDS-VALID             LOADCUST
C 033140          WHEN STATE-CODE (STATE-CODE-INDEX) =                 LOADCUST
C 033150                  STATE-EDIT-WORK                              LOADCUST
C 033160              NEXT SENTENCE.                                   LOADCUST

  22                    19.16.07        SEP  5,1978

  042120************************************************************** CUSTUPDT
  042130*                                                            * CUSTUPDT
  042140*  THIS MODULE EDITS THE CUSTOMER DISCOUNT. IT IS ENTERED FROM * CUSTUPDT
  042150*  AND EXITS TO THE D040-EDIT-TYPE-4-RECORD MODULE.          * CUSTUPDT
  042160*                                                            * CUSTUPDT
  042170************************************************************** CUSTUPDT
  042180                                                               CUSTUPDT
  042190 E020-EDIT-DISCOUNT.                                           CUSTUPDT
  042200                                                               CUSTUPDT
  043010     COPY EDDISC                                               CUSTUPDT
  043020          REPLACING CUSTOMER-DISCOUNT-TRANSORT2 BY             CUSTUPDT
  043030                        DISCOUNT-EDIT-WORK                     CUSTUPDT
  043040                 CUSTOMER-NUMBER-TRANSORT2 BY                  CUSTUPDT
  043050                        CUSTOMER-NUMBER-DISCEDIT-WORK          CUSTUPDT
  043060                 CUSTOMER-NUMBER-EXCP-WORK BY                  CUSTUPDT
  043070                        CUSTOMER-NUMBER-RPTWORK                CUSTUPDT
  043080                 FIELD-IN-ERROR-EXCP-WORK BY                   CUSTUPDT
  043090                        FIELD-CHANGED-ERROR-RPTWORK            CUSTUPDT
  043100                 TYPE-OF-ERROR-EXCP-WORK BY                    CUSTUPDT
  043110                        TYPE-OF-ERROR-RPTWORK                  CUSTUPDT
  043120                 U000-WRITE-EXCEPTION-REPORT BY                CUSTUPDT
  043130                        U000-WRITE-TRANSACTION-REPORT.         CUSTUPDT
C*034190     IF DISCOUNT-EDIT-WORK IS NOT NUMERIC                      LOADCUST
C 034200         MOVE CUSTOMER-NUMBER-DISCEDIT-WORK TO                 LOADCUST
C 034210                 CUSTOMER-NUMBER-RPTWORK                       LOADCUST
C 035010         MOVE CUSTOMER-DISCOUNT-FIELD-MSG TO                   LOADCUST
C 035020                 FIELD-CHANGED-ERROR-RPTWORK                   LOADCUST
C 035030         MOVE FIELD-NOT-NUMERIC-ERROR-MSG TO                   LOADCUST
C 035040                 TYPE-OF-ERROR-RPTWORK                         LOADCUST
C 035050         PERFORM U000-WRITE-TRANSACTION-REPORT                 LOADCUST
C 035060         MOVE 'NO ' TO ARE-TRAN-RECORDS-VALID                  LOADCUST
C 035070     ELSE                                                      LOADCUST
C 035080         IF DISCOUNT-EDIT-WORK IS GREATER THAN                 LOADCUST
C 035090                 MAXIMUM-DISCOUNT-PERCENT                      LOADCUST
C 035100             MOVE CUSTOMER-NUMBER-DISCEDIT-WORK TO             LOADCUST
C 035110                     CUSTOMER-NUMBER-RPTWORK                   LOADCUST
C 035120             MOVE CUSTOMER-DISCOUNT-FIELD-MSG TO               LOADCUST
C 035130                     FIELD-CHANGED-ERROR-RPTWORK               LOADCUST
C 035140             MOVE BAD-DISCOUNT-ERROR-MSG TO                    LOADCUST
C 035150                     TYPE-OF-ERROR-RPTWORK                     LOADCUST
C 035160             PERFORM U000-WRITE-TRANSACTION-REPORT             LOADCUST
C 035170             MOVE 'NO ' TO ARE-TRAN-RECORDS-VALID.             LOADCUST
```

Figure 6-68 Source Listing (Part 15 of 19)

```
23                     19.16.07        SEP  5,1978

043150*****************************************************************  CUSTUPDT
043160*                                                               *  CUSTUPDT
043170*  THIS MODULE EDITS THE LAST ACTIVITY DATE. IT IS ENTERED FROM*  CUSTUPDT
043180*  AND EXITS TO THE D040-EDIT-TYPE-4 RECORD MODULE.             *  CUSTUPDT
043190*                                                               *  CUSTUPDT
043200*****************************************************************  CUSTUPDT
043210                                                                   CUSTUPDT
044010 E030-EDIT-LAST-ACTIVITY-DATE.                                     CUSTUPDT
044020                                                                   CUSTUPDT
044030     COPY EDACDATE                                                 CUSTUPDT
044040         REPLACING LAST-ACTIVITY-DATE-TRANSORT2 BY                 CUSTUPDT
044050                   LAST-ACTIVITY-EDIT-WORK                         CUSTUPDT
044060               CUSTOMER-NUMBER-TRANSORT2 BY                        CUSTUPDT
044070                   CUSTOMER-NUMBER-DATEDIT-WORK                    CUSTUPDT
044080               VALID-MONTH BY VALID-MONTH-WORK                     CUSTUPDT
044090               MONTH-LAST-ACTIVITY-TRANSORT2 BY                    CUSTUPDT
044100                   MONTH-LAST-ACTIVITY-WORK                        CUSTUPDT
044110               DAY-LAST-ACTIVITY-TRANSORT2 BY                      CUSTUPDT
044120                   DAY-LAST-ACTIVITY-WORK                          CUSTUPDT
044130               CUSTOMER-NUMBER-EXCP-WORK BY                        CUSTUPDT
044140                   CUSTOMER-NUMBER-RPTWORK                         CUSTUPDT
044150               FIELD-IN-ERROR-EXCP-WORK BY                         CUSTUPDT
044160                   FIELD-CHANGED-ERROR-RPTWORK                     CUSTUPDT
044170               TYPE-OF-ERROR-EXCP-WORK BY                          CUSTUPDT
044180                   TYPE-OF-ERROR-RPTWORK                           CUSTUPDT
044190               U000-WRITE-EXCEPTION-REPORT BY                      CUSTUPDT
044200                   U000-WRITE-TRANSACTION-REPORT.                  CUSTUPDT
C*035180     IF LAST-ACTIVITY-EDIT-WORK IS NOT NUMERIC                  LOADCUST
C 035190         MOVE CUSTOMER-NUMBER-DATEDIT-WORK TO                    LOADCUST
C 035200             CUSTOMER-NUMBER-RPTWORK                             LOADCUST
C 036010         MOVE LAST-ACTIVITY-DATE-FIELD-MSG TO                    LOADCUST
C 036020             FIELD-CHANGED-ERROR-RPTWORK                         LOADCUST
C 036030         MOVE FIELD-NOT-NUMERIC-ERROR-MSG TO                     LOADCUST
C 036040             TYPE-OF-ERROR-RPTWORK                               LOADCUST
C 036050         PERFORM U000-WRITE-TRANSACTION-REPORT                   LOADCUST
C 036060         MOVE 'NO ' TO ARE-TRAN-RECORDS-VALID                    LOADCUST
C 036070     ELSE                                                        LOADCUST
C 036080         IF NOT VALID-MONTH-WORK                                 LOADCUST
C 036110             MOVE CUSTOMER-NUMBER-DATEDIT-WORK TO                LOADCUST
C 036120                 CUSTOMER-NUMBER-RPTWORK                         LOADCUST
C 036130             MOVE LAST-ACTIVITY-DATE-FIELD-MSG TO                LOADCUST
C 036140                 FIELD-CHANGED-ERROR-RPTWORK                     LOADCUST
C 036150             MOVE BAD-MONTH-ERROR-MSG TO TYPE-OF-ERROR-RPTWORK   LOADCUST
C 036160             PERFORM U000-WRITE-TRANSACTION-REPORT               LOADCUST
C 036170             MOVE 'NO ' TO ARE-TRAN-RECORDS-VALID                LOADCUST
C 036180         ELSE                                                    LOADCUST
C 036190             SET MONTH-DAY-INDEX TO MONTH-LAST-ACTIVITY-WORK     LOADCUST
C 036200             IF DAY-LAST-ACTIVITY-WORK IS LESS THAN              LOADCUST
C 037010                     FIRST-DAY-OF-MONTH-NUMBER OR                LOADCUST
C 037020                     DAY-LAST-ACTIVITY-WORK IS GREATER THAN      LOADCUST
C 037030                     NUMBER-OF-DAYS-IN-MONTH (MONTH-DAY-INDEX)   LOADCUST
C 037040                 MOVE CUSTOMER-NUMBER-DATEDIT-WORK TO            LOADCUST
C 037050                     CUSTOMER-NUMBER-RPTWORK                     LOADCUST
C 037060                 MOVE LAST-ACTIVITY-DATE-FIELD-MSG TO            LOADCUST
C 037070                     FIELD-CHANGED-ERROR-RPTWORK                 LOADCUST
C 037080                 MOVE BAD-DAY-ERROR-MSG TO TYPE-OF-ERROR-RPTWORK LOADCUST
C 037090                 PERFORM U000-WRITE-TRANSACTION-REPORT           LOADCUST
C 037100                 MOVE 'NO ' TO ARE-TRAN-RECORDS-VALID.           LOADCUST
```

```
24                     19.16.07        SEP  5,1978

045030*****************************************************************  CUSTUPDT
045040*                                                               *  CUSTUPDT
045050*  THIS MODULE CHANGES THE CUSTOMER ADDRESS. IT IS ENTERED FROM*  CUSTUPDT
045060*  AND EXITS TO THE D050-PROCESS-CHANGE-TRANS MODULE.           *  CUSTUPDT
045070*                                                               *  CUSTUPDT
045080*****************************************************************  CUSTUPDT
045090                                                                   CUSTUPDT
045100 E040-CHANGE-CUSTOMER-ADDRESS.                                     CUSTUPDT
045110                                                                   CUSTUPDT
045120     MOVE CUSTOMER-ADDRESS-MSTRIN-WORK TO                          CUSTUPDT
045130             OLD-MASTER-RECORD-RPTWORK.                            CUSTUPDT
045140     MOVE ADDRESS-CHANGE-WORK TO                                   CUSTUPDT
045150             NEW-MASTER-RECORD-RPTWORK.                            CUSTUPDT
045160     MOVE CUSTOMER-NUMBER-TYPE-3-CHANGE TO                         CUSTUPDT
045170             CUSTOMER-NUMBER-RPTWORK.                              CUSTUPDT
045180     MOVE CUSTOMER-ADDRESS-FIELD-MSG TO                            CUSTUPDT
045190             FIELD-CHANGED-ERROR-RPTWORK.                          CUSTUPDT
045200     MOVE CHANGE-MSG TO ACTION-TAKEN-RPTWORK.                      CUSTUPDT
045210     PERFORM U000-WRITE-TRANSACTION-REPORT.                        CUSTUPDT
046010     MOVE ADDRESS-CHANGE-WORK TO                                   CUSTUPDT
046020             CUSTOMER-ADDRESS-MSTRIN-WORK.                         CUSTUPDT
```

Figure 6-69 Source Listing (Part 16 of 19)

```
25                     19.16.07          SEP  5,1978

046040*****************************************************************  CUSTUPDT
046050*                                                               *  CUSTUPDT
046060*  THIS MODULE CHANGES THE CUSTOMER CITY. IT IS ENTERED FROM    *  CUSTUPDT
046070*  AND EXITS TO THE D050-PROCESS-CHANGE-TRANS MODULE.           *  CUSTUPDT
046080*                                                               *  CUSTUPDT
046090*****************************************************************  CUSTUPDT
046100                                                                   CUSTUPDT
046110 E050-CHANGE-CUSTOMER-CITY.                                        CUSTUPDT
046120                                                                   CUSTUPDT
046130     MOVE CUSTOMER-CITY-MSTRIN-WORK TO                             CUSTUPDT
046140             OLD-MASTER-RECORD-RPTWORK.                            CUSTUPDT
046150     MOVE CITY-CHANGE-WORK TO                                      CUSTUPDT
046160             NEW-MASTER-RECORD-RPTWORK.                            CUSTUPDT
046170     MOVE CUSTOMER-NUMBER-TYPE-3-CHANGE TO                         CUSTUPDT
046180             CUSTOMER-NUMBER-RPTWORK.                              CUSTUPDT
046190     MOVE CUSTOMER-CITY-FIELD-MSG TO                               CUSTUPDT
046200             FIELD-CHANGED-ERROR-RPTWORK.                          CUSTUPDT
046210     MOVE CHANGE-MSG TO ACTION-TAKEN-RPTWORK.                      CUSTUPDT
047010     PERFORM U000-WRITE-TRANSACTION-REPORT.                        CUSTUPDT
047020     MOVE CITY-CHANGE-WORK TO                                      CUSTUPDT
047030             CUSTOMER-CITY-MSTRIN-WORK.                            CUSTUPDT
```

```
26                     19.16.07          SEP  5,1978

047050*****************************************************************  CUSTUPDT
047060*                                                               *  CUSTUPDT
047070*  THIS MODULE CHANGES THE CUSTOMER STATE. IT IS ENTERED FROM   *  CUSTUPDT
047080*  AND EXITS TO THE D050-PROCESS-CHANGE-TRANS MODULE.           *  CUSTUPDT
047090*                                                               *  CUSTUPDT
047100*****************************************************************  CUSTUPDT
047110                                                                   CUSTUPDT
047120 E060-CHANGE-CUSTOMER-STATE.                                       CUSTUPDT
047130                                                                   CUSTUPDT
047140     MOVE CUSTOMER-STATE-MSTRIN-WORK TO                            CUSTUPDT
047150             OLD-MASTER-RECORD-RPTWORK.                            CUSTUPDT
047160     MOVE STATE-CHANGE-WORK TO                                     CUSTUPDT
047170             NEW-MASTER-RECORD-RPTWORK.                            CUSTUPDT
047180     MOVE CUSTOMER-NUMBER-TYPE-3-CHANGE TO                         CUSTUPDT
047190             CUSTOMER-NUMBER-RPTWORK.                              CUSTUPDT
047200     MOVE CUSTOMER-STATE-FIELD-MSG TO                              CUSTUPDT
047210             FIELD-CHANGED-ERROR-RPTWORK.                          CUSTUPDT
048010     MOVE CHANGE-MSG TO ACTION-TAKEN-RPTWORK.                      CUSTUPDT
048020     PERFORM U000-WRITE-TRANSACTION-REPORT.                        CUSTUPDT
048030     MOVE STATE-CHANGE-WORK TO                                     CUSTUPDT
048040             CUSTOMER-STATE-MSTRIN-WORK.                           CUSTUPDT
```

```
27                     19.16.07          SEP  5,1978

048060*****************************************************************  CUSTUPDT
048070*                                                               *  CUSTUPDT
048080*  THIS MODULE CHANGES THE CUSTOMER ZIP CODE. IT IS ENTERED     *  CUSTUPDT
048090*  FROM AND EXITS TO THE D050-PROCESS-CHANGE-TRANS MODULE.      *  CUSTUPDT
048100*                                                               *  CUSTUPDT
048110*****************************************************************  CUSTUPDT
048120                                                                   CUSTUPDT
048130 E070-CHANGE-CUSTOMER-ZIP-CODE.                                    CUSTUPDT
048140                                                                   CUSTUPDT
048150     MOVE CUSTOMER-ZIP-CODE-MSTRIN-WORK TO                         CUSTUPDT
048160             OLD-MASTER-RECORD-RPTWORK.                            CUSTUPDT
048170     MOVE ZIP-CODE-CHANGE-WORK TO                                  CUSTUPDT
048180             NEW-MASTER-RECORD-RPTWORK.                            CUSTUPDT
048190     MOVE CUSTOMER-NUMBER-TYPE-3-CHANGE TO                         CUSTUPDT
048200             CUSTOMER-NUMBER-RPTWORK.                              CUSTUPDT
048210     MOVE CUSTOMER-ZIP-CODE-FIELD-MSG TO                           CUSTUPDT
049010             FIELD-CHANGED-ERROR-RPTWORK.                          CUSTUPDT
049020     MOVE CHANGE-MSG TO ACTION-TAKEN-RPTWORK.                      CUSTUPDT
049030     PERFORM U000-WRITE-TRANSACTION-REPORT.                        CUSTUPDT
049040     MOVE ZIP-CODE-CHANGE-WORK TO                                  CUSTUPDT
049050             CUSTOMER-ZIP-CODE-MSTRIN-WORK.                        CUSTUPDT
```

Figure 6-70 Source Listing (Part 17 of 19)

```
 28                     19.16.07        SEP  5,1978

049070**************************************************************** CUSTUPDT
049080*                                                              * CUSTUPDT
049090*  THIS MODULE CHANGES THE CUSTOMER DISCOUNT. IT IS ENTERED    * CUSTUPDT
049100*  FROM AND EXITS TO THE D050-PROCESS-CHANGE-TRANS MODULE.     * CUSTUPDT
049110*                                                              * CUSTUPDT
049120**************************************************************** CUSTUPDT
049130                                                                 CUSTUPDT
049140 E080-CHANGE-CUSTOMER-DISCOUNT.                                  CUSTUPDT
049150                                                                 CUSTUPDT
049160     MOVE CUSTOMER-DISCOUNT-MSTRIN-WORK TO                       CUSTUPDT
049170             OLD-MASTER-RECORD-RPTWORK.                          CUSTUPDT
049180     MOVE DISCOUNT-CHANGE-WORK TO                                CUSTUPDT
049190             NEW-MASTER-RECORD-RPTWORK.                          CUSTUPDT
049200     MOVE CUSTOMER-NUMBER-TYPE-4-CHANGE TO                       CUSTUPDT
049210             CUSTOMER-NUMBER-RPTWORK.                            CUSTUPDT
050010     MOVE CUSTOMER-DISCOUNT-FIELD-MSG TO                         CUSTUPDT
050020             FIELD-CHANGED-ERROR-RPTWORK.                        CUSTUPDT
050030     MOVE CHANGE-MSG TO ACTION-TAKEN-RPTWORK.                    CUSTUPDT
050040     PERFORM U000-WRITE-TRANSACTION-REPORT.                      CUSTUPDT
050050     MOVE DISCOUNT-CHANGE-WORK TO                                CUSTUPDT
050060             CUSTOMER-DISCOUNT-MSTRIN-WORK.                      CUSTUPDT
```

```
 29                     19.16.07        SEP  5,1978

050080**************************************************************** CUSTUPDT
050090*                                                              * CUSTUPDT
050100*  THIS MODULE CHANGES THE LAST ACTIVITY DATE. IT IS ENTERED   * CUSTUPDT
050110*  FROM AND EXITS TO THE D050-PROCESS-CHANGE-TRANS MODULE.     * CUSTUPDT
050120*                                                              * CUSTUPDT
050130**************************************************************** CUSTUPDT
050140                                                                 CUSTUPDT
050150 E090-CHANGE-LAST-ACTIVITY-DATE.                                 CUSTUPDT
050160                                                                 CUSTUPDT
050170     MOVE LAST-ACTIVITY-MSTRIN-WORK TO                           CUSTUPDT
050180             OLD-MASTER-RECORD-RPTWORK.                          CUSTUPDT
050190     MOVE LAST-ACTIVITY-CHANGE-WORK TO                           CUSTUPDT
050200             NEW-MASTER-RECORD-RPTWORK.                          CUSTUPDT
051010     MOVE CUSTOMER-NUMBER-TYPE-4-CHANGE TO                       CUSTUPDT
051020             CUSTOMER-NUMBER-RPTWORK.                            CUSTUPDT
051030     MOVE LAST-ACTIVITY-DATE-FIELD-MSG TO                        CUSTUPDT
051040             FIELD-CHANGED-ERROR-RPTWORK.                        CUSTUPDT
051050     MOVE CHANGE-MSG TO ACTION-TAKEN-RPTWORK.                    CUSTUPDT
051060     PERFORM U000-WRITE-TRANSACTION-REPORT.                      CUSTUPDT
051070     MOVE LAST-ACTIVITY-CHANGE-WORK TO                           CUSTUPDT
051080             LAST-ACTIVITY-MSTRIN-WORK.                          CUSTUPDT
```

```
 30                     19.16.07        SEP  5,1978

051100**************************************************************** CUSTUPDT
051110*                                                              * CUSTUPDT
051120*  THE FUNCTION OF THIS MODULE IS TO WRITE THE TRANSACTION     * CUSTUPDT
051130*  REPORT. IT IS ENTERED FROM AND EXITS TO VARIOUS MODULES IN  * CUSTUPDT
051140*  THE PROGRAM (SEE HIERARCHY CHART).                          * CUSTUPDT
051150*                                                              * CUSTUPDT
051160**************************************************************** CUSTUPDT
051170                                                                 CUSTUPDT
051180 U000-WRITE-TRANSACTION-REPORT.                                  CUSTUPDT
051190                                                                 CUSTUPDT
051200     IF THIS-IS-THE-FIRST-PAGE OR                                CUSTUPDT
052010             NUMBER-OF-LINES-PRINTED = PAGE-SIZE OR              CUSTUPDT
052020             IS GREATER THAN PAGE-SIZE                           CUSTUPDT
052030         PERFORM U010-PRINT-HEADINGS                             CUSTUPDT
052040         MOVE SPACES TO UPDATE-TRANSACTION-REPORT-LINE           CUSTUPDT
052050         MOVE CUSTOMER-NUMBER-RPTWORK TO CUSTOMER-NUMBER-REPORT. CUSTUPDT
052060     IF CUSTOMER-NUMBER-RPTWORK NOT = PREVIOUS-CUSTOMER-NUMBER   CUSTUPDT
052070         MOVE CUSTOMER-NUMBER-RPTWORK TO CUSTOMER-NUMBER-REPORT  CUSTUPDT
052080         MOVE CUSTOMER-NUMBER-RPTWORK TO PREVIOUS-CUSTOMER-NUMBER CUSTUPDT
052090         MOVE SPACE-TWO-LINES TO PROPER-SPACING.                 CUSTUPDT
052100     MOVE ACTION-TAKEN-RPTWORK TO ACTION-TAKEN-REPORT.           CUSTUPDT
052110     MOVE FIELD-CHANGED-ERROR-RPTWORK TO                         CUSTUPDT
052120             FIELD-CHANGED-ERROR-REPORT.                         CUSTUPDT
052130     MOVE TYPE-OF-ERROR-RPTWORK TO TYPE-OF-ERROR-REPORT.         CUSTUPDT
052140     MOVE OLD-MASTER-RECORD-RPTWORK TO OLD-MASTER-RECORD-REPORT. CUSTUPDT
052150     MOVE NEW-MASTER-RECORD-RPTWORK TO NEW-MASTER-RECORD-REPORT. CUSTUPDT
052160     WRITE UPDATE-TRANSACTION-REPORT-LINE                        CUSTUPDT
052170             AFTER PROPER-SPACING.                               CUSTUPDT
052180     ADD PROPER-SPACING TO NUMBER-OF-LINES-PRINTED.              CUSTUPDT
052190     MOVE SPACE-ONE-LINE TO PROPER-SPACING.                      CUSTUPDT
052200     MOVE SPACES TO UPDATE-TRANSACTION-REPORT-LINE.              CUSTUPDT
053010     MOVE SPACES TO TRANSACTION-REPORT-WORK-AREA.                CUSTUPDT
```

Figure 6-71 Source Listing (Part 18 of 19)

```
31                    19.16.07        SEP  5,1978

053030****************************************************************** CUSTUPDT
053040*                                                                * CUSTUPDT
053050*  THIS MODULE PRINTS THE HEADINGS ON THE TRANSACTION REPORT.   * CUSTUPDT
053060*  IT IS ENTERED FROM AND EXITS TO THE U000-WRITE-TRANSACTION-  * CUSTUPDT
053070*  REPORT MODULE.                                                * CUSTUPDT
053080*                                                                * CUSTUPDT
053090****************************************************************** CUSTUPDT
053100                                                                   CUSTUPDT
053110 U010-PRINT-HEADINGS.                                              CUSTUPDT
053120                                                                   CUSTUPDT
053130     MOVE CURRENT-DATE TO DATE-HDG1.                               CUSTUPDT
053140     MOVE PAGE-NUMBER-COUNT TO PAGE-NUMBER-HDG1.                   CUSTUPDT
053150     WRITE UPDATE-TRANSACTION-REPORT-LINE FROM FIRST-HEADING-LINE  CUSTUPDT
053160         AFTER ADVANCING TO-THE-TOP-OF-THE-PAGE.                   CUSTUPDT
053170     ADD 1 TO PAGE-NUMBER-COUNT.                                   CUSTUPDT
053180     WRITE UPDATE-TRANSACTION-REPORT-LINE FROM SECOND-HEADING-LINECUSTUPDT
053190         AFTER ADVANCING 2 LINES.                                  CUSTUPDT
053200     WRITE UPDATE-TRANSACTION-REPORT-LINE FROM THIRD-HEADING-LINE  CUSTUPDT
054010         AFTER ADVANCING 1 LINES.                                  CUSTUPDT
054020     MOVE SPACE-TWO-LINES TO PROPER-SPACING.                       CUSTUPDT
054030     MOVE ZERO TO NUMBER-OF-LINES-PRINTED.                         CUSTUPDT
```

```
32                    19.16.07        SEP  5,1978

054050****************************************************************** CUSTUPDT
054060*                                                                * CUSTUPDT
054070*  THIS MODULE EDITS THE CUSTOMER NUMBER. IT IS ENTERED FROM    * CUSTUPDT
054080*  AND EXITS TO VARIOUS MODULES WITHIN THE PROGRAM (SEE         * CUSTUPDT
054090*  HIERARCHY CHART).                                             * CUSTUPDT
054100*                                                                * CUSTUPDT
054110****************************************************************** CUSTUPDT
054120                                                                   CUSTUPDT
054130 U020-EDIT-CUSTOMER-NUMBER.                                        CUSTUPDT
054140                                                                   CUSTUPDT
054150     COPY EDCUSTNC                                                 CUSTUPDT
054160         REPLACING CUSTOMER-NUMBER-EXCP-WORK BY                    CUSTUPDT
054170                       CUSTOMER-NUMBER-RPTWORK                     CUSTUPDT
054180                   FIELD-IN-ERROR-EXCP-WORK BY                     CUSTUPDT
054190                       FIELD-CHANGED-ERROR-RPTWORK                 CUSTUPDT
054200                   TYPE-OF-ERROR-EXCP-WORK BY                      CUSTUPDT
055010                       TYPE-OF-ERROR-RPTWORK                       CUSTUPDT
055020                   U000-WRITE-EXCEPTION-REPORT BY                  CUSTUPDT
055030                       U000-WRITE-TRANSACTION-REPORT.              CUSTUPDT
C*044040                                                                 LOADCUST
C 044050     IF (FIRST-FOUR-CHAR-CUST-NUMB-WORK IS NOT NUMERIC) OR       LOADCUST
C 044060        (FIFTH-CHAR-CUST-NUMB-WORK IS NOT NUMERIC AND            LOADCUST
C 044070         NOT VALID-CHECK-DIGIT-FOR-TEN)                          LOADCUST
C 044080         MOVE CUSTOMER-NUMBER-WORK TO CUSTOMER-NUMBER-RPTWORK    LOADCUST
C 044090         MOVE CUSTOMER-NUMBER-FIELD-MSG TO                       LOADCUST
C 044100             FIELD-CHANGED-ERROR-RPTWORK                         LOADCUST
C 044110         MOVE FIELD-NOT-NUMERIC-ERROR-MSG TO                     LOADCUST
C 044120             TYPE-OF-ERROR-RPTWORK                               LOADCUST
C 044130         PERFORM U000-WRITE-TRANSACTION-REPORT                   LOADCUST
C 044140         MOVE 'NO ' TO ARE-TRAN-RECORDS-VALID                    LOADCUST
C 044150     ELSE                                                        LOADCUST
C 044160         MOVE CUSTOMER-NUMBER-WORK TO                            LOADCUST
C 044170             FIELD-TO-BE-CHECKED-MOD11-WORK                      LOADCUST
C 044180         CALL 'MOD11CHK' USING MOD-11-PASS-AREA-WORK             LOADCUST
C 044190         IF CUST-NUMBER-DID-NOT-PASS-MOD11                       LOADCUST
C 044200             MOVE CUSTOMER-NUMBER-WORK TO CUSTOMER-NUMBER-RPTWORK LOADCUST
C 044210             MOVE CUSTOMER-NUMBER-FIELD-MSG TO                   LOADCUST
C 044220                 FIELD-CHANGED-ERROR-RPTWORK                     LOADCUST
C 045010             MOVE FAILS-MOD11-ERROR-MSG TO                       LOADCUST
C 045020                 TYPE-OF-ERROR-RPTWORK                           LOADCUST
C 045030             PERFORM U000-WRITE-TRANSACTION-REPORT               LOADCUST
C 045040             MOVE 'NO ' TO ARE-TRAN-RECORDS-VALID.               LOADCUST
```

Figure 6-72 Source Listing (Part 19 of 19)

CHAPTER 6

REVIEW QUESTIONS

1. Describe the similarities of sequential file updating and random file updating.

2. Describe the differences between sequential file updating and random file updating

3. Why isn't a new file created when a file is updated randomly?

4. Where are records stored when they are added to an indexed sequential file? How is a record found when it is to be randomly retrieved from an indexed sequential file?

5. What is the difference between a Rewrite Statement and a Write Statement?

6. What information must be stored in the nominal key field when a Read Statement is executed for random retrieval of a record in an indexed sequential file? What information when a Write Statement is executed for an indexed sequential file? What information when a Rewrite Statement is to be executed for an indexed sequential file?

7. Why is a Copy Statement used?

8. What does the Replacing Clause in a Copy Statement cause to happen?

CHAPTER 6

PROGRAMMING ASSIGNMENT 1

OVERVIEW – PROGRAMMING ASSIGNMENTS

The programming assignments in this chapter are designed to illustrate the random updating of the indexed sequential Multiple Listing Master file created in Chapter 5. Three programming assignments are explained: Programming Assignments 1, 1A, and 1B. A variety of approaches are possible when utilizing these programming assignments.

1. Only Programming Assignment 1 may be assigned. This approach results in the design and coding of a relatively small program that edits a series of Multiple Listing Update Transaction records and randomly updates an indexed sequential file. This assignment illustrates most of the basic concepts discussed in the chapter.

2. Programming Assignment 1A may be assigned as a maintenance program, in which case the assignment is undertaken only after Programming Assignment 1 has been designed, coded, and tested.

3. Programming Assignments 1 and 1A may be viewed as a single assignment and approached as one programming project. Utilizing both Programming Assignments 1 and 1A results in the completion of a program of the approximate difficulty of the sample program contained within the text.

4. Programming Assignment 1B may be assigned as a maintenance program, in which case the assignment is undertaken only after Programming Assignments 1 and 1A have been completely designed, coded, and tested.

5. Programming Assignments 1, 1A, and 1B may be viewed as a single, large programming assignment.

The method of assigning the program is at the option of the instructor.

INSTRUCTIONS — PROGRAMMING ASSIGNMENT 1

The Multiple Listing Master File created in Chapter 5 and stored on disk as an indexed sequential file is to be randomly updated by a series of transaction records. The transaction records are to be edited as a part of the update program prior to performing the update of the Multiple Listing Master File.

A program should be written to read and edit the Transaction Update Records and randomly update the Multiple Listing Master File. A Hierarchy Chart, IPO Charts, and Pseudocode Specifications should be used when designing the program. Test data to properly test all modules should be developed by the programmer.

INPUT

The input to the program is the Multiple Listing Master File created in Chapter 5 and a file of Update Transaction Records. The format of the Multiple Listing Master File is illustrated below.

Multiple Listing Master File

FIELD	POSITION	NUMBER OF CHARACTERS	ATTRIBUTES
Delete code	1	1	Alphanumeric
Parcel Code	2	1	Alphanumeric
Parcel Number	3-6	4	Numeric
Street Number	7-11	5	Numeric
Street Name	12-31	20	Alphanumeric
Town	32-34	3	Alphanumeric
Zip Code	35-39	5	Numeric
Selling Price	40-48	9	Numeric
Square Feet	49-52	4	Numeric
Features	53-66	14	Alphanumeric
Broker's Name	67-80	14	Alphanumeric
Date Listed	81-86	6	Numeric
Expiration Date	87-92	6	Numeric
First Mortgage	93-100	8	Numeric
Second Mortgage	101-108	8	Numeric
Yearly Taxes	109-116	8	Numeric

The blocking factor for the Multiple Listing Master File is 20 records per block. The file is stored as an indexed sequential file with the Parcel Code and Parcel Number (Parcel I.D.) acting as the key to the records.

Update Transaction Records

The format of the Update Transaction Records which are stored on punched cards is illustrated below.

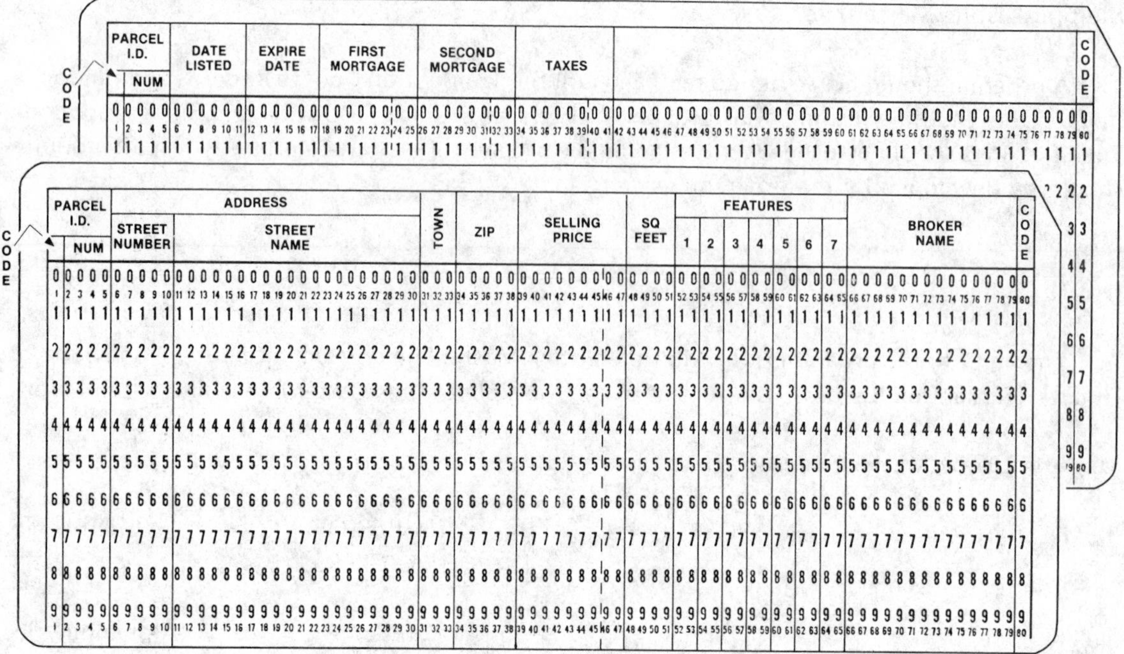

The Update Transaction Records will consist of records that provide for additions, deletions, and changes to the Multiple Listing Master File.

Additions to the file will contain all of the fields illustrated in the format of the records above and will contain, in Card Column 80, an Update Code 1 for the first record and an Update Code 2 for the second record. Thus, an Update Code 1 and 2 indicate additions to the file. For additions, there must be a record with a Code 1 followed by a record with a Code 2 with the same Parcel I.D.

Changes to the file will be identified by the Code 3 or Code 4 in Card Column 80. A transaction record with a Code 3 in Card Column 80 will be used to indicate a change in either the Selling Price or the Broker, as indicated by the fields contained in the first type of record illustrated above. A transaction record with a Code 4 in Card Column 80 will be used to indicate a change in the Expiration Date, First Mortgage, Second Mortgage, or Taxes, as can be seen from the fields present in the second type of record illustrated above.

A Transaction Record with the Parcel I.D. and a Code 5 in Card Column 80 will indicate that the corresponding record in the master file is to be deleted.

OUTPUT

The output from the Update Program consists of the Updated Multiple Listing Master File and an Update Transaction Report which contains a list of all errors in the transaction records being processed and a record of update activity including all additions, deletions, and changes to the master file.

The format of the Update Transaction Report is illustrated below.

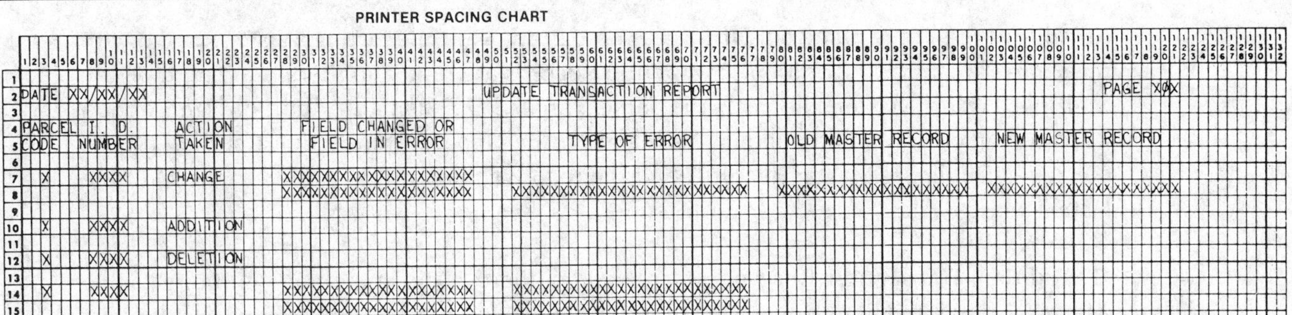

Note that the report contains the Parcel I.D., the Action Taken, the Field Changed or Field in Error, the Type of Error, the contents of the Old Master Record before a change has occurred, and the contents of the New Master Record after the change has been made.

PROCESSING

The processing which is to take place consists of editing the Update Transaction Records and making additions, deletions, and changes to the Multiple Listing Master File. The processing tasks are explained below and on the following pages.

Sorting

1. The Multiple Listing Master File is stored on the disk in Parcel I.D. sequence. The Update Transaction records must be sorted into Transaction Code sequence within Parcel I.D.

Additions

1. An addition takes place when a new record is added to the Multiple Listing Master File. The Transaction Records to cause an addition will contain a Code 1 in Card Column 80 of the first type of record and a Code 2 in Card Column 80 of the second type of record. For an addition to take place, there must be a record with a Code 1 followed by a record with a Code 2 with the same Parcel I.D. If there is not a pair of cards for an addition, an entry should be made on the Update Transaction, and neither record should be added to the master file.

2. An addition can take place only if there is no current Multiple Listing Master Record with the same Parcel I.D. If Addition Transaction Records are read and there is a record on the Multiple Listing Master File with the same Parcel I.D., then the Addition Transaction Record is in error; an entry should be made on the Update Transaction Report with the message "Duplicate Master Record," and the record should not be added to the Multiple Listing Master File.

3. If Addition Transaction Records are read and there is no matching Multiple Listing Master Record, the addition record should be added to the Multiple Listing Master File. Before the record is added, however, the records must be edited as specified under "Editing."

Deletions

1. A deletion can take place only if there is a master record with the same Parcel I.D. as the Deletion Transaction Record. If a Deletion Transaction Record is read and there is not a matching master record, then the Deletion Transaction Record is in error; an entry should be made on the Update Transaction Report with the message "Non-Matching Master Record," and the Deletion Transaction should not be processed further.

2. If the Deletion Transaction Record is read and there is a matching Master Record, the Master Record should be flagged by placing the Deletion code High Values in Position 1 of the Master Record. The only two fields required in the Transaction Record which cause a deletion to take place are the Parcel I.D. and the Deletion Transaction Code ("5") in Card Column 80.

3. The Deletion Transaction Record must be edited as specified under "Editing" before it can be used to delete a Master Record.

Changes

1. A change takes place when one or more fields in a record stored in the Master File are to be changed. Changes can be made to the Selling Price, the Broker's Name, the Expiration Date, First Mortgage, Second Mortgage, and Taxes. A Transaction Record to cause a change to take place must contain a Transaction Code of 3 for changes contained in the first record type, or a Transaction Code 4 for changes contained in the second record type.

2. A change can take place only if there is a Master Record with the same Parcel I.D. as the Transaction Record. If a Change Transaction Record is read and there is not a matching Master Record, then the Change Transaction Record is in error; an entry should be made on the Update Transaction Report with the message "Non-Matching Master Record," and the Change Transaction Record should not be processed further.

3. A Change Transaction Record must pass the editing criteria specified under "Editing" before it is used to change a Master Record.

Invalid Transactions

1. The only valid codes in the Transaction Record are 1 and 2 (Add), 3 and 4 (Change), and 5 (Deletion). If a Transaction Record does not contain one of these codes, an entry should be made on the Update Transaction Report with the message "Invalid Transaction Code."

Editing — Additions

The Update Transaction Records reflecting additions to the file should be edited according to the following rules:

1. In order to have a valid record to add to the Multiple Listing Master File, there must be a Type 1 record and a Type 2 record with the same Parcel I.D.

2. If a Type 1 and Type 2 pair of records with the same Parcel I.D. are found, the following editing should take place on the fields in the records. All fields should be checked in the records.

   a. Parcel Code — This field must contain a "C," "M," or "S."
   b. Parcel Number — This field must be numeric and pass a modulus 11 check digit test.
   c. Street Number — There must be a numeric address for each input record. However, the entire field need not contain numeric data. For example, the address 36003 is valid and so is the address blank-blank-360. As can be seen, the data is right-justified in the Street Number field. The data which is specified for the address must be numeric.
   d. Street Address — This field must contain data. If it contains blanks, it is in error.
   e. Town — This field must contain one of the valid Town Codes listed in the accompanying chart.
   f. Zip Code — This field must contain numeric data.
   g. Selling Price — This field must contain numeric data.
   h. Square Feet — This field must contain numeric data.
   i. Features Fields — Each of the seven fields may contain alphabetic data or may be blank. If the field contains alphabetic data, the data must be one of the seven special feature codes contained in the accompanying table.
   j. Broker's Name — This field must contain data. If the field contains blanks, it is in error.
   k. Date Listed — This field must contain numeric data.
   l. Expiration Date — This field must contain numeric data.
   m. First Mortgage — This field may be blank, or it may contain data. If it contains data, the data must be numeric.
   n. Second Mortgage — This field may be blank or it may contain data. If it contains data, the data must be numeric.
   o. Property Taxes — This field must contain numeric data.

3. The tables referred to in #2 above are illustrated below.

TOWN CODES	
Code	Town
ANA	Anaheim
CMS	Costa Mesa
FUL	Fullerton
GRD	Garden Grove
HNT	Huntington Beach
NWB	Newport Beach
ORG	Orange
STA	Santa Ana

FEATURES CODES	
Code	Feature
AC	Air Conditioning
DR	Dining Room
FR	Family Room
HR	Horse Property
OF	Office
PT	Patio
SW	Swimming Pool

3. If either record of the pair does not pass the editing criteria, then the record should not be added to the Multiple Listing Master File. Instead, it should be listed on the Update Transaction Report.

Addition records which do not pass the editing criteria or records which are invalid because of the lack of a pair of Type 1 and Type 2 records should be listed on the Update Transaction Report. The Field in Error messages should be descriptive of the field. The Error Messages which should appear in the Type of Error field are listed below.

Error Messages

INVALID PARCEL I-D
FIELD CONTAINS NON-NUMERIC DATA
NO ADDRESS PRESENT
INVALID TOWN CODE
INVALID FEATURES CODE
NO BROKER NAME PRESENT
TYPE 1 BUT NO TYPE 2
TYPE 2 BUT NO TYPE 1
DUPLICATE MASTER RECORD
FAILS MOD-11 CHECK

If the input record has more than one field in error for a given Parcel I.D., the Parcel I.D. should be group-indicated. See the printer spacing chart on page 6.83.

Editing — Changes

For the first record type, a change to the Master file will be indicated by a Code "3" in Card Column 80. These records will contain the Parcel I.D. and may contain either the Selling Price or the Broker's Name, or both. The editing which should take place for this record is described below.

1. Parcel Code — This field must contain a "C," "M," or "S."

2. Parcel Number — This field must be numeric and pass a Modulus 11 check digit test.

3. Selling Price — This field must contain numeric data if present.

With a Type 1 record, if the Selling Price is not blank and is numeric, the Selling Price in the Master Record is to be changed. If the Broker's Name is not blank, the Broker's Name in the Master Record is to be changed. It should be noted that a change for Selling Price and Broker's Name could appear on a single record or upon multiple records; that is, there may be a change record indicating a change in Selling Price and Broker, or there may be one change record for Selling Price and one change record for Broker.

For a Type 2 record, a change to the master file will be indicated by a Code "4" in Card Column 80. A Type 2 record will contain the Parcel I.D. and may contain the Date Expired, the First Mortgage, the Second Mortgage, and the Property Taxes. The following editing should take place for these records.

1. Parcel Code — This field must contain a "C," "M," or "S."

2. Parcel Number — This field must be numeric and pass a Modulus 11 check digit test.

3. Expiration Date — This field must contain numeric data if present.

4. First Mortgage — This field must contain numeric data if present.

5. Second Mortgage — This field must contain numeric data if present.

6. Property Taxes — This field must contain numeric data if present.

As can be seen, multiple fields can be changed by one Change Record; that is, the Selling Price and the Broker's Name can be changed by a Type 3 record and the Expiration Date, First Mortgage, Second Mortgage, and Property Taxes can be changed by a Type 4 record. If one of the fields in either of the records fails the editing specified above, it should not be used in updating a record from the Multiple Listing Master File. If, however, there are other fields contained in a record which are valid, then these fields can be used to change the Master File. For example, it would be possible to have a Type 4 record with a non-numeric Expiration Date which is invalid and a valid First Mortgage change. The Expiration Date should not be changed; it should instead be listed on the Update Transaction Report as a field in error. The First Mortgage, on the other hand, should be changed since it is a valid field within the Transaction Record. Thus, a single transaction record can have both valid fields which cause the Master Record to be changed and invalid fields which cannot be used to change the Master Record.

The error messages for errors in a field should be the same as those used for the Addition records.

Editing — Deletions

A deletion record will contain the Parcel I.D. and the Code "5" in Card Column 80. The editing for deletion records is explained below.

1. Parcel Code — This field must contain a "C," "M," or "S."

2. Parcel Number — This field must be numeric and pass the Modulus 11 check digit test.

Editing — Invalid Codes

If a transaction record does not contain a valid code, that is, a code of 1, 2, 3, 4, or 5, an entry should be made on the Update Transaction Report with the message "Invalid Transaction Code."

Test Data

The programmer should develop test data to thoroughly test the program.

Previously-Written Modules

Any editing modules written for previous assignments should be utilized in this program, if possible.

CHAPTER 6

PROGRAMMING ASSIGNMENT 1A

INTRODUCTION

At the discretion of the instructor, this assignment may be completed in combination with Programming Assignment 1 or may be assigned only after Assignment 1 has been completely designed, coded, and tested.

INSTRUCTIONS

A request for some modifications to the program in Assignment 1 have been received by the data processing department. The following changes should be implemented:

Additions

1. Editing of the Zip Code field should be changed so that the Zip Code is verified as being valid for a given town. For example, for the city of Anaheim (ANA), valid zip codes are 92801 through 92807. The chart below summarizes the valid zip code ranges and related towns.

ZIP CODES	CODE	TOWN
92801 - 92807	ANA	Anaheim
92626 - 92627	CMS	Costa Mesa
92631 - 92638	FUL	Fullerton
92640 - 92645	GRD	Garden Grove
92646 - 92649	HNT	Huntington Beach
92660 - 92663	NWB	Newport Beach
92665 - 92669	ORG	Orange
92701 - 92708	STA	Santa Ana

If the Zip Code is not valid for a Town, the record should not be placed in the Multiple Listing Master File. Instead, the error should be recorded on the Update Transaction Report.

2. The Listing Date and the Expiration Date must contain valid month values, that is, the month specified must be 01 - 12. In addition, the day specified must not be greater than the number of days in the given month, nor should it be less than 01. For example, the date 043178 is invalid. If the date fields fail this editing, the record should not be added to the Multiple Listing Master File. Instead, an error message should be written on the Update Transaction Report.

3. The Listing Date should not be later than the Expiration Date. For example, a Listing Date of 01/23/78 and an Expiration Date of 12/30/77 is invalid. If the date fields fail this editing, the record should not be added to the Multiple Listing Master File. Instead, an error message should be written on the Update Transaction Report.

4. The maximum Square Footage for a condominium or single family residence should normally not exceed 6,000 square feet. If it does, the record can still be added to the Multiple Listing Master File, but a WARNING message should be written on the Update Transaction Report.

5. The Selling Price for a piece of property should not exceed $90.00 per square foot. If it does, the record can still be added to the Multiple Listing Master File, but a WARNING message should be written on the Update Transaction Report.

Changes

1. If the Selling Price field in a Type 1 transaction record contains data, that is, the Selling Price in the Master Record is to be changed, then the Selling Price in the Transaction Record should not exceed $90.00 per square foot. If it does, the Master Record can still be changed but a WARNING message should be written on the Update Transaction Report. It should be noted that the square feet of the property is not contained in the Change Transaction Record; therefore, the Master Record will have to be retrieved in order to obtain the Square Footage used in this editing.

2. If the Expiration Date in a Type 2 transaction record contains data, that is, the Expiration Date in the Master Record is to be changed, then the Expiration Date must contain valid month values, that is, the month specified must be 01 - 12. In addition, the day specified must not be greater than the number of days in a given month, nor should it be less than 01. For example, the date 043178 is invalid. If the Expiration Date field fails this editing, the change should not be made to the Multiple Listing Master File. Instead, an error message should be written on the Update Transaction Report. It should be noted, however, that if there are other fields on the same Change record, they may be used to change the Master Record if they pass their editing.

3. The Listing Date in the Master Record should not be later than the Expiration Date contained in the Change Record. For example, a Listing Date in the Master Record of 01/23/78 and an Expiration Date of 12/30/77 in the Change Record is invalid. If the Expiration Date fails this editing, it should not be used to change the Master Record. Instead, an error message should be written on the Update Transaction Report. Since the Listing Date is not contained in the Change Record, the Master Record will have to be retrieved to perform this editing. It should be noted that if there are other fields in the same Change Record, they may be used to change the Master Record if they pass their editing.

Additional error messages should be defined by the programmer to handle the additional editing specified in these changes. Additional test data should be developed to adequately test these changes.

CHAPTER 6

PROGRAMMING ASSIGNMENT 1B

INTRODUCTION

At the discretion of the instructor, this assignment may be completed in combination with Programming Assignment 1 and 1A, or may be assigned only after Programming Assignments 1 and 1A have been completely designed, coded, and tested.

INSTRUCTIONS

A request for additional modifications to the program defined in Programming Assignments 1 and 1A has been received by the data processing department. The following changes should be implemented:

Additions

1. The Expiration Date should not be more than three months past the Listing Date. If it is, the record can be added to the Multiple Listing Master File, but a WARNING message should appear on the Update Transaction Report.

2. Property taxes should not be greater than 3% of the selling price or less than 1% of the selling price. If they are, the record can still be added to the Multiple Listing Master File, but a WARNING message should be written on the Update Transaction Report.

3. The sum of the First Mortgage and the Second Mortgage should not be greater than the Selling Price. If it is, the record can be added to the Multiple Listing Master File, but a WARNING message should be written on the Update Transaction Report.

Changes

1. The Expiration Date, if being changed, should not be more than three months past the current Expiration Date contained in the Master Record. If it is, the Master Record can be changed but a WARNING message should be written on the Update Transaction Report. Note that the old Expiration Date is contained in the Master Record; therefore, the Master Record will have to be retrieved before this editing can take place.

2. If the Property Taxes are to be changed, they should not be greater than 3% of the selling price in the Master Record or less than 1% of the selling price in the Master Record. If they are, the Master Record can still be changed, but a WARNING message should be written on the Update Transaction Report. Since the Selling Price is not contained in the Change Record, the Master Record will have to be retrieved before this editing can take place.

3. If the First Mortgage, or the Second Mortgage, or both, are being changed, the sum of the First Mortgage and the Second Mortgage should not be greater than the Selling Price. If it is, the Master Record can still be changed, but a WARNING message should be written on the Update Transaction Report. It should be noted that, depending upon the Field(s) being changed, the First Mortgage or the Second Mortgage may not be in the Change Record. If one of the fields is not in the Change Record, then the Master Record must be retrieved before this editing can take place.

New Report

In addition to the Update Transaction Report, created while the Master File is being updated, the Real Estate Listings Report should be prepared after the Multiple Listing Master File has been completely updated. The format of the report is illustrated below.

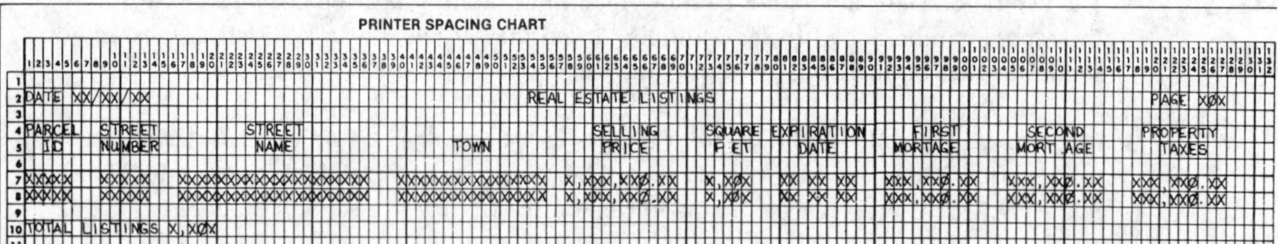

Note from the printer spacing chart for the Real Estate Listings that some of the fields contained in the Multiple Listing Master File are contained on the report. Note also that the Town field on the report contains the full-name of the town, not the abbreviation which is stored in the Master File.

Appendix

APPENDIX A

DISK AND TAPE CONCEPTS

INTRODUCTION TO MAGNETIC TAPE

Magnetic tape used with computer systems is similar to the tape used in audio tape recorders. Physically, the tape is composed of a plastic material normally one-half inch wide and coated on one side with a metallic oxide on which data may be recorded in the form of magnetic spots. The data recorded on magnetic tape may include numbers, letters of the alphabet, or special characters. Data is recorded in a series of parallel channels or tracks along the length of the tape. It is the presence or absence of magnetic spots on the tape that forms the representation of meaningful characters.

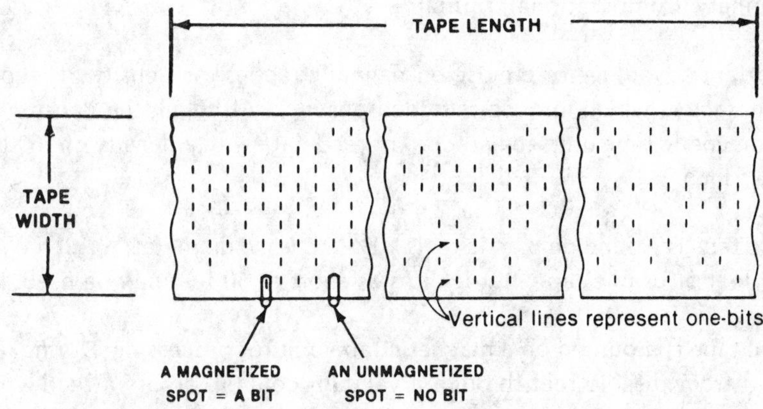

Figure A-1 Data Recorded on a Section of Magnetic Tape

Computers using the Extended Binary Coded Decimal Interchange Code normally use 9 channel magnetic tape. The tape consists of 9 horizontal channels with one of the channels reserved for parity checking. The following diagram illustrates the coding structure and bit configurations for 9 channel tape.

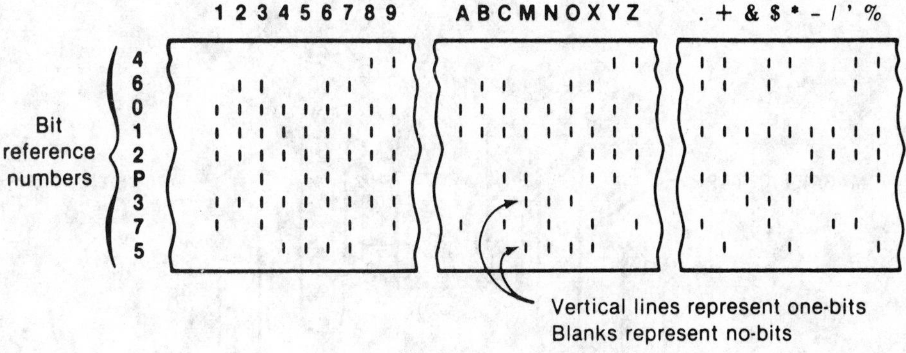

Figure A-2 Nine Channel Tape

The bit assignments indicated are based upon the coding structure of EBCDIC using the zoned decimal format. It should be noted that the bit assignments were selected for maximum reliability and performance. Those bits utilized most frequently in representing data are recorded near the center of the tape. The bit positions used less frequently are recorded on the outer edges of the tape where reading or writing errors are more likely to occur. The numbers to the left of the tape segment reference positions 0-7 of the byte. Note that position 7 of the byte is the second channel from the bottom on 9 channel tape. Bit position 6 is the second channel from the top, etc. For example, the bit configuration for the number "one" in EBCDIC is 11110001. This same bit configuration is contained on 9 channel magnetic tape by referencing the bit positions as indicated.

When using 9 channel tape, data may also be recorded in packed decimal (Computational-3) format or a binary (Computational) format.

An important advantage of the use of magnetic tape is the density of recording, that is, the number of characters which may be recorded per inch. Although the density of magnetic tape varies, most magnetic tape units may record or read data with a density of 1600 bytes per inch or 3200 bytes per inch.

Magnetic tape is wound on plastic reels 10½ inches in diameter. A full reel contains approximately 2,400 feet of usable tape, but lengths as short as 50 feet can be used.

Magnetic tape is mounted on a magnetic tape unit for processing. During reading or writing, tape is moved from the file reel through a vacuum column, across a read-write head, through another vacuum column, and to the machine take-up reel. Reading or writing takes place as the tape is moved across a read-write head. The tape-transport speed of the magnetic tape units varies from approximately 18.75 inches per second to 200 inches per second.

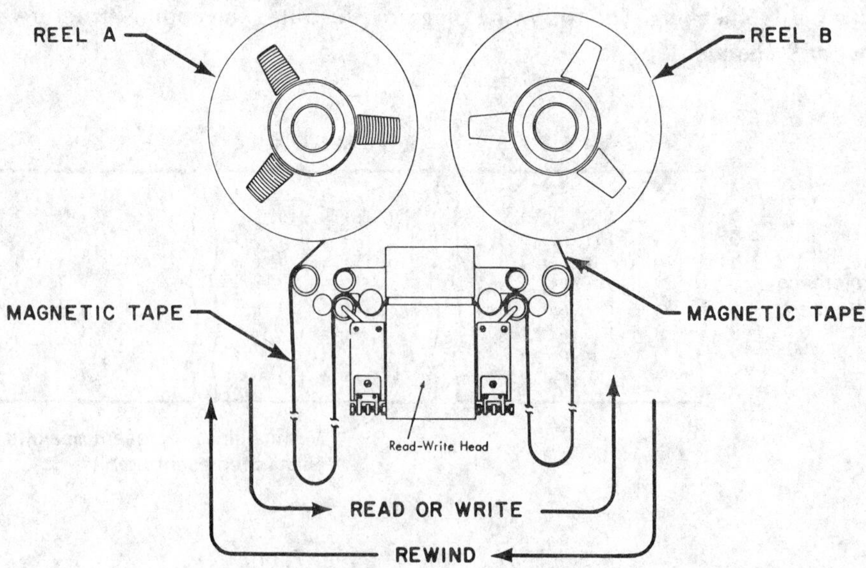

Figure A-3 Schematic of a Magnetic Tape Drive

Because of the density of magnetic tape and the speed at which the tape is transported past the read-write head, extremely fast input/output speeds are possible. To obtain the "effective" data transfer rate, that is, the speed at which data may be transferred to the Central Processing Unit from magnetic tape, the tape transport speed is multiplied by the tape density. For example, a magnetic tape unit with a tape transport speed of 112.5 inches per second, processing magnetic tape with a density of 1600 bytes per inch has an "effective" data transfer rate of 180,000 characters per second.

SEQUENTIAL FILE PROCESSING

Although tape drives operate in different modes, they all process data in a sequential access method. Sequential processing means that records are read or written one after another. Card readers and card punches operate in a sequential manner because cards are read or punched one after another. Thus, when using magnetic tape, records are read and written sequentially. In addition, the records stored on magnetic tape are normally arranged sequentially on the basis of some central field or "key" such as the employee number.

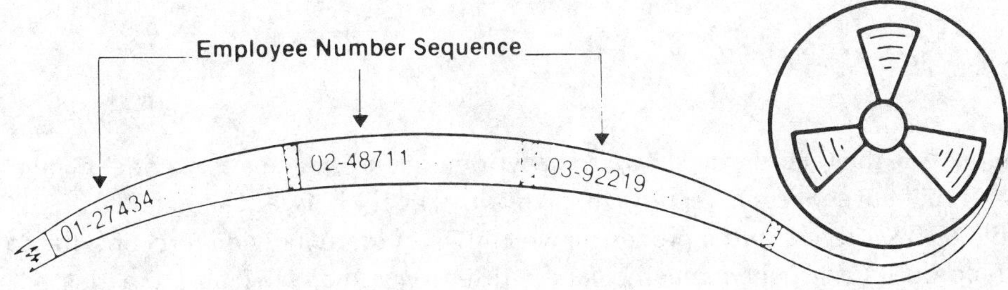

Figure A-4 Illustration of Records Arranged Sequentially on Magnetic Tape

After each record is written sequentially on a magnetic tape, there is an inter-block-gap (IBG) created (also called an IRG or inter-record-gap). This inter-block or inter-record gap is a blank space on the tape approximately .6 inch long and indicates to the magnetic tape drive that the end of the record has been reached. This inter-block-gap is necessary to allow for the starting and stopping, acceleration and deceleration, of the magnetic tape unit, and is required for correct reading and writing of records. Data to be read begins with the first character after an inter-block gap and continues to the next inter-block-gap.

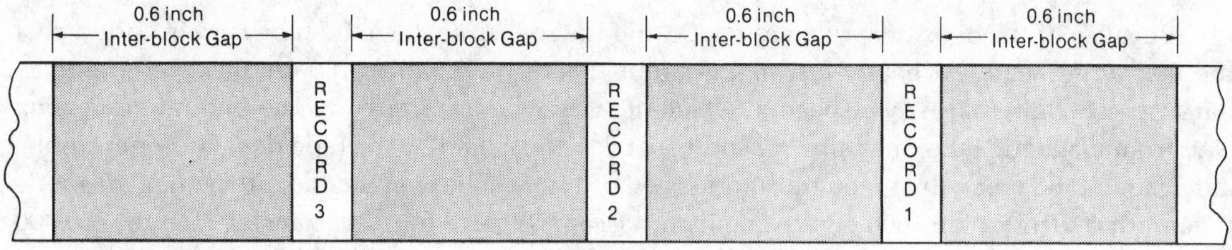

0.6 inch Inter-block Gap | 0.6 inch Inter-block Gap | 0.6 inch Inter-block Gap | 0.6 inch Inter-block Gap

RECORD 3 | RECORD 2 | RECORD 1

Figure A-5 Illustration of Records Stored on Magnetic Tape

When writing on tape, the records are written sequentially with inter-block-gaps between each record. During writing, the gap is automatically produced at the end of each record or block of records.

When all the records of the FILE (that is, the group of related records on the tape) have been written by the program, a special character called a TAPE MARK is written. When a tape mark is written on the tape, it signifies that the file has been completely written. Thus, when the tape is read by another program, the tape mark will indicate the end of the file.

BLOCKING

In Figure A-5, the records are shown to be written one by one in a sequential manner with an inter-block-gap between each record. In many instances, it is advantageous to BLOCK the records. BLOCKING refers to the process in which two or more individual records (referred to as "logical records") are grouped together and written on a magnetic tape creating a "physical record" or "block." (See Figure A-6.)

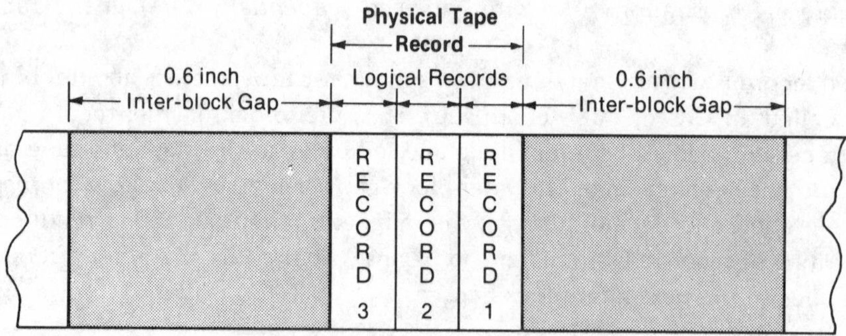

Figure A-6 Illustration of Blocked Records

Blocking has two major advantages: (1) More records can be written on the tape because a number of records are recorded between each inter-block gap, thus reducing the number of gaps on the tape; (2) The records can be read faster because two or more records can be read before the read operation is stopped by the inter-block-gap. The limiting factor in blocking records is the amount of computer storage available for input/output operations, as there must be enough room in storage to store the complete block of data to be processed. Thus, the larger the block of records, the more computer storage that must be allocated for storing the block. For example, if fifty 80 byte records comprise a physical record, then 4,000 bytes of computer storage are required when the physical record is transferred from magnetic tape to computer storage or from computer storage to magnetic tape. The programmer or analyst must make the determination as to what size block can be used so that there is enough storage available and the blocking is as efficient as possible.

The number of logical records comprising the "physical record" is called the BLOCKING FACTOR.

TAPE MARKERS

Magnetic tape must have some blank space at the beginning and end of the tape to allow threading through the feed mechanism of the tape unit. Special markers called "reflective strips" are placed on the tape to enable the tape unit to sense the beginning and end of the usable portion of the tape. The tape unit senses these markers as either the LOAD POINT marker which indicates where reading or writing is to begin or as the END-OF-TAPE marker which indicates approximately where writing is to stop.

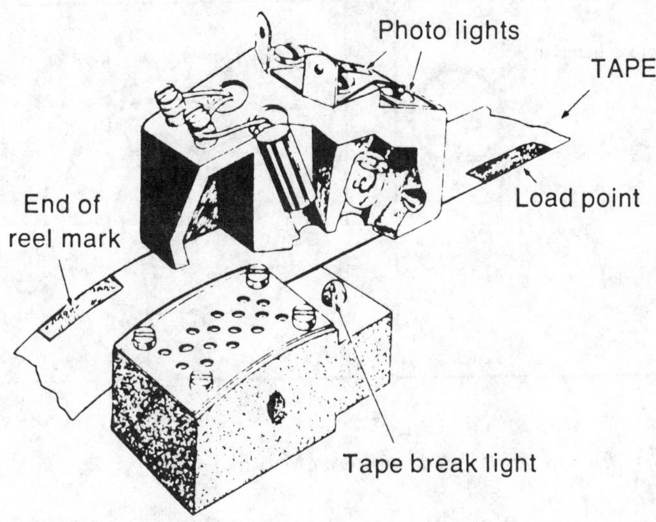

Figure A-7 Load Point and End-of-Tape Markers

The markers are small pieces of transparent plastic with a thin film of aluminum on one side. At least 10 feet of tape must be allowed from the beginning of the tape to the LOAD POINT marker, and approximately 14 feet are normally allowed between the END-OF-TAPE marker and the end of the tape.

TAPE UNIT POSITIONING

When a magnetic tape is loaded onto a magnetic tape drive, the tape is positioned at the LOAD POINT. As the tape is read or written, it progresses by being taken up on the take-up reel. Thus, when the reading or writing of the tape file is complete and the tape mark has been written or read, there will be tape on the take-up reel. Two commands are available to return the tape to the "user reel" — the rewind command and the rewind and unload command. When the rewind command is executed, all the tape on the take-up reel is wound back on the "user reel" until the load point is reached. At that time, the tape drive is readied and the tape is ready to be read or written again. When the rewind and unload command is used, the tape is wound back on the "user reel;" and then the tape is unloaded, that is, it is taken out of a "ready" status and it is possible for the operator to dismount the tape.

There are times when one file is larger than one VOLUME (that is, one reel of tape). When this happens, a tape mark is written at the end of the first volume and a second volume must be mounted by the operator so that the file may be continued. When this situation occurs, the file is called a MULTI-VOLUME file. It is also possible to have more than one file on a tape volume. This is called a MULTI-FILE volume.

FILE PROTECTION DEVICE

Because the writing operation automatically erases any previous information on the tape, a file protection device is provided to prevent accidental erasure. A plastic ring must be fitted into a circular groove on the tape reel to enable writing to occur on the tape (no ring — no write).

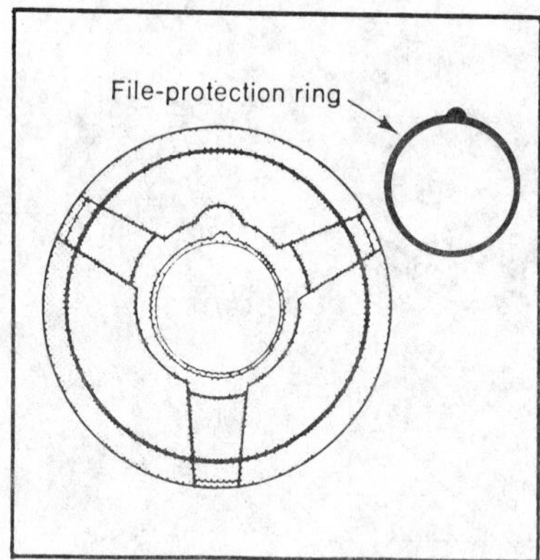

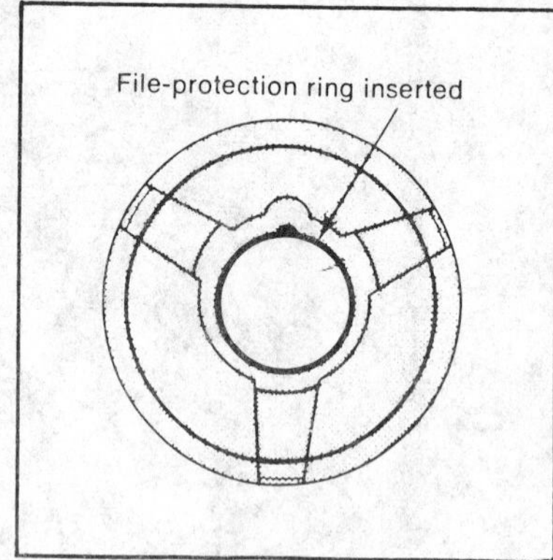

Figure A-8 File Protection Ring

When this ring is removed, only reading can take place. This technique tends to prevent accidental writing on a reel of tape as the operator must insert the ring in the reel for writing to occur.

MAGNETIC TAPE LABELING

Installations utilizing magnetic tape as a form of input and output normally maintain a tape "library." This library may consist of hundreds and even thousands of reels of tape containing the data to be processed. It is essential, therefore, that an effective means of identifying the individual reels of tape be developed. In actual practice, two types of labels are normally used to identify tape volumes or reels: an External Label and an Internal Label.

An External Label is written on some type of gummed label and is attached to the reel of tape. It normally contains information such as the volume number, that is, the unique number which identifies the volume or reel or tape; the "owner's name," that is, the programmer, department, etc., who is currently using the reel of tape; the date on which the tape may be "scratched" or used again; and a description of the contents of the data on the tape. Additional information may be included depending on the needs of the installation. This external label is used for identification purposes by the computer operator and the tape librarian.

An Internal Label is written directly on the tape by the computer. It is recorded in the same manner as data is recorded on the tape. It contains such information as the volume serial number, the data set name or identifier, the creation and expiration dates, etc. This internal label may be placed on the tape through the use of Standard Labels. These labels allow the user to uniquely identify each file or data set which is created on tape.

The format of an internal label or labels which are found on magnetic tape will normally be determined by the type of computer and the operating system which is used with the computer. Typically, however, the internal labels consist of at least three different types — a Volume Label, a Header Label, and a Trailer Label. An example of a labeled tape is shown in Figure A-9.

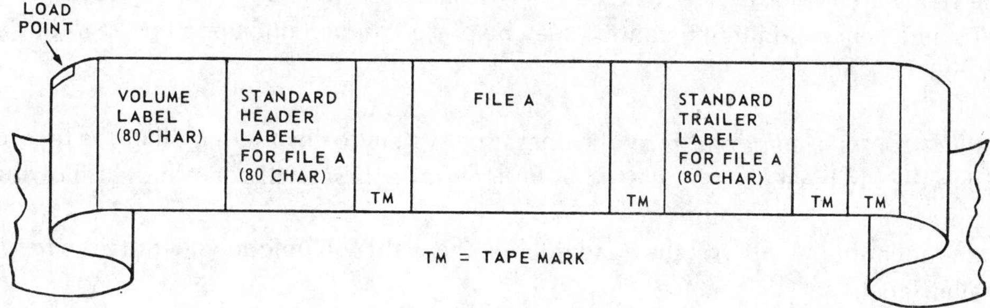

Figure A-9 Standard Tape Labels

The Volume Label is normally the first record on the magnetic tape volume and serves to identify the entire reel of tape. In most instances, the volume serial number which identifies the tape is written in this label; and there may be additional information dependent upon the needs of the operating system.

The Header Label which is written on the magnetic tape is normally used to identify each of the files which may be contained upon the tape. It will be noted that it is possible for more than one file to be stored on a single volume of tape; and if this occurs, then there will usually be a header label for each file which is on the tape. A header label will normally include at least the following information:

1. Label Identifier — This field contains a special value which identifies the record as a header record.
2. Tape Serial Number — This number normally corresponds to the serial number which is found in the Volume Label.
3. File Serial Number — This may be some unique number identifying the file, or it may be the same number as the tape serial number.
4. Sequence Number — This is a value which indicates the sequence of the file contained on the tape if the file consists of more than one tape volume (a Multi-Volume File).
5. File Identification — This is normally a unique name which is selected by the analyst or programmer to identify the file by name.
6. Creation Date — This field will identify the date on which the file was created.
7. Retention Cycle — This field will normally indicate the number of days a file is to be retained after it has been created or will give a date beyond which the tape may be used for another file.

These fields are basic to most header labels which are utilized in labeling tape files. Additional fields and, hence, additional control, may be present depending upon the operating system being utilized.

A Trailer Label is used primarily by the operating system to ensure that all of the records contained within the file have been processed. A typical trailer label will contain the following data:

1. Label Identifier — As with the header label, this field will uniquely identify the record as a trailer label.
2. Block Count — This field will contain the total number of physical records or blocks which have been written on the file. When the file is read as input, the number of records read will be counted; and after all of the records have been read, the number read will be compared to the value in this block count. If the values are not equal, it indicates that there has been a read error on the tape drive and corrective action must be taken.
3. Tape Record Count — This may be a similar count to that of the block count only it is a count of the number of logical records on the file, rather than the number of physical records.

Trailer labels may also contain any additional control information which may be applicable to either the operating system or the particular program or application.

NON-LABELED AND USER-LABELED TAPES

There is normally not a requirement, unless by installation standards, that magnetic tape files be labeled, although it is normally the best operating procedure to have labeled tapes. If labels are not used on a tape file or a tape volume, then the first record on the tape will be a data record in the file. The use or non-use of labels can be specified in the File Definition within the COBOL program.

There also may be provisions within the operating system being used which allow for user-written labels, that is, labels which contain any information which the user wishes to write in them. Special user label routines must be called in the COBOL program through the use of entries in the Declarative Section of the COBOL program.

RECORD FORMATS

Records on a magnetic tape can be of several formats. These formats are chosen by the programmer or analyst, depending upon the use of the record and what type of data will be contained in the record.

The two types of records are FIXED and VARIABLE. In addition, the fixed and variable length records may be BLOCKED or UNBLOCKED.

A FIXED-LENGTH record is one which always contains the same number of bytes. Thus, when a file is defined as having fixed-length records and the record length is 120, all records on the file contain 120 bytes. Normally, the fields in the record are defined in the File Section of the Data Division in the same manner used for the card reader and printer.

Fixed-length records can be blocked or unblocked. When they are unblocked, each physical record will be 120 bytes long. When the fixed-length records are blocked, the physical record contains more than one logical record. Thus, if a blocking factor of five is used, that is, there are five logical records for each block or physical record, then the BLOCKSIZE or block length would be 600 bytes (120 bytes/rec times 5 recs/block.)

A VARIABLE-LENGTH record is one which may contain a variable number of bytes in each record; that is, each record may contain the same or a different number of bytes. Variable-length records are used when different amounts of data may be available for each record. Variable-length records may be either blocked or unblocked, depending upon the application.

TAPE DISADVANTAGES

Although magnetic tape is an effective input/output media because of its high density and fast data transfer rate, the use of magnetic tape has several significant disadvantages. These disadvantages include the following:

1. Because records are stored on magnetic tape sequentially, transactions against master files stored on tape must be batched and sorted into sequence before processing.

2. Additions or deletions from a master file require that a new file must be created no matter how few the number of additions or deletions.

3. To extract a single record from a magnetic tape file (for example, the last record stored on a tape reel) requires that each record on the file be examined until the proper "key" identifying the record is found, at which time the record is processed as required.

4. In file updating procedures where there is little activity against the file, the use of magnetic tape is normally inefficient. For example, if a master file containing 10,000 records is to be updated but only 100 records are to be processed against the entire master file, the sequential file organization characteristic of magnetic tape requires that the entire master file of 10,000 records be processed.

DIRECT ACCESS STORAGE DEVICES

Another type of input/output device which is an effective storage media for many applications is a DIRECT ACCESS STORAGE DEVICE (DASD). Direct access storage devices may process files organized sequentially as with magnetic tape, but also offer the advantage of "random" retrieval of individual records from a file. Although a number of direct access devices are currently available, the IBM 3330 disk drive is representative of all direct-access devices and will serve as a general example for similar units. The 3330 disk storage drive is illustrated in Figure A-10.

Figure A-10 IBM 3330 Disk Storage Facility

The IBM 3330 disk storage facility allows the mounting of removable disk packs on a maximum of eight different magnetic disk drives. All eight of these drives are on-line to the computer at the same time. Each of the removable disk packs consists of eleven magnetic disks which contain 19 surfaces on which data can be recorded.

Data is recorded in the form of magnetic spots along a series of concentric circular recording positions on each disk recording surface. For the IBM 3330 disk packs, there are 411 circular recording positions per surface, with 404 of the recording positions available to the user and 7 alternate positions to be used in case one of the other recording positions is defective. Each circular recording position is capable of storing a maximum of 13,030 characters. Figure A-11 illustrates a schematic of the recording positions on the surface of each disk. The first recording position is referenced by the number zero and the inner recording position by the number 410.

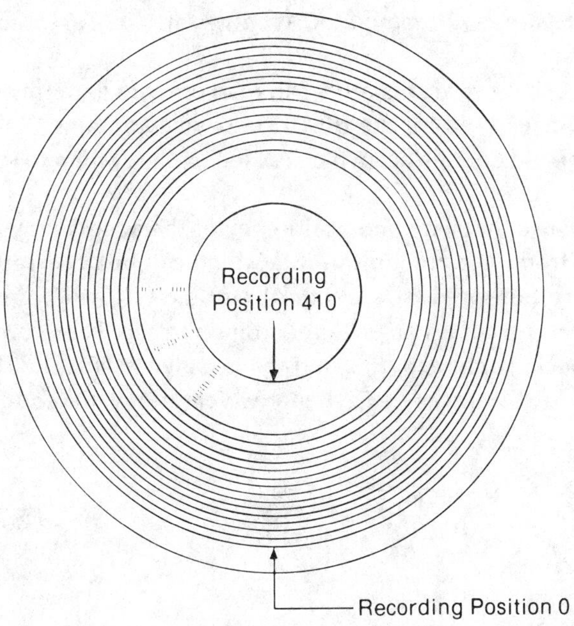

Figure A-11 Schematic of Recording Surface

As noted, the IBM 3336 disk pack which is used with the IBM 3330 storage device consists of 11 magnetic disks such as illustrated in Figure A-11. In order to access the data on these disks, a series of access arms moves in and out between the individual surfaces. This is illustrated in Figure A-12.

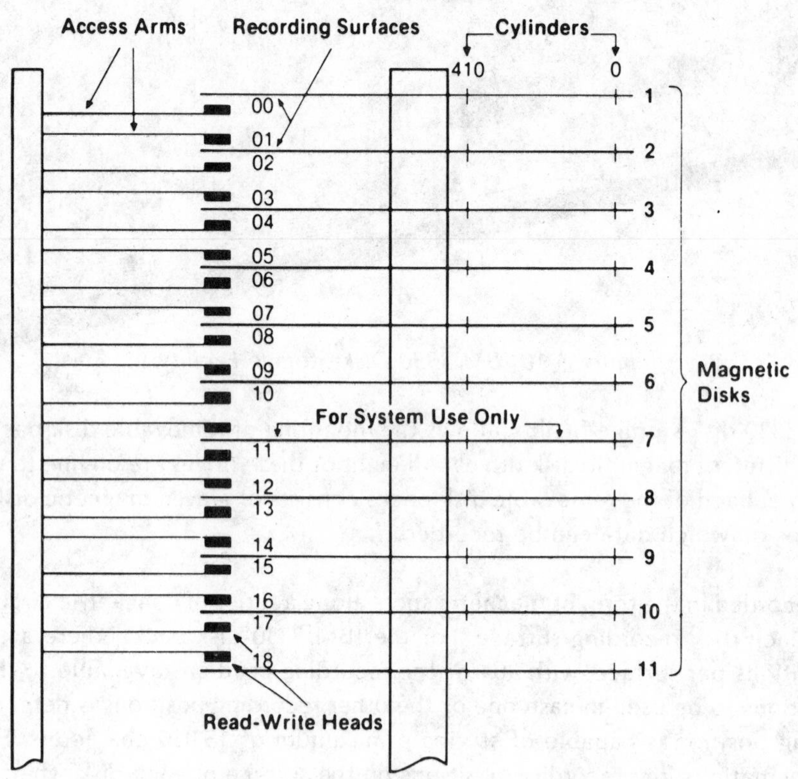

Figure A-12 Example of Access Arms and Disk Pack

Note in Figure A-12 that the access arms can read or write data from each of the surfaces on the disk pack. The disk pack used for the IBM 3330 device contains 19 recording surfaces which are available to the user and one surface which is used by the system to store control information.

It should be noted also that with one positioning of the access arm, all 19 recording surfaces can be written or read from. The amount of data which can be accessed with one positioning of the access arm is said to be stored on a CYLINDER of data. It will be recalled from Figure A-11 that there are 411 concentric circles on each recording surface. Therefore, there are 411 cylinders on an IBM 3336 disk pack. Each recording surface is called a TRACK. Thus, from Figure A-12, it can be seen that there are 19 tracks per cylinder which are available to store user data.

Each track on an IBM 3336 disk pack is capable of storing 13,030 characters. Since there are nineteen tracks per cylinder, a total of 247,570 characters can be stored on a cylinder of data on the disk pack and can be referenced by the access arm in one position.This is illustrated in Figure A-13.

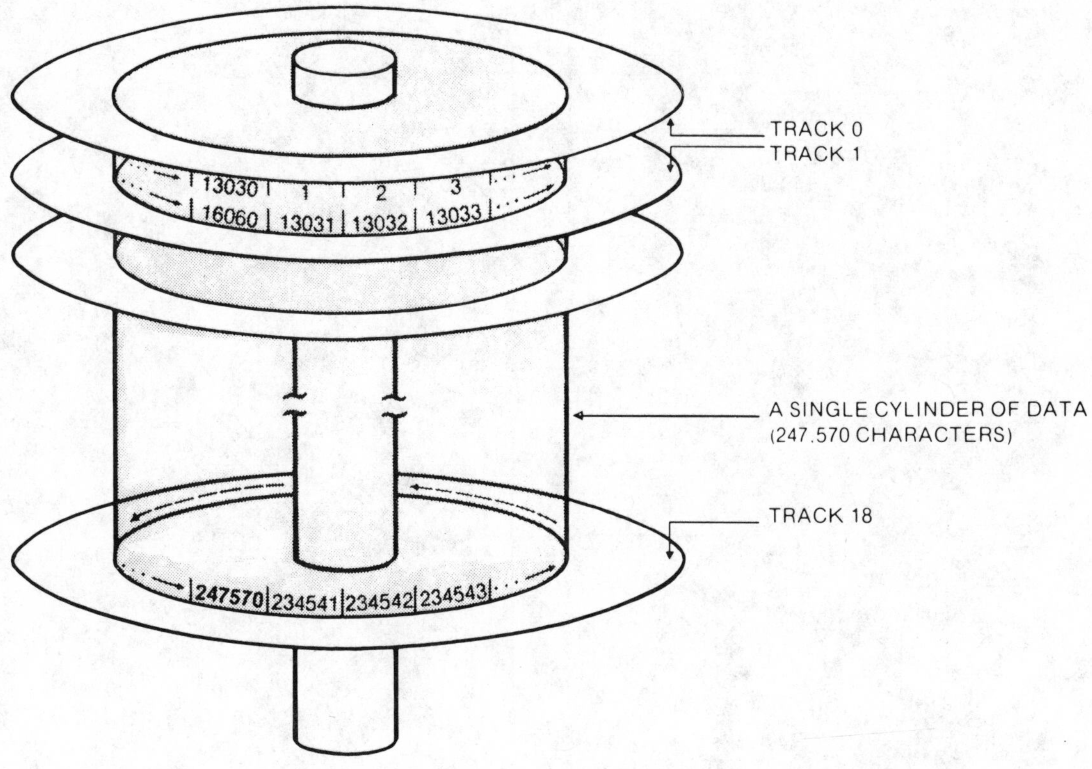

Figure A-13 Example of the Cylinder Concept

DISK LABELS

Labels are normally used for disk files. The labels provide the pertinent information about the disk file. They give the file a name, a creation and expiration date, the location of the file on the disk pack, and other necessary data.

APPENDIX B

PROGRAM CODING STANDARDS

Documentation of a program is material prepared by the programmer which is intended to show what and how a program does its work, how to operate the program, how to interact with the program, and, in short, everything one must know concerning the program. The most important piece of documentation for a program when it must be maintained is the source listing of the program.

When a program is to be changed, the maintenance programmer will usually read the program documentation to determine what the program does and how it does it. Even though a variety of forms of documentation may be developed, the most valuable piece of documentation is the source listing of the program because it is always up-to-date (whereas other forms of documentation may not be kept up-to-date) and because it specifies exactly what is going to take place within the program and how it is going to be done.

It is extremely important, therefore, that the source listing be an easily read document. Indeed, a source listing should be as easily read as any book which one would read. It is of little value to design a good program and then write it so poorly that no one can understand what the program does and how it does it.

In order to ensure that good source programs are written, it is necessary to establish and follow well-defined programming standards within an installation. The following guidelines are the standards used in all of the programs within this textbook, and they should be followed when writing the program assignments in this book; and, indeed, whenever COBOL programs are written.

Identification Division

The Identification Division in the COBOL program is used to identify the program; therefore, as much information as possible should be specified in the Identification Division. All paragraphs in the Identification Division should be completed by the programmer; and, in addition, comments should be included to indicate what the program does. This is illustrated in Figure B-1.

EXAMPLE

```
 IDENTIFICATION DIVISION.

 PROGRAM-ID.     LOADMSTR.
 AUTHOR.         SHELLY.
 INSTALLATION.   ANAHEIM PUBLISHING COMPANY.
 DATE-WRITTEN.   Ø1/Ø9/78.
 DATE-COMPILED.
 SECURITY.       UNCLASSIFIED.

******************************************************************
*                                                                *
*   THIS PROGRAM LOADS THE INVOICE MASTER FILE. IT READS THE     *
*   TRANSACTION FILE AND EDITS THE FIELDS WITHIN THE RECORD TO   *
*   ENSURE THAT THEY CONTAIN VALID DATA. IF ALL OF THE FIELDS    *
*   CONTAIN VALID DATA, THE RECORD IS WRITTEN ON THE INVOICE     *
*   MASTER FILE. IF ANY OF THE FIELDS CONTAIN INVALID DATA, THE  *
*   RECORD IS NOT WRITTEN ON THE MASTER FILE. INSTEAD, A LINE    *
*   IS WRITTEN ON THE INVOICE MASTER EXCEPTION REPORT.           *
*                                                                *
******************************************************************
```

Figure B-1 Example of Identification Division

Note from Figure B-1 that the PROGRAM-ID, AUTHOR, INSTALLATION, DATE-WRITTEN, DATE-COMPILED, and SECURITY paragraphs are all included in the Identification Division. These entries should be included for every COBOL program which is written. The comment entries to the right of the paragraph names should all begin in column 23 of the coding form so that they will be vertically aligned for ease of reading.

In addition, comments should be included which tell what the program does. The comments in the Identification Division need not be overly extensive, but they should define the purpose of the program and basically what it does. These comments should be enclosed in asterisks with spacing as illustrated in Figure B-1. Blank lines should be included as illustrated to improve readability.

Environment Division

The Environment Division also has standards which must be followed. These standards are specified below.

1. The ENVIRONMENT DIVISION Header will begin after three blank lines have been inserted following the last line of the comments in the Identification Division.

2. All Section Names (Configuration Section, Input-Output Section, etc.) shall have one blank line both before and after they are written.

3. Section Names and Paragraph Names will begin in column 8 of the coding form.

4. The Source-Computer and Object-Computer paragraphs will always be included in the Configuration Section. The programmer-supplied entries for these fields will begin in column 25, as will any other programmer-supplied entries in the Configuration Section.

5. Select Statements will begin in column 12. The first line shall contain the name of the file only. The second line of the Select Statement (Assign Clause) shall begin in column 18.

6. All filenames used will fully indicate the purpose of the file. Each filename will include the suffix FILE. The following are examples of acceptable and unacceptable file names.

Acceptable	Unacceptable
INVOICE-TRANSACTION-INPUT-FILE	INV-TRANS-FILE
CUSTOMER-MASTER-INPUT-FILE	CUST-MSTR-INPUT
INVOICE-EXCEPTION-REPORT-FILE	INV-EXCP-RPT
INVENTORY-MASTER-OUTPUT-FILE	INV-MSTR-OUT

A sample Environment Division is illustrated in Figure B-2.

EXAMPLE

```
ØØ2Ø4Ø ENVIRONMENT DIVISION.
ØØ2Ø5Ø
ØØ2Ø6Ø CONFIGURATION SECTION.
ØØ2Ø7Ø
ØØ2Ø8Ø SOURCE-COMPUTER.  IBM-37Ø.
ØØ2Ø9Ø OBJECT-COMPUTER.  IBM-37Ø.
ØØ21ØØ SPECIAL-NAMES.    CØ1  IS TO-THE-TOP-OF-THE-PAGE.
ØØ211Ø
ØØ212Ø INPUT-OUTPUT SECTION.
ØØ213Ø
ØØ214Ø FILE-CONTROL.
ØØ215Ø     SELECT INVOICE-TRANSACTION-INPUT-FILE
ØØ216Ø             ASSIGN TO DA-S-SYSIN.
ØØ217Ø     SELECT INVOICE-MASTER-OUTPUT-FILE
ØØ218Ø             ASSIGN TO DA-S-INVMSTR.
ØØ219Ø     SELECT EXCEPTION-REPORT-FILE
ØØ22ØØ             ASSIGN TO UR-S-SYSOUT.
```

Figure B-2 Example of Properly Coded Environment Division

Note in the example above that the coding in the Environment Division is written according to the rules specified. There is no excuse for the standards not to be followed when programs are coded.

Data Division

As with the other divisions in a COBOL program, there are coding standards for the Data Division of the COBOL program. These standards are specified below.

1. The DATA DIVISION header will always begin on a new page. This can be accomplished through the use of the Eject Statement or through the use of a slash in column 7 of the line before the line on which the Data Division header appears, depending upon the COBOL compiler being used.

2. All Section Names (File Section, Working-Storage Section, etc.) shall have one blank line before and after they are written.

3. Section Names, Paragraph Names, FD Statements, and 01 level data-names will begin in column 8 of the coding form.

4. In the FD Statement, each clause shall appear on a separate line and except for the first line containing the FD Statement, shall begin in column 14.

5. Each successive level of data-names (i.e. 01, 05, 10) shall be indented four spaces from the next higher data-name. This is illustrated in Figure B-3.

EXAMPLE

```
ØØ7Ø9Ø
ØØ71ØØ ØØ1  CUSTOMER-MASTER-OUTPUT-RECORD.
ØØ711Ø          Ø5  CURRENT-DATE-CUSTMSTR-OUT.
ØØ712Ø              1Ø  CURRENT-MONTH-CUSTMSTR-OUT       PIC XX.
ØØ713Ø              1Ø  CURRENT-DAY-CUSTMSTR-OUT         PIC XX.
ØØ714Ø              1Ø  CURRENT-YEAR-CUSTMSTR-OUT        PIC XX.
```

Figure B-3 Example of Level Indentation

Note from Figure B-3 that each level is indented four spaces from the previous level.

6. The data-name will be separated from the level number by two spaces.

7. Each data-name used in the program will fully indicate the purpose of the field or record being defined. The following are examples of acceptable and unacceptable data-names.

Acceptable	Unacceptable
CUSTOMER-NUMBER-TRANSIN	CUST-NO-IN
INVOICE-NUMBER-REPORT	INV-NO-OUT
HAS-AN-ERROR-OCCURRED	INDICATOR-2
TOTAL-SALES-ACCUM	TOT-SALES
INVOICE-NUMBER-WORK-AREA	INV-NO
CURRENT-DATE-WORK-AREA	DATE-WORK

8. No Level 77 data items will be used within the program.

9. No Level 01 data-name, with the exception of record names in the File Section of the Data Division, shall be an elementary data item. All data fields shall be identified by a group name. The following is an example.

EXAMPLE

Acceptable

```
ØØ6Ø1Ø
ØØ6Ø2Ø Ø1  PROGRAM-ACCUMULATORS.
ØØ6Ø3Ø         Ø5  SALES-AMOUNT-ACCUM              PIC S9(7)V99.
ØØ6Ø4Ø         Ø5  NUMBER-OF-EMPLOYEES-ACCUM       PIC S9(5).
```

Unacceptable

```
ØØ6Ø8Ø Ø1  SALES-AMOUNT-ACCUM              PIC S9(7)V99.
ØØ6Ø9Ø Ø1  NUMBER-OF-EMPLOYEES-ACCUM       PIC S9(5).
```

Figure B-4 Example of Level 01 Data

10. All Elementary Items within a Group Item will have their Picture Clauses begin in the same column and will use the abbreviation "PIC." If possible, the Picture Clauses will begin in column 40, but it is more important that all Picture Clauses begin in the same column within group items. This is illustrated in Figure B-5.

EXAMPLE

Acceptable

```
ØØ8010 Ø1  PROGRAM-ACCUMULATORS.
ØØ8020         Ø5  SALES-AMOUNT-ACCUM             PIC S9(7)V99.
ØØ8030         Ø5  NUMBER-OF-EMPLOYEES-ACCUM      PIC S9(5).
```

Unacceptable

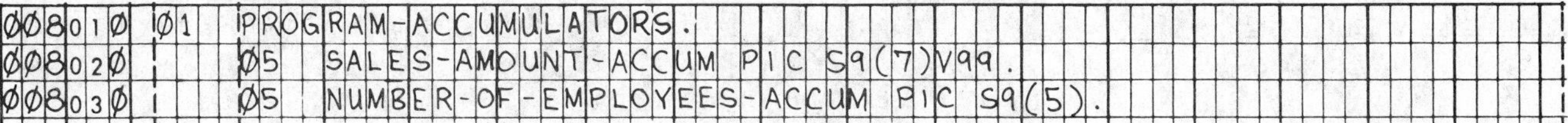

```
ØØ8010 Ø1  PROGRAM-ACCUMULATORS.
ØØ8020         Ø5  SALES-AMOUNT-ACCUM PIC S9(7)V99.
ØØ8030         Ø5  NUMBER-OF-EMPLOYEES-ACCUM PIC S9(5).
```

Figure B-5 Examples of Picture Clause

11. If more than three digits are to be contained in a field, then parentheses should be used in the Picture clause rather than a series of X's or 9's. This is illustrated below.

Acceptable	Unacceptable
PIC S9(5)	PIC S99999

12. The Value Clauses will be aligned within group items. If possible, they should begin in column 53.

13. If the value to be specified in the Value Clause is short enough, it will be specified on the same line as the Value Statement. If not, it will be contained on the next coding line, with the apostrophe one space to the left of the "V" in Value. This is illustrated below.

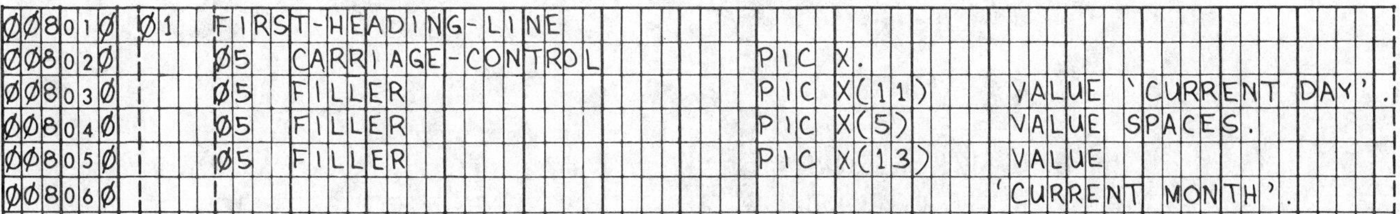

```
ØØ8010 Ø1  FIRST-HEADING-LINE
ØØ8020         Ø5  CARRIAGE-CONTROL            PIC X.
ØØ8030         Ø5  FILLER                      PIC X(11)    VALUE 'CURRENT DAY'.
ØØ8040         Ø5  FILLER                      PIC X(5)     VALUE SPACES.
ØØ8050         Ø5  FILLER                      PIC X(13)    VALUE
ØØ8060                                                     'CURRENT MONTH'.
```

Figure B-6 Example of Value Clause

14. There will be no continued values in the Value Clause.

15. If a value which is specified in the Value Clause contains more than two imbedded blanks, then a separate value clause must be used. This is illustrated below.

EXAMPLE

Acceptable

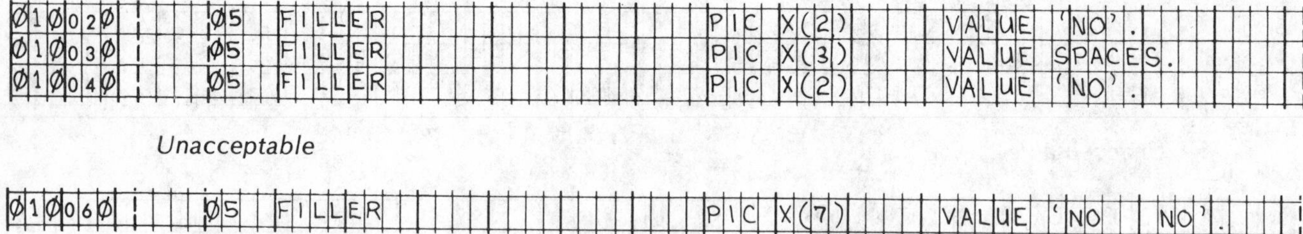

```
Ø1Ø02Ø       Ø5  FILLER                        PIC X(2)     VALUE 'NO'.
Ø1Ø03Ø       Ø5  FILLER                        PIC X(3)     VALUE SPACES.
Ø1Ø04Ø       Ø5  FILLER                        PIC X(2)     VALUE 'NO'.
```

Unacceptable

```
Ø1Ø06Ø       Ø5  FILLER                        PIC X(7)     VALUE 'NO   NO'.
```

Figure B-7 Example of Value Clause

16. The Occurs Clause, Ascending Key Is Clause, Usage Clause, or any other clause used to define data within a field other than the Picture Clause shall begin in column 53 of the coding form or in a column which makes the clause easy to read. This is illustrated in Figure B-8.

EXAMPLE

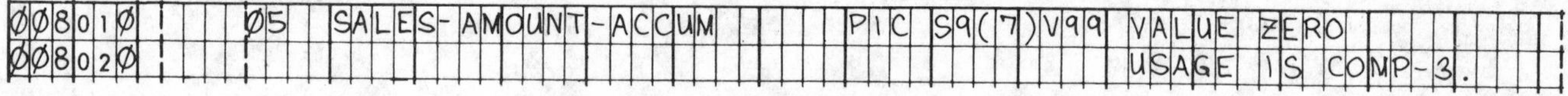

```
ØØ8Ø1Ø       Ø5  SALES-AMOUNT-ACCUM            PIC S9(7)V99 VALUE ZERO
ØØ8Ø2Ø                                                      USAGE IS COMP-3.
```

Figure B-8 Example of Usage Clause

17. Condition names (Level-88) shall be used whenever the value in a field indicates a certain condition.

18. Indicator names shall have their names be the question which is answered by the indicator. The following are examples.

Acceptable	Unacceptable
ARE-THERE-MORE-RECORDS	EOF
WAS-THERE-A-CONTROL-BREAK	CONTROL-BREAK-IND
IS-THE-INPUT-RECORD-VALID	VALID-REC

19. The only acceptable values in an indicator are YES or NO. Thus, all indicators have a picture PIC XXX.

20. All Level 01 data-names will be preceded by one blank line. In addition, blank lines can be inserted between other levels if needed for ease of reading.

In addition to these standards which must be followed, any additional techniques which make the Data Division more readable should also be implemented.

Procedure Division

The following standards should be followed when coding the Procedure Division.

1. The PROCEDURE DIVISION header line should begin on a new page. This can be accomplished through the use of the Eject Statement or through the use of a slash in column 7 of the line before the line on which the Procedure Division header appears, depending upon the COBOL compiler being used.

2. All modules will begin on a new page. The first module can appear on the same page as the Procedure Division header.

3. All modules will be preceded by comments (* in column 7) explaining the function of the module which follows and module(s) which call the module. In addition, the comments shall be enclosed within asterisks, and blank lines should be included as illustrated below.

EXAMPLE

Coding

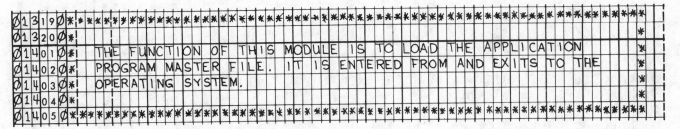

```
Ø1319Ø*****************************************************************
Ø1320Ø*                                                               *
Ø1401Ø*  THE FUNCTION OF THIS MODULE IS TO LOAD THE APPLICATION       *
Ø1402Ø*  PROGRAM MASTER FILE. IT IS ENTERED FROM AND EXITS TO THE     *
Ø1403Ø*  OPERATING SYSTEM.                                            *
Ø1404Ø*                                                               *
Ø1405Ø*****************************************************************
```

Listing

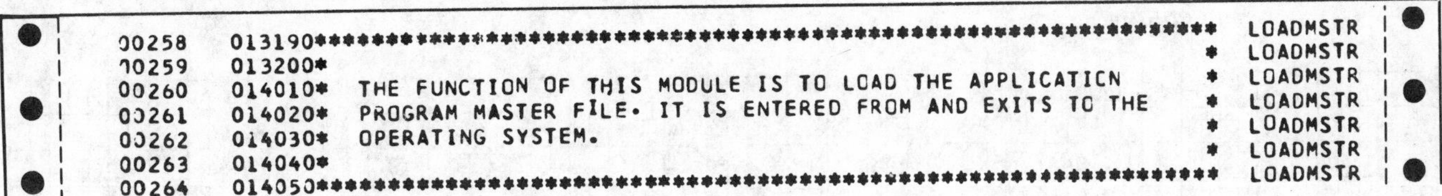

```
013190*****************************************************************   LOADMSTR
013200*                                                               *   LOADMSTR
014010*  THE FUNCTION OF THIS MODULE IS TO LOAD THE APPLICATION       *   LOADMSTR
014020*  PROGRAM MASTER FILE. IT IS ENTERED FROM AND EXITS TO THE     *   LOADMSTR
014030*  OPERATING SYSTEM.                                            *   LOADMSTR
014040*                                                               *   LOADMSTR
014050*****************************************************************   LOADMSTR
```

Figure B-9 Example of Comments in Procedure Division

4. All comments will be preceded by and followed by a blank line unless the comments begin a page. If this is the case, they need not be preceded by a blank line.

5. The name of each module will be the same as the function performed by the module. These names should be spelled out in full for ease of reading. In addition, each module name will be preceded by a four-digit field representing the placement of the module within the structural hierarchy of the program. The following are examples of acceptable and unacceptable module names.

Acceptable	Unacceptable
A000-LOAD-MASTER-FILE	LOAD-MASTER-FILE
B010-PROCESS-DETAIL-RECORD	B010-PROC-REC
C020-EDIT-CUSTOMER-NUMBER	020-EDIT
D010-CHECK-VALIDITY-OF-DATE	D010-CHK-DATE

6. If a separate paragraph is required WITHIN a module because of the use of the Perform Statement, the paragraph name shall be preceded by three blank lines. The paragraph will have a sequence number which contains the digits 1, 2, etc. in the low-order position, plus the sequence number of the module in which it appears. For example, paragraphs in the module B010 would have the prefixes B011, B012, etc. The paragraph name must be meaningful and describe the purpose of the paragraph.

7. All module and paragraph names within the program will be followed by a blank line prior to the first program statement.

8. Program statements which are not executed as a result of prior conditional statements or which are not continuation statements will begin in column 12 of the coding form.

9. All conditional statements or clauses within a statement which indicate a condition under which certain processing is to take place will be placed on a line by themselves. In addition, statements to be executed as a result of a condition's being true or not true will be indented three spaces from the position where the statement stating the condition begins. This is illustrated below.

EXAMPLE

Acceptable

```
015090     READ CUSTOMER-MASTER-INPUT-FILE
015100        AT END
015110           MOVE 'NO ' TO ARE-THERE-MORE-RECORDS.
015120     IF CUSTOMER-NUMBER-INPUT = SPACES
015130        ADD 1 TO BLANK-CUSTOMER-NUMBERS-ACCUM.
```

Unacceptable

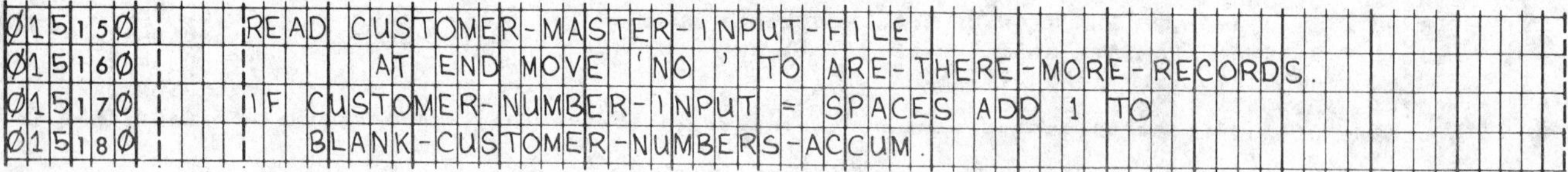

```
015150     READ CUSTOMER-MASTER-INPUT-FILE
015160        AT END MOVE 'NO ' TO ARE-THERE-MORE-RECORDS.
015170     IF CUSTOMER-NUMBER-INPUT = SPACES ADD 1 TO
015180        BLANK-CUSTOMER-NUMBERS-ACCUM.
```

Figure B-10 Example of Conditional Statements

Note particularly in the Read Statement that the AT END Clause is a conditional clause; therefore, it must be on a line by itself.

10. Any single statement must be on a line by itself; that is, only one statement can appear on one line. This is illustrated in Figure B-11.

EXAMPLE

Acceptable

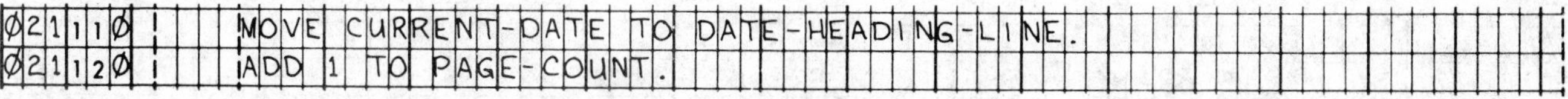

```
Ø2111Ø    MOVE CURRENT-DATE TO DATE-HEADING-LINE.
Ø2112Ø    ADD 1 TO PAGE-COUNT.
```

Unacceptable

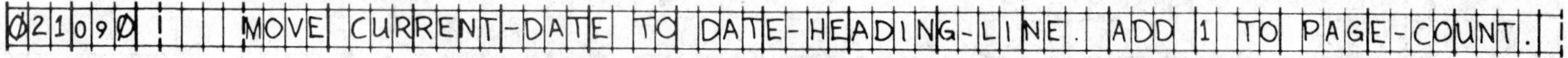

```
Ø2109Ø    MOVE CURRENT-DATE TO DATE-HEADING-LINE. ADD 1 TO PAGE-COUNT.
```

Figure B-11 Example of Single Statements

11. Any statement which must be continued to a second line will have the second line and all subsequent continued lines indented six spaces from the position where the statement being continued begins. This is illustrated below.

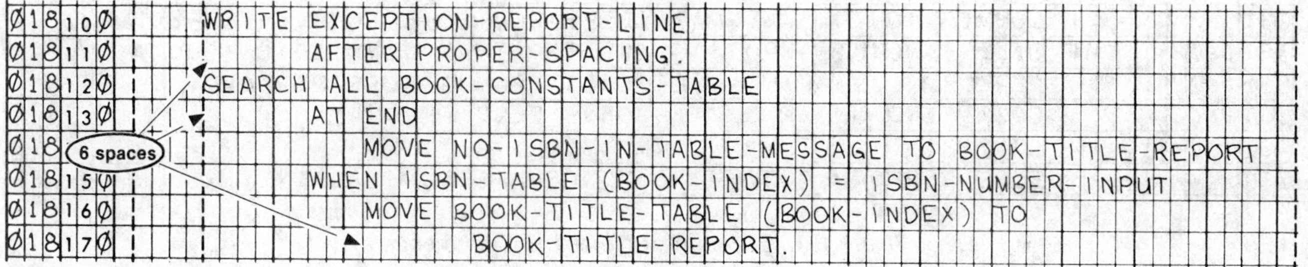

```
Ø181ØØ    WRITE EXCEPTION-REPORT-LINE
Ø1811Ø          AFTER PROPER-SPACING.
Ø1812Ø    SEARCH ALL BOOK-CONSTANTS-TABLE
Ø1813Ø          AT END
Ø18           MOVE NO-ISBN-IN-TABLE-MESSAGE TO BOOK-TITLE-REPORT
Ø1815Ø          WHEN ISBN-TABLE (BOOK-INDEX) = ISBN-NUMBER-INPUT
Ø1816Ø                MOVE BOOK-TITLE-TABLE (BOOK-INDEX) TO
Ø1817Ø                      BOOK-TITLE-REPORT.
```


Figure B-12 Example of Continued Statements

12. If Nested IF Statements are required to solve a problem, each IF and its corresponding ELSE will be vertically aligned; in addition, statements which are to be executed as a result of a condition's being true or not true will be indented three spaces in the same manner as any other conditional statement. This is illustrated below.

Acceptable

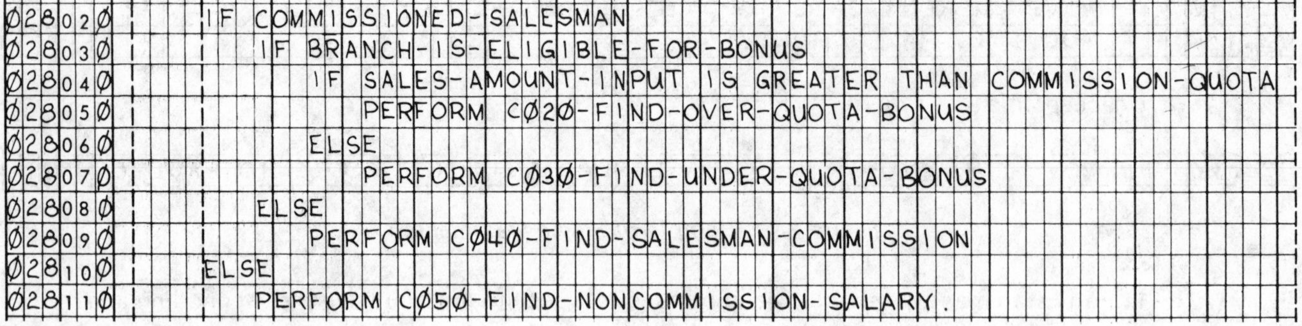

```
Ø28Ø2Ø     IF COMMISSIONED-SALESMAN
Ø28Ø3Ø        IF BRANCH-IS-ELIGIBLE-FOR-BONUS
Ø28Ø4Ø           IF SALES-AMOUNT-INPUT IS GREATER THAN COMMISSION-QUOTA
Ø28Ø5Ø              PERFORM CØ2Ø-FIND-OVER-QUOTA-BONUS
Ø28Ø6Ø           ELSE
Ø28Ø7Ø              PERFORM CØ3Ø-FIND-UNDER-QUOTA-BONUS
Ø28Ø8Ø        ELSE
Ø28Ø9Ø           PERFORM CØ4Ø-FIND-SALESMAN-COMMISSION
Ø281ØØ     ELSE
Ø2811Ø        PERFORM CØ5Ø-FIND-NONCOMMISSION-SALARY.
```

Unacceptable

```
Ø3113Ø     IF COMMISSIONED-SALESMAN IF BRANCH-IS-ELIGIBLE-FOR-BONUS
Ø3114Ø     IF SALES-AMOUNT-INPUT IS GREATER THAN COMMISSION-QUOTA
Ø3115Ø        PERFORM CØ2Ø-FIND-OVER-QUOTA-BONUS ELSE PERFORM
Ø3116Ø        CØ3Ø-FIND-UNDER-QUOTA-BONUS ELSE PERFORM
Ø3117Ø        CØ4Ø-FIND-SALESMAN-COMMISSION
Ø3118Ø        ELSE PERFORM CØ5Ø-FIND-NONCOMMISSION-SALARY.
```

Figure B-13 Example of Nested IF Statements

13. If multiple conditions are to be checked by one IF Statement, they must be continued on a second or third line. Each continued statement will be indented six spaces from the start of the IF Statement, and each line will end with the "AND" or "OR," indicating to the reader that the line is to be continued. This is illustrated in Figure B-14.

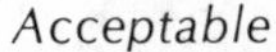

Acceptable

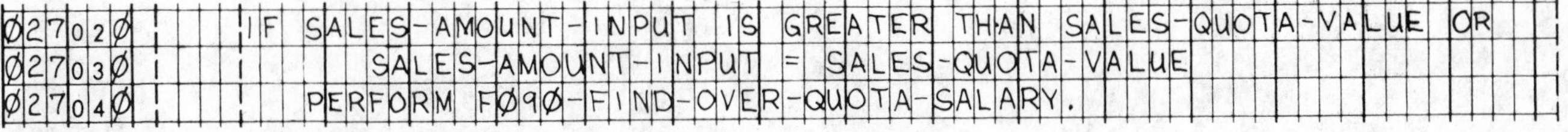

```
Ø27020     IF SALES-AMOUNT-INPUT IS GREATER THAN SALES-QUOTA-VALUE OR
Ø27030           SALES-AMOUNT-INPUT = SALES-QUOTA-VALUE
Ø27040        PERFORM FØ9Ø-FIND-OVER-QUOTA-SALARY.
```

Unacceptable

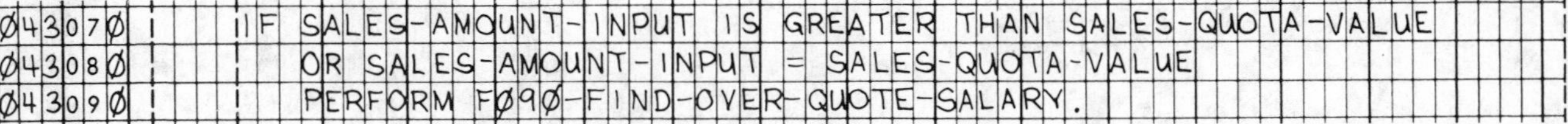

```
Ø43070     IF SALES-AMOUNT-INPUT IS GREATER THAN SALES-QUOTA-VALUE
Ø43080        OR SALES-AMOUNT-INPUT = SALES-QUOTA-VALUE
Ø43090        PERFORM FØ9Ø-FIND-OVER-QUOTE-SALARY.
```

Figure B-14 Example of Multiple Conditions

14. The PERFORM THRU Statement and the EXIT Statement will only be used when the GO TO DEPENDING Statement is used to implement a Case Structure. The Level-W Diagnostic "EXIT FROM PERFORMED PROCEDURE ASSUMED BEFORE PROCEDURE-NAME" is an acceptable diagnostic.

15. The GO TO Statement will not be used in a program except under unique circumstances, and must be justified to others in a walkthrough prior to implementation.

16. Page/line numbers (columns 1-6) will always be included for each source statement.

17. Program identification (columns 73-80) will always be included for each source statement. The program identification should be the same as the PROGRAM-ID specified in the Identification Division.

SUMMARY

The coding standards presented in this Appendix are not just good ideas; they are standards which absolutely should be adhered to. There is no doubt that some programmers will disagree with some of the standards which are specified here, but unless they propose a better way to code, that is, a way which is equally as clear to understand and read, then these standards should be followed to the letter.

APPENDIX C

COBOL FORMAT NOTATION

The following are the general formats for all COBOL Statements used in this text.

Identification Division

GENERAL FORMAT FOR IDENTIFICATION DIVISION

```
IDENTIFICATION DIVISION.

PROGRAM-ID. program-name.

[AUTHOR. [comment-entry] ...]

[INSTALLATION. [comment-entry] ...]

[DATE-WRITTEN. [comment-entry] ...]

[DATE-COMPILED. [comment-entry] ...]

[SECURITY. [comment-entry] ...]
```

Environment Division

GENERAL FORMAT FOR ENVIRONMENT DIVISION

```
ENVIRONMENT DIVISION.

CONFIGURATION SECTION.

SOURCE-COMPUTER.  computer-name [WITH DEBUGGING MODE] .

OBJECT-COMPUTER.  computer-name

    [, MEMORY SIZE integer {WORDS / CHARACTERS / MODULES}]

    [, PROGRAM COLLATING SEQUENCE IS alphabet-name]

    [, SEGMENT-LIMIT IS segment-number] .

[SPECIAL-NAMES. [, implementor-name

    { IS mnemonic-name [, ON STATUS IS condition-name-1 [, OFF STATUS IS condition-name-2]]
      IS mnemonic-name [, OFF STATUS IS condition-name-2 [, ON STATUS IS condition-name-1]]
      ON STATUS IS condition-name-1 [, OFF STATUS IS condition-name-2]
      OFF STATUS IS condition-name-2 [, ON STATUS IS condition-name-1] } ] ...

    [, alphabet-name IS { STANDARD-1
                          NATIVE
                          implementor-name
                          literal-1 [ {THROUGH / THRU} literal-2
                                      ALSO literal-3 [, ALSO literal-4]... ]
                          [ literal-5 [ {THROUGH / THRU} literal-6
                                        ALSO literal-7 [, ALSO literal-8]... ] ] ... } ] ...

    [, CURRENCY SIGN IS literal-9]

    [, DECIMAL-POINT IS COMMA] . ]
```

```
[INPUT-OUTPUT SECTION.

 FILE-CONTROL.

   {file-control-entry} ...

[I-O-CONTROL.

   [; RERUN [ON {file-name-1        }]
                {implementor-name   }]

                  {{ [END OF] {REEL} }                     }]
                  {{          {UNIT} } OF file-name-2       }]
           EVERY  {{ integer-1 RECORDS}                     }] ...
                  { integer-2 CLOCK-UNITS                   }]
                  { condition-name                          }]

   [        [RECORD    ]                                             ]
   [; SAME  [SORT      ] AREA FOR file-name-3 {, file-name-4} ...    ] ...
   [        [SORT-MERGE]                                             ]

   [; MULTIPLE FILE TAPE CONTAINS file-name-5 [POSITION integer-3]

       [, file-name-6 [POSITION integer-4]] ... ] ...   .]]
```

Environment Division

GENERAL FORMAT FOR FILE CONTROL ENTRY

FORMAT 1:

```
SELECT [OPTIONAL] file-name

    ASSIGN TO implementor-name-1 [, implementor-name-2] ...

    [; RESERVE integer-1 {AREA | AREAS}]

    [; ORGANIZATION IS SEQUENTIAL]

    [; ACCESS MODE IS SEQUENTIAL]

    [; FILE STATUS IS data-name-1] .
```

FORMAT 2:

```
SELECT file-name

    ASSIGN TO implementor-name-1 [, implementor-name-2] ...

    [; RESERVE integer-1 {AREA | AREAS}]

    ; ORGANIZATION IS RELATIVE

    [; ACCESS MODE IS { SEQUENTIAL [, RELATIVE KEY IS data-name-1]
                      { {RANDOM | DYNAMIC} , RELATIVE KEY IS data-name-1 } ]

    [; FILE STATUS IS data-name-2] .
```

FORMAT 3:

```
SELECT file-name

   ASSIGN TO implementor-name-1  [, implementor-name-2 ] ...

  [; RESERVE integer-1 [AREA ]]
                       [AREAS]

   ; ORGANIZATION IS INDEXED

  [                    {SEQUENTIAL}]
  [; ACCESS MODE IS    {RANDOM    }]
  [                    {DYNAMIC   }]

   ; RECORD KEY IS data-name-1

  [; ALTERNATE RECORD KEY IS data-name-2  [WITH DUPLICATES]] ...

  [; FILE STATUS IS data-name-3 ] .
```

FORMAT 4:

```
SELECT file-name ASSIGN TO implementor-name-1  [, implementor-name-2 ] ...
```

Data Division

GENERAL FORMAT FOR DATA DIVISION

```
DATA DIVISION.

[FILE SECTION.

[FD  file-name

    [; BLOCK CONTAINS [integer-1 TO] integer-2 {RECORDS   }]
                                               {CHARACTERS}]

    [; RECORD CONTAINS [integer-3 TO]  integer-4 CHARACTERS]

    ; LABEL {RECORD IS  } {STANDARD}
            {RECORDS ARE} {OMITTED }

    [; VALUE OF implementor-name-1 IS {data-name-1}
                                      {literal-1  }

        [, implementor-name-2 IS {data-name-2}] ... ]
                                 {literal-2  }]

    [; DATA {RECORD IS  } data-name-3 [, data-name-4] ... ]
            {RECORDS ARE}

    [; LINAGE IS {data-name-5} LINES [, WITH FOOTING AT {data-name-6}]
                 {integer-5  }                          {integer-6  }

        [, LINES AT TOP {data-name-7}] [, LINES AT BOTTOM {data-name-8}]]
                        {integer-7  }]                    {integer-8  }]]

    [; CODE-SET IS alphabet-name]

    [; {REPORT IS  } report-name-1 [, report-name-2] ... ].
       {REPORTS ARE}

[record-description-entry] ... ] ...

[SD  file-name

    [; RECORD CONTAINS [integer-1 TO] integer-2 CHARACTERS]

    [; DATA {RECORD IS  } data-name-1 [, data-name-2] ... ] .
            {RECORDS ARE}

{record-description-entry} ... ] ... ]

[WORKING-STORAGE SECTION.

[77-level-description-entry] ... ]
[record-description-entry  ]

[LINKAGE SECTION.

[77-level-description-entry] ... ]
[record-description-entry  ]
```

Data Division

GENERAL FORMAT FOR DATA DESCRIPTION ENTRY

FORMAT 1:

```
level-number {data-name-1}
             {FILLER     }

   [; REDEFINES data-name-2]

   [; {PICTURE} IS character-string]
      {PIC    }

   [; [USAGE IS] {COMPUTATIONAL}]
                 {COMP         }
                 {DISPLAY      }
                 {INDEX        }

   [; [SIGN IS] {LEADING } [SEPARATE CHARACTER]]
                {TRAILING}

   [; OCCURS {integer-1 TO integer-2 TIMES DEPENDING ON data-name-3}
             {integer-2 TIMES                                      }

        [{ASCENDING } KEY IS data-name-4 [, data-name-5] ...] ...
         {DESCENDING}

        [INDEXED BY index-name-1 [, index-name-2] ...]]

   [; {SYNCHRONIZED} [LEFT ]]
      {SYNC        } [RIGHT]

   [; {JUSTIFIED} RIGHT]
      {JUST     }

   [; BLANK WHEN ZERO]

   [; VALUE IS literal] .
```

FORMAT 2:

```
66  data-name-1; RENAMES data-name-2 [{THROUGH} data-name-3] .
                                      {THRU   }
```

FORMAT 3:

```
88  condition-name; {VALUE IS  } literal-1 [{THROUGH} literal-2]
                    {VALUES ARE}            {THRU   }

    [, literal-3 [{THROUGH} literal-4]] ... .
                  {THRU   }
```

GENERAL FORMAT FOR PROCEDURE DIVISION

FORMAT 1:

```
PROCEDURE DIVISION [USING data-name-1 [, data-name-2] ... ] .
[DECLARATIVES.
{section-name SECTION [segment-number] .  declarative-sentence
[paragraph-name. [sentence] ... ] ... } ...
END DECLARATIVES.]
{section-name SECTION [segment-number ] .
[paragraph-name. [sentence ] ... ] ... } ...
```

FORMAT 2:

```
PROCEDURE DIVISION [ USING data-name-1 [ , data-name-2 ] ... ] .
{paragraph-name. [ sentence ] ... } ...
```

COBOL Verb Formats

GENERAL FORMAT FOR VERBS

```
ACCEPT identifier [ FROM mnemonic-name ]

                           { DATE }
ACCEPT identifier FROM     { DAY  }
                           { TIME }

ACCEPT cd-name MESSAGE COUNT

ADD {identifier-1} [, identifier-2] ...   TO identifier-m [ROUNDED]
    {literal-1   } [, literal-2   ]

   [, identifier-n [ROUNDED]] ...  [; ON SIZE ERROR imperative-statement]

ADD {identifier-1} , {identifier-2} [, identifier-3] ...
    {literal-1   }   {literal-2   } [, literal-3   ]

   GIVING identifier-m [ROUNDED] [, identifier-n [ROUNDED]] ...

   [; ON SIZE ERROR imperative-statement]

ADD {CORRESPONDING}  identifier-1 TO identifier-2 [ROUNDED]
    {CORR         }

   [; ON SIZE ERROR imperative-statement]

ALTER procedure-name-1 TO [PROCEED TO] procedure-name-2

   [, procedure-name-3 TO [PROCEED TO] procedure-name-4 ] ...

CALL {identifier-1} [USING data-name-1  [, data-name-2] ... ]
     {literal-1   }

   [; ON OVERFLOW imperative-statement ]

CANCEL {identifier-1} [, identifier-2] ...
       {literal-1   } [, literal-2   ]

                    [ {REEL} [WITH NO REWIND] ]
                    [ {UNIT} [FOR REMOVAL   ] ]
CLOSE file-name-1   [                         ]
                    [ WITH {NO REWIND}        ]
                    [      {LOCK     }        ]

   [                   [ {REEL} [WITH NO REWIND] ] ]
   [                   [ {UNIT} [FOR REMOVAL   ] ] ]
   [ , file-name-2     [                         ] ] ...
   [                   [ WITH {NO REWIND}        ] ]
   [                   [      {LOCK     }        ] ]

CLOSE file-name-1 [WITH LOCK] [, file-name-2 [WITH LOCK]] ...
```

```
COMPUTE identifier-1 [ROUNDED] [, identifier-2 [ROUNDED]] ...

   = arithmetic-expression [; ON SIZE ERROR imperative-statement ]

DELETE file-name RECORD [; INVALID KEY imperative-statement]

DISABLE {INPUT [TERMINAL]} cd-name WITH KEY {identifier-1}
        {OUTPUT          }                  {literal-1   }

DISPLAY {identifier-1} [, identifier-2] ... [UPON mnemonic-name]
        {literal-1   } [, literal-2   ]

DIVIDE {identifier-1} INTO identifier-2 [ROUNDED]
       {literal-1   }

   [, identifier-3 [ROUNDED]] ... [; ON SIZE ERROR imperative-statement ]

DIVIDE {identifier-1} INTO {identifier-2} GIVING identifier-3 [ROUNDED]
       {literal-1   }      {literal-2   }

   [, identifier-4 [ROUNDED]] ... [; ON SIZE ERROR imperative-statement]

DIVIDE {identifier-1} BY {identifier-2} GIVING identifier-3 [ROUNDED]
       {literal-1   }    {literal-2   }

   [, identifier-4 [ROUNDED]] ... [; ON SIZE ERROR imperative-statement]

DIVIDE {identifier-1} INTO {identifier-2} GIVING identifier-3 [ROUNDED]
       {literal-1   }      {literal-2   }

   REMAINDER identifier-4 [; ON SIZE ERROR imperative-statement]

DIVIDE {identifier-1} BY {identifier-2} GIVING identifier-3 [ROUNDED]
       {literal-1   }    {literal-2   }

   REMAINDER identifier-4 [; ON SIZE ERROR imperative-statement]

ENABLE {INPUT [TERMINAL]} cd-name WITH KEY {identifier-1}
       {OUTPUT          }                  {literal-1   }

ENTER language-name [routine-name] .

EXIT [PROGRAM] .

GENERATE {data-name  }
         {report-name}

GO TO [procedure-name-1]
```

```
GO TO procedure-name-1  [, procedure-name-2] ...   , procedure-name-n

   DEPENDING ON identifier

IF condition;  {statement-1   } {; ELSE statement-2     }
               {NEXT SENTENCE } {; ELSE NEXT SENTENCE   }

INITIATE report-name-1  [, report-name-2] ...

INSPECT identifier-1 TALLYING

 {, identifier-2 FOR {, {{ALL    } {identifier-3}} [{BEFORE} INITIAL {identifier-4}]} ...} ...
                     {  {{LEADING} {literal-1   }} [{AFTER }         {literal-2   }]}
                     {  {CHARACTERS             }                                  }

INSPECT identifier-1 REPLACING

 {CHARACTERS BY {identifier-6} [{BEFORE} INITIAL {identifier-7}]                           }
 {              {literal-4   } [{AFTER }         {literal-5   }]                           }
 {{, {ALL    } {, {identifier-5} BY {identifier-6} [{BEFORE} INITIAL {identifier-7}]} ...} ...}
 {{  {LEADING} {  {literal-3   }    {literal-4   } [{AFTER }         {literal-5   }]}    }    }
 {{  {FIRST  }                                                                           }

INSPECT identifier-1 TALLYING

 {, identifier-2 FOR {, {{ALL    } {identifier-3}} [{BEFORE} INITIAL {identifier-4}]} ...} ...
                     {  {{LEADING} {literal-1   }} [{AFTER }         {literal-2   }]}
                     {  {CHARACTERS             }                                  }

  REPLACING

 {CHARACTERS BY {identifier-6} [{BEFORE} INITIAL {identifier-7}]                           }
 {              {literal-4   } [{AFTER }         {literal-5   }]                           }
 {{, {ALL    } {, {identifier-5} BY {identifier-6} [{BEFORE} INITIAL {identifier-7}]} ...} ...}
 {{  {LEADING} {  {literal-3   }    {literal-4   } [{AFTER }         {literal-5   }]}    }    }
 {{  {FIRST  }                                                                           }
```

```
MERGE file-name-1 ON {ASCENDING | DESCENDING} KEY data-name-1 [, data-name-2] ...

        [ON {ASCENDING | DESCENDING} KEY data-name-3 [, data-name-4] ... ] ...

    [COLLATING SEQUENCE IS alphabet-name]

    USING file-name-2, file-name-3 [, file-name-4 ] ...

    { OUTPUT PROCEDURE IS section-name-1 [{THROUGH | THRU} section-name-2] }
    { GIVING file-name-5                                                  }

MOVE {identifier-1 | literal} TO identifier-2 [, identifier-3 ] ...

MOVE {CORRESPONDING | CORR} identifier-1 TO identifier-2

MULTIPLY {identifier-1 | literal-1} BY identifier-2 [ROUNDED]

    [, identifier-3 [ROUNDED]] ... [; ON SIZE ERROR imperative-statement]

MULTIPLY {identifier-1 | literal-1} BY {identifier-2 | literal-2} GIVING identifier-3 [ROUNDED]

    [, identifier-4 [ROUNDED]] ... [; ON SIZE ERROR imperative-statement]

     { INPUT file-name-1 [REVERSED | WITH NO REWIND] [, file-name-2 [REVERSED | WITH NO REWIND]] ... }
OPEN { OUTPUT file-name-3 [WITH NO REWIND] [, file-name-4 [WITH NO REWIND]] ...                   } ...
     { I-O file-name-5 [, file-name-6 ] ...                                                        }
     { EXTEND file-name-7 [, file-name-8] ...                                                      }

     { INPUT file-name-1 [, file-name-2 ] ...  }
OPEN { OUTPUT file-name-3 [, file-name-4 ] ... } ...
     { I-O file-name-5 [, file-name-6 ] ...    }

PERFORM procedure-name-1 [{THROUGH | THRU} procedure-name-2]

PERFORM procedure-name-1 [{THROUGH | THRU} procedure-name-2] {identifier-1 | integer-1} TIMES

PERFORM procedure-name-1 [{THROUGH | THRU} procedure-name-2] UNTIL condition-1
```

```
PERFORM procedure-name-1 [{THROUGH} procedure-name-2]
                          {THRU   }

    VARYING {identifier-2} FROM {identifier-3}
            {index-name-1}      {index-name-2}
                                {literal-1   }

        BY {identifier-4} UNTIL condition-1
           {literal-3   }

  [ AFTER {identifier-5} FROM {identifier-6}
  [       {index-name-3}      {index-name-4}
  [                           {literal-3   }

        BY {identifier-7} UNTIL condition-2
           {literal-4   }

  [ AFTER {identifier-8} FROM {identifier-9}
  [       {index-name-5}      {index-name-6}
  [                           {literal-5   }

        BY {identifier-10} UNTIL condition-3 ]]
           {literal-6    }

READ file-name RECORD [INTO identifier] [; AT END imperative-statement]

READ file-name [NEXT] RECORD [INTO identifier]

    [; AT END imperative-statement]

READ file-name RECORD [INTO identifier] [; INVALID KEY imperative-statement]

READ file-name RECORD [INTO identifier]

    [; KEY IS data-name]

    [; INVALID KEY imperative-statement]

RECEIVE cd-name {MESSAGE} INTO identifier-1 [; NO DATA imperative-statement]
                {SEGMENT}

RELEASE record-name [FROM identifier]

RETURN file-name RECORD [INTO identifier] ; AT END imperative-statement

REWRITE record-name [FROM identifier]

REWRITE record-name [FROM identifier] [; INVALID KEY imperative-statement]
```

```
SEARCH identifier-1 [ VARYING {identifier-2 } ] [; AT END imperative-statement-1]
                              {index-name-1 }

    ; WHEN condition-1 {imperative-statement-2}
                       {NEXT SENTENCE         }

  [ ; WHEN condition-2 {imperative-statement-3} ] ...
                       {NEXT SENTENCE         }

SEARCH ALL identifier-1 [; AT END imperative-statement-1]

              {data-name-1 {IS EQUAL TO} {identifier-3             }}
    ; WHEN    {            {IS =       } {literal-1                }}
              {                          {arithmetic-expression-1  }}
              {condition-name-1                                     }

          [       {data-name-2 {IS EQUAL TO} {identifier-4             }} ]
          [ AND   {            {IS =       } {literal-2                }} ] ...
          [       {                          {arithmetic-expression-2  }} ]
          [       {condition-name-2                                     } ]

          {imperative-statement-2}
          {NEXT SENTENCE         }

SEND cd-name FROM identifier-1

                                        {WITH identifier-2}
SEND cd-name [FROM identifier-1]        {WITH ESI         }
                                        {WITH EMI         }
                                        {WITH EGI         }

    [                       {{identifier-3} [LINE ]}]
    [ {BEFORE} ADVANCING    {{integer     } [LINES]}]
    [ {AFTER }              {{mnemonic-name}        }]
    [                       {{PAGE         }        }]

SET {identifier-1 [, identifier-2] ...} TO {identifier-3 }
    {index-name-1 [, index-name-2] ...}    {index-name-3 }
                                           {integer-1    }

SET index-name-4 [, index-name-5] ... {UP BY  } {identifier-4}
                                      {DOWN BY} {integer-2   }
```

```
SORT file-name-1 ON {ASCENDING } KEY data-name-1 [, data-name-2] ...
                    {DESCENDING}

          [ON {ASCENDING } KEY data-name-3 [, data-name-4] ... ] ...
          [   {DESCENDING}                                     ]

   [COLLATING SEQUENCE IS alphabet-name]

   {INPUT PROCEDURE IS section-name-1 [{THROUGH} section-name-2]}
   {                                  [{THRU   }               ]}
   {USING file-name-2 [, file-name-3] ...                        }

   {OUTPUT PROCEDURE IS section-name-3 [{THROUGH} section-name-4]}
   {                                   [{THRU   }               ]}
   {GIVING file-name-4                                            }

                       [     {IS EQUAL TO      }           ]
                       [     {IS =             }           ]
START file-name        [ KEY {IS GREATER THAN  } data-name ]
                       [     {IS >             }           ]
                       [     {IS NOT LESS THAN }           ]
                       [     {IS NOT <         }           ]

   [; INVALID KEY imperative-statement]

STOP {RUN    }
     {literal}

                                                        {identifier-3}
STRING {identifier-1} [, identifier-2] ... DELIMITED BY {literal-3   }
       {literal-1   } [, literal-2   ]                  {SIZE        }

                                                          {identifier-6}
    [, {identifier-4} [, identifier-5] ... DELIMITED BY {literal-6   } ] ...
    [  {literal-4   } [, literal-5   ]                  {SIZE        } ]

    INTO identifier-7 [WITH POINTER identifier-8]

    [; ON OVERFLOW imperative-statement]

SUBTRACT {identifier-1} [, identifier-2] ... FROM identifier-m [ROUNDED]
         {literal-1   } [, literal-2   ]

    [, identifier-n [ROUNDED]] ... [; ON SIZE ERROR imperative-statement]
```

GENERAL FORMAT FOR VERBS

```
SUBTRACT {identifier-1} [, identifier-2] ... FROM {identifier-m}
         {literal-1   } [, literal-2   ]          {literal-m   }

    GIVING identifier-n [ROUNDED] [, identifier-o [ROUNDED]] ...

    [; ON SIZE ERROR imperative-statement]

SUBTRACT {CORRESPONDING} identifier-1 FROM identifier-2 [ROUNDED]
         {CORR         }

    [; ON SIZE ERROR imperative-statement]

SUPPRESS PRINTING

TERMINATE report-name-1 [, report-name-2] ...

UNSTRING identifier-1

    [DELIMITED BY [ALL] {identifier-2} [, OR [ALL] {identifier-3}] ... ]
                        {literal-1   }             {literal-2   }

     INTO identifier-4 [, DELIMITER IN identifier-5] [, COUNT IN identifier-6]

       [, identifier-7 [, DELIMITER IN identifier-8] [, COUNT IN identifier-9]] ...

    [WITH POINTER identifier-10] [TALLYING IN identifier-11]

    [; ON OVERFLOW imperative-statement]

                                                {file-name-1 [, file-name-2] ...}
                                                {INPUT                          }
USE AFTER STANDARD {EXCEPTION} PROCEDURE ON     {OUTPUT                         } .
                   {ERROR    }                  {I-O                            }
                                                {EXTEND                         }

                                                {file-name-1 [, file-name-2] ...}
USE AFTER STANDARD {EXCEPTION} PROCEDURE ON     {INPUT                          } .
                   {ERROR    }                  {OUTPUT                         }
                                                {I-O                            }

USE BEFORE REPORTING identifier.
```

```
                       ⎧cd-name-1                              ⎫
                       ⎪[ALL REFERENCES OF] identifier-1       ⎪
USE FOR DEBUGGING ON   ⎨file-name-1                            ⎬
                       ⎪procedure-name-1                       ⎪
                       ⎩ALL PROCEDURES                         ⎭

   ⎡    cd-name-2                          ⎤
   ⎢    [ALL REFERENCES OF] identifier-2   ⎥
   ⎢ ,  file-name-2                        ⎥ ...   .
   ⎢    procedure-name-2                   ⎥
   ⎣    ALL PROCEDURES                     ⎦

WRITE record-name [FROM identifier-1]

   ⎡⎧BEFORE⎫ ADVANCING ⎧⎧identifier-2⎫ ⎡LINE ⎤⎫⎤
   ⎢⎩AFTER ⎭           ⎨⎩integer     ⎭ ⎣LINES⎦⎬⎥
   ⎢                   ⎪⎧mnemonic-name⎫       ⎪⎥
   ⎣                   ⎩⎩PAGE         ⎭       ⎭⎦

   ⎡ ; AT ⎧END-OF-PAGE⎫ imperative-statement⎤
   ⎣      ⎩EOP        ⎭                     ⎦

WRITE record-name [FROM identifier] [; INVALID KEY imperative-statement]
```

Condition Formats

GENERAL FORMAT FOR CONDITIONS

RELATION CONDITION:

```
                              ⎧ IS [NOT] GREATER THAN ⎫
⎧ identifier-1             ⎫  ⎪ IS [NOT] LESS THAN    ⎪  ⎧ identifier-2             ⎫
⎨ literal-1                ⎬  ⎨ IS [NOT] EQUAL TO     ⎬  ⎨ literal-2                ⎬
⎪ arithmetic-expression-1  ⎪  ⎪ IS [NOT] >            ⎪  ⎪ arithmetic-expression-2  ⎪
⎩ index-name-1             ⎭  ⎪ IS [NOT] <            ⎪  ⎩ index-name-2             ⎭
                              ⎩ IS [NOT] =            ⎭
```

CLASS CONDITION:

```
identifier IS [NOT] ⎧ NUMERIC    ⎫
                    ⎩ ALPHABETIC ⎭
```

SIGN CONDITION:

```
                                ⎧ POSITIVE ⎫
arithmetic-expression is [NOT]  ⎨ NEGATIVE ⎬
                                ⎩ ZERO     ⎭
```

CONDITION-NAME CONDITION:

condition-name

SWITCH-STATUS CONDITION:

condition-name

NEGATED SIMPLE CONDITION:

NOT simple-condition

COMBINED CONDITION:

```
condition  ⎧ ⎧ AND ⎫  condition ⎫ ...
           ⎩ ⎩ OR  ⎭            ⎭
```

ABBREVIATED COMBINED RELATION CONDITION:

```
relation-condition  ⎧ ⎧ AND ⎫ [NOT] [ relational-operator ] object ⎫ ...
                    ⎩ ⎩ OR  ⎭                                       ⎭
```

Miscellaneous Formats

MISCELLANEOUS FORMATS

QUALIFICATION:

```
{data-name-1   } [{OF} data-name-2] ...
{condition-name} [{IN}             ]

paragraph-name [{OF} section-name]
               [{IN}             ]

text-name [{OF} library-name]
          [{IN}             ]
```

SUBSCRIPTING:

```
{data-name     } (subscript-1 [, subscript-2 [, subscript-3]] )
{condition-name}
```

INDEXING:

```
{data-name     } ( {index-name-1 [{±} literal-2]}
{condition-name}   {literal-1                   }

   [, {index-name-2 [{±} literal-4]} [, {index-name-3 [{±} literal-6]}]] )
   [  {literal-3                   } [  {literal-5                   }]]
```

IDENTIFIER: FORMAT 1

```
data-name-1 [{OF} data-name-2] ... [(subscript-1 [, subscript-2
            [{IN}             ]

   [, subscript-3]] )]
```

IDENTIFIER: FORMAT 2

```
data-name-1 [{OF} data-name-2] ... [ ( {index-name-1 [{±} literal-2]}
            [{IN}             ]    [   {literal-1                   }

   [, {index-name-2 [{±} literal-4]} [, {index-name-3 [{±} literal-6]}]] )]
   [  {literal-3                   } [  {literal-5                   }]]   ]
```

COPY Statement

GENERAL FORMAT FOR COPY STATEMENT

```
COPY text-name [ { OF } library-name ]
                 { IN }

 [ REPLACING { , { ==pseudo-text-1== }  BY  { ==pseudo-text-2== } } ... ]
                 { identifier-1     }       { identifier-2     }
                 { literal-1        }       { literal-2        }
                 { word-1           }       { word-2           }
```

APPENDIX D

TEST DATA

CHAPTER 2

INSTRUCTIONS

The following Athlete Decathlon Records may be used for all programming assignments contained in Chapter 2.

SCHOOL I.D.	ATHLETE NUMBER	ATHLETE NAME	COACH NUMBER	TOTAL SCORE	100 METERS	LONG JUMP	SHOT PUT	HIGH JUMP	400 METERS	110 METER HURDLES	DISCUS	POLE VAULT	JAVELIN	1500 METERS	
1 2 3	4 5 6	7 8 9 10 11 12 13 14 15 16 17 18 19 20 21 22 23 24 25 26	27 28 29	30 31 32 33	34 35 36 37	38 39 40 41	42 43 44 45	46 47 48 49	50 51 52 53	54 55 56 57	58 59 60 61	62 63 64 65	66 67 68 69	70 71 72 73	74 75 76 77 78 79 80

CHAPTER 2 TEST DATA — ATHLETE DECATHLON RECORDS

1 - 3	4 - 6	7 - 26	27 - 29	30 - 33	34 - 37	38 - 41	42 - 45	46 - 49	50 - 53	54 - 57	58 - 61	62 - 65	66 - 69	70 - 73
STA	101	Acosta, Victor C.	050	7280	0530	0900	0750	0700	0900	0800	0800	0810	0590	0500
STA	11A	Anchor, Joseph J.	050	7700	1000	0700	0500	0600	0500	0750	0750	0600	0800	1500
USC	233	Banks, Gregory A.	045	8110	1500	0500	0900	1200	0500	0600	0900	0700	0500	0810
USC	239		045	8100	0800	0750	0650	0500	0900	1000	0600	0900	0700	1300
UCL	352	Cady, Bruce C.	029	7525	0500	0925	0700	0900	0650	0750	0800	1100	0500	0700
UCL	355	Cannes, Timothy B.		7100	0700	1000	0500	0650	0700	0550	0700	0700	0550	1050
ORS	441		04F	9001	0600	0500	0550	0600	0550	0650	0650	0500	0600	0800
ORS	450	Davis, Paul L.	040	499H	0700	0700	0700	0900	0950	0800	1000	0550	1000	050J
UCB	539	Debow, Cecil L.	049	5000	0500	0500	0500	0500	0500	0500	0500	0500	0500	0500
UCB	540	Deese, Harmon C.	049	4999	0499	0499	0499	0499	0499	0499	0499	0499	0499	0499
WAU	544	Dodge, William C.	035	6500	0600	0550	0600	0650	0650	0500	0500	0550	0500	1400
WAU	555	Dredge, Ted D.	035	9001	0901	0900	0900	0900	0900	0900	0900	0900	0900	0900
WAS	575	Dryor, Keith A.	125	9000	0900	0900	0900	0900	0900	0900	0900	0900	0900	0900
WSA	582	Duty, Aaron D.	125	7200	0720	0720	0720	0720	0720	0720	0720	0720	0720	0720
STA	619	Evans, Harold D.	050	7500	0650	0600	0550	0750	0800	0650	0700	0800	1300	0700
STA	623	Fannel, George A.	050	7500		0700	0750	090C	1000	06A0	0550	05 0	0600	0700
STA	700	Foster, Albert A.	050	7590	0690	0650	0500	0700	0750	0600	0550	0600	0700	1850
USC	702	Franks, Edward G.	045	7200	0800	0800	0800	0800	0800	0800	0800	0800	0800	0800
USC	719	Frazier, Fred L.	045	7000	0700	0600	0800	0900	0500	0700	0700	0650	0750	0700
USC	732	Frye, Andrea C.	045	6799	0700	0700	0700	0700	0700	0700	0700	0700	0700	0499
UCL	777	Gable, John J.	029	7350	0650	0650	0600	0600	0750	0800	0600	0650	0700	1350
UCL	780	Gann, Todd P.	029	7350	0650	0650	0600	0600	0750	0800	0600	0650	1350	0700
ORS	788	Garlock, Donald R.	040	7200	0720	0800	0800	0650	0600	0500	0700	0800	0650	0980
ORS	800	Hamm, Richard C.	040	7401	2001	0600	0600	0600	0600	0600	0600	0600	0600	0600
ORS	810	Hart, Henry D.	040	9000	2000	1000	1000	1000	1000	1000	0500	0500	0500	0500
ORG	815	Johnson, Peter C.												
USC	825	Mendez, Ramon D.	045	8000	0800	1200	0800	0500	0500	0500	0500	0600	0650	1950
USC	850	Ngyuen, Guy E.	045	7940	0700	0790	0600	0900	0600	0700	0700	0650	0650	1650
USC	855	Ohms, Seymour A.	045	6900	0600	0700	0700	0700	0700	0700	0700	0700	0700	0700
USC	866	Racy, William B.	045	7200	0800	0800	0600	0600	0600	0600	0800	0800	0800	0800
USC	901	Raster, Billy I.	045	8000	1000	1000	0600	0600	0700	0700	0700	0700	0700	0700
USC	909	Samms, Gerald C.	045	5500	0550	0550	0550	0550	0550	0550	0550	0550	0550	0550

TEST DATA

CHAPTER 3

INSTRUCTIONS

The following Coach Identification File may be used for all programming assignments contained in Chapter 3.

COACH NUMBER | COACH NAME

COACH MASTER FILE

1 - 3	4 - 23
029	Tanner, Gregory C.
035	Raft, Felix A.
037	Short, Chester B.
040	Reynolds, Bruce D.
045	Yardley, John C.
049	Arnett, George M.
050	Webster, Tom F.
125	Smith, Harley D.

TEST DATA

CHAPTER 4

INSTRUCTIONS

The following Athlete Transaction Update Records may be used for all programming assignments contained in Chapter 4.

SCHOOL I.D.	ATHLETE NUMBER	ATHLETE NAME	COACH NUMBER		100 METERS	LONG JUMP	SHOT PUT	HIGH JUMP	400 METERS	110 METER HURDLES	DISCUS	POLE VAULT	JAVELIN	1500 METERS		CODE
0 0 0	0 0 0	0 0 0 0 0 0 0 0 0 0 0 0 0 0 0 0 0 0 0 0	0 0 0	0 0 0 0	0 0 0 0	0 0 0 0	0 0 0 0	0 0 0 0	0 0 0 0	0 0 0 0	0 0 0 0	0 0 0 0	0 0 0 0	0 0 0 0	0 0 0 0 0 0	0
1 2 3	4 5 6	7 8 9 10 11 12 13 14 15 16 17 18 19 20 21 22 23 24 25 26	27 28 29	30 31 32 33	34 35 36 37	38 39 40 41	42 43 44 45	46 47 48 49	50 51 52 53	54 55 56 57	58 59 60 61	62 63 64 65	66 67 68 69	70 71 72 73	74 75 76 77 78 79	80
1 1 1	1 1 1	1 1 1 1 1 1 1 1 1 1 1 1 1 1 1 1 1 1 1 1	1 1 1	1 1 1 1	1 1 1 1	1 1 1 1	1 1 1 1	1 1 1 1	1 1 1 1	1 1 1 1	1 1 1 1	1 1 1 1	1 1 1 1	1 1 1 1	1 1 1 1 1 1	1
2 2 2	2 2 2	2 2 2 2 2 2 2 2 2 2 2 2 2 2 2 2 2 2 2 2	2 2 2	2 2 2 2	2 2 2 2	2 2 2 2	2 2 2 2	2 2 2 2	2 2 2 2	2 2 2 2	2 2 2 2	2 2 2 2	2 2 2 2	2 2 2 2	2 2 2 2 2 2	2
3 3 3	3 3 3	3 3 3 3 3 3 3 3 3 3 3 3 3 3 3 3 3 3 3 3	3 3 3	3 3 3 3	3 3 3 3	3 3 3 3	3 3 3 3	3 3 3 3	3 3 3 3	3 3 3 3	3 3 3 3	3 3 3 3	3 3 3 3	3 3 3 3	3 3 3 3 3 3	3
4 4 4	4 4 4	4 4 4 4 4 4 4 4 4 4 4 4 4 4 4 4 4 4 4 4	4 4 4	4 4 4 4	4 4 4 4	4 4 4 4	4 4 4 4	4 4 4 4	4 4 4 4	4 4 4 4	4 4 4 4	4 4 4 4	4 4 4 4	4 4 4 4	4 4 4 4 4 4	4
5 5 5	5 5 5	5 5 5 5 5 5 5 5 5 5 5 5 5 5 5 5 5 5 5 5	5 5 5	5 5 5 5	5 5 5 5	5 5 5 5	5 5 5 5	5 5 5 5	5 5 5 5	5 5 5 5	5 5 5 5	5 5 5 5	5 5 5 5	5 5 5 5	5 5 5 5 5 5	5
6 6 6	6 6 6	6 6 6 6 6 6 6 6 6 6 6 6 6 6 6 6 6 6 6 6	6 6 6	6 6 6 6	6 6 6 6	6 6 6 6	6 6 6 6	6 6 6 6	6 6 6 6	6 6 6 6	6 6 6 6	6 6 6 6	6 6 6 6	6 6 6 6	6 6 6 6 6 6	6
7 7 7	7 7 7	7 7 7 7 7 7 7 7 7 7 7 7 7 7 7 7 7 7 7 7	7 7 7	7 7 7 7	7 7 7 7	7 7 7 7	7 7 7 7	7 7 7 7	7 7 7 7	7 7 7 7	7 7 7 7	7 7 7 7	7 7 7 7	7 7 7 7	7 7 7 7 7 7	7
8 8 8	8 8 8	8 8 8 8 8 8 8 8 8 8 8 8 8 8 8 8 8 8 8 8	8 8 8	8 8 8 8	8 8 8 8	8 8 8 8	8 8 8 8	8 8 8 8	8 8 8 8	8 8 8 8	8 8 8 8	8 8 8 8	8 8 8 8	8 8 8 8	8 8 8 8 8 8	8
9 9 9	9 9 9	9 9 9 9 9 9 9 9 9 9 9 9 9 9 9 9 9 9 9 9	9 9 9	9 9 9 9	9 9 9 9	9 9 9 9	9 9 9 9	9 9 9 9	9 9 9 9	9 9 9 9	9 9 9 9	9 9 9 9	9 9 9 9	9 9 9 9	9 9 9 9 9 9	9
1 2 3	4 5 6	7 8 9 10 11 12 13 14 15 16 17 18 19 20 21 22 23 24 25 26	27 28 29	30 31 32 33	34 35 36 37	38 39 40 41	42 43 44 45	46 47 48 49	50 51 52 53	54 55 56 57	58 59 60 61	62 63 64 65	66 67 68 69	70 71 72 73	74 75 76 77 78 79	80

CHAPTER 4 TEST DATA — ATHLETE UPDATE RECORDS

1 - 3	4 - 6	7 - 26	27 - 29	34 - 37	38 - 41	42 - 45	46 - 49	50 - 53	54 - 57	58 - 61	62 - 65	66 - 69	70 - 73	80
USC	100	Aaron, Randle R.	045	0600	0800	0600	0700	0800	0700	0700	0800	0600	0900	A
	352													D
	539			0850	0750	0550	0600	0550	0650	0650	0500	0600	0800	C
UCL	539		029											C
WAS	544			1100	0550	0600	0550	0650	0400	0500	0550	0500	1900	C
	575			0800	0800	0800	0800	0800	0800	0800	0800	0800	0800	C
WAU	575													C
	619													4
STA	700	Foster, Albert A.	050	0690	0650	0500	0700	0750	0600	0550	0600	0700	1850	A
STA	702	Frank, Edward C.	045	0800	0800	0800	0800	0800	0800	0800	0800	0800	0800	A
	710													D
	725			0600	0600	0600	0600	0600	0600	0600	0600	0600	0600	C
	777			0750	0650	0600	0600	0750	0800	0600	0650	0700	1000	C
USC	780		045											C
	788		037											C
	810		037											C
USC	923	Silver, Brent A.	045	0700	0600	0600	0600	0600	0600	0700	0600	0600	0600	A

APPENDIX E

RESERVED WORD LIST

The following is a list of the reserved words used in the COBOL language.

ACCEPT
ACCESS
ADD
ADVANCING
AFTER
ALL
ALPHABETIC
ALSO
ALTER
ALTERNATE
AND
ARE
AREA
AREAS
ASCENDING
ASSIGN
AT
AUTHOR

BEFORE
BLANK
BLOCK
BOTTOM
BY

CALL
CANCEL
CD
CF
CH
CHARACTER
CHARACTERS
CLOCK-UNITS
CLOSE
COBOL
CODE
CODE-SET
COLLATING
COLUMN
COMMA
COMMUNICATION
COMP
COMPUTATIONAL
COMPUTE
CONFIGURATION
CONTAINS
CONTROL
CONTROLS
COPY
CORR

CORRESPONDING
COUNT
CURRENCY

DATA
DATE
DATE-COMPILED
DATE-WRITTEN
DAY
DE
DEBUG-CONTENTS
DEBUG-ITEM
DEBUG-LINE
DEBUG-NAME
DEBUG-SUB-1
DEBUG-SUB-2
DEBUG-SUB-3
DEBUGGING
DECIMAL-POINT
DECLARATIVES
DELETE
DELIMITED
DELIMITER
DEPENDING
DESCENDING
DESTINATION
DETAIL
DISABLE
DISPLAY
DIVIDE
DIVISION
DOWN
DUPLICATES
DYNAMIC

EGI
ELSE
EMI
ENABLE
END
END-OF-PAGE
ENTER
ENVIRONMENT
EOP
EQUAL
ERROR
ESI
EVERY
EXCEPTION
EXIT

EXTEND

FD
FILE
FILE-CONTROL
FILLER
FINAL
FIRST
FOOTING
FOR
FROM

GENERATE
GIVING
GO
GREATER
GROUP

HEADING
HIGH-VALUE
HIGH-VALUES

I-O
I-O-CONTROL
IDENTIFICATION
IF
IN
INDEX
INDEXED
INDICATE
INITIAL
INITIATE
INPUT
INPUT-OUTPUT
INSPECT
INSTALLATION
INTO
INVALID
IS

JUST
JUSTIFIED

KEY

LABEL
LAST
LEADING
LEFT
LENGTH

LESS
LIMIT
LIMITS
LINAGE
LINAGE-COUNTER
LINE
LINE-COUNTER
LINES
LINKAGE
LOCK
LOW-VALUE
LOW-VALUES

MEMORY
MERGE
MESSAGE
MODE
MODULES
MOVE
MULTIPLE
MULTIPLY

NATIVE
NEGATIVE
NEXT
NO
NOT
NUMBER
NUMERIC

OBJECT-COMPUTER
OCCURS
OF
OFF
OMITTED
ON
OPEN
OPTIONAL
OR
ORGANIZATION
OUTPUT
OVERFLOW

PAGE
PAGE-COUNTER
PERFORM
PF
PH
PIC
PICTURE

PLUS
POINTER
POSITION
POSITIVE
PRINTING
PROCEDURE
PROCEDURES
PROCEED
PROGRAM
PROGRAM-ID

QUEUE
QUOTE
QUOTES

RANDOM
RD
READ
RECEIVE
RECORD
RECORDS
REDEFINES
REEL
REFERENCES
RELATIVE
RELEASE
REMAINDER
REMOVAL
RENAMES
REPLACING
REPORT
REPORTING
REPORTS
RERUN
RESERVE
RESET
RETURN
REVERSED
REWIND
REWRITE
RF
RH
RIGHT
ROUNDED
RUN

SAME
SD
SEARCH
SECTION
SECURITY
SEGMENT
SEGMENT-LIMIT
SELECT
SEND
SENTENCE
SEPARATE
SEQUENCE
SEQUENTIAL
SET
SIGN
SIZE
SORT
SORT-MERGE
SOURCE
SOURCE-COMPUTER
SPACE
SPACES
SPECIAL-NAMES
STANDARD
STANDARD-1
START
STATUS
STOP
STRING
SUB-QUEUE-1
SUB-QUEUE-2
SUB-QUEUE-3
SUBTRACT
SUM
SUPPRESS
SYMBOLIC
SYNC
SYNCHRONIZED

TABLE
TALLYING
TAPE
TERMINAL
TERMINATE
TEXT
THAN
THROUGH
THRU
TIME
TIMES
TO
TOP
TRAILING
TYPE

UNIT
UNSTRING
UNTIL
UP
UPON
USAGE
USE
USING

VALUE
VALUES
VARYING

WHEN
WITH
WORDS
WORKING-STORAGE
WRITE

ZERO
ZEROES
ZEROS

+
-
*
/
**
>
<
=

Index

—D—

—K—

—L—

—M—

—N—

—O—

—P—